Rainstorms and Rainbows

RAINSTORMS AND RAINBOWS

The International Library of Poetry

Catherine A. Burnett, Editor

Jessica A. Rapisarda, Assistant Editor

Patty A. Davis, Assistant Editor

Rainstorms and Rainbows

Library of Congress
Cataloging in Publication Data

ISBN 1-58235-542-8

Proudly manufactured in the United States of America by
Watermark Press
One Poetry Plaza
Owings Mills, MD 21117

The International Library of Poetry
poetry.COM

FOREWORD

Throughout life, we store information collected from experiences and try in some way to make sense of it. When we are not able to fully understand the things that occur in our lives, we often externalize the information. By doing this, we are afforded a different perspective, thus allowing us to think more clearly about difficult or perplexing events and emotions. Art is one of the ways in which people choose to externalize their thoughts.

Within the arts, modes of expression differ, but poetry is a very powerful tool by which people can share sometimes confusing, sometimes perfectly clear concepts and feelings with others. Intentions can run the gamut as well: The artists may simply want to share something that has touched their lives in some way, or they may want to get help to allay anxiety or uncertainty. The poetry within *Rainstorms and Rainbows* is from every point on the spectrum: every topic, every intention, every event or emotion imaginable. Some poems will speak to certain readers more than others, but it is always important to keep in mind that each verse is the voice of a poet, of a mind that needs to make sense of this world, of a heart that feels the effects of every moment in this life, and perhaps of a memory that is striving to surface. Nonetheless, recalling our yesterdays gives birth to our many forms of expression.

Melisa S. Mitchell
Senior Editor

Editor's Note

"Now the vicissitudes that afflict the individual have their source in society. Personal relations have given way to impersonal ones. The Great Society has arrived and the task of our generation is to bring it under control."
—Aneurin Bevan

All people share one trait—the need for social contact with other people. Whether it be a deep, emotional relationship, someone we admire, or an acquaintance, even the most remote contact has some effect on a person's life. Human contact does not necessarily come as a positive influence either; many times we have just as many negative as we do positive encounters. Any type of human contact can affect our lives, acting like food that nourishes our emotional well-being. The opposite is also true—distance hurts us emotionally. And yet, we continue to strive for any connection.

In "To Mississippi—From Massachusetts" (1), by Tay Sherman, the title punctuates the extreme distance that is shared by the two people at present. The poem itself is set in the persona's past and in Mississippi. The persona is surrounded by "liquor heat" and "unshaven angels of drunkenness." Alcohol is a prominent theme in the poem. At first, the persona makes excuses for the excessive consumption of alcohol:

> *liquor heat inside is the only release from*
> *sun and heat like a wall crashed into by cars.*
> *Besides, from a distance, Ma thinks it's iced tea. She won't catch us.*

The narrator claims that the alcohol warms the body to match the extreme heat of the outdoors, which in turn helps one cope with the heat. The narrator also uses as an excuse that "Ma" won't know that they are drinking liquor. The mention of adult supervision is juvenile and secretive, which lets the reader know the persona is young. Despite any excuses, we are told that the situation is not all realistic and clear: " . . . a pleasure of confused sweat drives them. Us." Pleasure denotes happiness, but the combination of alcohol and extreme heat makes one partially delirious or confused. This false happiness "drives," or motivates, the persona and his companions. So far, in stanzas one through three, the narrator has had contact with drunken and heat-beleaguered people, while keeping distant from "Ma." At the mention of "Us" at the end of stanza three, the narrator is excluding himself and his companions from the larger group—"them." Here, human contact is made significant and the type of contact is made clear:

Always, we fall. Together or apart, in heat
and disarmament . . .

The human contact in this poem is negative and destructive. The heat and alcohol disarm and corrupt the relationship between the persona and his companion, ultimately destroying it. Whether the relationship is one of a parent and child or a romantic one is uncertain, however the message is clear that it is a negative one:

We never meant for me to become like you, full of hopeless
love of drunkenness and humidity, full of patterned longing
for the strange hot dreams of summer that waste the skin slick.

A pattern repeats itself, carried on from one person to the next, which likely indicates a multi-generational relationship. Again, this stanza refers to the heat and alcohol, but they are mentioned here as part of the pattern passed on to the persona. Even in the midst of the pattern of alcohol and heat, the narrator recognizes the negative aspects of the situation. In the last stanza, we find the extremes of the relationship in the form of an addiction: "Mad of me to want the hands that strangled me and fed me poison." We are reminded that the persona still desires human contact, despite its destructiveness. He recognizes this contact as "poison," but still does not end it: "I could never stop you." Seeing the madness and not being able to end a negative situation is typical of an addiction, even if it is an addiction to another human being. The persona in "To Mississippi—From Massachusetts" became patterned after the negative characteristics of the person with whom he was involved.

In "Of Breaking Gently" (1), by Briana McDonough, human contact is reassuring and very comforting. Instead of using stanzas to progress from one description to the next, McDonough uses a paragraph form and allows her thoughts to flow from a certain beginning, expressing her point in the middle, and drawing a conclusion at the end. The initial image starts with "white porcelain" that gets broken. White is representative of innocence and purity. Porcelain supports this image of flawlessness. As are the beginnings of our lives, the beginning of this poem is pure and innocent. Throughout the next few lines, we have several references to imperfection: "crashed," "shattered," "pieces," and "showered." These words symbolize the sometimes painful difficulty of our lives after childhood. Naturally, as we grow, we have good times and bad. Lines four and six symbolize these rough edges in our lives. Between these negative images, line five represents the good times: "My feet bare, cold, and white . . ." Again, the mention of white reiterates the persona's innocence and goodness. The image of "bare, cold feet" also gives a hint of death, which foreshadows the end of the poem. Cold is often used as a negative symbol. Here it refers to a negative time in the persona's life. The comfort of the persona's mother is the only human contact in this poem:

> My mother's voices, sweetened by time and
> memory, echo wise reassurances . . .

The reader can confirm the comfort found in the pleasant words "sweetened" and "reassurances." However, "voices" is plural and those voices echo through time and memory, indicating many lessons through the narrator's life. The lesson voiced in this poem—"We don't cry over broken dishes . . . "—is about letting things go and not wishing to change the past. We cannot be "wishing the pieces upward softly, together again in one swift motion of redemption." Redemption is about recovering from a situation and gaining salvation from our actions. Everyone knows time cannot be reversed to put back together "[h]er anniversary plate, my baby cup . . . " or any material "treasure." Neither can we expect to reverse the loss of a loved one. Instead, the persona learns to let go of the past:

> But to open my hands, palms up—let it
> all fly freely out and away, accepting
> life's crash of finality with a spirit of grace.

The image of "hands, palms up" recalls Jesus' hands in the familiar religious iconography—an image of acceptance of all people and situations. As a person accepts loss, she must also find release as she lets go of loved ones. To "fly freely" reflects the release of doves as a symbol of freedom. Human contact teaches us these important life lessons. At times we desire more contact, good or bad, and at times we have to accept distance or loss. The narrator is learning a lesson by "accepting life's crash of finality with a spirit of grace." Death of a loved one is a difficult situation to endure; it is much like a shattering of our lives' tranquility. To learn to handle something so severe with any kind of "grace" or finesse is a valuable lesson.

"Mockingbird" (1), by Arthur Cambell, teaches another valuable lesson of human contact—the significance of seemingly unimportant human interaction and how we come to appreciate one another. "Mockingbird" is a relaxed sonnet that uses alliteration to express its point. In the first stanza, the persona makes references to sharp, harmful images: "slices," "rapiers," and "scissors." He does not appreciate the singing of the mockingbird and describes his songs as sharp, hurtful objects. Mockingbirds are known for not having a unique singing style, but for repeating the songs of others:

> He trills words of birds he's never heard,
> lyrics learned by ancestors, sewn inside his brain.

The mockingbird mimics songs or ideas of others, ones he never learned, but were inherently passed down through his family legacy. This is the mockingbird's only talent, and he is unappreciated by his peers:

> Close-beaked colleagues crouch on ragged branches,
> mutter that it is midnight, not a foggy dawn.

His peers find him foolish for singing at night and not in the morning; they tell him to be quiet, just as humans would get scoffed at for doing something out of the norm. The mockingbird mocks them, as well as mimicking their songs: "Mocking death, his rivals, human dreams." His real value is misconstrued, to be discovered later:

> Historian of squandered species, shaman
> of lost ballads, he knows one day we'll come
> to him and ask, "What was the bluebird's song?"

The mockingbird and the other birds—his peers—metaphorically represent different types of people. The mockingbird is a shaman, a historian and medicine man, the keeper of history who passes down important knowledge to his people. The same birds who make fun of him now will need him later to learn their own history. Historical facts are represented by the bluebird's song. The birds will need to be reminded one day of the bluebird's song, of their own history; the mockingbird will remember and not let the memory be squandered. This relationship parallels many in the human experience. Humans often initially misjudge the value of people they meet, but later grow to learn the true significance of human relationships in our lives.

As illustrated in all three poems, human contact can be positive or negative and can teach many lessons. Humans rely on such contact to grow and learn about life. Our memories are formed and our souls nurtured by human contact, which allows us to become who we are and tell our stories through poetry.

Each of the poems collected here serves as an example of communication at its most evolved level. I would like to extend special thanks to each poet whose work contributed to the wide range of material in this anthology. I encourage you to explore these poems, as well as the other poetry published on poetry.com, to discover the sentiments conveyed by each poetic voice. Congratulations to each of you on your ability to use words to express your thoughts and emotions to others in a most powerful way. Best wishes for continued success in all your creative ventures.

The publication of *Rainstorms and Rainbows* has been a culmination of the efforts of many individuals. Judges, editors, assistant editors, customer service representatives, graphic artists, layout artists, office administrators, data entry staff, and mail-room personnel have all given of their time and energy toward this anthology's successful production. I am thankful for their assistance and support.

Catherine A. Burnett
Editor

Cover Art: Leah Meirill, "As Yet Untitled"

Of Breaking Gently

Cool and slippery, the white porcelain flew
from my fingers, slid free from my grasp
(wet hands, damp towel)—
and crashed like glass rain to the floor.
My feet bare, cold, and white,
shattered pieces showered, spread like
dangerous confetti around them.
My mother's voices, sweetened by time and
memory, echo wise reassurances
(pulse lightly in my chest, through threatening tears),
"We don't cry over broken dishes...."
Her anniversary plate, my baby cup, no
matter the treasure, she tells me to stop
wishing the pieces upward softly, together
again in one swift motion of redemption.
But to open my hands, palms up—let it
all fly freely out and away, accepting
life's crash of finality with a spirit of grace.
                    Briana Ellen McDonough

Mockingbird

He slices me from sleep with roller-ball
sonatas, vaults from vane to chimney,
flinging rapiers of sound to pin
his kingdom's fringe, then squats
and sings his scissors at the moon.

He trills words of birds he's never heard,
lyrics learned by ancestors, sewn inside his brain.
Close-beaked colleagues crouch on ragged branches,
mutter that it's midnight, not a foggy dawn.

But he still unspools notes of warning,
mocking death, his rivals, human dreams.
Historian of squandered species, shaman
of lost ballads, he knows one day we'll come
to him and ask, "What was the bluebird's song?"
                    Arthur W. Campbell

To Mississippi—From Massachusetts

The southern heat sucks like a warm summer mouth
full of whiskey that distills life into grey shacks, black-
eyed peas, and browned, unshaven angels of drunkenness.

Liquor heat inside is the only release from
sun and heat like a wall crashed into by cars.
Besides, from a distance, Ma thinks it's iced tea. She won't catch us.

Mosquitoes crawl and dig like kudzu, then drop hot and bloated, wet
sand from the hand or crushed flowers in May,
a pleasure of confused sweat drives them. Us.

Always, we fall. Together or apart, in heat
and disarmament, in lazy dreams of release driven far
away by the immobility of heat. We say yes every time.

We never meant for me to become like you, full of hopeless
love of drunkenness and humidity, full of patterned longing
for the strange hot dreams of summer that waste the skin slick.

Heat is madness and drug. So were you, once.
Mad of me to want the hands that strangled me and fed me poison.
The other part was, well, the other part. I could never stop you.
                    Tay Arrow Sherman

Beaching It

Her facial features were arranged in a lively way,
As she squinted at the sun.

Turning away from me,
I could see her spine nestling
Into a portrayal of warmth and rest.

We remained silent.

The ocean looked heavy,
Nudging us away from its edge,
Tangling its legendary myths around our ankles.

Supposing our way along the shore,
We came upon a large rock,
A beacon of solitude,
Preventing us from continuing easily,
Begging us to stay a while longer.

She took my hand to steady me,
As I purloined steps over the mass
That was buried so deep in the sand.

    Sarah Cartmell

Organ

As the bird flies through the window of the old church
standing at the corner of Frost and Hughes
next to the warehouse boarded up for 30 years
where 200 people lost their jobs
and moved their families up north
in search of better homes and better schools
in a city where their southern heritage means absolutely nothing,
he chirps his beautiful song,
standing strongly on board the organ.

    Sharod Tucker

A God Awaits within the Menial Collection

I am a god mounted on the wall watching you.
I do not need belief,
just respect for my belly and fatted calf smile.
If you approach, I may allow you to touch my gold veneer.
Careful—
it flakes from my knees and elbows.
I rule over small, pliant things,
pencil erasers, tar in the road.
Even the jelly in the darkened pantry knows my name.
If you pay attention you may feel the
rubber band in your hair contracting, the
gum flooding your mouth with appled fear.
Stop before you enter the next room.
You are not a small thing, but observe me
a moment and tremble.
Not at what you know, but at what you do not care to know.

    Stacey Bandfield

Rain

Had the sky shed its final tears?
The rhythmic moaning of the sea boded a sad day,
The indignant sun, with an apron of scurrying clouds,
The wind sighing through the trees.
The air heavy with moisture,
Wearily, the heavens burst, emitting her fury,
Pelting rain, pouring down in cascades,
Sweeping, splashing, forming streaming gullies,
Eased of her burdens, she gave way to the brilliant sun,
Smiling victoriously, embracing the world,
Bestowing her light on my white washed village.
Her generous gifts exalted my spirits,
My world gave way,
My world was bathed in infinite beauty.

    Ruth Posner

No More Dot Coms

Every day another dream commits its suicide.
Childhood fantasies poison themselves with excess adrenaline.
What's left when everything in the world is wrong?
Girl standing straight legged all alone
in the company of hundreds.
She tries to run but voices always follow one step behind,
and in the air she so heavily breathes.
Plastic prom queens with pink plastic corvettes contain carcinogens.
Faces stained blue by television light radiation.
Girl thinks for three days—
What is my eyelash wish?
She takes a new path, unfamiliar to everyone,
but Alice thinks maybe inspiration will save us all.

    Rachel LeBlanc

Green Mango and Peppa' Sauce

It is the space between shoulder blade and neck
that is at once home and longing,
for this child whose eyes are like sunlight on the Essequibo
and sugar before it is burnt, black
who at three months has known the taste of her mother's milk
and the sting of her father's tears,
which didn't fall until later, after she was gone
back to the place where their navel strings were all buried
and whose freshness, even with baking soda, would grow stale,
except for moments, like at Christmas and
in death, always, in leaving
We were children for as long as we could be
I have stretched it out much longer than the other four
My sister is a woman now,
her hair is a river whose source is too deep,
too wide, and too thick to mark
She has walked bare foot down tarred street,
but there is never enough to cover the places she has to go
to find the space that is as familiar as the taste
of green mango and peppa' sauce

    Mark Anthony Williams

Shadows

Looking at the grey-haired man across the table
and his paunchy, balding friend talking,
thinking they are both eight years younger than I am.
Feeling as though I were pretending to get old
and wondering at the kindness everyone has shown me.
About how the woman pulled out a chair
and I sat down, feeling faintly foolish.
Noticing the smell of arms as they put plates
in front of me, perfectly, as I thanked them.
As though being served were part of the process
of becoming invisible.

    Bill Mayer

Untitled

I sometimes nail myself to the walls of my room
because it temporarily knocks the world off its axis
and in effect changes time for awhile.
However, eventually the nails fall out of place,
and the Earth returns to its uniform revolving motions.
You see, I have this hang-up with time—
it's always moving at undesirable speeds,
but it only spins that way in my mind,
because time is a constant that never changes pace.
So I sit and continually explode in my room,
leaving pieces of me on the floor,
and my thoughts on the walls,
until the sun goes down.
I'm tired as I pick up the pieces
and pull down the thoughts,
and attempt to reassemble myself once again.

    Breniman Green

Some Might Call It Dancing

Some might call it dancing
I call it stumbling closer to God,
the unrehearsed falling forward into love
as if the world was tipped.
Stuck dumb by ecstasy,
I have arrived by already being there,
lifted by my own breath
like a child in the arms of his mother.
It is here in this place of revival
that something in me moves, turns, reaches,
my body merely residue, a puff of smoke,
an awkward prayer whispered heavenward.
Operatic in my cells, I arrive again and again,
mute to the moment, mute to the pain,
where dancing becomes infinitely less about
movement than being moved;
for when the world is tipped and we,
drunk to our eyes in love's ballet, are willing,
there is nothing not dance, no one not dancer,
no place not stage, no breath not a standing ovation before God

    Mitchell Lewis Ditkoff

I Fell Asleep at Your Funeral

It's snowing phosphorus late afternoon-ish.
An essence snifter,
nice relaxer:
Bloody Mary and Klonopin
for my petite mal problem.
Curb your tired thoughts.
I need your wakefulness
(although I have crossed)
from the belly of this black shark of a car.

In a game begun
by a dead man on wheels
the headlights play a customary
follow the leader.
Were you here,
(and able)
you would sack the churchy creep delivering your eulogy.
Stir me when he has finished.

    Max A. Friedenberg

Night Hunting

The ducks conjure spirits in a circle close to shore
where the old women say they saw alligators.
Startled stars leap and fall on the water.
Spiders are weaving and reweaving
blankets to wrap around me every time I walk through,
and the wharf is my ship never reaching another shore.
Families are settling in the safety in the shelter of cypress trees
as the last duck's voice settles the dispute:
I should go in before I am caught.

    Mary Richert

Urbane Blues

Neon lamps and the concrete confusion singe
at night a tattered tomb
Fumes of a beaten window explode into a vacant carousel
Spineless hours slope elaborately slowly
Disintegrating bergs of snow submerge into the sea
As the alps of time discard to form a scourge of me
I strain to shackle every tock,
procuring shares of whirling rock
Abruptly snuffing diatribes I render
catalytic rides to landscapes that obtusely
slide from coastal planes to urbane blues
No aimless warrants there, exist
Omitting troops of remnant tracks that fix
beneath your shoes

    Jason Wyman

At Dusk by Sea

An iced-orange sun was melting by degrees
into the sea, leaving its liquid light on the
rough road sea surface, then dead-ending
where the waves stumbled onto the shoreline
in a muted explosion of orange sparks.
Behind, the beach was an unmade bed,
seasoned by the sodium sea-water—waiting
for the wind to pull tight its salty sand blanket.
Standing there, where the two met, I could
only wonder at the power of the living
ocean—pushing, then pulling, at this
lifeless land, as would fingers kneading a
lump of sand spoiled dough—plying it malleable.
Which would last longest of water or land,
of sea or sand? Would one surpass?
Innermost thoughts could barely suppose.
Innermost feelings found comfort in the hoped for answer . . .
neither.

    Constantine Nicholas Lambros

Observed/1

Flame-headed persona comforts another day
Trivializes herself for her appearance
Silence approaches . . .

She finds what she wishes inside her dream
Then drains it away in absence of esteem
The world is blurred by morning's first sight
Love squints away in endless light

Elegant lines: long running
But move with hypnotic energy
A chuckle and everyone stares fixated
A bare shoulder scatters thoughts to shameless wonder
I could surround her in my being
And she would look blindly beyond burning

    Robert Aaron Daniels

Forgiven

Salted, black, and brisk skies and I'll be home
about a quarter past eleven, your time.
It will be good to see you
now that the old wounds have mended
and my insides mean more than a Sunday morning confession.
I'm not the Saturday night for shot,
one hit wonder you elusively parted with in pale apathy.
I was deeply moved by your performance and mine.
Now, you might not recognize what you see
so take a second look.
Stare, touch me with your filthy hands
because it won't shatter the fact:
My fictional character was crucified this evening
and the blood is dripping down my body
leaving a trail of sweet mercy.
My name is forgiven.

    Sarah Barry

Venus

My red clay womanhood. Could be.
Pieces of me sliding deep down this spiral carnelian groove.
And I bring forth of myself. Without consort. Still a maiden.
My whole self being stitched up hatched over and over again.
Most perplexing! At least it seems so.
How my ballooning breasts thread down
And fumble the abyss of my groin.
How my hips track down in crescents to prowl my inadequate feet.
How the moonbeams seep through my blood nest
My womb lullabying my bubble eggs.
I'm gownless unaware of the secrecy of my filiations
Totally uncharted weaving the meshes of my otherness.

    Maria V. Rivas

A Letter Home from a Young Man Abroad

A few short words in a hurried scrawl,
penned on the cheapest of rag;
"Mother, dear Mother," the note began
(she is known by no name other)
"I have come to this field to die today.
I cannot pretend, my doom is here.
I only pray it's with honor I fall
and that of my death you musn't fear.
For know, dear Mother, that with my last breath,
I shall call out your name most dear.
Forever, with love, your Son," The words read,
on a field of blood and rust,
for folded it lay in his pocket creased,
waiting to return, like flesh, to dust.

Kenneth Bykerk

doozle

You always called me kid
and said you wanted me
until you went to jail.
(Drugs are bad, Brian.)
And I accepted 30 dollars' worth
of collect calls
from the correctional facility
and I waited and cried
for you.
I would have bailed you out
and now you're back with HER
(DIE, BRANDY!).
I thought you hated her.
I know it's illegal,
but because of you
I started singing Jessica Simpson songs—
"I think that I'm in love with you . . ."
Maybe you WERE too old, even though you could
buy me beer.

Beth Bagley

How Caverns Are Formed

They protest
(too strongly)
but he's seen these slow-dripping moments
way too many times before,
piling
like the dead cigarettes and desolates beer bottles
(one for each reason she left)
could gun down everyone here at the bar
but that'd be too easy
gimme another beer, he provokes

Mike Dornan

Borrowed Time

The artist
is unwilling to admit
to himself or to the world
that he has created his masterpiece
because he embraces a primal superstitious certitude
that once he has done so his continued existence
will no longer be tolerated by God.
This is why an unanswerable anxiety
scratches at the door of his perception
every
single
time
he
looks
at
his
daughter.

Scott Gardner Merrick

Grime

Evil, cigarette smoke-lacy early morning sunshine
And I feel it in my sleep-hungry and achy eyes.
Rise to a new day, rise to a new dawn.
Then to carelessly amble down the
Trash-canned back alleyways unseen.
Unaware of my movements, a sleeping city
Waits for some comfortable hour to wake.
Into an empty, all-night club I go,
For my breakfast of steak and beer.
An old body squeaks against the grungy,
Erotic pink vinyl seats.
Oh! My clumsy hand slips and agitated beer
Spills on the seat, adding to the sweat and
Indiscretions of last night's hustlers,
Hookers, winos, and losers.
"Anyone got change for a Dollar?
No one's got change?
Everybody broke in the Breakroom?
—Ah, another day at the Grind."

Christopher Michael Cyr

Mississippi

The sweet taste of blackberry pie touches my mouth,
and the sun hits my face like steam off a kettle,
Tankers move slow down the river like an old
man smokin' his pipe on the porch.
Mississippi Mud squishes between my toes,
with its cool sensation that tickles my senses.
The rain flows down in gallons and waters
the crops that stretch for endless miles.
Life in Mississippi slips by and can never be returned,
But the dream and passion of Mississippi lives forever.

Grant Emerson Cooper

A Fatal Attraction to Plath

Drowning in molasses depressions
and choking through life's trivia,
floating past the black on white signs
proclaiming the rich are pigs,
sex, just sex,
and acid's essential escape.
Only to be baited out of the oil spill
with prozac, hospital bracelets,
and a cute group therapist.

But you've got a swell window on the world.
Night strips and bares her black prophesies,
which you transcribe with iron clarity
and glass precision, that filters up
to grace mahogany shelves,
while your orchid face rests with the dregs.

Erin Lynn Cates

Tidal

Mother I believe you are an ocean.
The weight of your water exhausts me.
Sometimes I think you would have me
be your moon. I've been here too few years to direct your flow.
Mother I know how you sleep when you think you are alone.
Last night I heard you moan
over and over in the dark like a child or a lover.
I don't know how to hold you.
What unimaginable force could cradle the sea?
What monstrous pair of arms could take
the Pacific into their embrace and what voice
could ever carry over all that green-black
liquid to whisper
hush
hush?

Melissa D. Chandler

The Mug

Roy looked into the once frosty mug,
now it is old, tired, dirty

Just like Roy's life.

He had everything, a house, a wife, and a boat.
Now . . . nothing

he owned the biggest and best of everything
money could buy. Now . . . nothing

The mug had stolen his life in a dreadful turn around

He had paid for the mug
and HE HAD PAID FOR THE MUG

Still at the bar, Roy stared at the bottom
of the mug with guilt and odium,

and the mug stared right back.

Corey Micheal Sikula

Muriel Rukeyser's Voice

How she dwarfed her office, just sitting there,
large with sibyl knowledge: she knew who I was
and who I wasn't and what I needed.
She transcribed words, then forgot about them,
on a "virtually virgin" computer she gave Richard Howard.
His poem repeats her words, and now again she speaks to me:
The more you love yourself the more you are your own worst enemy.
Doing it is the only proof of ability.

She guides me, advice from the grave on tape.
It plays as I walk this smoky fall day,
when the air, like her office, smells of bread.

Marilynn Talal

The Two O'clock Rain

Gazing 360 degrees, look out searching, listening,
Falling and making a hollow sound against my jacket.
Amongst the trees is a steamy haze,
Where the only sound to hear is rain.

On normal occasions, a generator can be heard;
It's distracting, but not polluting.
Tonight, that same generator drips like one mere cricket,
Over 100 feet away.

Nature's song plays on; it ranks near the top of the charts.
For the first time in a long time, the night air has turned warm.
What I once despised is forever changed
An event worthy of the term, "Religious Experience."
Rain, in one session, earned a new-found respect in my life.

Phil Simpson

Royal Memory

Small hands patiently etch,
plotting a course of tradition.
Little feet stir gravels,
searching for rocks in perfect condition.

Tiny fingers testing texture, weight, and grip
slide two prime candidates into front pocket.
Tongue licks rosebud of upper and lower lip,
as arm slowly draws back, then tosses.

A smooth, flat stone lands in square number one.
Broad smiles break across faces of innocence.
Feet take turns jumping, first two then one.
A single leap clears a moon of no consequence.

Triumphant shouts carried indoors on the wings of the wind,
draw a crowd to my side at the window
—where watching brought flashes of a childhood friend.

B. D. Hensley

Ballade

Pale and clear as ocean water,
she looked at her green-as-of-late lover
and wondered why she fell in love.
That newly-met charm had long since faded
with none to take its place.
Where was the one whom she'd kissed
in the rain seems-like-years ago?
That hot spring rain that doused everything but their intentions.
Their wet clothes clinging like a second skin.
"It's OK," he whispers "but do not distance yourself
and say it's because my hands are empty.
They're as full as they ever were,
you simply no longer desire their contents.
We've changed, from violet to blue and red
and yes I'm sorry and no I don't hate and
maybe in a year you'll be under clouds and
I'll be in a valley and I'll think of you and smile.
But that rainy day has long since passed
and I refuse to fight with time.

Ricardo A. Vila-Roger

Lake Tahoe's Persistence

Past the Indian merchant who showcases his hand-crafted beads,
calypso music prances around my ears.
Past the petite Baptist church on the outskirts of Carson City,
ribbons of stardust dot the horizon.
Past the shy horse who grazes by herself,
the wind grows Herculean.
Past the questions of restless children on Jefferson Street,
my replies mosaic across my mouth.
Should I recycle my memories for tomorrow
or store them in my walk-in closet for my scrapbook?
Cilantro and oregano decorate the cabarets
and the Two Guys from Italy sign still seems brand-new
after the celebration of their 20th anniversary.
Circuses of pigeons wing their way toward the beach
as I leave the empty bench,
and snips of old-fashioned harmony satisfy my painting.

Lulu J. Yu

The Beneficiary

The dying trees sway in the gentle, toxic breeze.
The waters of a once beautiful stream slowly trickle by.
And a young child sits upon the shore and sobs.
An observer to the foul remnants of a land in desperate ruin.
As he looks on, his father takes a final, fatal breath.
So does he cry. A desperate, pleading cry.
Knowledge comes to him.
He sadly, reluctantly accepts his inheritance.
He has become,
The beneficiary.

Laura Lynn Place

Tribute to October

October fields lie bathed in Autumn sunshine;
Refreshed from Summer's heat by September's rain.
Orange pumpkins lie in fields
Waiting to be loosed from vines by eager hands,
And turned into spicy pies or scary Jack-0-Lanterns!
Apples, red and golden, are piled into baskets;
Some to be crushed into cider or find their way into a juicy pie.
But I intend to eat at least one that is still warm from the sun.
Shocks of corn dot the landscape in a field or two.
I know that the farmer who made them is sentimental
And is reminiscing earlier, simpler days.
The shadows are growing long, now, and the nip in the air
Reminds me of last night's frost. I will stay here until it's dark
And watch the harvest moon rise out of the eastern sky
And remember other years, long past.

J. Jo Ann Creitz

A Visit with Dad

Sign says; "St. John's, city of the dead."
Journey past the brownstone tenement district
as flat single stones signal stacked caskets
and weed encroachment masks identities.
Row-houses of stand up markers butt to butt
are followed by the high-rise condos
where caskets and urns, embedded in walls
have stone terraces for flowers.
Dad reclined in the suburbs.
His bit of the of the Olde Sod,
just big enough for his tomatoes and cabbage
had a clear view of the "Country estates."
There marble benches between Gothic columns
framed statues of Angels and Saints.
St. Anthony stood on the largest plot.
A little stone bird perched on His hand.
An apparent role model for Nature's own.
Dad thought it smaller than the Vatican,
but only because Popes had more money.

William R. Thompson

Liberation

I swim in a sea of black velvet
Floating on my back
Gazing up at the vastness I have created
I glide around gracefully, magically
Like a creature born to fulfill this destiny
No one knows about this different world, only me
And no one ever will
It's a secret I treasure dearly
Locked up in my heart with a gilded key
My own music box in my soul
The ballerina dancing only for me
And when the music stops and darkness envelopes
She just keeps dancing
The dance of someone not being judged
The dance of someone who has been liberated
It appears the box is closed and the music stopped
But I will never stop dancing
Gliding around in a sea of black velvet
Doing a dance only I can see

Lindsey Nichole Knutson

Dust

This poem is dedicated to the greatest of all healers, time itself.

I sweep dust streaks on the tiles,
shapes remind me of hands held,
time spent in a wistful world,
unlike those of Huxley and Bradbury.
Swept away,
it is a burden I still carry.

A light wind blows gently on the marble,
dusty images of memories mold,
the harder hours held onto fold,
into a dark day where you are no more.
Whisked away,
it is a burden that keeps me raw.

Rain, a quiet shower begins to fall,
dust-filled drops soon disappear
as the torrent trickle becomes quite clear,
past love and its leaving start to thin.
Washed away,
it is a burden that no longer keeps me in.

Grant Daniel Muir

Paradise

Mediterranean sea breeze
Flutters my soul within.
Ember sparks of lightening clash,
While wild horses run free at daybreak.
Thousands of mahogany butterflies
Course passionately throughout my veins.
Moonlight kisses smother me
In a faceless sky of rose petals.
Endless dragonflies
Whispering wordlessly in my ear.
Fervent rainbows endelved within
Each grain of sand I touch.
White, line bed sheets
Passionately waiting on a blood-red moonbeam.
Sweet surrenders of English-tea
Tempt me in my uncarpeted hallway.
Torrents of billowing smoke
Rage within each breath I intake.
A dying thistle pierces my every thought
Effortlessly consuming paradise.

Nicole Andrea Pusateri

Guinevere in Geometry I

With majestic grace
the demure maiden enters yet another squalid chamber,
heedless of her fawning blue-jeaned ladies-in-waiting
who bustle and giggle
and encompass her.

Suspended from a pallid throat on a silver chain
she wears the gilded crest
by which her first Lancelot has pledged himself.

With a lily-like hand
the golden band she nestles to her breast,
sighs, and dreams of misty cloistered trysts
and a gallant paramour . . .

Until the clattering of a brazen alarum
rudely awakens her to a stark present,
to endure alone the onslaught of unemotional logic
and chalk-forged angle edges,
honed for cleaving perfect dreams.

Manuel Mello

Choice to Ponder

Falling conscientiously,
chairmen of my own loss.
Doll, rag excuse for a girl,
in a thought too deep for bedroom talk.

Elbow as skinny as an antler,
chances to pierce gluttenous reality.
I make down-to-Earth,
a place where only spiders creep.

He calls me clown and dreamer.
He dislikes that I brush verses,
like a water horizon,
dancing on my own choices.

I set him to the side,
with pen, paper, and two thumbs to twiddle.
"Circle the thoughts worth hearing,
my sanity has a wanderlust."

Summer Alena Stapley

Remember

My Mother used to plait my hair
In the kitchen on a Saturday morning . . .
After it was freshly washed and pressed . . .

Royal Crown or Dixie Peach hair grease
she would use on her fingertips . . .

I remember the coolness of her fingers, as I sat
by the hot stove. My Mother used to plait
my hair for Sunday . . . go meet'in that's church you know.
And, she'd roll my bangs with a hot
curling comb. My Mother used to plait my hair
. . . in the kitchen as I sat on the chair . . .
with the heat of Summer and the smell of
fried greasy hair . . .

Royal Crown, or Dixie Peach . . .
my Mother, hot Summers, and me.

Urith Lynn Walker

His Absence Haunts This Cafe.   Discuss.

No one saw him leave, the thin and fragile
Carcass and the heave of broken bones.
Too long in exile from discussion was his
Downfall, stood still when he should have been
Long gone, back to talk with life of
Justice done instead of sucking all remains
Of Truth from topics since abandoned
By the rest. Thinking, often frightened,
Was what killed him, took him far from where
Acceptance filled him, leaving only
Dust upon the table where he ate,
Which no one could be bothered to remove.

S. McGregor Milne

African Violet

Seems like 100 years has passed
Velvety flesh has evolved into wrinkles
Black and Beautiful . . . as rich as cocoa
Ancestry of our Motherland, but now a native
of The Land of Liberty
Long shimmering locks . . . sparkles with specks of grey
African Violet
Glancing through her looking glass
the windows of the soul reveal years of
intellect . . . abstractions of ethnic unions . . .
When she walks she strides with grace from
years of performing the Juba dance . . .
Silk wrappings atop her head balanced with
perfect precision. . .clothed in a luxurious
afghan which holds rich hues of heritage . . .
Seems like 100 years has passed . . .
African Lady, Black woman, African Violet . . .

Lutisha Rena Corbin

Redolent Emotion

My hands are of brief and subtle endings
Torn by the choice taken entirely within
They caress the air (without absolution)
With wind beating softly against my fingers
With these hands are the epitome of my being
Never have I forsaken this hedonism
(curled up inside me like a ball)
For it has been too precious to throw away
This redolent emotion has contained me
Poured its wine into the blood of my veins
And with this provenance, found and spoken
I can keep my hands in the fold
(from which they keep)

Beth Anna Elderkin

The Old Photo

I thought I was invisible in a way that dogs
would not bark or even lift an ear—this was
when I got back from India.
I thought birds would not be afraid
and would land on my shoulders.
I was wrong about a lot of things. The rest is private.
At this point my only concern is the
seemingly endless rehearsal of Joy,
the mortal perfumed combat and the same
eternal story over and over
and over the way it was when we were seventeen.
They say it is a life wasted,
and maybe they're partly right,
but we all die soon enough.
So now we will again look at each other
in that shyly desperate trance,
and in the end it will be part of the same eternal Smile
written on the faded photo
lying on the kitchen table
taken just before the accident.

Mark Rudolph

Poem on the Fly #1

So I'm on the train and there's this
kid who started talking about Jesus to
a woman sitting down, him standing,
she kept saying, "Excuse me?"
Because she couldn't quite hear his soft crazy voice
Above the noise of the train his skin so black
so smooth, silken. This beautiful black man
He was a child once I kept thinking
She was a child once.
This guy sitting next to her avoiding the cadence of their
Nutty conversation he was a child once.
So there I am swaying and holding
on dreaming, dreaming,
holding on swaying
Listening to this crazy, crazy
Speak and feeling the rhythm of the
Train and all of a sudden,
I am flying above them looking down on them.
Free, not part of them, but rising outside of the
Metal confines of the train car.

Lisa Walsh-Miller

Train Fever

There's nothing sexy about them except the
way he has his hand on her knee. A heavy
silver name-tag bracelet hangs from his
wrist. Their faces are deeply lined with
the stories of their lives. What language is
it that they speak when they lapse away from
English? They lean close and do a crossword
book all through the long journey and laugh
together like adolescent lovers. She has
blue-veined legs. They smoke a lot. They
don't have much luggage, just one bag each.
I imagine them checking into some foreign
hotel 40 years earlier, using false names
easily thought up by passion-driven people
with secrets. I can't help but wonder what
keeps them together, at the rim of their
lives. And yet, there it is, the gentle,
sensual way his hand rests on her knee for
the longest time and how comfortable she is,
they both are, in full and public view.

Sam Fonte

The Lost One

"Chumbalala Chumbalalalaika . . ."
She dances through the streets
Empty eyes seeing nothing but sun glare,
Once girls voice screeches out of tune.
Old men shuffle slowly by.
Who are they? How, when, and why?
Nimble mind runs from confusion.
Aged and humbled feet stumble.
Struggle to keep up with the dance,
But refuse to give up the chase.
Her sightless eyes see firelight,
whirling gypsies, clashes of red wine . . .
Sudden focus reveals a concerned nurse.
What?
Faces flash behind her eyes,
Once a girl once a hag
Lost forever in an ocean of confusion . . .
flipping channels.
My lost one.
She sings: "Chumbalala . . . Chumbalalaika . . ."

Cecily Leokadia Ciezkowski

Shattered

We lived in a house of glass built on egg-shells,
and monsters' stomping timbre would shatter our fragile nest.
He roared out in a voice like thunder when he saw you, Mama.

Blood.

So much blood, Mama.
Look at how red I am.
You were so white that night. So pale.
I could see the tiny highways
of veins that mapped out your body.
I thought if I carved out a path on my own,
maybe I could have found you again.
Now, I am in your arms,
surrounded by a home of flesh and sinew
and vibrant reds and blues.

Don't let me go, Mama. I'll just sink . . .
sink into your softness and float away.

Amanda N. Tinnin

Driven

"I hate him," she said.
"Obviously," I said.
"Let's get the hell out of here," she said
as she tossed me the keys to her Toyota.
It was not my place to mention the remaining
hours of the workday, or that hate was not
the four letter word she meant to use.
We walked to her car. She grinned.
"What a mom!" she said, referring to me,
to him, to her, doesn't matter. "Let's go," I said.
And that was the first time we drove the demons out.

Melissa Lucey

Event

About last night,
my strength on the bedside table
like a slow clock,
a car hitting me without the slightest
indication of ruining its attractiveness—
by its taillights
it had robbed me of every
self-consciousness for making anger.
How can I hate myself
in being involved in such a cause-and-effect
revealing the beautiful machinery of the city?

Brian Fontanilla Brotarlo

Bulldozer

Rippers lowered into the earth thrusts
forward parting the dirt like Moses the sea.
An awesome force of metal gnawing along the surface.
A massive horsepower of energy pushing the
rubble into a growing heap of clay and dirt.
Fuming dust leaves a trail as the dozer
gouges its way into the heart of the ground.
The driver continually squeezing the energy
out of the machine to complete the job.
A man controlled beast of brutality toward the earth.
Synchronized reactions operate the depth of
the rippers and blade. A kinetic force from
man to machine to earth.
The surface around trembles as the mastiff
machine rumbles its way along.
And when it stops the silence is deafening.
The dozer rests like a prehistoric fossil
alien to the surrounding landscape.

John Boom

Roses

She thinks of love as she pours hot coffee
And adds nutrasweet,
Masking the bitterness,
An artificial sweetness
White woven in the black atomic lattice.
With his wine tinted roses by her bedside,
Once brimming with the vigor of life,
But now cracked and pale at the edges,
Spilling its life energy over the table top.
She drinks, cupping both hands around the mug,
As if the heat would be transferred,
Letting the steaming solution,
Travel down her throat,
Scalding the taste buds
'Til taste is reduced to the dull throb
Of liquid running over solid.

Lu Zheng

Life Companions

Sitting Indian-style in the growing green grass,
Faces to the sky.
Watching the powder blue sky with its white cotton candy clouds,
Fingers entwined.
Surrendering to the sweet smelling breeze that keeps things temperate;
Blowing his scent my way.
Courting alter, working children, grandchildren retiring,
Swinging lazily on the rusty porch chaise for two,
Faces to each other.
Exploring the lines drawn of wisdom and experience,
Fingers entwined.
Sipping on a sweating glass of iced tea,
Blowing our scent in the air.

Jeannie L. Koerber

Herself

She paints her words in purple across a vellum sky—
silly mouse, trying to mimic Monet,
when her tiny feet could spawn symphonies all her own
of bird prints—delicate, female strokes
of lavender, apricot, cerulean in the sand,
of cracks between floorboards cradling crumbs.

Her head cocked, she hears
how each mark chants her mouse's life.

Not wanting to think herself rodent or rat,
or even an Emily Dickinson mouse,
she scampers across blue-braided rugs
and hardwood bleached by the sun,
inside one house, one window, one wall, painting purple.

Kathy O'Fallon

Custer County Line

Lonely was the life back in 1809
where cattlemen struggled
and gunmen at crime.
Six months was their wait
for that Custer County Line,
perfumed baths scented the air
hot pack towels and a shave here and there.
Word had it then the main line was in
and the Custer County Line was running thin.
Oh!
That black belly steamer brought a lot of show
built up their business with women and gold.
As men drank hardy and fought for their play
the towns people suffered and stayed away.
Now,
time has drawn its end
from a day of crime and sin,
leaving in the horizon a feeling from within.
That only to blame now was the naked line
that man has built between distance and time.

         Joellen Dawson

Butterflies after a Long Sleep

Rust flakes off the hinges,
and cages wrinkle like stale clothes,
and summer hurts more than other seasons,
and the weather couldn't be brighter,
and hotter,
like chocolate
burning on the tongue.
And now it's exposed—
the dying porpoises, a crimson caloric intake,
adolescents sucking on bottles, a kissing of frogs,
forgotten closet doors and headless dolls,
an audience thrown on the stage
of your prying eyes
that represent the sun.
Wriggle around with sharp pins,
pierce the obesity, bleach the innocence,
sew the setting horizon
that still bleeds
like a fat leech.

         Bryan Nelson

The Infantry Officer

We came across him as we were laying wire,
a black flow on his tunic from his throat.
A good shot.
His right hand
rested across his breast
still clutching his field glasses,
his left hand outstretched
lain open to the sky.
On his face, at last, peace, as if in his
last moment he had seen Heaven.
He had surely known Hell.
The sculptor's hand could accomplish not
what laid before us in the Belgian mud.
Someone spoke up, said they had known him,
"A music teacher, I think, from Kent."
And none of us could help but wonder what
the Kaiser hoped to gain by killing a music
teacher from Kent.
And we continued on our way
laying wire as we went.

         Joe Gerard

Dimschor Street

There are no prophets reading scriptures
And the sidewalks are silver clean
As piles of glamour magazines intercept the sky

The nomads are throwing a party outside
Their cigarettes glow like a thousand small lights
Reflecting the stars above Dimschor Street tonight

Merchants sell photographs of other peoples lives
And there's a full garbage eclipse on the fourteenth floor
As old drunkards laugh and sharpen their knives
Outside the sickly liquor shop door

Late at night the curtains shut
And rain showers silence on Dimschor Street
Leaving behind no trace of any pain

I look back through the crystal window
As the bus fades away from a hidden land of sin
And sitting here I realize
Dimschor Street will never look the same to me again

         Daniel Levine

Blue in Green

Staring at the world through a windshield
darkened by droplets of jazz . . .

The first full notes won't resound at all
unless you love that piano
the way you love a favorite yellow dog,
the keys licking your fingers, notes that know every
groove and ridge of your fingertips
the way you know myriad eights and shades of touch
and force to coax cannonballs and ice or velvet smiles
from ivory for every note to lope and amble
in the tame and collaring sway of melody and empathy
for every chord of barrel-chested bass and piano
to dance in slow, casual gravity until the gentle
measured release arrives—trumpets unseaming
the heart's crimson curtain to coax dry the wet white
feathers of the uncaged soul, a brass, breathy angel
unballing itself, darting out past the hood ornament,
taking wing and fluttering . . .

         Michael Pacholski

Holocaust

Acres of pines ramrod straight; charred, barren, devoid of life
Stand as sentinels—weathered witnesses of a devouring heat
Raging flames and choking smoke, death and desolation
Reminders of the delicacy of life, privation and pain

Once a flicker, a smoldering ember
Formed by ignorance and indifference
Erupts into a fury, an all-consuming blaze
Dismissed as a mere inconvenience—transient and trivial
Eventual destruction unchecked by human interference

Too late, the war waged
Exacts the lives of those who combat the fire.
The flames extinguished, the damage done
Victory tempered by appalling loss,
A price paid in blood and tears.

Years later a rich carpet of green spreads o'er the forest floor.
Tender pines begin their ascent—life continues, nature rebuilds.
Stark against the cloudless sky scarred and battered pines remain;
Hoping the memory of past devastation
Protects the young woodland from a similar fate.

         Jolyn Twelves

Mr. Salt

He wears a peacock feather in an old mastic hat
Wearing red lipstick, sucking on a candy cane
He knew the devil intimately, for he wears the mask on his right cheek
An open black shirt, crucifix around his neck
Black jeans with a razor in his pocket, boots that look older than time.
He looks like he's been around the world exotic is his smell
Long black and silver hair tied in a ponytail.
He smiles at me my flesh begins to crawl
He is irritating the passengers on the bus
Passing on his words of wisdom, nobody's listening
Except for me, the words are weird, the language obscure
And the reality of his wisdom hangs heavy upon my heart
The bus stops and he set off, with a tip of his hat
But these nothing there, for the desert is wide and lonely
And before the bus moves on with its busy, restless people
I look back and he is nowhere in sight.
And I am not surprised.

Carrie Ann Kawa

Going On Four Months Now

Mom & I shelled the last of the beans Dad planted before his death
A truly awesome experience knowing that phase of our life was over.
Last weekend my sister weeded the remains of the garden.
She harvested the last Vidalia onions from last fall's planting . . .
That last harvest was gigantic!
From that time he spent with hoe in hand
And oftentimes on his knees . . .
Onwards 'til his death,
We marveled at the energy Dad mustered just to plant his garden.
None of us know what was in his heart, or on his mind . . .
We just know we benefited from the love he put into the soil.
He must have known his time was near
For he poured all his sweetness into those beans & onions.
None have ever come close to the texture and the taste of this love . . .
So tenderly nurtured by his hands,
in the composted soil he diligently
harvested, never wasting anything,
finding use in everything . . . for our benefit.

Gloria Gastellum Rapp

Silver Shoestrings

Thanks Chris, you've been so helpful.
You act in transparent hatred . . .
blinded by the fantasy of another piercing attention deficit—
I lied.
You told me that . . .
and I'm d*mn good at it, too . . .
I even believed my own little cucumber melon scented diversions—
You eyes are cheaply clothed with my sight . . .
my name still graces your balled tongue—
My ears are not forbidding to my mind, nor to my heart . . .
colored as your eyes are—
You are infatuated by my last move . . .
and so the lust for another grew in a temptress' eyes—
I'm your temptress.
Nevermind my body being the path once wondered down
and viewed as another go, if bluely desired.
Well, I'm not up for another spin . . .
I've found my go-round—
Hats off to you for making it happen.
And if you keep quiet,
I'll toss you a shiny nickel . . .

Amy Jennifer Peterson

Mountains

A mountain of shoes even scarier than the mountain of bones
Little feet walked the earth in those shoes
Pretty soon little feet became little bones and little skulls
I could taste the bitterness of hate here among the mountains

Anna Smushkovich

Careful Gwendolyn

The fire of the world burning
onto the pages of your journal,
your letters to lost lovers
who knelt to your written wealth,
mad from your distance and
direct assault on history and
human artifice and myth.
How wise you were at twenty-two,
how you knew that commitment was
criminal, that the artist must suffer
in arms of many.
Now, Osiris sits on a sphinx at the foot of
her bed, drawing out your magic,
a phone pressed to her chest.
Could Glenn be conducting his breath
or maybe the cries of Milt?
You listen and absorb and lie still
because your lips suck dry the bottle
of our undoing.

Brandon Flowers

The Peach

The fruit,
turned to fragrance,
invaded my body through my nostrils
and its nectar rolled on my tongue
with tales of late summer sweetness
and forbidden love.

He came to me first
through my eyes,
all golden,
glistening skin,
with the promise of treasures
in every pocket.

When he spoke,
I heard ancient voices
calling me to battle—
glory belongs to those
who brave the dragons.

And then
turned into a peach.

Marly Moil

Farewell Fanfare

And I'll play the last note,
and it will dance in the breeze—
a two-step, then a waltz.
It will prance out into the field
and catch a radio typhoon and boogie
across the northern lights, flipside
weaving through lost residents of
urban legends finding the tranquility
of the brook-streams to their liking;
and it will end up in a wooden house
with a picket fence of candy canes,
shingles of salvation—
and in this hallowed heaven
this echoing rhapsody will find
a pair of ears to soothe and caress,
and it will lie to rest
perched on top of your nose,
staring straight into misty black holes
of unmistaken, silent summer.

Amartya Basu

Sixpence

It is the sense of time passing.
I make the programme of the testament
Like the ones who burn, burn, burn

As falling on the floor.
A part of spontaneous melodies
That was hammering in my head.

It felt so surreal.
So the heart be right,
One could go up the hill of St. Lucy.

Looking for a elemental place,
How many people do look at themselves
In vain mirrors?

Botanical curved line, waved desert—
Those are all so alive.
The dew is my usual breakfast.

I do not need visionary things,
I carry all that in myself.
One copper on the tablecloth.

Yuko Ishii

Looking up at the Stars

Coca-cola on gracious ice
saltwater under the sojourning sun
black bikinis
skin starts to burn like a fantasy
protected from the wind by the glass

Blue and green eyes
the windows of the soul
Mexican art
thinking of a black witch
saw her soul

The ship in anchor looked like paradise
the bay was paradise like a sanctuary
a place to escape
red bikinis
Catalina Island

Another coca-cola
saltwater and love
if it were different the times
really beautiful eyes
looking up at the stars

George Pettersson

Empty Lullabies

Down long, sterile corridors
I followed silence—stony, cold
To automatic sliding doors
That expelled me into the black void
Of a night gone as lifeless
As the small, frail form
Lying somewhere beyond my reach
In the hospital's chill, foreign halls
The featherlike weight of the clothes he wore
Just hours before
When there was feeling
And warmth . . . and hope
Mocks the crushing emptiness of the void
That is my soul
I go home to piles of clothes
You'll never wear
And hum empty lullabies
While pieces of my shattered soul slide
As soft as you
Across my heart

Betty Sue Taylor

Lovebug Lore

Lo, amber-poled drift 'way,
Scurried 'long hot, late-summer breezes.
Quite peculiar, though, these they are,
And lead to question reason.

Black as pitch 'tween these crowns of amber,
Imbued by melancholy oneness.
'Tis naught sublime to be they are,
Whilst death ebbed a life: the treason.

And now he hangs 'til glory wind
Could try decouple pang,
Though mercurial gusts shall blow them far
Her trail remains the same.

She dies, ascribed, dead-season.

David Eric Thomas

Mexico

As I drove to Mexico
my father invaded my mind with
abstract notions of consequence

The periodic long shadows
of towering cacti did little
to shade my car from the paternal sun

Red and purple took over
the white haze of midday
as a sinking sun calmed me

Mexico became a fragment
in a larger dream of giants
and cool air surrounding me

The highway turned black
the howling absorbed my lingering father
final escape would come before dawn

Karen McBurney

Peninsula of Lost Souls

I climb 1,000 stairs
to the temple of the sun and
find nothing
but a stone idol stained
with centuries of virgin blood.
Beauty of place tempers alarm
at horrific deeds long past.
Would I dive into dark waters of a cenote
to reclaim hapless maidens
from watery graves?
It rains and I make a philodendron hat.

Sheila Panzone

Memories

Wrap tightly round your finger
A string of thoughts and words
Of kindness, love and laughter,
Of trees and flowers and birds.

Recalling love and beauty
Draws deep into our soul,
Uncovers dreams and joys we've had,
New goals sometimes unfold.

Each memory brings before us
The kind of life we've made,
Draws some into the sunlight,
Leaves others in the shade.

We can't go back and change those things
Nor how the world has turned.
We can be thankful for our lives
And all those things we've learned.

Gertrude May

Sin

I want to blacken you
dress you in ash
you said
spiraling galaxies in my hand
your eyes-amber and musk
my wrists locked
I want to blacken you
like a curse
you said
putting out your cigarette butt
on my endless yards
of canned snow
and I bit
my lip
hard
as blood roses
seeped lovely as sin
along my thigh
blacken you
as you'll blacken your vow

Gabriela M. Debita

The Shower

From the flat splash of morning's
unrippled basin, I rise
to an inflexible reflection.
I'm only halfway to halfway,
so they say, unless I fall prey
to terminal illness
or catastrophe.
I never believed in earthquakes,
but the man in my bones—
the flaking, crumbling man—
quivers and shakes
when he turns from the quick
to the dying
to hear how they speak.
The steaming shower has almost
shrouded the vulnerable
nude in the mirror. Faceless,
he feels delicate, mortal
and scrubs with unusual vigor
to get clean.

Scott Yung Kim

High Heels

Little girl from next door
in your mother's high heels
oceans too big for you,
yet managing somehow
to edge down the sidewalk.
Too soon you'll have
a pair all your own
to show off those legs,
leaving childhood behind
with the kindling shape of them.
Right now I want those small running feet
with the silk hair above,
the face full of wonder.
You'll be old soon enough,
your beauty a trouble
to all those who see you,
your manner self-conscious,
so terribly proud,
little girl going by
with the click-clack-clatter
of your mother's heels . . . .

Ghadi Al Jolen

Grown Up

Somewhere under my big girl bed
there is a forgotten child
with big brown eyes
and berry-red cheeks
that are feverish from climbing trees.
She plays with my old pink teddy bear
and my puzzles,
with only a few missing pieces,
and my board games
left in favor of Spin the Bottle.
She and my stiff-limbed,
ringlet-curled dolls
enjoy my cracked tea set
and the Easy Bake Oven
that didn't work
like the commercial said it would.

Billie Jo Bales

1942

A sea of handkerchiefs
hug the shore
little girls blow kisses
to sailors—
little boys,
perhaps just barely men,
puff out the chests,
wearing a country's glorified bravery.
A man with a short cigar
sucks at the juices of Patriotism
and jots down memoirs
that will later be translated
into a headline:
"America Gathers to Wish Her Boys Well"
accompanied by a flash,
so that the moment
is suspended
forever
in black and white.

Joey Lee Nicholls

Tropical Torrent

The rain fell slant-ways that day
Sending poisoned arrows down
Deep under my umbrella.
And lost in its onslaught, my heart
Was searching . . . searching
For a face in which to shelter.

All around in the dismal streets
The gathering pools of grey
Were reflecting their sadness upwards . . .
And the cold disdain of the wind . . .
The cold disdain of the wind

Left me to wonder:
What else is there in the world
But days that are too wet . . . too dry?
Days spoilt by love's sweet overflow?
Days spent without love's joy?

Emery A Cournand

Idol

You breed coffee-filter love.
It percolates and drips,
Spreads and permeates.
It slips through the filter
Into the empty mugs of the masses
Needing their caffeine-love fix,
Eager to drink your love,
A sip of you.

Amy Bragg

The Girl and the Trees

there is something
that is solemnly sad
about the girl
that stands amidst the trees
she bends to scratch
her legs
and remembers the lovers
that she once knew
the lover who drove
her to the park
and watched her walk amongst
the trees
there is something
so beautiful about the
trees
and her half-naked
back
as she bends to scratch her
legs and mingle
with the trees

Bridgette Acklin

Hidden Treasures

Every now and again
Maybe once in a lifetime
Fate offers you a wonderful journey
Offers you a new beginning
But Fate is a subtle creature
He will not offer it as a ticket on a train
Or a key to a door
But carefully disguise it
Giving you a chance to miss it
For Fate is also a selfish creature
He will present it to you in everyday things
You may find it in a smile
Or in the soft touch of a hand
You may smell it in a rose
Or hear it in a sigh of content
You may hold it in your arms
Or may feel it in a warm breath
Cherish completely these everyday things
For in them may lie the path to happiness
Hidden very carefully by Fate

Jeffrey Todd Taylor

Symphony Notes

Black and white, symphony notes
On ragged tattered pages
Carry weeping willow memories
That were lost
Along with my rain-cloud soul
They rise and fall
Becoming tides
Which ebb and flow
With the waxing and waning
Of the hunter's moon
While oceans of roses
Snow white, pearl pink
Crimson red, golden yellow
Laugh lazily
In the brilliant noon day sun
There will be no silence
As my internal melody and harmony
Go jetting through the Milky Way
And are uplifted
To the Gates of Heaven

Nancy Pawley

Olde(?) Williamsburg

The metered barricade of years
Becomes an open gateway when
Across the morning's sunlit green
Musicians call militia men.

Aroused, the ghostly regiments,
As in some secret spiral spun,
Quicken to familiar notes
To march again to fife and drum.

From shadowed vaults of days gone past
A phantom breeze unfurls a sigh,
Then stirs the leaves of yielding trees
In hushed memorial lullaby.

Now present scenes and those to come
In soft suffusion intertwine
With muffled hints of memories
In shifting streams of liquid time.

Thus history's longing for itself
Plucks threads from life's unraveled seams
And weaves on looms of yesterday
The fabric of tomorrow's dreams.

Marion Jean Blaney

Overtired

I'm tired of eating
grilled cheese sandwiches
in my Ikea chair and staring at
blank white walls of sadness.
I want to be noticed,
not for my auburn hair
or my pink flat lips.
I'm tired of pointless miniskirts.
As I walk down Morris Avenue
men in dump trucks are whistling
and tooting their horns.
Natural beauty is what I wish for.
I'm tired of forbidding my habits—
my fingernail biting and
twenty minute showers.
I'm tired of being considered a whore.
I dream in colors like black and white,
where makeup is an illusion,
and hair dye is not important.
I'm tired of false imaginings.

Beth Goldflam

Lebanese Music

Softly it strums across the heart.
It plays.
It gains momentum.
It dances in the air.
It exists.
The composer makes his song.
In Lebanon he makes his career.
He makes his art.
Christian and Muslim influences.
War and peace.
We want our children to be happy.
To live the good life.
The music is the human voice.
It gathers dreams together.
It swirls.
It sways, breathes, cries softly.
It rises like smoke.
How tiny the country is.
Like a prayer. Come, the music says.
Ascend with me.

Joan Eyles Johnson

Pursuing Home

Searching for shells on the beach
my mother settles one she likes
in the plastic drug store bag. At home
the new ones will be placed
with the baskets of others from year
after year in Sanibel. Once,
when I was young, I liked
a small yellow chip from a shell
broken in transit. Now,
each new batch includes
a perfect yellow shell, wrapped
carefully and given to me
on tissue. She doesn't see
it was the raw, unfinished
element that drew me; the edge
remaining hidden until the break.

Julie A. Damman-White

Beach Combing

Soloman's fingers
knit through disassembled sand
and only bother with the seashells
plucking nacre-cradled talismans away
finding treasures in gull-blackened shores
discarded homesteads of bottom-feeders
and slides them into his pocket
(that cradles the universe)

Chris J. Gyngell

Josepha's Hands

Josepha's hands
are worked to the bone,
fingers crooked
like the limbs
of a tree.

Josepha,
her hands bound to a Bible
and holy blue beads

Josepha,
a saint of sorts
a martyr of marriage—
a mother

Ann Gorman

Yet Another Surprise

We don't sleep much, you and me,
but link one moment to the next,
one breath to the last,
all night long.

And rising is our martyrdom,
our duty, by God—
the comforting toaster,
gentle ringing telephones.
It's about coarse hair in the shower drain.

We pull rabbits from hats
all day long.
Lately the crowd seems a little thin.
Where is your makeup?
I haven't shaved in days.

Like that night in the kitchen,
or your raven's hair wild
in the forced Sunday light.

No, we don't sleep much, you and me,
linking trees in careful solitude.
What welcome company.

Zachary Kelly

Little Tangerine

Winter's here
my only memory of sunshine
orange citrus globes
I relieve them of their loosened skin
juice slides down my palms
sharp sweet smell washes
over me in waves
I think happiness, and you,
and tea in bed, and noses red
from the cold air of our drafty house
All this memory in one such tiny fruit

Sat-su-ma, sweet torture
peeling one is
peeling the layers
from my heart.

Katherine Miller

A Child's Ignorance

The clicks and clacks of Plinko chips
turning and twisting, spiraling downward
like King Lear's fate into place.

Clapping hands applauding merely
for the cameras as blinking signs
dictate like Hitler
the behavior of the audience.

Dear old Larry's winnings,
like his debt-filled life
sum up to less than nothing,
bankruptcy filed after taxes.

Yet still young Davy's eyes are glued,
his mind nanvely drifting into daydreams
of being the next contestant.

Christopher M. Biscuiti

Judgment

Accusing gargoyle,
Seated high upon your pedestal
Of lies and deceit,
Haughty incrimination
Etched deeply in your cold facade.
Turn your judgment now to me,
For it is easier to find
Fault in others
Than it is to acknowledge
Your own.

Rachel Fielding

Agate Beach

The sea is an incessant flame
burning at man's shore,
fueling from its fracture.

Think, too, of a tree, grabbing
the ground, breathing in worm sh*t
while its branches lap up sky.

The fruit is semi-precious: agate,
jasper, jade—walnut-sized sand
on this, a Brobdignadian beach.

The hunters come in hordes, from
Ukiah, Eureka—they paint the stones
with hackneyed poems, sell them

from the ramshackle huts on Highway 101.
We bought a few for our aquarium,
thinking to bring a bit of the sea home.

Richard Hamilton Browne

lip treat

it's strange the way
the honey drips
from the corner of her lip
down to the golden pool
at her feet
and he laps it
feeding on the sweetness
drowning in the light
his hands and knees
in a cradle
the soft grass of God
a bright being
she can't see
her eyes glazed with the sap
she cries
thick honey tears
falling on the face of him
molding his features
in the pure state
of ecstasy.

Dezaraye Bagalayos

Fearful Love

Cherubim turn swords,
cast flaming fig leaves
on cursed ground.
With bruised heels,
we labor among the bitten,
festering fruits of our ignorance,
making thorns and thistles of our crowns.
In the sweat of our faces,
a pheromonic resonance.
In our dusty hearts,
skin clad, in cleavage,
we hope to live forever,
flesh closed upon itself,
conceiving sorrow.
Our trees are pleasant to the sight
of gold and onyx stone
and every beast and fowl has its name
except for our nakedness.
In a garden of talking serpents,
cool days, and lying Gods,
I betray you to the voice and hide.

Sam Vaknin

exam!

brief beams stream through my
bamboo shades, a new day dawns,
swarms into my soul . . .

television
laughs at me as I scurry
through bun, coffee—flee!

steadily falling
rain streaming down my lifted
face to taste the wind . . .

slashing winds rip me,
I bow into pure chaos
spring in Chicago . . .

blossom pushes through
broken glass, sad detritus,
ancient glory shines . . .

eyes glued to the screen,
fingers tremble on the board,
my brain must work now . . .

Delphyne Woods

Eliminating Karma

I am always three.
There's no fun in watching,
but it's all I ever do.
I can't explain it, complain it,
any better than that.
Maybe . . . I should cut in,
take the dance away,
run out of the church with bride in tow,
showing courage and confidence,
eliminating karma,
doing what I know is right—
rather than what I believe is right.
But while everyone has their days,
I'll be alone at night,
running out of the church with bride in tow,
showing courage and confidence,
eliminating karma.

Patrick Anthony Giusto

Goddess

She stood before the moon
In awe of its magnificence
Wishing it could be Hers
The moon told her story
as she glided into
the night sky of cobalt
She knew the moon smiled at her
and would follow her only
when kissing the water-sparkling
Making the flow dance with light
When she made love,
to her favorite lover,
the moon disappeared
leaving the sky to the stars.

Danielle Cary Morrison

A Repository for Rusty Nails

I am a repository for rusty nails,
for some reason, I can never throw
them away. They gather
intertwined, chipped-off
flecks of brittle iron collecting
in my bowels. Plaster adhering
to some, sawdust to others,
some end up jotted down
in journals, but most work
their way toward bone, forgotten
eventually but always present.
Always threatening tetanus,
communing with hemoglobin,
becoming indistinguishable from memory
or reflex, from all the redundant
genetic material intertwined
within every cell of my body,
because I cannot throw them away.

Bradley Earle Hoge

Aviary

At breakfast,
I sight a hummingbird at the feeder,
flitting and sipping, nipping
its beak into my sugar water,
strutting its ruby necklace
and velveteen cap.
My daughter bounds down
the stairs—home for the weekend—
coffee only—
wings beating faster than
my eye can see—she sips
and goes.

Wendy Kelly

Tobacco's Last Dance

Tattered tobacco sheaves
hang like antique ladies' dresses
browned with age
and gently dried in brittle folds,
lined up in the bureau barn.

The farmer's glowing pride:
A new ancient collection
of prized crop-gowns,
once worn by his fields,
now waiting to be sold.

They sway with quiet dignity,
The wind stirring up only
a few rustling rumors,
counting down the warm days
they have left before burning away.

Rachel Vater

The First Time

It was not
as they said it would be
those who slide so easily
into bed, into each other

Those who sing that
irresistible duet
the one song that
everyone wants to learn
the um, the oh, the ah

It was
an unexpected struggle
like singing with
a swollen tongue

Jacqueline Nadiger

Underwater

Strength
From barbells
And leg lifts
Could never prepare
Your skin
To hold yourself
Together
When the world around you
Is falling apart
Wiping your tears
Like hands
In a ocean
I drown
To the very bottom
Swimming to the top
Is a joke I told myself
So I guess
I will learn
To breathe underwater

David Armenta

Spiders

It's a good thing
these spider plants don't spring to life,
because if they did,
they'd probably be really p*ssed that
no one ever watered them.

And they would creep into our rooms
at night while we're asleep
on all eight legs
and suck our brains out from our ears.
That's just how I see it happening.

Lisa Wise

Yellow Heat

She stood in the doorway
Of the room he left
A bed and a furnace
Of imperialism

American boys
Took a vacation that year
From courtship
And music concerts on the lawn

To work for the devil summer
In the south
While fathers were proud
And lovers were glad for a cause

When she stood in the doorway
Of the room he left
A bed and a furnace
Satisfied

Scott Donnelly

Travelsick

Bleary with rain
And stations
Obligations running to a tight schedule
I'm sitting even tighter
On this strangely intimate situation.
This standard fare
As jostling the jagged baggage
Of each other
Faceless, nameless
Fellow travellers
Dream of destinations
While dodging the flicker
Of opposing eyes.

And do not sneeze . . . Please!
"Infections go 'round and 'round
On the Circle Line"
(say vital statistics).

And I'm just in this game
To catch a train.

Bernadette Mary Reed

A Voice Undenied

Martyr . . . No,
you did not die
for anyone else,
nor did you part the sea
or make the clouds divide.
There in sandals,
you spoke of honey
and utopian ideals,
red-lettered words
that keep me occupied.
Zealot . . . Yes,
naked in the rain.
Alone, speaking in tongues
foreign to most ears
a voice undenied.
Your visions alive,
colorful still images
flicker across my mind,
though it's been years
since Lenny Bruce died.

David Perry

A Poem for My Husband

For years we went our separate ways,
Living alone in a prison of days,
And at our speaking we both did see,
That with us together, we'd both be free.
Free to live and laugh and love,
At ease with each other as hand in glove.
Truth was allowed to give us our start,
Love will keep us from breaking apart.
I can hardly begin to tell you dear,
How I've longed for love year after year.
A love so kind and gentle and true,
The kind of love I get from you.
I've so much love in my heart to give,
And it's all for you, as long as I live.

Marie Getts

I Hope

For Bill

I hope you find time for smiles today—
    To share a laugh with a friend;
I hope you give yourself something special
    To help your heart continue to mend;
I hope you remember people care about you
    And want you to treat yourself right—
I hope that your intuition lets you feel
    All the times I hug you tight.
I hope you take the opportunity today
    To relax and let yourself be;
I hope that you find a moment
    Where your heart and soul are free.
Please, find the time for smiles,
    For laughter, and self-care
And look within yourself and see what I see—
    Someone very special there.

Dorothy E. Boyden II

My Hiding Place

The stream flows gently, effortlessly
dancing with grace and beauty.
I sit beside it to contemplate
the twists and turns of this life.
It soothes me like a mother rocking
her baby to Brahms' Lullaby.
It's cold and sweet on warm summer days
and twinkles in the sunshine.
It gives life to all things and nourishes
the soul with healing and love.
My quiet hiding place renews me to
continue life's long journey.

Carolyn Pratt-Elliott

Farewell to the Friend

So gently, gently
Sailing off and on a cloud
Started to muse the moon

Farewell rhymes
I wanted to write on the fan
It crashed in my hand

And what would we need more
The sun shines all the time
And it is to us
Not to see it

Those who see
Fly like swans
On a free path of the sun

Swans that fly the endless path
On infinite wings
Have a nice flight little butterfly of mine

Biljana Tripkovic

Earth Gifts Surround Us

Earth gifts surround us
I see the ocean so blue
Beauty of the waves

The majestic hand of God
Mountains so high
I see the sea gulls passing by
I hear the voice of angels singing
Love is in the air

The smell of evergreens
Beauty of a flower
God is everywhere
Whispers of the wind
Freshness of the country air

Reflections of the sunlight
bringing peace throughout the land
stars shine like diamonds in the sky
these are the blessings of God's eternal light

Laurajean McDowell Barbato

Mind's Eye

For Judi, Chuck, Hillary, Rachel

What is it that one does see
Inside one's mind, so private indeed!

What images does one's mind surmise,
Without the world to swiftly revise?

What fantasies quickly come to mind
From daily activities, different in kind?

Perhaps the way one wishes to be perceived,
Interacting with circumstances easily foreseen.

Perhaps a great ruler in days long past,
Perhaps great victories, peace to enhance!

Perhaps a champion skating on ice,
Perhaps the gold medal, not once, but twice!

Perhaps to travel far amongst the stars,
Meeting new life forms well beyond Mars!

Perhaps to travel through space and time,
Perhaps to observe the change in mankind!

To imagine one's life, other than it is,
Better than the best while one did live!

Back to reality where one must see
That better than the best indeed is thee!

Mary Ann Burney

Missing

Where has all the laughter gone?
And all the cheerful music?
All my friends have gone away,
And left me all alone.

The radio still plays,
But the songs seem sadder now;
The house is still and empty,
Just memories left to remind me of bygone days.

I am so lonely now,
My life is so empty.
I have everything I really need,
Food, shelter, & clothing.
I even have a boyfriend,
Even tho' he'd rather watch TV than be with me.

Yet there is something,
Something I cannot name—
    missing.

Caril Crosby

Give It Time

The special people know who they are.
Inside and out you are beautiful
There's a point of view in your mind
Even though you search everywhere
Sometimes it can be hard to find
The only thing you can do is give it time

We share the bond of friendship
Although we want something more
Sometimes against the grain
Will deeply cut you to the core
I guess the only thing we can do is give it time

Inside and out you are beautiful
Don't ever forget who you are
Stand as tall as you can and be counted
Don't let them, your spirit scar
One day you won't have to give it time

Give it time to heal your wounds
Give it time to grow anew
Give it time and you will see
There's a place in my heart for you and me
Just give it time
            Wayne Tink

The Clone and I

What a freaky world this would be
If I saw you as you saw me

There would be no distinction between I and you
For identical faces provide no clue

A reflection has brought me to this conclusion
I'm lost in a world of mass confusion

I inquire out of sheer curiosity
Is that you or is that me?
            Betsy Gilliland

Life's Sugarplums

To my children, who make life sweet
Life's irony, with its twists and turns,
While following our dreams, the lessons we learn.
Choices we make define our paths.
Fate takes its hand; we are at its wrath.
So many times, we are drawn toward,
Only to find the attraction deters.
Searching over and over, time and again;
How many times before we can swallow the truth?
Everything in life tastes bittersweet.
But knowing, and understanding—that's the real treat!
            T. Scheuers

Seeking the Answer

I stand in a land that is said to be free
But when I walk with a bop, people judge me.
By what they see, an unspoken creed of fear
Because they can't lead me into the path of thee.
Controlling with inaudible signs, trying to get mines
So I string these lines of words.
Hopefully y'all won't say how absurd
Because you can hear even when it's not given.
Wrapped in a package with a ribbon
Us and this world we live in will have a discussion;
So that we'll proceed to better our own lives
Without the jive 'cause I think we've had enough.
Too rough, because we don't want clouds
And we want it now but I can't say it loud.
So hush . . . and bring your mental collection
No seekin' the answer without the question.
            Hastings Lloyd

The Visit

I guess it was the Grim Reaper who knocked on my door that night,
I couldn't be sure or it could have been a vampire who stalked me.
All I know is, a pain that I can't endure has possessed me.
I don't know how death found me.
Oh, why, Lord, have you forsaken me?
Because I smell the stench of death around,
how foolish I was that I didn't see
the darkness that reached out to me and how
my ignorance would lead me to my grave.
So on my deathbed, I remember now,
my mistakes and regret all—nothing will save
me from inevitable fate,
close my eyes and for the darkness I wait.
            Monique Sarmiento Francisco

The Boy on TV

I have a secret.
I love someone who is famous.
Everyone knows his name.
But I love him for different reasons.
I see his intelligence, his kindness,
and his sincere ability to bring out the
best in others.
I see more than just a gorgeous face.
He's on TV
He's in the movies.
But I will always see him
as this boy who I want to give my heart to.
Could it happen?
Would he love me?
Oh! Why did I fall for the boy on TV?
            Fayla Harrington

A Cold Day

Just like Dante, I too, seek salvation
Here on the bottom, I've found motivation
I feel empty, living for no reason
Cold and lost in the eternal winter season

Wandering through snow, I begin to freeze
The pain and fear force me to my knees
I look up for the sun, searching for light
I start to believe in His glory, His might

Please forgive me Father, for I was wrong
I realize, without you, I'm not as strong
I have locked you out of my heart and mind
My fear of you returns and tickles my spine

So I close my eyes and sleep in the snow
Not really knowing where my soul is to go
I quietly rest and I do not fear
With my new found faith, I know you are near
            Tony Macko

My Heart Talks to You

I sit here with the wind blowing gently in my hair.
With my mind blank and at a pretty hard stare.
I remember all the special things I use to do,
But the best seems to be of a special girl, you.
I think of the times we spent together.
Will that time come back—no never ever.
It is now time to say good-bye.
And it hurts worse than I'm going to die.
These are the last words I am going to say
To a girl I was going to marry one day.
    These are the last words you will ever hear
    From this man you once called dear.
    For today is the day he decides
    Today is the day he died.
            Randall Kalbaugh

The Thought of Losing You

I'm going away with an aching and broken heart,
Sad and lonely, not because I'll miss you.
But the thought of losing you, I can't bear.

I knew from the very start
that I have no place in your heart.
But still I showed you in many ways
my love and affection.
That was all ignored and cast away.

What else can I do?
Nothing but cling to my instinct.
To hope, to trust that maybe one day,

I may find a place in your heart.
When you can no longer
feel the beating of my heart.
For I am gone, gone forever
to my resting place.

Fanny Huxley

Inspiration

Sometimes it's so hard to see just how much you gain,
At times all you feel is misery and all you see is pain,
Yet somewhere in that darkness there's a smile and a ray of hope,
And you know deep down within you there is a way to cope,
Look deep inside your heart where your strength grows,
And find a way to make it that no one knows,
No one can help you out better than you can,
Not another living soul that is known to man,
You have a light that is there to make you see,
That nothing is impossible unless you let it be . . .

Amy Stiles

At Last It's Twilight

At last it's twilight when the calamity and devastation
of darkness and night comes face to face with the soft
ambient brightness of the sun and placid amicable light of day.

Even as the sun accelerates toward its place in the sky
it fails to reconcile the harmony of man, or even remotely
animate the fatigue of body, soul or mind.

In these final minutes I resigned myself to no more fear.
No more pain. I succumb to the level of unconsciousness.
I saw myself arise to the clouds, bright clouds of silver
linings. I saw towns and I saw cities, I saw friends long
ago lost, there were clouds like daffodils and oceans
of many hue continents, oceans and universes
filled with harmonious bliss.

No more fear, no more pain, no fatigue of body
or mind, for my soul succumbs to serendipity.
"At last it's twilight."

Ruby Dennis

Silence

The sound that flowers make when they're growing.
The sound of a bird soaring up near the clouds.
You hear it at dawn and at dusk.
If you listen hard enough it can be loud.
The sound the world makes when its children are sleeping.
Librarians say it's golden.
Silence

Diana Dekajlo

If to Say

The summer warm breeze embraces him as he walks.
The sweet essence of blooming flowers wrap around him
Soft and purple like a winter quilt.
His body too old and torn to walk as he did, once.
Those ways long forgotten, drifted from memory
Like the ebbing tide, lost in a sea of memories.

His slender arm extends to a gnarled fist clutching
an equally gnarled staff,
Worn, it whispers of journeys made long ago.

The faint chirp of a morning sparrow echoes through the forest
The melody so simple
Yet beautiful causes him to stop and linger,
Each note wafts through the shaded forest
Illuminating the very essence of tranquility and life.

Each tree reaches beyond the sky, as if to touch the sun
They are the silent, immovable citadels of the forest.
They loom above the old man giving him their shade
As if offering gifts to an old friend.

And as if to say thank you, the man puts down his staff and rests,
In the mother like embrace of the forest.

Niklas Jackson

A Special Silhouette

My shadow on the ground, that feels my steps,
I know that you feel my pain, with your depth,
Your love is so true, I know, all by heart . . .
My personal spirit, even though we're apart.

If I see a star fall, a wish, I would make,
To have you beside me, when dark nights break,
Or maybe, you'd speak up, to demand a fair right,
Please ask for the moon, that shows you at night!

Life wasn't kind, when it placed you below,
It should have reflected, your image to show.
We reflect in mirrors, and waters below . . .
But shadow, your special, we journey and go!

Maybe shadow isn't pictured, with details keen,
But pictures deceive, and your heart left unseen.
Reflections show age, as time runs a race,
Dear shadow, don't worry, you're blessed without face!

Your shadow needs attention, it's a best friend,
The mirror gets too much, the time you two spend!
I love you my shadow, I know, you are me,
My sensitive nature, made me feel your plea.

Helen Nadeau

Debbie

(Death Enters Bored Beings Innocently Enough)
Sleep enters my being in a fool hearted way,
Entrapping the life of my soul;
In a maze of unreturnable corridors,
I journey through the black, the deep, and the cold.
A ray of light reaches and grasps my hand,
With a vise-like grip, never to let go.
The door of death has been opened,
Allowing me to enter; I tremble upon the threshold.
I reject with deep repentance.
There are no second chances.
My choice has been made.
The thick threads take hold.
My sweet breath of life is gone.
My loneliness has been left to a world no longer mine.
A world who deserves the torments of loneliness.
A world with no feelings or pity.
My master takes hold . . .

Anita Pastier

Do You Believe in Miracles?

I sometimes wonder if life is real
With all the pain and suffering we feel
How strong must we be to keep up the pace?
How weak are we if we lose the race?

Confidence is our strength in living
Love is our hope of constant forgiving
But there must be something more to this life
That cannot be changed by the twist of a knife

Without our dreams, we have no scope
We would fall apart and lose all hope
So have some faith and you'll get by
If you believe in miracles then so do I

they say no one's perfect, this may be true
Everyone has faults so what can you do?
If an ideal world were to call
Then we wouldn't believe in miracles at all.

Brendan Conti

Wolves

Believed to be a magical breed,
they humbly fall into place while one leads.
They dance a magical way
through the playgrounds of wilderness.
Their ears keen, eyes sharp, they possess an intuitiveness.
Howling to the silvery moon,
talking to the other side,
teaching spirits so they learn
how to run and hide.
Run from the wickedness that enters their domain,
Hide from the evil one who comes in search of their game.

Nancy Schnarr

I Cry

Some call me baby, too sensitive, over emotional, well maybe.
I look at faces of survivors when a loved one has passed.
I feel the pain in married couples when love just doesn't last.
There is joy in seeing God's good work, the sky's all painted blue.
The beauty of this great green Earth in the morning dew.
Suffer do unwanted pets, they wander for some scraps.
Suffer do the children, they just want up in your laps.
It's sad when love is lost and parents go astray.
The children suffer from their faults, and live another way.
I watch my family grow and grow, then slowly fall apart.
Don't tell me you don't feel a thing, it's got to break your heart.
We go through life; we cause this pain, and do it to each other.
What is it that we have inside that rips into another?
So sadness, I do, see this way, my heart is hard to lift.
But others say go on and cry because you have a gift.
A sympathetic ear I have, you will not cry alone.
For compassion is a gift from God, to some it is unknown.
So I Cry.

Linda Lamberson

Never Satisfied

When hot, I seek cold.
When cold, I seek heat.
When hungry, I seek food.
When too full, I seek relief.
When lonely, I seek companionship.
When surrounded by people, I seek solitude.
When at peace, I wonder why.
When in turmoil, I seek peace.
When in love, I fail to nurture.
When love is lost, I desire another chance.
In all that I do, I'm never satisfied.
Will I ever be content?
God only knows.

Rosalind Simpson

Verse for a Halloween Night

Soft moonlight shines upon the knoll
While in the distance church bells toll
An evening train, its whistle blows
The sounds of frogs and crickets, crows
As sunlight fades upon the hill
An autumn breeze will break the still
And send leaves flying, stripping trees
With sounds foreboding 'cross the leas
The trees once filled with autumn bloom
Now blend with darkness, twilight's gloom
Simple sights and sounds of day
At dusk, bring fears one can't relay
Despairing moods, dark thoughts take over
On this last night in gray October
One's pathway home, once pleasant, calm
Now draped in black, conveys alarm
As moonlight gleams on distant rill
The night takes on an eerie chill
When trepidation and awe convene
To celebrate on Halloween

Karen MacDonald Tanguay

The Present

Gazing at the phosphorescent screen,
Searching for the words
    that will open my heart.

Assimilating wisdom of the ages.
Hoping to find the magic message
    that will wake me from my fitful
    longing.

Searching, ever searching
    for the light.
Hoping, like a child the night before
    Christmas to be able to open the
    present of my life
    and get a glimpse of my soul.

But all the while having a sneaking suspicion
    that the words I search for
    are the words I am writing.
That the present I so desperately search for
    is the gift of this present moment
    covered with the wrapping paper
    of my endless thoughts.
Tied with the ribbon of constant trying
    and knotted with my doubt.

Michael Saathoff

Music

Music gets you hyped,
comb out your pockets for a CD or tape,
vinyl record for your crate.
Music, the one thing everyone listens to.
WHY?
Because music speaks to you,
talking about the good and bad
you can relate to.
You love music because music is in you.
It's true,
that's why Jazz is so blue,
instruments so classic,
rock 'n' roll so spastic,
R&B full of soul, hip-hop and rap,
worth millions in gold.
You sing music in the house,
in the car, at the bar, on the road,
on a flight, hanging with your friends,
stopped at the traffic light.
No matter where you are or what you do,
Music is always in you!!

Andre' Morton

My Tribute to My Children and Grandchildren

When I was a child I'd sit and I'd stare
I needed a reason why the stars were up there.

I'd play with my dolls when I was alone
I'd pick up some leaves and each precious stone.

As I grew older I put up the toys
My life was now busy with all of the boys.

As time went on, I became a wife
Things started to change in my once simple life

I soon had my children, a boy and a girl
My already hectic life was now in a whirl.

Each day they grew older, our time was so short
They laughed and danced and played every sport.

Now they have their own children, a girl and two boys.
They really are darlings, and I'm back to the toys.

My lifetime is getting shorter, but I really don't care
'cause I finally know why all the stars are up there.

Judy Cagle

Praise God

There could be peace on Earth if man decided
he is not the soul leader;

If man could make the moon rise or put
the stars in the element, or make the clouds
bring down rain, or make the wind blow
then man could take over.

Praise God, because God is still holding
the world together.

Mary L. Williams

The Caskets

There's a leaden casket down in my heart
That is heaped with heavy things:
The stones I have gathered along the way,
The thorns I have plucked from day to day,
And the heart's own broken strings.
But I've hidden the casket low and deep
From the guess of day and the reach of sleep
And snapped the lock on the somber keep
And thrown the key away.

There's a golden casket down in my heart
That is full of a treasure glow:
The smiles that have greeted me on the way,
The roses that bloomed and, sweeter, stay
In a scented afterglow,
And the treasures break from this golden keep,
Through the risk of day and the guess of sleep,
And I slip the lock and I spy and peep,
For it's open night and day.

Walter C. Bruno

Name Your Poison

Mom drinks diet cokes; they must be caffeine free
She is always on a diet because that's the way it has to be
Dad prefers a bottle of gin; that's the way it's always been
He drinks his gin with tonic, because it makes him catatonic

Sis prefers a daiquiri; won't put any liquor in it
She likes bananas and cherries, or any kind of berries
Junior takes his bourbon straight, and his scotch on a rock
He doesn't like the taste; just trying to be a Jock

I don't claim to be a lady; folks say I'm kind of shady
I drink my beer from the bottle, and I like a sip of whisky
It makes me kind of frisky, and I like Salty Dogs

Mary B. Britton

Funeral

Ashes to ashes, dust to dust
I wonder if what we had was love or lust.
As I watch them throw dirt into your grave
I remember the times in our secret cave,
When it was just you and me and ocean breezes
With no rashes, or colds, or hay fever sneezes.
I recall the times we laughed until we were sore,
And the times you tickled me until I couldn't stand it anymore.
Oh, say, what about the time we went running hand in hand,
Or when we built small castles in the sand?
And now the ocean has swallowed our dreams,
And someone has put an end to our schemes.
All around me people wearing black are crying.
Why is it when you are young you never think of dying?

Tammie R. Trail

Behind a Child's Eyes

I have looked behind a child's eyes and saw a soul so pure,
True innocence and wonder, yet insight though unsure.
Young in age and wise in heart his little soul cried out,
To all who ever loved him—to be sure and without doubt.
That he is still their loved one and always to the end,
For he has lost someone he loved, a future father and dear friend.
He said his heart was broken with profound dignity and grace,
And wondered if it was common among the human race.
To lose a special part of you and wonder where it went,
And also wonder if the years you had have really all been spent.
I looked into a child's heart, which showed upon his face,
And all the stoic self he portrayed to keep his tears in place.
To protect his mother is his goal and never let her know
That his heart is breaking deep inside and he will not let it go.
A secret from his mother and a prayer to God above,
That he will never ever feel the loss of another's love.

Rita Falsetto Whalen

When the Time Comes

Living is a joy, each day a blessing
When family are near, the day is refreshing.
The problems that we can't sometimes seem to solve
Appear to be manageable when loved ones get involved.

We climb our mountains, rise to many occasions
We struggle, but go on with great anticipation
Making the best of every situation.

We often put inner feelings aside and go with the flow
For life has taught us to take things in stride.
Yes, we have learned to weather our storms
Regardless which way the winds blow.

Sometimes our every effort to make others understand,
Just falls a part in the palm of our hands, and
It's then we realize the master plan—
Our destiny lies with He who created man.

So in the event that you feel defeated
And you are the one who's always mistreated,
Don't give up and waste your life away
For your time has come too fast and pray.

Carol Y. Hinnant

Translation of Aloha No Aina

Placed on high misting cliffs,
The Lei of heavenly stars,
The full moon of the night,
Touch the love of the land,
Bringing the warmth of the sun to the cold.
Comforting the heart.
Pikaki and Maile Vine
Your fragrance is born
Infusing my very being.
Love of the land is ours!

Umiokalani Edmo

Children's Lessons

Oh, little children, hear me true,
Some things you must not do.
Do not believe all that you hear,
Do not allow yourselves to fear.
Do not lie, cheat or steal,
Try your best to be what's real.
Do not want what others have got,
Do not pretend to be what you're not.
With each new person that you meet,
At home, at school, or on the street,
You must at all times be aware,
Not every one of them will care.

Please keep in touch with all your senses,
for you alone can mend your broken fences.
When you count on others all the time,
You're allowing them to control your mind.
The only way we can be free
Is holding love inside of we.
To stand firm, alone, when times seem hard,
Will always give us the top most card.

Vera Benusic

Late

Ring. Ring. Ring.
When I woke up,
There was a scream,
I was late for a meeting.
I rushed as fast as a cheetah out of my bed,
And pondered in my head,
Why am I always late?
All of a sudden,
I ran to my closet, as quick as a rat trying to get some food,
What am I going to wear?
Should I wear the red dress or the blue dress over there?
The red dress is as old as my grandmother's 1950's organ,
and my blue dress has a stain on it.
Well, I guess I'll wear the blue dress and keep the stain hidden
Because it's time to go,
But, Oh, I stubbed my toe.
Man, Oh, man, did that hurt!
I slipped some shoes on just like Cinderella
Because I didn't know what was in store,
I just knew I had to get out that door!

Monet Bagneris

Elegy: The Bed (The Day Mom Died)

Rest your weary bones against my frame.
Know I the long years wear heavy
On sinews and shoulders,
Once firm and supple,
Now sloped and thin with passing age.

Share I your dreams and fantasies
Through long, lone, languorous nights.
Evening tears on pillows tell
Of friendships forged and betrayed,
Of promises made and unmade.

Rejoice I your many-born,
Anchors of hope in life's tempest tossed.
Hopes, aspirations and pains,
I will cradle as I have cradled yours.
Life fulfilled in autumn years.

Hearkened! Come now!
Night's velvety net cast.
Time once more for new dreams.
Let me embrace your memories;
Let me becalm the day's unjust.

Weng F. Chew

Eternity

Eternity goes on forever,
It never, ever ends.
Eternity, unceasingly,
Where there is no time, my friends.

Eternity,
Consider the universe and never-ending space,
Not temporal nor conditional,
Where there is no commonplace.

A different state of being,
Not like anything we've ever known,
Not as mortal human beings,
Our bodies we'll disown.

Imagine this place called eternity,
We do not know of now.
How will we spend eternity,
A question never ending . . . how?

Contemplation, imagination,
Perhaps we'll discover once we are there.
Just what this place eternity is like,
And will there be any solace there?

Evelyn Ann Dolas

Twisted Mind

You're playing with my body, playing with my soul.
I cannot understand it, no way I can say STOP!
Why?
Why not?

It can happen soon, maybe never . . .
My mind is twisted, my heart can never rest.
I want you both, if only for one night.
It might never happen, heart and soul, in a giant fight.

Why not try?
You say no.
What about our friendship? It might be destroyed.
Is it worth the risk?

You both look beautiful.
My heart goes to one, my mind to the other.
WHY DO I EVEN BOTHER?
It will never happen—I believe that for sure.

A first time for everyone, a first time for me.
I think we would like it. How can this be?
I think I know, from the bottom of my soul.
I want you, both of you . . . so?!?

Stein Roessaak

What I See . . .

These beautiful surroundings.
The attention to detail. The furniture, first rate.
The toys. There are more toys, from more
sources than can be counted.
Clothes. They are carefully selected. The colors
are dazzling, and there are more items than
can be used. A lot still need to be grown into.
The food. It is fussed over as if someone
had hired a gourmet chef.
There is a lot of love that goes into
such a superb home.
It is truly what every child on this Earth deserves.
But what makes this life so special are the people.
The Parents, Grandparents, Aunts, Uncles,
Siblings, and some Friends. They all have so much
to offer. Caring, mindfulness, compassion, wisdom,
love, reasoning, discipline, and always humor.
Growing up to be no one's fool is a certainty.
I do believe that this is just how
God intended it to be.

Nick Mortellaro

Declaration of Love

I have power, I have money,
But without you I don't have everything I desire.

I desire all the riches and the power
that only you can give with your love.

It doesn't matter going through trouble to love you,
Because anything with value has a high price
and for me the price is your love!

Wilberto R. Fernandez

Musty Old Attic

Musty, old attic, reveal your secrets today!
Tell me your stories of small girls having tea parties,
Of little boys on rocking horses acting
Out the tales of warriors long gone.
Tell me the stories you alone have been witness to,
Of plays put on in long out-of-style gowns,
Of play houses amidst your dusty wood trunks,
Of young children hiding from chores,
And great-grandmothers hiding from approaching Nazis.
Tell me the tales that your walls alone have heard,
Stories told on a stormy Hallows Eve,
And of fantasy princesses riding atop unicorns.
Tell me these stories and more, musty, old, attic.

Sheena Pennell

Wind

Wind, guide me through this dark place in which I am in
Wind, sing me your song of nature to calm my fear
Wind, tell me a story to keep me in attention
Wind, remind me why I am here and alone
Wind, remember me as you leave this dark place

Jose Raul Medrano

Jeanne

I saw you last night in your little dress with purple flowers
and puffed sleeves; I reached out to touch the fabric and
you smiled and hugged me; my heart melted into happy satisfaction.
After all the pinning, tucking, taking off and getting back into,
sewing and snipping, it fit, your favorite color!
You look like an angel with your long golden curls
and dark brown eye lashes that touch your eyelids.
And I saw the twinkle in those beautiful green eyes
and I tried hard to fall asleep once more to pin another tuck
in your little dress to see the sweet smile
I've missed and make you stand still
'til you fall into my arms, laughing once more.
You were five then, that was so long ago.
I wonder if angels wear purple?
I wonder if God allows angels to wear robes with purple flowers?

Jo Jamman

My Love for Thee

The fierceness of which I love thee
burns within the heart
The devotion of which I give to thee
Will last and never part
The words of love I told thee I meant
Them with fierce desire
The feelings of love I showed thee
Were meant to lift thee higher
High upon a pedestal is where I place thee
High upon a pedestal is where we both should be
The feelings of love I've shared with thee
Are etched upon my heart
Never to be erased from me
I've loved thee from the start

Brenda Richards

Life

The meaning of it is not determined
By the house you live in, or the car
You drive, but in the kindness of your
Heart and the feelings in your soul.

Life,
Such a big word, such a broad meaning.
The value of life is priceless.   What is
Life? Is life a feeling on the inside, showing
On the outside, or does life live in our soul?
Maybe life keeps the soul alive.

Life,
What is the difference between your life and
Your soul? Do they correspond, or are they
Two different, very different things?
Is life priceless? To some, yes, yet, to others, no. Why
Do people take their own life? Maybe they don't.
Maybe they take their soul. This question can
Be answered by one judge. Do you judge yourself?
If not you, then who?
Your soul will answer that question.

Andrew Lovegrove

Just Riding

When life cages me in, like a prisoner behind bars
When people get to be too much

And the problems never seem to end
I can get on my bike, and just ride

Riding breaks all those chains that tie me down
The sound of the motor beneath me says,
"I'm taking you away"

The wind blowing through my hair
Tells me freedom is very near

The winding road asks,
"Where do you want to go?"

Embracing the horizon before me it says softly,
"Follow me, I'll take you there"

A chill is running down my spine, my blood runs faster
As the horizon wraps its endless arms around me

Softly, I hear, "Don't look back"
As freedom takes over, the chains have snapped

The problems fade into the sunset
The people are swallowed by the road
Freedom reigns, if I'll just ride!

David L. Adkins

Blood and Tears

Come thee to this life in blood and tears.
Crawl, then walk, then run through years.
Learn thee always from cradle to ground.
Talk and laugh and fill time with sound.
Color paper and fabric, and tint your skin.
Paint orange sunrise mornings and pink sunset ends.
Swim with the current when life's water is warm.
Float and tread swells as you wait out the storms.
Find thee good work, good music, good friends.
Sweat and struggle, yet all the while sing!
Find peace and quiet within your own mind.
Give comfort and solace.
Help others to find the beauty in loving and living. Be kind.
Praise God in the morning and thank Him each night.
Study His word. Keep Him ever in sight.
Let His teachings guide your every path.
Choose compassion, forgiveness, and justice, not wrath.
May God's wisdom live in you, and His vows calm your fears,
'Til go thee out of this world in blood and tears.

Betty Jones

If I Had One Wish

If I had one wish,
I would go to the moon.
I would go to the moon and make room for you.
I would go to a fancy ball,
But if you weren't there,
I wouldn't wish at all.
I would ask you to go with me,
On a trip to Hawaii,
But you're gone,
We said farewell.
The song that was just playing
Rang a bell.
I love you Dad,
But . . .
If I had one wish,
I would go to the moon.
I would go to the moon, and make room for you,
I would go to a fancy ball,
But if you weren't there,
I wouldn't wish at all.

Jillian Owens

The House

The house of my childhood
poses placidly on the hill like a haughty dowager.
Stately and composed, dressed in white with black trim;
she sits surrounded by the green, clipped lawn
and shaded by the huge Silver Maple.
Within her corridors echo voices raised in elation and in anger—
Over time, three generations of our family
lived within her spacious rooms, strode these halls,
had company conversation around the dining table,
fed harvesters heaping plates in the kitchen,
listened to "Ma Perkins" and "Grand Ole Oprey."
The creaking stairs led to six big bedrooms.
Up another set of stairs to the ample attic—
Retreat for dolls and games, the old typewriter,
and large portrait of Aunt Alice in a white dress.
Picture books shelved below the window,
Lincoln logs fence in plastic cows, sheep and chickens.

In memory, squirrels still spring from maple branches,
a dog barks, cows move steadily in from the pasture.
The John Deere tractor rumbles through the green cornfield.
I walk past the scent of hay, clover, ripe tomatoes.
And I find this house of my childhood
still gathers me within her walls.

Rosalie Nelson

Ocean

She is movement in her stillness.
Chaotic, quiet, fluid strength
knows no form but that of her container.
Shifting hues of blue and grey and
glowing green,
she is mystery.
What lies beneath her churning hair,
her beckoning wetness, her threat of life,
her promise of death?
She is paradox; she creates it.
You go to her, and yet you are afraid.
She aches to consume you,
to take you into her, to envelop you,
to take you back.
But she cannot have all of you,
for she is not of your world.
She is formless flowing
pure power,
raw naked
love.

Joann Siravo

Smile

You see a little girl smile
What is she thinking that makes her so happy
Maybe she can share her happiness with me
What will happen if I smile
Do I feel better
Do I feel complete
Why yes, yes I do
You should try it

Isabel Mandelkern

What Does Love Mean to You?

Is it the sand between your toes at a day at the beach?
Or the clouds in the sky that one day you'll reach?
Are they the angels that surround you each day?
Or is it fun in the park, on those early days of May?

What does love mean to you, do you even have a clue?

Is it that guy who you can never stop thinking of?
Or the sky, so beautiful and blue above?
Are they the looks your dad gives your mom,
when she glances his way?
Or is it always having a friend there, knowing just what to say?

Is love friendly and honest, but most of all true?

Is it the shimmering stars you wish on each night?
Or is it having someone there when things aren't quite right?
Is it the way two souls are meant to be?
Or is it just the fact that life is a mystery?

Love is all of this and much, much more
It gives you hopes and dreams on which you can soar.
So what does love mean to you?
I know, and now you know too!

Jessica Bond

My Little Man

My little man is sweet and kind, he means the world to me.
He makes me smile when I am sad, just by the things he does.
When we were all alone one day, he said these words to me.
"Mommy! Mommy! Come and see, the picture I have drawn . . .
It looks somewhat like a clown . . . but then it looks like Dad."
It made me laugh so very hard, the words that he had said.
To think that doggie on that board looked so much like his dad.
He's such a cute little man, and you would love him just the same.
No matter what he said to you, you would adore him even more.
That's my little man, you see, who means the world to me.
He makes me smile when I am sad, just by the things he does.

Sheila D. Dwiggins

An Answered Prayer

I bid you goodnight
for again we must part
forever grasping needed hope
you will never go far
As we say tomorrow
again we will be together
With heart felt sincerity
I pray to God you will love me forever
The love we feel and share
even the most beautiful words could do no justice
But can be explained
with our most passionate kiss
I let you leave
with sadness assured
For when you return
I will know a happiness that can only be found
when a prayer is answered

Jacob Pytlik

Grandma

I lie alone in the dark, thinking of you,
wishing you were here.
To help me through everything.
As I face the problems of life each day,
I pray that you were here.
Decisions are put before me, and I don't know what to do,
because you are no longer near.
I pray to the beautiful heavens above,
for I know that you are there watching over me.
Never a day goes by,
that you don't cross my mind.
Your presence on Earth was so much adored.
If only I could talk to you one last time.
What I wouldn't give to smell your precious scent,
to touch your old, used, worn-out hands one last time.
To know that you are happy,
would fill my heart with overwhelming joy.
Until the day I see you again I can only pray,
that you will give me the strength,
through your spirit to get through each day.

Lindsay Pflaumer

Thoughts of a Broken Heart

I think to myself, bitter are my salt tears
lost on a lonely sea, surrounded by thunder,
lightning, and darkness below.

With every second that passes, my heart is
a little closer to drowning in this sea of pain.

The constant unknowing of my fate is almost
too much for my mind to bear, and even so, my
mind draws conclusions of what my heart hopes
will come to be.

Robert Craft

Forever Will I Be Yours

To Bill . . . I love you, Baby
Whenever you put your arms around me,
I feel your love enfold me and make me feel warm.
Like the sand is enfolded by the sea,
Your words and your smile around me do swarm.
When you tell me my eyes are pretty,
Something inside me starts to glimmer.
It makes me feel gorgeous and witty.
And when your blue-green eyes start to shimmer
My heart starts to beat faster, my soul sets fire.
As our lips touch chills are sent down my spine.
A mix of hot and cold of which I won't tire.
And while around you I have no reason to whine.
You've showed me the way to life's open doors,
And for that, forever will I be yours.

Katherine Turner

Have You Been through the Process?

Have you been through the process?
I'll tell you how you can tell: have
All your weaknesses been exposed?
Have you been through the process?
The process in which only God can shape
And mold.

Have you been through the process?
Now able to accept your greatest defeats,
While you humble yourself before the Lord,
As you bow before his feet.

Have you been through the process?
Let all the truth be told, that you have been
Through the process, and now know how to stand
Abase and Abold.

Angela Dew

God Is

Take a look around you at this beautiful land
God is the only one who could have made it
the only one with the plan

The mountains, trees, land, animals
and of course you !
Such magnificient designs
intricate through and through!

God is the master and it shows in all of these
If He is not the Divine One
Then by all means show me who is please!

Laura Armstrong

Senses of My Heart

I see magic in your eyes,
and that comes as no surprise,
I've felt something all along,
in an enchanted, silent song.

I hear passion in your heart,
almost a classical work or art:
that has grasped my very soul
and makes me feel completely whole.

I feel captivated by your gentle stare,
a mystical look for us to share.
The perfect kiss placed on my lips,
your face I touch with my fingertips.

For all the joys you've given to me,
I'm like a child just beginning to see;
you are my most treasured friend,
we'll never say good-bye; there'll be no end.

Yehara Raddalgoda

Simple Pleasures

A new puppy's whine, a baby's sweet giggle,
Mexican jumping beans, see how they wiggle.
Balsawood airplanes thrown at the sky,
lie on your back and watch the clouds sail by.
The smell of fresh cut grass, squishing mud through your toes,
bright yellow dandelions to rub on your nose.
A castle of sand with a genuine moat,
homemade ice-cream for a big rootbeer float.
Bobbing for apples, a trip to the fair.
Waking up Christmas, knowing Santa's been there!
A Valentine shoebox, fireflies after dark,
holding hands with your sweetheart, a walk in the park.
Rainy days in the house, tracing your hand.
Cards in your spokes, a lemonade stand.
I don't want more money, don't need a degree,
Life's simple pleasures are plenty for me.

Ray Hubbard

Sometimes and Others

Sometimes when you're here, you're really not,
And sometimes when you win, you really lose.
And when in life you must decide,
You find you cannot choose.

Sometimes when you love, you really hate,
And sometimes when you dream, you're wide awake.
And when an issue is so small
There's so much more at stake.

If today is a gift, why must it be so harsh.
And if a statement seems so vague, it's usually a clue.
Sometimes the message depends on the reader,
And right now the reader is you.

Andrew Wilcox

Hear My Cry

Don't punish me Oh, Lord
In your anger of heat.
Pity me Oh, Lord, because,
I am weak.

My mine is fill with apprehension and gloom.
Please Oh, Lord, rescue me soon.

Come Oh, Lord, rescue and make me well,
Don't let my soul rest in Hell.

I am worn out my pillow wet with tears.
Waiting on you Lord and your good will.

I know you keep your promise
I know you are near.
I am waiting on you to wipe
Away my tear.

Channie Pettway

Paradise

One day I'm gonna find happiness
It's gonna show me everything that I've missed

I might find love, I might even find a piece of mind
But what I'm truly looking for is my own paradise

Ever since I was a kid
I've dreamed of that day
It's like my heart yearns for something better
Better than what this present day offers me

I might not have much to live on
Much to push me along

But I do have my dreams, I have my song
What I'm looking for shouldn't be to far along
Maybe I'll find something to stop the cries
Maybe I'll find a piece of paradise

Gabriel Gutierrez

Separated

Tonight must come without asking,
Like a darkened black shadow over a field.
It comes like a black cat in waiting,
Looking for that tenth life to steal.
It will hover like the web of a spider
Waiting to catch its last prey.
Tonight will last a thousand more years,
Then a hundred and a day . . .
Millenniums and millenniums creep with the
tick of the clock.
The moon snickers, "The day is near," as he
grins at me and mocks.
Yesterday's love and your images,
catapulting in my head.
The loneliest journey I'll ever travel is
the only one ahead.

Denise Jo-ann Joseph

Pages

Life is a book whose pages have only begun to be filled
A new chapter written with the passing of every day
Another lesson learned with the turning of each page
Emotions and experiences compiled and bound together
With threads of discovery and wisdom
The common onlooker may form prejudices
Based solely on the outward appearance
Blind to the text within
Only proving further a proverb which has now become cliche
Though it may be . . .
Never judge a book by its cover

Elise Rosenberg

Be Together Live Forever

I wish I knew where you were,
But to you it didn't occur
That you didn't know how I felt
When my heart started to melt
Because you left me.
And I think that shouldn't be,
We could be together and live forever.

But you don't want me "Oh, nnnnooooo,"
And you know that I love you "ssssooooo."
I wish we could be together and live forever,
Be together and live forever in each other's hearts.
We could buy each other gifts, my love, Trevor.
Now you put something in my heart—darts.
Please, we made a start, now we're apart.
We could be together and live forever.

Taryn Bartscher

Try, Try, Try

I try so hard 'cause you're the one I want
When I ask, you say you don't.

Having you as my lady would really be great
But when you say no, that's what I hate.

Times are hard without you near
I think if you're there, there will be no fear.

I admire your personality so much
That on my heart holds that special touch.

My love for you is so strong
But, the desire travels in my mind so long.

Words just don't express the love I have for you
I try so hard to prove my love is really true.

Our time has yet to arrive
But I wonder how much longer can I survive.

Dreams do come true!
But will this one, too?
My love for you is so real,
But the real question is,
How do you feel?

Your move!

Shaun L. Lewis

The Promised Land

The promised land is inside you
Your great, quiet voice from within
Is telling you how to get there
Knowing you don't know where to begin

A wondrous, glorious place for you
The world said it doesn't exist
I wouldn't listen to those who don't know
That your spirit wants you to persist

Your promised place is calling you
Where the sun shall shine forever
Stand firm through the storm before the calm
You can make it for you are quite clever

My promised land is beckoning me
To get there at any cost
I have to go the distance
To see paradise found and not lost

The promised land entices me
For certain I heed her call
At last I can embrace her
There's a winner in me after all

Laquita Moore

Out of Fate's Hands

I never believed in love at first sight
Until that one sweet day turned to that one sweet night
I heard it calling, fate's loud cry
it was always a sign I couldn't deny
My time was fleeting, the night was cold
But you gave me a feeling I never had known
Life showed me the way, fate opened the door
It was just too good, not to ignore
We opened each other to life's ecstasy
Almost as if God answered my plea
Your friends wouldn't have it, just like mine
Almost as if forbidden by time
We couldn't be saved from falling apart
I was losing my mind, it was breaking my heart
I was leaving that day, looking ahead
But when the news broke I was better off dead
I admit I want more, though we work well as friends
But ours was definitely out of fate's hands
There's no beginning without an end
But ours was definitely out of fates hands

Rob Luzhak

Betrayer

I hate her. She is a betrayer.
Why did she do that to me? She was a friend turned enemy.
I want to pull her hair out! I want to scream and shout!
I can't believe this.
She's a snake that goes, "Hiss!"
She came one day and tried to trip me.
Then she hid behind a big tree.
Good thing I didn't fall
For in front of me was a wall.
"Don't flatter yourself," she would say.
(Don't worry. One day you'll pay.)
I told the teacher what she did.
The teacher said she acted like a kid.
Immature is what she was.
Hurting my feelings is what she does.
She's not the friend she used to be.
She flies like a butterfly, stings like a bee.

Katherine Bernal

As One in the Skies

Eagle of my life
As the eagle soars the skies, his life is his own,
free as the wind, yet powerful and controlling.
Beauty, grace, and pride show as he soars the heavens,
power and strength give him the ways to survive.
Seeking and uniting with only one mate for life is unique,
until nature takes that one life away.
Bound into captivity will only destroy this powerful life,
breaking it down to a simple bird of the sky.
Escaping its bondage will bring back that rare quality,
returning it to the skies with all its grace, beauty and pride.
Only memories will be left of how one can only wish that this
was his way of life.

Phyllis Berg

Alive & Died

Why do people say that living is the best thing ever?
I don't see nothing good about living.
You are just there.
The only thing that ever happens is you see people dying.
Is that why people live to die?
I don't see nothing good about living if you are just going to die.
I prefer being dead than alive.
When you are alive you go through Hell.
When you are dead you are just there.
You won't get hurt because you're dead.
So why do people say that being alive is so great?

Otilia Galindo

Constitutionalized

Have you ever heard of the unheard,
Or ever told of the untold?
Mouth carries the power of word,
And forms my immaculate mold.
Have you ever been lost in thoughts—
Saddened by their vanity?
Never thoughts of seeing someone shot,
But slowly losing sanity.
I was happy my whole adolescent life,
And now I'm living in bliss.
Every day I seem to encounter strife;
I thought there was more to life than this.
Raised in a world of falsified information,
Continuing the path of descendants.
As is told in America's declaration,
Being forced to follow someone's amendments.
Unable to find the meaning of existence,
And slowly losing control.
Never falling down without resistance,
Now enter the presence of forbidden souls.

Aaron Hulit

My Father

A wonderful man throughout the years has shared my life,
Always there when needed, never once caused any strife.

A man that I cherish with much respect in my heart,
It's hard not to see him, as often, since we are miles apart.

He is one who has taught his children well,
Even when at times they did deserve a little Hell!

I have much love for him that he needs to know about,
I may not tell him enough but there should be no doubt!

This man could never be replaced by another,
Because you see—this man—he is my father.

Holly Ann Waite

Just a Friend

No one knows that I sit and cry,
I think to myself I'd rather die.
I tell myself it's OK,
And it'll be better someday.
I'm felling so alone, you never even call me on the phone.
I try to keep you off my mind,
But I remember you were so kind.
We used to say our love will never end,
But now all you are is just a friend.
I'm so mad,
I didn't understand what we had.
I wish I had a four leaf clover,
So then our relationship wouldn't be over.
Four leaf clovers are supposed to bring you good luck,
So then my relationship with you wouldn't suck.
I miss you so much,
I'd give you anything for your loving touch.
I wish my dreams would come true,
So then I could be there with you.

Rachel Johnson

Roger

The pain is really something when you lose your best friend,
My brother went and shot himself, i thought it was the end!
I don't really understand what made him so sad,
Was it the childhood we lived or the home without a dad?
No one really knows who or what to blame,
All we really know is his children feel the same . .
So if you're considering that word that's so hard for me to say,
Please get some help so you can live another day . . .

Lori Foster

My World of Fantasy

The real world is closing in on me, and I must
escape into my world of fantasy, where there are
no if's or but's and can't's and don't's,
where nothing is forbidden.
You can let loose from chains, from walls,
from borders, from boundaries. You can be free!
You can drift like the wind, flow like a river,
fly like a bird, blossom like a flower, bathe in
the sunlight and the moonlight; you can float
on a cloud and get to the skies and the stars,
or swim like a fish in the sea and the ocean.
It's a world that knows no age, no time, no limits;
a world that knows no tears and pain and loneliness
nor hunger and thirst, only an abundance of joy,
of love, of affection, of care.
It's a world that closes the gaps of distance,
of separation, erasing gaps in heartbeats, so thinking,
and feeling, and breathing, and throbbing can be one.
It's a Shangri-La of a world that can last forever.
Come . . . escape with me into my World of Fantasy.

Aida A. Joshi

Reflections on a Spring Morning

Do you see the lowly marsh-reed
that only serves to mar the landscape?
Like some old person tottering on unsteady legs,
along a broken sidewalk filled with youths.
But wait!
This reed is necessary to keep the soil from eroding
and to serve as a safe nesting place for shellfish and fledglings.
So too, our senior citizens provide stability,
comfort and safety for the very young.

Julia Phillips

So Much Pain and Poverty

It pains my heart when I look around and see
The destruction crime and drugs
are bringing to our community
Mother against daughter father against son
Problems solved by pulling the trigger on a gun
So many people homeless living
and sleeping in the street
Begging for a handout so they can
get a bite to eat
Drugs and poverty are taking their toll
Our young are dying before the old
Whatever happened to love thy
neighbor as thyself
Instead of helping one another
most of them are seeking fame and wealth
When will it stop and peace and
brotherhood begin
Only when we stop sinning
and allow Jesus Christ to come in

Jackie Rivers

My Sock

My sock rocks like a clock, tick-tock.
What a clock!

But it is made out of chalk.
I knock on the clock and it only goes tick-tock.

What a stupid clock. I really want a new
clock. Tick-tock goes the clock.

My sock hates the chalk clock. What a dumb clock.

I always have to lock the chalk clock or it
will rock! Tick-tock!

Zachary Yates

The Friend

Running with the mushy sand slapping beneath synchronized feet.
Salty, clear water lapping like a dog.
And soon to be raised up, golden in the setting sun.

Leaping in. Swimming out. Stopping. Floating on my back.
Calling with the soul. Listening for that graceful, that finishes
with a billow of water, splashing, leap.

Now sitting on a sleek, moist, rock . . .
But I had not realized the affectionate, lifting, touch
that had come to be.

Wait! No! Not a rock!

See the never-weakening smile.
Of the Friend.
The click, whine, and whistle.
Belonging to the Friend.
Giving in to the swift, agile, and stream-lined swimming.
Belonging to the Friend.

Katy Balog

Forever

I remember your skin upon my touch,
And the kiss of your lips that I long for so much,
The taste of wine so tender and sweet,
How the earth trembled beneath my feet.
As we lie together intertwined in love,
How the world cannot separate two hearts from above.
My heart would ache to let you go,
I would rather die before it be so,
So promise me now that here we shall be,
Forever in existence for you and for me.

Irene Flores

Visions of Love

Visions of Love are visions of hope
Attached to your heart they're strong as a rope
Visions of Love so tender and warm
Are just like the sun that follows the storm
Visions of Love are visions of joy
The feeling that touches a girl and a boy
So never let go how intense they may be
Of those visions of Love let your soul set them free
Visions of Love I'm seeing them clear
They join us together they make us come near
Come open your heart and feel free like a dove
Then let them all in there those visions of love
Get carried away with those visions so true
Those visions of love for me and for you

Alexander Hoffmann

Street Walker

I drink, I'm drunk, therefore I am
A vision of rags, an advert for man,
I walk the streets, hidden, subdued,
Reeking of life from the spirits imbued
An alley of garbage surrounds my bed,
Whilst a river of numbness flows through my
                                        head
I am your father, your uncle, your son,
I am the Street Walker, the person you shun.
I steal the warmth from the cold cloak of
                        night
I cherish the sun and its first ray of light,
I exist on the fringes, society's damned,
Living on handouts, soooo generous a land
The mists of my mind, whirl and descend,
Crushing my dreams, forcing an end
I am the banker, the plumber, the priest,
I am the Street Walker, on famine I feast.

Justin Beserk

Out of Touch

Your missing presence in my world
Has broken my heart in two.
And everyone told me it would soon happen,
But the pain is worth the time I spent with you.

The bond that we both shared and treasured
Is no longer going to be there.
I love you so much, little one,
That missing you will be hard to bear.

You made me smile, and you made me laugh,
You brought so many beautiful things to me.
You're a very important part of my life,
And I understand why you can no longer be.

All I have now are pictures and memories,
because you're so far and out of touch.
And I know it wouldn't hurt this bad
If I didn't love you so much.

I know as time goes by for you,
I won't be anything but a faint memory.
You're just too young to hold onto that,
But you'll always and forever be a part of me.

Melanie Walker

A Poet's Lament

I thought to write as one of those.
Those that rhyme, time after time.
They've a creative bent, they write paths where others have went.
They treat minds to wordy treats, they perform grammatical feats.
We savour the flavor of their . . .
but wait, there's something else here at stake.
Brain hits wall, thinking shrinking, mind seems blind.
A block of our brain as our thoughts, are for nought.
Struggle and struggle 'til hope is but lost.
Light creeps in where darkness was lurking,
energy, thought, brain cells a'jerking.
Ideas rattle, from nothing to chaos,
confusion reigns but gradually wains.
Again it comes clear, what should be written here.
Closing words would be kind, alas a poor reader
who may wish they were blind.
Leave not a harsh word to ravage a mind,
but a kind "Thank you, for lasting this long" behind.
So ends the meanderings of this mush of a mind,
to return again sometime with some words to unwind.

Phillip Isabell

Remembrance

Dedicated to Christina Carrasco, we will never forget her.
We walk among others, alike in our ways.
Our sisters and brothers, 'til end of our days.
We work with each other, not knowing our fates.
We think nothing of it, until it's too late.
Each night we would see her, each night we would greet.
Not knowing that this night was the last that we'd meet.
How clear I remember her voice and her face.
Only moments before, had lived in this place.
But now there is silence, her voice heard no longer.
We drift into sadness, although we grow stronger.
Her face, known so well, shall grace us no more.
Our hearts now grow heavy, and regrets shall now pour.
We wish for a chance to say our good-byes.
And hope she's at peace, wherever she lies.
We'll never forget the days which we spent.
And nights full of laughter, each one Heaven sent.
Still another day passes, though never the same.
Even though we'll not see her, her spirit remains.
Still we walk with each other, though she may be gone.
In our hearts may she rest, and there shall live on.

Chris Young

Rejoice My Heart

The April rain has left its mark of beauty on the land.
Dew drops of crystal, lace the limbs of the dogwood tree.
Beads of crystal strung through out its branches
The blue spruce is bedecked with silver crystals too.
Everywhere I look, the world outside is a picture book.
Like pages unfolding flowers and droplets of dew,
In morning splendor.

I drink my coffee and dunk my toast, while
Drinking in the beauty of my host
Thanking God for blessings given.
For my eye sight and gifts from Heaven;
Six A.M. in the morning daylight is arriving
Fast I know this beauty will not last

The sun has arisen from the night; daylight is
Drawing night glistening dew drops, now
Turning into jewels of crystal bright
Sparkling like diamonds in the morning light.
I must be living in a fairy land, what a joy!

Florence Mick

Take Time

Take time for yourself,
It relaxes the mind.
Take time to smile,
It enhances the face.
Take time to share,
It brings appreciation to someone else's life.
Take time to dance,
It brings pleasure to the body.
Take time to read,
It empowers the mind.
Take time to love,
It brings joy to the soul.
Take time to be you,
Because you can never be someone else.

Enid Pryce

Christmas Time

Christmas is very very near,
it comes only once a year.
Christmas is a time for children to sing,
songs of happiness that Christmas bring.
Christmas is laughter, hope and joy,
filling the hearts of every girl and boy.
For Christmas is a birthday for Jesus above
but more than anything Christmas is love.

John H. Davis

Eroticism Is Not Love

The word "love" is misused and misapplied by many people
Eroticism (and all that is related to it)
Is commonly referred to as love
And the two are not synonymous
Indeed they are not related in any manner
One can love without including eroticism
And many people actuate eroticism yet love not
Eroticism is fleeting and those who seek it
Do find that it is inconsistent and does not last
Yet they continue to emphasize it in their activities
It is not needed although many people
Accept and insist that it is required
There are many who know and live
That eroticism is not necessary
And they do far better without it
For they do not interrupt their flow of love-energy
When they do not include the erotic
Because love-energy can be expanded without impediment
When the blockage of eroticism is kept away.

Guen Chappelle

Mother Nature's Medicine

A two-acre pond lies quiet and still
By a grove of willow trees;
It's somewhere near the top of the list
In my book of memories.
Even in the slow-paced days it had
Such calm and luring appeal,
So calm at times I wondered if God
For awhile said, "Time be still."

An old cane pole, a straw slouch hat,
A can of red wiggler worms,
And if anyone wanted a piece of my time,
It had to be on my terms.
Today it's still what life's about,
Enjoying the gentle ease,
With saltine crackers, a can of sardines,
And a plug of red rind cheese.

So when I'm stressed, I allow my thoughts
To drift back to this peaceful bliss,
Because I know Tom Sawyer and old Huck Finn
Never had it any better than this.

Johnny C. Mauldin

The Reel Truth

My life seems like a movie,
I never know what is real (which reel?)

It had the opening credits and will surely have an end.
What happens in the middle is still in the writer's hand.

The plot is forever evolving,
The good, bad and ugly always revolving.

I'm the star of this movie,
I produce, direct, film and edit.

I'm responsible for the story line,
So I can make it a comedy or drama anytime.

Whether it's tears of joy or sorrow,
I decide which path the plot will follow.

So no matter what my critics say,
I can win an Oscar every single day.

Because no matter how mundane or thrilling my life might be,
I'm the one who gets to live it,
Not you, only me.

Tim Ward

My Pocket Holds Only Paper Dreams

Small circles of copper wishes and larger circles of silver faith
reflect in my infant eyes as though issuing my future
from beneath the blue blue water whose ripples remind me
of my loved ones who've lived and died.
Ripples wrought from the last withered hands that clutched and in a
severely held breath released a pocketbook full of copper wishes.
She smiled and sighed as her wishes fluttered and sank silently
to the marbled floor.
My pocket holds only paper dreams.
I place one green dream on the blue blue water's surface,
like a child sailing her first ship after a spring rain.
I step away and with one final glance over my shoulder,
I leave my dream behind, soggy and floating.

Rielle Vobi

Love

Love is cold, Love is also hot.
Love is the feeling any person should have a lot.
Love is a scream, Love is a whisper.
Love is when the person is gone and you miss her.
Love is a man, Love is a woman,
And love is that thing that holds them together.

Fred Williams

The Limitations of Man

What can man write with words,
Or paint in pictures.
Or express through feelings,
Or use his greatest wisdom to describe, the things he knows not of.
He cannot know the fullness of God's great power,
He cannot see infinity.
He cannot sense the duration of eternity.
He cannot see the splendor of God's glory.
He cannot feel the magnitude of His love.
He cannot control the elements,
He cannot emit light, and life, and love in invisible waves
throughout the universe, as God does.
God reveals much to man in His word.
Who can but know the full meanings?
For man is given only glimpses,
For he is shrouded in veils of unknown mysteries of life.
For man's understanding is not God's understanding.
Man can only seek and yearn for these things.
But they can never be his, until he becomes
a complete oneness with God.

Joan Di Fabio

Dear Mom

You gave birth to me on a hot summer's eve,
And named me after an angel that fought against the fires of evil.
You could not have known, at some point in my life,
I would burn the feathers from my wings.
You stood by me and helped me mend the wings I singed,
And you proved true what it is to be a mom.
Your angel is a man now, Mom,
Flying high to complete his tour.
Dear Mom, I could not have done it without your faith,
And belief in me.
The angel you named,
Michael.

Michael Moreno

Julie

I climbed no mountain high
Nor vistas did I see
But 'til the day I die
I love the woman who loves me

Did Rembrandt in a vision see her smile
Did Mozart in a future echo hear her sing
How else could they the world beguile
And turn the winter into spring

With love and play with words to teach
She comes to city, comes to children small
So they will wish a star to reach
For she's the mother of us all

I learn from her a giving heart
That giving is an ecstasy
And when this world I must depart
I'll ever love the woman who loved me

Lou Guttman

I Am Special

I may be a child, and very small,
Or I may be an adult, all, sturdy, and tall
I may be rich, with money to spare,
Or I may be poor, with nothing at all.
Whatever I am in this place called Earth,
I know that I'm special because of my birth.
For God made me in the "image" of Him
So, I can be all that He wants me to be.
I'm special, I'm special; can't you see,
You are very special just like me.

Frances L. Henry

The Wall

An old-fashioned farmhouse, weather-beaten with age
Stands like a picture from a storybook page.
The doors from the hinges are leaning a bit,
The porch, though it's sagging, says, "Come now and sit."

Oh, the memories we have of that grand old place,
Seem as warm and as gentle as an old friend's face.
But the one thing I'll tell you, that says it all
Are the pictures Mom hung on the living room wall.

There's Grandma and Grandpa, God bless their hearts,
There's Momma and Daddy, never apart
There's my sisters and brothers, myself and you know
There's the grandchildren, too, how Mom loved them so.

If that old wall could talk, what a story she'd tell
Of the wonderful times we remember so well.
Mom's gone now, but still, she recorded it all
By the pictures that hung on her living room wall.

    Shirley Frazier

Melt the Walls

Melt the walls, melancholy and encompassing,
Winged whispers of song.
Passions of your heart fill the solitude,
Perfect the truth of your path.
Fragile as you may be,
Combat imagined horrors: your frailty.
Caress the pulse of surging breaths.

Lift your Spirit from powerful depths.
Breathe in your gifts from Heaven's bright surf.
Ripple in your blissful spring
Through limitless dimensions;
Stretch upward on silent feathers sail brilliant waves,
Sanction blossom and burst forth creations.
Enjoy flowing rivers through the valleys,
Flourishing rewards of wealth.
Melt the walls, bright with promise.

    Karina Bridget

Valentine's Last Stand

There will be no romance for me
Come the day of Valentines,
As my destructive but productive verse
Rains on parades with new rhymes;
Moving my poetry in major ways,
Hoping to see better times.
I've watched a lifetime pass by through a
Puddle of tears;
Each drop of saltwater adding on to the
Countless bitter memories, inherited over the years.
I cannot help but notice, that as a man's
Wallet stacks fatter with capital,
Greed feeds off of scandalous women
As if it were a vile parasitic animal.
Take my votto up in Michigan City, for instance;
A violent night laced with insults and pitch forks,
Can send a man crawling back to his primal instincts.
The root of all evil and broken hearts go hand in hand;
Thus Valentine's last stand.

    Ed Snyder

Memories

As I lay in bed at night,
I heard a baby crying for all his might.
I heard the mother saying, "Hush,
don't cry, for I am with you tonight."
I wish I had a mother to hear her say those words to me.
Or a father to bounce me on his knee.
Or a husband to tell me good night.
All I have are my memories to last me through the night.

    Sherrill Milazzo

Rippling River

Rippling river how beautiful you are.
The sunlight dances on you
and whirlpools form as you flow along.
Where are you going?
Where did you begin and where will you end?
You are dancing and singing merrily today,
nothing harsh, just soft
relaxing melodies playing
on the stones and earth below.
You are a sign of peacefulness.
Flow on.

    Peg Feiler

On Parenthood

Though I be dragged to death
'neath rocking horses,
I will deny that I am ever bored.
House bound, within my own enchanted walls,
I own a freedom long denied the horde.
Even racked upon the jungle gym and tortured,
I won't confess to less than fascinated.
Escape from threatening choo-choo wheels
can have aesthetic worth
to those indoctrinated.
Only when the ruby-valued rites of nap
o'erflow my cup, will my admission
(made in mindless bliss)
concede that, briefly, I evade
this day's perdition.

    Nan Reid Lorentzen

The Children

It was spring
The flowers were in full bloom
Children's laughter echoed through the parks
As they played joyfully.

Then the Nazis came,
Our hearts were filled with sadness
As they marched and sang
"Deutschland, Deutschland uber alles."

Then there was no more spring,
No more flowers,
No more laughter
For the Jewish children of Hungary.

Without mercy,
Without regret,
They were destroyed
In the gas chambers of Auschwitz.

Fifty-six years have past, I still cannot forget
That my two little brothers did not come back.
Who can forget? Who can forgive?
For those who cannot speak.

    Violet Ibi Unikel

Fate's Betrayal

Shaken by an epiphany
as I listened to my true love speaking.
The one entity which gave me light,
blew out my flame in one breath
causing my body to shiver
in the coldness of reality.
Never had I felt so in-tune with a friend,
nor had I been in sync with a lover.
Glorified in its essence,
a love bathing in its perfectness,
torn apart by our desire's odd direction,
betrayed by fate's deceit.

    Erryn M. Jordan

Outside

Outside the sun is shining bright in the sky . . .
The sky is a lovely shade of blue . . .
The birds are singing songs for two . . .
But as you walk inside . . .
You see clouds form around a heart so true . . .
You see the sadness I'm feeling without you . . .
My sadness is the feeling when you won't talk to me . . .
The sadness from not being able to walk with you . . .
The sadness from not being able to hold you . . .
Wishing I could be back home with you . . .
so I can feel the magic that's outside with you . . .

Dawn Rhodes

Frozen Spring

Someone has frozen my sun
I've felt a lifetime of pain
And I've only just begun
Tears burning my cheeks could substitute rain

My spring is so cold
All the flowers have died
The last butterfly floats
On a raindrop I've cried

As I drift on a glacier
In a world so ice cold
I fight to stay young
As my body grows old . . .

Jyllian Powers

A Night to Remember

It started with a party; doesn't it always start that way?
"It will be fun!" That's what they always say.
A car full of kids, happy and drinking,
I was the driver and I wasn't thinking.
I saw despair and I heard the cries,
Death sometimes comes with a sudden disguise.
What would happen next was expected least,
When a car turned the corner the loud laughter ceased.
Squeals of the tires as the car loses control,
I brace myself as the car starts to roll.
Twisted metal and glass being shattered,
Two seconds later my thoughts were all scattered.
A pounding in my brain overtaken by crying,
My best friend two feet, from where I was lying.
But I look back that confused look was right,
She died on the cold pavement, that black lonely night.
I killed my best friend and one other kid,
Driving that night I won't forget what I did.
So there you see what happens when you drink and drive,
It ruins friendships and destroys lives.

Arianne Hummelle

Sunset and Sunrise

The twilight sets in
The star studded sky wears the evening star on
its forehead
The night wears a soiree of glistening stars
The Moon sees its image in the mirror of the lake
The sun light pours its vermilion on the forehead
of the night sky
The birds twitter as dawn breaks in
The sun glistens over the noon sky
The twilight sets in
The star studded sky wears the evening star on its forehead

Shyamali Chaudhuri

Day In, Day Out

They say that you are as wise as your years, your days
But all I see is salty dry tears, the ones you cried
Because the memories, the burn, a part of you has died
As you walked along the path of life without a turn
The wear and tear, grind constantly
The feelings have you in a vise, a bind, you expel these feelings
But not all the way, a reminder, a reminder
Every day when, at last, you think you can see
You look in the mirror and you is actually me

Billie Jo Christensen

Bah Hum Bug

Don't sing me "Oh, Tannenbaum"
And don't jingle my bells.
Because I don't want any snow at Christmas time
because it's cold as Hell.
So don't wrap me any presents and put them under your tree
Because Christmas time is just another day in the year to me.
I won't put up any twinkling lights or decorate any pine trees
Because I would just as soon see Tiny Tim on his knees.
So Joy to the World and Fa La La
I just have to say La De Da.
Don't ever think about decking my halls with boughs of holly
Because you can bet I'm not sitting around waiting for Mr. Jolly.
Oh, Come All Ye Faithful and walk in my Winter Wonderland
Because Christmas in Florida is full of sand.

Jeffrey Martin Blancett

Treasure Love

Such a treasure is his mind
Gems are his thoughts
Precious is his intellect
Such a treasure is his heart
Rich in love for me
Diamond, his innocence,
beneath the roughness of his wisdom
Such a treasure is his soul
A gold that complements my silver
Rare and precious, his energy
Such a treasure is this person
A pearl among pieces of coal
A unicorn running with mules
And so I cherish what is mine
and dream of the treasures within,
the treasure I will have

Christina M. Zera

Separated

I thought they were happy
I guess I was wrong
They don't want to be together anymore
Yet they've been together so long.

Their fake smiles of happiness
Were not true to the heart
So now they have decided to separate
And become apart.

They didn't talk to each other
Silence was all I heard
From sun up to sun fall
They didn't speak one solitary word.

The silence between them
Was too hard to take
I tried to help them as much as I could
But between them love I could not make.

I guess they weren't meant for each other
That's just the way life is
Maybe next time they'll find someone
To live much happier lives with

Stephanie Rae Jones

My Family is a Roller Coaster

My family is a roller coaster

My mother is the brakes that stop me
from doing anything I want that might be dangerous.

My stepdad is the chain that pulls my family up the hills.

My half sister is the screaming people who always demand more.

My stepmom is the loop that scared my family apart.

I'm the track that everyone always tries to run over.

Stephanie R. Beach

Color of Words

I draw my pictures with the color of words.
I weave their meanings to create a tapestry of thought.

Touch me; I teach you to see as I do.
Feel me closer as you nudge my heart by uncovering my words.

Open yourself to know me.
Understand the comfort I have found in my own discovery.

Let me touch you with the words.
Breath gently, let them move your fragile circumstance
as they already have for me.

Touch love with the adjectives of imagination.
Color in your own world for this is not only my canvas.

Choose your words in careful contemplation.
They can both erase and create.
Know me deeper as you read this precious art of words.

Annette Marie

Around Midnight

When the clock strikes twelve and people are sleeping,
There comes the sound of crying and weeping.

Our souls come out for a glance and a dance
And if we awaken at midnight, by chance,
We're frightened out of our wits at the sight
Of this most bizarre spectacle, around midnight.

This sometimes is known as the witching hour.
These souls bounce about and try to devour
Our feelings of joy and the sweetest of dreams,
And always, just about midnight, it seems.

They play on our heads and taunt us and haunt us,
These poor tortured souls who are lonely and aimless,
Who appear around midnight and ruin our sleep.
But we own them forever; they're ours to keep.

So, if about twelve you rise from your bed to
Witness your soul playing on your head,
It's only a dream, though it doesn't feel right
And it only happens around midnight!

Gretchen Kane

The Path

The world is but a myth we live in,
with love, fear, deceit, and sin.
What we do leaves an imprint,
leaves a message that is already sent.
A trail that we have followed,
but is sometimes a place in which we might have wallowed.
For now the trail could be sweet,
but possibly gone by the end of the week.
And sometimes we stand in the path unsure of how it is,
wondering curiously if there is unmistakable fizz.
For now I shall stay in this part of the trail,
no matter what, a change, shall never fail.

Jami Byrley

Hear God

Listen, hear God whispering, don't you hear
the wind blowing through the trees.

Listen, hear God singing, can't you hear the birds
song of the new spring.

Look, see God smiling, see the beautiful
spring flowers blooming in the field.

Look, see God playing, watch the squirrels as
they race up and down jumping in the trees.

Look, see God working, behold the honey bees
as they busily buzz around their hive.

Look, listen, God is everywhere.
Feel his sweet presence in the warmth of the sun,
in the scent of the honeysuckle as it climbs the mighty oak.
Shhh listen, what is God saying to you?

Aletha Winstead

The Note He Left

A wilted bouquet on my dresser drawer,
A tattered note torn on the floor,
A girl with tears running down her cheek,
A boy with another girl to seek.
Don't give me flowers, they'll only die, why tell
Me you care if it's only a lie, I don't need that kind of affection
Or that kind of play, just leave me alone, as you've always done.
You hurt me too much to be the one!

Jennifer Jones

Reflection

Oh, how time passes by and you think
memories have gone good-bye.
Then suddenly a stranger can open that box
of memories without your permission,
one stranger after another,
each giving you a look once again into the past.
In my heart I said good-bye,
yet what I thought was silent in my heart
and mind have resurfaced
and I try not to hear those memories,
Oh, how I wish I could turn off my ears and that projector
that runs without my permission.
I speak to my memories and I tell them, "Go away,
good-bye, I'm done with you."
And when you think they have understood,
here comes a stranger, the box opens, and my ears start
to hear and the projector runs without my permission.

Frances Jurado

What Must Be Written

A burgundy ribbon
across a blank, white page.
The shadow of a butterfly
against a textured wall.
The sunlight in an empty room.
What do you say to yourself
in an empty world?
My mother always wanted to go out
and travel. She also talked about how this
had so much to do with being rooted.
She made sure I could write letters.
"Wherever you go, you must know how to
put it down in your own words."
Her Japanese fan. Her hometown
in an island. These are all
going to become words in a story.
She said it was no use being so far away
if there wasn't anyone at home to write to.

Justine Camacho

Lord Send Me an Angel

For so many years I've just wanted to be loved!
I have so much love in my heart and soul to give
Lord, send me an angel!
I've prayed for You to please send me my angel to love me
For eternity . . .
To love all my hurt away . . .
To love all my loneliness away too . . .
To love me for me as I will love him . . .
To love me with all my goodness and goodwill
And yet I still pray
Lord, please send my angel!

La Tanya R. Hammond

He Is, but He Is Not

He stands before you,
a smile on his face.
The gentle look the same, the eyes the same,
the look the same,
but he is not the same.
He does not know you;
his mind has erased the past.
The terrible shock of him not knowing—
the years erased to nothing—
is not bearable. It is not right.
Something is very wrong.
It can't be; it is so.

What is there to do? The truth is so painful—
a loved one has disappeared,
but he stands before you,
living, breathing, talking.

You learn a new life of thanks—
he is still with you.

Jack Gordon

A Baby . . .

To my baby, Kristine

You watch over me when I am asleep
And gaze into my eyes with loving warmth
You ponder over tomorrow and hope
That I will always be safe in my journey

You clothe me and feed me, shower me with kisses
When you hear my cries echoing in the midst of silence
You wrap and cuddle me in a thousand ways
To ease my miseries and wipe away my tears

I know not how to thank thee for thy goodness
My hands are too little and feet too wiggly
Pardon my moments of awkward gestures
To utter my first words mama and dada

Every so often you worry about me
And wish you could seize each moment
I smile to let you know
That Someone is watching over you, too . . .

Elenita M. Obille

The Grave

I had a dream one night
Of a grave in moonlight
An empty grave no writing on the stone
Yet something chills me to the bone
The grave starts to fill with sorrow and sin
The more it fills the more I want in
I remember the grave and it makes me mad
I remember my feelings and it makes me sad
Will I be placed in that grave I don't know
Hopefully it will shrink as I grow

Robert Otto

The Mist Ball

In the cold, bare field the mist,
As illusive as angel hair,
Dances and dances, in order to keep warm,
Until the sun, taking its inspiration from Rumplestilskin,
spins the mist into gold.
Then, being thoroughly warm, the golden mist
slips away, until another cold morning
calls the mist to dance, once again.

Suzanne K. Beckley

Little Miss Mariah (Mon Petite Fille)

You scared us when you came too soon,
Drawn to the light, it was dark in the womb.
You insisted on coming early,
And in your own darling way,
To change our lives a little
Each and every day.
And, sweet little munchkin,
You've done that, my dear.
For none of us you've touched
Are the same as we were last year!

Ruth A. Holley

They Bleed Red, Also

Two young boys playing in the street one day,
One boy is white and the other is black
The boys play and play and play all day,
The little black boy runs and trips and skins his knee,
A little trickle of blood runs down his leg
So the boys continue to play
The white boy's mother comes out and sees the boys playing together
She calls out to her son, Billy come over here. Now!
So the boy runs over to her
The mother says, don't you know you're not supposed to play with him
But Mom,
No Billy, they are not like us
But Mom,
No buts Billy, I don't want you playing with him
But Mom he bleeds red, also

Robert L. Allen

I Am Your Child

I am your child, give me love
Wipe my tears, when I am crying.
Hold my hand, when I am scared.
Give me strength, when I am weak.
Show me the right way, when I am wrong.
Speak for me, when the words seem not to come.
Hug me when I need it, and even when I don't.
No matter what we go through,
I am your child, give me love.

LaFranza Bennett

She

She has been stripped of her will
She has been stripped of her freedom
She has been stripped of her pride

As she stands alone, cold and naked
The tears run down her cheeks
Her hair a mess, her flesh pale and cold
As she surveys the room for help all she
Sees are the people who did this to her

She begins to sob as she realizes
She is now a shell of a person who was once whole
She realizes she has become a statistic
Like so many others before her, she has
Fallen from grace with no one to catch her fall

Sarah Deck

Beware

May a flower bring lightness
While a smile brings wickedness
Flowers come in different shapes
Smiles come in different faces
Poison ivy can deceive you with its beauty
Smiling faces can stab you when you're not looking
Red roses bloom
Red blood drips
Petals fall
Tears drop
Flowers give pollen
Smiles give laughter
Dried up flowers give a scent
Smiles can pretend
Flowers, you can expect their ways
Smiles, you can't detect
Flowers, so soft and tender
Smiles that won't surrender
Wild flowers multiply
Smiles will divide

    Jacqueline G. Salinas

My Child

To my child born unaware
Of a life he'll have to bear

He will be born unable to speak
With a strong mind but no use of his feet
He'll be bound to a family so full of ties
To fight for his life they'll all have to try

Through his brother's eyes his life be lead
To run jump and play his spirit be fed

For mom and dad are always there
To help him through the Hell he'll bear

He will learn of love through a family of pride
Never be afraid or feel a need to hide
All of life's trials he must endure
He'll overcome all that's for sure

To love the child unable to speak
Our hearts seem full of total defeat

Although he'll never walk or talk
He'll go through life as God intends

To be conceived was the choice above
For God has given a blessing of love.

    Robbin Brewer

Gift

It's something that comes
from only the heart,
It's something one never truly finishes
Once they start.
It's a gift given to very few,
A gift that must grow deep inside of you.
It's a want so great, a need so bad,
A yearning to seek the patience,
You never thought you had.
Standing at that line, ones heart feels so weak,
Nerves so alive,
Concentration so deep.
But once that line is crossed again,
With a strength one never knew,
There, lies an exasperating comfort,
To look back at what you have gotten through.
With many races behind,
And many left to go,
A sense of pride is felt, that can only come
From deep within a runner's soul.

    Tarah Sobodas

Heaven in His Eyes

The first time we danced,
I looked into you eyes,
But what I saw was something strange.
As I took a closer look ,
I saw something peaceful,
I thought to myself for the whole dance,
But when I realized what I saw,
I said aloud, it was Heaven,
Heaven in his eyes.
From this day on, when I see him
In the school halls, I am reminded about
That special place,
That special place in his eyes called
Heaven.

    Rebecca Mcmenemy

My Tunnel

What is that, which lies ahead?
'Tis but a faint glimmer of light.
Ever moving forward, yet further away.
Seems that the closer one gets,
the further it goes.
Every step a stumble, every leap a fall.
Yet still getting up, trying to move closer.
I ponder often, will I ever reach the end?
But alas, I cannot give in,
For my love travels next to me.

    Jim Loftin

Perfect Love

Sometimes I don't know what to do,
Life just seems so meaningless without you.
There is this feeling so deep in my heart,
And there's no way to find where it starts.
It doesn't begin or end,
The feeling doesn't twist or bend,
It never breaks or fades,
There in my heart it stays,
Growing stronger and stronger each day.
It gets me up in the morning
And keeps me going all through the day.
It makes me happy that I am alive.
The feeling helps me survive.
I hope it's there to the end of time,
Because then, I know you will always be mine.
Deep in my heart I know it is true,
Because these feelings I have
Tell me how much I Love You.

    Michelle Campbell

God's Greatest Creation: "The Black Woman"

Black and beautiful, created by thee, drug free and
Alcohol free, God's most powerful vessel is she.

Gainfully employed, family orientated, and domesticated,
These three, black and beautiful, for God-fearing is she.

She is respectful, honest, and true, all the qualities
Which are necessary as well as important to you.

She is first a child, then mother and wife, she is
God's greatest creation in life.

Black and beautiful, she is a gem, a precious jewel,
Her stock is more valuable than a diamond mine.

She is truly man's treasure chest, his holy blessing,
God's greatest creation, she's one of a kind.

Your search is over, she is standing next to you,
Love her tender—love her sweet, love her forever.

    Janice T. Houston

A Correction Pen for Everything

Many people correct their mistakes using white-out,
But to me this is not what white-out is all about.
I think of white-out as more than something used to erase ink.
To me this white-out is symbolic and meaningful, I think
It represents humanity's sorrows and our various attempts
To erase a dreadful past and live out dreams that we once dreamt.
It represents our goals towards perfection,
And our thirst to become number one.
White-out represents our attempts to the bitter end,
To achieve our goals and our failures to transcend.
It represents our chances to start our life anew
And to comprehend everything that at first we misconstrue.
White-out is symbolic of our trials and our strife
That we try to overcome to brighten up our life.
Yes, but then again white-out is still just a correction pen.
But you must look beyond the substance . . .
And recognize symbolism now and then.

Latrisha Desrosiers

Holy Oak, the Druid's Path

Oh Holy Oak so big and strong,
You make me feel that I belong.
By time of day and time of night,
You give me strength and give me might,
So I can go on, 'til I see the light,
At the end of the tunnel, which tells me I Died

Wim-Jaap Modderman

In My Little Mind

In this little mind you can find.
All my little feelings I have kept in mind.
From the time I thought I liked you.
'Til the time I knew that I loved you.
Also in my little mind,
I have kept this one thought in mind.
That this one wish would come true.
But then I thought in my little mind.
How was I so blind not to find,
That my wish had come true.
Now I know since I found you.

Jared Wiekamp

The Dreamer

She was born a dreamer; her life was full of promise
She dreamt of becoming wise
She dreamt of becoming famous
She hoped of being loved
She thought of helping those in need
She dreamed of a life that was fulfilled and happy
A life with meaning and cause
She dreamed and dreamed and dreamed . . .
Until one day she woke up
Running around frantically trying to fulfill those dreams
Doing instead of dreaming
Fighting instead of hoping
Working instead of wondering
Pulled apart not knowing where to start
With time running out she had to stop!
She closed her eyes trying to think things through
But it was too late
She realized that she dreamt her life away
She was born a dreamer and she'll die a dreamer
And she fell asleep again

Cynthia Alfano

When I Think of My Mother

I think of the woman who created my life;
Who gave me love, warmth, and nurturing to help me grow
into my existence.
She believes in me and encourages me to use my mind.
This I know is why I've succeeded, instead of falling behind.
I think of the woman who taught me value & respect;
and along came with it her patience, tolerance and understanding.
I think of the everlasting bond that could of only come from
within a caring, giving soul.
I feel comfort, security & peace knowing
there was a purpose for my belonging.
The wisdom she instilled in me gave me "trust
in my happiness & faith for my dreams."
I see her as my guardian angel adjusting my wings.
She is always there to guide me, to protect me from evil,
teaching me that kindness is God's will for all people.
I feel sheltered from the world's dishonesty
and I know through every step I take I feel
proud to be her legacy.

Lori Comstock

The Ole Cowboy Prayer

Eternal Father up in the sky.
Have mercy upon this cowboy, before it comes my time to die.

You gave me this range on which I roam.
For many years now you've let it be my home.

I know I don't talk to you as often as I should.
Although I know your word is, I always could

You gave me a horse that is more like a friend.
He will be with me until the end.

Lord, I'm not complaining about the job I have done.
You help me round up all them strays, each and every one.

I felt your warmth in the fire last night.
I felt your presence, Lord, in the first light.

Yes, Lord, if you will, consider this old cowboys prayer.
When I say, "Father" will you always be there.

Then, Lord, when it comes time for my roundup in the sky,
place your loving arms around me and quickly let me fly.

So when they read over me, they will say, "This one did his best,"
Now Father into your arms, let this old cowboy rest.

Wayne H. Moore

The Wonder of It All

I sometimes think of all the things the world is made.
The soil in which we eventually will be laid.
The sky so incredibly white and blue.
It does us good at times, our blessings to review.

The wisdom of making us a nose in order to smell.
Trees and flowers and the rain to make them grow so well.
The ability to speak certainly is no small wonder.
The creation of senses to feel and hear I often ponder.

Can you imagine someone loving us so much
We were given feet to walk and hands to touch,
A heart to keep us going, and a brain to tell us what to do,
The miracle of our eyes, so everything we can view?

I look around this vast world so great,
It should only be filled with love, never hate.
How anyone could not believe in God I cannot understand,
For every small detail he so wisely did plan.

We take so much for granted and forget our thanks to say
For the air we breathe and good health day after day.
He knows we are sometimes troubled and weak,
But He is always there, simply reach out and seek.

Edna Loving

Lost in My Thoughts

Lost in my thoughts, with you on my mind.
Seeing you there, all of the time.

Seven children, all that you had.
Now you're gone, no more Dad.

March 1, 2000, seeing you there, lying on the floor.
How I wish it wasn't true.
Tears pouring down as I walked through the door.

My dad this isn't true, it can't be real.
Your pain has stopped, now it's my turn to feel.

Hurt, angry—I can't get it straight.
Father's Day came three months too late.

I love you, I miss you, I wish you were here.
Standing at your grave was my biggest fear.
Out in the cold, looking down.
How could my Daddy be in the ground?

How can it be, why is this true?
Oh, God, Oh, Dad, I just miss you!!

Shelly Brobst

The Golden Sea

The wheat fields were waving,
Like a golden sea
Far from a city or even a tree
The children were dolphins
Roaming carefree, upon the Earth's golden sea
As day passed, the sea grew still
The night wind made waves
Upon its will
In the morning the dolphins
Will see nothing has changed
In their still golden sea

Jennifer Dyer

Branded

Down in the cotton fields way back home.
The nights were cool and breezy
The days scorching hot and ever so long.
Rise up early in the morning
Cotton bowls filled with dew.

Fill that old cotton sack
With a hundred pounds of cotton.
Lord it's hard on my poor aching back
But I know I can draw two.

Run child, run fast as you can
Fetch a bucket of cool drinking water
From the spring and the river's end.
I hear the master's whip a crashing, upon my back

Burning, hurting stinging blows he is lashing
A few stolen cooling moments under the shade of a tree
Has Branded me 400 hundred years later still
A liar. A thief, and lazy

Gerri Darrisaw

Nature's Goodnight

As the fiery sun slowly went down behind the ocean
The stars began to glow one by one each twinkling
The moon reflects off of the calm ocean
Bringing out night crabs
Scurrying across the wet sand
Dolphins jump out to catch a glimpse
And dive back down traveling, traveling
The waves crash against the shore
As if to say goodnight to all

Julie Reinert

Alone

Alone
All alone without a soul in sight
No one but me to internally fight
There I stand, all alone
Standing there, chilled to the bone
Listening to the street top sounds
Letting my mind go . . .
Further
With ideas no other mind can comprehend
The multitude of foreign voices to completely blend
Confusion is all that is left
But yet I have not slept
Yet no one is there to lend helping hands
So I am left on my own
To walk in memories past out-grown
And to die slowly in the ever-quickening sands
The sands of time

Aaron Ross

Prayer

In my own world I have seen
Not much of roses, peaches, or cream.
Tough experiences from an early age
Filled me full of hate and rage.
Must the past be repeated, my soul defeated?
Creating my own living Hell, in misery dwell?
Without concern for others, or even spare
A loving look at you, nor for myself care.

In my own world I have seen
Not much of roses, peaches, or cream.
In my own way I paid the price.
A bad roll of the dice.
Can this pain be gone now?
Through faith in God and strong belief?
Where, my relief?

Adam Colonna

Unicorn

Thou exist in thy heart, thy mind and thy soul,
Thou freedom is sacred,
Thou beauty is infinite,
Thou heart is pure,
And thou wisdom is unforetold.

Through time thou travel,
Spreading truth, justice and love,
Thou presence is foretold,
Thou are the saviour of the innocent,
The holder of truth,
The bearer of justice,
And the symbol of love.

To thou I kneel,
To thou I pray to save thy soul,
To no longer fear the cry of pain, the cry of the innocent,
To live as thy soul was born to live,
To live in freedom

Jacqui Turner

Unanswered Prayer

Dear God, please whisper in my ear,
Must men wage wars and die?
Has all life lost precious value?
My Lord, please tell me why.

War brings on constant death
And makes our loved ones cry.
Are we filled with such hatred?
My Lord, please tell me why.

Herman Guy

Love

Love sometimes last
'Til death do us part
Love can hurt especially if
Love walks out of your life
You may have friends
Love is a hug
For two people
Love is friendship
Especially if it is a dog or cat
Love is a family
As well as a home
Love is laughing at a good joke
Even when you have a mountain of problems
Love is mom and dad
And their guidance
Love is grandma and grandpa
And their stories of days gone by
Love is love itself

Jackie Morris

Feeling Lost Again

As the east wind kicks up its
heels from the Columbia Gorge,
the pines surrounding his house
dance madly with abandoned freedom,
creating a comforting sound.
While alone in his bed,
shared only with the 2 1/2-year-old
black lab, Bubba,
who loves him unconditionally.
He remembers . . . two very different loves.
A perfect wife with an imperfectly
scarred body, which fit his own.
Two years, three months, twenty-three days ago
the brain tumor won.
Now it's 16 days, 17 hours and 20 minutes.
after diabetes finally stopped his mom's heart.
She gave him his love of music and poetry,
and his wife's deaf ears loved him for
simply sharing both with her.
And I am . . . feeling lost again.

C. V. Woodard

Photographs

Thinking of the past with you is very hard to do
So I go through my photographs and find the ones of you
They are my precious memories sweet visions of the past
They show me how we used to be and make the moments last
They take me to another time when life was so carefree
When I was there with you and you were here with me
I wish that I could go back to those moments in our lives
But life only goes forward and our memory survives
Photographs are memories they're visions of the past
They show us how we used to be and make the moments last
I'm glad I have these memories of when you were alive
Although you are no longer here your photographs survive
Photographs are memories that keep our past alive
But they were made by human hands which means we never die.

Richard Wayne Love

Melody Man

If I could hide behind that musician's ears
Maybe I would feel the way he feels
When those sounds hit him like waves crashing on a deserted beach
The perfect curl of his eyelashes
Would be an ideal shelter
On days of blindness, when I need a different perspective
And when I would be too tired to sleep
I wish I could hang on to one of those notes he sings
And be carried away by the wind

Maysan Marouf

Prelude

A light rain faintly taps at the window
while the awaiting storm is still a whisper above the clouds.
Lying next to you, I vaguely ponder
this moment that has unfolded.
The heat of day has become the warmth of night,
as moonlight spills into the room.
I turn my face to yours and watch
as soft slumber silently embraces you.
I let my hair fall over your chest
so that I may listen to your gentle breathing,
and still I can feel that relentless ambition
pulsing through your body as you sleep.
Knowingly, I smile to myself, passionately believing
that you have wind in your blood and fire in your soul.
Delicately, I kiss your lips.
Softly, you answer with a smile
that unlaces a thousand mysteries
that lie within the canyons of my heart.
And as I nestle deeper into your arms,
unaware, you nestle deeper into my heart.

Lisa Niewinski

Ethereal Memorandum

To one of my shadows
Like a ghost in the darkness
made of mist and of time
The thoughts are chaotic and senseless
feelings it gives are purely sublime
Chronologically displaced
Pure in direction
Always and never
Not a man nor a woman
or a spirit of abstraction
An idea
Often unprovoked
May get worse, may get better
Like the past regurgitated
made of truth but stranger
Twisted by the perspective of the rememberer
To learn
To treasure
To honor
A single ability out of many
Separates the intellect from the orthodoxy

Heather L. Makar

Time—The Eternal Peneplain

To my Son, Alexander David Fanshawe
Unending as a peneplain, where level
land, undisturbed by crustal cracks,
moves, imperceptibly, to some
parameter of evolution
From an object defined by its
properties at a particular moment
in time, to the notion of a state,
or, to the way things are—
What we call space and what we
call constant time space, is space-time.
The problem of time
is that it Vanishes and only God
withstands its ravages.
No clock is perfect, for "now" has gone.
The future is a feast
of possibilities, the past—
a multifarious range of
genuine infinitesimals.
Time, the emerging concept,
a clepsydra of endless possibilities.

Jude Croasdell

In the Aftermath of Disease

For the love of all my patients, especially Norine and Samuel
Raging soldiers marching in with missions of deadly destruction.
Aggressive warriors invading cellular barriers, unseen in the night.
Unveiling their presence through subtle pangs of deterioration.
Their untimely visit, thrusting unsettling fear into thy soul.
Denial and confrontations with reality consume thee.
Uncertainty of survival ricochets off the brick walls of thy being.
Harboring feelings of an unjustified sentence in an unwanted war.
Waving white flag in hand, surrender seems to be the only recourse.
Unaware, thy internal command post is activated.
Armies of fight or flight rescuers emerge.
With sudden renewal, the broken spirit surmounts.
Standing fearless now, staring straight into the eyes of fate.
Retreating soldiers are now unseen.
This war is aborted and life triumphantly marches on.
Peace reigns in thy soul, bearing messages to those spared.
Always keep thy will alive like a warrior with upheld dagger.
Fear not the unknown enemy.

T. L. Scheuers

Merry Christmas?

For the victims of Lockerbie
Flight one-o-three, the papers said
two hundred and seventy or more feared dead.
Just hours before they all were fine,
all heading home for Christmas time,
but now they lay on floors stained red.
Two hundred and seventy or more now dead.
So sad the tears that line each face,
where relatives gather to hear their fate.
No "Happy Christmas" waits for them,
their lives destroyed by heartless men.

Martyn Passey

Spirit Bound

Deep within this human clock
Dwells a spirit bound by social grace.
Dare I ever to unlock—And face contempt
From my fellow race.

Time is receding,
Closing in . . .
Shackled bound my thought within.

I've witnessed spirits roaming free
Uniting their souls in harmony.
The price for this too high for me;
For, while Earth-bound, it can never be.

Annette Clarke

She Is Still a Slave

This is the twenty-first century and this
Black woman is enslaved by her black brother!
Yes, he may say that he loves her.
He may even feed and clothe her.
Yet, he also scolds her!
Then he beats her 'til she's black and blue!
He scares her!
What can she do?
Maybe she should call the police
And incarcerate that black man.
She has that option!
She really can.
No, but she can't!
He has her like a maid.
She is his black slave.
He has not only just scarred her physically,
But he has scarred her mentally as well.
Does this pain inflicted upon you, the black woman,
Ring a bell!

Deidre Davis

You!

To my best friend and my inspiration, Kimberly Manuel
In the midst of the night
my heart sings a melody
only for you to hear.
As it begins with a soft elegant tune,
filled with the softest bids of good night.
It then emerges to the lonesome cry
from my heart to yours.
Then ends with a solemn, sweet tune,
filled with the essence of love.
Just as the first ray of sunlight beams of the day,
I am astounded by the beauty you have become.
To awaken to your presence
sends with me the whole day through
a simple, but sweet, reminder of you.

Penney Doss

True Intentions

A start not intended for the suffering but a declaration
for new ventures into a life as one. My, how words
you do twist and fade into questionable doubts,
doubts to be made conveniently available for
a never ending time and to be recalled when
your way is not the way things done.
Why do you ridicule this intent? 'Tis not your reasoning
with harm, but of my reasoning with honesty and true
intentions. There lies not a hidden treasure of
twisted meanings to everything one does.
The heart does hold an abundance of
truth and, as well, a conscience
to keep it ever so level, as
not to spill over the pain
and tears of the past.
Open thy heart and see what I see. Is love so blind
as it masks the very dreams and true intentions
of tomorrow with the fears of our yesterdays?

Phillip Teresi

Little Butterfly

How enchanting you are to me, little butterfly.
With each soft flutter of those tiny intricate fans—
Your canvas wings (an explosion of the
Utterly infinite gamut of hued emotions sprinkled
Upon a surprisingly minute and finite space)
—What delicate, tender winds they bring forth,
Caressing, mesmerizing my whole being
Until I am utterly taken—enraptured, captured.

With the syncopated magical rhythm of your flight
You slowly cocoon me into your world—your mystical thread
Intertwining with my skin,
With my soul and the blaze of your heart,
In a graceful dance of endless pirouettes, taking flight
Into mine.

I could do nothing but be a willing captive,
Powerless in the clutches of your sheer fragile beauty.

Jason Vincent Cabañes

Half Past

Half past a life time, you will find me still loving you,
Standing in the very balance of all that I know to be true.
In the still of the darkness, silent hours when I am alone,
The clock that sits on the mantel, eases time with a single tone.
My heart can hear you breathing, a soft mist that fills the air,
The very essences of you so near me, such tenderness you share.
You may be but an illusion, some Prince without a Princess,
But you came to me like none before you, filling all my senses.
I will linger in the unity of this oneness that we have made,
A simple love that will not leave me, nor will it fade away.

Katherine Raborn

Fate

He saw her one day, looking pretty and sweet.
Oh! If only he wasn't tongue-tied.
But suddenly, then his heart skipped a beat;
Fate smiled this day, so he tried.

It was simply a "Hi," she smiled back, "Hello."
He thought she looked like a queen.
She liked him too, didn't want him to know
That she was just newly sixteen.

After that it was movies and walks in the park;
They seldom were ever apart.
Until soon they both knew that very first spark
Had become an affair of the heart.

They made plans to wed, but fate took a hand,
As it had in their life once before,
But this time fate gave him no choice but to stand
And fight for his country in war.

A year or so later, the telegram came;
Before it was opened she cried.
She never would know who was really to blame;
Fate frowned that day, so he died!

Art Bott

Life Isn't Easy

Life isn't easy, it has many changes.
Sometimes the whole thing just rearranges.
We go through life with many emotions.
You make it through it with a lot of devotion.
To the people we love and the things we believe in.
You make a promise not to deceive them.
You love them and care for them all your days through.
Don't worry about the little things life brings to you.
Because life isn't easy, it has many changes.
Sometimes the whole thing just rearranges.

Vicky Lynn Fuller

Theater of Life

It is a cloudy night,
maybe later will rain
and maybe later I'll die
to find beauty behind my pain.
Giving life to a clown,
scared of laughter or tears,
dressed like a crow
flying out of here.

All the promises I made
are gone in a glass of wine.
All the characters I played
my lines in this theater of life.

Excuse me if can't make you smile
but the comedy's end is calling my door.
Nothing to give, but a remaining while; then,
excuse my death when you don't smile anymore.

Carlos Morales

But

They say: "No two snowflakes are alike."
But, science has proof there's only five snowflake types.
They say: "Lightning never strikes the same place twice."
But, people and places have been struck 3, 4 or more times.
They say: "I love you and will never hurt you."
But, the pain they cause can be too great to bear.
They say: "Walk silently but carry a big stick."
But, not speaking up or violence only creates larger problems.
They say: "Hello. How are you? How are things going?"
But, they mean, Hi, I don't really care or have time.
They say: "Best Wishes, Merry Christmas & Happy New Year!"
But, get upset and curse you if you didn't buy them an expensive gift.

Dusty Watson

Always and Forever

As I look back on my life I see very few bright spots in it.
You were one of them
You brought so much happiness into my life
We were so young but I know we were in love
We would talk on the phone for hours
Hang out with each other almost every day
But then came the day we stopped talking
I forgot all about you and went on with my life
But now I think of you, hoping that we can become friends again
But our lives are so different now
Different towns, different friends, completely different lives
But in my mind that's okay because
I still have the memories of us together
Always and Forever

Dara Roxlau

He's Gone

My mom called.
Told me to get dressed quickly.
I waited and waited.
Then she finally arrived.
She said to hurry.
She had spoken to the nurse.
The nurse said he was fading fast.
If your kids want to see him before . . .
We arrived at the hospital.
We ran as fast as we could.
We didn't run fast enough.
We had gotten there too late.
The room was dark and closed.
I felt my heart being crushed.
My mom ran to ask the nurse.
My mom walked back over to us.
Her with tears in her eyes.
She lightly spoke out two soft word's.
That will live in my memory forever.
He's gone.

Catrina Haase

What Is Your Imagination?

Your Imagination is a world
that gives you creative ideas to work with

It is Mt. Everest
filled with adventure

Your Imagination is a question mark
that only you can understand

It is a color
painting pictures in your head

Your Imagination is a dream
where you go every night

Stacy Patrick

Remembering You

As I watch the rolling sea from a distance,
My mind is filled with thoughts of you.
The memories are as warm as the sun,
Creeping across my face from behind the clouds.
When I close my eyes, I can feel you,
Oh, so close.
Arousing all my senses within,
Music is playing in my head.
I can smell the sea,
Taste the wine,
And feel my fingers in your hair.
At this moment, time stands still.
Nothing can interfere.
When we are apart,
I am remembering you.

Kimberly Graham

The Ocean

The orange glow of the quickly fading sun
Reflects off the clear crystal blue ocean,
Making it seem larger than life.
The high white-capped tides
Crash upon the sand and rocks,
Bringing hidden treasures from below.
Seashells of different shapes and colors
Glisten from the clear water.
A starfish, longing to be back
In the waters of the deep blue sea,
Rests upon the pale sand,
Waiting for another high tide to come so
It can be carried back home into the water.
While I am standing on the sand,
Overlooking the ocean,
Seeing the tides coming in and out,
And life forms bringing their dazzling bodies
Up out of the ocean into the sunlight,
My heart is uplifted,
And all of the troubles of the day disappear.

Tina Enochs

The Gift of Salvation

He paid for me.
Yes, He paid for me.
He paid for me on that wooden cross . . .
In Calvary.

He bore my sins, though He had none
He conquered death, the Victory He won.

He paid for me with His life
With His death, He paid the price
Sturdy nails pound through his hands and feet
Yet through the pain, there was no defeat.

For hope is what He brought that day
To people desperate for a better way
To rise above the darkness of sin
And bring a sense of peace within.

Kathy Creek

Joys of Spring

In spring the leaves begin to sway,
As the breezes blow throughout the day.
The birds and bees are busy then,
I wish that I could fly with them.
Oh, the joys of spring.

The geese return to their former place
Near fields, of course, ample food to taste.
Gophers are popping up and down
From tunnels they've dug way underground.
Oh, the joys of spring.

Early spring flowers give us their beauty
With wisps of fragrance and color a plenty.
Trees are sharing their place here too
Giving shade for me and my old dog, Blue.
Oh, the joys of spring.

Diane Fredette

Funny It Seems

Funny how a flower grows,
Then slowly ebbs away.
And think of all the butterflies,
That live but for a day.

It seems that good things have a way,
Of going by too fast.
And then the worst things leave their sting,
To linger in the past.

Robbie Freeman

Appreciate the Colors

Do the colors speak
to us in a gracious way?
Burgundy, magenta, and amber.
Do the colors
have something to say
when they are put
so delicately in the
objects we see every day?
Rubies, opals, and emeralds.
For without these
divine colors
there would be no sunrises
for our eyes to gaze upon,
No crescent moons to dazzle us,
No rainbows to bewilder us.
We shall never be able to appreciate this beauty
Until we can see no more,
For only when we are blind,
We shall be able to see what we lost.

Miguel Halling

Regret

I looked at my feet
as I walked down the street.
To look up, I didn't dare
'cause I knew she was there.

I walked past her and she said hi!
But I couldn't speak; I was too shy.
She probably thought I was insane,
and indeed, there was something weird in my brain.

But I found out she was sick,
and that no medicine would do the trick.
Why was there nothing I could give,
just to let her live?

I've felt bad ever since she died,
and God knows that I have cried,
because I didn't say hi!
the day she walked by.

Magnus Sveinn Jonsson

Waiting for You

I never thought I could ever fall
in love with you
it has never crossed my mind
that you could be mine
because you were the kind of guy who was just my buddy
It has always been for both of us
nothing but friendship
but things have changed my way
And I'm madly in love with you
while you don't even notice the change
so here I am sitting here
waiting for a love that I'll probably will never have
If only you could notice my love
but apparently I'm in your eyes nothing but a friend
so I'm sitting her waiting for the day that you'll be mine
even if I know that day will never come
I'll always be waiting for you

Francesca Giola

A Friend Like You

As I walk down the trail of life,
I thank God for the privilege to meet you,
A friend so kind and willing to listen,
And one who is very encouraging.
How wonderful it is to walk down the trail of life,
Knowing I have a friend like you.

Judy Hammel

Love at Second Sight

Through the halls crowded.
All in an uproar on to their next destination.
I follow and lead.
They shot through me with a certainty.
The aim was perfect,
like an arrow splicing an already centered arrow.
Her eyes brought memories that will never evaporate.
I was helpless.
At the time I was holding the hand of another.
I could not help but to gaze back at her.
We were locked. Many thoughts lingered.
My past was striking me without pity.
I am in love with this girl.
As eyes unlock, confusion sets in.
The new one beaten out by the old.
I was surrounded but really alone.
should I respond? Or should I walk away and live in grief?
I love the new one too.
Never as much!

Duane Belcher

The Rose

"What is wrong?," she asked of me.
"Nothing," I answered.
"But I see pain and sorrow in your eyes," said she.
"Look deeper," I answered,
"And you will see love there also,
for the thorn that pierced my heart came from a beautiful red rose."

Enid Tate

Best Friends (Pets)

Most have four legs, but some have two;
Some have none; just fins will do.
But each one does their very best
To take the pressure off your chest.
They slow you down and make you smile;
Then you relax and rest awhile.
You scratch their ears or watch them swim;
Forget the day as your troubles dim.
Troubles fade: life's not so bad,
Whatever the pet,
they make you glad.
Slither, swim, crawl or fly,
They help your every day go by.
So just remember, man's best friend
Is always with him to the end.
Feather, fin, scales or fur,
For the stress of life they are the cure.

Derek Wright Sherlock

Have You Ever?

Have you ever caught a glimpse of someone,
And said, "I wish you were mine?"
Have you ever met someone, and thought,
"For you I'd put my life on the line?"
Have you ever fallen asleep at night,
And noticed no one else crossed your mind?
Have you ever had a touch
That was so gentle and kind?
Have you ever felt
A tremendous pounding within your chest?
Have you ever realized,
Without that person you couldn't ever rest?
Have you ever made a wish
On a clear crystal night,
And had this beautiful feeling
That things would turn out right?
All this I have endured, now I am at peace.
So let me tell you no matter what,
My love will never cease!

Christy Petersen

A Father's Love

I watch your eyes twinkle as you watch your boy.
I see he fills your heart with pride and joy.
You want him to learn and you want him to grow.
You want to nurture his heart and soul.
No greater love does a father have to give,
Than the kind, caring words you whisper in his head.
When he gets hurt, you kiss his pain away.
You want to protect him but let him find his way.
You try to teach him everything you know.
You want the best for him and it shows.
I've seen you cry when he was taken away.
A father's love was abused and betrayed.
When he returned, justice was done,
Because of a love a father has for his son.
When you see your son's eyes and his tiny little face,
His love for you`is evident and can never be replaced.
So in times of turmoil, in times of despair,
See your son's smile and never fear.
Your fatherly love creates a strong bond,
An unconditional love between a father and son.

Jolene De Young

Imagination

In the darkest forest, amidst the green ravine
I find myself ruinous, running, dodging
False objects flying from the enemies arms
The feeling or power of being someone, other then myself
Being myself, filled with ambition and strength
Aries, Orpheus, Zeus, Athena
All convene into one beast
Rages of hope and fear dance through my remains

The power of pretending

Sitting like a dead man's toe
Thoughts, dreams, people flow
Accomplishments and pain
As you grow most things fade
Soon everything drains
When imagination ceases all you have is
Day after day of endless drudgery
With no escape from reality

The power of imagination

Megan Mutch

The Lighted Path

Through the darkness I search for direction.
No Light.
There lies a light within.
Too Frightening.
Others try to lead me down their lighted paths.
No footing.
I fall into the darkness.
Discouraged.
I look before me, there is no light.
I stumble.
I look behind me, my path glows.
Brightly lit.
Many paths cross mine, sometimes widening it.
Added brilliance.
Other paths intersect, even collide.
My path is uncorrupted.
My inner light speaks. My path is now lit.
I understand.

John Favors

Love by: Crazy

Oh, to be in love
is such sweet pain.
Hard to imagine something so
beautiful can drive you insane.
But I can't complain, for my feelings
remain the same.
Love is complicated, far from plain.
Who's to blame?
What kindled the flame . . .
The flame of passion and romance.
I didn't stand a chance.
Love forms a bond that's thicker than steel.
Words can't express how I feel.
Love, what's the deal?
The more I try to understand . . .
The less I know.
Is love a friend or foe?
Do not take love lightly.

       Chad Beall

The Bond of Our Love

To my Loving Wife, Tracy

Together we have explored many worlds
and have discovered untold treasures.
We have molded our hearts of the purest gold
and have paved our path with only the finest gemstones.
Since the night we met,
I knew that we were meant to be together.
Now I thank the Lord for a Love like yours
because I know that it will last forever.
I still can't believe that all of my dreams
have finally come true.
I am so in Love with you and I just have to let you know.
I have got to get it out.
You're all that I ever think about.
It's something that I have to say
because your Love has overtaken my heart.
Soon you will receive the bond of my Love,
a gift from my heart to yours.
My heart has hand crafted this bonding token.
I give it to you with the knowledge
that no evil will ever break this Bond of Our Love.

       Steven Fordyce

Betrayal

One lie, one tiny betrayal;
If you only knew what they did,
What havoc they wreaked:
The broken heart,
The destroyed trust,
The battered soul, the lost relationships,
But you never thought.

I am sorry;
I have no buttons to push
Enabling me to forgive and forget.
To forgive I need to forget,
And to forget, I must leave it all behind me,
Everything that is a reminder of my pain,
Whether it is a memory or the real thing.

I wish you joy and life,
Though I cannot share them with you.
For our lives are no more bound by ties,
Ties which you shook
And which I must now break.

       Meryam Dabhoiwala

Woman in the Willow

I once hung from that windswept tree.
My ankles entangled by its wisps.
Limbs twisted: knobby trunk.
My nights and days full of
marching shadows.
Others seek safety from the squaw vine
that runs across the softened Earth
searching to entrap that which stalks the tree—
to burrow itself into the deepening
crevices:
to suck life through
its roots.
Their clawings mar the bark.
My fingers reach to grasp the
cunning red berries.
I am
the
tree.

       Elizabeth Fecto

Golden Memory

Watching the delicate petals unfold
In the morning sun, a delicious gold,
Makes me recall a time long ago
When I first met and got to know
The person who has guided me throughout the years,
Saved me from despair, and banished my fears.
I can remember their face in every detail;
Eyes so wise and skin soft and pale.
I wish to remember the way they were
When we were together and life was a blur.
Now it has slowed considerably
And they are no longer here with me.
So now I sink back into despair and I mope
Because with them gone, I've lost all cause and hope.

       Jomarie Kusner

A Mother's Love

Dedicated to Reba Green, my Mother, who was a dynamic poet.

A Mother's Love will last forever.
A Mother's Love will never die.
A Mother's Love will last forever,
Whether she is near or far.
Cherish your Mother—she is the one
that taught us to Love.
She learned that from our Father above.
When you are born you are inside of her.
When she is gone she is inside of you.
A Mother's Love will last forever,
even if she has gone to be with God.

       Trudy O. Payne

I Cannot Let You Go

These eyes are fixed and distant.
Nature's sighs abound.
Unwanted rays of sunshine linger.
This mind utters not one sound.
My lids feel sadly moistened.
Your essence drifts not near.
The casket's silhouette blends with nature.
And dirt pours on a heart so dear.
Two tense arms carry my last offering.
No multitude of flowers suffice.
How will my being survive your absence?
My crying, stifling soul will die.
Inner light and peace you radiated.
Untold tensions you transformed to hope.
Your caring love evoked my passion.
I cannot let you go.

       Evelyn Biskeborn

What Is Friendship?

Friendship is a link that joins two or three or more people together,
Each one having his or her own feelings as to the strength
And the commitment that keeps
The friendship together, in spite of varying degrees
Of personality, culture, or social status.

True friendship never ends, it may have its highs and lows,
But there will always be one of you to say
I'm sorry if you hurt or laugh with you if you're happy.
Friendship cannot be measured by a yardstick
But is measured by the sincerity, loyalty, love, and respect
Shared by the parties, thus binding the friendship together.

True friendship allows each party to keep and
Maintain their own space.
True friendship can be described as the wanting
On the part of each other; to remain forever friends,
In spite of their individual differences.

Pamela Willock

Left Behind (But Not Alone)

My mother and father had to go away before it was time
My father died when I was nine.
I had my mother for a few more months, and then,
She went away when I was ten.
It was hard to understand why they had to go
Leaving small children behind, with yet so much to know.
But I guess God knew there was someone who'd step in and do
Someone who would watch over us as we grew.
Someone who would teach us right from wrong
To be there as long as we needed her, until we grew strong.
It wasn't just me, but two younger sisters, that were left behind
A better person to watch over us you couldn't find.
The three of us are grown now and gone our own way
But we love our "bonus" mother for giving us love and a place to stay.
Thanks for all the things you've done,
For putting two families together and making us one.

Brenda R. Anderson

Winds of Change

Peacefully, she rocks the decrepit limbs of dying trees,
comforting them, lulling them to sleep.
Then, with their death, sorrow overcomes her.
Moaning through the broken panes of an abandoned building,
her pain echoes through empty rooms with hollow cries
that cause the shack to shudder.
But the agony's too much to bear and frustration overcomes her.
Renting her anger, she forces dust devils to dance madly about,
biting into homes, tearing the caps from their heads
and tossing them carelessly through the air.
Bitter cruelty, until she can wrestle no more.
And so, she whispers through the pines, apologizing for her brutality.
Asking forgiveness by gracefully sweeping through fields of wheat
until she herself is breathless as day succumbs to night.
Until next time, for her breath is eternal.

Anita Faye Dyck

Introspection

Lone tree in a barren desert, no rain here to nourish your roots,
no wind to rustle your leaves, but that hot wind carrying gusts of sand
to expose the thin veneer of your trunk, raw areas holding exposed memories;
patches of life, desolate, scattered hulls of spent friendships,
silent skeletons haunting.

Thoughts crash against the door of your mind; dark night moving fast,
taunting and whispering,
"Move on, keen and wail, poor lost soul; no matter . . . you have no goal."

Reach deep within your soul;
in retrospect, nothing would change.
Words exchanged in anger, expressions softened with time, interpretation tucked close.
Night drape drawn, dawn softens offering peace.

Melinda Sellers

Reason Not to Give Up

I am surrounded,
I am blind,
I can't breathe.
I hear voices,
They echo,
My head hurts.
I am tired,
I am restless,
I want to give up.
Then I remember
The reason
I am here.
I believe in myself.

Ruby Sethi

Inside the Sea of Me

Among the dwellers of the sea
There sounds a cry of agony
An emotion that dispels
A feeling from thyself
As the tides cease to carry
Suddenly a feeling scary
Deplores an eager fit for me
To forever dwell amongst the sea.

Rechelle Flave

Homework

I hate homework,
I hate school work,
Math work is the worst,
Because it's so hard,
I think I'll burst
I don't care, put me in a cage.
Just don't make me do
one more page.

Abby Deniken

Time

In the quiet, watching snow,
where did all the flowers go?
Will they bloom again in spring?
Time moves forward, echoing.

Eugenia Veley

Old Fashion Curfew

Daddy didn't need a clock
Must have had a mental block.
Rather an archaic way
To come home without delay.

Not allowed at night to roam,
Must be safely in our home.
Be at home before it's dark,
Was the curfew he would bark.

Would not listen to a reason,
Sunlight varies with the season.
Still the same as we depart,
Be at home before it's dark.

When the days were very short,
Home by dark, was his retort.
Even when it's dark by 4:00
Better be at your front door.

Eastern, Central, Pacific Time,
Still the same consistent chime.
Be at home before it's dark,
Listen or sleep in the park.

Silvia Tsoutsouris

The Wardrobe

Ominously, it stood in the corner of the empty, old, back bedroom
Thick double doors stained a dark brown hue
Black knots, as if silent eyes, to watch your every move at night
Standing tall with only enough room to don a cobweb crown

Who knew what this cavernous passageway could lead to
Or what creatures lurked within its dark, mystic domain?
Surely, inside were nameless, faceless ghouls
And silent, rapid, repetitious, black-and-white nightmares

Inexplicably, some unseen force bolted it to the old house's wall
A shrine, a temple, lodging the dwelling's soul and indigenous spirits
Forbid that its gates be shut behind the entering inquisitor
Would it be too late for retreat? Or would one submit to newfound environs?
Victim or victor? For better or for worse?

A place of solitude and rest where dreaming is and wishing was
No restrictions, no limitations, no apprehensions
Where solutions come and problems go
Ignorance alienated and ideas grow

Or would dreariness prevail, a bitter foretaste of a predestined Hell
Can no one hear you pounding the door?
The sound just travels inward because a two-way path is known no more.

Joel P. Powell

The Alley

I awaken, and look at myself.
My hands are dirty, bruised, and covered with calluses.
The filthy rags that adorn me offer little protection from the icy winds.
I peer through the holes in my shelter,
and I am disgusted by what I see.

A long, dark corridor littered with cardboard boxes,
beer cans, broken bottles, graffiti, spoiled food.
The ragged bodies of my eternal companions
lie strewn across the hard, black asphalt.
I gaze at these souls, and I know Fate has looked upon them harshly.

We are slain soldiers left to rot in the battlefield of our lives.
We were once respected citizens
Lawyers Doctors Politicians Businessmen
But we were greedy and led evil lives
Now, as I stumble through this long, dark alley
And I hear the pleas of the fallen to ease their suffering,
I know I will spend an eternity questioning
how I could have, should have, lived my life.

What could I have done to be a better person?
As a child, we are taught Hell is a place of fire and demons,
But in truth, Hell is merely an alley

John Connelly

Nightmares or Dreams?

An event happens to you every night.

Sometimes it makes you a little bit scared.
At times it makes you blissfully happy.

Trying to get past the truly BAD or TERRIBLE events that happen in your mind,
Attempting NOT to center on the MAGNIFICENT things at the same time,
Searching for that middle ground that we all know is there.
We may not like what it holds up for us, like a gift.

We try our best to receive it with a smile.
Honestly we do our best.

Sometimes our best may not be good enough.

E. Guido

Talking To God

I talked to God today
And he told me I was strong.
I wanted to trust his words
And I knew I was wrong.
I wanted to move on
I wanted to smile,
But all I could do
Was be sad for a while.
He brightened up my heart,
And took all of the clouds away.
I could breathe again.
I was good that day.
My eyes shown bright,
And relief took me away.
I knew everything was alright.
I was sad up until that day.
God told me she was safe;
She was in His arms now.
He kindly excused himself
And took a bow.
I walked away
And took a sigh of relief.
It just happened;
It took away my grief.

Tiffany Leclair

Week

Hurricane Dennis, August 1999
Monday morning, workers yawning
Trudging down the hill.
Tuesday's dawning, weather's warning
Of a major spill.
Wednesday comes round all too soon,
Best day of week, at least 'til noon.
Then Thursday's hurricane
Pays us a call.
Friday's present is a storm
Way beyond the average norm
When trees and street signs
Take a major fall.
But Saturday the calm returns
With buzzing bees and mild sunburns
And children's cries of
"Let's go shop the mall."
Sunday's set for rest and play
At least that's what they always say.
But everybody knows it's just
The day before Monday.

Matt Ryan

Equus Rex

Dark scent of sawdust and sweat
      Massive power-heavy
         Stomp stomp
            Steps
      On the too-solid ground

All white desperation
   His eyes are as
      Up up
         He rises
      Slow-mo'
         Hooves
            Kick out
               Strike
      Out

Plunging down and on
   Into the green-blinding-bright
      Prancing proud

Katherine Gardner

My Mother's Love

I can always tell you love me, I know because you're always there,
To show, even in the smallest ways how much you really care,
Though I may not realize it at the time, I look back and see,
That thought I did not understand, you were only caring for me.

The kind words you say, the words spoken softly when I've had a bad day,
Show me even if no one else likes me for who I am, you love me anyway.
For your love sees beyond what any other's eyes could ever see,
You don't look at what's on the outside, rather what's deep inside of me.

A thank you could never be enough, for words are only play.
So rather, I'll try to be like you, and show my love every day.
The things you do, when at the time I don't understand,
Is what make you such a special mom, and the son that I am.

With that Mother's love you warn me, about things that you've been through
And even though I push it off, that's how I know your love is true. You've always
been there when I am down, ready to give some advice,
To show me what to do and point me in the direction that is right.

Thank you, it's not much to say, but I mean it with all my heart,
Even though I may leave you, I hope to never grow apart,
So on this Mother's Day may you always know it true,
That always and forever I will, with all my heart love you.

Nathaniel P. South

The Shore

You're like the ocean shores
where the sea gulls and other beauty soars
like the sun on the beach
waves where people and kids play
'til the end that makes the stars begin
in the big dark sky above
that makes my eyes sparkle when you are near
and near so I hope you can be my ocean
and stay close to me always.

Susan Winkler

Love of a Song

The black battered case sits there alone, quiet
The shape of the case reflects the man that played the guitar inside
He played the guitar with a passion so great it could put any star in its place
He might not have made it to the Grand Ole Opry, but he knew it wasn't to be
He never quit playing because he loved the feel of the strings on his fingers
Many times I was awakened by the strum of the guitar
He was always singing his song, holding his guitar like a newborn child
His music touched the hearts of many, with no holding back he opened his heart

William Ross

Weeping Heart

I woke up in the middle of the Valentine's night
Moaning with a pang of pain, strangled with a weird feeling,
I tried to weep; instead I bled inside with a strange fright.

Yesterday, I wish I knew what happened,
The sky was dark, wind whispering, restless bouncing tree,
I shivered, suddenly with a flush of pain; the sky burst into tears,
Setting the dark cloud free.
It was a kind of sad rhyme, but a chill crept into my spine,
My heart banged savagely against my rib—it was not supposed to happen,
Shuddering with apprehension, I crept into my room.

Suddenly like a siren, the telephone rang,
A faint broken voice, far away from a distance,
Drifting across the waves of pain, whispered, "He has left us, he is gone."
I shivered again with fear, and a shrill scream
tried to burst through my vein, "What did you say?"
The voice kept echoing, "Luther is gone, he has left us for Heaven."

I didn't know how I supposed to react, nor did I knew how to deal,
Devastated and with a throb in my heart, cold and drained,
Drowning deep into my sorrow, I realized how sorely I would miss my friend.

Dora Noor

You and Love

Love is an endless feeling,
That we have always shared.
To love you is my special way
to show you that I care.

We may have been down
Some dark and lonely roads.
But when we say we're sorry,
The love we share is whole.

My heart is so full of love;
As full as it can be.
I love you very much!
And I know that you love me.

We were meant to be together,
(that is why we are)
I know that I can tell you
Everything that is in my heart.

I will always love you.
This, I swear to you.
I am very thankful
To have someone special . . .You!

Kara Allen

Who Findeth Me

When life is dark,
And the way in dim,
I put out my hand,
And walk with Him.
When I am weary,
And do not care,
He comes to me,
My burdens to share.
On pages of the Bible,
On wings of prayers,
When I need Him,
He is always there.
(Living for each other,)
His great love to share,
We climb the steps of Heaven,
Joyously He is there.
It's not hard to find Him,
In stable, garden, fields, or home,
When helping hands and seeing hearts,
Do not let you walk alone.

Renee Oberreich

An Animal Tale

I have a monkey in my pocket
And a lion in there too,
As I walked along the road
An elephant jumped up on my shoe.

When the bear climbed up my arm
I was as frightened as could be,
Until I spotted a large pink hippo'
Resting quietly on my knee.

When I looked into the mirror
What do you think I saw in there?
It was a long necked giraffe
Dancing softly on my hair.

Then I noticed something else
Curled up tightly on my chin
It was a shiny yellow snake
Looking at me with a grin

I am finished with my story
I think I'll sit and rest a while
But not before we're joined
By Joe the friendly crocodile

Terry Hofmann

A Letter to Remembering Moments of Falling in Love

Hello lover, who are you today?
Yesterday you were a moment when I saw what my future held for me.
One day you were the seasonings I used to flavor my dinner;
yet, when that taste left, I found a way to preserve what might have been lost.
I remember the time I fell in love with the color of the sky
and when I took a second glance, clouds started moving in and that color had changed.
Driving down a curving road with the top down, as the leaves changed consistency and tone,
and the day is not as long as it was a week ago, is a time I remember falling in love.
The day I came home after being gone on vacation for three months,
I entered my place only to find the next moments to fall in love.
I met a beautiful lady in passing and we shared a stare and a smile;
we never spoke a word or saw each other again, but for that moment, we fell in love.
Seeing the sunrise over the lake when the water is calm and the sky is clear
asks me a question, "Are you falling in love yet?"
I went to a local bar one day and just sat, observing all that surrounded me.
When my date arrived, she noticed a certain look on my face.
I looked up at her before saying hello and I asked her, "Did you fall in love today too?"
I read a book entitled, "Confessions of Lifetimes in the Fountain of Choice"
and something in those stories showed me just who can fall in love.
This letter is to anyone who chooses to read it and I hope you understand
that each moment in life is meant for someone to fall in love with someone or something.
Falling in love is so much more than a gift;
it is also a choice that only takes a moment if given a chance.
The only place this moment can last is a place in time that we all hold in our spirits.
Sometimes falling in love feels like an illusion because we wonder, "Will it last?"
The greatest illusion ever put before man is his own flesh.
This vessel of flesh is a transitory as the day itself,
when there are so many other wonders to fall in love with.
Piece by piece, the whole wide world is my lover.

   Better to know falling in love for a moment than live in hate for a lifetime.

    Anthony E. Hinton

The Broken Heart

I guess I'll never understand you,
or the things that you do,
but never will you understand the things you put me through.

I've been played for a fool more than on time,
and many times you're the one responsible for the crime.
Many times it seems as if things might start,
but, always in the end, I'm here picking up the pieces of my once again broken heart.
I'll never understand why I keep bouncing back,
I guess determination is one thing my heart does not lack.
But someday you will see,
the one with the broken heart won't end up being me.

I guess you'll never understand the things you put me through,
But one thing you must understand is..
I'll never go back to you.

    Jennifer Bain

Faith

Faith is something that we can't see,
but, Oh, what a wonderful beacon of light, it can be for you and me.
Faith is something that can be felt so strong
that it can radiate from us to others our whole life long.
Faith, Jesus said, is meant to come flowing from our mouths as water does
from a fountain, and all it takes is one droplet of faith
to crumble the biggest of mountains.
Faith is something that can mean so much
that often people can be healed by one
whose faith comes through their touch.
Faith is something for us to draw upon when we feel low;
if we tap the spigot enough, it can sustain us to stay on the go.
And, finally, though faith may not be something that we humans
can drink or eat, it is, in the end, what really need to feed our bodies,
not alcohol, sodas, or meat.
And though faith is not something we can always see or touch,
it still is the same powerful cure for one's soul as it was when Jesus
walked through the world and it still means so much!

    John Chinn

Dry My Tears

To My Family
Emotional
That's how they describe me
Full of tears
That's what I am
I don't know what to think anymore
I don't know what to feel.

What has this world become?

Why is it that when someone's happy
Something bad happens
In exchange for that happiness
Why do people have to suffer?

These questions are not new anymore.

Dry my tears
My inner soul
Clear my mind
My cluttered being.

    Lara Mia Veronica Garcia

Tired of Trying

I'm tired of trying
Been trying all my life
I'm tired of trying
Don't want to think twice
Tired of trying to please
Trying to make it
Need to relax
My mind can't take it
Trying to help
Trying to make happy
I'm tired of trying
Tired of surviving
Tired of trying
I'm tired of trying

    Karen Randolph

Lost People

Fear of losing identity,
values troubles a lot,
Though body only perishes,
fear of losing loved one scares me,
Even though nation means people
I feel the loneliness of prosperity,
By leaving fate on time, with past
wonderful memories still searching
for unanswered questions.

    Amarnath Ramasubramanian

Unit Number Nine

Inaccessible yet inescapable,
I lack the vision
needed to shut the doors of life.
I choose not to.
I choose not to open,
but I am unable to close.
I choose not to see,
but I am unable to turn away.
I choose not to speak,
but I am unable to dim the noise.
I give up my right to individuality
and let a greater force tell I'm wrong,
and sit alone waiting for a
burnout
blowout
blackout
whatever.
Faulty units can always be replaced.

    Anne Bruun Jensen

Life Is a Continuous Struggle

For many years we tried so hard to occupy
our space, home, work place, children and spouse.
We try for laughter, joy, living, loving, and caring.
Sometimes we find as the years go by that some things we thought
were special become dreams, and distance is drawn between them.
Not because of love, not because of caring,
because it's too late for enduring.
We say not because of love and caring,
Because our children are our blood, our strength, love and our caring.
Sometimes we take for granted for what we have,
no thank you, no sorry and no love.
We look at life, no joy, no peace and no happiness.
We try to correct this emptiness.
We look at life from here to there, instead of there to here.
Remembering no laughter, no joy and no living.
We pick up the pieces and go on.
Then an awakening as if in a deep sleep.
There's a new face, a new heart, peace and happiness, a new life.
Everything you have love and caring there's a new
meaning, an abundance that sets the heart aglow.

Cindy C. Estill

Angel

He was a kind and loving man, the kind everyone wanted on hand.

He touched our lives within our hearts,
Of joy and happiness right from the start.

He always knew just what to say to brighten up someone's day.

His heart was true, loyal, and understanding, so strong and free and undemanding.

He made us laugh when we were crying,

He never gave up, he always kept trying.
So energetic, free-willed, and compassionate,

Funny, caring, truthful, and considerate.
So full of life, trust, and smiles,
He touched everyone throughout the miles.

But now he is in Heaven, shining down,
Still making sure no one goes on with a frown.

His song will be heard throughout each day,
To give us strength and help us pray.

Death is tough, sad, and yet unfair,
But his love will stay true through each day, I swear.
His memories will last forever, his word will never fade,
You see, he is the reason all this love was made.
His spirit will go on and his love will never quit,

For it is him we love and miss, our dear angel, Ricky Allen Whitt!

Stacy McElhaney

The Wall

The wall was built by me and you
It was built to keep us in and them out
but the wall was not built of stone or wood or brick
It was built by the dying soul in each of us
It was built of nightmares and fears, of blood and tears
It was built by shutting people we love out of our life
and of profane words we say to one another
This wall was built of hurtful abasement
This wall was built of judgment towards others
of hurtful words and actions towards us
Block by block, memory by memory, this wall was built
Laid around our hearts and souls for eternity
And if by a miraculous chance one day this wall does fall
its stones still lie around and its imprint will be on the ground
and it will start building itself all over again
Because maybe love tore it down, but there can be no love without hate
no hate without hurt and no hurt without healing.
There can be no healing without a calming peace
and there can be no peace on Earth without a compromise

Polissa Danielle Tidwell

Dad

Through all the years gone by
With seasons that have passed us
We have always been together
Although miles keep us apart.

From the bottom of my heart
There's still time to make a start
When I hug you I feel closer
Which words can never say.

My promise is to love you
To always be by your side
Because I'm your loving daughter
No matter where you are.

Time will help us through
No matter what we do
'Cause I will always love you
This I know is true . . .

Lisa Langdon

Life in a Shoe

What can you do
When you live in a shoe?
We really can't stop
Onward we must walk.
First of all, we choose it
To get the right fit.
Then we decide for awhile
On the color and style.
This all takes quite a lot
Of wise decision and thought.
Our life is what we choose
It's kind of like buying new shoes.
The shoes must be comfy and just right
It's the same with our life.
If life isn't peaceful and right
Then our shoes must be too tight.
What can you do
When you live in a shoe?
Tie it up, but not too tight
Leave ample room for comfort and light.

T. Cochet

The Unemployed Dragon

When you look at him
What do you see?
A dragon of hope
For you and me.

The ladder he climbs
Will be strong,
To give us the strength
To carry on.

The parasites are here
To thwart his quest.
Soon they'll learn
Which way is best.

Helpfulness will show
Them how
To care for others
In the here and now.

Compassion can only
boost this state,
Making jobs for others,
before it's too late.

Understanding and love
are intertwined,
When we think from our hearts
as well as our minds.

Lillian Davis

The Only One

I stood out in the wind today, a box of leaves was blazing,
and by myself I placed three flags to burn them all as I was gazing.
It's not my first choice to burn them there, but to bury is such a worry.
Can't stand the thought of that wonderful flag being down and torn and dirty.
Why can't our government make a place to send old flags, like Ol' Glory?
So I don't have to stand and watch as the flames destroy her and make me feel so sorry.
As the flames burned so hot, my tears ran like a river.
And as I looked into the flames its history made me start to quiver.
How many men died to keep her there and flying, morning after morning?
So we could see, that we are free, so the wind can proudly keep her soaring.
I stood there 'til all I could see was only metal rings in the ashes.
The fire was out and I had no doubt of her memory burning from passion.
I remember being told how she flew so high, as the bombs around were falling.
And here I burned the thing that stirred, and kept their hearts still yearning.
From freedom's call or to the mall, our flag will never waver.

    Karen Jo Stewardson

When There's No One Else, There's You

I hear people talkin' sayin' I'm crazy for having a dream,
but they've apparently forgotten that not everything is exactly what it seems.
All I've really ever wanted is just a helping hand,
but all I ever get is some put down and another selfish demand.
I will never be able to figure out how and where it all went wrong,
and I know that Jesus said that the weeping in the night won't last too long.

If I'm crying at night while I lay awake in bed,
when all I can manage to hear is the static in my head.
When there's no one else there's you.
Whenever I get lonely and I feel empty and incomplete,
You are the one who finds the way to get me back on my feet.
When there's no one else, Jesus; there's you.

They could be a little more patient and give me the chance,
instead of always thinking what they do from taking only one small glance.
They would see that is you who leads my way and will always be,
and that I was once blind, but it was you who made me see.
Too many people are so shallow that they could never dream of letting you in,
but if they'd just turn to you, you would be there to help them.

    Judith Anne Barnett

Divine Blessings

For the creator has giving each creation
An special instrument,
That of great magnitude, on the behalf of its defense;
He gave the turtle,his shell, and the first settlers, amexem, to dwell
He gave the rabbit, his cleverness, as for the conscious, he set in Heaven's mist
He gave the porcupine, its needles, and to the quickening of speed, the cheetah
He gave the rhinoceros, its horn, and to all mothers, a new born
He gave the zebra, its stripes, for to the days, its nights
All the creators' creations were blessed with its own defense
For the most of all, he gave woman and man, their common sense

    Kwesi El

Memories

Sometimes we lose people that we love suddenly.
We may have lost you,
but your memories will be with us forever.
You brought joy and laughter to our lives,
you were always there.
Now that you're gone I just feel so all alone.
My heart feels so much pain that it feels like it will bust.
No matter where I go or what I do your memories will see me through.
I feel so empty and all alone now that your gone.
The tears I've cried and the hurt I feel, chills me to the bone.
You brought me so much joy and laughter,
just being a part of my life.
Now that your gone I don't know what to do.
Your memories will always be there helping us make it through.
No matter where I go or what I do I will always think of you.
Even though you're gone your memories will always be in our hearts helping us through.
When I feel like I can't go on, I just stop and ask myself what would you do.

    Scarlett E. White

Moon Tea

i drank the moon one night
as it sat pale and fat
on the dark lake like a tea bag
it tasted as i always
  imagined it would
cool with a rusty grain
like well water from a tin cup
or like iron rich river water
so cold that it
  burns your teeth raw
familiar and distant
i still held its aftertaste
in the craters of my face
when the sun came to
  sift through the dregs

    Lance Molis

A Broken Mirror

A broken mirror
A thousand shames with blight
Comes back much clearer
Reflecting pain, sorrow, and plight
Won't you hold me dearer
Than the sun holds its light
I want you nearer
And it's the only thing that's right
To me now that I know
What I've been living for
You came to me
You opened the door
I feel liberated
I've never felt more
Invigorated
And now I am sure
I've lived life alone
Through all the Heavens and the Hells
Still, I'm alone
And in my soul that loneliness dwells
Somehow, I'm always alone
Like a tide that recedes and swells
Will I always be alone?
And will you be alone as well?

    John Hedges

Numb

My mind
frozen,
not a thought
provoked
by the simple nature
of your presence.
Forgotten moments
once enjoyed,
are lost,
discarded,
and I can see the anger
my distance affronts.
Crying out,
help!
reach me
despair;
yet you stand so still
in the face, of desperation.
Leave me
alone now
to deal with my
solitude,
I'll miss your company,
but not my pain.

    Cristie Thurling

Can't Stop a Storm

The sky in color was a grey-blue
A storm was really beginning to brew
Wind, rain, tornadoes, and snow, they make a dangerous crew
But sometimes it's the best time for a great view

So much is hidden in every storm that passes by
And we only see so much of it through our eyes
Some will fight so hard to survive,
And for some it's like an energy booster, which puts them into drive

Storms are cool looking in the daylight
And the clouds block out the sunlight
But then again, storms even look cool into the night
With lightning flashes so magnificently bright

The rain and snow will come down
And the wind will have a loud whistling sound
And the tornados will come around
Pulling trees and houses from the ground

Trees and debris all over the roads
Piece by piece, escaping from the mother load
Destroying fields that just have been sowed
And just think, it's too bad we can't stop a storm with some kind of code

Lourie Passmore

Lady in Chains

Who is this lady whom once men cherished like a new bride,
this wonderful and amazing lady, for whom many men would risk their very lives?
This lady who was protected by God's own hand?
Her struggles were hard, and sometimes long,
but she seemed to prevail as time went on.
Who is this lady that the world would has come to envy,
jealous of her kindness, and her riches untold?
Who is this lady that once held the key to unlock the door
to freedom for all mankind to enjoy the fruits of their labor?
Who is this lady, always giving and yet there are those who seek her demise?
Though still young and beautiful, she has found herself bound in chains,
by the corruption of her court, who once protected her, but now mocks her.
This lady who man has taken for granted without slightest thought,
as she silently weeps, her caretakers become apathetic as she grows tired
and weary, while her court sells her off like a prostitute of the night.
While her people sleep, her court seeks to destroy her
and slowly wait like wolves to devour their prey.
As her children are brainwashed and slaughtered,
her only hope is that God will unchain her before she is consumed.

Steven W. Lunsford

From the Moment We Met

From the moment we met, I saw your smile.
from the moment we met, I knew it was love at first sight.
from the moment we met, my heart went pitter-patter.
from the moment we met, I got cold feet, they wouldn't move.
from the moment we met, you took my breath away.
from the moment we met I knew I wouldn't be able to sleep.
from the moment we met, my dreams were of you.
from the moment we met, I knew I would miss you.
from the moment we met, I didn't want to leave your side.
from the moment we met, I knew I couldn't live without you.
from the moment we met, you placed a kiss on my cheek.
from the moment we met, you said I will be your next wife.
from the moment we met, I knew it was meant to be.
from the moment we met, there is only you.
from the moment we met, Oh, I wanted to say I LOVE YOU.
from the moment we met, you said I am stuck with you.
from the moment we met, you played our songs:
("Wherever You Go" & "Nothing in This World is Gonna Separate Us")
from the moment we met, you said I am yours and you are mine forever.
from the moment we met, I knew no one could win my heart but you.
from the moment we met, today, tomorrow, and always,
Larry, my love is only for you.

Sharon Garrett

My Mother Died

In a breath
the wind carried
her thought
far from its place of birth

And in a grieving moment
she bent to face the Earth
and the Earth held her there
so the wind would pass

She fought the Earth
and whispered to the wind
return to me and set me free
lift my feet and carry me

The wind heard her words
gently picked her up
and soared with her
when she glanced back, one last time
the Earth smiled back at her . . .

Sally Ferguson

Time

When time comes
we will Always know . . .
When time goes it
will Always show.
So use your time wisely,
before you grow old!!

Maria Bannon

Down Deep

I see your tears,
and hear your fears,
but I hide mine down deep.

I know your pain,
but I can't say how,
'cause I won't let you down that deep.

You know my fears,
'cause you know your own,
but you can't stop to help down deep.

So I'll sit and sigh,
and smile so sleek,
'cause I know my pains down deep.

And I'll keep it hid,
so you can't see,
'cause I'm only weak down deep.

Misty Beddoes

Night's Companion

despite the fears and
   the blackest thoughts
of fitful, sleepless nights
tears reside
   unshed in their wells
cushioning anguish
despairing of pain
dreading the next bout of
   unforsaking torture
awaiting the spark
   the lightning bolt
to unleash the torrents of
   the brewing storm
to release the dammed-up
   whirlpools of anxiety
to explode in orgasmic respite
   from the nightmarish
torment of flesh and soul

Maris Mohr

A Little Secret I Have

Run—come, come
Come here to where I am,
Put your hands all over me
like a baby playing in the sand.
The way you make me feel you'll probably never know,
But whenever we do what we do, you know how I like it, whatever you do don't go slow.
Whatever we have is something not so real,
But does that all really matter as long as we know what we feel?
The words you speak sound so sincere,
Though we haven't even met I feel you near
Are we just something that I made up,
Or did I just wake up from dreaming and got struck by luck?
Is this all a little secret? Hmmm . . .
I guess they'll never know.
And if about this we are ever questioned, we'll just smile and tell them
I don't think so . . .
This secret in my heart is one I'll always keep.
This secret in my heart, so little, yet so deep!!!

Yvette Cruz

A Mother's Love

From your mother who loves you with all her heart,
all of you so wonderful, nothing else can set apart

Know one could love you more than I, so deep in my heart like the bows of the Earth
so radiant, felt like the sun in the sky

You'll never know what a blessing you've been to me,
you're the reason for my happiness, happiness that has set me free

I've seen you all mature and become the wonderful people that you are,
this outweighs anything in my life by far

You've given me such joy and filled my heart with such love,
my gift of you wonderful children is a gift from above

So my dear children, I've let you know what's in my heart today;
may the Lord Jesus fill your hearts with the same peace and love,
in this I pray.

Nancy Surette

Rule of Law

The lecherous, lawless liar and his Waco Butcher
join together to stand on Rules of Law to force a
boy unto the rule of one who claims that "He belongs to me!"
to be returned to a place where no one has a Human Right
to Life nor Liberty nor Choice nor to belong to any but the State
its iron fist clenched in hate for US
Where forty years of nuclear fission
threatening brewing volcanic emissions sulfuric-threats
Affairs-of-State nearly spewing just to clear our slates.
It all creates far too heavy tortuous weights for the
six-year-old shoulder to bear.

Ina Rogers

Loss of My Beloved

Quin skin so beautiful with a chocolate tone
Left for school one day and never made it home
Three years, two months since I've seen . . . my baby girl
clothes still fresh with the scent of my eight-year-old pearl!

Jah! Almighty king, break these chains, that hold me captive in this house
I have no strength, no voice, for it has shrunk to that of a mouse

I'm breathless as the sun shines down on me
I'm speechless, for the love of his grace will set me free
The tree swaying, birds chirping as I hang her clothes out to dry
Breeze sent such a fine scent through my nostrils
Squeeze my eyes completely shut . . . as I began to cry

I hear the Lord calling me, telling me it's time to rest
For the burden of my beloved's death has been lifted off my chest!

Rosan Ferguson

Respect

As I sat one eve in solitude
And gazed upon the dawn
My dreams were interrupted
When a friend just wandered along
Our thoughts were quite different
We pondered the meaning of life
We gained respect for each other
We stayed 'til early sunlight
His heart was filled with pride and joy
His step was very light
He had to make a perfect star
He toiled through out the night
We left understanding each other
Our own paths along the way
An alien came into the garden
And wiped my friend's life away
Life belongs to everyone
Not just a chosen few
So if you think you are inferior
Remember it could happen to you

Judith Chapman

If I Could See behind Your Eyes

If I could see behind your eyes
What wonders would I find?
A raging sea? A sky of blue?
The world you left behind?

If I could see behind your eyes,
What secrets do you own?
Perhaps a secret love of old,
Or maybe a Queen's fine throne.

If I could see behind your eyes
What magic would I see?
The way you have of seeing through
To the innermost heart of me?

If I could see behind your eyes,
Would I then understand
A little more about your love
For me, this petty man?

I wish that I could see behind
Your eyes, so full of pain;
There's so much you're not telling me
I wish you'd let me in.

John E. Thomas

Death

Death comes suddenly
Like the shot of a gun
In the dead of night
Death is peaceful,
Or so we think
For all we actually know
Death could be as painful as
Torture is to live humans,
But who knows
Though for now
I would rather believe
That death is like
Petals on the wind
Beautiful, yet painful to those
Left on the ground
Like the thorns the petals leave behind
When they fly away
To me Death is like
Grasping a rose
Painful
Yet . . . beautiful.

Leanne Mosher

Contemplations

He looks out to the stormy waters,
A vast of emotion, adventure, and mystery,
As what he is admiring slowly comes to a calming sea . . .
Sending a chill up his spine . . .
A gentle breeze through his hair . . .
His eyes a passionate pale gray with a dazzle of green . . .
Yet he starts to realise it is he who is the stormy waters,
He who must come to a calming vast,
And he who must discover the mystery within the mystery . . .
Which he has finally perceived that . . . he is but the mystery . . .
He whom has discovered the reflection of his yearning . . . restless heart.

Misty Russell

If I Ever Go to Heaven . . .

Then let the birds sing all day
Then let the swallow tweet all night
Then let perfumes run through the air
Then let the ground be covered with violets
Then let the maples dance in the breeze
Then let the roses bloom with love
Then let the waters be crisp
Then let the winds be sweet
Then let the mountains be tall
Then let the paths be hidden beneath the wild tops of enchanted woods
Then let me be surrounded by the ones I love . . .
Then let the stars be pearls
Then let me drink the honey
Then let the flowers shine like gems
Then let joy and sorrow run through the land
Then let the creatures be peaceful
Then let the fruits be ripe
Then let the palace be majestic
Then let me be surrounded by the ones who love me . . .

Dasha Velichko

While You're Away

Each time we say good-bye, I get a feeling that I can't bare.
One last look to let you see how so deeply that I care.
One last kiss to feel your love, to know it's there each and every day.
Every day that we are apart, I know it's always here to stay.
So strong was the pain, to hear your voice, but not to touch.
But the words that I heard most was how you missed me, Oh, so much.
I miss your smile and the little things you do. It hurts so bad,
But I feel that I will always love you.
I know the day will come that we can be together.
I just had to say, I love you today, tomorrow, and forever.

Rondal Sessions

Love Story Eight Thousand Miles Away

To send sweet notes across the Pacific Ocean eight thousand miles away;
To travel half the world someday to see his lady and take her away;
To dream of fooling in the snow with his Princess like Preppy and Jenny . . .

Or fishing in Vermont on a summer day
Or driving to New York City to see the high rises and the Statute of Liberty,
Or sharing the Connecticut Yankee life with a little brown pearl from the Orient seas.

If I were this Princess in his waking hours daily,
Must I not pray Prince Charming will come
Today, Today?

Miriam Day

Love Is . . .

Love is like a flower—the more you tend to it, the more it will grow
Love is like the sky—it will last forever if you believe
Love is like a circle—if you follow it, it will never end
Love is precious—if you cherish love, you will live happily ever after

Patricia Jewett

Rue Words

The words that I should have said
Bother me somewhat
But what bothers me a lot
Are the words I said
That I wish I had not

Beatrice L. White

The Art of Salvation

The art is the human on Earth,
A true fruit of love.
The love from one person to another.
A branch from God above
Not to be blown away in the wind.
So stand firm in all that you do
For the world every day is new unto you.

Diane Holder

A Melody of Tolerance

Please let me be me
For once the me is no more
I'll fade away
Into the abyss of anonymity
Consumed by a ruthless inferno
Of an amorphous monotony
'Til the voice of harmony
Resurrects variety
Lifting us differently together
Beneath the smiling rainbow
Blending our differences
In a nurturing chorus
Of a melody of tolerance
Mindful of a timeless thought:
Together we are better
Because we are different!

Etheldredah N. Voyi

My Shadow

Hopes, dreams, ambitions, goals
Vanished, destroyed, along with my soul
Dominating, controlling, dingy, and gray
My shadow has always stood in the way

Restraints, chains, locks, and ties
Unknotted, loosened, cut so I can fly
Now there is light and I finally see
My shadow has no control over me

Jennifer Vredeveld

When the Peacemakers Fall

Someone cried out for freedom,
and a shot rang out.
The bells, Oh, how they wept,
across an ash-colored sky.
White doves and candlelight,
frankincense and myrrh.
What's the method to the madness;
when will it ever end?
With star-spangled eyes,
one asked, "Why?"
"Where's the glory and freedom?
Where's the peace and harmony?"
We don't need war and oppression,
sacrificial lambs of innocent lives.
Freedom and peace can never be had,
never bought nor sold.
There are no more voices,
when all the peacemakers fall.

Gary S. Potter

Silver against Deep Blue

Effect: from Latin, to do, to make
As the sky runs clear beyond the clouds

As across the terrestrial stage we move—howsoever—to
awareness of an essential humanity,
of a practical effectiveness for "what works:"
awareness that rings sure and tests true and
challenges us to rise and clear the clouds,
Then do we better appreciate the mystery of our
private worlds of reality, and the freedom—beyond poetry—of
our efforts for what really works best.

We lead each closer to the essence of what s/he loves best,
together closer to open expanses of human endeavor.

As freedom becomes us

As effectiveness increases, we rise anew to meet the day:

the task, the chore, the challenge, the sacrifice, the promise,
We lead to secure the beauty in the worlds we hold and choose to make.

With each move—*against deep blue*—
We are the beauty in the worlds we make.

Hrand Saxenian

Inspired by Desired Thought

"They say it takes inspired thought to make a poem know.
A winter's beauty, a majestic city, or flowers in full bloom.
Some happening, they say it takes, to get words in one's mind,
To show exquisite, innocent beauty, in something as plain as lines.

Desire is all, it holds the key, to worlds and realms unknown.
The way to say just how you feel, when what you feel cannot be shown.
You have to sit in silence, contemplate, and think, and brood,
But desire to say just how you feel is how you start with that first word.

When spoken words can't seem to cope, you just write and let words flow,
Until through simple black and white, the other, your feelings know.
And then, though some may criticize, and others praise and laud,
It matters not, for it all started with one thing, desired thought."

Brian Ball

A Moment's Grace

The warmth of a smile softens another's heart;
Someone's gentle healing touch means so much.
Inspiration from our dreams gives us the courage to succeed.
Moving so quickly but so slow, we find ourselves and achieve our goals.

Friendships we build and friendships we lose;
So many moments so precious and few.
Patience, self-worth, and love will endure.
Courage to keep going and faith to believe.
Memories keep coming and carry us through.

In despair the darkness falls.
A teardrop that trickles for our broken heart.
Lost in the dark the light shines through;
Blessed in the peace that is renewed,
Beams of forgiveness shine through and through.

Terri Veinotte

Loneliness

Loneliness is like a highway in the night, barren and alone.
No one is there, no one knows you are there.
Time does not exist; it just floats by.
You turn a corner and you see your whole life pass you by.
Memories come and go then totally disappear like dust.
The future, your future, seems to be as dark as the night sky.
You know you will last, though—you have to.
Then you see a twinkling star;
You finally remember that you are not alone.
You had just forgotten a few things while on the highway of your loneliness.

Kathryn Oldewurtel

Missing You

Do you know how much
I've been missing you?
I know you probably do,
and you must miss me, too,
but don't be sad and blue,
for the good Lord will comfort you.
Your work here was through,
it was time for something new.
You're at a better place,
you just needed a change of pace.
Once more I wish I could see your face,
but that will be at the better place.

Karen Owings

Our Country's Heroes

Veterans are admirable,
Loyal, and true.
They are blessings
For me and for you.

They fought for our country
So boldly and brave.
They are our heroes
Today and always.

Some gave their life
As they fought hard,
For their job wasn't easy—
It was very hard.

Others became disabled
As they fought, too.
For what they believed in,
It was the honorable thing to do.

Our prayers are with them
Each and every day,
Because we know
Memories never fade away.

Dona Goodnight

You are Very Special and I Love You

You are special and I love you,
I love your smile,
You make me blush,
I am shy of you,
I would like to be true,
You are so special
You tickle me pink.
No, I am not a fink,
Again, you make me blush,
You love to give a wink
You make me blush.
No, I am not in a rush,
As long as the sky is blue.
You are special and I love you.

Edward Bayer

Trapped Emotions

Feelings of hatred
left unsaid
Bottles of tears
left uncried
Bags of laughter
no one to make me laugh
I feel so alone
all these feelings and emotions
locked inside my head
Everything so weird
my heart just died.

Edythe Furmage

Can You Hear the Footsteps

Can you feel them coming nearer and nearer?
Do you hear the voices calling your name?
Do you see the forgotten stranger appear before your eyes?
And just when you think you're awake,
Do you feel the presence of tomorrow?
Does the sun grab at you?
Does the warmth invade your mind?
And if the sky should fall, would you be there to see it?
The buzzing sound is more incessant, and so is the light around you.
You begin to fall forward in time.
You start to feel your physical self.
As like any other person, you realize that you have to face the world.
But the question is, when you wake up, will you still be in it?

Vanessa Gal

No Boundaries

I call few people my friends.
Have many sons and daughters throughout the world, they call me mother
I've learned from them, they've learned from me. Why can't the world be.

Every country learning form its brother, what we have done,
what they have done, what we can be.
Each country antiquated in the past, crying for the future what will we be.

Big or little, walking and climbing upward helping one another.
Amplifying what we can be.

I love my children, can't you see, when we can grow up we can all be.
This millennium has no boundaries.

Valerie Brooks Hellstrom

'Til the End

I'm not the same person that you once knew,
I've changed so much, and it's because of you.

I've grown up, not only mentally but emotionally inside,
it has been from the lack of your presence by my side.

It is difficult leaving all my memories of you behind,
Resignation and peace with myself, is what I'm trying to find.

Although it is difficult to forget, as you well know,
Believe me I am trying to move on, to let go . . .

Only time will tell what will happen while we wait,
Although unfortunately, it might be too late.

Just wanted you to know when you feel alone,
Don't hesitate to call me, on the telephone

I know it sounds as if I am contradicting myself,
But for once, think of me, and not of yourself.

Whatever happens between us, remember me as your forever friend,
I'll promise you my unconditional love and understanding, 'til the end.

John Bier

Indignation

I will not laugh while others laugh
Nor weep while others weep
Or smile a smile because they smile
Or speak because they speak
I refuse to imitate the pack though some will hold that I'm mad
But this life I'm enduring is all my own in spite of dreams you've had
I do not pray to a mystical being
To relieve me of my sorrows
For I firmly believe this intransigent man
Is responsible for his tomorrows
And so I quote from my realist mind
To all others with powers and pelf
That I pride myself on the controversial fact
That I'm answerable to none but myself!

Nathaniel A. Woods

Rhythm Without Rain

Out to walk
lands of clay
this rock
warm summer day.

One frog's echo
a butterfly
silver and lace,
another butterfly
metallic blue
flicker away.

Peace comes
with joy,
soft green,
bare
feet
on this splendor day.

Carolyn C. Spily

Mother

A mother's smile is the warmth
Of the sun that comes down from above.
She's a beautiful flower
That grows from God's Earth.
The glow from her being,
Lights up the way.
Like the Heavenly star
That shines in the night.
Rebecca, mamma dear.
A person alive can't
Reach your heights!

Bennie Goldman

The Angel

I asked God to send
me an Angel today,
And he did, in the
most unusual way.

There was no fanfare,
no glorious light,
simply a little old man,
stepping out of the night.

His words were few,
and yet so strong.
He merely said, "Keep on smiling,"
and then he was gone.

Debora J. Ewaniuk

Fat Cat

What a terrible and fat cat,
He smells like a stinky bad rat,
He sleeps all day dreaming away,
About food and a mouse named Matt.

Even though he will never play,
I guess you could think he's OK,
Well he's not he'd rather sleep,
Occasionally he hunts for prey.

Into his chair he'll always creep,
He'll climb right up without a peep,
He'll snuggle in without a sound,
And snoozes in a sleep too deep.

Don't wander to his hunting ground,
For sure you will be stalked and found,
Be careful, somewhere he's around,
Be careful, somewhere he's around.

Braedy Mckay

Spilt Pink Blusher

Watching fake fur slipping softly round your shoulders—
Singing softly past the neon Marlboro man who offers you a cigarette,
but you refuse him.
Who are you to scoff at men that leer from giant pictures
with a golden smoky torch at their command?

Now I offer you a cigarette to light you on your way
and you take one from a girl! (Why I never thought you'd be so fey)
But nothing in your eyes was ever wicked
'til I slipped on shiny silver drawn obliquely on my pale blue eyes.

Tearing off your jacket falling down onto the floor—
The crowd upon the telly seems to break up in a roar
But I can't see their faces, see their toes scrunched coldly into trainers
Only see your faces, with SPILT PINK BLUSHER at my side.

Then when the dancing's over, your hand slips warmly into mine
Child—when the dancing is over, your hair falls softly into mine
And this carnival of city living becomes my finest wine
(Becomes the sweetest of times)

Anne Booty

In the Darkness

In the Darkness I lie watching you,
hearing you breathe, cherishing every word you say.
I lie here with you in the darkness, holding your body close to mine.
Hoping the love we share will stand the test of time.
This night in the darkness, tears fall upon my pillow
as the cherished love we shared seems to slowly slip away,
no longer hearing you breathe,
no longer being able to cherish every word you say.
I lie here in the darkness, the sheets on the empty side of the bed
feeling cold against my skin; I wonder where you are, I wonder how you've been.
My heartbeat echoes against the cold hard wall as I lie here tonight, alone,
alone in the darkness.

Rebecca Battin

A Better Day

Abandoned, neglected, abused, used, totally rejected.
If you are raised this way, will it stay this way.
Should this be what I get, or is there more in life to expect?
What is normal for me, is not normal for you;
So how do you define normal?
It is more important how you deal with life, than what life dealt you.
Overcoming obstacles is what makes life worth living,
adversity breeds strength.
You truly can turn the other cheek, be a better person for trying,
and never give up that which you strive for.
A bad beginning does not a bad ending make,
there is always tomorrow, make it a better day.

Peggy Terrien

Search for the Undying Love

As each day goes swiftly by I can't help but have tears in my eyes,
Tears that choke your throat silencing the muffled cries.
I lay down alone at night,
and the tears stream unchecked in the filtered moonlight.
The longing hidden deep in my heart burst forth into the silent dark.
It's the lonely ache,
that can only be put there from a missing Soul mate.
Where are you? Comes the sobbing plea.
I've searched everywhere and still find only me.
Through the crowds I walk,
In the rain I stand, searching for a glimpse of a man.
Where could he be calls my unbidden thoughts?
I must find him I know,
for what good is one half when it should be a whole?
So I'll keep searching high & low,
and maybe someday this lonely half will become a whole.
Then once and for all,
I'll experience the undying love I've lived a lifetime to know.

Bonita Richardson

Wandering

Wandering life aimlessly
   Looking for a love I can't see
Comes a girl true and proud
   Making my heart scream aloud
Sitting under an old oak tree
   Talking a little carefree
Trying to make the moment ours
   While basking under the stars
Turned to her kinda shyly
   Said I love you kinda mildly
She turned to me with a smile
   Which made my heart jump a mile
And when she says that she is mine
   Our love will last for all time
Until this dream of mine comes true
   There is nothing I can do
But wander life aimlessly
   Looking at a love I can see

Shawn Fehl

Mario

There once was a boy from Ontario
His name was super Mario
He love to go ski
But he had to pee
Because of his scary scenario

Natasa Zivanovic

How Do I Forget?

*To all those who have lost
someone you truly loved*
Forget the betrayal?
Forget the hurt?
Forget the way you rubbed,
All my love in the dirt?

Forget the love that,
We were meant to share?
Forget the way you said,
You'd always care?

Forget that when we touched,
My heart would always melt?
Forget the wonderful way,
That, by your side, I felt?

Forget the night you left,
Myself to sleep I cried?
Forget all this and so much more?
How do I forget your love for me has died?

Sunshine Brabazon

This Night

This is the night for a million dreams,
a million thoughts, a million scenes.
And as my head spins through the mist
of people known and places been,
of mosses touched and landscapes seen,
I seize upon an image past
and pray to God that it should last.
For against all warning I have dared
to keep that image and to keep it fair.
So fair an image, the romantic's dream,
with tender touch and eyes that gleam.
The image kept, my fairy queen.
A girl so fair beyond design.
A vision plagued upon my mind.
So again this night I lie alone
and all to ease this pain it seems,
is a single thought and a single dream.

Peter Corson

My Love for You

My love is the Universe and You are the Earth,
forever being surrounded by my Infinity of love's embrace.
Just as the Night is filled with the Stars, so is my heart
filled with the love I have for you.
Just as the Milky Way appears to leave an everlasting impression in the Sky,
so does my love for you.
Just as the Atmosphere surrounds the Earth,
so does my love for you.
Just as the Universe that has no ending,
so does my love for you.
And as the Universe that has held the Earth for many years before
and continues for many years to come,
so has my love and will continue to do so for YOU.

Yvonne Perkins

The Lifetime Kid

I've seen life and I've also died.
I've seen what was once inside.
I've seen millions of people even lie, 'Cause I am the Lifetime kid.
I've seen tears, also smiles, walking 'bout a million miles.
I've seen good and bad and even vile, 'Cause I am the Lifetime Kid.
I've seen peace, I've seen war.
I've read every story and lore.
I've seen shoplifters at the store, 'Cause I am the Lifetime Kid.
I've played every sport, every way to have fun.
I've even seen convicts on the run.
Please don't stop, I'm still not done.
'Cause I am the Lifetime Kid.
I've heard every song and sung every beat.
Seen homeless kids on the street.
They talk and scream sometimes in discreet.
They say, "Please don't leave us, Lifetime Kid!"
But people don't listen, only forbid.
Every man, every father, everybody, every bit.
But I always listen, watch and understand, 'Cause I am the Lifetime Kid.
So look back and remember.
Don't close your mind's lid.
What was it like when you were the Lifetime Kid.

Antonio Barrientes

Everlasting Love

Words can never say how much love for you I have inside.
You have given me happiness and brought me one step closer
to that everlasting perfect light.
When I close my eyes thoughts of you come abruptly to my mind,
you always used to bring me joy and never once did you even try.
Even now that you are gone, I will remember you with a delightful smile,
and the memories I hold close to my heart of the time when you were here,
unfortunately now that all belongs to yester year.
I will never forget the joy that you brought to everyone's life that you touched,
nor will I forget all the sorrow and pain from that mournful day that you left all of us.
You are now in Gods' grace and he will carry you home,
so from now on your memory we'll hold.

Cathleen Kumberger

On Wives

Few things are as wonderful
As the blessings you can know in life,
As when God the Father looks down
And smiles on man and joins him to a wife.
She provokes in him emotion of loyal protection of such strong commitment,
That until he fulfills her every dream, he just can't find contentment.
He'll meet the challenge, he'll run the race, from no obstacle will he abort
Just because he knows she's there with her loving, caring support.
She's a mother, a counselor, a confidant; on her you can depend.
And next to salvation in Jesus Christ she is your dearest friend.
I stand in awe of the consideration that went into His plan,
When God created the gift of a wife, just from the rib of a man.

Guy Beaty

Un-known

For Jewels B.
It's not a question,
But more a mystery.
Searching for clues
To my un-known misery.

Every night,
The same harsh tears,
Pouring from
My un-known fears.

When I sleep,
My mind they haunt,
When I dream,
My mind they taunt.

The depression comes,
And, Oh, how it's grown.
I overcome it as . . .
I step into my un-known.

Jb MacMullen

Four Letter Words

Words all play dirty
Can't make them behave
Ask for a whisper
They rant and rave
Try to explain
They work hard to confuse
Are serious and sober
When I try to amuse
Laugh right aloud
While I pray for sincere
Scoff at my goblins
Exhibit no fear
But ask them to stand
Their feet turn to clay
They stumble and fall
Limp lamely away

Myra Bourne

Quintessence (Butterfly)

Emerging from shelter of cocoon
stretching her wings
into immediate flight
from clover-to-clover
from flower-to-flower
form the adeptness
of Nature's arms
on the gust
of Mother's breath
drinking only
the nectar necessary
to command dominion
over her own
determined duration
living in each
moment's fragrance
with the significance
of perpetuity.

Sidona Marie Hunsberger

The Love in My Heart

It's not the road too long;
But the life too short,
It's not the Day too short,
But the hug I didn't give,
It's not the hug I didn't give,
But the Love in my heart
As long as I live.

Carol Farar

But, a Messenger

Of three parts is man comprised mind.
body and soul as has been surmised.
The eternal soul, as energy within the heart
gives us life, right from the start.
The body, with all its skin
Is just a vessel for the energy within.
The complex mind, with all its closed doors
God's plan, from beginning to end, within, it stores.
Science will tell us, it's all just "A State of Mind"
But in some areas, they tend to be rather blind.
It is a matter of Heart and Soul
That brings us out of our sleepy lull.
For once the mind is opened by the essence of who you are
You become so much more by far and may even rise to be a star.
The expiration of the vessel, no longer will be of such great concern.
For now, one knows, that in another life one will return.

    John A. Krol

Wish You Well

I am the wish-you-well wishing well.
I stand at the side of the road, in a very barren place.
I give freely, the cup of kindness to all who thirst.
Yea, I am the one, which all the others, call on first.
Yet, not one cares—to replenish me; suddenly I, am very dry.
The sweet water, meant for living, has ceased to be.
Rust comes, poisoned dregs.
Now pours a bitter cup.
Think twice, before you, too, greedily suck the life
From your own wish-you-well wishing well
Learn to balance your cups.

    Rhonda S. Galizia

Who's Who in Education

I am a red apple.
Bite a forty-two minute chunk out of me
And uncover a limerick of life.
Perhaps you are on a nose-dive.
Groundzero . . . S.O.S!
You know my number—the expectations:
Learnyourthreer's, reachforthestars, uncoveryourscars
Nothing new here? Everything you knew to hear.
You may be more wrong than you know.
I am a bookbag, filled with papers
Waiting to be graded, recorded, filed,
And hung up on some grateful refrigerator door.
I am the air, necessary yet unnoticed,
Life-giving yet unappreciated.
I am your teacher.

    Richard Schwartz

Being Alone

When clouds cover up the sun, I feel saddened and have the urge to run.
I think of all the days gone by and the sad memories that make me cry.
The tears flow gently down my face,
I long to feel your sweet embrace.
If I whisper, will you listen?
I call out for help, but no one is there, being alone again is my deepest fear.
Alone in the darkness, afraid of the unknown.
If I asked you to stay, would you run away?
If I told you I loved you, what would you say?
I must know what lies ahead, I need to know what will be.
Will I be your lover? Will I be your friend?
I need to be with you until the end.
Throughout this life and all eternity, will you be with me?
When it begins to rain, will you kiss me gently to ease the pain?
Will you hold me closely to take away my fears, and all my pain?

    Cory Lovelady

Houston

Blackbirds take flight
Into the bliss
Divine beauty and symmetry
Dare not miss.

Remote clouds foreshadow
The glorious sun
Halos encircle skyscrapers
Of what is yet to come.

Omens to confiscate freedom
Permeate the air
Lurk inside skyscrapers
With imminent despair.

Demiurges scout the land
With deferred freedom games
Dare not reveal
Their syndicate names.

    Kathline Wells

Life's Unkind Infliction

Oh, Life! How you tease me

With your incessant breath!

When the enemy has poisoned me

With his odour of mortality

You linger still 'round me;

Laughing, holding me tightly!

Will you not let me go?

For only when you do,

I can see you face to face

And enjoy, at last, Eternity!

    Victoria S.N. Perez

A Virus for the Mind

Thoughts
One thousand thoughts a theory
One theory
Inspiring ideas
Ideas spreading
Cascading, falling and tumbling
Creating change
Freeing a mind
Developing
Thoughts.

    Matt Smith

Sense of Love

Smell of cologne

Feel of a heartbeat

Taste of salty skin

Sight of a beautiful smile

Sound of soothing words

The smell of your body next to mine

The feel of your arms around me

The taste of your sweet lips

The sight of your eyes gazing into mine

Your spoken words—

I LOVE YOU

    Deborah Newcom

Ajean smile

It's been done,
    The new revelations,
So we stand, on
    Stood ground, begging
For renewal.
    The days expired,
There's mold on her lips.
    Six strings snap
And we become silent.
    The road is silver,
Shiny-long . . . lost patience,
    We sit
Swoop seagull, borrow my love,
    Digest my fear
And be gone.

She walked right by.
    Robert Crooks

The Flock

We've flocked together
just like birds
"birds of a feather flock together"
together we have gone many places
some of us have broken from the flock
some of us have joined
together we've been through
rain, snow, and sun
but once we get older
we will break the "V"
we will fly our own way
and soon we will join other flocks
lead flocks
and even make flocks
    Trista Marlow

Goodbye to a Friend

From the moment that we met,
I knew that we'd be friends.
We got along so well,
We always made amends.

You were always there,
When my pain was just to much.
I cried upon your shoulder,
You had the loving touch.

I tried my very best
To be the best a friend could be.
I tried to always be there for you,
Like you were there for me.

I know that even though you leave,
You never really go.
But I must say goodbye to you,
And try not to let my pain show.
    Jennifer Keener

My Brother, Derek

Derek is a person that's special to me.
I just have to accept one thing,
That will always be.
He will never be normal
In a physical way,
But in my heart he is.
That, I can say.
Normal or not,
He will always be my brother.
I love him always,
Like my father and mother.
    Daphne Zimmer

What We Are

Winds of Change Forever blow
On their clouds we do grow
To twist and weave into any form
To live and survive, it is our norm
A helping hand, a goodwill token
Dangerous Mind, Crimes unspoken
Steel and granite Rise up high
Metal birds that soar and fly
Mountains Conquered, Rivers Tamed
Strip mined land, Horridly maimed
Dry harsh deserts, Frozen Wastelands
This planet's fate in our hands
But we will learn, and then go far
Humanity, it's what we are
    Dennis Michael Pechmann

Reflections of You

I could live an eternity
and not find what I have now.
A warmth, a glow that radiates
And yet I know not how . . .

How could I be so lucky
to have found such precious a jewel?
A joy that cost me nothing,
yet fills me with life's fuel.

Fuel of desire and passion
that stokes my lonely hour.
Within my darkest desert
the solitary watering tower.

Tower of strength by your side
I shall always be.
For I can never replace
the very essence of what you mean to me.

Me, the smallest part
of an exciting future life
Shared with my cherished three
my friend, my love, my wife
    Gavin Lilburn

Memories

A lock of hair neatly tied with ribbon
First tooth to fall, very well hidden
Shoes, size zero, for feet so small
Together all placed inside

Hand sketched picture of days gone by
Cards of good wishes to cherish

A dried rose from our first night
A locket from you with us inside

All of these I keep safe within reach
For my memories run deep
The love we shared and the life we lived
Now just a memory
I keep safe within my heart
    Claire Currier

Waking

She, the moon goddess,
    white beneath a diamond beauty,
whispers of shadows a moment gone.
    (Still sweet in their shining void,
        no language could recall them.)
Her arms, elaborately languid,
then smooth away their death,
And, like a cool wind,
    She moans their symphony.
    Suzanne Cole

You Take My Breath Away

Sometimes when I can't sleep
and the house is quiet
in my mind I go to a beach
that Hannah showed me once.
I take your hand
and I walk with you there.
On Hannah's beach
the wind was blowing
so the wind always blows there.
It musses your hair
the way I always wanted to do.
Even with mussed hair
you are so beautiful
you take my breath away.
    Debra Burton

Glee

dancing around
i go up then down
on my face just a frown
on top of my head a crown
i am king "i will never die"
need a queen
don't know what i mean
never happy
feel a little crappy
lost interest anyway
i hate today
no time that's fine
just wandering around
look at me
an upside-down frown
what can i say
i hate today
    Chuck A. Gifford

Not to Have You

Why do I have a heart
only to be broken
Why do I have eyes
only to cry an ocean

Why do I have hands
only not to touch
Why do I have a mind
only to miss you so much

Why do I have ears
only not to hear your voice
Why do I have a mouth
only not to have a choice

Why do I have dreams
only not to come true
Why do I have anything
only not to have you
    Beth Richardson

How Wonderful It Might Be

How wonderful it might be,
If I saw you and you saw me,
From the inside out,
And we had no doubt,
I in you, and you in me.
There is but One,
And like the Sun,
Its rays are everywhere.
Its warmth for all to care.
What's inside is the same,
No matter what the name.
    Charles D. Geddes

Wonders of the Sea

Sea of colors, sea of wonders,
Sea of all that you discovered.

Green, red, yellow and blue,
Orange, brown and purple too.

All the colors that you want,
You have seen them just like that.

The way they glide, the way they glow,
And shimmer inside.

Their graceful pride, their loved soul,
And yet, the way they feel is untold.

The way we feel is more than great,
But, how about them, is it too late

Grace A. Conley

The Old House

The old house echoes
With voices from the past.
The child within me
Still hears the clang
Of horseshoes,
The barking of the dog
The laughter of all those years.
Now, so many years later,
The House is empty.
Yet, it still speaks to me,
As if it has a life of its own.
Those I loved
Are now all gone,
Yet, I can still feel their presence.
Who I am
Comes from that house
And will remain
With me forever.

S. E. Saar

Church Women after the Funeral

I pretend not to notice
the old church women
crowding my lonely home.
Their incense, and preaching
nurse my mood.
They rearrange possessions
into one room, lock it shut,
hide the key.

They want to talk,
but nothings slips beyond
my mask of silence.

When night falls
they go back home
and louse around,
calling one another to gossip.

Not noticing,
They make their beds
with my sorrow.

Rhonda Benson

Your Power

Total control, awesome power
every minute in passing hour
days to be, gone and here
chance be taken, fun, no fear
world like this, near and far
take it now, the way we are
love not gone in all time passed
left to fly, it's way to last

Susan Carroll

Friends

Josh and Pooh go everywhere,
together they explore life.
Day to day, without a care,
no stress, no worry, no strife.

For the world is wide
and wonderful, big as can be.
They travel it from side to side
to see what they can see.

Josh and Pooh go everywhere,
exploring their world.
At the end of the day, the boy
and his bear, in their bed are curled.

Bob Cail

Passing Through

A moment in eternity,
A time to build and grow,
A chance that God has given us
To love and care and know
The pain that comes in being,
The struggles that we face,
The choices we must daily make
To earn eternal grace.

The Father understands our faults,
He hears us when we call.
And even though we fail again,
He'll never let us fall.
There is a higher power that
We simply can't deny
And we shall know the Master's plan
In his time, by and by.

Marion Williams

I Love You

For Seda
I thought I saw love in your eyes,
But now I see that those were lies.
Sweet and cruel lies that burnt
My heart, my soul—pain I learnt.

You say there's no hope for us,
But I can't go on living thus.
I loved you the moment we met,
And you said you weren't ready yet.

Now you say there's someone else.
I don't think he also tells
You that he loves you the way I do.
I just say that "I Love You!"

Karen Souren Sarkissian

Traits of a Family

Dedicated to the Wong Clan with love
The unity in one
The clan
Trust, that never will be undone
Hope and togetherness
Traits that binds the soul
And leads us all to an ultimate goal
To be or not to be
The tread that hangs in the balance
The destiny that is our essence
For it unites us all as humans
The everlasting flag to rally
To be what God foreordained
A family

Shawn Quah

My Poem?

My Poem?
What did you say?
tick,
tick
I ask, turning numb.
Her eyes glare at the TV set . . .
kick
SCRATCH
SCREAM
Is it my poem?
silent ashes burn my mind
tick,
tick
IS IT MY POEM
or
just me you don't like???
it must be
me.

Mara Beitzel

Mary Jane

She never asks of anything
Or tells me what to do
She never hides her face from me
Or fails when I am blue

The future's sure to know her
As past years can attest
As time goes by I know that
It's truth that she possessed

Her origin's unknown to all
Yet many know her well
They find a certain peace within
A lasting magic spell

Many names disguise her
With untruths there to fool
Some use her for their body
Others for a mind's tool

Mother Earth is part of her
Deep rooted in the seed
Close relations you could say
Earth wind fire and weed

Bjorn Stokes

The Man I Love

There is this man I love,

He is more beautiful than
any angel above.

He gives me a love that is
so special to me, and treats
me all so tenderly.

The bond that has been made
between us, is of true love
and not of lust.

We have an understanding
between one another . . . I'm not
his mother and he's not my father:

The feeling we receive from
holding each other can only
be experienced between two lovers.

When the time comes for us to
part, we will both be grey-
haired and known as old farts!

Carol Jones

A Heart Unopened

A flower unborn, a book
Unopened.
A fruit with seeds unharmed.
A path without marks, a house without
Doors.
Lack of pain, perfume to gain.
A landscape without dirt,
A treasure unconcealed.
This is the day that God
Awaits,
Beyond the land's mystic plates.
Preston Dilworth

Sight Unseen

She has a quietness about her
That enchants me
Her gaze speaks of many things
Her eyes read volumes of me
In an instant
My soul smiles back
From this awkward position
I have arrived
Trying to decipher
Her quietness about me
Amy Guala

Love

Love in your heart
wasn't put there to stay

Love isn't love
until you give it away.
Belinda Voyles

Daddy's Little Girl

I was daddy's little girl
'Til God took him away.
I didn't know what to do,
And mommy said I should pray.
So I said, "Why did you take my daddy?"
And God said, "Because he was sick.
So I took away his pain,
And made him all anew,
So he could always be
Your guardian angel
And could take care of you."
So I thanked my Lord above
That He had healed my daddy,
And I thanked Him again when I was done.
Because of His great love,
He sacrificed "His only begotten Son."
Edna Murphy

A Friend You Are

A friend you are
A kind soul you'll be
A world of love
You offer to thee
You brighten a blue day
I'm glad we've met along the way
You give so much joy
Like a kid with a new toy
I'm glad our paths crossed
For I no longer seem lost
I no longer need to hide
You've taken away all my lies
I'm so glad you're my friend
You've carried me through to the end
Rhonda Heckathorn

The Little Angel

A man walks down a lonely street
in the middle of the night
Not knowing where he's bound to go
or where he'll sleep tonight
The morning breaks as the man awakes
startled by the world
He squints his eyes at the sudden sight
of a beautiful little girl
She is the most peaceful thing
he's seen in quite some time
The little girl now takes his hand
she's delicate and kind
As they are walking hand in hand
a peaceful silence arose
The man looks down at the little girl
who's adoring face now glows
The precious voice of the little girl
now whispers in his ear,
"No longer will you be alone,
for He has sent me here."
Elissa Michelle Lonsdale

Silent Night

Dedicated to my best friends:
Fannie & Sylvia
Silent night
Dawn so well
Morning glory
Noon arrives
Born to live
Live to love
As carrying a suitcase
Suitcase of memories
Memories of you
You, I love
Spit the bitter
Taste the sweet
The space is wider
In the sea They meet
Love is my unspoken word
Diamond is my ungiven gift
Novita Harianto

Missing You

Lying against the wall
Watching other people have a ball
How come I don't cry?
Instead I just dry my eye
You've been gone more than a year
I haven't shed one tear
If I could
I would
Turn back the hands of time
I'd spend more than a dime
Just to see you again
I can't go through this pain
Lying against the wall
Watching other people have a ball
Cinnamone Harris

Lost Rose

My soul was famished
From the stark invasion,
A rose that had vanished
From another's persuasion.

Once had a garden
Quenching hunger with bread,
My neglect please pardon
For the words not said.
Pablo Ceballos

I Love the Way You Look at Me

I love the way you look at me
You must see things that I don't see
The way I feel when I see me
Brings such awful memories
The lines, the pain, and such despair
When I think back, I just don't care
I love the way you look at me
You must see things that I don't see
When we lie down, you hold me near
Your love releases all my fear
I love the way you look at me
You must see things that I don't see.
Dinah Berry

Spring

New leaves cover branches
beating the rhythm of life
into air, maybe with diffused effort
making happy. Life too unfolds daily
hope to make oneself, others happy.
Leaves leave, memories remain
of things left behind.
Effort builds upon them
the tangible joyful, wonderful world!
Madhukanta Sen

Love

Love is not what you buy,
or something that you learn;
Love is what you feel
when your heart begins to burn.
We feel it in our hearts,
and may even see it with our own eyes.
And when the feelings come around,
our stomach is filled with butterflies.
We search long and hard for this,
and sometimes the search is long,
but when the search is over,
we feel like we're part of a love song.
Everything feels so great,
and every day is just the best,
for problems are not as bad . . .
and are easily put to rest.
Take it in with open arms,
instead of running and trying to hide;
Hold tight and hang on . . .
for it is one terrific ride.
John-Ruben Aranton, Jr.

Doing It My Way

It's easy to relax,
I'm so very content.
I had to learn who I am,
All my anger to be spent.

I've loved you so long,
I still feel it every day.
Now, I'm doing all I can,
and doing it my way.

I've learned to live without you,
I even dream of a new tomorrow.
You're still a part of my thoughts
But no more tears, no more sorrow.

Now my days are much brighter,
I sometimes laugh and play,
Now, I'm doing all I can,
and doing it my way.
Betty Russell

Tears of Sickness

Tears fall down upon my cheeks
A finger wipes them clean
Sorrow fills my heart sometimes
It hurts beyond all pain
I ask myself the questions of
Answers hard to make
I feel like my soul is empty
A feeling I can't stand
The day comes to an end and I sleep
Restlessly
A short calm overtakes my guilt
Of feeling so alone
I love who I am
But not what I have become
For it scares the Hell out of me.

Lisa Bales

Mindscape

The hills have matured
Through the valley gushes a stream
The grass green and lush
Smells of the first spring rain
The trees wear yellow blossoms
The clouds cast a blue veil
The wind caresses with a song
The sun a warm haze
The birds come chirping
The fishes sail
The bird watchers stir in their nests
The boatmen fish in vain
The hunter strangely walks alone
Hunted by his prey

Suresh Karunakaran

Vanity Destroys

She stands in front of the mirror
leaning across the sink
slowly applying her makeup
careful not to blink.
Vanity has taken her soul
she has left, emptiness in a case
spending so much time on the outside
no one can get past her face.
Freely spirited as a child
the soul inside, strong and bold
now has been torn down
her spirit, not even enough to hold.
The emptiness has taken over
as she stands, staring at herself
not even noticing what's inside her
she is left, a dusty book on the shelf.

Jill Zanella

In Love

My heart is full of joy, my Lord
That I can't do without
I like to sing about your love
It shows me where I'm at
I am so full, yet I see
There's something more to do
Nothing short of doing your will
Could make me happier still
But only you give truth, love, and hope
That tells me where I'm lacking
When I drift away pull me back
And show me the where and why
You treat me with a purest love
I'm always seeking after
'Til by your side, my Holy Dad
I'll know I've come full circle

Carol A. Ross

Clouded Views

I sit on death row
day after day
Watching my life
waste away.
Yet I think back
on a life I once had.
Where times now,
don't seem so bad,
thinking of all
the love I had.
But the drugs surely
clouded my view and
ruined my life and others too.

Ronald W. Clark, Jr.

Life

It was the stone of life
She was stepping on.
Her life was moving faster.
A life now stepped upon.

Why would someone make her
Live it day and night?
Don't make her live again
Through contention, dissension, strife.

Now her stepping stone was moving,
Moving through her dream.
Her stone was getting smaller,
Anguish at the scene, the dream.

A dream flashing, flashing in her life.
She can't remember being!
Was it life or was it just a dream?

Bette Merrill

Arrows and Hearts

See the brave archer
Golden bow at his side
Is he unavoidable cupid
Or some wolf in disguise

See the exquisite maiden
Flowing locks of auburn flame
Upon her white stallion
Her desire impulsive as the rain

The battle of love engages
Upon the chosen field
With no mercy shown
To those who might yield

The battle is forever
The players dramatically scream
For life is the great stage
And love is the great scene

An echo in the night time
All souls begin to hark
What does entice them
Arrows and hearts

Nick Nunley

What's

What's words
Spoken in my ear
What's written on a screen
What's words in motion
Whisper with no fear
Of best beauty ever seen
Passing so much emotion
What's the confusion of words
what's the loving words?

Bob Sande

Neglect

Here you are
There you go
Always in a hurry
Always in a rush
Come on, slow down
Sit down for a minute, just one
That is all I ask
Up and down
In and out
Here and there
There you go again
Who knows where to, or how long
Will I ever see you again
Will you ever have time for me
I don't know you
All I know of you is
No time for this
No time for that
No time for me
And I am your son

Jeremy Haley

Angel

Angel of Mercy
Angel of Love
I'll Always Be With You
My Darling
My Love . . .

Alberto Rodriguez

I Am with You

In the darkest night
I will see you

In the coldest wind
I will hold you

In the warmest afternoon
I will shade you with love

In times of need
I am your foundation
Built from bricks of hope

When you are sad
I am your grinning fool
With conical and bells
Tinkling through the lonely night

When you are scared
I am your strength
A tall oak tree with leaves
Tattooed with color

When you are alone
I am close
A footfall away

Brian A. Bachar

Remember

I remember
I remember
You so warm and dear.
And through all kinds of
Weather I will always
Want you near.
Through rain and snow
Through sleet and ice

To me my darling
Mother, you will
Always be so nice

Mary Dolores

Here in Prison: For Now and Forever

Here in prison
For now and forever
Nothing left
But boredom and punishment

The sickening smell in the air
Dirt on the ground
The food that only makes me puke
A chill that I just can't shake

All alone
Nothing to do
But wait
For nothing

I could kill myself
But what good would that do
I'd probably go to Hell

If only I had another chance
I wouldn't do it again

But it's too late now
I'm here in prison
For now and forever
                Ray Pefferman

Spirit Wind

The wind,
Force of nature that I love,
Blow hard, blow soft,
But don't stop.
Whistle through the pines
Rush down the canyons
Bring the breath of the mountains
Cool, clean air
Just blow.
Disperse the seeds
The dandelion fluff
Rustle the grass
Scatter the autumn leaves
Ripple the water
Travel with the river
Roaring as the rapids
Carve the land
Run the race
Wild and free
Untamed, the wind.
                Brenda A. Wentzel

The Frame

How can love be so cruel, so dark,
That sometimes it embarks
Upon a course of lies and schemes
That tears its world apart?

So often done to those around
I never thought that I . . .
Would be the one within this Frame
Of those who wonder . . . why?

A frame so large and old as time
Wrapped 'round the heart of man,
That houses tears it holds inside
Like tiny grains of sand.

I view this Frame now differently
I see it from within
Where hearts held captive for awhile,
Think on what might have been.

Though having loved has put me here
Inside this lonely place
I still believe in "One True Love"
And that's how I'll escape!
                Vicki King George

Thoughts of Youth

Years ago I was young and free,
Without a care or a need,
At the thought of a whim,
I loved and I lost;
Without even counting the cost.
Now I am old and ready to go,
Recounting the things that I know;
I'd gladly turn back the hands of time;
And recant the actions that were mine.
                Kay Bragewitz

Be Like an Apple

When an apple falls,
You can pick it up,
Or let it be.
One thing for sure,
You can't put it back,
To grow on the tree.
Will you let it lie,
To rot and waste?
Or take a bite,
And savor the taste?
An apple is useful,
Don't let it die.
Put it in salad,
And bake it in pie.
Gather the apples,
Shine them up bright,
And then cut them open,
And take a big bite!!
                Dottie Britton-Thornburgh

Streaks of Red

Streaks of red
Pass my eyes
In a feeling of dread
Though my mind wishes to wander
It can't help but stay
On the vision it doesn't wish to see
In front or behind
Streaks of red
Cover me
I begin to weaken
In strength and in mind but I
Strive to pull through and
Streaks of red
                Tristan Pirak

I See You

Arriving home, very late, tonight
about to climb the tall
lonely stairs to my apartment
I looked up . . . and stopped
I could see the stars
twinkling
I smiled
for in those most radiant stars
I could see your eyes
sparkling
And then I looked over
I saw a brilliant moon
shining
I gleamed
for in that perfect, caressing moon
I could see your face
glowing

It's good to be home . . .
                Lare Austin

Unconditional

Gaze upon the morning sky,
and out across the meadows,
for where the sun touches the rye,
I will be there, waiting.
When you look out your window,
and the rain is falling fast,
just focus on the memories,
of love past.
Once upon a midnight blue,
across the waters, there was you.
You looked so fair, you looked so fine,
I knew I had to have you mine.
If ever there was a time to shine,
if ever a time to be,
if ever there was a time to love,
that time is now, that time is we.
Being there is just the half,
loving you the other,
my love is unconditional,
I love you like no other.
                Chad Crider

Revision

Another day,
one of contradictions
Another way,
to underline man's restrictions
Another choice,
to make the right decision
Another voice,
saying, it needs revision
                Natalie Hartgers

Like an Old Ragdoll

Like an old ragdoll
you picked me up.
I was happy,
But only for awhile.
Like all toys,
I was thrown out.
You tossed me out.
Because you'd had your fun,
and then you gave up on me.
Like an old rag doll.
You broke my heart.
Yet you treated me like an old ragdoll.
An old ragdoll.
                Holly Neimeier

Thinking of You

My cries are like,
a thunderstorm;
with a darkness surrounding me.
My heart bleeds for you . . .
My suffering is like,
an earthquake;
shattering apart.
My heart bleeds for you . . .
My loneliness is like,
a blackout;
not knowing where I am.
My heart bleeds for you . . .
My screams are like,
a hurricane;
spinning away.
My heart bleeds for you . . .
My anger is like,
a volcano;
burning inside of me.
My heart bleeds no more . . .
                Margarita Torres

Dreams

We blink, veiled in reflection
Monsters of dispossessed loss
No Albatross or wreath
To cast once there
  Samuel B. Sharpe

The Old Water Tower

It stands a symbol of
  bygone days
Here in this almost
  forgotten place.
Lonely, rusted, never again
  to give the town
Life saving water
  pouring down.

Yet there it basks
In the glorious sunlight
Of a warm summer day
Standing tall, it asks
For you and me to delight
As morning's sun beams
  around it play.
  Johnsie Allen

For My Daughter

Where have all the years gone?
It seems like yesterday
I watched you from the window
As in the yard you'd play

Now here you stand before me
A young lady fully grown
Ready to face the future
But never on your own

For I will always be here
As a mother and a friend
With a hand outstretched to help you
Or an ear you wish to bend

We've sometimes had our ups and downs
And both have shed some tears
But through it all—we had our love
And made it through those years

Now just because you're "grown up"
Doesn't mean my role is through
For you'll always be my "little girl"
And I'm always here for you.
  Christine Tetrick

Like the Snowflakes in the Winter

Like the water flows so gently
  Over the pebbles and the rock,
  So the love of Jesus flows
  Into every Christian's heart.

Like the stillness of the summer
  As beauty adorns the Earth,
  So is the peace of Jesus
  To those who hear His word.

Like the snowflakes in the winter,
  Each one drifts down with grace,
  So like the child of Jesus,
  He gives each one a place.

Like the sun, the stars, the moon
  One differs from another,
  So are the gifts that Jesus gives
  Each one to help each other.
  Betty Mann

Song Writer

I know a man
who sings
so beautifully that
women are
drawn
to him.
I know a man
whose life
experience
has left him
embittered
but inspired.
I know a man
who writes
so beautifully that
a woman is
arrested by a
glimpse
into his soul.
  Lois Strangemore

cupid of the night

darkness falls down into the night
strangers walk below my feet
i am high above the sky
flying and grasping the city heat
my passion is at its peak
evening desire deep in my lust
drifting on a cloud to ecstasy
surrendering to the night i trust
i am invincible with the wind
soaring like an eagle in flight
no resistance can stop me
for i am the cupid of the night
join me to Heaven 10 clouds above 9
there is my home where all love dwells
every cupid has a hand to hold
come with me & ring my desire bells
the night has called me down to you
to take you in the cradle of my wings
for i am your cupid of the night
the only angel to make your heart sing
  Joey Rosario

Plastic People

So afraid am I

Afraid to be near
for I may be hurt
Afraid to stay afar
for fear of loneliness

So Plastic I became
so no matters, mattered

Ah, but did I forget
Plastic melts and has no form

Who am I?
  Michael Elterman

Fireflies

What if . . .
there really are no stars
shining in the night,
only the shadows of fireflies,
gathered from hundreds of thousands
past summers' twilights,
their lives remembered only
by the twinkling
of their lights.
  Charles Lunsford, Jr.

Emotional Decisions

it is a story of the funny girl
her hair were shiny, black & curl
she was in her early teens
her age was hardly sixteen
she started loving a boy
and he used her as a toy
when she strongly urged to marry
the boy refused her to carry
what happened then was bad
the poor girl was sad
castles of her dreams were demolished
alas! the lovely days she polished
emotional decisions in brief
usually lead to a grief
  Asif Iqtidar

Angel Kiss

Kiss me angel, I do take heed,
Lest I should fall in love divine.
Kiss me angel, my soul be freed,
Angel kiss, your lips are mine.
Kiss me angel, and I shall know
The truth of all I've dreamed.
Angel kiss, the wind does blow
And sends your kisses to lips redeemed.
Angel kiss, my soul cries out
Angel kiss, my heart does cry
Angel kiss, my mind does shout
For angel kiss, your lips defy.
Angel kiss, was all for naught,
For all the pain your lips have brought?
  Thomas Epps

Whenever

Contented Sigh.
Blueberry Pie.
Shirt and Tie.
You and I.
Sun and Sky.

Old and New.
Not a clue.
Many and few.
Me and You.
Honey Dew.

Goose feathers.
Pirate treasures.
Beautiful weather.
Us together.
Whenever.
  Chason Ishino

The Corner Stool

Working hard all day
She spends her nights alone
Not one to hold her
Not one to care
Alone in a crowd
Is her home away from home
From a corner stool
She watches the world go by
She hides her loneliness with style
And the pain behind a smile
From that corner stool
She whispers "Nothing lasts forever"
But where is her Prince Charming
Perhaps across the room
Watching the rest of the world go by
From his own corner stool
  Mary Wright

To Be Manic

Infused with Fire
Licking my brain
Unrelenting and fierce,
What passionate flame
Is this; as Irony's
Child—was I
Created for Life,
Or born to die?
My hunger creates
To tame this Fire
Keeping my pain
From climbing higher
Spewing my Madness
On paper, on keys
A needle thrust in
The pressure to ease
So if my creation
Moves you in part,
Don't burn yourself
On my Fire in Heart

Marion Johnson

The Northern Light

The rainbow of the stars
like a river in the sky
floating towards unknown adventures.

Melkorka Sigurdardottir

When You Smile at Me

When you smile at me
I could swear the sun is in your eyes
And when you laugh with me
It's then that I realize
The friendship that we share
Means more to me
Than all the wealth in all the world
I believe that if the Earth fell
And the sky rained tears of sorrow
If I were all alone
In a place where peace is unheard of
If I could hear you say my name
If I could see you smile—
The sunrise in your eyes
The world could fall apart around me
And I would be happy
Much wealthier than the kings themselves
Because the thing that makes me happiest
Is the smile of joy I feel inside
When you smile at me.

Jennifer Ott

Love Me Not

I reach out to touch you,
But I feel nothing but air.
I long to hold you close;
You pull away and stare.

You said you loved me,
Then you treat me this way.
I never know what to say;
Words fall on deaf ears.

Why is nothing ever right ?
Everything has to be so unkind.
Feelings, words of pain,
Emptiness inside my heart.

False words and lies
Buried deep inside me
Too painful to forget;
But life goes on instead.

Marilyn Jean Duncan

love

love i see forever in your eyes
i can see Heaven in your smile
and when i hold you close to me
i don't want to let go
because deep in my sole
i know girl you're the only light i see
your love means everything to me
i know we'll never be apart
you'll always be in my heart
you're like an angel from above
sent here to shower me with your love
and you'll always be the one i love
for now and forever will i love you
and be true

Brian Epchook

To the One I Love

The night is dark and cloudy
yet the stars they shine so bright
you're one in a million stars
and you're mine to keep tonight

I'll put my arms around you
and never let you go
surround you with my love
'cause darling don't you know?

Shining star—I love you so.

Jane Jensen

Darkness

My passage through depression
Darkness caves in on me
the feeling of me and everything
agrees mutually

Not one of love, the opposite feeling
hate is all around

My only path is a scary one
no yellow brick road is on the ground
this path is black and not much fun.

It takes me to a place I know not of
Murky trees, dead and dark
I realize now, i have no love
I had it once but it left on a lark

My path may see bright days ahead
Or it may lead to my awful end

But I will know where I am led
Is not my choice, and I can mend.

Christi Niermann

Relationships

though you i promised
through infernos (these walls my mind)—
although i would
give you all nights
of stars and moonshine bright,
too late tomorrow i find
in stopping far short of perfection,
once again through what Fate divined,
i confined myself to isolation.
you in desperate happiness
afflicting only yourself;
you, wishing to permeate my senses
with happy juice,
you tritely informed me
how imperfect all we are,
while suggesting options more—
you are always the one for me.

Megan Small

Shamrock

Clover is indeed a colorful plant
With hues of green and white and red.
It started when time began,
So it has been said.
It graced the fields of Eden
When this very Earth began,
And occupied the garden
About the time of man.
When Patrick preached in Ireland
His converts were many and free.
He used the little shamrock
To show one stem with three.
They listened, heard, and believed
How the Father, the Son
And the Spirit were one,
Like a Shamrock . . . the Holy Trinity.

Joseph F. Kamalick

Last Words

I, who has been a friend to solitude,
Embrace death, at last, in gratitude

Friends I had when most alone
And never more when with death I'm gone.

Anthony Njoroge Muhia

Omnipotence

Upon the stars I am sitting,
watching the Earth below.
Pondering about the destruction,
and where humanity will go.
Whatever happened to principles,
lessons, manners, and morals?
Valuable liaisons are cheated,
lied to, and toiled.
Cursed I am only to look
upon this ignorance and plight.
Isn't it obvious to them,
that what they do isn't right?
The entire truth is somehow miscued
when no one is around.
Love has lost its meaning since
we have fallen so far down.
So finally the question remains,
as I sit in this lifeless stare.
With all the pain you have made me feel,
How or why do I even care?

Scott MacDonald

Take Time Out to Pray

Man is so busy relishing
The raptures of each day,
He doesn't take time to notice
That the end is on its way.
The pestilence and the famines
That are taking over the land,
The earthquakes and volcanic eruptions
That are taking full command.
Oh, sure man talks and gossips
About it every day,
But it's just his conversation piece
To pass the time away.
He doesn't really notice
What the Lord is trying to say,
He's giving man a warning
Not to lead himself astray.
Because it really won't be long, you see
Before it's Judgement Day.
So heed these words of wisdom, and
Take time out to pray.

Travis Miller

While

These summer pollens
irritate my petals.
I sway con amore
with the relentless breeze,
believing those wings
could take you
far deeper.

Like the monarch butterfly
that you are, traveling across
the mile long tendencies
of greed,

knowing that
I will still be
waiting for you
to come out of your chrysalis,
to fly across vast meadows,
across boundless petals

into me.

Carlo Saavedra

In the Winter

In the winter
You don't get a splinter.
Outside it's very cold
Inside the fire is strong and bold.
Snowmen built out in the yard
The snow is packed down hard.
Numb fingers, cold toes,
Cocoa with marshmallows.
Winter is great, winter is fun,
I can't wait 'til the next one.

Sabra Estabrooks

The Fairy Day

Modes of colored blossoms,
Hues of rainbow skies,
When sunset brings the moon,
Here the fairy lies.

He is majestic ruler,
Above all spirited fairies,
And he begins the midnight feast,
On the blue blossomed berries.

Then among the eastern stars,
Light is shining through,
Purples, pinks, orangy reds,
Night is bidding the fairies adieu.

The fairies end their starlit play,
And say goodnight to the fairy day.

Jenny Grest

The World

This world is kind
we make it unkind
when we forget why we are here.
To love one an other,
to care for our children,
and to remember our past.
Our past and our present
one day they will meet:
when, face to face,
our creator we meet.
He won't ask if we black . . .
he won't ask if we white . . .
he will solely ask:
Did YOU love one another?
did you remember your past.

Amalia Dirazar

I Am Rage

I am rage, I can no longer contain it
It threatens to burst forth
From the crumbling walls around it

A caged beast of pain and destruction
Seeking to wreak havoc
On the world around me
And one in particular

I scream with the beast
Our pain is one
I pound the walls of my prison
I want to be free, FREE

Yet muzzled I am and trapped I feel
A pressure inside that will destroy me
If I don't set it free
And unleash it upon the world

I can hear myself scream in anger
I can feel the pain and anguish
I can see the walls hemming me in
I am still, I am silent, I am blind

I am rage

Jane Phillips

The Hour of Amber

Let this moment be a jewel
Glowing on my memory's string
Seal the time in golden silence
Dream
Day by day our hearts grew harder
'Til they fossilized in sorrow
Excavate the gem from rubble
There is tomorrow
There is sun of ancient ages
Captured in past's honey depth
Spark of hope and light of wisdom
I saw it—I wept
In my veins primordial pine trees
Finally crystallized in amber
Share the sweetness of this hour
Remember
Let this moment . . .
. . . last . . .
. . . remember

Anna Nadgrodkiewicz

Great Poetry

High school taught me poetry,
Showing how lines ought to be;
Full of meaning, complications,
T.S. Elliot compilations.

E.E. Cummings has no rhyme,
Meter rough, no "beat" in time.
Kauffman "sings" of smashed "giraffes,"
Hidden meanings are their crafts.

If I laboured long enough,
Those works showed such depth and touch.
Sorting through strange metaphor,
Hardly made me pine for more.

Gone the joy I used to feel,
Lines that sang, because they're real.
Juicy verse that used to please,
Poems I understood with ease.

Then I saw what I must do,
Love those simple lines I knew,
I'll embrace that old cliche,
"Keep it simple," that's the way.

Brian W. Kelly

The World

I was afraid to venture out yonder

For Life seemed too deep

This World too long
But Oh! How I learned

You must earn your stay here

Never again will I shield myself

From thy thirsty eyes

Never again will I hide from thy
Stinging, sting

For Oh! Finally, dear world, I know

You are round

Carlton Johnson

Kitchen Memories

Floured hands kneading bread,
Apron faded and torn,
Remembering what her own mother said
In the house where she was born.
Sifted flour, measured oil,
Memories of Mother's toil . . .
Did she sing while cooking there?
Did she whisper morning's prayer?
Did she mind her daily task?
These are questions that I ask
In my kitchen while I cook.
I hang my apron on its hook,
And wonder who will remember me?
What fond memory will there be?
Will they remember I loved them well,
And think of me through taste and smell?
I brush the flour from my hair
And knead the dough with loving care.

Janet Diane Frey

Sorry

In dedication to David and his parents
I'm sorry
About your loss
I'm sorry
That I can't help

I'm sorry
That he's gone
I'm sorry
For everything else

I'm sorry
That I'm not there to comfort you
And I'm sorry
That he was so young

Amanda Henderson

Along the Coast

In summer's time of mist
and wayward fog
Along an ocean that shares
with us its eternal self
We stop in movement,
and stand in silence
To feel what came and
swept all around us
In a gentle but knowing way
our love with this, the sand and sea
To become one, and yet be free.

Tim Costa

Mother, My Perfect Companion

Who is our perfect companion?
Can it be a tiger on mother?
They glisten like ruby red gems
And twinkle like twinkling stars.
They guard us from fear and harm
And will always cherish us like charms.
Who is our perfect companion?
Our mothers, of course,
So elegant in charm.

Iman Ahmed

Lovers

Good times and bad
Happy or sad.

Laughing, talking, smiling
Enjoying each others time.

Sharing secrets, stories
Remembering the past.

Leaning on each other
For strength and understanding.

Lovers are you and I
Making it last forever.

April Sullivan

The Wall

Walk softly on this ground.
Show reverence and respect.
Honor all whose names you see.
Remember and reflect
Young men who went to battle
To give their Country Honor;
Young men who lived next door,
Or just around the corner.
Think of all their dreams,
Their hopes, and their desires
Torn and cast asunder
By wars bitter fires.
This ground is now Holy,
Blessed by blood they shed.
For if we do remember
They never shall be dead.
Walk softly on this ground.
But please! Do walk tall.
Walk softly on this ground.
For you stand, before, "THE WALL"

Charles Bantos

The Eagle

See an eagle in the sky,
A man shot it down, why?
A free spirit in the sky,
Tell me why it has to die?

Did the eagle attack the man?
Why couldn't he understand?

The eagle's spirit in us grows,
Just like the old Medicine-man told.

Now the eagle's lying on the ground,
And his spirit's free and says to me,
Fly with me to shadow land,
Fly with me to promised land.

Now the eagle's free
And says to me,
Just like the old Medicine-man told,
That an eagle's spirit in us grows.

Kjell Pedersen

My Mother's Love at 70

My mother's love is like a rose;
A thing of beauty to behold.
From early days nurtured, growing
Ever stronger, ever showing
The way to Heaven,
Both in direction and in soul:
Fragrant, beautiful, and whole.
Each aspect, each petal, stem and leaf
Combined as one in strength, yet sweet,
With thorns should any come between.

My mother's love is like a rose;
Ever stronger through the years
Constant, through sunny days of joy
And summer showers of tears,
A bouquet of life, and hope, and peace.

Robert E. Graf, Jr.

Santa's Heaven

Oh, Santa, if you hear me
don't bring me any toys
just take me up to Heaven
with the other girls and boys

Don't bring me any bats or balls
don't bring me any train
just take me up to Heaven
so I don't feel the pain

My mom don't mean to hurt me
I always make her mad
she says that she is sorry
now I'm feeling very bad

Oh, Santa, can't you hurry
she's hitting me again
I want to come and be with you
so all my pain will end

Charlene Kelly

Fallen Angels

"Where is my halo? Where is my halo?"
No longer a pure innocent white.
Now a dirty brown or black.
Mud-splattered and torn.
Picking up the pieces
And groping around in the dark.
Light has faded.
You cannot see.
Do not laugh—do not cry.
You can't.
Don't pray.
You have forgotten how to.
Do not live.
You do not belong to this world.

Marisa Wikramanayake

The Struggle

Burro, Wing, carries the wood,
C-lump, c-lump, c-lump,
His feet move down the dirt path way.
He lets out a breath,
Tired of walking he sits,
His owner, Wan, stands him up,
Once again the grueling path goes on.
Being led down the pathway,
Wing bows his head.
His tail swatting the big black flies,
Wing falls down,
Tired, old, too old to be doing this.
He looks at Wan as if saying,
"Good-bye old friend."

Amber Inman

Golden Drops of Dew

Down in the valley,
Under the sky blue,
I sit alone,
Thinking of you;
Soon,
The sun will go high.
And
The day will pass by,
But
In my memories
Will always remain fresh.
The moments passed with you,
As fresh as
On a morning flower,
Golden drops of dew.

Naren Israney

You May

If You Run
You May Walk
If You Yell
You May Talk
If You Live
You May Die
If You Give
You May Get
If You Stand
You May Sit
If You Kill
You May, No You Will Pay . . .
Well That's The Way It Would Be,
If I Had Things My Way

Alex Beisler

Horse

Riding the rugged trail
with me upon your back
Thy sky looks like rain
The afternoon is perfect
Walk, trot, gallop, run!

Every time I ride you, horse
Such amazing discoveries
Horse and I together ride
A new road each time
Completely alone.

Your warm wet nose
Your gentle neigh, neigh!
Your powerful hoofs
Your soft brown mane
Your leather saddle

The perfect place
So far away from everyone
Except the one that you love
The ride with the horse.

Donna J. Flynn

Passion, Desire, Forever

Caress her heart and you
shall fill her soul with
Passion.

Feed her passion, and you
Shall become her hearts
Desire.

Touch them both and
You shall have her love
Forever.

Belinda Tillotson

Sweet Blue

The spring sun
The winter breeze
The light sky
The summer squeeze
A perfect day
All evening's light
Sitting in the sun
And daytime's night
It all adds up
All for you
We sit and wait
For the sky's
Sweet blue.

Audrey Nieto

Beating Hearts

Lying lazily in a field
Of dewdrops, in the
Subtle shade I lie.
Here am I, sipping herbal tea
And surrounding myself with incense.
Here am I comfortably,
As a solemn-by-myself
Person watching the
Decline of moral values,
Ethics of my native people.
Come hear the steady
Beat of the drums.
Come sway with the
Strumming strings in
Tune with your soul.
Come dance around my fire,
Come gaze upon my flame.
Enrapture yourself in
My aura and thou shall
Never feel the same.

Constance Lupton

Missing

In the complete silence
the leaves start falling
one by one
to hit the mirror water
to float down stream
into an unknown target
of a desperate dream
what's done is done
faces of stone
I hear you calling

Synnove Tilrem

Because They Know

We all laugh at those people
Who try so hard to be accepted
But do we really know why
They try so hard.

Is it because they just want friends
Or are searching for companionship?
Is it because they need advice
Or someone to rely on?

Why do they fight so hard,
Always trying to be a great friend?
Is it a result of a troubled childhood
Or in reaction to a failed friendship?

Why do some people try so hard
To be what we all want?
Because they know what it's like
To see the pain in a mirror's eyes.

Jennifer Krall

Falling for You

I'm falling, I'm falling for you
the love I feel is as deep as the
sea and just as dark and blue.
When I see your face, my eyes
fill with glee, I wish that you
would be with me. I'm trying
to convince myself that it's a
waste of time, but whenever I
turn around and see your smile,
I feel fine. I can't explain to
anyone what's going on inside my
mind, but I know my life would
be no use with out you intertwined.

Ashley Marshall

Solid Light

Carrying the cross
He had lost
People once with Him
Now against Him
Getting beatings
Getting denied
We all had died
People yelling
People crying
Something He didn't deserve He took
With a cross
Crown of thorns
Nails in hands and feet
He paid for our sins
He loves us this much
SOLID LIGHT

Lucy Kenealy

Tree

See that tree
it stands so tall
God made that tree, after all.
And like a man
that tree will bend
then it straightens up again
like an umbrella
it protects from the storm
it covers you
with its outreached arms
"come close," it seems to say
"storms too
are part of God's day"
and when the rains cease
and the sun breaks through
I whisper
"thank you tree
for being you."

Dollie Cook

Your Embrace

You will never know
What your embrace
Did to me because
You were my life
You were my soul
You were my day
You were my night
You were the glue
That held me together
You were the song
That gave me life
You were my sun
My everlasting light

Antonia Pastor

Summer

Summer is the best time of the year.
In summer you don't feel any fear.
You can jump in a lake.
Or eat juicy steak,
Which is my favorite part, I must say.
I'll swim in my pool.
For hot dogs I'll drool,
An not once will I think about school.
The fun's just begun.
I'll lie in the sun.
Oh, no!
Summer is over.

Brittany Liford

Loneliness

Lonely is what I feel
I wish it wasn't real
I feel so empty inside
With not a place to hide
I don't feel like seeing anyone
Or having any fun
I don't want someone new
I just want you to feel the way I do
I'm trying really hard
To heal my broken heart
But every time I try
I only start to cry
Tears fill up in my eyes
Hoping soon you will realize
You really, truly care
And all the dreams we can share
So when I'm feeling lonely,
I just start to think of
You, the one I love!

Gina Caruso

My Messenger

God came to me this morning
Through the voice of a bird,
As I listened through my window
'Twas a song I've never heard.
I listened so intently
So I could hear the words.

It seemed to say, "Good Morning.
How are you today?"
I whispered through my window,
"Hello, please don't go away."

I ran to get my little boy
So he could come to see
This beautiful specimen
Saying things to me.
This morning now I realize
God sent the bird to me,
So I will be more cheerful
For my family.

LaNell Dodson

you're loved

i love you this much.
how much?
enough!
i love you forever.
how long?
indefinitely!
i love you now and here.
when and where?
this moment this second!
i love you unconditionally.
thank you! thank you!

Sharon Kirnon

Native Sun

When Council Fires
burned across the land,
And the eagle soared its
Width and breadth,
We offered our knowledge
To young and old alike.
Those times are gone and the
Fires of Council are few now.
But we are still the People.
We are no less, because we
are fewer.
In our hearts, the spark glows
brightly;
In our minds, the truth echoes;
In our hands we raise the pipe
to the Creator
And then as one we know . . .
Though it is night
Our Sun will rise again.

Nasnaga Russell

Imagination in a Maple Tree

Old Lady Maple
Sits down to tell a story
Of times long passed.
Two young children
Climb her broad trunk
To sit in her lap.
Long, dry limbs
And large bony elbows
Surround a boy and a girl
In a leafy embrace.
Adventure and safety,
Life beneath her green cloak.
A boy in red shorts
On a hot summer day
Becomes Peter Pan.
A girl in her favorite tutu
Is a fairy
Living in the treetops
Among a colorful canapy;
All
As
The
Story
Unravels

Katherine Andersen

Oh, How I Wish

Oh, how I wish I could write
A book of poetry,
The beauty enclosed within its pages,
To all of the world from me.

Oh, how I wish I could give
People a really nice rhyme,
Sharing some of my innermost thoughts
In such a creative time.

Oh, how I wish I could see
The words that are yet unwritten,
For while I love many things in life,
In poetry I am smitten.

Oh, how I wish I could bring
A smile to every face,
To touch people deep in the heart,
And find their special place.

Oh, how I wish to complete
A book of poetry,
The beauty enclosed within its pages,
For only you to see.

Sally Bolwell

Without

Oh, how bleak the world would be
Without the sun, sky, and seas
Without the stars to shine at night
Without the moon that glows so bright
Without flowers in the spring
Without mountains and trees
Without love, peace, and harmony
Oh, how bleak the world would be
Heavenly father from up above
I praise you for your perfect love
On the day when I must leave
I pray to thank you personally
For all these gifts you given me

Marie Maloy

Pragmatist

What I want, I want,
So don't tell me I don't.
What I can't, I can't,
So believe that I can't.
What I won't, I won't,
And it's true that I won't.
What is free, is free,
So do let me be.
What I can, I can,
So please understand.
What I do, I do,
And what is that to you?
What I think, I think:
In this, I won't blink.
What I see, I see,
And this defines me.
What I know, I know,
And that's how I go.
My world is my world—
What else can be unfurled?

Theresa John

i believe i can die

i believe i can die
i got shot by the fbi
all i wanted was an onion ring
from mcdonalds or burger king
i was tired of waiting
so i punched a man in the eye
and joined the fbi
then i grew into a butterfly
flew up into the sky
and dropped into an apple pie
i believe i can die

David Oloula

phantom carrion

ours are the dead ones

the living have left

we the alive

noting the space

hurting the selves

on account of the nothing

the gone

and ours is the stolen

not any thing

that ever was ours

Jenny Vega

Never Again

I was stupid and I was blind,
I could not see clearly,
Into your eyes,
I thought our love was fine.
Now I am being told,
All different things,
This makes me feel cold,
This is the heartache that life brings.
Now I build my concrete wall,
I will not feel love any more,
Even If you try to call,
Just now my heart is an empty core.
As time goes on my heart will mend,
I will never love again,
so don't even try to send,
your love to me ever again.

Christine Rolston

In Memory of Michael Dale Gobeli

She says I love you,
He needs her too.
He fills his nights
With thoughts of you.

Warm moments,
Side by side.
Happy memories,
Tears they have cried.

They danced that night
To a fateful song,
Creating memories,
Their whole life long.

They have so much to give,
In so many ways.
But most of all hon,
Have I told you how much
I love you yet today?

Jennifer Gobeli

The Beautiful Tree

See the tree as it flows,
Rays of Sunlight all aglow.
Sway the branches side to side,
Tired heavy are my eyes.
Calm as gentle breezes pass,
Feel the tranquil time at last.
Smells of green in all its grace,
There is no other like this place.

Lorraine Sepulveda

One Moment in Time

One tree can start a forest,
one bird can herald spring.
A chosen word can lift a soul,
so happiness can ring.

A friend to keep your secrets,
you know they're good and true.
Choosing them or finding one
is not an easy task to do.

Think about the heavens bright,
each star a lost soul in the sky.
Looking down to valley's deep,
the mountains rise to ask them why.

So life is just a fleeting moment,
it looks so crystal clear at night.
But for every star that's shining,
one poor soul will see that light.

Peter Cowan

Autumn

Pine cones
Settle on the ground,
Autumn wind
Makes gentle sound

Clear and clean
The air is cold,
Leaves now fall
From growing old

Colors collide,
Magic alive,
Summer is gone
No longer will thrive

Fire on hearth
Warmth from blaze,
Stars appear early
From fall shortened days

Snow coming soon
Autumn so fair,
If I had just one place
I'd always be there

Charles Banks

The Shadows Grow Longer

With the setting sun
casting gray shadows
on my writing pad
I sit.
Fallen branches are
strewn across the
broken sidewalk of
once good intentions.
My lady has come and gone
and I am left sauntering solo
through the crumbled remains of
the crackling embers that burn still.
Onto the threshold
of a new beginning.
A car ride begins
the journey back
to innocent egocentrism.
Drown out the cries
of that beautiful mess
I left so long ago.

Sean Hart

Ragdoll with No Eyes

I feel as though I'm in a box,
which sits upon a shelf.
I'm taken down and opened up,
but cannot see myself.

I am what others play I am,
what ever they decide.
I have no voice in decisions,
my thoughts I keep inside.

I have no say in what I do,
nor what I want to be.
I'm dictated to by others,
they tell me what is me.

They make me just what they want me,
adhering to their rules.
I am just a helpless ragdoll,
But Oh, those silly fools . . .

Repairing me for perfection,
they'll get a big surprise.
No longer a helpless ragdoll,
when they repair my eyes!

Janet Ebert Handleton

Fairytales

I really did believe back then
that fairies took my teeth,
I'd carefully lift my pillow
and slip them underneath.
I really did believe on time
that sleigh and deer could fly
and once a year on Christmas Eve
old Santa crossed the sky.
Then my fairy tale began
one chilly April night,
a true-life prince(or so it seemed)
came after his Snow White.
My life was in a state of sleep
but with your kiss I woke.
I soon believed your words of love
and everything you spoke,
But cheating eyes can lurk beneath
a pair of loving eyes.
If only I had learnt back then
that fairytales were lies.

Katie Gibson

These Are Times

To the one who has kept me smiling . . .
for D.S.I.
There are times when life seems cruel
and people don't seem to care,
Though in your eyes there holds a love
that only I know is there.
Sweet times we have together alone
with no one else to hound,
These are the times we truly have
for our love shows all around.
And in your dark black pools of eyes
I know your emotions are strong,
As you have seen mine
which have always been there,
caring for you all along.

Stephanie Kar-Leng Lee

Self-Inflicted Injuries

I live . . . sadly,
Haunted
By memories of what almost was;
Taunted
By dreams of what might have been;
Treasuring
The hours of what can be;
Measuring
The years of what cannot be.

I die . . .slowly,
Hearing
The music of what should have been;
Fearing
The silence of what never will be;
Tormented
With the cruel reality of what is;
Demented
With the wish that I were not . . .
. . . And wondering why I am.

Vivien Feeger

Morse Mail

The telegraph was invented by Morse.
Communication was faster than by horse.
A letter was slow,
But as we all know
E-mail is fastest of course.

Tarik Ozumerzifon

A Haiku Offering

In soft shadowed wraps
Of morning's unopened day
Reclothed . . . nimbus creeps.

Marie D. Meyer

To the Gods

Forest deep and dark of night
The Old Ones gather for the rite.

The clock stands high, time winds down
All the blessed form the round.

Salute the corners one times four
Between the worlds open the door.

The witches invoke the powers
Of earth and air, fire and water.

Candles dressed and burning bright—
The Wiccans dance in the fire's light.

Within the circle feel the power
So much to do in the witching hour.

Burning candles, weaving spells
Salt the circle, ring the bells.

Incense sweet, the rite complete
Go in peace until again we meet.

Penny Keiser

For Beth

Little known
little seen
not alone
though I have been
who could have told me
I should have been warned
I long to be free
though the free man is scorned
the life that I know
in the time that I have
maybe I should throw
away that love, that healing salve
I can't say I did
'cause I loved him too much
my feelings I hid
'cause of egos and such
I swear that I know what it's like
though I can't show you how
to have love's problems strike
here, there, later, and now

Sarah Brand

Behind Those Loving Eyes

Behind those loving eyes
are all the cold dark lies
and the promises broken
even when nothing was spoken.

All the things you said to me
just because I was too blind to see
that nothing I could do
would ever get through to you.

I've cried so many times
you've committed all the crimes
you broke my heart in two
and nothing you said was true.

Even though you lied to me
I just couldn't see
life with any other guy
even though you made me cry.

DeAnn Jackman

Anticipation of Your Arrival

We are counting down the days to be with you;
Mommy and Daddy are very scared, but excited too!
So much preparation has gone into to your arrival;
Building a crib, stocking up on diapers for baby's survival.
Soft snuggly blankets of blue, pink & yellow;
Await to wrapped around you to keep you warm and mellow.
Little rattles and lots of plush toys;
Here for you to smile when they make noise.
We wonder what color will your eyes be?
Brown like Daddy or could they be blue like Mommy?
Will you have thick dark curly locks of hair?
Or will you have fair golden tufts here and there?
I can't wait to hear your soft cry;
Hold you, rock you, and sing you a lullaby.
Each day our anticipation grows much stronger;
So please come soon; we can't wait any longer!

Andrea Loescher

Remembrance Day Prayer

On this special remembrance day,
Let us count our blessings on the way.

In this beautiful country in which we live,
a great land that God did give.

We live in peace, our freedom preserved
by 116,000 Canadians; for us they served.

On foreign shores their lives they gave
to keep us free and not enslaved.

To express opinions with fear for naught,
to raise our children for whom they sought,
and strived to give a better life.
For this they paid the highest price.

A country rich, a land imbued,
with overabundance they paid our dues.

To our U.N. peacekeepers far from home,
their humanitarian duties for this they roam.
To war-torn lands and points unknown.

For those who served, and those who died.
We thank our God on their behalf
that we could write this epitaph.

Patricia M. Burley

Rose Petals

Petals of the rose are falling
Signs the fall is due
Petals of the rose are decomposing
Means the cold is coming soon
Buds pushing through the branches
Signals spring is here
When the scent of the rose permeates the air
And the wind blows gently by
Take this time to smell them
They do not last forever
Like us they bloom wilt and die
Roses touch my heart strings of
Lost loves and pain
Also of their beauty when covered with dew and rain.
Oh, the dew drops scented tell a story each,
Of life and death preceding over the ashes of the earth.
They lie in silence sleeping until they root and bloom
Just like life dust to the wind.

Diana M. Reath

Two Views

Two walked in my garden at soft, sunny hours,
One saw my weeds, one saw my flowers.

Michael Wells

Myself

Sometimes I like myself,
At times I feel I'm worthless.

Sometimes I know I'm right,
Other times I just guess.

Sometimes I'm proud and strong,
Other times I'm weak and shameful.

Sometimes I'm good and loving,
Other times I'm mean and hateful.

But all the time I'm living and feeling,
All the time I'm hoping and breathing,

And all the time I need MYSELF.

Betty Daniel-Lanie

Dash's Time Out

David's dog Dash came over one day,
Because Tracy and David wanted to play.

Chess was boring and Dash saw Tamona,
The cookie she was eating had a great aroma.

So Dash went forward and started about,
He ate her cookie and she started to shout.

Tamona put Dash in the bathroom for time out,
The door was locked so he couldn't get out.

The neighbor's bathroom Tamona needed in a while,
The neighbors gave them a nail file.

So they used it to unlock the door,
Now Dash wasn't in time out anymore.

Daniel Evan Kaplan

The Name of Jesus

The name of Jesus is one of a kind.
It gives us salvation and brings peace of mind.

Showing us love like no other,
Representing one that's closer than a brother.

Giving us life that we might live,
Telling us clearly: "You must forgive."

Righteousness coming through belief in His name,
Showing us that life is not just a game.

Comforting us in our times of trial,
Always seeming to make us smile.

The name of Jesus is one of a kind,
The purest one you'll ever find.

Ginger Reeves

Abortion Kills Children!

To Jackie Carl
Mother, let me live, let me live!
Can you hear my cry of plea?
Mother let me live, let me live!
You are throwing your dream into the sea.
Mother, let me live, let me live!
Do you know my love for you?
Mother, let me live, let me live!
I am begging for you to.
Mother, let me live, let me live!
Who knows how I might affect your life?
Mother, let me live, let me live!
Could you, for a moment, set aside strife?
Mother, let me live, let me live!
Are you listening in the den?
Mother, let me live, let me live!
ABORTION KILLS CHILDREN!

Alicia Brozovich

Spectrum

Grandiose magenta softly highlights luscious purple sky . . .
Striking, how Art can create worlds in brush strokes
And how I find that I
Almost resent the vivid scene that soaks

Me in, threatens my demeanor, takes joy in luring
Me into fantastic imageries and uninterpretable hue,
Away from reality's reassuring
Clasp, this dull, dim confine causes a conflicting milieu:

Harmony and dissonance, sanity and lunacy—
If I could unravel the chaos, reassemble it all
Lay out a synchronized spectrum of emotional simplicity
Then how it all would crumble, how the world would fall

Angel Ali

Mother, I Love You

Mother, you, my angel,
You, my eternal friend;
Your arms have been my favorite cradle,
And your voice, the only lullaby I remember.

You took care of me for so long
And you never asked anything;
Today, I grew up and I just understood,
I never gave you anything.

One day perhaps, I'll have children,
And that day I'll be proud to show them
To you, Mother, who never forgets me.

Mother, I love you,
And the bunch I couldn't bring you,
Accept it by thoughts because it comes from my deepest heart
As thanks for past and as hopes for future.

Mother, I loved you, I love you
And I'll love you forever.

Wafa Al-Nachar

Never Let You Go

I sit and stare at the blank and lonely wall
I wonder what it would be like
If you were to suddenly appear,
Walk through the door and surprise me unexpectedly.
What I would do, just to see your face,
To look deep into your eyes and see deep into you.
Deep into your soul.
I'd look deep to find you, your feelings, your love.
Just to see what you like.
I'd run my fingers through your hair,
And let you know just exactly how much I really care.
What I would do just to see you smile at me and say . . .
"I love you and I never ever want to be without you."

Michelle Hoyt

The Grandfather Clock

Some time ago, I knew a tallish man,
And I don't know how you and me can
But this tall thin man just used to stand,
All day and night he used to stare
He gave no sign that he should care
But although he stared, we got the time
And exactly every hour it chimed
My Grandfather loved him like a son
He bought him from the fair of fun
It stayed with him for 90 odd years
And he and his son went through many fears
But on the day my grandfather died,
It seemed to me the clock had cried
So much it did that in his sorrows,
He never woke up for another tomorrow

Anosha Saleem

Sisters

One day I was walking, sad as can be.
I had no hope inside of me.
After making a phone call,
God had blessed me connecting me to the Sister Program
so they could support me.
I'm proud to be in the Sister Program so I can be free.
They share their experience, strength, and hope with me.
Now I can live just for me.
Thank you Sisters for reaching out to me.
Sisters spread love, Sisters share joy.
The Sister Program means the world to me.
Thank God for unconditional love.
If you want love and generosity,
I encourage you to become a Sister like me.
Join the Sister Program and have a second chance.
No more drugs and alcohol, but women holding hands!
To care is to love, to love is to share, to share is for real.
To join the Sisters is to live.
To become an inspiration is good for you and me.
So come join the Sister Program and recover like me.

Jacqueline Carter

Moving On

As I look out my window,
I see the world through new eyes.
This window shows me opportunity
To live and love again.

My life has been like a pillow;
It's been hit, fluffed, and tied.
I try to be happy
While growing with the pain.

I have learned to see more clearly
And have dealt with my past.
But, sometimes the future is wrapped with history,
And I don't think I can last.

Time is supposed to heal all wounds.
I wonder if that's true.
I would love to continue
Instead of being so blue.

Life goes on,
I know and see.
It's time to move on
Over you, over me.

Kathy Berden

We Were Lovers Once

We were lovers once

Our eyes reflected the waves of passion
That surged incessantly
Against the shore of our souls
Beating the rhythm that united our hearts
With sweet music
Merging—Blending—Orchestrating
The blazing fire of our love

We were lovers once

Our spirits tangled
In molten tide of ecstasy
Fusing—Flaring—Consuming
Those timeless visions
Fanned by our flame

We were lovers once

A golden thread woven in intricate promises
Now seared with the dry ice of indifference
Frayed—Marred—Lacerated
We bled and died

We were lovers once.

Sharon Williams

Would You Love Me If I Sent You Violets?

Would you love me if I sent you violets?
If I gave you my joy, heart and life
I spilled my soul to you
Honestly let you peer inside my heart?
If I let you see me smile
I allowed you one glimpse of my emotions
Hide even my shadow deep inside nameless darkness?
Would you love me?
If I told you how dreams of you float through my consciousness
Like a fog on a cold, damp ground
If you were to see my image of you
And I were to tell you how the mere thought of your existence
Fills every fiber of my being with such inspiration
It tempts me to sit on a riverbank, and weep
If I sacrifice my necessities on the altar of love
Would you love me then?
Would you love me if I sent you violets?

Jen Lapekas

Every Other Night

Every other night
The needle penetrates my skin
Every other night
I almost forget I have it
Every other night
I get sick and can't sleep
Every other night
I look at the bruises
Every other night
They won't go away
Every other night
I pray they find a cure
Every other night
I know it's this—for the rest of my life
And every other night
A tear comes to my eye
Because every other night I realize
I'm not like everyone else
And I'm scared

Elizabeth Rose Engelhardt

You Will Be There

You're like a ray of sunshine that looks down on me from afar.
Wherever I go, whatever I do, you're always there watching over me.
I may be bad,
I may be good, but it never matters what I do; you will be there!
I'm lucky to have a friend and mother like you,
because no matter what happens, you will always be there.

Laura Gooch

It's Time to Say Goodbye

Goodbye, my love, for your face is only a shadow
I search for something more
And find great comfort when your smile
Surfaces in the forefront of my mind.

Goodbye, my love, for I cannot hold you close
Except in my heart where you will always be.
Death claimed your life, took you away from me
To a better place where we shall meet again.

All of your worldly possessions now are gone,
A heartbreaking task, I hold them one last time
My mind, it wanders to the happy times
When you were here with me, but are no more.

Goodbye, my love, your spirit lingers here
To give me strength, to get me through my pain
I must go on without you at my side
Please guide me, Bob, it's time to say goodbye.

Elizabeth Tower

This Much I Know

Even though I don't know you . . . this much I know
Your smile
makes any day a day to remember
Your lips
so soft and full they are perfection
Your walk
graceful in design only Heaven could create it
Your eyes
shine like stars that light faraway planets
Your mind
is like an ocean no one knows its depth
Your heart
is like a treasure worth more than pure gold
Even though I don't know you
I know enough to know this

William Evans

It's an Old Idea

It's an old idea, of course to remember,
that the stars, the sky and minute snowfalls, belong to us;
all marked with glorious adventure and notable achievement.
It's an old idea, of course to remember that love,
not fame or popularity, bridges the gaps of life.
It's an old idea, of course to remember that redemption is wherever
and whenever one person takes time to be understanding.
It an old idea, of course to remember.

Pamela Perkins

Have You Ever Danced in a Fairy Ring?

Have you ever danced in a fairy ring?
Did you ever pick a clover just for luck?
Have you ever heard a whippoorwill sing?
Did you ever stop to hear a wild duck?

When did you last see from a bird's-eye view?
When did you last feel the sun upon your cheeks?
Where did you last taste freshly fallen dew?
Where did you last enjoy Mother Nature's sweep?

You take no notice when nature cries,
And fail to observe when she is merry.
Life is too short to wait until we die,
To relish Mother Earth's fruits and berries.

Material things will come and go . . .
But Nature's beauty will always show!

Richelle Speilman

Two Tiny Souls

Two tiny souls, asleep in the hamper.
Oblivious to time, the date doesn't matter.
Four tiny eyes, closed tight as a fist,
Two tiny heads, inviting a kiss.
Two pairs of ears, perked high and alert,
Two dusty coats, a thin layer of dirt.
Eight tiny paws, running through dreams,
Down through the fields, across shallow streams.
Two tiny hearts are so full of life,
Perfectly peaceful, absent of strife.
Two tiny souls, asleep in the hamper,
Oblivious to life, Only dreams matter.

Josh Morris

Restaurant (Dinner at Eight)

I just wanted to tell you that I feel kind of forgotten
A quiet man sitting in the window of a Chinese restaurant
Alone watching traffic
I could take my picture a thousand times

B. Macdonald

Hope's Journey

Valentine sentiments in blossoms of red
So many words yearn to be said.
Past loves lost glimmer as wishes
A primal dance of many sweet kisses.

Standing in front of you and your past
A creator who's holding the best for last.
While hearts quicken at yet another chance.
Our lives, our souls will be richly enhanced.

Standing in front of you with feelings so new
Frightened and fearful can this really be true?
Out of the past she comes to stand
Never having known such a wonderful man.

Whispers entwined in sensuous caresses
Speak to the heart of the one she addresses.
Lovers scintillated by thoughts of each other
Drift in two hearts and there they will hover.

This February month of Valentine kisses
Fulfill our hopes, our dreams, our wishes.
As sentiments tug at our mind and our heart
Two souls journey together on a beautiful start.

Patricia M. Wolf

Caged Beauty

For quite some time now you've been gone
Somehow I knew it all along

That some bird's feathers are way too bright
To be caged up night after night

You seem so happy for this I'm glad
I'm not jealous, and I'm not mad

Yet still I miss this bird's great song
And still I wonder what went wrong

You were too young, and Oh, so cold
I too warm, and Oh, so old

Some dreams broken, some dreams tattered
The life I loved, is somewhat shattered

I have survived, I will move on
Yet still I miss this bird's great song

Inside my heart, brews a stormy night
For some bird's feathers are way too bright

Rich Johnson

the godless god

the godless god
a being without heart
a being without whom most could not survive

the godless god
infects our judgment
insults our intelligence

the godless god
whose actions defy explanation
whose actions cause much endless debate

the godless god
mystical
or mythical

the godless god
really imaginative
or really a figment of the imagination

the godless god
why has thou forsaken me
or is it I who has forsaken thou

the godless god
wherever I may roam

David Blasucci

Memories

It was an old song from an age long gone
An age that she would always cherish so
The music was still fresh like roses at dawn
And it took her thoughts back years ago
She remembered the blooming meadows in spring
The grass hid jewels of red and yellow fair
She picked the best flowers, happily singing,
And made florid wreaths for her golden hair
She remembered the mountains and the sea
The lofty peaks were the home of her dreams
She could still smell the fragrant pine tree
And hear the waves and the whispering streams
She remembered Kyle, her loving sweetheart,
Calm romantic nights and eternal happiness
Living without him tore her tender heart;
The flame of his soul had faded into darkness
Those days were wonderful, with no tomorrow
Oh! Remembrance is such sweet sorrow
The ghosts of her past, joys and miseries,
Were all she had left: her sweet memories.

Randy Nahle

Delicate Flower

There she lay, peacefully abed
Dressed in a white satin gown
On her chest her arms folded
And her face showed no smile nor frown
Between the four walls stood the crows
That uttered shrill cries for the dame
But her eyes saw no friends nor foes
And her ears couldn't hear her name
For her soul belonged to the undertaker
Who had cut a hibiscus with his scythe
Leaving behind a stem with no flower
And a poisonous juice that gives no life
Rainfall fills my saddened eyes
As I let go of her motionless hand
Her soft skin was pale as the sky
And why she had to go I couldn't understand
For her I will fight the force of darkness
But even with Athena's guidance
This battle was meant to leave me powerless
So, delicate flower, live without turbulence

Frederick Agyeman-Duah

Kisses

I sit and watch the snow fall,
Wishing it were your kisses,
Soft and pure and Oh, so sweet.
If kisses were snowflakes,
I would want at least two feet.

Lisa Clark

Someone I'll Always Remember

You're someone I'll always remember!
Through June, July, August and long past December.
The days and months now pass me by,
growing older with the twinkling of an eye.
It won't be long 'til age makes my body tremor,
you're someone I'll always remember!
One day my working days will be done,
I'll be retired and too old to have fun.
My eyes too weak to give off a glimmer,
you're someone I'll always remember!
Someday I'll lay down for my final nap,
a little shorter and big belly in my lap.
I know life's not meant to be forever,
but you're someone I'll always remember!

Glenn Gay

Novella

My present is immobilized
in a straightjacket bathrobe
that restrains my arms from flapping.
A tedious past
burns a novella of regret on the insides
of my eyelids.
Who knew so many melodramatic chapters
could fit on such thin skin?
But I can read them with my eyes closed,
if my future shines through the parchment.
I can lie on the sofa
and read
and read
and read.
This book is easier company,
its pages so much more familiar,
and this cozy atrophy less menacing,
than watching everything around me either
promise to effloresce
or threaten to implode.

Brian Tacang

The Storm

I think about the storms every night of the week,
I cry over the storm when I hear him speak.
When I hear the storm I step outside.
"Touch my soul, let me know you're there!" I cried.
Then one night that is what I yelled with the slap of a belt,
And the storm is honestly what I felt.
The lighting came down and carried me like a baby,
Then I heard him tell me I've turned into a nice young lady.
A second is all I spent in the sky,
And I promise, I tell you no lie.
At first I was scared when I went above,
But then I realized it was just a touch of the storm's love.

Brandi Stansel

Hand in Hand

Two figures seen on the beach yonder,
Down by the surf thoughts start to wonder,
Two souls on horseback trotting by the waves,
No words are spoken; they're both in a daze,
They stare into each other's eyes, wind in each face,
Their hearts skip a beat, and start to race,
The waves roll in, and crash on the shore,
If only this moment could last ever more,
Nobody else could ever understand,
The feeling they feel as they ride hand in hand.

Elizabeth DuPree

I Am

I am a little football player
I wonder if I will go pro
I hear the whistling wind
I see the end zone
I want to run so fast, that no one can catch me
I am a little football player

I pretend I am soaring
I feel the wind blowing in my face
I touch the sky
I worry if I will get hurt
I cry if I get hit too hard
I am a little football player

I understand I'm not the best
I say don't give up to myself
I dream that we will win
I try the best I can
I hope to go unbeaten
I am a little football player

Nathon Sellers

Falcons

The eyes of the falcon
See more than we could ever imagine
They see death on the wings of flame
They see the anger of sharp steel
They watch the fury of guns on the street
They guard the resting place of ancient trees
They wheel away from smoke
Not needing to pass through death
To know what it is
They see the blood of victims
Yet they also see
The meadows of dancing butterflies
The towering forest of green foliage
The peaceful horses browsing the grass
The water twinkling off worn rocks
The laughter of kids sledding down snow banks
Owls calling to the stars as they leave the safety of their nests
Cats lounging in the warm sunlight
The flower buds beginning to open as new life

Kara Clissold

I Saw You

When I was born,
I opened my eyes and saw the skies,
Heavenly clouds
and shades of blue.
The angels came through and I saw You.
All through my life came joy and pain.
I looked to the skies and I saw rain,
Heavenly rain to wash away my feelings of blue.
The angels came through, and I saw you.
When I died, they closed my eyes,
and I saw the skies, Heavenly clouds and shades of blue.
The angels came through and I saw
You.

Linda Robledo

My Enemy

I approach this enemy of mine
you do not attempt to run or hide.
rage and hatred propel me across
to grab you by the neck
I raise you above me
preparing to end it all . . .
the bottle is grabbed out of my hands
my family stands behind me holding the bottle of alcohol
the bottle smirks at me saying
"I told you so."
tears of sadness and pain fall as I collapse
defeated by the bottle
wishing I was as innocent as a newborn
never knowing of this thing called alcohol
which has stolen my family from me.
My enemy.

Pauline Littledeer

Disguised

Feeling as if I am hidden from family and friends
Like I am the hunchback of Notre Dame,

Not telling them what happened,
Not saying why I'm depressed

I feel as if I am an embarrassment
and shunned upon

I try to make sense of it
as if it's no big deal

I try to understand my life
whether it's fake or real

Danielle Goodwin

Feelings of Rain

It's raining!
Droplets running down my face,
As I stand with my eyes cast up to the heavens.
It's raining!
Each like a diamond held up to the light,
They are peaceful yet strong.
It's raining!
The smell of wet leaves,
Of clean, fresh air.
It's raining!
I catch them on my tongue,
They taste like the sky.
It's raining!
I hear them pattering on the roof,
Like music to my ears.
It's raining!
It's raining at my house.

Erin Bailey

New Beginning

O thank You Lord for the new beginning
Starting out new no more sinning
O the time has come for us to start winning
O the Lord has chosen us to be
soul winners to represent his gospel
To all sinners
O thank the Lord we are qualified
Special witness today to bless
His little children and show them
the way we won't the whole world
to know that we have found the clue
Lgive the Lord back the glory
That He is due.

Sue Robinson

Come on 2 Me

If Something Between Us You See
I Want You To Come On 2 Me
If You Think We Have A Chance
I Think We Should Have A Dance

Fulfill Your Fantasy
Come On 2 Me
Turn On Your Sexuality
And Come On 2 Me

Are You Undressing Me With Your Eyes
Is That A Smile I See, Or Just A Disguise
If You Desire Me, You Don't Have To Say
Just Come On Over, And Take Me Away

Unleash Yourself Passionately
Come Over And Come On 2 Me
Become Sexual Energy
Turn On And Come On 2 Me

James Yancey

First Broken Heart

It's hard for me to get up every day.
I still can't believe I let my first love get away.
I acted like I didn't care.
Now all I do is think of the love that we shared.
I've cried tears of joy and I've cried tears of pain.
Now that you're gone, I don't know if I'll love again.
Now when I lay me down to sleep,
My heart slightly begins to creep
Down through my chest and into my gut,
And I know that I love you, no matter what.
I still wish that we didn't part,
'Cause you're my first love and my first broken heart.

Jesse Arlo Jorges

My Many Collective Friends

I am your Brother
who will cut your throat for pocket change
I am your Comrade
who will stab your back to impress the boss
I am your best Friend
who admires you with a cannibal's smile
I give you my life, for I covet yours
We are all Equal, all one and the Same
Sacrifice the Few to save the Millions
Liquidate the Thinkers to feed the Dross
And Voltaire's head is on the chopping block
For "the Revolution has no need for Geniuses"
Hail the supremacy of mediocrity
The great collective is waiting
Welcome to
Hell

Robert Sternberg

Without You

The loneliness and sadness
The fear the anguish
The emptiness and blankness
Is all I feel without your presence

The pointless reassurance
The feeling of just coldness
The simple notice of life's meaningless
Without anyone like you to bring happiness

The reaching for something so helpless
The hugging only darkness
The crying for what's so pointless
Just wishing for us two

The praying for your hand
The begging for any way to stand
The knowing I have no chance
I just keep hoping to be with you

Tabitha Alcorn

Unbroken

In the heat of the night
As the passion gets deeper
I keep getting closer to you
So close it scares me to death
Can't you see, is it getting through?

With our world it's dangerous
Feelings and emotions become one
Adrenalin pumping through our veins
Confusion becomes clear
As the climax becomes reached
We are there, holding on for dear life

Yet I feel so safe
And I believe it's true
With a love so strong, we will always belong

Trust is there to see us through
The love is there to pull us together
As the day breaks with the sun, lying together,
It all comes to an end,
With a bond so strong and unbroken.

Lori Armstrong

Remember

Remember well and bear in mind,
a true friend is hard to find.
When you have one who is tried and true,
Never trade an old one for a new

Melvin Arnold

Blue Light Special

Ha! Ha! Ha! Ya gotta laugh
at what women want in a man.
Oh, he's gotta have blue eyes!
No, girl, he's gotta have a good job.
Ya'll just don't get it . . . he needs Jesus.

Strolling down each lane of Love-Mart
we check our coupons while searching
for the best bargain . . . man style.
Tall, short, phat and skinny.
Salsa flavor, red beans and rice, oriental
Checking his brain, wallet, and pants.

Deep in the back of the store, the lights flash.
Here I am, blue light special! Love 4 sale!
Rushing to the fast lane to gleefully make our
purchase. As we hungrily open our man prize,
we realize that we've lost the receipt.

Sheila Williamson

The World's Beauty Lies in the Children

Special little boys and girls
Prancing all around the world
Perfect right from the start.
Lucky are the ones to receive
Disabled are those who don't, and
Disgusting are those who take advantage.
Like mystical creatures
Who cease to exist
Babies are just so hard to resist.
Do everything right—
Even the wrong
Eased to sleep with
Just a song.
At peace with themselves
And all the world
These perfect people deserve
Their needs to be met and
The best they can get!

Christine Dopico

Scared

Sometimes I wake up in the middle of the night,
Holding a flashlight giving a beam of light.
As I creep down the hall,
I think I hear
Behind me the sounds of a snarling grizzly bear.
But when I turn around to look,
Are my eyes fooling me?
How foolish I must be!
For I see nothing there!

Phyllis Wang

The Answer

From mountain tops my Saviour sees
the world spread out below.
How mortals living here on Earth
keep running to and fro.
They run from this and they run from that,
not knowing what they seek.
If only they would look and see
Him on the mountain peak.
He, who would guides their every step,
and give them peace and rest.
For He alone is always there
to lead in the way that is best.
To you who are weary and worn in heart,
look to the mountain peak.
The Answer is waiting there for you,
the Answer for which you seek.

Mildred M. Wilkins

Peace

I face a tormented world
Bitter with hate
Contaminated with faulty futures
Simplistic ideas that leave only remorse
Even too complex for the ordinary being
Spirits torn by ravaging sadness
Puritan ideals turned into salty sin
The concise precision of Satan's hands
Tying our arms behind our back
Pounding us in the gut with iron hands
Leaving welts around our eyes
And tumors in our minds, souls, and bodies
Only deepening our conception of "peace"
A sexual "peace," a violent "peace," a vulnerable
"peace," an addicted "peace"
Contradicting predictions
Stereotyping "the girl next door"
The one with the smile
The bright teeth
But what lies in her room?

Stacy McKenney

My Church

Upon this rock I will build my church,
And the gates of Hell shall not prevail against it.
St. Matthew 16:18

My church triumphant stands,
Because her Sovereign reigns.
Her theme throughout the lands,
Behold! A cross with stains.

My church has an open door,
To receive seekers of his love.
Joy and peace will outpour,
Thanks to the Lord above.

My church joyfully sings
Of Jesus' blood and power.
The message of hope rings
In this, her finest hour.

My church offers much prayer,
Entreaties to God are made.
Supplicants soon become aware
Of the price Jesus paid.
My church? No, not really mine.

D. E. Watts

34 Children in 7

I will always remember 34.
Blessings through providence
even 3 plus 4 being 7 is divine perfection!

34 became a perfect gift.
Instructing 7 years olds who I sang the song of childhood with.

Outrageous and adorable in presence
Their future is worth marveling at;
Yet, of becoming wholly helpful, only God fully knows.

To them, my prayers stretch across the globe
Arching, from Earth to Heaven and back, as a rainbow
Hoping for a spectrum of blessings to shine upon their souls.

May each young mind explode into awareness!
Receive treasures of knowledge through listening and
Fortunes of understanding by doing.
Yes! Goodness and skill are developed through godliness.

I will always remember 34.
Frolicking together, contagiously happy
And observing, in all ages,
God's Spirit is youthful within hearts that care.

Gregory S. Hochman

What You Do

How do you do just what you do,
Making me to love you?

You look in me like no other.
You're my heart's very own cover.
You see me not just outside, but inside, completely.
It's almost as if you can read my thoughts so deeply.

Without you I wander aimlessly, lost,
But for your love there is no cost.
My heart would never let you go
Only because I love you so.

Take my heart now and hold it tight
Because somehow I know it's right.
You hold the key that unlocks my heart,
And no other could ever play that part.

I never want to lose you
Because I know now what you do.
You make me whole and so complete
Because our love runs so deep.

Diana Kessler

Reflections

Reflections, the only token of the past,
Are over me like a cast.

They make me ruminate,
And the forgotten feelings they fabricate.

A mirror of the days gone by,
The days that can never be said goodbye.

The images of which being vague,
But the passion deep and awake.

A gallery of the moments we treasure,
The moments of pain and so of pleasure.

Seemingly real and ever so near,
But just a mark of the gone-by years.

Some giving exhilaration to the heart,
The remaining filled with misery of being apart.

The book of emotions buried deep in
Is opened to reveal the words within.

The only thing which we carry all the way,
'Til the tomb are the reflections of each and every day.

Rekha Bhanuchandran

Why Did You?

Why did you leave me,
With no sign,
With no reason why,
With no last words goodbye?

Why did you love me so,
With no conditions,
With no motives,
With no problems?

Why did you choose me,
To carry on your legacy,
To carry on with your dreams,
To be nobody but me?

Why did I hold it in,
Thinking I could tell you later,
Thinking you weren't going anywhere,
Thinking that I had all the time I needed?

Why did I not shed a tear,
Holding back my fear,
Wishing you were here,
Knowing that you're gone?

Jamar Alphonse Logan

Mother, on Mother's Day

Growing up, you were always home,
And for that, I never felt alone.
Each day I'd walk through the door,
Greeted with a hug and kiss, always getting so much more.

Over the years we've grown so close, like best friends.
Our relationship is like a circle; it never ends.
Maybe you never knew what you meant to me,
So close your eyes, I'll tell you what I see.

I see a beautiful woman full of grace,
With an honest and gentle face.
I see a woman determined to do things her way;
An inner light shines from her as if to say:

I can do anything! Mountains, move out of my way.
It is just the beginning; it's today.
For the strength you've given me over the years,
There's always been much laughter and some tears.

I think back on my life; I pause and smile,
Thinking how much I want to be like you all the while.
You are a large part of my life, my heart, and there's no other,
My mentor, my friend, the one I call mother!

Lisa Autuchiewicz

Abrasion of the Heart

My surroundings melt from sight
As you run rampant in my mind
Enhancing my craving for your presence

I close my eyes
Letting you run through my veins
Chasing you, like chasing the dragon.
I inhale the sensuous smoke of your spirit.
Addicted to the thought of you,
I slip into an altered state of consciousness

I want to feel you inside me,
Our souls intertwining,
Absorbing each other's thoughts and emotions
Your euphoric being taking me over,
Relinquishing the unworldly desire that plagues my existence.
My desire for you

Tormented by my own thirst
I'm not unlike Tantalus,
Struggling to touch her lips to the water.

Damned to hunger for the sweetness
Of that which she shall never taste.

Alana Branson

Dream

It was a clear, starry night.
I closed my sleepy eyes tight.
I fall asleep in my big comfy, bed.
And then a dream pops into my head.
I dreamt I flew high,
Up into the sky,
Far above the rooftops.
I flew up to Heaven,
And counted shooting stars.
I saw exactly seven!
I gazed down at the Blanket of lights below,
As the sky lights up with their golden glow.
I turn around
And say good-bye to the moon.
And then I fly,
Back down to my room.
Through my window,
And into my bed.
And that is the dream,
That popped into my head!

Jess Connors

Good-Bye

It's hard to say good-bye.
It's hard to think while you cry.
It's hard to try when you know you'll die.
I try to fight the fear away.
I try to brush the tear astray.
I could've stayed another day.
I left it all behind.
But I knew they would never find,
The reason I took my life, for I was blind.
My family and friends who loved me dear,
I knew would live their lives with a tear.
But what's greater was my fear.
My fear that I wouldn't be
What everyone hoped from me.
But now it must be.
I loved my family dearly,
And my friends sincerely,
But I showed my love for them merely.
I guess it's over now.
I've taken my last bow.

Brandi Sims

When You Look at Me

Look at me and tell me what it is you see;
Do you even know the person that is me?
Do you see the love I feel for family and friends?
Do you see the loyalty that never seems to end?
Do you see the compassion I feel for fellow man?
Do you see uncertainty when I try to make a stand?
Do you see how much I need the love that comes from you?
Do you see without it my heart is void and blue?
Do you see the sorrow for mistakes made now and then?
Do you see the fences that I can never mend?
Do you see the person that I have grown to be?
Do you see me crying with my heart upon my sleeve?
Do you see the pain that comes from years' strife?
Do you see the dignity in which I've tried to live my life?
Do you know the question I long to ask of thee?
What do you see exactly . . . when you look at me?

Angela Kellems

Toys

When I play, I make a big mess.
I have to 'cause I'm playing my best.
Old toys are spread all over the floor,
Along with new ones brought from the store.
I play with one and end up with ten.
I just never know when I've reached the end.
When play-time is over, I hear, "Girls and boys
Ok. Now, lets put away those toys."
When the toys are gathered in a neat pile,
I can expect my teacher to smile.

Toni Wilson Smith

Love

It twists and turns like a nightmare fantasy,
And hurts and burns forever and eternity.

It lifts you up and breaks you down,
a lonely person in a crowd.

It rages on, yet burns out quickly,
Like a furnace rising and flickering suddenly.

It fades away and leaves you cold,
Used, unwanted, rejected, sold.

It kills inside and eats away,
Yet still I crave it every day . . .

Love.

Helen Spink

Today I Pray . . .

Yesterday I prayed for today's health,
Never will you recall me praying for wealth.
Also that you would show me the way,
I will always pray in your hands I will stay.

Today I pray
In my heart you will lay,
Please help me Lord to stay this way.
I want so much to feel your touch,
If it takes giving up all my bad ways I must.

Tomorrow I pray
When I die and laid in my grave,
I thank you Lord for showing me salvation's way
Now as I lay here all in peace,
I know my body I only leased.

Cindy Benfield

Shepherd's Bond

Although I am but a child of this universe,
I have found necessity to act as a parent as well.

My fellow children, my peers, my people; all equal,
In my mind and in my heart—they give me purpose.
When those of my flock seek guidance, I shed my role
As one of their number, and don my shepherd's cloak,
Doing all that is in my power to keep them on their course.

I have assumed the role of teacher in the past,
But only for those who have asked to be taught.
I cannot say that I teach absolutes, but rather truth, as I see it.
And in the course of my teachings, I myself learn more
About myself, about my people, my flock, my world—
Than I ever could by simply learning on my own.

Michael Rich

The Homeless

Oh, God, guide them from
the harm in the street
and Lord, help them
get back on their feet.

You see them there and everywhere
and it's very hard to bare
people see them and ignore them,
those are people that don't care.

If you should ever stop to greet one
you'll find they're human like you and me,
you'll also find that, that's the way
our Lord God wants it to be.

These are people that have problems
that has let them to go astray,
why don't we render our hearts
and help them find the right way.

Antonio Plaza

The Broken Pieces of My Heart

My world was shattered
Like pieces of glass
My heart broken
Never to mend
A friend, a companion
I lost in you
A life too short not long enough
Yet my life goes on
But my spark is gone
I feel your presence
I know you're here
Remembering that what we had
Cannot return, neither today, tomorrow, nor the next day.

Sally Bernstein

Kris Kringle

Jingle jangle jingle, rock it with Kris Kringle.
Rock around the Christmas tree.
Have a holiday—it's almost Christmas Day.
Sing along with me.
Sleigh bells keep on ringing while
The choir keeps on singing;
Listen to the sound they play.
Ding-a-dang-a-dong, dance and sing along.
Have a merry Christmas Day.
We're going to rock around the clock at night.
Celebrate until Christmas night,
We're going to swing along and have some fun
Until Christmas Eve is done.
Jingle jangle jingle, rock it with Kris Kringle.
Rock around the Christmas tree.
I look in the sky while the reindeer go by.
Merry Christmas to you, from me.

A. George Dave Prince

Breaking

In the depths of solitude,
You can find comfort.
Though in tears one can find pain,
But there can always be warmth as the shadows
Are washed by the rain.
And in the days
Of woe and despair,
Amidst the darkness
Of a cry that flares,
There will be sighs
For the hurt, fleeting
Relief and joy for
A heart again beating.
And as the waves crash
Against a heaving chest,
Know that a soul's cleansing
Forever comes best,
Not when the sun makes the waters run dry,
But when the rain
Becomes tears as you cry.

Anna Foz Castro

Depth

It was a tear from a mermaid of deep
The churning blackness, the darkened love
Where rays glide where none can reach
And the only dance is of the red seaweed
Bled from a mermaid's heart.

Jeremy Chong

To My Friend

May God bond us together forever.
To thank you for your help is just not enough.
When I needed an angel there you were.
Telling me how important I was and supporting me.
I needed you, but you didn't know how much.
Your kind words were welcomed with hesitant arms.
In a time that I thought my life had no charms.
There was no light at the end of the tunnel, only death.
Your heart was opened and offered healing to the weak.
Unlimited, unconditional, supportive and positive.
Pure, innocent love and concern is so rare to find.
And ever harder to keep in this world.
But I believe in my heart we have met for a reason.
I'm sure God has a plan for us in many future seasons.
I will pray in every prayer that God keep us close.
In our hearts, our minds, and in our souls every day.
And if we ever part ways I want you to know.
You have changed a woman's and a mother's life in a way.
That no amount of thank you's could ever repay.

Brenda H. Clayton

Untrue Love

When it comes down to it
After all the pain I feel
Pain so deep and so intense
That it doesn't seem real
And after all the untrue love
I felt for you is stripped away
And, Oh, how I untruly loved you
I see that it's better this way
'Cause we were doing something wrong
Our love could not defeat our fate
And it was not near strong enough
But we found this out much too late
And now I see why it had to happen
'Cause we were in such untrue love
That we would have spent our lives together
And something false be thinking of
But we have found a second chance
To find true love and all its charms
And we should make the best of this
Though we won't be in each other's arms

Elisha M. Cooper

Seasons

And once again the fall season is here;
The leaves fall rapidly on to the hard ground.

The ants, bees, and bugs are in fear;
Disappearing are summer's sounds.

Now it is winter's time to shine;
Snow has fallen on the dead, cold leaves.

Wild animals have retreated to their dens;
This season brings on the early eves.

Now the season is glorious spring;
All the animals emerge from their homes.

The songs of many wild animals ring;
Elders say this is the time of gnomes.

Summer is here and all the children cheer—
This is all of their favorite time of year.

Aubrey Myers

Blind to Love

I have been so blind to love
For I have treated it as a mere possession
But once this love was lost and gone,
It turned out to be my only obsession.
If I could somehow make up the future
Or turn back the hands of time
I would treat this love more as a beauty
And not commit such a selfish crime.

David Kujat

Dear Mr. Kennedy

Dear Mr. Kennedy,
Although we've never met, and probably never will,
Like your parents before, word of your tragedy gave me chills.
But only long enough for me to recognize
That death is only history wearing a disguise.
Some discuss what you would have become,
But I know greatness and death only come early to some.
You've made smiles all over the world, this I confess,
So it would seem only natural that God too was impressed.
So join your parents now in your after life mystery,
Listen for you name in the conversations of history.
As for me, I've only ever been impressed by a few,
Malcom, Martin, your father and now YOU!

Oscar O. Carter

Mom

All through my life, all down the years
you've been there while I cried my tears.
You watched me grow up big and tall.
You have helped me make it through it all.
You taught me about God and
His never dying love.
And about His son Jesus,
He sent down from above.
You taught me how to be obedient.
And that minding Daddy was
The main ingredient!
My mom was never there to care,
So now my life with you I share!
I love you Mom!
In a very special way
And no one could make those feelings go away!

Jasmine Livingston

What Seems Is Not

What seemed so distant is now up close
What looked so foreign is now so common
What felt so odd is now so usual
And what was supposed to stay, left
And now the pain is mine

If the world was not unjust
It would grant me some pity
And spare me a few minutes with you again

Life is just but an empty dream
It is harsh and cold
With no way out and no escape
This is the world in which life is a dream and death is the waking up

Lea Udler

Happy

Happy was—I guess,
One summer's day in the south of England,
when the sky was as still and blue
as it always seems to be
in cinematic portrayals of the phoney war.
Not yet aware of my own mortality,
Content in the knowledge
that my parents could save me—
from anything,
and too young to puzzle
about anything other
than when I would be able
to ride a bike
with no hands . . .

Richard Evans

Autumn

God not only took Sunday to rest, but all of Autumn to paint.
The leaves fall softly,
Patchwork quilt upon the ground.
Greens turn pale, then into
yellows, reds and browns.

The harvests are in
As the air rings crisply cool.
Wrap warmly your cloak about you.

The birds wing silently to the south
With the seasons ever changing mood.
While the squirrel gathers his winter stores,
The bear leaves his domain
To winters hollow calling
As he looks to slumber in some hidden den.
With the Earth's changing colours
Comes a serene and lasting peace.

Robert James Tucker, Sr.

The New World

It seems as just yesterday,
The day when I began to pray
That everything would be all right,
And I too would live to see tonight.

This is the pinnacle of our childhood,
I would go back if I could.
Things always happen for a reason;
A tear runs down my chin as I put the tassel
on my hat.

Where did it go, as if to vanish forever,
This is the new beginning of The New World called life.

Cory McCorkle

what is heaven?

what is heaven, is it a circle of light?
what is heaven, is it something bright?
what is heaven, does it make things right?
what is heaven, is it as exciting as flying a kite?
what is heaven, is it a beautiful sight?
what is heaven, is it the howl of the wind at night?
probably not as painful as a snake bite,
is it as beautiful as a rainbow?
is it as frosty as snow?
what is heaven, no one knows.

Nicole Vonbulow

Mothers

Mother's Day is one of the days designated as
"A required day to fly Our Nation's Colors."
Mother brings some visualization to everyone.
To some, a protector, to others a confidant.
Mother was the great healer.
She has even been known to mend broken hearts and/or spirits.
She can fix hurt feelings in no time.
The toughest time comes when all seems lost,
When Mother is with us no more.
Then we have to go up the chain of command to God
To seek comfort from this, often times, devastating loss.
We hope that God sends a comforting Angel
To all those who have suffered the loss of their Mother.

Richard Armatrout

A Teenage Girl

I cry out for help with no words or tears to sound,
My feelings are deep inside and cannot come out, I've found.
But look into my eyes, into another world of misery and pain,
My feelings are angry and hurting; Am I sane!
Someone, please, who cares, just a little, take the time,
To look into my eyes and find the feelings that I mime.

Michelle Acton

Silent Tears

First thing morning i felt pain
First thing evening i saw the tears roll down my face
You are blind you have been blind
You cannot hear them, you are deaf to the sound of my tears
They are silent
Alone in our room, you have never seen past
my voice, nor my smiles
Nor whatever lies beneath me
I am the Great Pretender
Nobody but nobody hears the sound of my tears
They are silent
No more the Great Pretender
First thing morning i say goodbye
First thing evening i feel happiness

Akua Asamoa-Krodua

Girlish Dreams

And when the little girl grew up
And the boyfriends she did date,
The dresses worn, the parties attended,
What would be her fate?
For marriage floated in her mind,
A single girl is she,
To find the guy to help her out,
In life they would be.
A loving, laughing, caring couple,
For many years to share,
To help each other in happiness and despair,
Wouldn't that make a pair?
My wishes that I send you,
The warmest kind they bring,
That both of you go through life,
With a lovely song to sing!

Stefanie Coburn

She Is . . .

In the dawn's early glow She glided
through the bluegrass
softly, softly humming
she knew she was the essence of being,
through the clouds of gold & silver she came
seeing, hearing, feeling, knowing, loving
In the dawn's early glow she is the light,
she is the dawn, She is . . .
through the grass she walks in the dawn,
in the spring,
in the light of life
loving people see her gentle light
like the mist, a thousand colors burst forth
melding into the cascade of the forest gently humming,
she is the light, she is the dawn
SHE IS . . .
Life, celebrate her!
in the dawn's early glow She Is . . .

Crystal Resonari

Before I Rise I Must Fall

Before I rise I must fall
But yet I still give to all
Between dusk and dawn the sun does rise
It's the in between which I despise
To see the sunrise the sun first must fall
Same as my life I can recall
My hopes and dreams still linger in the air
Attached to my heart waiting to share
When the next one comes along lucky if he
Understands my language within the deep sea
And so I bow to he who tries
And look over my shoulder for the next sunrise

Jillian Forster

The Path

Life's mysteries travel one path.
All you experience, all you meet,
And where you end up,
Lies within the path you choose.
My path has been crooked,
Even deceiving at times.
Never has it been easy,
But it always was prevalent.
The valleys I have traveled while on this path,
And the rocky road I walk endlessly,
I would travel a thousand times again.
For along this path,
I found you.

Christina Likomitros

My God

Guide me in all the things I do,
Help me do these things for you.
Stay close to me, I need you near,
With you by my side, I've nothing to fear.
I must remember I was made for you,
I must never forget how you love me, too.
I need to want what you've got,
It's as simple as that, a game it's not.
I'll fight to the end, it's you who I trust,
To place you first, I know I must.
I have to forget this life for a while,
And begin to fight this thing that I am.
I need to think about your things to change,
I want to hurt, I want to feel the pain.
Help me be strong with all that I see,
Let me remember you're helping me be free.
Let's call this a start, this is my prayer,
It's a comfort to know you're always there.

Steven Carlson

We Are One

We are one in spirit with God,
One in unity with each other.
Although each one of us is different,
We are one in spirit.
We received the gift of life and
The opportunity from God to share our love.
We are living our lives as spiritual beings;
We're doing our best,
Being our best.
We are one in spirit.
We always do what we can for others,
Knowing that we can do so much more.
One day our blessings will come
As long as you know in your heart
That we are one in spirit.

Wayne K. Barkley

Starlight Tears

The glowing moon and twinkling stars,
Bring their reminder to me from above.
Spread your shimmering light through these prison bars,
These bars that are the bondage of my love.
So dark, the light of love is not found here.
Outside love's light shines, here it's never felt.
Starlight fell from my eyes as single tears.
One look from you my hardened heart would melt.
Oh, heart! Oh, heart! Tonight we must forget!
Now! Here in the bondage of love's neglect.

Jill Phillips

Mothers of the Next Generation

We are the mothers of the next generation.
Raising our children with pride
Going through good times, as well as the bad
Progressing with every stride.

Dealing with people who are in doubt
Saying "it can't be done."
We're proving to them and to ourselves
By raising our daughters and sons.

Although we are young, we'll never give up
Our confidence will always grow.
For it is our children that motivate us;
We love them with heart and soul.

As time goes on, we see them prosper
Fulfilling their wants and needs;
For we are the flowers in which life begins
And they are the precious seeds.

Ruby Jennings

Lost in Time

I constantly think about you,
The way you were always there
when I needed you the most.

And yet, when I need you the most,
now,
you don't come and comfort me anymore.

I'm lost in time, somewhere in the past, waiting for you.
But you are not lost in time.
You are living in the future,
not waiting for me to follow.
I'm lost without you.

Erika Schuh

The Cross

The Cross I Bear is Mine Alone.
I Would Suffer in Silence. Not let anyone Know.
I Would be Strong, Oh, Was I Wrong
Are the Tremors Going to be Worse Today?
Will I Freeze in Mid-Step?
Can I Stand up Straight and Walk Without Stumbling?
Ah, Blessed Sleep, Will it Come Tonight?
I See a Miracle Happening in the Eyes of my Family.
I See Great Concern, Love, and Caring.
In many Unspoken Ways They Show Me,
My Cross is not Mine Alone.
Oh, Was I Wrong!
They Share it With Me and Make it Easier to Bear.
I Count My Blessings Every Day.
I Thank God for The People Who Make The Cross I Bear,
Not Mine Alone.
I'm So Glad I Was So Wrong!

Darlene Quinn, A. Parkinsonian

Maid of Mullaghmore

Mist rolling over purple mountains,
the wind swept, colorless sea turning.
Cold felt by awkward seals, graceless in entry.
Golden tranquility broken by strangers.
Red coated stripper wrapped tight against the
wind and rain,
cheeks red with natures rouge,
eyes and skin alive.
Vibrant maid of Mullaghmore.
Naked, but for clothes, exposed beyond belief,
hiding from the darkness offers no relief.

Davy Hutton

My Dream

When I dream
I dream of a land all so green
with beauty colors blue and yellow
glittery rainbow peaceful and mellow
purple roses silver daises
Green daffodils butterflies chasing
crystal waterfalls, juicy fruit trees
As the wind kisses paradise with a breeze
And in this beautiful paradise dream
I walk barefoot in a sparkly stream
As sunshine caresses the shimmery waters
My sand footprints appear with botanical flowers
Bathing myself in the waters warm springs
scattered scented Rose petals caressing my silky tanned skin.
Wind songs whispered softly in my ear,
Humming: "nature has its special charm especially when you here."
Finally my dream ended under the cherry moonlight
Hoping to see my dream in another fantasy life.

Diana Torres

The Bench

It stands alone as a symbol of strength.

A structure of mortar and wood
Made to carry the weight of guilt,
And in its lap,
Somehow cradles all that is good,
Between two lovers.

It stands awaiting an infrequent visit.
Existing as their sole retreat from separation,
And in its lap
Somehow ebbs a quiet desperation,
Between two lovers.

It stands as a monument to patience.
This bench which acts as a bridge
That spans a lifetime of romance in waiting,
And in its lap
Holds their chance at a future of happiness together,
Aching to begin
Between two lovers.

Philip DiMartino

A Family Is Love

A family is a circle, a circle of love.
One's sent to each other from God up above.
Sometime's they laugh, sometimes they cry,
But it is each other on which they rely.
Blessings will come, blessings will come blessings go.
But their love for each other, will grow and grow and grow.
Sometimes there's two, sometimes there's three,
Sometimes there's more, Oh, yes! And always
There's one that we cannot see.
He is with you, He is with me.
He is the greatest in a family.
If you are one all by yourself.
You can become two if Jesus is with you.
All you have to do is just ask Him to.
A family for me, a family for you.
In every family there should be at least two.

Sandra L. Koshinsky

Moment of Truth

When the inevitable wheel of fate doth turn
  And a message upon our souls doth burn
    When that which you thought you loved the best
      Has shattered to bits and been laid to rest
        And the things are gone for which you fought so hard
        And you sit hoisted upon your own petard

What now?

Alike for those who bemoan their fate
  And lay their souls at yesterday's gate
    The shroud of the past over their future is drawn
      Their life will be sunsets—never a dawn.
        Where to—will you look to find a new way,
          Or will you sink back into a long yesterday?
          This can become your finest hour
            A time of sunshine, joy, and power—

Your choice!

William E. Bailey

Deep Silence

The love for you is more profound than our world's oceans;
though it may not have been evident to bring you near,
my only witness was the heavens above whom knew my fears.
The years have passed and the silence remains
with the exception of my inner self which screams in vain,
my love—my love—my love.

Milagros Rosario

Some Stairs

I climbed to the top of some stairs,
I thought went nowhere.
One thousand and ten there were.
I climbed to be on top of the world.
I had closed my eyes while I stood there,
and felt a warm breeze, brush past my skin.
In the distance, I heard angels.
I assumed they sang to God,
In the heavens, in the sky.
Slowly, I had taken a deep breath.
All that I inhaled was fresh.
I smelled sweet grass in the air.
I felt delighted to be there,
In all that beauty.
I was alone with nature,
and for the first time . . .
I had known true happiness.
With that peace, I had found a freedom.
Again, I will climb those stairs . . .
I now know, go somewhere.

Jessica Bouchard

Once More

Walking in despair on this temporary path
I'm showered with dreams of past tense
In contempt of what once was
I dread the rising dawn
Confused of what has yet to come
I witness the birth of beautiful grace
as the mist reveals today
Just another day of words unsaid
Just another day of songs unsung
Just another day of prayers unheard
Just another day created for loneliness

Jeanette Vrelits

Kelly

I cried a tear for you, for you did so much for me.
I know not how you knew, but you must have heard my plea.

I needed a hug of love and so you did respond;
as gentle as a bird, you gave this caring bond.

I wanted someone to hear for the feelings I have been handed;
you gave me an open ear, with nothing in return demanded.

Only you said the words that made me feel as one,
your voice as free as the birds, and your smile warm as sun.

And when I needed to grieve, your shoulder wet with tears,
my side you did not leave, through the minutes felt like years.

I owe so much, my friend. You would do it all for me.
My heart that you mend will finally be set free.

So now I am living well and my troubles are through,
so when you go through your Hell, I will be there for you.

I love the way you make me smile, the way you make me feel.
I just want to know—is this for real?

Michael Varnes

Tomorrow's Dream

I have tomorrow in my dreams of today
I am the future, I'll find a way
You are yesterday, gone like the sun
You are the memories fading one by one
Today when I saw you, I remembered our past
We shared something wonderful, it just did not last
I can't stay any longer, I have to move on
o look for the future for yesterday's gone.

Mayuri de la Cruz

My Mom

My mom was great and loved by all.
When you looked at her, that smile said it all.
I loved my mom with all my heart . . .
Too bad we had to part.
Mom and I went everywhere.
Even with her friends, I was there.
And in my heart my mom will always be.
And that, no one can ever take away from me.

Helen Cingolani

Rising

Up these mountains and through these caves
is where my ancestors were slaves. I stand
and breathe the air, nothing in this world
could ever compare, how women were brutally
raped and the men were treated like apes,
monkeys, just plain animals. I stand tall to
tell you all how proud I am of what we
have accomplished as a people. It still may
not be equal, but to see how far we have come,
I know there will be a sequel.
So you can say by standing here makes me
feel free and full of life, even though
I feel a darkness come over me because
I know my ancestors paid the price, but
still it's nice to know when I'm long gone
the next generation has a place to call home.

Courtney Wallace

To My Darling Daughter

It's your first Christmas,
And I'll always hold it dear,
For I hope it's the first of many
To come for you each and every year.

My only wish this Christmas
Is for your happiness, health and love,
To keep it close to my heart,
As God meant for you from above.

My darling, Merry first Christmas
Remember, mommy and daddy love you,
For if anything you desire will we will try and get
To make your dreams come true.

I hope you'll have all you desire,
And get everything life has to offer
I will always help you get there;
You can count on me in times of trouble.

So Merry Christmas Victoria,
My love for you is never-ending and strong
You are my life's most precious joy,
You are what keeps me going on.

Sheryl J. Walker

Location Is Everything

I could drink up
In a paper cup,
That big lake of water . . . from here.

A meek little mouse,
Might frighten his spouse,
With a low enough candle . . . behind him.

That road up ahead,
That's thin as a thread,
Will be wide as two cars . . . when we get there.

The troubles we anticipate,
If they don't first dissipate,
Will contain solutions within . . . when they come!

V. Gene Clark

Journey

Life for me has not been a tranquil journey.
The road to success I have not yet reached.
But there are many obstacles I have passed along the way.
Twisting roads. Dead ends.
Road blocks. Intersections.
I have seen them all, yet I managed to conquer them all.
So far, I see my light at the end of the tunnel
Like a diamond in a coal mine.
But I am not quite there yet.
And I will never cease to stop until I grasp the light.

Jennifer Jaworski

When I Dream

Dreams are for the inner endless dimensions of the mind
Vast and quiet

I hear and see what my soul seeks
Inner peace
Timeless

Dreams are for the moments that I pursue my Destiny
Private and secret

Intimate recollections
Ever present

Dreams reveal myself to myself
True
Without Distortion
Silent

And through my dreams
I know the light of God

Samuel A. Eriz

Man in Red

Who is this in red and a beard?
Always the one to bring Christmas cheer
Like the three who are wise,
could he be an angel in disguise?
To come in the midst of the night,
begone by the earliest of light.
Once a year he comes this way
maybe to remind us of the one in the hay.
Not only to bring a sack full of toys,
but the birth of Jesus to all girls and boys.
When you open your gifts and before you start,
give from yourself, a gift from the heart.
And this is why your Christmas is spent
with the man in red, that God has sent.

David Denman

Streets

Through the streets of suffering,
Across the paths of agonizing,
I try to find my way.
Is there?
Through the road of bliss,
Across the alley of laughter,
I try to make my day.
Can I?
For life is so complicated.
I feel so disoriented.
For death is so close,
I can see it almost.
Is it coming now or tomorrow?
Should my life be wide or narrow?
Is it here today?
Would it end my way?
Questions flood my dark, dry uncompleted soul
And I can't find the answers
Before drowning in its hole.

Erez Bialer

Mystery

It's a mystery the way that I feel
A strange way of life that seems so unreal
So absorbed in a dream of some strange fashion
But a beautiful dream of hope and of passion
Pain and despair give way in a moment
To joy and peace and almost no torment
How can one change in the wink of an eye
From happiness to a wish that he'd die
It's a story they say as old as man's life
His quest for a mate, a lover, a wife
Never easy this task of finding the truth
Yet we pursue it . . . we start it at youth
Older now and wiser it seems
Still and all we must keep our dreams
So here it is and will remain always with me
This feeling I have that love is a mystery

Andrew Cantatore

Song of the Windmill

At night the wind carries a tune
To the old windmill out side my room.
I lie and listen as they carry on,
The wind and the mill have a wondrous song.
I like to believe I know what they say
When the moon is high and as bright as day.
But on the darkest night, when one can't see,
The wind and the mill sometimes frighten me.
But I know when I hear that wondrous song
That the wind and the mill are still carrying on.

Lois Wineiger

Everything Is Beautiful

Everything is beautiful when you look to the sky
With those fluffy white clouds
That move through the sky

He made the trees
That make us shade

He made the grass
Which is ever so green

He made the birds that sing to us
That sound like a song from the heavens above

He made the ocean
With its waves
Softly blowing in the wind

That is why everything
Seems so beautiful to us

If we could see God we would say
He is beautiful too

Anthony P. Galasso, Sr.

For God and Country

Red—was the rose that lay on the table,
A long stemmed beauty.
Red as the blood of our dear Savior Jesus
White—as the pure innocent lamb.
The rose was dappled with pearly white dew.
Blue as the Heaven above—from where our
Lovely Lord Jesus descended,
and where we'll ascend to one day.
Red white and blue—old glory's colors.
Believe in Him, believe in the flag
for which our soldiers died and believed in.
For God and country, for God and America:
Believe and be born again.
Long may America live—the home of the brave and free!

Gene W. Hawley

Dear Friend

The message in my mind.
The message in your eyes.
It's as inspiring as the tide,
Through something as simple as your stride.

And just when I start to forget,
I catch your eye and once again let
everything stir inside and set;
and remember every single life long debt.

Then suddenly I look to the ground,
or everywhere else around.
I hear your voice, it's in the sound!;
that has the soft sweet comfort I have now found.

I pray that this is not the end.
And I tell myself on you I will not depend.
Thank you is now the message I send.
So thank you so much, my very dear friend.

Alison Stewart

Hope Restored

Restore yourself if you've faced defeat.
Revive yourself if your enemies have beaten you.
Rebuild yourself if life has broken you.
Redeem yourself if you've made mistakes.
Regain your footing if you've slipped a time or two.
Recapture your pride when circumstances have shamed you.
Regain your courage though at first you were fearful.
Recover your smile though at times you were tearful.
Replace hate with love and vengeance with
patience; and only then will you see, what the
Lord has in store for you.
A perfect destiny!

Malcolm Palmore

Longing

I don't regret having liked you
I don't care if you don't like me at all
I wanted to forget you
But I couldn't resist thinking about you
The more I try to convince myself
That we can never be friends
The more I wanted us to be
And the more it hurts inside me
Because I feel that we can never be
I just wish I never met you at all
I wouldn't have gone through
This painful realization and disappointment
I have to live with each day of my life
I don't know how long I can carry the pain
I don't know how long I will hold on to my dream
All I know is that I'll always love you, my friend
And hope you'll love me back just the same

Dulce Narvadez

Commitment

To commit means to give in charge; place as a trust,
Not to pretend to love or treat as lust.
To commit means to do or say something that
will involve or pledge one,
When you are able to do this, the long,
painful race you have won.
Commitment is strong words, it means a promise, pledge,
It has its tendency of running people off the edge.
Commitment is not meant to be complicated just natural for life,
But most men are afraid to say, "Will you be my wife."
If it is meant to be it will happen in time,
So just let your heart shine.
Keep letting the other person know you care,
And in time your lives you will share.

Maria Peel

My Wishes for the World 2000

In my 2000 I don't want to see
any fighting or wars all around me.
In my 2000 I don't want to see
anyone breaking the laws, especially me.
In my 2000 I want to see joy and happiness all around me.
In my 2000 I want to see a clean and cozy place for me.
In my 2000 I don't want to see a horrible and dirty place for me.
In my 2000 I don't want to see a messy and black colored sea.
In my 2000 I want to see animals playing joyfully.
In my 2000 I want to see snowflakes falling softly.

Aimee Torkington

The Building Blocks of an Inmate's Life

The compound fragments of my huge domain
intricately fall apart
and reveals a presence unwanted by all
yet created by many.
and the debts left unpaid disappear
as easy as midsummer dew,
just visiting for awhile,
but becomes an illusion
when the sun breaks the sky.
Painstaking hours invested needlessly,
venturing to places unknown
reaching insurmountable levels,
but endowed to achieve so much more.
while life passes by those
who choose to remain on its highway,
as a raging river demolishes all opposition.
those who are separated from the results
notice the forces of good and evil
ready to be harnessed
even in the most demanding situation.

James Pasmore

Rainy Night

Sprinkles of rain falls down on my face
I hold this moment, not wanting it to be erased.
But then I'm cleaning up each trace that it makes.
The cool wind blowing through me like ice,
melted into a soft, chilled, but warm liquid
breeze, swallowing me hole, with each blow I receive.
Rain softly tapping the streets,
causing a beat, I move my feet.
Hoping the rain never becomes weak.
Spinning around, becoming one with the rain
and the wind, creating a human tornado, that
only brings relaxation, meditation and
concentration to my mind.
As this night untwines, I leave behind the
sight of this ever so peaceful
Rainy Night.

Shano Daye

Mother's Day

Mother you have been there for me every single way,
That is why we celebrate Mother's Day.
Ever since I was born
you loved me and kept me warm,
so I want to thank you for helping me.
You are the best mom that could ever be,
and you're the best I have ever met.
When I'm naughty I will regret.
Every hug and every kiss
When I grow up I will miss.
I love you so, so much
when I'm hurt what helps is your special touch.
I only have one thing to say,
I love you more every day!

Sarah Trudelle, age 9

teenage puppy-love

my energy yielding carbohydrates
with your random acts of music
I am taking a crash course suicide
your random acts of protection
dance with lightning
my lovely crash course
you and your speeding dream
I tried to sit myself in your passenger seat
we must get to the dark
to find the light
but there is a cloud of purple beeping
blocking my tongue
I wonder
will you put me in your box of toys
or shut me in your drawer
just leave me on your desktop
I will send you a reminder once a week
or
you could add a check and just delete me . . .

Crystal Weber

My Wife's Balance

For Ross-Anne

Yeah . . . My Wife is the Butter on my Popcorn.
She's the Starch in my Shirts
The Candy in my Cotton Candy
The Static in my Static Cling
The Play in my Horse Play, but the Business in my Monkey
Business.
My Wife's the Cheese in my Macaroni and Cheese
The Seldom Wrong mostly Right in my Right and Wrong.
My Eternal Companion and Full Time Partner
She's the Cake in my Cake Walk and the Piece in my Piece O'
Cake.
My Wife's the One and the Only in my One and Only
She's the Improved in my New and Improved
She's my Yin & Yang, Up & Down, In & Out, and Left & Right.
My Wife's the Mediator, Moderator, Dinner Maker & Clothes
Folder.
My Full Service Support, Often Over Looked and Under Estimated
Sometimes not Appreciated, but Always Relied On.
She's the Quiet and the Peace in my Peace and Quiet.
My Wife is my Every and my Thing in my Everything.

Yeah . . . My Wife's Balance

Scott David Gibson

Of Thee I Love

Never again shall we return together
or stand here together looking at the sea
or smell the faint smell of heather
under the shading of this wind-bent tree

Autumn will come with grey rains and wind blowing
and winter with a thin melting cover of snow
spring will break with red flowers
and full streams flowing
though you and I will not be here to know

But far across the blue wide shining sea
that whispers gently now below your feet
when April comes in another place we will be dreaming
how soft the grass and how the berries are sweet

And this is lost to us
the calm expanding blue
the drifted downs
the wind-stressed trees

Still in your eyes I shall see
the white cliffs standing
and hear your voice in the low pulse of the sea

Donald Robinson

Strings

Sick and prickly a good while
Small and serious, sensitive and resilient
She's unaware she's destined to be the pillar

A brother, two sisters follow
And lastly a baby named Danny
The birth was flawed and he too . . . some

Mother gone too early at 42 . . . father three years later
She meets a soldier who takes her heart
And moves to his town so far away . . . 10 miles
Danny delivers open hearth baked bread door to door
And frequents local firehouses and bars

Soon a child arrives and another 3 years later
These were the good years . . . some say
Danny so happy with people and life parties on
'Til one December night too much . . . too much
One slip on the stairs, the next day he's gone

A grandchild arrives . . . so special . . . so light
But all is not smooth

She still lives with the old soldier in his town
But almost alone, most all are gone

Andrea Faleshock

The Loss of a Daughter

If I could turn back time,
I know you know I would.
Then you'd still be here with me,
Loved the way you should.

I hope someday you'll understand,
This decision wasn't ours.
And I hope that on that day
Your heart's not full of scars.

When you go home, they'd better be ready
To face the consequences.
Because if something happens to you,
They'll be left with no defenses.

Anyone who's ever lost a daughter
Should know what we're going through.
But others are unsympathetic,
And they don't care about you.

Many said that they did care,
But if they really did,
They'd take a little more interest in
This poor, young, innocent kid.

Kevin J. Kowalski

Biography of a Poet—Hello Louie

They still gather in the mall in town
Ever since Frank's Pool Hall shut down
It's two forty-five
The first person arrived
And after all these years I still recognize Louie
A battle raged in my mind
Fearful of what I might find
There were things I didn't know
From a long time ago
And Louie still has the key
I walked across the floor
And right out the door
I turned and said, "Hello, Louie"
He was puzzled at first as he looked at this nurse
Then I mimicked the time
On the telephone line
A slight nod, he still remembered me
I just wanted to say
I got the tickets that day
And I saw that last show—was it '73?

Marjorie Henderson

My Husband

There was a man that I saw
That I could cherish, love, and adore.
Through the years he has changed—
His appearance, his ways; does he still have the same name?
This is a man that I thought I knew.
We have changed, we both have grew.
Now we went through 15 years of marriage,
Four cribs, and baby carriages.
He is not the same man that I fell in love with once,
He is the same man that I fell in love with once more.

Gina B.

The Clown

A painted face with a cherry red nose
An old torn top hat and raggedy clothes
A pair of white gloves to cover the hands
And oversized shoes fastened with rubber bands
Now with the disguise all in place
He's ready to enter onto center stage
He hears the beating of drums
Which tells him his time has come
He begins his act with stumbles and falls
For he is a barrel of laughs after all
As he plants his feet firmly on the ground
He takes his first bow and looks around
Many people have gathered from town
To see this happy-go-lucky clown
He weans his way into their hearts
As he merrily plays his small part
One final leap into the air he suddenly knows
His act is done and back to the dressing room he goes
As he sits removing his disguise
He sadly finds he's just an ordinary guy

Kathryn Zawadzski

And the Angels Sang

Softly colored rosebuds sprinkled the Earth
The sweet scent of tulips intoxicated angels
A smooth gentle wind embraced the trees
O', God, why is this day so perfect?
And the sun deep dark and gold,
Shined brightly upon the ground this day—
The day of your birth

And the angels sang gloriously
While cobalt flowers smiled
Little fingers smooth and soft
Pushing the fields of youth
And in your time of hurt and sorrow
The angels wept with stinging tears

The sound of your voice radiated the stars,
As your charm made others drunk with desire
Swift and sweet your flame burned bright
And now, as we are standing facing each other
I can still hear the angels singing
now and forever

Jeffrey Wang

Real Love

One feels part of the other without reason.
Time seems to escape too soon.
Life is too short to have difficulties.
Gratefully embracing the next day with each other.
Finishing a thought without words.
A friend, a partner, a part of your own life.
Love is real without hesitation.
Love is thanking God for every moment of life together.
Life is to be savored.
Real Love cannot be explained, it just is.

Kathleen Bates

Persistence of Friendship

One year of joy, laughter, and fun,
Ended on the phone, and all seemed done.
No more secrets, parties, sleep overs too,
One year wasted, our friendship was through.
She'd move far away soon that day.
No one's left to wipe my tears away.
I cried nonstop. My best friend was long gone.
I had no idea what I had done wrong.
Surprisingly my tears had stopped.
Now I knew our friendship had not "popped."
How, you might ask, from my mother of course.
Her words of wisdom were the right source.
She said even though we don't go
To the same school we will still show
We are still friends forever. We'll still talk.
We'll still have sleep overs and write songs that rock . . .
WE'LL BE BEST FRIENDS FOREVER!

Randi March

In the Heart of the Night

In the heart of the night,
When the pulse of the world is still
That's when you come
Slipping through my dreams
Stealing in on wings of darkness.
I feel your touch on my skin
Stroking, caressing
Your lips on mine
A knife edge of pain
Tearing through my heart
Burning tears
Staining my cheeks and pillow as I wake up
Alone.

Siobhan Densley

Beach Death

Footprints once marked a place in the sand,
Children once ran along the shore,
Waves once crashed upon the rocks,
Sea gulls once danced above in the sky,
And the sun once shown through the marshmallow clouds.

Footprints no longer mark the sand,
Children no longer run along the shore,
Waves no longer crash upon the rocks,
Sea gulls no longer dance in the sky,
And the sun no longer shines through the marshmallow clouds.

For the only thing that fills this sand, shore,
rocks, sky and clouds,
Are the horrors of technology,
Man is uncaringly killing our beaches without even realizing,
The beauty is gone and the darkness has set in.

Stephanie Cosentino

Heaven

The stars sparkle and shine so bright,
Like glitter on dark snow;
The silvery moon casts its eerie light
On the Earth below;
What is it about the night
That frightens people so?
This myriad of other worlds—a fantasy flight
For those who know;
And yet people try with all their might,
To forget and deny and say "no"
To this everlasting sight;
While deep inside their loneliness starts to grow,
As they realize how insignificant their plight.

Stephen Thomas

She Wants You To Know

She walks alone in a crowded hall;
they all see her but thinks she's too small.
They don't care what the real person is like,
they only see all her bad sides.
She may not be the best looking girl,
but sometimes she is all she has in this world.
She may not be like the rest of the school,
but all that matters is that her heart is pure.
She wants to know why they treat her that way,
Does she deserve this?
Is there a crime she needs to pay?
Sometimes she's close to picking up the knife,
and taking away a privilege, not a strife.
She needs to know that someone cares,
she needs to know that someone's there.
All she wants is to hold her head high,
and not be ashamed and bow her head down and cry.
She wants a normal life where she will be loved and admired,
but down in the end she is just lonely and tired.

Anastazija Burazin

I Am . . .

There can be beauty in sound . . .
As well as in silence.
Welcome to my world.
This is me . . . I am . . .

ART WORD LOVE HIGH LOW NEAR FAR
GIVING LAUGHTER WARMTH GODLINESS

I am ART, for we are all a work of creation
I am WORD, formed by many characters
I am LOVE, for it is the reason for existence
I am HIGH, in pursuit of my dream of fantasy
yet I am forced to sink LOW
into this world of materialism and realism
My physical existence among you
people brings me close to you,
but my introvert nature makes it such that
I am NEAR, yet FAR.
I am GIVING, for I have in me graciousness
I am LAUGHTER, for it brings happiness to my soul
I am warmth, for you can never find coldness in me
I am GODLINESS, for my name is Michelle

This is me. I am.

Michelle Ng

what is love

to stephanie schermerhorn
love is caring, honoring, and cherishing
looking into each others eyes,
like shining stars throughout the night,
taking our new relationship to a new height,
i admire u from head to toe,
i wonder sometime what direction to go,
with your guidence from your heart,
i am with a girl who has very much intelligence and smarts,
slipping an engagement on her finger,
fits like a shoe just like a slipper,
in gods honest truth i am with to night,
just the truth is she really knows i love her

i solely know that i do love her,
i hope to tell her i am very proud of her,
just to know my dear stephanie i do love u,
that is why i dedicated this poem to u,
to prove that i love u

this poem is dedicated to stephanie, the love of my life!

love always,
ikie hamilton

Jack Hamilton, Jr.

Music—That's the Thing

1930's—the beginning of swing
1940's—swing is the real thing
1950's—rock 'n' roll at its best
1960's—really put us to the test
1970's—Oh, my it's real hard rock
1980's—my ship still isn't at the dock
1990's—now it's rap you can't understand
2000's—maybe they'll bring back bandstand
As you can see, music is my thing
But make sure that it's old rock or swing
The metal craze is not my cup of tea
And rap really leaves me out to sea
Rock 'n' roll, good jazz, big band sound
That's what makes me go 'round 'n' 'round
Music, music, music that's the going beat
Don't you know it is really neat.

Lila Manley

Revelation

To all still suffering in their addictions
It is not the flame that burns us,
but our fears, anxieties, and our pride.

It is not our tongue that lashes out,
but our frustrations, our anger, and our innermost thoughts.

It is not the sun that scorches us,
but our guilt, our pain, and our self-loathing.

It is not our eyes that blind us,
but our prejudices, our preconceived ideas, and our judgement.

It is not the Earth that weighs us down,
but our negativity, our depression, and our misery.

It is not our mind that is not open,
but our beliefs, our trust, and our hearts.

Rebecca Mills

Graduation

Today I say goodbye to you
For the memories we share will never fade.
Your friendship has left imprints on my heart
And your love has enlightened my soul.

Today we begin a lifelong journey
To explore the unimaginable
To face the unpredictable
To accomplish the impossible.

Although we must go our separate ways,
We take a part of each other,
For each friendship represents a world within us.

So I say to you, this is the end of the beginning.

Jenny Spinelli

Every Moment and Forever

I sit here thinking of my heart's betrayal,
how it opened the door for me to be so in
love with one so far away.
My soul fills with pain as both my mind and
body remind me that you are not here.
I pray each moment that some miracle would
strike that would bring us together.
I think of your velvet skin touching mine,
your breath on my neck, entwined together,
enjoying the peaceful sleep of lovers.
I toss and turn reaching out for you,
looking for you, but you are not there.
Exhausted, sleep overcomes and I dream of
days with you by my side, feeling you
touching me every moment and forever.

Debra Elaine Ennis

I Can . . .

swim across the sweet sea of grass
live in the future and change the past
make the raged beast shed a river of tears
make the blind see, allow the deaf to hear
stop a lightning bolt dead in its tracks
cast a spell on life to change the facts
burglarize banks and museums without going in
dig a coal mine with a shovel made of tin
make the sociopaths become conceited and rude
end all world hunger with one can of food
thaw the arctic with the warmth in my heart
make the smart so easy and the easy smart
kill the colorful flowers with only one touch
bring them back, because i love you so much
memorize the books of fiction, make them true
do nothing so wonderful unless I'm with you

Christopher Pullen

Remember Me?

I look in the mirror and who do I see?
A women, middle aged, is that really me?
I feel so vibrant and so alive!
Why in the mirror do I look so old?
When did my life start to unfold?
Kids grown and on there own, my marriage through.
What does a middle aged woman do?
We put on a smile and do all we can to help others who say,
Is that really me?

Susan Lovitch

Be Strong Knowing Love

Love has no boundaries
It has no nationality
It is meant for you and me
Only time will tell
When we will be together
Be assured
Know that love is patient
It does not know time
Permanent is what it is
Our bond is forever
So do not worry
There is no need to be scared
Love does not harm
It only knows good
A life of love is waiting for us
We must be strong and know that it is there
Let us reach for it, grab it
and never let it go

Deborah Miller

To Sierra

My darling daughter, I love you so.
I watch in wonder as you grow.
Still so tiny with eyes so clear.
What will they see in the coming years?

Eyes of slate and hair like down.
Rosy cheeks, so soft and round.
Long slim fingers, legs and toes.
You even have your brother's nose!

You're quiet and calm, but, Oh, so strong.
We named you Sierra, it seemed to belong.
You're second name Jade, so precious and rare
So you'll always remember just how much we care

I watch you sleeping, and still can't believe
That such sweet beauty came out of me.
I'm writing this poem 'cause I want you to know . . .
my darling daughter, I love you so.

Viki Jo Johnston

A Day in June

Guess what I saw today?
Four baby birds at play.
They flew from chair to chair . . .
On my patio . . . They had such fun there.
One walked up on the chair's seat.
Another flew over to the table
Which was quite a feat!
Mama bird was sitting nearby . . .
Chirping and encouraging them as they learned to fly.
They peeped as they flew from place to place.
I had such a huge smile on my face . . .
As GOD sends us pleasures to start our day
Did you notice any as you went on your way?

Ann Marie Pedersen

Question Is

Can't seem to realize
Nor at all materialize
What our culture quite is.
None of it makes real sense
Nobody seems conscious
Of who our Mother is.
It seems that everyone is quite lost
And willing to understand at any cost
What a good economy is.
And civilization seems so uncivil
When even over the love of God we quibble
And never question how good our nature truly is.

Nan Kavanaugh

The Queen of Broken Hearts

As she steps into the spotlight,
shimmering light surrounds her face
The picture of an angel here, from another place

Her hair as gold as sunlight, her smile as warm as wine
Her voice comes straight from Heaven,
but with a tear in every line

For all her fame and fortune and undisputed wealth
Her songs all cry of heartbreak and love that went all wrong

She knows a bit about it, for she has lived those hurting songs

She left us far too early, but her legacy lives on
In the hearts of those who loved her,
and that tear in every song

Maureen Melong

Soul Mates

Love deeply felt with tenderness
You see is true love, a reality.
Touching souls with precious and most
High quality is to live life in God's
Realm with each other, in certainty.
Feelings so pure and true is God's gift
To me and to you.
To each other our love we give knowing
In our hearts God's love stands long
And true, just as your love is for me
And my love is for you. Steadfast and
Vigilant so protected we are, from within
Worlds we each live, so deep and
So far. What time is best, my love, for
You and me? Only God knows, for our
Love will last through eternity.
With love so pure and so true,
We stand at His gates with love so
Sincere, as
Soul mates

Sandy Gividen

The Shadows of the Night

We have travelled here on the great wings of time,
swimming through the depths of hunger and pride.
While the loneliness tries to hold on to this heart of mine,
I fight this war, to have you by my side.

Deep in the darkness of the night, my soul cries out for you.
My desire a flame burning hot, burning slow.
The feeling of longing growing with each thought of you.
Your smile, your kiss, your gentle touch,
is all that I need right now.

I would pay any price, any ransom, to have you by my side.
To be surrounded with the essence of you in the air that I breathe.
And in the shadows of the night I call out your name.
For my love is drowning in the depths of your stormy sea.

The moments that I see your face are the most precious to me.
And the heartaches from the past are quickly fading away.
In wanting you close to me, I am finally free.
Because it is you that I need and want, tomorrow and today.

Christina Clements

Courage

Loneliness swallows my soul like a wild beast
About to make its kill on the helpless prey
As it stands there and cowers with no one to help it.
The prey needs courage; some say courage comes from within.
But where? I need courage to fight battles of life and reality.
Where do I find it?
In my lonely soul, in my heart, where?

Tracy Wiedel

Ave Vita

To Camilo and Rafael
Mama died today or was it yesterday? Not with a bang but a whimper.
Of all those who breathe—only one will truly live.
The Threat—from hollow lips—is not to have:
cafe; vinho porto; sixty seconds worth of run; aficion; loss.
Don Quixote da la Mancha—doesn't he, too, fit in the values?
To breathe: full of sound and fury, is to regret.
To regret: is to die. To die—perchance to dream.
A dream—a nightmare—where no memories will come. Om!
To Regret: windy suspiration of breath.
To breath: is to have lived not wisely nor too well.
A dream—a whimper—not brilliant only perfect. Om!
To play: with direct eyes, is to defeat the shadow.
To live: in the here and now—ay, there's the rub!
Those inconclusive experiences, memories—bangs—brilliance. Om!
To Lie: is to be cursed with a hundred years in solitude.
A Lie—of having raindrops on roses, and warm woolen mittens.
Ave Vita to he that not once looks up, but does it for himself.
"Om!" Says the river. "Because it is my name!"
"Om!" Says the river. "Because I cannot have another in my life!"
"Om!" Says the river. Ah! There's the respect.

Craig Alan Johnson

The Next Level

Mental attraction we have achieved . . .
So what else do we need?
Physical connection; chemistry at work . . .
Motions moving, minds wondering, tongues flickering . . .
Our bodies engulfed in pleasures . . .
Unknown are physical barriers . . .
No need for scars to surface . . .
Licking each other's wounds.
Under the moonlight we'll be together . . .
Caress constantly, holding gently . . .
Whispering softly . . . tender words carefully . . .
Mental level at its peak.
Now's time for physical attraction . . .
The next level we seek.

Travis Smith

Broken Wings

When hopes are low,
And sadness grows
When darkness prevails,
And sorrows sail,

That is the time when I remember our friendship,
How you were beside in every hardship
When there was no one to share,
You were always there

I remember how you showed me the paths
Where the happiness was sure to last,
Whenever I was woe-begone,
I always had your shoulder to cry on

The bird which wanted to touch the sky
Has no longer wings to fly
Now she weeps and never sings,
For no one can mend her broken wings.

Syeda Bokhari

A Crack in My Armor

Her vow of love
Burns me to the core,
And with a passion I never knew I had,
I let her in my soul.

I know that I am vulnerable,
But I can't help myself,
Because now there is a chance
That I won't have to be alone anymore.

And then, with a laugh,
She turns her back on me
And rips my heart and soul in two,
And with an uncaring shrug
Leaves me shattered and broken.

Bemoaning my fate,
I just let myself go,
Hoping I will die,
My life's blood flowing into the gutter. . . .

Michael Martin

I Loved You!

For Jordan Howell
I loved you and you turned away.
I was all alone with no one who cared about me like I did you.
When I told my friends they thought you were a jerk.
I told them you would come around.
The next dance you asked me to dance.
I was really happy when we started dancing.
Now I have found myself loving you again.

Christina Klann

My Special Companion

For years you were at my side,
Then the Lord called, and you died.
I would give anything to have you back.
As you well know, you always kept me on track.
All our future plans are gone,
And I am trying to get along.
You promised to save a place next to you in Heaven;
I hope you are able to save a seat
Until we once again meet.
I would marry you again, and be asking while at your feet.
You were my hopes and dreams, and now
I remain like a bird missing a wing.
Honey, I'll love you forever and look
Forward to our being together.

Harry H. Collum

My Expression of You

When I look into your eyes
I see into your heart.
It is then that I know
there is nothing to keep us apart,
I feel your warmth, and strong embrace,
I see your love when I see your face.
You taught me things
I did not know.
You showed me things
to help me grow.
I appreciate all you've done for me, and
I will be grateful to you for all eternity.

Jennifer Ashbrook

A Dolphin's World

I am swimming and giggling with the sea,
hoping for someone to play with me.
I see a boat and beam with delight;
I do turns and show how great I can be.
Diving beneath the deep blue sea,
I discover the wreckage underneath me.
Those sunken boats left silently:
pieces of wood and metal shaped exquisitely.
Coral and seaweed and rocks as far as I can see.
Schools of fish swimming happily.
This is my world, the deep blue sea.
This is where I feel completely free.

Kylie Harrald

Suicide

Thoughts that were tamed and quiet
now unleashed wild and frantic.

Python desperation squeezing at the throat.
Heart pounding like a racehorse.

Sweat forming perverse rivers seeking every
crevice of the body.

Once, understanding and judgment reigned.
Now pain's throne rules over reality.

Darkness violates the light of the inner
child of innocence.

Hopelessness screams silently at the mind.
A bottomless pit awaits to embrace misery.

Life's sea tossing from one tragedy to another
has ceased to exist.

Suicide has claimed its victim cast down
at Mercy's feet.

Sandralee Mason

The Sonnet

I need to write a sonnet fair tonight.
I have tried so hard but my mind is blank.
But nothing seems to come to mind quite right.
I would rather walk on a long slim plank.

A sonnet is so hard to write, it's true.
The rhyming and the timing is so hard.
If I have to write one again I'll sue.
I would rather write to you in a card.

Help me, Will Shakespeare, to write this sonnet!
Help me write this and I will be grateful.
So grateful that I will ride a comet.
Right now it's so late that I am hateful!

William Shakespeare is now under the sod.
I am done now with this sonnet, thank God!

Robert Williams

My Love

Dedicated to Tony Hamel
You have always been my friend
Given me advice, and one I can always depend
Your shoulder has always been my pillow
In times of sadness and in sorrow
You brighten even the gloomiest days
With your humor and your joking ways
You will always be my one and only
Thanks to you I will never be lonely
Now is my promise to you
In front of our friends and family too
I will be your happiness when you are sad
Be your good when things seem bad
I will be your shelter in case of rain
Heal your wounds when you are in pain
I will be the brightest star on those dark and cloudy nights
That ray of sunshine, making things bright
I will always protect and stand by your side
In me, you can always confide
My love for you is here to stay
For today, tomorrow, and every day.

Laura Rykers

With Only You

We Fly amongst the clouds to a sea of blue
out of darkness with only you
I clutch your hand I hold you dear
I fail to understand your deepest fears
to a lost paradise that we must find
for eternity if you don't mind
hand and hand to find a light
I pray to God He keeps us bright
I walk the moon with only you
I keep you near for the rest of life

Henry Blan

Inspiration

Lonely is the sea,
Lonely like me at 3 a.m.

Suddenly I see,
What the heck could it be?
A little bird!

A little white feathered lover walking on the beach,
Singing and dancing lonely, but carefree.

The little white feathered lover said hello to me.
And now we are all friends, I, the lover, and the sea.

Peter Dimopoulos

A Plea to the Ignorant Multitude

All men who have reduced their lives to dust,
Heed! Stop! I beseech you; pray, do wait!
You may live this life if you must,
But, pray, heed ere 'tis too late.

If you waste your precious lives in this way,
Tell me, what have you to gain?
God will still forgive you, so pray!
Else you'll never escape the pain.

You have trodden on the wrong path,
Mistaken hideousness for grace.
Do you want to incur His wrath?
If not, in Heaven will be your place.

Redeem yourselves whilst there is time,
Pray, do come into His glory.
Temptations come a dozen for a dime
But, salvation? 'Tis another story.

Nirmalya Ganguly

Black Woman

My hair is nappy and dry
my skin is dark as night
my eyes shine brightly
like the morning sunlight
some say I am headstrong
others say I am manly
why do I always play the mammy?

I have an eighth grade education
my intelligence is not so high
I got pregnant at the age of 16
my boyfriend left me out to dry
I work for Mrs. Johnson
I am a maid to her you see
I pray every day that the Lord
will come and set me free
I am a black woman.

Slavery was ended about 90 years ago
you say we are equal, then why am I still poor?
I work night and day doing the best I can
I get all fancied up
and still can't find a man
I am a black woman.

Kimberly Wilson

A Vision to See

If I could wish upon a star that comes out at night,
If I could go a mile or two, and everything will be bright,
I would go to the uttermost parts of the world,
for I will reach magnificent shore,
If I had wings and fly away, and that will be a glorious day.
When look to the hills, which cometh my help.

The vision to see, I ponder never to forget.
Ever presence, omnipotent power that I felt
I looked in the mirror, just an image of my face,
Somehow my heart gave me a beautiful embrace,
I have gotten lost on this journey and could not see ahead.

Because my vision was blurred and my tongue was slurred.
Each day there is a prayer that hold me fast,
Not a day goes by that I would pass,
I talk to my heart and asked the question why?
Is there a reason to see the vision of my eyes

The answer came to me in a dream!
Why I can't see, I must first believe there is a mind vision in me,
Focusing for good things to happen, think positive, and be grateful,
For what you can be, it's a big picture of love

Lou Ann Morris

Mom

Your boys came one by one,
So you thought that it was done.
But to your surprise you gave birth
to the cutest little girl on Earth.
Just fifteen months later another one came,
tiny and sweet, she was just the same.
You didn't stop—there were two more boys,
surely your life is filled with joy.
In all there were eight kids;
raising us was not a whiz.
The girls didn't cause much worry,
'Cause we grew up in a bit of a hurry.
Now for the boys there were some woes,
Boys are more hard-headed as everyone knows.
As a Mom you're above the rest;
Lord knows we put you to the test.
Times we were in trouble you stood in the gap,
for your prayers and love we stand and clap.
There's just one more thing I'd like to say:
Hey Mom, have a great Mother's Day!

Brenda Landram

Love of God

The love of God is like a breath of air
refreshing my soul within
with His gentle care.
He forgives my deepest sin.
Love Him as He loves you
in all that you say and do.
You are loved today and every day.
In prayer He will show you the way.
So open your heart to the Lord,
He will listen with merciful love.
Spill out your weaknesses across the board,
just give them to God above.
God is patient, loving, and kind,
when you get angry He doesn't mind.
Trust in Him in all that you do,
even when things go wrong
He will never stop loving you.
Just sing of Jesus in a song.

Mary Jane Ferreira

Run to the Mountains

What a magnificent sight to behold,
Visions appear both vivid and bold.
Their strength, their beauty, ever enduring,
Reality is Hell, the lessons I'm learning.
My mind is ready, so ready to go,
The tears, my eyes, won't stop the flow.
The vastness of ranges will set me free,
Now the past must let me be.
If I begin now, I'll have a head start,
Before it engulfs the whole of my heart.
The ghost of darkness just holds me and grins,
As I dream of running, running to the mountains.
There are no chains, no shame, no fear,
That's why I run to get so near.
One day my journey will find its end,
On that day, I will find a friend.

Charmaine M. Heimes

The Cold

The bitter, biting, shivering, cold wind
Gives me an icy slap, and piercing cold
Awakens senses dulled by slumbrous warmth
To cognizance of winter's full import.

The tragicomicality of life,
Unseen in warmth, is seen in winter's cold.

Just as the trees and shrubs are stripped of leaves,
The characters become denuded of their facades.

Nature, alive with summer's color, dies,
Except for evergreens and sunset skies,
As winter comes with deathly pall of gray,
Necrotic colorlessness rules the cold.

Ally Windsor Howell

Sea Bound

For rocks and sea, locked in a timeless duel,
Salt mist, bird shriek, and freshening breeze,
Sea-fevered longings never cool.

The golden plains stretch out their arms to me,
But ardently my troth long since was plighted.
I'm bound forever to the sea.

The rock threw back the foaming wave.
For one brief moment waters calmed.
The mermaid green of silent sea was seen.

There from the streaming, battered rock
The jewel green depths did call me down.
Sea-trusting into emerald cool I slipped.

Virginia C. Von Colditz

The Empty Cross

Why do I see those tears falling down?
Why do you kneel there on the ground?
Why does that cross have meaning to you?
Is there something for me to share there with you!

Answer me, answer me, what have you found!
Why do you kneel there on the ground?
Why does that cross have meaning to you!
Tell me all about it, let me share it with you.

The empty cross on Calvary,
The empty cross means so much to me!
The empty cross, Christ died for me.
The empty cross, Christ set me free.

The empty cross, the blood stained tree.
That's where Christ lived and died for me.
He carried his cross day by day.
And poured out his blood to wash my sin away!

That's why you see these tears falling down.
That's why I kneel here on the ground.
That's why that cross means so much to me.
Come kneel here beside me, and Christ you will see.

Lawrence E. White

Song of the Unknown Soldier

I am the boy who was called upon to fight,
And die in a far-away land.
I fought for my country,
I fought for what was right,
and fell with a gun in my hand.

Yes, I am the unknown soldier
Of everlasting fame.
I've earned the name, "America."
"America" is my name!

I fought in the jungles, I fought upon the sea.
I fought in the trenches of Hell.
I won every fight, and I died for liberty.
My final resting place is where I fell.

No victory parades for me;
No garlands for my head.
My only decoration is my tunic stained in red!

Yes, I am the boy was called upon to die,
And earn everlasting fame.
They call me the unknown soldier.
Remember, remember my name!

Edward J. Barrett

The Bug

Thank you for letting me know,
   that I am not a pesty bug.
Maybe I am a good bug,
   and if I was,
I know where I'd hang around all day,
   on your shirt.
I would crawl up your ears,
   and whisper kisses.
And buzz you 'til you notice,
   I'll stare 'til I melt.
And when I get tired will crawl,
   in your pocket for a rest.
Warmth of your chest,
   and close to your body,
Will keep me from winter chill.
   close by your heart,
Is where I rest! While your heart beats,
   playing music to my ear.
So my sweet don't block me out,
fore this is where I want to be.

Nirja Leon

Mother's Day Wish

This Mother's Day wish is just for you,
hoping you day is happy and not at all blue.

It's for everything you do or have not yet done,
so these words are especially for you, hoping you have lots of fun.

I love you for always being there,
wether it was for fun or my time of despair,

I love you for being the mom you are,
and taking care of me, near and far.

Thom Whitney

Waiting to an End

Rosebud was our cow on the farm.
Wild raspberries smell and taste so good.
I wish Life was so sweet and good.

There's a locked up building dark and cold.
That came from my childhood.
Where's that Funny Little girl?

Shyness seems to have stolen her.

Dancing, singing in my mind,
Hoping nobody heard it rhyme.

Sweet blissfulness of thought
At least there I won't get caught.

Forgiveness is sweet as candy.
Maybe it will come in handy.
Allowing me to stop waiting for it to end.

Julie A. Nord

Eye of Life's Storm

No clouds were in sight. It seemed like an ordinary day
until it started to rain so hard you couldn't see ahead of you.
Then, just as quickly, the sun came out behind the clouds.
It's strange how the weather is intermingled in God's
plan for His Creatures and Creation.
The eye of life's storm knows what is in store for us
because this eye is God.
Thunder is another way of His communicating with us to
let us know He is never far way from us. He is as near as a
whisper of a prayer, a kind word, song of praise,
even the very thoughts of our hearts.
The streaks of lightning are His beacon in our darkest night
to make us aware of God's promise that He will never
leave or forsake us.
Should we promise less to Him?

Mary Allen

Life's Strength

You dream about a future so full of success,
That you are driven to become the best.

Working to get to that point in life
Where you can be comfortable
And not have to think twice.

You set a path for yourself to follow,
Without knowing what may stand
In your way come tomorrow.

Don't let the challenges in life
Distract your direction,
For the challenges are only
For your protection.

Don't move too fast,
Take it slow,
Follow your heart,
Your dreams will show.

R. A. Carter

Warm My Heart

I open my heart to the chilled winter breeze
it whispers to me of the past worries,
heartbreaks, and wounds to my pride I rush forward,
away from the whispers on the wind
and begin to see promises of the future
dreams fulfilled, healing of wounds,
and love I want to stand still
and enjoy this new feeling as the wind cools my skin
with you to warm my heart

Misty Pierson

Journey

In every journey there is a mountain to climb,
In every journey there is a rough road and a smooth road,
In every journey there are storms and there are sunsets,
In every journey there is sorrow and there is joy,
In every journey there is failure and there is success,
In every journey there is weakness and there is strength,
In every journey there is work and there is play,
In every journey there is confusion and an answer,
In every journey there is noise and quiet moments,
In every journey there is fear and there is hope,
In every journey there is a stop and a go,
In every journey there is an end and a beginning,
In every journey know that God is carrying you in the palm of
His hands—through life's mountains. . . .

Chona Cruz

Life's Storms

In the midst of the storm the billows toss high
And my boat seems, Oh, so small.
I'm tossed about by every wave;
It seems I'll be drowned by all.

With frightened gaze and windswept hair
I rush to the pilot's room
"We're bound to die!," I fairly shout.
I'm stunned by the depth of his calm.

"'Tis nothing we've not been through before.
This vessel will weather the storm"
And somehow knowing He's in charge
I suddenly feel safe and warm.

'Tis the same through life's many stormy tests,
'Though Satan threaten to harm
When it seems I'm about to go under and drown,
God shelters me with His arm.

Carol J. Newbraugh

Chess Game

I guess I'll enjoy life while it lasts,
Got one chance, better enjoy it before I pass.
'Cause if you ain't prepared to die for something
There's no reason to live, nowhere to be going.
Life is a mystery to be lived, not a problem to be solved;
A billion questions, no answers, just fight 'til ya fall.
So do what you can to reach fortune and fame
Just keepin' perspective, just a piece of a chess game.
A person's life seems like an obstacle course,
Blind folded, so you get hit hard not knowing the source.
Just about to climb the wall, but I need a helping hand,
Reach up, get kicked in the face, fall back to the land.
It really hurts, but I get up and try harder
Always getting knocked down, but I keep getting smarter.
Getting closer each and every time,
I'm gonna make it, keep being tough, Lord, it's all fine.
When I get there, you'll push me and I won't move,
Pain and suffering is a part of life, finally understood.
Like X, my work still ain't done, I still have fears,
Gotta look past now, after the fears, come the cheers.

Fred Green

Mother Night

What lies out there?
Who knows what evil stares?
I look into the dark,
Right before the day completely parts,
And as I look through the trees,
I feel there's something staring back at me . . .

It gets darker . . .
I can now see the moon and stars:
So beautiful and bright.
I see the Big Dipper, Pegasus, and Orion,
But wait . . . I hear something.
No, it's just the wind and leaves rustling.

I feel someone dangerously close,
I turn around, maybe it's a ghost.
Someone's calling my name.
Who are you? I say.
Daylight approaches, my child.
And I reply, I'm coming, mother night.

Brandi Cunningham

This Place

I live in my town right here, in this place
beware, they say, it's not all ribbons and lace!

In a brick house, one in a row,
Out back there's a place for my flowers to grow!

Neighbors are friendly and helpful to me,
there's just no other place I want to be.

Each day I look to the Heavens, and pray for grace,
that people will find the good in this place.

Here in this town, built up with "faith"
this is where I want to live.
Right here, in this place!

H. Renee Meiskey

Don't Grieve for Me

Don't grieve for me for now I'm free
To follow the path already laid for me,
I took his hand when I heard him call,
I turned my back and left it all.

I could not wait one moment more,
It was time to follow those that have gone before.
Tasks left undone must stay that way,
I found true peace at the end of the day.

Be not burdened by your sorrow,
I wish you all the joys of tomorrow,
My life's been full, I've savored much,
Good friends, good times, a loved one's touch.

So, I ask you again not to grieve for me,
For I'm truly where I longed to be.

Valerie Honey

Notorious You

You are notoriously splendid
Nothing less than gratitude intended.
The mere luck of chance
To set my boundless soul to dance.
You fill my smile with chattering mirth,
To rest my body through a timeless birth.
Do you feel what I feel?
And to know that these feelings are real!
All the fame and fortune may be glorious,
But it is nothing without you, notorious.
Your whole being is truly mystique;
That's why you're so wonderfully unique!

Beatrice Hall

What Dreams Are Made Of

An ocean's a dream, or it may seem.
A place known to man, a place where you can.
A reality fantasy land.

A warm gentle sweet smelling breeze.
A brilliant bright gleaming ray of sun shining upon the open sea.
Children of all races at play on a crystal, clear blue ocean day.
Adults, young and old, holding hands and walking along the way.

Kids playing in the snow white sand, in depth that has no end.
Crushed colored shells and white ocean foam in between your toes.
Sand castles so sweet, not a care we need meet.
It must be a dream, for here there are no woes.

So take who you can, a stranger to this land.
Hold him, love him, cherish him, show him.
That this is a place where dreams are made of.
No other place like this can be found.
Open your eyes, for Heaven is all around.

Susan M. Cebula

The Storm

The storm stood over the hills,
Sending ahead of it cold and chills,

The wind shook the tall trees,
And bent the pines upon their knees,

The clouds descended down the mount,
The sun's shine was blotted out,

The air became frigid, freezing and cold,
The wind blew on, fierce and bold,

Showing forth His awesome power,
God, from who's anger the creatures cower,

The snow was let loose in a blinding rush,
Blanketing every branch and bush,

The wind whipped and howled and moaned,
The trees snapped and cracked and groaned,

But suddenly, the storm abated;
The earth seemed breathless as it waited,

The wind kept blowing on,
And soon the storm was gone.

The valley looked glad to see it go,
As the sunshine sparkled on the fresh fallen snow.

Jenny Terhune

The Summer I Grew Up

I was eleven years old last summer.
My mother was sick and needed my help.
My silly sisters would remain children,
But I would become an adult.
My mother had brain surgery.
I became "mother's helper."
I tried in every way
To be supportive and encouraging.
I did many chores—cleaning, cooking, and making beds.
I played with my sisters to keep them busy and quiet.
I walked to the store for bread and milk.
It would hurt my mother to say this,
But I wasn't a child that summer.
The grueling pain that she went through
Was like knives stabbing in the back.
I felt the misery that she endured,
But I learned from this experience.
I saw life in a whole new light.
I saw hope and encouragement, patience and courage.
I learned this all from the best—my mom!

Kelly Leonard

My Diamond Necklace

First, the sweet baby smell and loving hugs and kisses
fill your heart with wonder.
The small snuffling sounds . . . the soft
cooing hang in the air like beads of diamonds.
Too soon, the children's cries of delight, coming home from school.
Cookies all around. Each sound a precious gem.
As they grow older, each with their own identity, to hear them
laughing together as they bond in some communal work effort.
This is music to my ears.
The pride and joy of their accomplishments is the silver
thread that strings the diamond beads together.
No one may beg, borrow, nor steal the diamond necklace
they have formed and stays in the safety deposit of my heart.

Evelyn Hunter

Life

The pain, the misery, the loneliness
all reach out to grab me,
to grab me and pull me down to my dungeon,
my dungeon where my pain and sorrow hide,
the sorrow that no one can stand,
sorrow that no one should have to live with,
the pain that constantly tortures me,
pain that drives me to my death,
life.

Trisha Specht

No One to Turn to

What do you do when things go wrong?
Who can you talk to ease the pain?
A feeling overcomes you like you don't belong
It drags you like a ball and chain

Who do you go to for advice?
Is there someone who you can trust?
Will they turn their back and be cold as ice
or blow you away like bits of dust

Is there no one to turn to?
Will I always be afraid?
Of what's ahead of me, will it come true?
Shall I wait hoping the problem may fade?

Why must life be so blind
That no one knows where it takes you
It's like a game; it plays with your mind
God give me the strength to get through

Catherine Craft

Love's Afraid

She left her wings in Heaven
to be reclaimed again one day

She flew down to be with me
She landed in my arms

She glows with innocence
never has a smile gleamed so bright
never has a hand as soft as clay
reached for me in this way

She's like a living flower
Delicate and pure are not good enough for her
Sunsets, stars nor precious gems can compare

Love is afraid to describe her
She is beyond what love can offer

Beauty weeps with sorrow in envy of her

She is sent to me as a gift.
I am past complete
I am terrified with happiness

Teresa Tebib

Poor Little Moon

Satan's fire rampaged through cities, cascading from town to town,
burning everything down. Nothing remained but the ground.

The Earth lay scorched in cinder, its blackened face;
for every creature that ever lived, once a magnificent place.

It was gone like the wind and knew no more;
the rage of mankind had deadened its core.

They came from the pits of Hell:
Man-made demons released from their shells!

Bulleted casings twenty-feet high,
stabbing as thousands arced across the skies!

The instrument of destruction was on hand,
built by the "brilliance" of man.

They ran and they ran, but no one could escape
the inferno that swept through as "Auld Lang Syne"
played on. How ironic, the end was near.

Some laughed, some cried, some played, and some tried,
and only the little ones knew better.
But the others they lied and because of that, we all died.
The end was here. Poor little moon.

   Mike Kotowski

Where Do You Go

Where do you go.
Where do you go.
How could you know would it be that I should grow.
You wanted me when I was new,
the care you gave to see me through
Where were you, where were you.
When I found you was it only me,
an image, a farce that only I could see.
Reality my cell shall ever be.
Padded forever, inseparable for our eternity.
Forgiveness but by whom this key
is needed for my room in order that I may grow.
Where do you go, where do you go.
All alone in our cells, side by side shall be dwell.
Each is a motionless well and in our minds is our Hell
please help me release the spells.
Thirty years have I wept. Why am I so inept?
The time for you has crept, while I have just stepped.
Your bars shall be my rail, your clouds and the gale.
For now I will sail for I can never fail
I can never fail.
Where do you go, where do you go.
Forgiveness, but by whom?
This key is needed for my room.
In order that I may grow, where do you go.

   Eric A. Olsen

Is There?

Who believes in something after death?
For what to justify the pain and suffering!
Is there something after death?
Will we be just another rotting corpse, life distilled?
Hollow after this Hell on Earth we spend.
Those that say our soul is released to go anywhere
And everywhere, no different than you or I.
Do we go where one's human mind has always wanted?
Realms life a fairy tale, or space, an endless episode
Of stars and Mars, the field
Of dreams our elusive mind left us with,
Or are we stuck in time right when we die?
Who can say? No ones been there,
Done than, and come back to tell the tale.
Peace be at one amongst us all,
For one day we all hear the call.

   S. Vincent Johnston

Twisted Agony

It started out with calling names
Just a little fun and games
Humiliation reddened her face
Always the one put out of place
She closed her eyes and began to pray
Perhaps she would fit in another day
Teardrops fell upon her bed
As crazed thoughts ran throughout her head
Whisper, whisper, little voice . . .
Dare to listen? She had no choice
See the darkness, feel the burn
In this black hole, there's no return
Stepping through the gates of all infinity
Trapped in thoughts for all eternity
What more can be achieved in life?
Held her breath . . . pulled out the knife
Pain and suffering dripped to the floor
Of which she would suffer no more
Words we say sink into the mind
And hateful hands can truly bind

   Bethany Hargett

For Matt

When I look into his blue eyes,
I see the wonder of his first Christmas.
When I see his smile,
I remember his sweet grin with only 4 teeth.
When I touch his dyed black hair,
I feel his strawberry-blond baby fuzz.
When I hear him speak,
I hear his first words.
When I look up to see his face,
I see his face looking up at me.
When I see his size 13 feet,
I remember his first steps.
When I look at my rebellious Teen,
I see the little boy he was,
I see the man he will become,
And I wouldn't have it any other way.

   Teresa Arnett

I Remember When

I remember when; full moon, snow falling,
Christmas coming, memories of you.
I remember when, tight hugs, deep kisses,
You said come on, but I went home.
I remember when, cushion line, together alone,
Yellow dog, Christmas presents.
I remember when; 10 years later, we met again,
GM picnic, never forget each other.
I remember when; fantasies fulfilled.
Broken bed, sunrise in your window.
I remember when; sleeping 'til noon,
Crazy about you, all the reason's why.
I remember when; your letter goodbye,
My broken heart, memories of you.
I remember when; the best sex I ever had,
The love I still feel for you, I will always remember.

   Helga I. Cavender

We Below Need Something Above

We below often think we can buy anything
But we can't buy love
Love is a serious thing, incomparable to a fling

Love's a beautiful gift from God above
If we had no connection to love
Life would be empty and a meaningless thing
Obviously we below need something above

   Spark Lee Gold

Is It Worth It?

Sometimes I sit and wonder why,
I even bother to try.
Nothing ever goes my way,
No matter what I say.
School and work are just too tough,
And as for sleep I just don't get enough.
New babies are born and people die,
And we all have to go wondering why.
The meaning of life no one will know,
Except for what others tell us so.
Am I the only one who feels this way?
Does it keep getting harder each passing day?
Is life really worth all the pain?
Is it possible to live and not go insane?
I guess in the end the pain is worthwhile,
Take the extra step and walk the extra mile.
Do something to bring a smile to someone's face,
Live at your own speed because life is not a race!

  Kristina Gonzalez

Quest of the Eons

My mind must wander through life's rough path.
To see the future or events elapsed.

To know its secrets and feel its pain,
To hope and pray all's not in vain.

It's who you are and how you'll be,
A life imprisoned without its key.

The key of life is in one's soul.
You must not look, you simply know.

So hold your memories within your heart.
It stirs your soul and oceans part.

  Rachel Glennie Collier

Faded Glory

Second hand, always ticking
Leading to the next minute
Every which one chipping
Chipping away at your life
Cutting through the years
Just like a dull knife
Though your pain and strife
Second hand, never stops
If something done wrong
You can't bend time, no matter how strong
Make no mistake,
Your life is at stake
Something done right
Frozen in time, never forgotten
Second hand, one-million times fold
You're getting old
Down to the nitty gritty
Father time have pity
Second hand, still ticking
Make good while you're still kicking

  Johnathan L. BullComing

A Greater Friend

A greater friend could not be mine, had I
With trembling fingers shaped your form
From the still earth
And the salt air, and the
Smell of the pine-forest rising with
The blue jay's jagged song, high in the boughs of the seas
Hesitant—in the days when the Earth
Was young, and the stars not born
In the morning.

  Robert W. Whitworth

Lonely Without You

With days so long and our meeting so near,
I wish I could hear your voice in my ear.
How I miss you, I miss you, my dear.
Lonely am I without your words.
Your letters make me fly like the birds.
So here I sit, my mind does wonder.
Thoughts of you are all I ponder.
Across one Ocean and a Sea.
I will meet the person I dream to see.
Her voice is so soft and pleasant to hear,
Just a small part of why she's so dear.
We will walk together on the beautiful beach.
Our eyes will tell more than our speech.
With great hope the chemistry is right.
We look at the stars under a soft moonlight.
Fate is the path soon to unfold.
Time is the wait for words untold.
So until the wait is no longer here.
I miss you, I miss you, I miss you, my dear.

  Richard Todd

Flight

I traveled up high, high up out of reach
way beyond sadness, fright, and speech.
Away from the pain, the fear and their touch,
somewhere it just wouldn't hurt so much.
I left the cold ugliness behind,
I started to leave, a new place to find.

I became light, light as air,
free from worry, pain and care.
A happiness surrounded me,
of freedom very few will see.
A feeling, there are no words to tell,
a freedom from this Earthly Hell.
An answer sent from God to me,
to help me survive, to help me see.
He gave me a choice, to leave or to stay,
he let me choose, to have of my way.

I said to him, "I can't leave now,
they need me here, to help somehow,
to find a way to fix this mess,
and lead us to some Earthly rest."

  Valerie Mick

The Thoughts that Come with Silence

I sit here in this room in the silence of the day,
While my hopes and dreams seem to drift to far away.
There they go, my dreams, out the door,
I dread this silence and I can't take anymore.

I sit here alone, alone in this room,
Can you tell by my face that my heart's filled with gloom?
The silence of this place makes it even worse,
The love of my life has just given me a curse.

This love of my life who I'd love through and through,
Makes the hatred and anger begin to stew.
I'd love him forever and would have never let him go,
When he's nowhere near me, my life seems so low.

The tears are coming now and it's hard to keep them back,
I feel so very lonely now, because it's his presence that I lack.
I'd do anything in the world to feel him next to me,
But I guess this sadness comes for a reason,
That reason is we were not meant to be.

  Heather Skene

You

You are born into this world
with everyone loving and hoping for the best.
You are raised with loving brothers who become a piece of your heart and soul.
You grow up together, caring and loving each other,
having fun and a few fights.
You go on dates together and help them pick their life long mates, you think.
You move away from each other, a happy and sad time,
but we are all growing up, we are no longer nine.
You all start families of your own, all get busy, even to telephone.
You get a call, your brother's dead, it's John, cancer in his head.
At 33, how can that be, no one knew.
You cry, you get angry. After a while you let him go.
But remember him in your heart forever so.
You go on with your life, and you get another call,
your brother Steve, who's 38, is gone, and you think, how can this be.
Car crash, he flew fifty feet.
You go into shock, you cry, and after a while, you let him go,
But will forever remember him and love him so.
You go on with your life, you have kids of you own,
and a lot of times I just want to be alone.
You jump every time the phone rings, 'cause there is never any good news.
You have to go on living, but you think, how can you!
Then you hear the phone ring.
Nancy Ellen Ludwig

Lifetime

Dry leaves falling, fewer, fewer.
Wind whipped branches leaning, swaying.
Softly, footsteps walking, walking.
Daylight bringing wailing death near, stalking
nighttime fading into sunlight. Still no chances being taken.
Babe at last, head emerging, balking.
cold November, early morning. A child is born.
Holding back, despite all the pushing, rending labor,
wants no part of cold November. Dreads a world all asunder.
World now out of ugly war, new sheathed sabre.
Thrust unwilling into breathing on a cold November morning.
Calendar leaves flitting, flitting. November mornings passing fast.
Years are days and days are years. Babe no longer, youth gone yonder.
Woman living, working, being woman. Solemn wonder.
Gave herself a few new lives in labor, gave a few days to the past.
Nor a moaner or complainer, smiling, laughing, dreading thunder.
Wondering why? Wondering if it all was for nothing, much, or everything.
Cold Novembers bring anew old questions. Who will tell her?
Answers then nor ever coming. Waits and listens for the ringing,
tolling bells to tell her . . . time has come, the task is done.
Did I do well? Did I fail? Will the bells the answer tell?

Dry leaves falling. Fewer, fewer. Cold November wind a'blowing . . .
Bonnie Cullens

And God Whispered

Within the overgrown weeds in a dirty alley way red roses bloomed,
Changing the color of my day.
And God whispered . . . It's because I love you.
A large pastel rainbow changed the dark, blue stormy sky.
It filled my eyes with awe.
And God whispered . . . It's because I love you.
This man touched me with love so warm and so sweet.
We became one and my heart was complete.
And God whispered . . . It's because I love you.
Then a baby soft and new smiled in my arms as I held it close.
I thought this is perfect.
And God whispered . . . It's because I love you.
I heard the sounds of laughter from the yard as my children played.
Then they ran up to hug me with dirty smiling faces.
And God whispered . . . It's because I love you.
Through tears and wonder I realized your Son died for me all because
you wanted to set me free.
And God whispered . . . It's because I love you.
Deborah Yeryar

Nora

Mother of Ruben, Sebastian,
And Stephan
Who loves me much
Who gives help when needed
And takes care of me
Who brought me into this world
Who has faith in me
Who does laundry
And makes breakfast
Who encourages me
Ruben Caballero, Jr.

Love

I miss you
but you're not even gone yet
I think you're so special
but nothing has happened yet
I think you're sexy
but I don't know you yet
I still remember you
but nothings happened yet

You're a guy in my dreams
In my dreams you are so real
I will meet you one day
I'm getting so impatient
I really hate to wait
When will I finally meet you?
I want to know who you are

I miss you
Jamie Lewis

Clowns

If clowns should rule society
I'd have to run and hide
They'd scare me half to death, you see
I'd always stay inside
Their makeup and their squeaky shoes
Subduing everyone
They'd terrorize our cities with
Their clowny, rowdy fun
They'd transform children everywhere
To grow up just like them
And all our schools would turn out fools
Who copy clown mayhem
Our handshakes all would have a shock
Our flowers all would squirt
And if cream pies ran out, I'm sure
We'd end up throwing dirt
Be happy that the circus traps
Those pasty, smiley clowns
Our world is better off when it
Intelligently frowns
Sean P. Dudley

Catching a Wave

Current of the river
take me away.

Let your stream make the
safest way.

No more worries,
No more fears,

I can see my home
right over there.

You did well, I must
say; don't worry
I'll be back
another day.

Joshua Uriah Rodriguez

The Blessing of a Child

Teddy bears, rocking chairs, and toys galore,
Ice cream, Jell-O, and Kool-aid are only part of the repertoire.
Little things that tell you that children are around,
But there are far more important things concerning children to be found.
They are precious gifts from God; a blessing you might say,
From the day that they are born we love them more every day.
God expects us to train our children in the way they should go
By putting him first and letting him show!
This is an awesome task for parents you see,
Because we have to not only tell them but show them what they need to be.
Their small eyes are always gazing at us from afar,
For when others are fooled—our children know who we really are.
The Bible is the only instruction manual for raising children today
And it is of utmost importance we read it and we pray.
Without God's love and guidance in parent's lives all the way along,
Our children are destined to a life of eternal wrong.
Tell your child you love them and that Jesus loves them too!
Show them by the life you lead and example you set too!

Connie Brantley

A Meadow of Thoughts

On a cool spring morning as I gaze upon the meadow,
I see a million daisies all shining bright and yellow.
I feel the slight breeze as it blows across my face;
I don't think I'd rather be in any other place,
I caress the soft petals of the beautiful flowers;
I could lie here and dream for hours and hours.
I dreamily gaze at the bright blue sky
As my whole life flashes before my eye.
At times I see people who helped mold my life.
My parents, teachers, and friends were there for me
in moments of joy and strife, I see my grandmother as she passed away;
She told me to never go astray.
My grandfather taught me to always be kind,
And to always keep a good heart and mind.
I began to realize how these people influenced me;
If it weren't for them, the Lord only knows what I would be.
As I woke from my dream, all the flowers had ceased.
All things around me had no soul, no peace.
It occurred to me then that life is so short.
Like a flower, after death you rise no more.

Kara Mullican

My Dad

Some call you son, brother and friend,
We call you husband, papa, dad 'til the end

You've touched so many lives in so many ways,
I'll forever miss you for the rest of my days.

I'll miss so much about you, your jokes,
Your laughter—most especially those hugs,
The people who knew you, will remember your love.

Some say you're in a far, far better place,
Dad, you know me, I'm selfish, I just want to see your face.

People say God needed you, to help him out,
I'm not sure what all the hurry was about.

Dad, I thank you for always being there for me,
I wish I could have one more moment, but I know that will never be.

And I thank you and mom for teaching me good from bad,
I love you, I miss you, I'll be forever sad.

My heart has been broken in so many places,
I'll always remember your advice, your laughter and funny faces.

You made me a better person by being in my life,
I promise to take care of my mother, your partner, your wife.

I'll never hear you call me poochie again, I'm proud to call you dad, my father, my friend.

Lynn Nordland

Civil Star

Psalter of the sea,
Magic of the wand;
Courses life through me,
Victory be won.
To the bitter end,
Through the grief and woe;
Silently we send,
Message far to go.
Cannon shots be hurled,
Sing the last refrain;
Banners all unfurled,
Blood will make the stain.
Endless trails of night,
Light of day to come;
Aid us in our flight,
On our way back home.
Sail on through the veil,
Flow the silent run;
Stars be on our trail,
Majesty undone

Kelly Ford

Last Call

Birds singing, harmonizing
Warm, cool air rising
The sun hammering into our bare skin
Causes our thoughts to revel in sin
The clear, blue skies
Serenely reflected in eyes
Waves crashing
Hearts thrashing
Fever escalating
Thoughts of mating
Dreams reincarnated
Futures fated
Time whizzing
Energy fizzing
Early evening, sun setting
Soft petting
Moonlight comes
Soft, gentle hums
Nightfall
Last call

Patrick D. Edwards

Lesson of Love

Love knows nothing of distance
Love knows nothing of time
It only knows the feeling of
Two hearts beating in perfect rhyme,
It knows no race or color,
No creed, no boundaries, nor laws
It's sometimes unexpected
for whom your heart falls.
You may fight it for awhile
You may ponder on how you feel,
In the end you'll find it useless
And surrender to its will.
There are those who may be judgmental,
Close-minded, and often cruel
But allow your heart to love its love
And let happiness be your only rule.

Sandy McDonnold

You Are

Your hair is as black as night.
Your cheeks are as red as a rose.
And you are as sweet as an angel.

Taja Rebecca Towne

On Losing the Love of My Life

Arching my body forward, I search frantically for
you beside me on the bed.
I long to feel your comforting grip, your reassuring touch.
I long to smell your natural, freshly-shaven face.

As I clutch the shadows of nothingness,
I gaze aimlessly at the barren wall
Somehow it manages to connote captivity!
I am entrapped in this cold empty room.
I am becoming more claustrophobic by the moment!

Clinging to the sheets, I still keep an eye open,
my last hold on reality.
My breath comes in spasms.
This nightmare is overwhelming and I long for daybreak,
when I can rule this intense ordeal as fiction.
Yet the longer I wait,
the more I am beginning to realize that you are truly gone;
that no matter how much hoping and praying that I do,
you will not take your role beside me, not lie beside me again.
Sleep finally pervades.

Somewhere in my subconsciousness,
I come to realize that human beings thrive on the tangibility of things.
Our minds completely evade mystery.
This is why I find solace in my sleep, that never-ending sleep.

Deon Campbell

Scripted

An absentminded doddle
On the scrap of a forgotten artist's book.
I am amorphous, definitionless.
Awaiting pencil to contour limbs, confidence.
Voiceless without dialogue written, edited, approved.
Paralyzed without calculated and commanded action.
Searching for a character to animate, a plot to execute
A genre rendered certifiable by critics and pleasing by audience.

A fabricated life with directions, cast, climax, completion
Pre-assembled sense, pre-validated purpose—
A guide for the unwitting or backbone for the diffident,
A reservoir of peace for the
Ever-searching, wondering, calculating, preparing, planning, hoping mind
                                        to drown in.

Hilary C. Forster

Anamllovr

There was a baby bird that fell from its nest
and could not fly back, though he tried his best.
He searched for food and warm cover,
when other critters told him of the Anamllovr.

He pecked and he fumbled, stumbled and fell,
then happened upon a wishing well.
He drank until his thirst was quenched,
then looked up to see an old woman sitting on a bench.

She was surrounded by cats, dogs, and critters he'd seen,
but had been warned, those with four feet could be mean.

He was fragile and frail, so young to be alone,
he just wished he could fly right back to his home.
He needed help, you see, he broke his wings flying into a tree.

He watched the old woman as she fed all the critters,
and thought to himself she may not get bitter
at feeding a broken baby, as he, so he could get well and fly home free.

As he approached he felt a bit sad,
as if his idea might have been bad.
But the little old lady gave him a crumble of bread,
with a smile on her face and a kiss on his head.

Ramona M. Hammes

Missing You

Once we laughed together
by the Riverside.
And watched the little waves
lapping the shore.

Now I walk
along the banks
the waters very blue
and I am watching the waves
and missing you.

Judy Carole Harbin

I Wonder

What happens to the words I write
that goes beyond the type?
Are they far and few
and get lost in the hype?
Will I ever know the last few thoughts
that are absorbed in the night?
I wonder; I wonder
and can't help but imagine
the dreams that are cast
into the night.

Joseph Coniglio

Ghetto Girl

She's not your average girl
She struts with confidence
Sporting one white shoe
And one black boot

This girl puts others to shame
All the while controlling her domain

In a loud voice
Not a whisper
She shouts to the world
"This is my world, mister."

As she goes through her day
With a smile on her lips,
With a swing of her braids,
And a sway of her hips

There's flash in her style
No designer can fake
Because a Ghetto Girl
You cannot duplicate!

Joseph Mwanza Sumbi

One Lovely Rose

One lovely rose in the garden
Its fragrance so pure and true
Standing there in the sunlight
Reminding me of you

From the moment you entered this world
I loved you right from the start
I know I'll see you again someday
I believe it with all of my heart

And though you are no longer with us
Your memory will not fade away
You'll live forever in my garden
In my heart you will always stay

So for now rest quietly in my memory
And if ever the tears start to flow
Remember my heart is your private garden
And in it you will always grow

Carolyn S. Geeting

Who Am I

I stand in the driveway filled
With hesitation
Thanking the lord for one more visitation
who am I
As they looked through their window
And wave goodbye—I turn away and begin to cry
who am I
My god given right or, so I thought—
Reduced by the hypocrisy and rules of court
who am I
Their wants and needs drive me to achieve
Their innocent curiosity and questions lead me to seek knowledge . . .
So that I may provide answers—
Which may help them to discover understanding
who am I
I am and always will be . . . daddy

    Richard Serrano

Lifeline

I've climbed mountain tops and swam the ocean deep
I've birthed children, a love that's for keeps
I've witnessed breathtaking sunrises and the shimmering moon's glow
I've heard the sweetest songs and viewed the finest shows
I've tasted gourmet cuisine and drank exquisite wine
I've achieved momentous honors and had my time to shine.
I've walked deep valleys and swam mightily upstream
I've experienced rejection and lost sight of my dream
I've felt heartache and sat lonely many nights
I've heard deadly silence and seen appalling sights
I've pained with hunger in order to pay the bills
I've known embarrassment and humiliation more than my fill
Yet all is not lost Just part of the cost Of being refined through the fire
Which strengthens me when I tire
Memories making us bitter or better
Choices shaping or breaking our future
Simply existing, surviving, or truly living
Keeping to yourself or freely giving
I choose to fight the good fight and run the race to win,
One foot in front of the other, just begin.

    Vickie LaFlower

letter to my savior

why does it seem that bad things always happen to me?
all i want is to be truly happy.
i say that you are in my heart but my life continues to fall apart.
is it because my love is not true? is it because i don't have faith in you?
that's not true because i do. is it because i use your name in vain?
is it because i only come to you when i'm in pain?
if those are the reasons then i will change; my priorities will rearrange.
instead of looking for love in a man, i will look for love in you.
you have always loved me and i know your love is true.
i apologize for what i have done. today my new life has begun.
hand in hand i will walk with you. i know all my dreams will come true.
i realize why there was so much stress. you were just putting my faith to the test.
it's good to know that i passed and i assure you my faith will last.

    Brandi Holmes

Marriage Eternal

What will you think of me when you see my soul laid bare on the surgical tables of Heaven?
Disguise of flesh discarded in death,
disrobing all of my thoughts and deeds.
In your eyes of night and body of stars, will your disgust show,
I wonder?
Perhaps instead, compassion for my state will soothe the sunspots of emotion my
unclad soul exposes to the universe.
Will you be with me in death as we are in life?
Will we explore the depths of the next realm as we suffered greatly through the first?
Bathe me in your truth and heave me into the Abyss,
or keep me with you forever. Judge me now, my Love.

    Brian Schroeder

Where's the Love?

We are disrespecting our sisters
Back stabbing our brothers
Just one simple question
Where's the love for one another?
Many homeless people in the streets
Only a few call the shelter their home
It's good to help out others but
Where's the love for our own?
Parents no longer stay together and
Instead try to forget what they did
Someone was born to that union
Where's the love for our kids?
We want to be so much in life
At times we can be greedy
Little satisfaction with just enough
Where's the love for the needy?
Although each life has a different path
It's best to try and do right
The one above can solve it all
Where's the love for Christ?

    Tamura Freeman

The Art of Imagination

The art of imagination
Is nothing you want to lose
So consider this and be careful
When it comes your time to choose
Childhood, well so they say
Lasts only through your teens
But I believe, 'til your last day
It remains, if only in dreams
Whether you are 3 years old
Or a grandpa, very great
Imagination—in any form
Is kept—it's never too late
So express it somehow
And let it show
If you don't now
No one may ever know

    Megan Dawn Miller

Blossom and Grow

There's a person inside me
So desperate to grow
A flower ready to bloom
And it's beautiful, I know

I need to make my own mistakes
And to know I will survive
And to know above all else
I am good and I am alive!

I need to know I'll manage
And make it on my own
I need to know I'm good company
Especially when I am alone

I need to get to know myself
And come out from behind my mask
I need to be accepted as me
Is that too much to ask?

    Marlene M. Presnell

Soulmate in Time

Will I never find the love I seek
Will I never fill my soul that aches
Will I never feel a warm embrace
Will I never hold a hand
that so perfectly fits mine
Will you just be around the corner
or always pass me by

    Suzanne Nowak

A Journey from Nowhere

I've walked this road so much that I have sores on my feet, yet I refuse to quit;
there's a candle along the path that my Savior has lit.
Sometimes I tire and stray along the way;
I throw caution to the wind, yet I find myself the next day.

I know my journey ahead is still filled with pitfalls and tribulations,
yet this time I'm sure to reach my destination.

A place with many trials, with Heavenly bliss,
and now I see it was my inner self that, until now, I've missed.

The streets aren't paved with riches of gold,
but the greatest journey to travel is the finding of one's own soul.

  C. Douglas

The Clothed Servant

The sun has left the day
The transient moon awakens the night
half-hidden amongst the Heavens
drawing each spirit closer to God

So vivid, so near
Its dark recesses lay bare imperfection
revealing a servant, such as I
aspiring to Heavenly purpose

Poised, face to face,
the naked moon and I, hold our face toward God,
hoping to capture His Beauty
to bask in His love

Unobstructed by clouds
Free to cast off light
Assured that when clothed in the fullness of His Glory,
we can illuminate the sky

  Michelle Tayloria Kenner

The Poet

Like ancient, spoken chants, your words, they seem to dance.
The passion that existed inside of you was original and true.
Distant and hidden, your meanings were forbidden.
Your eyes were open to unimaginable sights,
but not to your inner most fights.
Drugs you did to expand your mind, answers that you could not find.
You were a legend in your own generation,
and in this one, a lasting sensation.
Forever your words will go on, as with each and every beautiful song.
Such an extraordinary poet and singer, your memory will always linger.
You've left an impression, like footprints in sand,
your legacy lives on by your voice and your hand.

  Candice Lee Smith

O' Sea Shore

O', Sea, O', Sea
The beautiful and wavering sea shore.
Far, far across the hillside a beautiful shore.
O', shore, O', shore beautiful shore.
Rise far beneath the eastern shore.
While listening a wind came up above and beneath the shore.
O', Sea, why is thy beautiful shore far? Far away the wavering shore.
Wave high the wilderly Wave.
Tall as a scenic mountain top the wave rose high.

O', Sea, O', Sea
Far, far away I saw the tiltering shore.
Quietly come a colorful wave wandering ashore.
Shore high, shore low with a soft thundering wind sound.
I heard a sea shore. Wilderly whispering far beneath the shore.
O', Sea, O', Sea, beautiful sea. The charming far shore.
I love the far, far wavering shore.

  Ozella Crusoe

My Heart Finds Rest

A couch soaked with my tears
I wrap myself in a blanket of fear
Afraid no one will be there
Wishing someone was here
As the end of my heart draws near

In my weaknesses
There remains your strength
Through all calamity
Comes rushing your peacefulness
For I escape
Yes, I escape
Into your holy presence
Lord, I thank you
For your faithfulness

At your cross
I find my resting place
I listen and learn of your grace
With my heart I seek your face
I now bow and give you all praise

  Michael James Cornett

Of Trying Times

Pure emotions flowing
Lingering through the day.
Bewildered of knowing
What to say.

Though things appear concealed
Sorrow will not stay.
The spirit will reveal
Love in a special way.

Even when, night falls
God of glory divine.
Will wipe away all
The tears, of trying times.

  Bernice Shaw

The Man Who Stole My Heart

In August 1999, a man stole my heart
He's one of a kind

Is a jack of all trades
He is king of all kings
Has a very gentle touch
Never let us part
Is always on my mind
This one is sharper than blades
Doesn't have a swing
I carry a special torch
We sit on the couch
He has a back porch
Is very wild
But now very mild
Also very huggable
He is very lovable

He is very smart
The man that stole my heart
Happy New Year's.

  Alice Stockner

Night Waves

Midnight moon upon the water
Waves reaching to one another
Going in their own directions
God's creation, his perfection
Curls and foam with darkness there
A peaceful feeling the world can share

  Linda J. Bridges

Children

When I look into my child's eyes, I'm overwhelmed with glee—
The sweetest little girl in the world, that is what I see.
She's Daddy's girl; I long to hear her laughter.
Happiness always for her, that is what I'm after.
So to all you parents, have you told your child you love them today?
They need to hear these words; it's the only thing to say.
God has blessed us, for the children have become our souls—
They look for our guidance, one of our primary goals.
So hug your children, be all that they may need—
It's our job to provide, it's truly the daily deed.
May all your loved ones be joyous, be thankful for this special gift—
Don't be weighed down with other problems, for families are the lift.

James Rollo

The Cowboy

The first chance meeting I had with the cowboy,
It was love at first sight.

He was quite a travelling man, with no intention of settling down.
He thought he had to make every rodeo around.

I never dreamed we would eventually marry,
or that his child I would someday carry.

He put the rodeo life behind him at the birth of our child
and became a loving husband and dad ever so mild.

The cowboy stays at home now,
but he still has his dreams of what might have been.

He reminisces of his past rodeo life,
but now the important things to him are his child and me as his wife.

If you ever by chance meet a cowboy beware,
because like me, you will come to care and for him to always be there.

Cindy Pace

My Invisible Soulmate

Whenever I take short glances at you
I see desire within your eyes burning so deeply
When I touch your skin lustful feelings try to creep in me
When the time comes for me to have to let you go
My legs are saying leave but my heart tell me no
When I hear your everlasting voice speaking so humble
It causes my hand to shake and my spirit to crumble
I dream of you daily and nightly as I try to sleep
But then I feel lonely knowing that you're not there makes me weak
Your love casts spells on me
and my heart is trying to make me rebel from my good ways
Nearing to be with you every hour, all day
All the passion I take in makes me want to endure
The capacity of your spirit looking like a dove, so pure
My love is forever with you and always will it be long
If you continue to be yourself and love me our love will forever be strong.

Shareka L. Campbell

Thank You, Daddy

Thank you for knowing when to say no despite my childish anger
and when to say yes despite my teenage reluctance.

Thank you for the lessons of hard work, honesty, and friendship.

Thank you for staying close enough to hear me call when I needed you
and far enough away to let me try my wings.

Thank you for asking about my day and my life
and for not offering unsolicited advice, guilt, or obligations.

Thank you for the memories of childhood,
the guidance of my teen years,
the freedom of adulthood,
a model for grandparenting,
and the serenity of aging.

Phylis Cranfield

Celebrate

Celebrate the "Young Love"
That brought your hearts together
Those early days were magic
The vows you made forever

Celebrate the "Demanding Love"
When children now share your lives
With hardly a moment for each other
And still your love survives

Celebrate the "Respectful Love"
You developed along the way
The sacrifices you each did make
To bring you to this day

Celebrate the "Comfort Love"
The golden age is here
Rejoice and count your many blessings
Embrace and call each other dear

Marcia Amonette

MS Musing

I am like a cliff swallow

fluttering about
on fragile feet

swaying
and
stumbling

but I can still sing

listen to
my song

Karen S. Allen

God's Child

Did you know you are God's child
you're made from His love
so soft, and so mild
He gave you a body
to walk on this Earth
He gave you a soul
to determine your worth
through your spirit
your faith He will test
and through your strength
your prayers He will bless
in your walk
many struggles will lay
but God is there
to help guide your way
and when on Earth
your time is done
you will be with your Father
and He with His son

Angela Michelle Biddle

Children

Children laugh
Children cry
They run
They jump
They sing
They play
Children dance
Children love
Children hurt
Children are
Precious angels
On loan from Heaven

Doris J. Foutch

My Life

I dedicate this poem to my family and friends who believed in me.

My life is a story of its own
No one understands or knows
The pain and sorrow I had to encounter
And the things I go through every twenty-four hours
Things I went through in the past
I bet some of you wouldn't last
No one could endure the pain I once had
Even if you had the chance
Because you would have more common sense
Not to fall into those kinds of traps
Like lost love, best friends, different things like that
My life is a big story
That is still untold
But few people know
What I really think inside and when it's questioning time I have to lie
All people see is a protective shell
A few special people can tell
Achieving for excellence is what I'm encouraged to do
My mother, father, sister, and brothers, too
They tell me go on to prevail, trust in the Lord and I will never fail

Laura Ann. Teixeira

Desert Rain, Here I Am

I carry on in life, yet one image prevails,
with thoughts of flight unable to carry
my images of desert rain in its trail.
Why is this so, I ask.
Not even a lover could find one's love behind a mask.
Is it myself in the desert, bent down on my knees,
with rain pouring over my face and strands of hair with no despair.
What does it mean, I often ask with a broken flask near
with no answer to calm my fears.
I'm no painter, or so I believe.
I'm no photographer, or so I believe.
I'm no film director, or so I believe.
I'm no writer, or so I believe.
Yet here I am, or so I believe, in a desert down on my knees,
with no answers to relieve my needs.
Yet here I am, with no rain, praying to God, who I've never believed.
Yet here I am, regaining faith,
when rain begins to fall from the Heavens above.
An angel appears to say but one thing.
Believe, for here I am.

Dion H. Hughes

The Image

October 31st is tonight, it's a night of fright and frills.
I am staring down a dark street, when I suddenly start to get chills.
The wind is howling, the leaves are rustling, going 'round and 'round.
From what I feel and what I see, the strong gust is north-bound
Then there was a sound that was so odd it stood out from all the others.
My instinct told me to run inside, and climb under the covers.
I was frozen there. I couldn't budge. I had to see just what it was.
My heart asked me, "Why?" My mind answered, "Because."
It was the sound of someone walking; their shoes tapping the cold street.
As I thought of what it could be, my heart began to skip beats.
I stood on my porch in the dark of night, hoping that I would see some lights.
All of a sudden the sound dropped, ten seconds later, the sound stopped.
I squinted my eyes where I thought the image would be,
then I saw something I wish I didn't see.
The image stood at my bottom step, and slowly towards the porch it crept.
In the middle of night, creeping in the dark, it was so silent it hushed the dog's bark.
I stood there, freezing, with curiosity, wondering,
"What did it want with me?"
Then it opened its mouth and said, "You! Now go to your loved ones, and bid them adieu!"
My eyes widened, and I choked on my breath,
Then I realized what the image was . . . DEATH!

Patrice McDonald

Multiple Sclerosis

Tell me your secrets, all and now!
for you're a ghost to the afflicted
who, in multiple relapses, dwell
until your life comes to light;
for humanity will no rest know
'til succor and success come.

Tell me your secrets, all and now!
for as therapy and symptoms contend,
and hope from funds smiles,
comfort in distress comes forth;
for humanity will no rest know
'til succor and success come.

Tell me your secrets, all and now!
for later, though, sooner than later
extinct'll your outcrops be,
and memories'll linger no longer;
for humanity will no rest know
'til succor and success come.

Theophilus Alozie

Demands of Death

Death must be joyful.
It must be peaceful.
It must be gentle.
It must be kind.
It must be restful and easy.
Death cannot be empty
and black
and wild
and boring.
Death must be as the wind,
gently flowing and free.

Cecilia McNelis

The U.S. Today

That Cuban boy Elian
Is not a big deal
But what is, is that
Poor people need a meal

In other countries
Kids are getting malnutrition
But instead of helping them
We're making gas price decisions

But what about Senior Citizens?
Why aren't they treated fair?
Why can't they ever get,
Decent health care?

Why do young kids join such
Wild, violent gangs?
Maybe they want the money,
"Ice," girls and fame

What's up with the U.S. today?
It's not ever safe for kids to
Go out and play.
What's happening?

Brittany Solomon

Innocence

Too much hurt, too much pain
Innocence in the eyes of a child
The black eyes, the bruises they hide
Innocence in the eyes of a child
A single tear, a hope of love
Innocence in the eyes of a child
All is quiet, the crying has stopped
We bury the innocence of a child. . . .

Betsy L. Walker

Psalm of the Winds

The mystical choral of the ascending winds
bloweth thy divine prophecy
Through the most desolate and lonely depths of the world.
The wind, speaks of thy deliverance, Oh, Lord,
who receiveth the perishing soul into the vastness
of thy waiting hands.
Swiftly, on great invisible wings, the wandering wind passes
through remote and strange silent regions of mountains; far
over distant plains forgotten, except for the constant shining stars.

The futile heart, in dreary despair and withered hopelessness,
is already accepted in the splendor of the courts
of the highest of kings.
The hushed silence of eminent rocks and princely snow-adorned trees
remain in waiting reverence of thy omnipotent majesty.
Every longing soul, though cast down into the fearful longness
of night is cherished in thy watchful sight.

Prayer is the only consolation to the waiting soul.
The most highest glittering snow crowned mountain, even unto
the meek and lowly hills, kneel beneath thy supreme scepter.
Why should the trembling heart then be fearful of the shadowed valleys
which are cast by the tremendous wings of thy realms of angels.

If all things of nature devoutly proclaim thy perfect divinity,
The glorious power of our minds should be more exalting.

Andrew Clarke

A Man's Weaknesses

Her giving up on our love was unspoken.
My cry out was of a heart . . . a heart now broken.

Our last words to each other were of our feelings.
We parted . . . I closed out . . . no time for healings.

Yes, we parted ways—
Now once again I'll be lonely . . . lonely for days.

What I miss the most is her gorgeous brown eyes.
Of her leaving me . . . now my love and passion dies.

Growing from boy to man, I never did shed a tear.
She has came and left from my life . . . and now I feel a sense of fear.

My heart feels heavy and weak from sadness;
I fear now of never loving, despair, and a streak of madness.

I sense now what was a loving heart will now die,
And now for the first time in my life . . . I sit and I cry.

Mondre Lee Wilson

Clare Marie

Every day, when my daughter calls at 6:45 a.m. and says,
"Father dear, your loving daughter," I realize what a lucky man I am.
She always says, "How are you?"
Now, that may not seem like much to you, but since I have
no one else who cares about me, I look forward to her call every day.
She's now with child and that in itself makes me very proud.
However, I wonder if she'll still have time to call her dear old dad.
I sure hope so, for she's all I have in the whole wide world.
But when God makes her a mother, will she still have time for her father?

Well! The baby's come and it's a girl, a beautiful six-pound baby girl.
She's probably going to be the most loved baby
in the whole wide world, and spoiled rotten.
I'm so proud of my daughters, a son, and a big black dog.
So I gained rather than lost, and that's good as it should be.

Now the Lord's taken my daughter with Him up in Heaven.
She doesn't call every day and I miss that very much.
But evidently God needed to be served, and eternal happiness
is everlasting for her. My love had grown stronger with her passing
and we do talk every day, and that's what a father needs.

Robert J. Pivec

Listen All!

Listen all to what I say
and choose wisely what to do.
The Earth is falling all apart
and you ask this is the fault of who?

You, my dears, must right the wrongs
of those who have come before
and clean the rivers and the skies
and never ask what for.

The Earth is precious to one and all
and must be treated properly.
if not for you and not for me,
then for our children to see!

Brandy McCall

Mother

I often reflect, to what you say.
How we can't go back in time,
not even for one day.
It's okay you wouldn't love me anyway.

With a heavy sigh,
I look up relieved.
To say goodbye,
Having no tears in my eyes.

Friends and family ponder why.
Gazing in disbelief.

But, remember;
Big boys don't cry.

Chester Mark Clough

No Rest

Today I sit and wonder,
So many things to dream,
A million thoughts to ponder,
A million thoughts it seems!
Running through my mind
At a pace I cannot keep,
I wish I could catch just one of them,
'Cause then I'd steal its sleep!

Nikki Brugnone

Flowers

Beautiful
Fragrant
Blossoms
Delicate
Petals
A gift from God.

Lisa Smith

Pure Love

Eighteen years today have passed
With the woman I love
I'm meant to last . . .
So many things
We've been through in life
The good, the bad
We held strong a fight . . .
Memories of joy, sorrow, and fear
Together forever
We'll still beat them, dear . . .
A short note may I add
For time still to come
I'll love you forever
And forever as one
Happy anniversary, dear

Sal Gianni

Angel Boy

Gift of life, the world his footstool, small and precious this Angel boy of mine.
To school with trust giving teacher's a hug or touch, quarrels with
others, tears flowing, rising like the rolling sea, aching eyes,
raw pain, forgive me please.
Camping under the stars the sky for his blanket and the warm earth for
his bed, moonbeams covering his face, gleaming on his hair, touching his
brow with a grin. Dreaming of castles and secret passageways,
foreign countries, other planets and friends.
Awaken to the soft sound of rain, mud puddles, frogs,
a rolling lake and fish jumping high.
Climbing mountains, gathering wildflowers, kicking rocks and watching birds fly.
Winters snow pure and white, building a snowman and borrowing Papa's
favorite tie. Drawing a beautiful masterpiece just for Nanny,
knowing no self-defeat, always reaching.
Whispering his love for his baby brothers and mother, his example they
share. Profession of Faith, water cool, the family watching as God
smiles with love and care. Life is but a shadow, a revealing shadow, as
my Angel boy grows into a young man,
the Great Giver of Life, with love overflowing, holding ever so tightly to his hand.

Jo Rogers

My Heart

By the grace of God;
for the nine months I carried you buried inside of me
as you grew and developed, He placed you "beneath" my heart.
When you were born into this world, upon my first hold of you,
I placed you "on" my heart.
Through many playful sessions we encountered
I would raise you above my head,
smile up at you and got laughter in return
as I placed you "above" my heart.
Looking back over the majority of the photographs that we took together,
you were always placed on my left to be "next" to my heart.
As the years pass by and you mature and become independent of me,
once again with the grace of God, until my last breath is taken and my
contractional beats cease, you can always find your place "in" my heart!

Sherry J. Walls

The Paradox of Ascension

Of sour dreams and misbegotten fantasies
What use of imagination if it's shackled to time?
Like Atlantic ships without buoyancy or earthbound ravens tasting sky . . .
What may become of this withering mind?

Of all its reflections and indoctrinated perspectives
Which ones were the teachers that made him its student?
Which lessons were worth his sacrificial blood?
All of them I imagine

James K. D. Cole

Race of Life

It seems as if I lose again, every time I try to win
Even though I never cheat in the race I always get beat.
I'm always last to get picked in the race of opportunity
Instead of looking at my achievements, you look at my failures.
Instead of looking at what I have become, you look at what I used to be.
Instead of helping me achieve my goals you try to steal my pride.
Instead of trying to build my courage you try to hurt my inside.
You never want to face the fact that one day, I will beat you.
And I will take everything you've become
And use it as a peaceful solution
When I beat you I will surely succeed.
And all the unhappiness you will heed
But I will not kick you when you're down
I will extend my hand and lift you off the ground
And in this race of life I will,
I must, and I will
Forevermore use my speed.
And in doing so I will succeed.

Ashanti E. Barber

I Keep Walking

The night is dark and unforgiving
The day I stepped out of daily monotony
The darkness surrounds me like a shroud
I closed my eyes and started to dream
A dream like no other
The darkness slips in to my soul
It pollutes my mind and being
I start to cry as I see visions
My mom, my kids, my whole family
I turn and walk away from them
From everything I know
From everything I love
As machines ring the sounds of the end
I keep walking into the darkness
And cannot turn back
My lungs breathe their last breath
I keep walking into the darkness
Never looking back to my life.

Erica Christine Jagust

Full-filled

Amidst the clouds and subtle winds,
A hawk is soaring high,
And then my restlessness begins,
Oh, how I wish to fly!
It may not be a flight in air,
But just to steal away,
And if I ever choose to dare,
What place, my head, to lay?
I neither sleep, nor seem awake,
My mind a muddled daze,
I cannot find the path to take,
The air is thick with haze.
Many dreams lie unfulfilled,
Inside my shaken core.
Is it what my heart has willed,
Or should I want for more?
All at once, my reverie,
Is broken at the glance,
That my tot's upon my knee,
And she has filled her pants!

Catherine M. Rosine

Nature in the Sky

A deer and a doe are dancing in the sky.
Jumping and leaping, I wonder why?
I lay on my side all the day,
Because the beauty took my breath away.

Brandon Aaron Elder

Seasons

In the springtime of our loving
When everything was new,
Mid High School fun and classes
I fell in love with you.

In the summer of our loving
Those busy hectic years
Of marriage, home and children
And war—with lonely fears.

In the autumn of our loving
We filled our empty nest
With hobbies, friends and travel
And a new home here in the west.

Now 'tis the wintertime of loving
With memories old and new,
After all our years together
I still reach out to you.

Alice R. Marks

To Marry a Friend, To Love a Wife

At times I wonder immersed in bliss, where you hide your wings.
An angel gave you to me, to love above all things.
A task simplified by my love for you.
Love is a pain I gladly endure, my life I'll give up for you.
To hold you close is never enough, nor is life without you.
I often wonder how could it be, greater my love grows for thee.
Show not your eyes to mine, for my heart aches with love for you.
Eyes cannot endure beauty meant for the heart.
Your eyes are so gentle, your smile so true.
God says, "It's perfect, my son, this gift I give to you.
So hold her close, and love her as I do."
I will my Lord, for I love her too!
For if grace could ever walk this Earth, by my side I know it stands.
Forever we walk through this life, together hand in hand.
If God should ever ask me, did I enjoy my life,
Can I look past the tears, the pain, the sorrow, and strife?
I would proudly stand before him, always knowing one thing is true.
My life was well worth living,
Because I spent it loving you.

Eric Coleman

My Heart Refuses to Say Goodbye

Sadness embraces every crevice of my heart,
Constantly reminding me of a love torn apart.
It's easy to say it's over, but much harder to realize,
Just when you thought you've won everything, you see you've lost the prize.
Your mind may not remember, but your heart still holds the memories,
From every loving moment, to your last heartfelt pleas.

It's difficult to say goodbye when you're still holding on,
To every kiss goodnight, to making love at dawn.
When all that seems important just doesn't mean as much,
Being angry with your self for still remembering every little touch.
It's easy to say goodbye when your heart doesn't know such a lie,
In truth my heart refuses to say goodbye.

Chari Fulton

Things I Am Thankful For

Four walls around me windows to let the sunshine in a door to the outside
to see God's beautiful creation, legs to walk on with help and that I can
still go outside sometimes, a heart full of Jesus and His love—friends
to share him with—a family that loves me as much as I love them. For my
church, I'm thankful that I can still take care of my personal needs and
cook my food sometimes. God has been so good to me, he answered so many
prayers, and he never leaves me.

I am thankful that I have one good eye to see and can still read some and
enjoy living so much. Even though there is great physical pain sometimes I
am thankful for relief when it comes.

Only God knows all the things in my heart and how thankful I am for His
guidance and love in everything.

I can't begin to tell the half of it. How God could love us so is beyond understanding.

Alma Baker

Look into My Eyes

The eyes are a window to your soul

They can't lie about who you truly are

So look into my eyes and see who I am

See past the man I show you and see the boy I am

As the layers unfold you will learn things that I never told you

You will understand how I see you and how deep in my heart you are

You will understand like never before and once you get past the fear

You will accept what I have told you and take me into your heart

Then I will be truly happy

Joseph Andrew Spadaro

The Pond

The pond is like looking glass
With life on both sides
The mirror for a surface
Reflects what we have inside
To see all its beauty
That is around at anytime
Now that is a blessing
Not to is a crime

The life below its surface
Has its own tiny world
I watch the little fish hide
Where the algae is curled
So much like out here
They try hard to survive
To me this pond
Is very much alive

Elizabeth Cannafax

Love

Love can happen
anytime or place.
To anyone
no matter your color or race.

Love can be gentle
and beautiful too.
It can be meaningful
to each of you.

Love is an emotion
that everyone can feel.
And someday you'll find
that what I say is real.

Nancy A. Edwards

The Jester

The princess is not in
Her castle destroyed
Her moat blood red
From tears she has shed
Of lost love and hate
Of friendships unreal
The princess confused
How should she feel?
She turns to court jester
Masked hate
He beckons her smiling
She holds his hand
Swept into a world of terror
All she sees is jester
Making her laugh
When she's really crying
But he leads her into the confusion
Not letting go
But when she is finally at the peak
She finds herself alone

Kathleen Shaw

Life

As the seasons change . . .
Life changes.
As the leafs fall from the trees,
like the tears rolling off my face.
As the sun goes down a little earlier,
darkness fills my soul.
As the summer days turn to winter haze,
depression starts its journey.
Walking though my head . . .
The fog rolls in and I can't find my way.

Deatra Young Duncan

Questions of a Lover

Where does your mind wander,
when it is overcome with passion?
Or is it subject to passion at all?

For whom does your heart long,
when it longs for someone?
Or does it long at all?

What governs your body,
when it pulsates with love?
Or does it love at all?

Follow your heart!
For it is powerful and conquers all.
The object of your affections desires you;
do you desire him?

Open your heart!
Fill his soul, his thoughts, his body.
Acquaint him with the taste of your passion,
your longing, your love.
You shall not be taken for granted.
Permission grants ascension.

Andy Barbo

A Walk on the Beach

I traveled through life going the wrong way
thinking will I get a promotion, will they increase my pay
can I afford a new car or a house by the bay
because next to the ocean is where I'd like to be
with the sun shining on my face and the sand under my feet
yes walking on the beach that is the place for me

How could it be so easy to give up these things for he
it wasn't so hard when my mind was made up you see
because after it was all said and done I knew I was free
now I realize I gave up nothing but gained everything
even without these things I still have the same name
I don't travel the wrong way anymore that's all that's changed

Because after I think about it I can still get the same things
I already got my promotion and when I'm gone I'll get the increase in pay
I don't need a car because I have wings living in God's house by the bay
now Heaven is my ocean and the sun shining is my faith
I still walk on the beach with the sand under my feet
but now I have the son of man walking next to me

Shane Tucker

The Desert

This sunset is not so cold it is warm, often exceedingly warm
And it is not so lonesome here.
The wind still howls true! Sometimes by day and by night,
But, I find not so much as a hair out of place.

Where I have arrived only today is truly a happy habitat
Would the images all yellow and pink and green tell me otherwise?
At dawn, and as well at twilight's glow
Purple shadows appear to have a tinge of gold though ever so slight,
Like fine gold-leaf collectibles, not the bright and shiny jewel-like
Gold, so common in the crowns of the kings of yesteryear.

The flowers abound too, mostly crimson, sometimes covered with sand
And can be known to stay until tomorrow, perhaps many tomorrows
Even days beyond that to be enjoyed one by one
But only by one?

The loves and friendships once shared in other places
Dwindled by time the thief who knows no boundaries,
Grabs and picks out favorites be it friendships, loves, flowers.
Yet, it makes no difference at last I'm at home in the desert.

Rosemary Riberdy

A True Friend

A true friend's hard to come across
Especially these days
One who doesn't criticize
The error of your ways
But gives you hope and understands
That flesh can sometimes yield
Although you try to do your best
On the lifelong battlefield

Each day brings many blessings
When a soul's at one with you
Someone when they are blue
You can fire their faith anew
So now I want to thank my friend
For loving selflessly
And having the maturity
To speak with honesty

Ruth Price and Bill Ellis

What I Love

*To my dear mother, S. Saraswathy, for
showing me the path to love*
The stars I love.
Signals they send
from some lost home.

Silence I love.
In it I find
the mind of God.

The spring I love.
Her blossoms bright
bring us some hope.

Good hearts I love.
Meaning they give
to life human.

This life I love.
A chance to choose,
be and become.

Prabhath P.

World of Sorrow

In the cradle of the sea,
Dolphins, fish, and manatees,
Seals, urchins and anemones,
All facing extinction.
A precarious disease.

Beneath a canopy of trees,
Snakes, birds, and monkeys,
Perching on a wooden trapeze.
Disappearing forever trees.
Please hear their silent screams.

By use of flood or fire,
Forests and creatures expire.
Yeah, the situation is dire.
So can we save them?
These, our primitive squires.

Paul R. Smith, Jr.

Who Cares

I do
Who you
Why
Because God cares for me
So I care for you
That's how it should be

Bonnie Kuffler

The Night Magic

Twilight, skylight, sunset delight, all the colors of the rainbow are
within you tonight, your beauty is more becoming so right,
the perfume leaves the smell of your lingering love so bright.

When we dance in the night in the moonlight so bright, with a twinkle of
stardust you move Oh, so right, and the cool midnight air is so pleasant and fair,
all my dreams just came true because you are still here, you're my hope
and my wish so please don't disapear, if you did all my longing of dreams would dispare,
I know how you feel and I can tell that you care,
so give me your time dear we'll both be on air.

Because of this night, and magic so right, this dream I have got should
never be stoped, so let us dance on in the moonlight so bright,
and keep going on upward to the heavens of flight.

Until the sunlight meets the night of the cool morning air there will be no despair,
as we twirl in the mist of the dew on the ground around here,
the star of the morning is in our sight, tells me to stop dreaming 'til
dust of tonight, 'til all the luster is gone from the night sky up
Above we have lustered in love,
as we come to an end of this dance we have made we
will always remember this night of twinkling starlight.

Jeanine Bilger

My Eyes See

You can't see what my eyes see
out of them I see the recognizable smile of a friend,
and behind that, all the beauty deep within
I see grace, love, sincerity and joy.
I see to the very soul of a scared little boy.
You warn me to stay away, that you will only cause pain,
that I should run before I point the blame.
In front of your eyes you only see the rain.
I look into your eyes and see true light behind
that there's someone living in there who knows how to love right.
I don't see some secret waiting to unfold, dirty secrets you don't want told.
I long to know the character you possess as it draws me in,
I lay awake at night eager for the lessons to begin.
My eyes see purpose in your face.
I hold the hope that can't easily be replaced,
I don't want to run and escape this place.
I look in your eyes and I cry.

Deirdre McCray

Observations in a Laundromat

Sitting in my laundromat chair . . . lulled and wakened by the unique symphony
of Wash, Rinse, and Spin, Acutely aware, yet feigning ignorance of the
kaleidoscopic intimacies of strangers . . .
Tumbling about in see through dryers, stacked one on top of the other.

A slight, not quite elderly woman, sitting in the corner, savoring her
nicotine treat . . . Smoke-filled years etched across her kind face. A young
Latino couple, perhaps high school sweethearts . . . quitely donning matching
jerseys (though not in a corny way)—their Downy balls all neatly in a row.

The man with the carefree curly mane—strangely dissonant with his somber
features, serious stride, and dress shirts hung precisely in pristine array.

Who are these strangers amidst the sheets, jeans, and fruit of the looms?
They seem so different from me, yet is the chasm as wide and real as it
appears? Like mine, do their brains hum the tune of Sesame Street, blaring
on the laundromat TV—reminiscent of innocence past? When they see me,
do they also fashion curious imaginations in their minds?

Ahh, the similarities may not be clear, but one thing is certain . . . Were
it not for the beautiful differences, life would merely be—How should I
say? An uninteresting load of whites.

Lizbeth Strack

Smell of Sorrow

The smell of sorrow,
The touch of pain,
The fear of forever,
The thoughts of being sane.
The truth is lurking,
To the side of your heart.
Do you want to know?
Or will it draw you apart?
Wishful thinking
Of a better tomorrow
But always remembering
The smell of sorrow.
Is there burning in your body?
Does anyone understand?
I understand your hurt,
I will hold your hand.
Does dreaming of it make it better?
Does wishing about it help the pain?
I'm sorry you feel this way,
Please don't go insane.

Lisa Diane Wallace

My Journey

Everyone who helped me through my journey
This is my journey through grief,
Let me experience my pain now.
Don't tell me what to do.
Only I can know how.

If I'm talking about something
It's because I want to.
Please don't stop me—
Just listen.

If I'm crying it's because I have to.
Please don't try to make me feel better,
I will when I'm done.

Don't tell me "you know how I feel"
There is no way that you can.
Only I can know what I need
And how I need to deal.

I do what I need to do
At the time I need to do it.
Don't worry—I'm getting through,
I have my faith—and I have you.

Beverly M. Badore

Dark Dreams

I dream dark dreams
Though they come in day's light
Dark dreams of a dark man

And in a grey background
Dark music fills me

And through the smoke
I believe I see the face of the man
A dark man in dark dreams

Is that him there in the doorway?

There in the doorway of the mausoleum
The scrape of stone against stone
And it causes my flesh to move

The feel of his breath excites me
How I long to taste his skin
To feast on the dark red river
Which courses through his veins

In silence of rapture forbidden
A whisper of pleasure is heard

Gwendolynne Ann Longenecker

The MS Girl

I am a 32-year-old single mom with M.S.
And on some days, my 7 year old son gets PMS!
But that's ok, 'cause if it wasn't for his way
Mine would be to stay in bed all day!
And just when I think I can't go that extra mile
All I have to do is turn to my son and see his big and beautiful smile!
So all in all, when life gets me down I have to remember to be a clown!
This I do for my son 'cause he's the only one! So look out M.S.,
'Cause you can keep your mess, along with your stress!
And so I'll be fine,
because I know my son's love for me will always be mine!
His love will always be in my heart for me to cherish and always keep
So, M.S. you can go take a flying leap!
'Cause there's no time for me to weep or to wonder why,
But it's just time for you to say bye-bye!

Donna Mandala

Spirit Dance

I hear the sound of thunder like the beating of drums
in the far off Sacred Mountains,
and my Spirit longs to dance.

As I listen, I become the Drummer, the Chanter, and the Dancer.
As I drum, my heart beats in time with the pulse of nature,
and I learn that if I am to live in Peace,
I must become one with all Nature.
As I chant the songs of the Old Ones, I am singing in
praise of the Great One from Whom all words come,
and I feel the Love He has for all His Creation.
As I dance within the "Sacred Circle," I celebrate the Great
Mysteries of Life: birth, death and the living that comes between.
In dancing I honor those who have long past departed the Sacred Circle,
as I hope to be honored when I am no longer counted among the dancers.
In the doing of these things, I know I have done well.

I hear the sound of thunder like the beating of drums
in the far off Sacred Mountains, and my Spirit longs to dance
and It does.

Randall Harvey

Voices of the Past

So much to do, so little time to do it. I know that my job is to pursue it.
I must record for posterity and tell the tales of yesteryear.
I hear their voices telling me,
It's your work to record for those who are yet to be.
Tell who we were and when we lived,
Who we loved and what we believed in.
No one else has told the story so it's up to you.
When you come to us in glory we will thank and love you.
The good, the bad, tell all you can gather.
For we are just the people who lived before you.
Our blood and yours run together and will pass on to other generations.
Who we were is what you are and part of the rest to come.
It matters not, of royal birth, of just a common man.
Just tell our story of the past the very best you can.

Mae Ellen Sawin

The Game of Life

Dedicated to Stephanie Geber

Life is not a game you can play around with.
You can't pick it up when you want and put it away when it bothers you.
People come in and out of it, play their level, and leave.
We are always stuck waiting for the next round to come along.
It always seems like someone else has control over the joystick your game runs on.
Life seems like a game, an endless cycle, that is so hard to win.
The levels repeat on you, and you go right back to the beginning.
If you are lucky, your game will be picked up by someone who knows how to play.
When you do find that person, hold onto them, whether they are a friend, a lover, or both.
For when you find someone who knows how to play, you will always win the game of life.

Jamie Roitman

Own life

Late class come early
while conversations
procrastinate the
weather's change.

All the ritual routine
are halted by lack of
cigarette funding,
and Short-hair
tells me that television
is how she schedules her life.

Michael Wohlgemuth

Reflections

See the young girl score
the winning point with a slam dunk.

See the new mother pushing
the stroller through the park.

See the grandmother serving
milk and cookies on the back porch.

See the young woman flirting with the
young man two offices down.

See the beauty, joy and mystery
each woman posses.

See the gifts and challenges
each one of us can find at
anytime in our lives.

Michelle Lynn Garcia

Untitled

Trampled into a world of loneliness,
Only I can save myself.
From the silence of nature,
I hold true.
It was never the end,
Beauty has only begun,
The strength of mind,
To love yourself,
must be divine.

Bridget A. Jones

January Weather

On a cold winter day
Snow flakes and icicles are best seen
From the warmth of the barn.

Frieda Henson

innocent boy

i thought i knew
the boy that went away
but now i suddenly know
that he is no one i know

the illusion i saw
was quite seen
who would have known
that this innocent boy
would turn into a vicious man?

surely i did not
and i bet
the survivors didn't either
but somehow we got him back

although it has been hard
only a couple days later
i'm sure we all will make it out ok!

Kate Elizabeth Anness

Since You've Been Gone

There was a time when I thought that you would be here forever
I never thought that such cruel fate would take you away
I was a fool to take you for granted and when I turn around you were gone
I wish I could turn back the hands of time and make everything alright
If I could I would take away all your pains
and make you happy as you've never been before
But I can't and time have already sifted away
leaving only shadows to whisper on the wall
All that is left are memories of you that tears can't erase

I never had the courage to come and say I love you
And now I wish I could have told you so long ago.
I regret not telling you just how much you mean to me
Now everything is so different and life seems incomplete
There's a hole in my heart which no one could ever replace
Was it your laughter I just heard or is it just the wind blowing on the trees
How I yearn for you to be here so I can call proudly your name

    Nina Lee

My Brother

Here you lie in this hospital bed for a long three weeks, today.
I speak to you with words of wisdom, for there's so much to say.
Just let me start by saying, I love you so very much,
And when I touch you day by day, I hope you can feel my touch.
Our mother, Celillus, and our sister, Brenda, we pray for you every day,
And all of our friends and family send love and prayers always.
Just keep on trusting in the Lord, for he's the power of all things.
Just let him work his miracle, for he knows what the future will bring.
So as you lie here, getting stronger, remember who's in charge of us all.
For God has the power to heal and the one who makes the last call.
So keep on trusting in the Lord, no matter what people may say,
And soon your troubles will be over and we'll take you home one day.
Until that day finally comes there's so much more to do,
But, "Ted," we want you to know we give thanks to God for you.
So, my brother, just be strong and keep holding on,
For there will be tougher days but we must all keep our faith
And give thanks to God always!

    Susan Hinds

The Storm

Gray darkness all around, nowhere is there any sound
Birds are quiet, animals still as if awaiting some violent will
The breeze blows steady, soon conditions will be ready
Off in the distance far out of sight,
the storm approaches with all its might
Dark clouds roll and tumble, but as of yet we hear no rumble
Piling high the storm clouds grow, soon nature will put on a show
Here and there a chirp is heard, of course, it's only a nervous bird
Softly now the sprinkles fall, next will come the mournful call
Flash, the sky is now ablaze, sending us through a visual maze
Seconds now we mark the time, to find the distance to the crime
Thunder travels across the miles, letting us know if we have a while
Once again a flash is seen, this storm could prove to be mean
Now the thunder again is heard, closer than the last it is feared
Some do dread this forceful gift, I myself feel it's a lift
Watching and waiting alone, I sit, am I scared? Not a bit
Soon I know this storm will pass, and leave behind just cold wet grass
Then I will once again wait, and hope next time the storm comes late.

    Dorinda Marie Pedersen Truax

Do You Remember When?

Do you remember when the time seemed to pass so slow?
Do you remember when you were, Oh, so impatient just to grow?
Do you remember when your heart was touched to hear a robin sing?
Do you remember when your days were spent in happy dreams?
Do you remember when you had your special star at night?
Do you remember when everything in your world was so very bright?
Do you remember when one day you looked back and time had passed by?
Do you remember then how it shocked you so that you had to cry?

    Katie Hayes

wishing . . .

wishing you would
only if you were here
how much I would show
how much that I know
how far apart that we've been
wishing you would
as when we were near
glow with that glow and show
just how much you know
all that I've seen
wishing you would
tend what I say,
and not wend away,
from that one else
who knows;
amongst and between
just how much so
we've been wishing
"you, wherever you are,
are wishing me"

    Wilfredo Escobar

Forever Waiting

As I lie down for the night
Remembering first time I saw you
As I looked into your eyes
You had a smile, a smile Oh, so bright
Will your smiles shine for me tonight

Voice of an angel
So sweet and full of life
To hear your voice
Again for me tonight

A touch that's so gentle
As gentle as the night
To feel your touch
Just for me tonight

As I lie down tonight
Only wishing for you
To be with you tonight

    George E. Tucker

Grandma

The day Grandma died
Was so full of sorrow

As I lie in bed now
I pray to see tomorrow

My cheeks are tear-stained
As I think of the past

If only the day Grandma died
Wouldn't have been the last

She had a special way
Of making me smile

By getting me a cute gift
Once in awhile

And I'll never forget
The great bear hugs she gave

But it saddens me to go see
Her beautiful grave

I know now she is living pain-free
In a happy place watching down on me

But Grandma, I want you to see
That I will always be your little Katie-B

    Katie Reimer

THE MANY LESSONS OF LIFE

T ough it's not to make a choice between right and wrong
H elpless I am to the fact there are killers I live among
E vil has a delightful ring and a decent taste

M an's self destructive, and crying is a waste
A way to the magic kingdom, the place of again
N ever will I ever lie, I'm immune to all sin
Y ou say that I'm crazy, I never claimed to be sane

L ove has a melody, it's the creator of all pain
E nemies are in the dark, and there are shadows in all light
S uspicious of all who trust, what gives them the right
S oldier on a mission, who's trying to find a cause
O ff to a better place, if there ever was
N obody else seems to know, communication is man's ruin
S ecrets are conspiracies, and no one knows what they're doing

O f all the crimes of the world, greed is number one
F orget the poor, feed the rich, 'cause the rabbits got the gun

L ittle man in the moon, I would love to hear your story
I nstinct tells me to be scared of the proud man's glory
F reedom's just another word that evolved from hate
E verybody has to die and Heaven's got a gate

Scott Islam, Jr.

I Am the Resident

I am 30, I am 60, I am 80, I am over 100 years old, I am the resident.
I'm black, I'm white, I am rich, I am poor, I am the resident.
I know my rights, I have no rights, I am the resident.
I understand what is being said to me, I am confused, I am the resident.
I can take care of myself, I am totally dependent on others,
I am the resident.
I am happy, I am lonely, sad, angry, tired, and scared, I am the resident.
I have lots of visitors, I have no visitors, I am the resident.
I am wise, I have lots of knowledge to share with you, I am the resident.
I am ready to die, I am afraid of dying, I am the resident.

When you care for me, remember, I am all of these things,
but most of all, remember that one day not so long ago,
I was not a resident. I was just like you.
As you come to care for me, know that at any time
something could happen and you may become a resident. So care
for me with the same dignity and respect you would like, because,
who knows, maybe one day I will recover, and I will be caring for you!

Cheryl J. Wilson

Attitudes

The cruel and condescending way that others' energy puts you off
is a problem in itself.
If the world is on a cycle, as man states,
who is he that he knows the answers?
You tell me what to believe and I'm supposed to follow without questions?
We are all numbered, don't look for 666.
Keep your beliefs true. True to your heart.
They want to have total control.
My reply, "It's not yours to have."
Come out and let all see what your intentions really are.
It's not harmony of nature. Why battle human evolutions?
You only use ten percent of your brain.
I'm wrong because you said so. I don't think so.
Treat us differently.
So you know everything and won't listen to the different.
It's all about you and what makes you happy. I'm on this Earth too.
There are tears for tomorrow that shed like rain today,
caused by the lakes symphony of the ocean.
I needed help to get me through the day.
When you came in the way of rain.

Marcia L. Douglas Howard

Ode to the Violets

Oh, violets spread in the sun,
Your beauty beckons me
To come and smell the sweetness,
To watch adoringly.

The summer's sun upon your face,
Your petals fresh and new
Are the color of the evening sky,
The deepest, darkest blue.

I lie across this bed so soft
And gaze up at the trees;
I realize now the beauty
That attracts so many bees.

And when the winter's cold has come
To wash your scent away,
The memory of your loveliness
In my mind will always stay.

Emily Krahn

Earth

Earth
Precious, giving
Water, air, food
There is only one
Earth.

Susan Rosamund Cooper

A Mother's Nest

She sees me fly
 I am a bird
She sees me fall
 I am still young
She hears me chirp
 I have much to say
She hears me choke
 I have uncertainties about my thoughts
She sees me fly

I am just like her
 She is my mother
I am my own person
 She is my complete opposite
I know she loves me
 She says I am a gift
I know I am a burden
 She regrets much
I am just like her

Tina Novello

Freedom

To love . . . to truly love
we must set free;
Allowing you to be you
and me to be me;
Uplifting one another
to . . . mutuality!
Surrendering obstacles . . .
hindrances in our way;
Bringing hearts together,
truly caring . . .
gives joy to our days!
It is then . . . we finally see,
in opening our subconscious dreams
of hope . . . for reality;
Just finding truth . . . so it seems;
Embracing love unconditionally,
with understanding . . . sets us free!

Joyce R. Berentz

Jerry's Kids

There is a bug that stays hidden
That cripples and leaves kids bedridden
It is a crippling disease
Until it's cured, we'll never be at ease
It's known as muscular dystrophy
Always on mom's mind, but still a mystery
So let's give this thing a kick and a shove
Let's destroy this thing and show the children our love
With all the contributions to Jerry's cause
This dreadful disease has started to dissolve
If I've keep up the good work and pray
Maybe one day, Jerry's kids will run and play
So if we want our kids to laugh and play
Let's destroy this damn thing today
So away with this mystery
So our children may rise up and shout, no more dystrophy
Let's try something different today
We've been watching other kids do it, I think it is called run and play
Oh! It's so much fun to be out in the sun
From all of us to Jerry, our thanks we've almost won.

Thomas L. Crist, Sr.

Ever-Darkening Dream

The light is coming back to me,
No longer can I see the cruel darkness.
Drifting away, I carefully walk along.
Sweet music, angelic voices.
Charming light illuminates my darkened world.
Beautiful sounds, joyful explosions of color.
Never will I leave, never will I leave.
This sweet angelic excursion, never will I let it go.
Flying, laughing, no darkness, no darkness.
I will never see the darkness again and I don't miss it.
This world entrances me, sweeps over as a river over a rock.
May I never leave this Heaven,
May I never traverse through the darkness again.
Be with me always, let me live in you.
Then the darkness is coming yet again.
Flowers of many colors die and wither.
Black lightning rips through, leaving it all in shreds around my feet.
Weeping, I turn away, back to the ever growing darkness of reality.
May I never forget the joy of this place,
May I never forget my dreams.

Kyle Wilson

Lemon-Aid

Oh, here I lie again, so often as I do,
for doctors, surgeries & hospitals aren't even a "déjà vu"
From head to toe, I've been mowed, nothing left, I suppose
From birth to 28, I've had my share of aches
From physical to emotional illnesses, I have seen. Having one
behind the other isn't one's future dream
Each new year I take with strength, only to deal with illness again.
Should I make this my new best friend?
Kind of funny, yes, it sounds strange, but what else is there to gain?
I strive for good health but, Oh, again, I'm poked by jagged ends
When, Oh, when will this so called party end?
For my parents are always there devoting love & care
Oh, what will I do, if, ever I lose you?
Chills are sent up & down my spine, while tears embrace my face,
just imagining this taking place
Could the lemon tree from where I came make thee whole again?
For what surprise remains before my eyes?
But to find keloid scars revealing the pain,
to this child they call lemon-aid

Dana Liebert

Too Many Butterflies

She flies by
I hold her for an instant
Why should I cry?
I see another in the distance
Why should I try?
Too many butterflies

She lands on the sill
I reach for her
Will I keep her? I haven't the will
She flies off in a blur
I love the thrill
Too many butterflies

Birds don't sing
Weather grows cold
Soon it's spring
I get old and still
Too many butterflies

Ralph A. Elio

Firecrackers

Brain exploding like
firecrackers on the 4th of July,
this is no celebration, it's madness.

Pacing angrily, ranting obscenities,
smothering in a cocoon of rage,
I am waiting for Godot.

On a floor named, "Elopement Risk,"
encapsulated in a padded room,
I find a piece of my mind.

Eunice S. Whiting

Epitaph for Scattering Ashes

Where wolves howl in the forest,
where wild birds sing in a tree,
where coyotes drink from a stream,
set my spirit free.

Where flowers send seeds in the wind,
where mountains push peaks to the sky,
where great pines lay down a carpet,
let my spirit fly.

Where waves wash over the sand,
where rain makes the riverbeds flow,
where swirling dust gathers and soars,
into the clouds I'll go.

As morning fog rises in vapor
and clears the coastline, I'll be
the sparkle in shining sunlight,
and melt into foam on the sea.

Carol Hammond

Life Is Black

Life is black,
I wish I could go back.
Life is red,
I wish I were dead.
I am tickled pink,
I wish I had a drink.
Life is yellow,
I will go fix some Jell-O.
Life is blue,
I think I will go shop for some shoes.
Life is green,
Time to go to the latrine.

Myra L. Haas

To My Husband

When you reach out and touch my face
Or gently stoke my hair,
My heart begins to swell with pride;
I'm so very glad you care.
As you continue to stroke my skin,
My worries slip away.
The pleasure that you bring to me
Grows stronger day by day.
What once was a consuming fire,
A hot and burning flame,
Has mellowed sweetly through the years
To a depth you could never name.
Your love has become my very life;
I've given all to you.
And I'll not regret one moment,
When my life on Earth is through.

Jo Dansby

Father of the Bride

Father, you are my protector,
My guardian angel you might say.
I look to you for guidance,
That's why you're giving me away.
You've always stood beside me,
No matter right or wrong.
All the love that you've given me,
Will last my whole life long.
You have taught me things,
Only a daddy could ever know.
I would give up my life for you,
Just because I love you so.
I remember spending summers,
In my "Daddy's World."
Just to share some memories,
Because I'm his little girl.
Our special bond will carry us,
As the years go by.
You will always be my hero,
Until the day I die.

Shannon Stadey

Wings

Cup O' Java
McCartney sings
Brisk air at dark
My heart grows wings

Jamie Powers

My Partner in Life

To men in love
Each day you put a smile on Me,
I want you to know, I surely see—
All the things, that we do—
Let's me know why I love you—
Everything that you share,
Shows to me, that you care—
And even when it's dark and gray,
I know that you are here to stay—
When my heart is feeling blue,
You touch my soul, and make me new—
And if we're ever far apart,
I always know you're in my heart—
So when you stop and think of me,
Know that I'm a part of thee—
You've touched me in a special way,
You always seem to make my day—
It's always better when you're with me,
That's why you make me feel carefree—
I want you to be my wife,
I want you for my Partner in Life.

Mark Bennett

the woman who birthed me

where did you go?
where is your heart?
our souls, no longer in sync,
weep over what keeps us apart.

dear woman, I am you—your flesh.
I am you— perhaps too much
of your dreams and aspirations
crushed
into a new being.

I miss the woman who birthed me.
perhaps she misses her child.
maybe we miss each other
while we're really standing side by side.

Romya Turner

Pieces of Rain

As they scurry from the top
They make the fall drop by drop
Quickly how they hurry down
Just to crash upon the ground

Richard Henry

Just Passing Through

Where did the time go?
It's passing by so quickly.
Just yesterday when I was 10
I faced the world so meekly.

Where did the time go?
I guess I have lost track.
Just yesterday when I was 20
I ran and never looked back.

Where did the time go?
I haven't got a clue.
Yesterday I just turned 30
and I've got so much to do.

Where did the time go?
I heard them say, She's old .
I can't be old at 50!
My hand's too good to fold.

Where did the time go?
I haven't done that much!
At 65 I'll start again
And this time I'll skip lunch!

Jan Wright

Dreaming

I see you in my dreams
and long for you in
morning light.
Your eyes are deep and
dark brown . . . they melt
my resistance and my heart.
Your smile draws me in and
captures my lonely soul. Your
touch ignites the passion of
my heart. Your voice sends tingles
over my skin. I long to tell you
of my feelings, but am too afraid,
so I live for the nights when
we become one, if only in my
dreams. Soon I will tell you
and my dreams will become
reality. Morning won't be lonely,
for you will hold me in your arms.

Rebecca Anne Johnson

Through Eyes of Love

*To family and friends who have encouraged
me, thank you!*
Through eyes of love
I look and see
The world through reflected light.
In rainbow hues, with colors true,
In the midnight shade of night,
All colored by the light of love,
Behold the beautiful sight.
The prism glows, as friendship grows,
Turning darkness into light.
Through eyes of love
I look and see
Your face smiling back at me . . .
Through, eyes of love.

Kimberly Wiggins-Beardsley

Rose

The fragrance of this rose released,
It whets accepting sense,
I host the symptoms in excess,
Because of luring essence.

Van A. Behrendt

Runaway

While walking down a country road,
I met a man in passing.

His face was weathered from the sun,
hands worn from "many-a-planting."
This road ends just up ahead.

"It won't take you anywhere
but, it'll take you back home again."

I had no choice but, to turn around
to the direction from whence I came.

And side by side we walked,
me and the man without a name.

We talked about a place called "home"
and the folks who were waiting there.

Where "love" could still be found,
in people who really cared.

Norma Jean Combow

Mask

*To Jason: You are the light that guides
me . . . You are my life.*
As I look into your eyes
I see my life reflecting,
like a mirror to the windows of my soul.
Helpless, I sit back and watch
as your body grows old.
I remember your happiness
and I've felt your pain,
I once was your shadow
before the sun became the rain.
I share your memories of the
present and the past,
I see the heartbreak you hide
behind the mask.
So, as I search your eyes
and see my life reflecting,
I remove the mask to see
whose heartbreak it's protecting.
Behind the mask I know who I will see,
for this mask is protecting
a heartbreak deep within me.

Kylie J. Edwards

Pretend

If you have any questions
If you have any doubts
I want to hear you speak loud and clear
Get it all out.
If you don't know where we come from
You don't believe in Heaven on Earth
Take a good look around you
I'll tell you what it's worth

It's more than black and white
It's more than meets the eye
There's so much in disguise
It's more than you and me
This is our destiny
What are you trying to hide deep inside
It's killing you

Pretend that you know me
Pretend that you need me
Pretend that you really care
If there's one thing I'm sure of
I can't get more of I'll be there.

Jason Imlays

Opposites Attract

My lover is shabby
And never quite kept.
But his heart is a matchbook
Which I strike against.

All our days are a bonfire
Of joy and dissent.
And the ashes are precious
Souvenirs of warmth spent.

Marguerite Pileggi

Beer

I think that I shall never hear
A poem as lovely as a beer
Brew that Joe's bar has on tap
Golden column, creamy cap

Beer the drink I sip all day
Until my worries melt away
Poems are made by fools I hear
But only Coors can make a beer

Jerrold W. Dean

Stars

The stars in the sky
Just look at them all
Not one is the same.

Some twinkle, some do not
Others dance, others do not
They shine bright in the sky
Sparkling diamonds in the sky.
How many do you see?
Sometimes, more than you can count
Other times, only one or two
Who decides how many will shine?

Sometimes they come out to play
But never during the day!

Some form shapes
Some even have names

Some burn out
While others fade

All to put on a show
When the sun goes to bed
And the moon comes out to glow.

Kelley A. Maginnis

My Apology

I didn't mean to start the arguments
I didn't mean to start the fights
I didn't mean to be selfish
You tried to love me
You stood-up for me
ever since we met
I took you for granted
I'm sorry
When you walked out that night
it took me by surprise
I cried all night
I should of given you
more respect and appreciation
Instead I gave into my own greed
I awoke the next morning
and over my coffee cup
I cried
Because I didn't mean
for you to leave without
saying good-bye

Jessie Ann Janson

Sing

Sing in the sunshine or the rain
Or whatever brings the day

Sing and let no one
Take your song away

Sing when you're riding high
And down in the valley still

Sing until the melody
In you has been revealed

For once it's been discovered
And you know it as your own

Sweeter grows your melody
More beautiful your song

Roslyn M. Jordan

Shyness

I saw shyness clearly
She was weak and quivered
when people talked to her
She turned and walked away slowly
I saw her with a tear running down
her pale skin
and heard her talk to herself quietly
and I felt bad

Nicole Browning

I Am a Bird, I Fly Away

I am a bird. I fly away.
You try to catch me.
I fly away.

You throw stones. I move away.
You shoot at me. I go away.
I see my friends locked up
in cages. I fly away.

Then someone feeds me,
talks to me, plays with me.

You try to make me go away.
You yell at me.

I fly away.
You should be nice to
all animals on Earth.
I am a bird. I fly away.

Lisa Torelli

The Unknown

I fall
So easily smitten
I fall
To deep unknown depths
I fall
Into strong unknown arms
I know
Of rights and wrongs in life
I know
of pains and frustrations
I know
of the strong unknown arms
I fall, I know
of love

Debby McIntire

Moments

Bubbles in the sky sweetly drifting.
I lie and watch as one by one,
they float undeterred and aimless.
Then in a tranquil blink they are gone.

I try to grasp the meaning of this,
but it slips away.
I sense an opportunity has been lost,
but when I close my eyes, I smile,

and I know it must have been beautiful.

John Kim

The Fire I Seek

The soft glow from the candle,
Reflects the pale gold of the moon.
But the soft glow in my heart
Is nothing like the raging fire I seek.
There have been brush fires in my heart,
Here and there, along the path
Called my life.
But still I search.
I seek a romantic life,
Full of violins at sunrise,
Travels through exotic lands
Into myself.
A wanderer seeking haven,
In the arms of another wanderer,
The other half of my soul's light.
Hold up you candle, Love,
So that I can find you
In my darkness.

Jennifer Marie Monnens

Psssst . . . I Love You

Please, will you take my heart and soul,
Come dance a jig with me?
Hold me tight to your breast
For the whole world to see.

Time well spent can bring us joy
And laughter shall never end.
'Tis surely true, two hearts in love
Into one they shall blend.

No thunder, wind, nor terrible storm,
Can shatter our bonds of love.
For there will always be the calm,
Like the cooing of the lonesome dove.

Nestle close to me,
Your tender lips on mine.
Tell me that you love me
And let out hearts entwine!

Ronald J. Knowles

Something's Missing

I am nothingness . . .
My reign never began.
The helpless fools outside my walls,
They beg for my mercy.
I can't hear them, however,
Due to my not really living.
I'm scared of being alive.
A great pride once fluttered inside,
But now, it's gone forever.
I've killed my game.
A friend speaks of this loss,
And he reminds me of what I once was.
He speaks of a youthful man
That's now become an old fool.
I miss what I used to be . . .
I loved being it . . .
Now there's only one problem:
I don't know what's missing.

Tony Fraley

A Friend Like You

Daphne

A friend like you is someone who
is there through thick and thin.
You're someone who I'd gladly help
in a fight you could not win.

A good friend knows exactly what
to do when one is sad,
and listens to everything that's said,
even when one is mad.

A friend like that can cheer me up
by giving a simple smile,
and make the trials and tribulations
all the time worthwhile.

A friend like that is easy to keep,
but really hard to find.
A friend like that everyone meets
but once in a lifetime.

Paul Michael Daniels

Home

Strangers drawn together,
Sharing time and space.
Helping one another,
Speaking face to face.
Living life together,
Never on their own.
Creates a strong foundation,
Welcome to our home.

Danny Crandell

Paper, Pencils and Ideas

On paper one pencil's in lines
with thought turning gears.
A good plan is like magic
It could last years and years.

VCR's advancing
CD's brilliantly clear
Space age technology
An idea some people fear.

Paper, pencils and ideas
shaping our times.
Paper, pencils and ideas
Educating our minds.

Kristerpher Pal

Loved by All

Loved by all they were,
They never had a care in the world.
Always laughing,
Always smiling,
Loved by all they were.

Loved by all they were,
Nobody could ever compare,
Sweet Langdon and Sam were,
Everybody loved them so.
Loved by all they were.

Katie Sellmeyer

We Are One

As long as I am
Secure in your love,
Nothing can harm me.
You mean everything to me.
Your love carries me
Through good times and bad.
My future only
Exists for you.
We are one as long
As you love me.

Linda M. L. Morris

Have You Ever?

Have you ever lost something
That you cherished so dear?
Have you ever found the courage
To dry somebody's tears?
Have you ever found the heart
To give out all your love?
Have you ever found the wings
To fly high like a dove?
Have you ever made a wish
That you realize cant come true?
Have you ever found something old
That still feels like it's brand new?
Have you ever felt the pain
When you lose something you love?
Have you ever had someone
Who enclosed you like a glove?
Have you ever had a feeling
That makes you cry inside?
Have you ever had an angel
That you know is there to guide?

Amy Garno

Strawberry Blossoms

Strawberry blossoms
In summer fields of gold . . .
I'll be with my baby,
Whom I love and dearly hold.

In a web of dreams
So sweetly spun . . .
We'll be together,
Forever as one.

Sing you to sleep,
Then kiss you good night . . .
Holding you close
'Til the morning light.

Mommy misses you so
And is trying to be brave . . .
As she lays strawberry blossoms
On your grave.

Jennifer Letizia Diogo

Even When

Nothing makes me happier
Than snuggling with my Nikki
Whenever I make eye contact with her
Everything else becomes a blur

Nothing makes me prouder
Than to walk with her hand in hand
I could always find my way to her
Even if I could not stand

Even when the world stops turning
Even when the sky is not blue
No matter whatever happens
I'll never stop loving you

Even when the day I die
I'll be smiling down on her
From Heaven as she cries

Adam Uplinger

I Lost My Shoe

I looked under the bed—
not there,
so I told my brother Ned.
Ned didn't care—
that's what he said.

I told my mom I lost my shoe;
she said it would cost me
to clean my room.

I cleaned my room.
I even used a broom.
My dresser drawers
sparkled like the moon.

Just when I was about to give up
and tell my mom I had no luck,
I looked across the room,
and there lay my shoe,
on the floor, near the door,
where I left it before.

Kimberly McNeill

Reflections and Hope

Those were the days when life was lazy
Then showers moved in and it was hazy.
Hollyhock and Black Eyed Susan
Burst their blooms in great profusion.
Robins cocked their heads to hear
if there were bugs and earthworms near.
Noisy lawn mowers weren't around
Song wrens made the only sound.
Porches were the place to be
to watch the squirrels in the tree.
Wicker rockers held the key
to easing stress, anxiety.
Kids were happy, life was good
Christians lived as Christians should.
Games and toys were all inventive
Giving children great incentive.
Life's progressive, we all know
But where did all those good times go?
So, smell the roses, help a friend
Money's nothing in the end.

Nancy Scharf

Awaiting

I, here, awaiting
awaiting alone for someone
someone alone awaiting
awaiting somewhere for I.

Kantikarn Husdaja

Not My Religion

Preach now from your Koran
Recite psalms from God's Bible
Adam, Eve, the 40 day walk
Is this your religion?

Go to your own temple
I'll stay and worship the sun
Venus, Zeus, and Hades' Hell
What is your religion?

Don't think my thoughts for me
Don't shove your words down my throat
What goes 'round comes 'round
But it's not my religion

Marianne Lim

Sonnet No. 5

Alas, my sweet love,
Do I long to hold you tight,
These long winter nights,
I know I could not have you,
We were not for each other,
But I pray,
We are not against each other,
Heartache and heartbreak,
Is all that I have felt,
These cold and lonely winter nights.

Jason Bland

Memories of the Heart

They say home is where the heart is
Maybe that would explain
Why my torn and lonesome heart
Seems a thousand miles away
The laughter and tears so vivid
Gone without a trace
The warmth of the sun
The cool of the breeze
The feeling of rain on my face
The memories I hold so dear
The life I can't forget
The pictures in my mind so clear
Why can't I go home yet?
When will all my torture end?
When can I be
Safe at home in my own bed?
When will my heart be set free?

Amy Birdsall

On My Husband's Death

I awoke with a start!
Was it just a bad dream?
I reached out a hand,
There was only the bed.

How can I go on
Without you beside me?
For fifty-odd years
We two have been one.

Our children, now grown,
Have lives of their own,
They can't interrupt
For my sake.

"But I am with you."
I heard a voice say.
Yes, God, you are here,
So I will not despair.

Ina S. Fitzgerald

To Let You Know

This is to let you know
The feelings I need to share,
And for me to finally show
How much I really care.
If I had just one day,
With you is where I want to be.
If I had one thing to say,
You're the perfect one for me.
I don't care it's too sappy,
These things that are true,
But it makes me happy
To show that I love you.
In the end I hope you see
How much you mean to me.

Seth Adam Peterson

For BW

The curve of her wood,
The strength of her steel,
Waits patiently for your touch.

With the caress of a song,
She can breathe through your heart,
Let her do this for you, she's waiting.

Play her loud, play her soft,
She will be there in return,
For she forgives, she loves and adores!

Become one with the curve of her wood,
And the strength of her steel.

She's there—She's REAL—

WOOD—and—STEEL!

Kay F. Hassing

This Love

A stream flows through the forest.
Its water runs strong.
The warm water soothing to the touch;
It's this love.

Flowers grow on the forest floor.
Their buds bloom proud.
The colorful petals brighten the day;
It's this love.

Birds nest high in the forest.
They sing their songs merrily.
The music sounds sweet and symphonic;
It's this love.

Jack Stewart McArthur

Spoiled

Wandering fingers
Caressing all boundaries
Tempting what's forbidden
Lost in confusion
Purity spoils me

Overwhelming pleasures
Cruel expectations
Fulfilling my destiny
Leading to my destruction
Innocence spoils me

Uncontrollable satisfaction
Blanketed silence
Unforgiving desires
Exhilarating freedom
Love spoils me

Francisca Higuera

Ode to Jeff Jewelry

I'm over the hill,
So I'll take a pill.
Life isn't such a thrill,
So I'll sit by the window sill.
And then you ride to me,
On your mustang of ebony,
Like a knight of chivalry;
My heart belongs to Jeff Jewelry.
I have a rush in my heart
That races as fast as
Your new engine starts.
I dream of us together . . . forever!

Louise M. Lehmkuhl

Death in My Heart

From the moment of my birth,
I have wondered what my soul is worth.
Is it love, or is it hate?
For this answer I must wait,
'Til the day I go down,
Six feet under, in the ground.
Until the day that I die,
I will wonder who, when, where and why?
Who, when, where and why?
I don't know, so I die!

Devon Linder

Too Late

It's too late to
say goodbye
I wasn't thinking
about you
when I was out
drinking
I couldn't even
tell you how
many I drank down
I got in my car
happy as a clown
I couldn't even tell you
How sorry I was
when I looked down
and saw your motionless face
I only heard a man say
How many did you have
I was lead away
I didn't even say
Goodbye.

Margaret Gomez

Handprints

Happy Mother's Day
Handprints, handprints,
Upon the wall.
How did they get there?
Was it my will?

"Mommy, Mommy,"
I can call.
Quickly, she walked
Through the hall.

"Look, look,
Upon the wall!
Handprints, handprints,
Just like mine!"

Helping hands
Grow so fast.
It won't last.
Soon, it's past!

Sue Harding

When Death Comes Knocking

When death comes knocking at your door
There's nothing you can do
So go ahead, let go my friend
And let the light shine through

They say the light is beautiful
A sight beyond belief
It fills your heart with joy and peace
And puts an end to grief

I know that God is standing there
He's come to take you home
He's holding out his hand for you
To lead you to his throne

So when the angels come for you
Don't be afraid to die,
A better life is waiting there
So go ahead and fly.

Gale Woolems Alvey

Thoughts on Space

Somewhere There
Another sits as I do,
pondering questions
without knowing,
Gazing perhaps
upon a wild bird fiery,
Hearing old thoughts
on the starlight glowing.

Rosa B. Lester

Ocean

She seems to
weave more water
every day under the hot,
sticky sun.
OCEAN
She tosses and
turns in the night,
alone in the black,
freezing cold,
and the stillness of the DARKNESS.
OCEAN
Her long, glistening,
smooth, and elegant coat
of water gleams in the
warmth of the sun's rays.
OCEAN
When she is
furious she
screams an endless
cry of PAIN!

Georgina Rai

Fueling

A love I once had is
Now gone from me or was
She really there?
Motionless with no passion
My miserable self goes
right along with no path to walk on.
What is was to touch her
Not just with pale emotions
I knew but hers as well
Not for long was it pale
Or passionless but the paleness
Of emotions bonded us.
Fueling

Erica W. Short

Be Your Own Strength

In this world there are
very few things that we can rely on,
But one thing is for sure the person
you see in the mirror is yours alone.

You can tell this person
anything and they will always love you,
You can be guaranteed that
this person to you will be true.

They will always give
you the support you need through life,
Never stabbing you
in back with a knife like others might.

Be faithful to this person
in the mirror and they will be there,
And a more worthy friend
than this you will find is rare.

Sherryl Chilcott

Beyond

Cynthia
beyond the fields we have sowed
for so many a lonely night
beyond the whispers we hear
and deeply yearn for
yes beyond our very youth
the oldness of our days
that which makes the grey of our souls
turn whispers into shouts
beyond the hollow echo
of tears on aged cheeks
wind snow dried
frozen in mid-thought
in the blackness of the night
love shines with cutting radiance
bright,
bright,
bright

Dr. John R. Feeney

On Pondering

What is life . . .
Does anyone know?

What is peace . . .
But a contented soul.

And love . . .
Isn't that life's goal?

Jo Marie Ramirez

cloudy day

dark skies.
no birds fly by.
the sun is gone
in gray marshmallowy puffs.
thick air
the strong smell of rain.
the clock ticks.
we wait.
then it comes, slow at first
with a tink, tink, tink.
then it beats hard on the roof
like millions of people dancing.
then it stops, after hours.
hours of wet drippy sky.
the clouds clear.
then lay a starry sky.
i lie on the moist, grassy ground,
starring at the beautiful sky.

Heather Donato

Where'd You Go

Oh, where, Oh, where'd you go
My friend, my companion, my bro'?
Slathered in sin
she connived you in,
then handed you a scroll of death,
then left.
Fifty years for taking your life,
sure came cheap.
Confounded in strife.
Now I have no sleep.

Fay Sedore

Where Is Love

Where is love, when you need it most
Lost in space, without a host
Try as I must, to get it back
I'm at a loss, I'm not on track

Oh, help me now, to find where it went
Give me the strength, borrowed or lent
I try to open up, to let love in
To get it back, to win, win, win

Where is love, that I once had
Out there in space, that's really sad
Help me now, to see the light
Help me now, to do it right

From outside in, to inside out
It's out there now, out and about
Can you help me, Oh, please say you can
For I'm at a loss, I need a hand

Deborah Kolsovsky

Runaway

Whose child is this
so all alone?
Has he no parents?
Has he no home?

In his time of need
he feels so unloved
Does he seek guidance
from someone above?

Alone and homeless
In need of hugs
His home, the streets
His parents, are drugs

Earla Ritz

Time

Time is slow.
Time is fast.
Time will never ever last.

Laura (Hill) Jackson

Life

Life
The Seed—Love
Watch it bloom
Sprout—Spread its glorious wings
Sail through time
Lingering
Blind, baffled, blundering blot,
Vanished from Humanity
So precious, yet exploited
Veratrized
Devastated
Still

Arthur McCoy

You

Your name makes me smile
Your smile makes me weak
When I am near you
I just cannot think
I know it's not love
Still, I don't understand it
For some reason I need you
My heart cannot stand it
I want to give up
To go on my way
But I can't
My heart begs me to stay
So I wait.

Lynsey Pollard

Cornerstone

A wish made in the dark.
A dream sent to the sky.
A hope lit by the light
Of a thousand starry nights.

A memory that keeps on turning.
A nightmare that keeps on burning.
A feeling of yearning.
The world keeps on turning.

The stars keep changing.
The soul is raging.
A drug that changes the mind.
A heart that is feeling.

The cornerstone of human existence.
The thing that kills.
The thing that thrills.
The fresh breath of freedom.
It quenches the soul.
It's what makes us whole.

Ben Baker

A Moment

Carried aloft on a warm summer breeze
the furry dandelion took flight.
I watched it dance away from me
dipping and soaring as it goes.

I held my breath as it almost dropped
into a puddle in the street
and just as quickly rose again
high and out of sight.

And I knew a moment out of time
when nothing was more important to me
than the fate of that little weed.
Just a brief moment.

Just one of those moments
  when God smiled
    my heart sang
      and all was right in my world.

Judy Thornhill

With All My Heart

With all my heart and all my soul
I will never let you go
Though times may change
And people, too
I will never forget you
Your smile, laugh, and eyes
I guess it's no surprise
you live on

Amber Johnston

Clover Lake

Crimson waves ebb and flow
On a swelling sea of green
We drift on a raft of happiness
Sailing the meadows of our daydreams

Gauze feathers of pristine white
Tickle a canopy of azure blue
Soaring with the swallows
Our lives refreshed and new

Fall with me, my love
Into the cool clover lake
Fall with me, my heart
Fragrant love we'll make

No grays, no blacks, no angry reds
No browns, no haze, no murky depths
The storms and snows and floods recede
Disappearing from out mother's breast

Sunshine sparkles and rainbows dance
The oceans and rivers and lakes sway
The night song permeates our love
The new song brings another day

Lisa Hale Kennedy

Timeless Love

To my brother, with all my love,
I miss you more than you know.
To this day my heart still aches
Because I love you so.

The voice has since diminished,
Your face I can barely see,
I feel I've let you down
Because you've lived through me.

I can't wait to see you,
There's so much to talk about,
Time and space are between us
Heaven must never be in doubt.

For one day the Lord will come,
He'll take me on my way.
We'll meet each other in Heaven
Beyond the Pearly Gates.

Until we come together,
I'll bid you farewell.
Please always remember
Where in my heart you dwell!

Clementine B. Watts

Her Love—It Leads Me

Her love, it leads me like a song
Of never-ending melody,
And all the notes they dance along
The bars of recent memory,
United with a rhythm strong
That lifts my heart to revelry.

Her cheerful verse with simple scheme
Moves my soul to a pleasant state,
Where intoxication is the mean
And melancholy thoughts abate.
To fragments from forgotten dreams
That leave the soul to postulate.

The gentle lyrics are her own,
Calling me from this callous place,
While distant measures lead me home
To all her tender, loving grace,
Where music frees the mind to roam
And I am lost in her embrace.

Harold W. Peterson

Love Is

Love is me
Love is you
Love is in everything we do
Love is right, love is light
Love is the sweet wind that blows
On a summer night
Love is the joy that you bring
Love is everything
Love is the baby that cries in the night
Love is the way you hold him tight
Love is the words that you say
Love is what makes him feel OK
Love is what lets him sleep all night
In his heart he knows that
Love is alright
Love is in every word you say
Love is what gets me through the day
Love is the way you care
And that is how I know love is there

Annie Lawson

Heaven Sent

To ride the wind so warm and sweet
Upon a cloud there we shall meet
And in your eyes I see the sun
Telling me that I am the one
For you are an angel in my eyes
Peering down through endless skies
Yet you shall come to steal my cries
Then like the sun we both shall rise

Douglas R. Thomas

On Hearing Beautiful Music

How is it then, that man
Could in this world
Of stone and digging
So rise above his needs
To touch eternal beauty
And put down with pen these notes
That satisfy our lives.

God then must live within us,
For beauty seen
Can but predict the quality
That is expressed
In these most vibrant tones.

Our longing for such meaning
Comes in full waves
That hold no loss or lack
But sends the soul
Onto its winged way,
That it may find
The purpose of its being
In this, our Earth-born day.

Kathleen Brady

meditation

Heaven inside me
calm, clear, quiet, and free
contacting with all
breathing the Love
healing the heart
joyful as can be
drunken the spirit
with invisible wine

an eternal bliss
no one to miss

Mitra Kamali

Without You

Without you I am nothing,
  scared, defenseless.
Without you I am lonely,
  worried, restless.

Being away from you,
  will never be easy.
Being with you,
  has never sounded so pleasing.

I know I shouldn't fear,
  nor shed a tear.
I know you'll be alright,
  even if I worry every night.

Wait a few weeks,
  back in my arms—I hold you.
With you again,
  our love will never have felt so true.

Andrew Paul Salvatore

A Night of Rain

Immaculate rain,
Wash away the pain.
Teardrop stains,
Against my window pane.
Emptiness inside,
This shattered heart of mine.
Every drop of rain,
Washes away my pain.
Inflicting pain,
Intruding its way in,
Enclosed to this window pane,
What can I do? It's driving me insane!

There is loneliness outside.
He's staring at me!

"Immaculate rain,
Wash away my pain!"

Iniquities inhibiting my soul.
Evil thoughts!

"Immaculate rain,
Wash away my pain!"

Hemory Caban

Dolls

Friends, or make them what you
want them to be. Imaginary names
fall from the air, and we play happily again.

Florence Camp Jackson

Garden Haiku

Bumble sneaks a peak
of flowers yet unopened.
Buzzing, snaps his cheek.

Cricket rubs his feet
for next sun's heated warning.
Rubbing, falls asleep.

Inch worm seeks a treat
of raindrop's dewy nectar.
Sipping, finds relief.

Hatchlings cry and tweet
for morning's taste of glory.
Singing, stretch their beaks.

Garden's mighty fleet
brings never-ending story.
Blooming, makes life sweet.

Shirley Amitrano

Never Again

As I crawl into hiding,
Thoughts race through my head.
Scared and crying,
Wishing I was dead.

Never again!

Paralyzed with fear,
The room at a stand still.
Except for the trickle of tears,
Which wash away my will.

Never again,
Will I feel the blame.

Never again,
Will I feel the shame.

Never again.

Melisa Billings

You & Me

You and me sitting here,
And there's no one near.
You holding me in your arms.
Hypnotized by your charm.
The water crashing upon the shore.
We are laying here on the floor.
I want to be with you forever.
Do you think we will always be together?
Nothing could be better than this.
Holding each other and then we kiss.
You can do anything you want to.
I want to show you how much I love you.
Watching wave after wave.
Touching you is what I crave.
I will do anything to make you happy.
I'll show you right now and you will see.

Terah Hoxey

X-Country

Crack.
and I lunge
away from myself
the one before me flees
the beast following pursues
Anger and Need and Fear course
    over my head and
    in my limbs and
    under my feet
As animal strides thump and pound
animal hearts stretch flex and pump
    we flow and gasp
    in pride and desperation
where none but ourselves sees
who falls and who is held aloft
by the mechanism
of hot muscle on rigid bone.
am I the hunter or the prey?

Laura Musich

Bridge in Winter

A bridge in winter,
a siren whistling from
icy girders and frosted spans,
luring winter gusts from
brittle treetop and frozen meadow,
snaring and torturing her victims
who, in agony, leave howling,
hunks of wind-flesh still
clenched in her teeth.

Wayne R. Hollis

I'm Far Away

It doesn't seem right.
This shouldn't be the way.
Why am I here now?
Why didn't you let me stay?

You dropped me off here,
In this place of misery.
You didn't tell me why.
You left it a mystery.

You won't let me come back,
But you don't have a reason.
You won't say why,
But you hint it's for treason.

I decide I don't care.
I decide I hate you.
I will never come back.
I will try to forget to.

Rachel Hill

Crazy Mind! (A Haiku)

This crazy heart,
yearns for more;

The chattering mind,
goes on and on . . . .

Sushil Bhatia

War Souvenirs

The fragments from a blasted bomb
Have now adorned the fireplace
The destroyers of peace and love
Are preserved by the afflicted race

These souvenirs of a horrible war
These remnants of a sad retreat
These children of scorn and hate
These broken symbols of defeat

They made us walk on the path of hate
And led humanity to disgrace
Their place is under the burning wood
And not above the fireplace

Yusuf Rahat

Our Wedding Day

Before us lies a journey,
Bringing what, I do not know.
We'll walk that road together,
Because I love you so.

My heart is yours forever,
A truth you must not doubt.
To love, honor and cherish,
That's what life is all about.

To stand beside you in the good times,
When joy is all around.
To comfort you in the bad times,
When sadness will abound.

I hope you will remember,
These words I share today.
When beauty has escaped us,
And we are old and gray.

Today you become my husband,
And I will be your wife.
Today I want to tell you,
I will love you all my life.

Christina Bondesen

Shouldn't Have Loved You

Since I met you in July
I know I've never felt fine
I thought that you're deeply in love with me
And I thought that I was right
But then here comes a day
I can feel that your love it starts to fade
Instead of the three magical words you used to say
All you would say is just, "How was your day?"
And then here comes the Valentine's
That day I thought that I was blind
There was no card from you nor anything
Just to let our love shine
I've expected to get as much as I give
Now I realize I was as silly as a kid
I'm only a part of your contact list
And your heart has never been the place I live
I love you dearly, I always have
But I can't stand the pain no more, no I can't
Although I know I need you so bad
I've decided to let go, I won't regret

Juliana Kung

What If

Dedicated to my mother, Barbara Jean Vines 1951-1980
So many words not spoken, no mother daughter talks.
For you left without being given that chance.
I never talked to you, just cried to you.
You once held me close, but only for a while.
We were together, mother and daughter,
but now we are far apart.
I've grown up without you, but never has the thought
escaped my mind of "what if?"
Our time spent together was special, but memories
I cannot remember. I was just a baby and you,
my mother—taken from me, your daughter.
"What if?"

Elizabeth Vines

Wishing

Much love I have for my Darling it's true
Please tell me why do I have to be blue
Worry and Fear I still have every day
Wondering is today the day he will say
Sugar, I'm sorry, I love you so much
Please don't you worry come here let me touch
Got lots of trouble I can't seem to cope
I always burst your bubble, I know I'm a dope
You worry each day if he's a little bit late
You know what he'll say when he comes
through the gate
Sugar, I'm sorry, I love you so much
Please don't you worry come here let me touch
No sweeter a man you ever could meet
When sober he is he just can't be beat
I can't stand his drinking I sure wish I could.
He wants to stop drinking he knows that he should.

Shirley Hancock

untitled

When you don't notice me, this is how my heart feels.
picture of a broken heart bleeding

When you say you don't care, this is how I cry.
picture of an eye crying

When you say you want to kill yourself, this is the gun I see.
picture of a gun

And every time you say good-bye, this is the memory I hold inside.
picture of a cross with the word R.I.P,
standing in a doorway and the sun shining down upon it

Marina Mendez

Grandmother's Eternal Love

Your love is so special, it's kind and gentle
It is like no other, your hugs are warm
Your kisses are soft, you care so much
Nothing can destroy it, nobody can take it away
Times are hard now, I know soon it will be time to say goodbye
It is the hardest thing to do
I love you so much, I know I will be OK
Someone so special touched the lives of people you knew
Your heart reaches out in long ways of comfort
I know your scared, so am I, it's your turn now
For our hearts to reach out, to comfort
To hold and to love
You will stay in everyone's heart and soul
We know you're safe in the skies above
You will be an angel to guide love and protect us . . .
I love you mom-mom

Renee Abrams

Free

How long must I pretend to have fun?
Could this be over, is your game really done?
Can one's troubled soul try to move on
and fly freely through an endless dawn?
No I cannot with undying nights and no sleep,
because all this pain lies with me so deep.
Now I cannot laugh, just cry.
Why is it so hard to even try?
Don't worry I will stand, my heart won't let me die.
Still puzzled and longing to find another day,
I let you fool me, I let myself stay.
Maybe true love was not meant for me,
and you and I were never meant to be.
You should have let your heart see,
so you could tell me you needed to be free.

Sarah Mae Briggs

Interior Fantasies

Luck, Lucks of puss.
Grotesque to the core.
Larger than most, steadily stepping down with
each puff of a dreamy debut.
To the point of despair,
I can taste my own wear.
Inconstant impulses.
Do you visit often?
Don't have the time to stay.
A slither of slick,
A bit of a lick for
my temp to taste.
And while a lesser would falter,
I'm the lesser man.
Soothe his ways, yet
touch his pain.

Drew Robinson Parks

To Move On

However reluctant I may be about letting you go
I, also, realize that sometimes,
growth only occurs when one is given the room to expand.
When growth does occur, change is inevitable.

I realize that things are changing between us,
and not knowing what lies ahead is frightening,
but for either of us to benefit,
I have to let you go.

If nothing else, at least I'll know,
that I allowed us the opportunity to change,
and reach out to new horizons.
As individuals, this will allow us to grow and learn
with hopes that we'll both be richer from the experience

Anita Worthey

Mommy

Mommy of mine, please tell me again
Where did I come from?
In Heaven with the angels
My sweet child
One evening as I prayed for
A child to hold, my dear
An angel appeared by my side
So very near
These things it said to me
While on my bent knees
On this day I bless you with a child
God sent me to answer your pleas
A child it shall be
With eyes the color of a soft, blue sky
This child shall have the hair color of golden wheat
Do not be sad and no longer weep

Cheryl Rae Leach

My Sister's Face

Sometimes I'd sit and watch her
Her face so sweet and kind
Sometimes I'd just watch her
Knowing, we had so little time
Her life was slipping slowly
I prayed, I begged the Lord
Don't take my little sister
My very, very best friend
I held her weakened body
I kissed her pretty face
But God just didn't listen
He took her anyway
They say it's for the best
She's in a better place
But where God has taken her
I cannot see her face. . . .

Margie Diane Benoit

Then Came You

As years go by I spend my time with
someone who I tried to change like you,
someone who I know could never be you and
someone who only made me miserable because it wasn't you.
I found myself alone one day not thinking of you
and found that I should love myself
before God would bring me someone like you.
As I grew to love myself and others and be
on my own to prepare for the love that God
would bring me. Then came you.

Lucy M. Urrutia

Fine Wine

In my land there is a vineyard that
Produces the finest wine. I farm it and
Harvest it, though it was never mine. It
Was never tread upon nor devoured by cows.
And in this vineyard that I planted, the
Sweetest love grows. The field is tended by
Cherubs, the loving type they are.
Seraphim, they age it far sweeter than any
Star. Twenty and one years it waits for the
Keeper of the key. She can only be let in
By the Gatekeeper, me. No lips have tasted
It's content, no hands have caressed its
Golden form, only the sun's gentle beams
And the rain drops of the storm. Until the
Owner appears, only my feet shall touch its
Grounds. Only the birds shall see it,
Singing their glorious sounds.

Gerald Vincent Sutherlin

As Clear as Water

I find you to be as clear as water,
I can see your feelings,
I can feel your life,
And most of all,
Above everything I see in you,
I can see you love me,
And it's your love that sets me free,
When it comes to water,
It is necessary for sustaining life,
When it comes to you,
You are the one that sustains me,
Showing me what I have to do
And giving me all that I need,
To me,
I find you to be as clear as water,
And for letting me see again,
I love you . . .

Kin Lee

Quaint or Modern

A modern American girl of today
Believes in having her own way.
A girl in the days of old,
Always did what she was told.
A dress of today might show her curves,
But, the girl of yore lowered hers.
The American wife of today
Can work in the business world outside,
But, alas, yester-year's spouse,
Didn't dare to work out;
Her place was in the home,
Cooking, washing, and sewing.
The girl of yore had fun and care,
And was hardly ever called a "square."
But today, U minus Sage,
Are considered as belonging to an Aeon Age.
Now my lasses, tell ME this,
"Would you prefer, if you had a choice,
to be a QUAINT or MODERN Dish?"

Katherine Pearl Drewry

amaze.0 (the addict's lie)

The little brown round,
That little pill rides again.
Drowning, drowning,
In your own cathode tube.
Shoot the plastic,
Over the orange counter top,
Into that darkness void again,
I still love you, for the fool rides again.
Into the red, A small glitch,
Twitching around in this cynical world.
Sarcasm is your only escape.
Worldly. Worldly.
3 iron spikes,
Love is indeed a brutal exception.

Ryan Bishop

Taken Away

Too much life to be taken away
I don't want to go but I know I can't stay
amongst the shadows, which never end
soon enough my pain will descend
walking away from the river of life
away from love and all its strife
away from the pain I can't escape
away from the love that was once at stake
so much I cared for
so much I'd die for
so much I ended up giving my life for

Sara E. Mead

Glouster Point Pilot

There was a warrior from this ancient shore
Who fought in the second and last great war.
It was a simple police action when he signed up;
He spent four long years a prisoner of Germans begging sup'.

He had an old tea machine of matches and foil;
He made Red Cross tea with a bellows, wadding, and oil.
He smoked captured Russian cigarettes in nineteen and forty-three,
And choked at paranoid thoughts of his Virginian sweetie.

Two broken legs and no teeth in his smile,
He came home with tales that humor would beguile—
Of Germans running around in a broken coo-coo clock;
Tanks turning against the homeland, with Hitler to mock.

Over a thousand young souls died in his camp in those years,
Yet my uncle is always full of positive cheer.
A pilot he was and a pilot he is now,
Dreaming, living conquest with American power.

Berryman Green

The Wind Surfer

Somewhere between the deep and the sky
Alone I sail
Skipping over waves, flying through air
Pitting my strength against God alone knows what
As the wind and spray hits my face,
I'm filled with an exuberance that takes me to
heights unknown only by another wind surfer.

Louise P. Birchmire

The Lamentations of a Student

Cursed woe of toil and sorrow
From which children hate the morrow!
In which some people are so cruel
Inside the tortured depths of school.

Weekends only are students glad.
And only Monday are they sad.
Tuesday through Thursday students are
Hoping for the weekend so far.

Though weekends come and weekends go,
On Monday waiting is the woe.
Oh, how bad must the student feel;
Learning torture goes in a wheel.

Although they say it's good for you,
There must be a better way to
Teach students what they need to know
Without them thinking it's a woe.

When you turn eighteen you are free
To do what ever you darn please.
And if you survived the past pain,
Then say, "`So long, I've caught my train."

Chris Sauer

Nobody Knows

Nobody knows what to say it's hard to feel your sorrow.
Nobody knows what to do to prepare you for tomorrow.
Just keep your faith in the Lord, your life is in his hand.
Each day he gives you drops from it, like a grain of sand.
Nobody knows how many grains the Lord has in his hands.
Nobody knows how many days, 'til we leave this precious land.
He takes us up to Heaven all we need is faith in him.
Nobody knows the exact time when our Earthly life will dim.
We pray, "The Lord be with you," through many grains of sand.
To give you strength to walk alone and hold you by the hand.
Nobody knows what to say—but I know that tomorrow.
The Lord will strengthen you to handle your present sorrow.

Charles W. Smith

Soul Mate

I hear my name, yet it's all the same.
You're not the one I should blame.
This hate filled world has taken its toll
on one not knowing life's goal.

Never feeling love—out of the dark you make
your mark, for if love is true it's
because I found you.

Follow your heart into mine—as we twine
isn't this ever so Divine.
Our love so strong this can't be wrong.
Just sing this song—In this time of despair
I'm coming ever so near, don't you fear.

Shatter your hate before it's too late.
Faith is coming to be our date.
For finally I found my soulmate.

John Christpher Lesner

Come Follow Me

Come with me, love, to a land so divine
Where the living is easy and there is no time.
Feel your mind wander, it won't be so hard
Sit with me now, let me see who you are.

Come follow me, our dream is set to start
We'll lock our thoughts together and keep them in our hearts.

Play me a song, one that's filled with love
You'll hear the birds sing in harmony above.
Flowers are swaying as they dance to the beat
It's wild, maybe crazy, but we can make it complete.

Come follow me, many mysteries await you,
While the bright sun still shines, see where it takes you.

It's a steep hill to climb, but it's easy to try
At the top there's a castle made of gold in the sky.
You'll wear the crown, and I could be your queen
We'll sing and dance and live in our dream.

Come follow me, you could by my king,
We'll make this our world, only your love to bring!

Dolly Schuller

Unity

Your hands caress my face
like the gentle breeze of summer
warm and graceful
they make me drift to another place
entwined with you
we are one within this embrace
how I do not want to ever leave
I open my eyes to see your face
that of an angel, warm, soft, full of grace

William M. LaBarge, Jr.

My Angel

Need I compare you to a glorious morning?
For You are far more wonderful,
Not a moment of your life is boring,
You make the day bright and heart full.
The way you look at me,
When you're drifting asleep,
Is enough to make me fall to my knees.
And silently yet truthfully weep.
The smiles you give,
The giggles you share,
Makes me so glad you live;
For you I will always be there,
Oh, how I wish I were your mother,
I love you so much, my little baby brother!

Julie Scroggs

Your Dream

A lost young petal and many wondering and wandering souls
I see the dream you seek.
Follow me please, if you dare.
The dream is here for you not me.

I return by your side with a heart in my hand.
My heart is like a dancing flame of fire,
dancing to the beautiful music turned
by your beautiful eyes,
Your eyes that shine as bright as the morning sun.

Now that your dream has come true,
My innocent heart that was once as smooth as ivory
has turned to an ugly sulfur.
I retire my heart full of love, tears, and happiness to you.

I hope you will keep it warm and full of love as I have done.
You may not and may never love me,
but I care and cry for you and your beautiful soul.

Love her as I have loved and continue loving you.

Deseray Solis

God's Plan

I rose to meet you this morning,
The birds were singing their song.
The roses were blooming so brightly,
And my heart was singing along.

I sat by my window just thinking,
What would I do if you were not there
To remind me of all of your blessings
In this glorious world that we share.

The trees bowed down as the wind blew,
And petals from my roses were strewn.
My pathway seemed almost too perfect,
'Til I realized your plan was my gain.

You answered my prayers as I prayed them,
And even gave more than I had asked.
Many years I had struggled and wondered,
If I would ever be up to the task.

God's plan had always been shaping my life,
To prepare me for work of this day,
And now I look back and see how his hand,
Made me willing to do things his way.

Alice J. Mathews

If I Could

If I could, I'd hold you every time that you felt pain.
Dry your tears. Calm your fears.
Make sunshine out of pouring rain.

If I could, I'd embrace you while you slept so tenderly.
Watching the rise and fall of each breath.
Wishing your woe could be shared by me.

If I could, I'd laugh the most joyous laugh in the universe.
Just to share in each triumph would be my part of victory's purse.

If I could, I'd fight with the greatest passion history's seen.
Just a guarantee for me that yours is a pasture of infinite green.

But "If I could's" and "Wish I would's,"
And wants for all that's good and true
Will never be enough, my love,
To prevent life's hurts from touching you.

I have no magic potions. No enchanted words to share.
The greatest gift I offer you is myself on knees in prayer.

And as silly as I may sound and a zealous as I may be,
I know this gift of prayer for you is life's greatest guarantee.

I still may try to cry your tears and endeavor to halt your rain,
For "If I could's" from the heart of love are never done in vain.

Tina Haning

Life

It is such a waste to worry
Such trying times to hurry,
Life—such a treat
Oh, so very sweet.

Stop to taste, not in haste
Your fleeting and joyous youth.
it passes beneath your feet, but wait—
Age also runs at a certain gait.
What is your pleasure my dear?
Why are you still here?
Have you not learned as yet,
the pace is yours—you earn what you get.
Run from age and you'll get there faster,
make friends and you'll be the master.
What ever you have you wanted,
be clever in your endeavors,
life is yours, you wanted it.

Lou Langston

Dear Lord

Dear Lord, I don't mean to waste your time,
but I need to talk to someone kind

I need to know what it's like to die,
all the nights I think and cry.

Is there a Heaven up above?
Are we your children for you to love?

Will it hurt and will I feel pain?
Or will I hear an angel call my name?

If there is no Heaven, where do you go?
Do you fade into nothingness buried below?

If and when my life should end,
will I be reunited with my friends?

Is there a way I can see them now?
If there is, I beg, tell me how.

Well thanks for your time and patience to,
I have so many questions I wish I knew.

I guess these answers you can't explain
Unable to know I'll suffer the pain.

Pain of not knowing that endless fear.
I hope it is gone when my time is near.

Angela E. Butch

Buster

This is my dog,
Resting on a white and blue pillow.
He is in my room with white carpeted walls,
Yet he is fairly small,
Though he will not be here for long,
For his nap will be gone until night falls.

Ericka Jennings

Four Little Angels

Four little angels, yours and mine,
sent from Heaven for us to love.
They were sent with love so
precious and dear for us to share our home sweet home.
We'll build a little cabin down in a green valley
and there we'll live for ever more.
Our four little angels will go to school,
they'll learn to read and write, they'll go to church
on Sunday morn to learn of God our maker.
Four little angels yours and mine.

Florence L. Barnes

Hidden Crush

You touch me with angel hands
That seem to glitter in pain.
Hand marks written on my body
Are the only remains.

Shattered hope wears down,
As you turn your eyes away.
I choose to be ignored and follow
Your footsteps left in my way.

Mistreated love wanders off,
In my valley of death.
When I lie down and look above,
I see your face as I hold my breath.

Now my suffering is distracted
By your sparkling smile.
I would give a thousand pieces of my soul
To see that last awhile.

Nicole Mobley

Where Are You?

I don't know, Lord, where are you?
I feel like things are just falling apart
And I don't know what the next step is.
Lord, I've never felt so alone, so scared
I know what I need to do, but I don't know how
Lord, this is what you have been preparing me for
Now that it's here, all I want is to run away from it
Lord, you have to help me out with this one
I don't know if I can make it on my own
I don't know Lord . . . where are you?

Ivette Ntumba

Life

Life is a wheel that goes around and around.
Never stopping, or touching the ground.
Always has a beginning, middle, and end.
It's like a long story, that has a never ending.
It's something you can't hide from, or run from.
You have to face it eye to eye.
It has excitement and adventure all at the same time.
It ends when another one begins.
Life is a wheel that goes around, and around.

Gayla Morris

When I Was Just a Little Girl

I sit here this morning, not knowing quite what to do,
'Cause everywhere that I look, all I can see is you.
It's right here beside me, a vision before my eyes,
And it all seems so clear, like an angel in disguise.
I can see the joy that you gave me to carry in my heart,
I can see the strength that you gave me when we had to part,
I can see the hope that you gave me when I felt alone,
But of everything you gave me, it's the love that keeps going on.
It's deeper than the ocean and it's wider than the world,
And you gave it all to me when I was just a little girl.
Now as I sit here I know exactly what to do.
I look deep inside myself at everything I learned from you,
And I say it with lots of love and I say it with pride.
Thank you, dear mother. for the things I don't have to hide.
I thank you for the joy that you gave me to carry in my heart.
I thank you for the strength you gave me whenever we had to part.
I thank you for the hope you gave me whenever I felt alone.
I thank you more than ever, Mom, for the love that keeps going on.
It's deeper than the ocean and it's wider than the world,
And you gave it all to me, Mom, when I was just a little girl.
Yes, you gave it all to me, Mom, when I was just a little girl.

Melissa J. White

What a Father Means to Me

To my father Clifford K. Thatcher
Now that I have lost you, life is not the same.
I often cry for you in the night just to help relieve my pain.
I know that tears and sadness is not what you want to see.
I just feel terrible that you had to lose your life for me to see.
What a father means to me.
This has made me cherish seeing your smile, hearing you laugh.
It has made me remember that when you were happy,
you had an unmistakable twinkle in your eyes.
Why I had to lose you, I don't know why?
There is no one who can replace such a special guy.
It just hurts so much, that it took this for me to see.
Just what a father means to me.

Dwan Thatcher

Yes, I Am Eighty

Slipped on an oil spill breaking my arm
Made privy to the doctor's mindset

Are you often dizzy

Dizzy? Not in this life

Then came the insult: Do you know what day this is?
Must be Halloween the crocuses are blooming

In bed I request a newspaper
Eccentric me involved in the world
She says I'll bring you one
Of course it never comes
Why would an old woman want to read a paper?
Clearly wasted money should sleep or watch TV

Hear me now twenty-thirty-forty
When misfortunes come to haunt thy days
Interpret thine as mine
. . . if you can remember

Ruth Roland

Love

The word is used so many times!
Used to portray the heart, body, and mind.
A spiritual, verbal expression
To unfold life's expectations and ambitions.

Perhaps, an over-used syllable to say the least
Often recorded to save the peace.

A word sometimes found only at death's hour
Yet, with others, they sing about
it while taking a shower.

Check it out with your Family Tree
Without Love, where would you or I be?

Remember the Man? The Tree?

I'll remember you
Please don't forget me.

Annie Warren

Temptation

The moment was very tense;
we talked for hours about setting the soul free.
But as it became clear to the soul it broke the spirit.
I've never known the true concept of being a priceless jewel—
something you put away and watch the value increase.
I've had small taste of what life offers to people for lifetimes,
but too many times I contemplate
on the experience of others as to want the same.
Praying in God's name.
I once forgot who I was, as it was stolen and not replaced.
Lost again in this same running race, with nowhere to go.

Shirley Rogers

I Will Be There

When things get tough,
And you feel you just can't go on.
When life gets too tough,
You have my shoulder to lean on.

You can always count on me
I will be there.

Just when you feel all alone,
And it seems nobody cares.
And even though we're miles away
From one another right now,
We always have all the sweet memories
Within our hearts of all the wonderful times
We shared.

Call on me
I will be there

If you ever feel lost in life at any time,
And there's nothing but strangers near.
The highest mountain, I will help you climb
Without any hesitation or fear.
Just look for me I will always be there!

Sherry M. Moser

My Beautiful Rose

My beautiful rose,
As big and brilliant as my toes,
Painted as red as a bright red nose,
But now my beautiful rose has died,
I will wait for my beautiful rose to rise,
To bloom and become my beautiful rose,
As big and brilliant as my toes

Melissa Kreiser

Dreams

Dreams are made of happiness and love
With those who are friends 'til the end.
Dreams are made of kisses and hugs
From a love that helps your heart mend.
Dreams hold memories of years lost in time.
They hold the moments you let love pass by.
Dreams show you the paths
Of hearts you left shattered.
Up 'til the day you find
That lost love really mattered.
Dreams can show you that friends are forever.
And life is too short for friends to say never.
Dreams are there when no one else can be.
Dreams reflect your feelings
About things no one can see.
Dreams will allow what life will discourage.
But dreams will teach you
IN LIFE YOU CAN MANAGE.

Mandy Renee Edwards

A Look at the Bible

Turn to Romans three, verse twenty-three;
Read it carefully and you will see
We all fall short. There is only one perfect one
And that is Jesus, God's own Son.
Look now at Romans six, verse twenty-three;
Think of your life . . . will you live eternally?
Read First John three, verses sixteen and seven;
To love your brother, you must love God in Heaven.
Back to Romans—chapter ten, verses nine and ten;
Jeus Christ wants the hearts of men.
Turn to verse twelve of St. John, chapter one;
God gave you the power to be His son.

Trudy Carole LeVrier

Angels Soar So High Above

Angels soar so high above energized in the beautiful sky

A beautiful dove flies next to you
and shows you how your dreams come true

An angel then does appear singing

gently in your ear listening just to you

keeping you safe and happy too.

They listen to us all day long never judging
whether we're right or wrong.
Their spirit is pure and true with so much love in them too.

They're miracles from God

that's definitely true
never allowing us to feel blue.

Leona Parker Scannell

Have You Ever?

Have you ever felt the pain in life
Is like a large knife
That strikes you in the heart
Whenever you're falling apart.
There it remains,
and it drains
the life out of you.
The life you thought you knew.
Day after day
it pulls you away.
Away from the world's happiness
and it always leaves you helpless
Have you ever felt as though you've had plenty,
or are you still empty?
Have you ever felt like you had enough,
so you held your head up high and fought tuff?

Irma Samson

The Scheme of Things

It all fits like a million-piece jigsaw puzzle.
The scope so incomprehensively unique.
How history and life coincide is completely a mystique.
How Pharaoh, Hitler, and Jeff Davis failed in the scheme of things.
How poor souls perished from disease, and
yet cures were found, all in the scheme of things.
How, amidst calamity, chaos, and destruction
decency prevails, all in the scheme of things.
Is it Christian, Moslem, Jew, or Buddhist?
I'm not sure, but it all fits in the scheme of things.

Anthony Lewis Thornhill

Friend

I did not mean the things I said
and I wish I did not ask
I hope you can still accept me as a friend
you can least tell me if our friendship will never last

I'm sorry for saying those things
I know I wonder too much
I was only curious of those things
to see how you are

I only wish to get to know you better
but my chances have faded away
I only wish for a friend
and love in a friend way

I'm sorry for asking those things
I did not mean harm
I thought it was no wrong
to see how you are

Josh Cameron Marshall

Giving

Giving is the most important fact of life—
That no one can deny.
It is there to be known when it is felt by one's heart,
When you give from your heart.
Giving brings about change in one's attitude within a person.

Giving makes the stony heart melt within,
re-creating new life to a dying soul.

Giving never makes one tired of feeling like
you are losing by giving all the time.
Most importantly, giving pays off.
With eternal life for one to continue sharing,
with the gift giver of life, Jesus Christ, the author of giving.

So sleep on, Mother, until you hear the Master say, "Well done!"

Terrie A. Burford McGhee

Standing Alone

Standing alone in the night,
I wait, for him my pulse
races and my heart aches.
My eyes burn for tears
of longing and despair,
but I cannot weep.
I shed no tears,
now, no matter how I want to.
The chill of the breeze makes
my longing grow ever so slightly.
I cling to memories as if they were him,
but I can only hope that he will return to me,
and for me alone.

Sayeh Tehrani

Addicted to Familiarity

I seem to have a great investment in the perpetual need for sadness
I'm not as transparent as I thought I was
My eyes like blue chiffon in a warm and misty breeze
Lonely Oh, so lonely
For a divine being to see my shadow soul behind them
Reaching out to my hand of eternity
My life like a mirage
Intangible as the coastal fog
Did I die and get stuck in a linear dimension?
I don't feel real
Are my feet on the ground? Am I invisible?
I watch the world unfold around me.

There's so much going on
Have I disappeared in the light of the sun?
Am I the salesperson who was too honest to sell?
The seer of human flaw?
Wrapped in my cloak of sadness
Wrapped in my cashmere of pain
Dancing in a silver slice of the moon
Sadness in my tears like a warm and roaring rain.

Lori Heuer

I Finally Found You

I was lost and lonely, I felt empty inside,
with nowhere to run, and nowhere to hide,
There was no one to turn to, no one to care,
But then I remembered you were there.
But I couldn't find you anywhere.
You weren't beneath, above, or behind anything.
I felt like I was missing something, a very special part,
Then that's when I found you, right there in my heart!
But how could you forgive me, when I've done so wrong.
How could you save me, when I've waited so long.
Then finally, at last, someone told me the secret,
All I ever had to do, was just ask!

Vickie Reilly

Myopia

Beauty is talked about, limits imposed.
Standards are set up, knowledge supposed.
Rules make right wrong, borders proposed.
Eternity's timed, faith's indisposed.
Truth is made abstract, values opposed.
Have supplants wanting, needing's disposed.
Life gets false meaning, death's decomposed.
Emotions get sorted, feelings composed.
Thought taught without thought, wonder's reposed.
Honor is tainted, pride carefully posed.
Magic joins science, seeking's disposed.
Justice gets blinded, yes, unopposed

Daijo Akutagawa

Blinded

As the sun sets,
darkness is upon us,
always looking to find our way.

Walking around blind,
most of our lives,
always missing what is in our path.

But, when the sun reappears,
we ignore what is true.
Living our lives blind, both day and night.
Open the eyes of our hearts,
Where the sun never sets,
only then will we see . . .
what is true.

Theresa Skolen

Valley View

A cool breeze blows through
On a mountain in Valley View
Big tall trees shade the sun
A vision of beauty, artistically done
The hills look like a patchwork quilt
Roads and gardens, homes people built
The colors blend a spectacular show
Your eyes behold, nature's best below
Butterfly wings in the wind
Softly blowing as the trees bend
All these things are new
Sitting on a hill in Valley View
A place to sit and think things through
What to finish, what to do
I guess this is what you would call a retreat
It looks like Heaven, the air is quietly sweet
Lovely place with the right name
The wonders will intoxicate you just like champagne
I'll be back and I can't wait
To see this again in "Heaven's gate."

Mary Thom Carpenter

Forever and a Day

Forever and a day means that I want to spend
every day of my life with you. Forever and a day
means I'll give you an everlasting love
that's honest, sincere, and true.
Forever and a day means that I'll give myself
to you unselfishly. Forever and a day means that
I'll give you my all throughout eternity.
Forever and a day means that just as I loved
you yesterday, just as I love you today, I'll love
you just as much tomorrow. Forever and a day means
I'll always give you the best of everything I have to offer.
Forever and a day means that we will always be together.
Forever and a day means I'm so much in love with you,
and I want to make it last forever and ever.

Johnny Kendricks

O.C. and Me

They give you a hard hat and a red vest too,
When you start working with the County Crew.

You're up in the morning, an hour before dawn,
Packing your pail to work the day long.

You're out on the road throughout the whole day;
Trying to make a dollar so bills you can pay.

In the spring it's a job without much class;
You're pulling out fence posts and picking up trash.

The summers are hot, muddy, dusty and dry,
Why a man spends his life here, I do not know why.

In the fall we are busy, doing all kinds of things,
Shouldering roads and putting on wings.

The trucks and the graders are ready for snow;
We will soon get a phone call to say when to go.

I've had some good days, some bad ones too,
The older you get the tighter the screw.

I've worked with many throughout all these years;
Heard lots of stories and had a few beers.

When I am gone and no one thinks of me,
I'll still be glad I worked for the County.

Larry G. Rohloff

Milk

I drank some milk that tasted sour
And I sat there drinking hour after hour
Finally my eyes fell on the expiration date
November 9, 1988
The information didn't process so I drank some more
Then my head said, "This is a bore"
Then Mom came bursting in
"Don't drink the milk in that old carton"
"Too late," I said with a foolish grin
And I pointed to it in the garbage bin
To the hospital we went running
Our old carburetor was a-humming
Code blue the doctors and nurses said
Jamming needles into my head
When I woke up I felt like gook
In my stomach there was a hook
Now I know I made a mistake
Always look at the expiration date
Unless you would like to take a trip
To the hospital where every nurse needs a huge tip

Ariana Barusch

No Means to an End

Look around and there's nothing there
Your world is collapsing, all is suddenly bare
Groping for something to hold on to
Look in the mirror and you're not you
He's not your soul-mate, not even your friend
She's acting different. There is no end
To the disappointment and the heart-ache
Is everything masked, is everything fake?
Try to get up, don't let yourself fall
Obstacles will increase, you'll hit brick walls
The wells in your eyes will run dry
You'll want to just lie down and die
There's one remedy, though, which hasn't deceived
You just haven't tried it, you don't believe.
Trust and believe that you're never alone
Trust and believe nothing's written in stone
Trust that everything happens for good
Trust that you won't, even though you could
You're being protected, God is always there
Trust and wave a hearty goodbye to despair.

Yaffa Mieror

Another Day

Every dawn becomes a new day. Every dusk
another night. Every heart beats a new race
in this endless fight. But another day has
gone by and I'm still in your arms tonight.
Every wish goes unanswered. Every dream kept
with a prayer. Every question remains
unanswered and it's just not fair. But another
day has gone by and I'm still lying there.
Another day, another dream. Every moment
without you there is like a million years.
Every whisper that my heart makes seems to
be screaming your name, and when you're by my
side I feel so much more alive.
So love me for another day

Joe Mathew Like

The Power of the Priesthood

The powers of the priesthood given to every priest
at the moment of Ordinations is an awesome reality,
which takes place at the moment of transubstantiation
when Jesus, hidden in this veil of secrecy,
is present in all aspects of His Divinity and humanity.

The many miracles of the Eucharist proves this truth,
although there is no need of proof, as Jesus, their true Messiah
gave this power to His Apostles at the Last Supper,
which marks the beginning of Christianity.
Let this be an incentive to every student
who comes to the realization of the
great value and purpose of this vocation,
and the reward which awaits them in Heaven.

Sarah Gracie

Say Peace

Say peace, what a wonderful word it is, say peace,
The Holy Word that Jesus gave to His disciples to say, peace!
He said, upon entering say peace!

What wonderful joy it brings, say peace.
Can you believe that all things work together
For good for those who love peace?

Just try it brothers and sisters, say peace! We must love
One another, say peace. Don't be so critical of each other,
Say peace! Stop your back biting, say peace! Be a better
Example for your children, live peace, just say peace!

If you want to be closer to God live the word "peace."
God will help you off of your sick bed, say peace.
God will make your enemies leave you along,
Think peace, love peace, say peace!

God will calm the angry sea, just say peace, think peace, live
Peace! The Earth will be still say peace, live peace.
Stop your worrying, say peace, think peace.

God will make everything alright for you just,
Love peace, live peace, say peace!

Zelia M. Champ

It's OK

Sometimes I am lookin' right raggedy
Sometimes you will notice I walk a bit slower
Sometimes my speech is a little slurred
Sometimes I repeat myself
Sometimes I forget my train of thought
Sometimes I have no thought.
You may notice some or all of these things
In me and they may have nothing to do with MS
It may just be I'm gettin' old
So take that strained look off your face and
Give me a hug. It's OK.

Pat Long

Your King Has Come

Bride of the Lamb most blessed art thou,
rejoice and shout for the time is now.
Your years of mourning and sadness have ended,
for the feet of your King have finally descended.

In justice and truth He will establish His reign,
the end of all war, starvation, and pain.
Redemption is here for those who've believed,
and those who've endured will no longer grieve.

Creation exalts at the sight of the new dawn,
for the curse of man's sin is finally gone.
Death and destruction that recently plagued,
is conquered forever by the blood that now saves.

And now we can laugh at times long ago,
at the tears that were shed and heartaches we've known.
We will finally be rid of the flesh that entices,
no longer fooled by the devil's schemes and devices.

Now the omnipotence of Christ is revealed,
Satan is defeated by the sword that He wields.
Every man on this Earth will surely bow down,
but only the holy will be blessed with a crown.

        John Delamar

Bird

Sometimes I wish God would make me a bird
So I could fly free
I wouldn't be left alone
Just one of my own
When we try
To have people hear
The system fails
And we are all in tears
If nothing happened
Where would we be?
I would be a bird
Flying extremely free
Hear the sobs of society
Hear them lose in a game they choose
A battle that kills with a knife
Of a game called life
Mmm, Mmm, I don't know
Mmm, Mmm, why I can't let it go
My thoughts are tangled to deceive
I wish I was a bird, so I could fly free

        Elizabeth Anne Stollings

My Heart Longs for You

I had this dream that I would find happiness with you
The reality was that you distanced yourself from me

But no matter what,
You gave me the Strength
to continue to move forward
You gave me the Hope
that one day it would be like my dream
You gave me the Love
that I knew was there but always doubted
You made me smile
Even during our darkest moments

And even though I'm not here with you
My Heart longs for you
Though I'm happy standing where I am
I still feel the need to be close to you

Tell me how can it be
That with the happiness I feel now . . .

I still want you.

        Tania Guzman

Never in Her Presence

What I'm dealing with now because of her, I've found
the perfect cover for manly pride refuses to let her see
the effect of her words.

Just outside my window it rains profusely, but I will
not stand in your presence in pain.

But she has hurt me, for she stares into my soul in
search of the reward she thinks is deserving of her.

I refuse to allow her to discover why it is I stand
smiling as I walk into the rain.

But just outside of her ability to comprehend this
smile, the rain allows me to do what I would not let her see.

        Anthony L. Anderson

I Seem to Be

I seem to be quiet but inside I'm loud.
I seem to be weak but really I can show you.
Some think I'm not good at sports but look, I am.
I seem to be neat but really I can be sloppy.
I seem to be good in art but really that is true.
I seem to be always friendly
But sometimes it's the other way around.
I seem to be funny but believe me I could.
Some think I'm this and that.
But really I'm that and this.

        V. Rajski

It's Great to Be Me

Hi, my name is Kati
And I'm a young lady.

I just turned nine,
I'm my dad's Valentine.

My favorite game is Scrabble.
I can spell words like "game" and "babble."

My mom says I'm a good cook.
We get all our recipes from her cookbook.

My dog's name is Jumper.
Sometimes we tie him to our bumper.

This assignment is a bore,
I'd like to throw it out the door.

        Kati Rudy

The Holocaust

It was a time of war and strife,
when an old man could do nothing but think of his wife;
it was known by few but felt by more;
this was known as the dying war.

 In a time of righteous agony and rampant fear,
the soldiers strove mightily not to hear
the screams of the dying, told truths untold,
then slowly died out, into the cold.

 It was the death of dreams and the killer of life,
their voices rang out in the streets and cut like a knife.
The lack of mercy and the absence of right
made it easy to pick out the many bodies in the dying light.

 When the smoke cleared and the dust settled,
no one knew how many had died.
All around there were broken men.
They said it wouldn't happen. They lied.
You could hear the cries, you could smell the fear,
but good fortune that day was mine,
and it occurred to me that the heart of a good man,
it seems, is hard to find.

        Clym Aleel Gatrell

Advice

Hear the wisdom
I speak from the Peak Valleys of my heart
Let me break you off some Knowledge
From the chocolate chip factory
Words that dig the soul deep
Words making complete logic
One can dance
From broken chances
Slam doors
Missed opportunities and mistakes
Find your way through tenderness in eyes
Let the angels of mind
Be comfort to your yearning
Giving you strength to move upward
Faith will heal the invisible pain hidden
Resurrect the direction of your path
Changing left turns
Into right passages
Call possession of power to side
Wipe the mud from your eyes and see

Vanessa Anderson

Fusion or Fission

Does one dare question the thought
That one will be consumed
If the continuance prevails?
This love that torments
And falls possibly, forever, on cannot be.
It seems to be stimulating 'tis true
This, morosity, but perhaps also creativity.
. . . And how so consumed
By the fires of coupling souls and spirits
At last released in fusion or fission?

Catherine A. Rich

Through Baby's Eyes

Mama's only sixteen and in a little bit of a fix
She has some decisions to make for someone so young and usually sick
She'll see the doctor today to check out her options you see
But mama's not been herself, no time to care for me.
The doctor just said he could help her today
If she'd sign these papers to take me away
It will only last a while he told her you see
The pain won't last long, but what about me?
"You'll have another change without baby," he said.
So now it's decided they're going ahead.

I'll be with Jesus today, this one thing I know.
I'll be with Jesus today, I know He loves me so.
My life is taken away before I am born
But my new Daddy's arms will be secure and warm.

My mansion's ready for me in this City of Old,
Oh, the streets up here are made of pure gold.
Now, I'm in my new daddy's arms.
I'm His bundle of joy, 'cause I'm in Heaven now.
And I'm my Daddy's bouncing baby boy.

Gary G. Williams

Precious Life

I woke up this morning and wiggled my toes,
I wiggled my fingers and touched my nose.
I opened my eyes and I could see.
I thanked the Lord for blessing me.
I jumped out of bed and I could walk,
I could smell the coffee and I could talk.
I could say the words and I could read.
How lucky I am that I came to be.
I swam the fastest of all those tadpoles,
I burst through that egg and low and behold
God had created another great soul.

Mary L. Burch

Fallen Tower

There is this place between bliss
and rock bottom.
It's knowing a Vietnam Veteran on sight.
At the bus stop today, I saw him.
Millennium Moses standing amidst
the sand of his newly-parted sea.
A sunflower in a field of snapdragons,
towering, pseudo-defiant, crumbled.
Haunted.
It was his eyes;
the unattainable sapphire fury
of Heaven and Hell combined; like my Father's.
Hair, long and unattended,
he drooled from lips
that hadn't been kissed in years.
His make-shift shrapnel clothing
wreaked from a pain that I will never know.
Sea of faces stared in pity. In fear.
I looked on; saw my Father,
and needed to hold him.

Roshelle L. Amundson

The Planet Body

the sky is my hair
the wind is my breath
there is a volcano deep inside me
it is my heart
a river of lava flows inside me
my blood
an earthquake occurs when my skin is ruptured
there is no need to look at the stars
when there is a planet to be discovered in
YOU
and
I

Chrystel Lynn Justice

Pages of You

You make the hours burn like the sunrises
Pages of you
Torn out
burned
Thrown away and lost
through shame
Pages of you were thrown out
Pages of yesterday
and feelings long gone
and lost.

You make the hours
crawl slowly on begging knees
You make the moonlight
drip
slowly though the window pane
the pain . . .

Lisa M. Martin

Where in the World . . . ?

Colors, shapes, people, Earth,
Many colors of the Earth are green.
Green is the way of life,
Life is like a fantasy.
Fantasies aren't always nice,
Nice flowers maybe, but not reality.
Reality is like a wonder world,
In a wonder world you don't know what's happening.
What's happening is what's going down around you,
You are a time bomb that is waiting to go off.
Off the Earth and out of this world.
Where in the world are you?

Daniele Lee Young

Dear Daddy

I understand what MS is
and in my book it says
you will live for a long time
I know you know that there are a lot of different people
who have different kinds of MS
so don't worry you will be just fine
if you acted like mom did when she had cancer
then you will be just fine.
We all are on your side and you will make it through this.
And you will live forever
I love you Daddy.

      Lacy Jo Bates

My Prayer

When MS reaches a person,
And starts its heartrending works,
It makes no difference who we are.
Young, old, teenager, female or male
In the nature of it all, MS causes pain.
MS destroys our quality of life

Whenever God can get all of us together to
fight for a goal a cure for MS
Would you say this could be the miracle?
Yes, with all my heart, for all His people.

      Marie Puckett

The Beginning of the End

We are at the beginning of the end
The secret, power hungry few
Are gaining more and more control of our lives
We have always believed the myth
That we were masters of our own destinies
Wake up—big brother is not coming
He is here.
There are no freedoms, no choices
They lay out our lives and make us believe
That we're doing what we want to do
When a voice comes along to speak the truth
They snuff it out
We don't even question anymore
We protest for a little while
And then we accept
They sit in secret with their fat, well-fed bellies
Their money and their power
They have no compassion, no love,
No feeling at all
Except the insatiable appetite
To rule the world

      Geraldine Jacobs

Jazz on a Raining Afternoon

As I gaze with a silence mood at the steady rain out my window,
thoughts invade my head with a harmony of serenity.
A misty flow of raindrops cascade off my windowpane,
as I'm captured in my day dreams once again.
Turn up the volume to let the soothing sounds tenderly rapture me,
that I'm infatuated to be captivated in a trance of hush tunes.
A jazzy melody to relax my sense of being.
Take me there on a raining afternoon.
A smooth composed sound that's killing me softly
with whispers of enchanting and fascinating flavor
that are, Oh, so delicious.
A cool groove that examines my purpose as an observer
of appreciation of life from my point of view.
To feel this, to respect the one with a design of positive vibes—
an untainted clarity of perfection.
I respect a higher one who keeps me striving to be true to oneself.
I will continue to maintain this feeling on a raining afternoon.

      Glenn Pope

Not That You'd Care Anyway?

When you walk down the street, do you see me?
No, not the preacher on the corner or the girl on the bench.
Yeah. Right there. The guy looking for food in the trash can.
You see the tattered trench-coat I wear,
those filthy, cut-up gloves and dirt-covered cap?
Did you ever walk by and drop your spare change in my cup,
or give me a sandwich, or drop off a blanket?
What about helping me with a job, or letting me stay at your place?
Do I remind you of the decay of society;
am I what you don't want to see?
That's OK, I'm used to it—not getting a chance, that is.
I always see you, with your sports car and fancy suits.
You probably live in a mansion with a pretty wife and cute kids.
There's probably a lot of food in your fridge.
I wonder what would have happened if I had a chance;
would I be in the office, or maybe I'd have a house and family?
Maybe I'd at least have some food.
Oh, well. I guess I'll never get a chance, not in this life.
Maybe next life?
Not that you'd care anyway.

      Nicholas Close

I Remember I Love You

I remember your laugh, I remember your smile,
I remember the way you told me it's alright,
When I look back and think, I remember your hugs,
I remember your voice, as soft as a teddy bear,
I remember when it would rain, you held me tight,
I remember, grandma, I remember.

Now I'm here without you, I miss you grandma,
I want you here, not there,
Not far from me, but close to me,
I remember you and I love you,
I love you grandma, I'll never stop loving you,
Not even if the world tumbles on top of me.

Straight from my heart, straight from my soul,
I love you and I know that you love me,
So don't forget me, I won't forget you;
I'm telling you now, we'll always have each other,
In our hearts, in our souls,
I miss you grandma, I'll never stop,
Until you come and be home with me,
Don't forget this: I remember I love you!

      Susana Evelyn Navajas

Uncontrollable Desire

Desire . . . when I think of you;
when I see you at a distance;
when I hear your voice;
when I walk next to you;
when I sit near you;
when I stand behind you . . .
at times I walk away.

When I stay, the intensity increases as I talk to you;
as I look into your eyes,
as I catch your smile . . .
I feel my body responding.

Soon the pleasure becomes too much . . .
we move closer;
you touch my hair, my face, we kiss.
You say things that feel so good . . .
I want to stay.

You have the power to move me
to another place in time
where you melt my body from the inside out;
where I can experience pleasure
in new ways and forgotten ways.
When I have to walk away . . .
I want so much to stay.

      Margaret J McDowell

The First Bite

To my grandnephew
I heard you got bitten the other day
by a little girl with whom you play.
The bite was hard, the bite was swift;
You should have stayed in your crib.
The first bite is a warning of the things to come.
They'll do it often, they'll do it very long,
so get used to it and take it all in stride.
Put up your chin, don't let it hurt your pride.
It's a woman's job to bring you misery.
It's been happening all through history,
so welcome to the world and don't have a fit.
You've come from a long line of men getting bit.

Tom Graham

Mist of Our Dreams

In the morning mist of dreams
Where lives unknown are liven
Where thoughts are unspoken and
Promises are unbroken
And those that are . . . forgiven.

In that morning wash of wakening,
The mind is fooled—the heart is fueled
With unbidden desires . . .
Bodies tremble with fires
And the depth of our meaning is pooled.

Our minds strain to believe
What the night left behind;
Was it wish, was it lust,
Was it wrong, was it just?
Or will it always remain undefined?

A regular interval of unconsciousness
Takes hold of our fate, so it seems.
Do we really make our own choices?
Do we speak with our own voices?
Or is it really just the mist of our dreams?

G. Smith

Life

Life in the crevice of the rock
Flower in the midst of the sand
The foaming waves talk
Conveying the hardship of the land
The sun scorches those who dare
To engrave their memories in rocks of time
Forever standing there
Even after its maker crosses life's time line
Waves angry and judgmental
Ever raising their demands
Burdening those whose monumental
Pleasure is in the scorching sands
Yet the peace of life's serenity
Abounds here in this place
Where every emotion presents itself
With a slightly different taste
From the flower with no water
Isolated and alone
To the critters that here loiter
With only the waves to call home

Amy Arita

Skyward

Together they stood 'neath the azure sky
Watching the birds soaring on high;
Each man wondering, "Why can't I
Sprout wings that I too may fly?"
In a voice as soft as a father's sigh,
God whispered . . . Orville, Wilbur . . . Try!"

Dorothy Gilbert

My Life Is in the Hands of Destiny

Every day I hope and dream
That my future will be secure
With happiness and health it would seem
I shall gratefully endure
If I shall find the one true to love me
If I should remain dignified and alone
Whatever happens my life will remain free
My heart my spirit and my home
Wherever I go and whatever I do
I'll live life until it is through

Laurie Lindgren

Love Across the Miles

The time that we were apart
My feelings for you grew stronger
I missed hearing your voice
And seeing your smiling face
But I just remembered the time
that we spent together before I left
To make me feel happy
Every day you tell me you love me
and I start to trust you more
My heart belongs to you
and I love you very much
So you don't have to doubt my love for you
I will stay true to you
No matter what happens
and I will stand by you always
Through the good and bad times
The laughter and tears
and whatever life has in store for us

Koren Nishida

Yoswimitee Pam

Yoswimitee Pam was the kind of fish
Who some folks thought was quite a dish!

Her color was red,
But she wanted blue.
Now what do you think she was going to do?

She searched hard for some blue.
She wanted that blue hue.
(hmmmm . . .)

NOW she knew what to do!
STAY RED!
That's what she'll do.

Ann Alley

Life Is . . .

Reflections on the eternal question
Plague the mind of generations and more
Driven to madness by quests gone astray
None closer than those before.
Inundation of provoking news
Spawn cries and confusion of all
Tempered by this communal bond
But shaken by the fall.
And the question shifts from fringe to center
Carrying the weight of the globe
Few step forward to shoulder the response
Easier to wait and hope
But when I go to sleep at night
And have her to hold in my arms
Lost in her eyes and captured by her heart
Safe for the moment from harm
I understand it all
Like a glorious light from above
The question eluding predecessors
Has been answered . . . life is love.

Mark Connelly

To the One I Will Always Love

A love so pure can never be wrong
For God knew I was weak, not very strong
He saw the pain that was deep in my soul
He knew without help this pain would only grow
My heart in chains at the devil's front door
God held out his hand and said, "Cry no more"
He sent a gift—that gift was you
His plans for us only He knew
You released the chains from my heart
Giving me a second chance, a brand new start
No more darkness, no more tears
Your love destroyed most of my fears
My mind at peace, my heart can now sing
Only you deserved to wear this ring
I love you more than you will ever know
You're a wonderful part of my soul
Hold on tight—our days are not long
A love so pure can never be wrong

    Pamela Gail Stennett

Dear Dad

This isn't a letter, nor a threat at best.
It isn't a promise either, it's merely a request.
You say I ruined the family, but you're the one that did it.
You had an ideal model, I just didn't fit it.
At my graduation, don't dare show your face.
Don't walk me down the aisle, it's definitely not your place.
No matter how things change, there will be no more hugs.
Your actions have been harsh, and I'm gonna hold a grudge.
I'm gonna have some kids, don't ask if they can play.
Things could have been different, but you had to be that way.
You're ignorant and shallow, immature and selfish too.
I'm thankful for one thing, I didn't turn out like you.
If I die before you, have no grief to give.
'Cause when I was alive, you wouldn't let me live.

    Kathleen D'Amico

Oh, My Precious Tiny First Born Girl

On a cool August eve,
You were given to me and you were taken from me,
And taken to Heaven,
My Precious, Tiny First Born Girl.
But in the few moments that I held you,
They meant a lifetime to me and to all who love you.
We held you so tenderly,
Oh, so tenderly.
And we know in our hearts it was meant to be,
So when we look to the sky and the stars,
We will always be looking at you,
My Precious, Tiny First Born Girl,
So rest in peace, our little loved one.

    Kathern Louise Hille

My Father

Some people find it hard to love
This I know is true
You closed your door on me and I closed mine on you
There were no Father's days, no Happy Birthdays,
no parades or calls just to say . . .
I never said goodbye, we just parted
You gave me life and I made lives you never even knew
Of all the people I've loved
Daddy, I needed you, I loved you
And now that it is too late
I'll miss you
In my heart, in my mind, in what makes me who I am,
I know deep down in my heart that you loved me
and I loved you
Goodbye, Daddy, and God bless you

    Catherine Lee

I Had a Dream

I had a dream of times gone by,
When little things would make me cry—
Like tangled hair or skinned-up knees,
Dead frogs or a sudden swarm of bees.
But now "just past" the prime of life
I understand a greater strife—
An adulterous spouse began my tears—
His betrayal after twenty years.
And then he worked his deceitful schemes
To take with him my kids, my dreams.
Therefore I've learned what true grief entails—
Much more than a kite that never sails.
It's a broken heart, a shattered soul,
A flow of tears only oceans could hold.
Living alone, sharing no love.
My only lifeline is God, above,
Who tells me that He is on my side,
So in that promise I faithfully abide.
When this grief ebbs, then I'll cry o'er a stubbed toe
Or seeing a lightning bug's silent last glow.

    Diane Tennihan

Life's Garden

There is a delicate pink rose
Whose fragrance is so rare;
It whispers in the wind,
And beckons to the air;

"Come join me in my dance"
Soft petals for a season;
My floral swirls enchant,
Love's treasure is the reason.

We float down moonlit paths,
Radiant clouds beneath our feet;
The fragrance of the rose makes pale,
Other vapors that we meet.

Drifting high above the heavens,
Hearts blooming as we fly;
Fragrant illumination of song,
Memories of angels as we pass by.

When the soft, fragrant dance grows dim,
Thorns rain and storm clouds start;
But the rare pink rose re-blooms each time,
Love's memories fill our hearts.

    Diane F. Iacopi

Look at Me

Look at me.
Tell me what is there.

Look at me.
Will you stay or run?
If you stay that shows you care.
If you run remember to look behind you for I will follow.

Look at me.
Am I walking or in a wheelchair? Do you mind?
Will you still love me?
You should, because I'm still a person.

Look at me.
Do you love or hate?
If you love is it true? If you hate, why?

Look at me.
Do you look at talents or my heart?
What if I have no talent, will you turn away?

Look at me.
I am a child.
Please love me for who I am.
For I love you.

    Megan Helferich

Shattered Dreams

I can't believe it, Andre is dead.
Walking to the store, he was shot in the head
A young black man fallen victim to violence;
All this black on black crime doesn't make any sense.
Broad daylight and no one saw nothing,
 Afraid to talk, someone has to know something.
If he were their friend, they would be the first to talk,
but he wasn't, he was mines, so they just stare at the chalk.
If it were up to me, there would be no violence in the world.
So tell me, who is going to explain this to his little girl?
She now has to grow up without a father in her life,
it's like cutting her heart with a double-edged knife.
Who will sing to my children when I'm dead and gone?
And when they go to sleep, who will sing them their song?
Will the world ever become a better place?
Will there ever be a smile again on his daughter's face?
It must be the end of the world, or at least it seems.
So many broken promises, so many shattered dreams.

Rhonda Nicholson

My Father's Gift

My father has given me many a thing,
For Years I glided upon his wing,
He showed me love and withdrew me from hate,
And as I got closer to the adults gate,
He nudged me a little,
and then pulled me through.
Not even knowing If I would come through.
life can be bumpy and life can be tough,
but with my fathers help, I made it through stuff.
Now my father, finally needs Me,
and I'm hoping, that I can help him to see,
That all of his love and all of his care,
has boomeranged back for both of us to share.

Maureen Moncrieff

Love Anew

Our love is a precious gift from God above
Which takes flight within us like a graceful dove.
It appears that our hearts flood with joy,
As we anticipate a life meant for every girl and boy.
Though our love is new it can be described uniquely,
We feel afraid because it arrived here so quickly.
One thing we realize is that we don't want love to leave,
Because it is Happiness we're trying to achieve.
We begin and end each day sharing and bonding,
And next year our love will be described as astounding.
Rings of love will follow after a while,
However, our true symbols will be seen in our smiles.
People will notice the difference; they will stop and stare,
Since we're starting life anew; we won't care.
Many will analyze our love and put time restraints on it,
But whatever they decide it just won't fit.
We'll realize they are not ready for the experience of,
Sharing with us in this special intimacy we call LOVE.

Patrice Tidwell

Nurani

Nurani, you make my heart skip a beat!
Nurani, you are my world!

Nurani, I love you so!

Nurani, you make me dream again!

Nurani, I will always love you 'til the end of time its self!

Nurani you are a shinning star in my night!

Nurani a person that will live forever in my heart and mind,

you are a gift of God!!

Paul Dean Marlowe

The Leaf Falling off the Tree

The leaf slowly fades away,
Holding on to her last breath.
Holding on to the branch with all she's got,
But the wind betrays her.
Falling slowly to the ground,
She wonders when she'll reach.
Days pass by and she's still falling.
She's patient, though,
Knowing the end will come.

Lisa Thornton

Sitting by the River

Sitting by the river
with the breeze in my hair
Sitting here watching the ripples come to me
I wish that I could run free as the river I see
I wish that the ripples would wash me to you
And the breeze would blow you to me
We'd meet in the middle
Somewhere in the trees
We'd fly away and finally be free
I'd like to seize the moment
and keep it in my heart
If I'd seize the moment
We would never be apart
But for now I'm just sitting by the river
Thinking about you
But for now this scene will have to do
'Til I find you

Adam Lingenfelter

Forbidden Lovers

Two lovers engaged in a forbidden passion of love.
Both know how they feel about the other
But no one understands the two lovers.
Is it a crime for them to love one another?
No, it is only natural; a part of nature.
But some think that it is unnatural for the two
And they try their best to stop what is happening.
Little do they know that for all of their ambitions,
They are pushing the couple closer than before.
When the time is right,
The couple will embrace each other
And announce that their forbidden love
Is no longer forbidden.
For they have taken the final step
A step that sealed their fate
As LOVERS FOREVER.

James Parrish

Ultrasound Vision

There it is, up on the screen,
the most beautiful face I've ever seen.

Yes, the monitor is color.
Yes, the picture could be too.

No, the film was black and white,
but, Oh, my lord, what an enchanting sight!

Some people say they just don't see it,
some people say it's so alien.

I see my grandson, granddaughter,
generations to come.

I see myself and my parents.

There it is . . .
the past, the future!

Janet Harrison

Beauty

If a smoky blue genie happened my way
And offered me one wish, I wouldn't ask for pay.
I would wish a wish for the whole universe,
One that would never be seen as a curse.
I would ask that all things beautiful and good
Be seen, appreciated, and understood.
The morning dew shimmering while the sun rose,
That golden brown deer frozen in a delicate pose,
The harmony that floats when a young woman sings,
That flash of blue on a brush jay's wings.
All things lovely, near and far,
Would all be recognized for the jewels they are.
So maybe some would stop and admire
Instead of just rushing by on spinning tire.

Kaila Finlayson

Ode to a Lover Not Yet Seen

You are not here, yet you have my heart to
the full just the same.
I've not laid sapphire eyes on you, yet I
know no other beauty save that of your name.
I hear music in all God's creation, yet it is
your voice that veils me in starlit
wonder's dream,
and it is you, and you alone
can enter here,
claim that secret sacred place,
and reign its king.

Bethany Richelle Cramer

Imbedded

Imbedded deep within Mother Earth
She has long since established herself
Alone and unique
Aloof or so it seems
Her arms outstretched waiting to nurture
Though once vital and limber
Are now withdrawing
Still seeking, coveting a personal touch
She reaches and discerns
The warmth she despairingly needs
No longer passionate
But within the solace of the memory
She encourages the discourse
The loneliness subsides
She is once again fulfilled
As daylight ebbs
The stillness of dark is actuated
Stealthily across her vista
She remains stoic, recondite, waiting.

Alberta Risner

Life

We all have to learn
That everyone makes mistakes
Everyone has many different masks
Our goal is to see what's under those masks
When you find that
You find yourself
Once you find yourself, it's time
Time to live
Experience things
Know things
And love things
'Cause with love you find happiness
With happiness you find peace
When you put that all together
You find the meaning of life
What is the meaning of life?

Cheryl Ann Nielson

Reality

As night is here the clouds seem a hundred
feet straight up; every now and then there
is a clearing in the fast-moving clouds
and I catch a glimpse of a angelic star; its
brilliant light illuminates the sky;
accompanied by a trillion others, their
presence lay a carpet of peace atop the
night; I hear the continuous sound of an
orchestra of crickets, as well as
an occasional chirp from a nearby humble
bird; the night is young as a breeze brings
comfort to this hardened body; from afar,
the sound of the city brings me back to
the realization that I'm not in the paradise
that I've tried to mold myself into; the
sound of a jet streaking through the sky; how
it jogs my thoughts to attention; for the
future is now the present, and the present
now the past.

John-Isaac H. Brock-Hines

You Should Have Known

I look at you through glassy eyes
though tears get in the way
I can't see but I'm not blind
I can't withstand another day
I sit in silence and weep in sorrow
who knows what we'll be by tomorrow?
by then I wonder, will you see
how very much you mean to me?
if you can't, you're in denial
I've felt this way for a while
or will I lie in a puddle of my own
with a note saying you should have known
never to be awakened again?
I ask you now, are we still friends?
I ask you now, so tell me true,
what does that word mean to you?
I'll stand by you through thick and thin
my love for you comes from deep within
so hear me now and believe, because it's true,
when I look in your eyes and tell you I love you

Kim Ann Klang

Anger

I can't see through the darkness.
I cannot extricate myself from this anger.
I tried to scrutinize myself to find out
 what's wrong.
But all I see is pain.
I tried to embellish myself with laughter.
I tried to talk it out with friends.
But all I see is darkness.
Will this pain ever end?
The fire in my eyes can show you how I feel.
But all I can do is keep it real.
Try to hold it all in, until my dying day.
Hopefully it's not today.
Even though the darkness doesn't leave,
I will pray, and I will believe.

Candace A Green

My Aunt's Spiritual Legacy to Us

One day at a time, O, my God, is all I can do
Let me join my suffering with you
Limited in activity, still let me be
A loving presence to all who come to visit me
While trembling and shaking often tear me apart
The world's intentions I carry in my heart!

Mary Joan Meyer

Seas Song

Misty mornings lullaby across the ocean blue
As the siren sings her lilting song
Beckoning me to sea!
She sings come with me, come with me,
To the deep blue sea.
Where you and me will sail away across the gentle rocking waves,
And the sea maidens fair will caress you there
Out in the deep blue sea.
So come along, you and I
Across the ocean blue,
Bobbing to and fro we go
To the deep blue sea once more!

Valerie Melton

Love Sonnet 23 (To Vala)

Deeper than outer was her inner space,
where her thoughts formed the substance of her lair;
deep I dove to explore that dreamy place,
fingers to run through her silk-crimson hair.
She's seen through a watery medium,
where things are not as close as they may seem;
I struggled on through the depth's tedium,
to reach her, to hold her, to grasp her dream
But the currents held me just short of her,
as I stretched and reached and begged for her hand;
—What would she do with this strange voyager?
—What made him think that he might understand?
And as I was gasping for my last air,
She reached out and took me, our dreams to share.

John Joseph Cox

Heavenly Agenda

Millions of eyes view the twilight horizon
Oblivious to Venus lounging in full glory
Guiding her radiance into a cave
Where Mars completes a study & review
Of parchments annotated with galactic codes
Illuminated by love's mistress of the heavens
Her golden tresses blowing in the solar wind
Like the flame of an oil lamp on a breezy night
Sharing a soulful delight in desire's manipulation
Deceiving & misleading with the most charming of airs
Directing cares to the Golden Mean
To create sights unseen, but so very welcome
A star seed incubates in Jupiter's orbit
While Venus & Mars prepare the field
Neptune & Pluto wait on the back burner
Anticipating the finale spotlight
Whose beam will make their roles more pronounced

Barry Tingle

The Arrival of Spring

One day spring came and so did you.
My garden blossomed and you did, too.
Your first hello is what I long for,
And your first smile is what I remember.

April's life is easy and love is easy.
Roses multiply so effortlessly,
With various designs of shapes and colors,
Inviting flows of winged creatures.

I wake to watch birds dance and sing,
Holding you close each May morning.
Parted we're obliged from dawn to dusk,
Love's simple not but it's a must.

Then June and July I tend to forget.
At night I wish she's in my bed.
I hope she knows love is for her,
But it's your first smile that I will remember.

Dara Ung

I Love You

I remember everything you say.
You're a part of me that will never go away.
I stare so deep into those eyes so green,
I stare so deep that my image is seen.
But it's not me that I'm looking at,
It's the way you look at me back.
Thoughts unseen, things unheard,
Yet the silence is broken by those three words.
You say, "I love you," and I ask, "Why?"
You say, "Because your beauty is as endless as the sky."
It feels like a dream, something so unreal.
For the first time I know what it's like to feel.
All my emotions run through me at one time.
I now know that I'm yours, and you're mine.

Jenny Rachel Reese

Softly, as in a Summer Morning

Softly, as in a summer morning
You come to me
But only in a dream
And touch my cheek the way you used to
And run your hands through my hair
And look into my eyes . . .
That remind you of an ocean
So deep you get lost in them
And put your arms around me
And tell me how much you love me
And how much you care for me
How could I have been so callous?
To throw your love away
Now I know things can never be the same between us
But softly, in my dreams
You're still with me
Please don't wake me
Just let me go on sleeping. . . .

Daniel P. McGrath

Love Has No Boundaries

Honesty reaching out,
With an outstretched heart,
Your mind like a sighing forest,
Secrets on display,
Need not whisper their scent,
As it is carried to me,
On your sweet breath
and crystal eyes,
Which project me the key,
To another world,
In which I already entered,
Following the twisted limbs of ancient trees,
And direction of the stinging winds,
And the cold, sombre stone of
another millennium,
All leading me home to you,
Somehow, a timeless mystery,
Beginning from the inside out,
Your love shone from darkness,
Like a moon lit sky.

Sarah Elizabeth Taylor

Heartbreak

I'm physically and emotionally drained,
I just won't wallow in this pain.
The hurt is so deep inside my heart,
I wish we could have a brand new start!
It's over for him, the feelings are gone,
Why is it for me ever so strong?
I have to let go, I know that is true.
It's time to move on, but I'm still feeling blue!

Pam Milligan

Summer

Gentle breezes at night
Sun-filled picnics at day
Friends blossoming every any way
Shorts and sandals, sipping lemonade
Sit underneath the oak tree under its nice, cool shade
Frogs and fish a-swimming
Coyotes howl to the moon
Thunderstorms come banging, boom, boom, boom
Sleep-overs full of laughter, friendships buzz about
Summer really is the best season throughout

Amanda Cedrone

Our Shining Star

You, dear Dad are our "Shining Star!"
We watch with honour wherever you are.

We follow your footsteps along the way.
We'll be just like you some day.

As we walk, the path of life.
We don't mean to cause you grief or strife.

Our mistakes are not errors in your eyes.
Just a way of learning, you realize.

You guide us with your golden heart.
And from your teachings we will not part.

Day by day, you share your light,
So one day soon we too, can shine bright.

We're so happy that you're our Dad.
Our days with you are the best we've had!

Memories of you our whole life through
Will be of love and peace and happiness too!

Barbara Hacking

Love in the Fast Lane

Who would suspect you in a bowling alley?
Bowling is fun but you go there to dally
The ball rolls down, you hope for a strike
He's watching! Wondering what you'd like

What's in your mind as you give him the eye
How will you get him? Is he bold? Is he shy?
He stands at the line, a good-looking guy
If you make a pass, will he say bye-bye?

Is he straight? Is he gay?
What's his religion? Does he like to play?
He scores a perfect 300 and asks for a date
He wants you and he to go celebrate!

Commitment? Forget it! Too early to say
His masculine ego likes it this way
So go on the date, and come what may
Remember my words: "Don't get carried away"

Sylvia Kogel

My Most Special Friend

Dedicated to Ernest Weber

Sitting high in the clouds, gazing down upon me,
He was always there in times of need,
My Most Special Friend.
The night I went to visit.
He lay there in bed all night,
drifting off slowly.
I'm sure he's in Heaven, keeping an eye on me;
He must have been there when I thought no one could see.
I'll miss him forever and I pray we meet again,
For he wasn't only my Grandpa,
he was my MOST SPECIAL FRIEND.

Charles Robert Stevens, Jr.

My Visits to Grandma's Place

Today I am going to Grandma's place,
To her warm, friendly kitchen with curtains of lace.
The smell of home cooking will tickle my nose.
I'll visit her garden and pick her a rose.
Yes, today I am going to Grandma's place,
With its simple charm and elegant grace.
We'll sit and chat o'er a cup of tea;
She'll tell me of days that used to be.
I treasure those days spent at Grandma's place;
Her smile is so sweet, so soft her embrace!
My eyes fill with tears and my heart swells with love
When I think of her now with the angels above.
Though years have come and years have gone
I cherish the memories that will always live on.
Yes, I still make my visits to Grandma's place
When I look in the mirror and see Grandma's face.

Elaine Harvey

Open Eyes

I look at you with open eyes,
my being there for inspection.
I look at you but see
clouds I cannot fathom.
Your being is hidden from my knowing.
You are closed to my searching for who you are.
The veil in your eyes won't let me see
your pain or your joy,
only the body you're wearing.
Take down the veil, open yourself to me,
I want to share in all that you are.
Your pain and your joy can be shared;
your sorrow eased, your joy increased
when two can look
with eyes of peace.

RoseAnna Newlove

One Thousand Years

If we could live one thousand years,
Maybe that's time to reduce the world's tears.
One thousand years with hope in your heart,
To end the things that rip this world apart.
No more pain, sadness, or starvation,
When the dream of man is to see the salvation
In living together as sister and brother,
To have nothing but love for each and another.
All things are possible, at least they say,
But it doesn't seem so in what we do today.
So let's strive to do better with our time here,
Every day in time brings your end ever so near.
Just do your part to align the world's gears,
And maybe it will be better in one thousand years.

Harold Vaught

In Your Eyes

What Color do you see? What lies lie ahead?
What is it we must do to get past this mess?
Who is it you will turn to? When it's
time to face these lies? What is it you're
going to do when it becomes judgement time?
Why is it we insist to categorize a topic,
a color leaving behind a heart that dies.
Do look beyond this stupidity and begin to
realize that behind every man is a heart,
soul, and mind. Give us a chance to show
you what our world is all about it's not too
different from yours and surely that's no
doubt. So when you look upon me the very
next time just remember the same hopes and
dreams that lie in your heart could just as well be mine!

Juan Enrique Torres

Heartwoe

In my heart I feel many things
sometimes pleasure
sometimes pain
I prefer the pleasure to the pain
but I have yet to see a heart unstained
heartache and misery are a part of life
I know this is true for I am a wife
pushed away and torn apart
I must have the strongest heart of hearts
I carry on though beaten and tattered
he looks at me as I never mattered
I scream inside Hey I'm still here!
somewhere down deep through all the fear
I'll hold my head high 'til the day I die
until' then silently I'll cry.

Martha A. Gifford

Home Again

When I woke up today I went out on the porch.
Looked up in the sky to the white puffy clouds,
birds in the trees, a warm summer's breeze.
The birds were singing a simple tune
It was the first day of summer middle of June.
The wind swirled, I started to fly
it carried me up to the sky,
when I saw an angel gliding by.
The sun glowed all around so bright,
she was, a miraculous sight.
She reached for me, I grabbed her hand
she pulled me up to the Promised Land.
I wanted stay, but I had to go,
they said when it's time they would let me know.
I smiled, I knew one day my angel would come,
and I would know my work here was done.

Dori Theresa Slota

See the Three

See the old lady who sits alone,
she's gone through life all on her own;
she has had no one to love,
so she prays to God above.

See the little girl on the swing,
watch as she flies into the sky and sings;
she has only herself as a friend,
but her happiness will not end.

See the young mother,
and her children without a father;
listen as the people whisper about her,
watch her as she turns her face when her eyes blur.

You see these three;
to them all a friend you could be,
but you turn your back,
and still a friend they lack.

Jessica Dawn Poepping

How We Died

With eyes and hearts full of forgetfulness,
we travelled into the grey winter.
Clouded only by our own inner chaos,
we lost sight of the way and became jaded and cold.
Our flesh became dry and hard.
Our eyes saw nothing but falsehoods.
Our ears heard nothing but lies.
Our tongues spoke nothing but hatred.
Here our hearts died
and were scattered into the wind.

Vanessa Croteau

Once Again . . .

From the moment of birth on mother Earth;
There was an unfilled passion deep within;
A voice in the wind beckoned me,
I followed that voice to the mystical sea.

While on my watch late at night;
I filled with awe at the sight;
Of what God created for you and I;
The heavens above the waters below,
I felt a peacefulness , all should know.

When my spirit moves on, my dust will remain;
Take me back to the waters once again;
The water spirit still beckons me;
I yearn to be a part of the mystical sea.

Sue E Wendell

Whose Grandma Are You?

Though her eyesight has faded, her eyes twinkle blue.
I tell her my name but she asks, "Who are you?"

The housecoat is flowered and bright like the sun.
Every time that I see her it's always this one.

To find part of her story was my game plan.
We just sit and she smiles while holding my hand.

Her hand is now gnarled, the stroke's done its harm.
She smiles and pats me and says, "Your hand is so warm."

God gives just a moment of His wonderful grace.
I kneel beside her and she smiles, stroking the beard on my face.

Does she see her son, her husband, or maybe her dad?
The moment soon passes; then comes a sigh sounding sad.

She looks out the window, I think, toward a tree.
Whose face is that? She giggles, "Oh, it's me."

Though her eyesight has faded, her eyes twinkle blue.
I tell her my name but she asks, "Who are you?"

Gary R. Meller

Heaven Has My Father

Heaven has my Dad,

Missing you day and night.
I never thought we were EVER this tight.

You being my father, a very special man,
I will never forget you on this land.

Always there to guide me through thick and thin,
I can't believe this; this is a sin.

I love you so much,
It's so hard to live without your loving touch.

Ever since you left I have became much stronger,
But I wish you were here just a little longer.

Watching over me as I sleep, to be with you, a dream I keep.

Amanda Rose Campbell

The Image in the Mirror

There's an image in the mirror
A familiar face of someone I thought I might have known.
This face looked a little tired, and wrinkled
from the caring that she had shown.
Her hair, was streaked with silver
She looked twice at me, but had nothing to say
I thought, her eyes looked a little older
Her smile somewhat a little colder.
The image that I had seen wasn't just another being,
It was me looking in the mirror . . .
And my mother looking back at me.

JoAnn Lemmon

Arks

I am an ark. The child
piles creature upon creature in my lap
and, looking on through Laura's dancing eyes,
I see my lapful spring to life:
The plush converts to fur, to feathers, scales,
and vivid eyes intensely meet my own.

The image shifts. What if,
in far-off corners of reality,
these bears, this owl, these turtles in my lap
were dispatched by their breathing ilk
with silent messages for us?
With soundless pleas for rights, for space
amidst the rising deluge of mankind,
for help in finding gangplanks to their ark?

I hold the child, hold Laura, and we talk.
Perhaps it is a step.

Susanne P. Moyer

The Shot

Every night as I go to bed,
I see that ball way ahead.
Flying flying through the air,
I close my eyes 'cause I cannot bear.
To see my shot miss the hoop,
I long to be part of a special group.
Going to the championship game,
Going to the hall of fame.
Then I open my eyes to see my fate,
I start to freak like my friend Nate.
Then the ball hits and rides the rim,
My face turns pale, then I start to grin,
As the ball falls through the rim.
Jumping and screaming I am so, so happy,
I am no longer feeling so, so crappy.
I am on my way to that walk of fame,
'Cause I made that shot in that perfect game.

Michael Weber

Fools in Black and White

Playing the I am better than you game
Feeling cheated in life looking to blame
Sanctimonious thoughts about race and color
Prejudgments passed down one to the other

Raised to be little and always criticize
Glazing eyes of suspicion a fools selfish pride
Facades of power wealth and righteous name
All chains and shackles of mistrust and pain

Cynical patriotism defiance of laws
Holier than thou fanatical walls
Hopelessness, disillusion, anger and strife
Hatred and bitterness paralysis of life

In this passage our father will ask
How can you love me whom you cannot see
And not love your brother whom you see every day
Because God made us all in his own image
To reason with love and not to diminish

Praise God because we are all the same

Henry W. Morgan, Jr

I'll Dream

Though beauty fades and places grow old,
You, I'll keep and tend with care.
You, I'll treasure beyond compare.
For with you, I'll go to places never seen.
Thanks to you
I'll dream!

Cheryl Muhr

No One Even Cares

See that man over there,
Standing on the corner?
No one even cares
How long he's been standing there.

Does he go to sleep?
Does he even dare?
If he goes to sleep,
Will the nightmares be there?

We can sleep at night;
We don't have to fight the nightmares.
No one even cares
That he was sent there.

His name is our brave soldiers
Who went to fight for peace.
Doesn't anyone even care
How many died over there?

There's more than one way to die.
They give up the fight to be alive.
Doesn't anyone even care
There's one standing at the corner over there?

Julia K. Strickland

Reflections on the First Day

The silence and the beauty engulf me like
the fog on a cloudy day, wraps me in its
magic and wisks me away on its journey

To look in falling, flowing water splashing
over rocks and twigs to its pool of memories

To peer at the gentle breezes playing with
the treetops and hear the soft, misting rain
falling in an Irish meadow

To watch the endless flutterings of a
hummingbird as it wonders at me
through a glass window

To admire the deep serenity and conviction
of a doe for her fawn as they nibble at the
blades of grass 'neath their hooves not
knowing or caring that they are observed
with envy and awe in their solitude

A short distance away lies the difference
between relaxation and frustration

But at this moment, as time stands still, I'm
living in fairy land and protected by beauty

Jane George McMurry

Sister to Brother

Well Bro, I'll tell you
Life for me ain't been no game
It's had winners
and losers
and places with all
Disappointing
But all the time I think of you
I've been a winner
and I got a prize
and I feel so happy
and sometimes sad
Where there's a winner you're always there
So Bro, don't you change
Don't you quit being a player
'Cause you are always a player to me
Don't you forget me
For I'm still yours
I'm still cool like you
and life for me ain't been no game

Teri Jeanne Pierson

Imperfections

The vessel was cracked and tossed on a pile;
It seemed that its life was to end.
Its beauty destroyed by misuse in the world;
No potter could take it to mend.
An elderly man picked it up as he strode
Through the alley-way where it now lay;
He handled it gently and carefully looked
It all over, then went on his way.
He took the old vessel down into his shop
With a lamp he examined its hue;
Then on the inside he shone a bright light,
And the cracks let the brilliance shine through.
The man closed his eyes and thought of his life
Like the vessel with cracks all a-twine;
Remembering back through his earlier days,
Through his weakness, he let God's light shine.

Jan Kaye Tritapoe

Life

A journey through life's many, many avenues
May you always meet each new day beginning
With the hope of obtaining greater heights, without
Looking at yesterday with sorrow or regret,
And not let greed be your aim.

Love not for what it means to you,
but what it has in store for those few whom are found
worthy, and it will certainly direct your course.

And if it should by chance, life takes you to
the land of the Nile or Far East, with all its
enchantings, melodies, remember, in others it
can sometimes bring out the best, if only
We care enough to show our very best.

Olive Williams

Thoughts of an MS Patient

Another new day and what will it bring?
Tremors? Blindness? Most everything.
When I think this over and ponder it all,
I'm thankful for living. It makes me stand tall.
I may be quite different from others you know.
Still, I will push on and stay on the go.
Someday soon I'll have to slow down,
But until then I'll keep running around.
You may think it's sad, this thing I must fight,
But I'll struggle on with all of my might.
Don't pity me or the way that I look.
I'm someone special. I'm not by the book.
I may walk funny and sway once or twice.
Still, I'm very blessed, so take my advice.
Be thankful for family and the blessings of life,
For children and spouse, whether husband or wife.
We all have demons that we have to face.
I'll still make it by God's mighty grace!

Betty Poarch

Brayden

Heaven sent us a precious angel, to fill our hearts with joy
Brayden was the name he took, our precious baby boy
He touched so many hearts in the short time he could stay
Until his third day here with us, Jesus took him away
Your beautiful face, your tiny hands,
we were filled with so much love
The angels must have sung beautiful songs in the Heavens up above
You'll remain in our hearts forever more,
our beautiful bundle of joy
Now in Heaven, wrapped in Jesus arms,
our precious angel boy

Penni Doran

Visionary

I lift my eyes unto the hills and let them
rest on the horizon as the dreams of my heart
and soul meet and dance to the voice that
sings to my spirit and gives me life

On my knees I clutch my belly overwhelmed
as I feel my spirit stir with life;
I envision the other side of tomorrow

Here under the blackness of the midnight sky
A place where life begins, I pray a thousand
words that fall out of my mouth like little
drops of honey that entice the angels to
descend from the heavens on high and taste
the meditations of my heart

I lift my eyes unto the hills and let them
look past the horizon and catch the falling
star as my dream comes to life

Jennifer E Dukes

Angels

Because we have yearned for redemption
Perhaps because the love within still shone
You have come in numbers to lift the souls
Of who ever was readily waiting.

In fate, sometimes we do not see
The simple necessity
For her daughter, you've heard of Destiny!
So in the midst of all disturbing commotion
Perhaps you could search how you'd change the tone
Of the emotions that drag you down between the poles
Of dual certainties and of those fatalities
Unnecessary baggage, really just limiting.

So come and tempt us into ecstasy
We'll drop our robes of irony
We'll shine and pray that we'll dare see
How easy it is really, to be!

Dominique Meunier Stolow

Once upon a Time

I once was a bird that flew so high
I once was a fish that swam far and wide
I once was a tree that swayed in the wind
I once was a cat with a mischievous grin
I once was a dog with no cares in the world
I once was a cloud that danced and twirled
I once was a hurt little girl with no where to go
I once was a big girl that couldn't say no
but now I am nothing but words on a page,
and people on paper don't grow with age.

Melanie Melrose

He Weeps

As the whole world sleeps, He weeps.
He weeps for the diseases we've spread,
For the things we've killed, for the paths we've tread.
He weeps for the morals we've lost;
For our infidelities, for the lives we've tossed.
He weeps for the lies we've told;
For our tales of violence, for our greed of gold.
He weeps for the war we've wreaked;
For our fountains of blood, for our prey on the weak.
He weeps for the terror we've instilled;
For our rape of faith, for our hate revealed.
And still, when the dawn breaks, He smiles.
He opens His arms, He closes the miles.
He spreads forth His light from above.
He fills us with peace, He offers His Love
And, as the world sleeps, He weeps.

Rea K. Griffin

Grave Prince

I long for youth—dreams that exist only
In dreams, yet I've tasted dreams and know to
Wait for them fully, though the hourglass
Spills and my young heart beats itself to death
And trees mock me when wind caresses them
Beneath stars and cats stare up at me to
Be let inside, informing me of our
Alliance with the night and Milky Way.

Fool. Alone. Still dreaming. Duped and seduced
By romance, cursed by time and glories past.

Let's breathe each other for the sun will soon
Explode. Shakespeare will vaporize and our
Words of love and life and sound and fury
Will have to be rewritten by things in
Golden ships, who will spy my bone in the
Upper crust and see my skull with liver—
Eyed stares and wonder, "What did this one do?"

Mark J. Williamson

Forecast

Slate sky overhead
gunmetal blue gunmetal hot
no cloud cast its shadow
on the ground
still bright air
taste of dust smell of burnt flint
drying nostrils scorching lungs
tight stretched skin
sweat popping out
disappearing before it beads and rolls
dust devils lying exhausted by the road bed
pitiful eddies kicked out of retirement
by shuffling feet
too dehydrated to step over them
trees limp defeated
in the distance a faint tinkle
wind chimes pouring sweet notes
into air too still too bright
a-a-h-h-h the promise of a breeze
the promise of rain

Sheron Hinson Roberts

Shadows Dusk

As the dusk of day rolls into night,
shadows slowly creep upon one another
Inner lurking through the passages of darkness,
A dismal siren of helplessness can be heard
from the echoes of a wailing child.
Cries filled with fear, shame, and often hunger.
Each tear a memory of something soon to be
replaced by another beating, or maybe
another touch, or even another day without nourishment.
Nourishment needed to keep spirits above the level of sanity.
A sanity in an insane illusion of what is supposed to be.
However it may differ from what is.

Brenda Dale Burton

My Bunny

My bunny is funny!
It has lots of money.
Its brother's name is Sunny.
My Bunny's full of honey.
Its nose is always runny.
Can you guess what kind of Bunny that is funny,
has lots of money, its brother's name is Sunny,
its full of honey, and its nose is always runny?
It's a honey filled chocolate bunny who someone bit off its nose!

Megan Catherine Karkoska

Dandelion Seed

A rush of wind, a cloud of white,
The dandelion seed has taken flight.
A tiny vessel, a glider plane,
Swirling; a pilot, gone insane.
Floating crazily through the air,
Its landing place?
I know not where.
Will it be soil, or cracked concrete,
To merely be trampled by a passerby's feet?
It's about to land! But a sudden gust
And into the air, the seed is thrust.
And then the wind stops,
No more sound would it yield,
The seed, it alights in the open field.
Upon landing in dirt, will the seed even grow,
Into a bright yellow sunburst,
With its radiant glow?
A truly amazing thing, this dandelion seed,
To make a whole field of flowers,
But still, just a weed.

Aaron Douglas Twiddy

Love Well Read

Though confined to no image,
My beloved remains.
Unmistakable.
His raven verse gives hue to pallid settings.
Absorbed through my eyes,
His silent voice echoes throughout my mind.
Indulging in his gift to revisit yesterday,
He does so, time and again.
Often he journeys to land unexplored,
Yet he lingers.
Resting safely in my hands.

Jane Suzanne Bebar

Light

the world is big the world is round
the beauty i see is only with sound
i have so little yet i have so much
you gave me fingers in which to touch
i'm like a flower something to behold
for roses are beautiful so i've been told
thank you for my feelings and giving me a sound mind
because as you know dear God that i was born blind

Jeannine Ann Malone

Cancer

She feels like she is in a cage
Always going down in age
Surrounded by the ones she loves
Waiting for the angel's above

As the days go by
Everybody says goodbye
she hopes and prays for the day
When the angels will come and take her away

As she gets weaker and weaker
Her life starts to get sucked out of her
Her body is starting to shut down
Always with a smile and not a frown

Going one day at a time
Always thinking she was fine
As her pulse starts to weaken
We wonder, "Will she make the weekend"

As the cancer devours her body
She lays there with her family
As they go home to bed
Wondering if she will be there in the end

Dawn Therese Tremblay

Saying Goodbye . . . Duchess

You came to me, but not for long.
God took you back where you belong.
The wind was up, with moon so bright,
I knew, with foreboding, cursedly proven right.
It broke my heart to say goodbye,
I know it was right, but still ask why?
Why so sick, so soon it came,
Why must there be so much pain.
To pray for you, to pull through,
then to pray, for god to hurry and take you.
Petting you, held close to my breast,
until that final gasp to eternal rest.
You were only a puppy, with lots of love,
but God said he needed you up above.
A hunter was lonely up there,
and needed a puppy's love to share.
Duchess, you're now free,
now lacking your misery.
You're happy, healthy and running free.
Don't go too far, Please wait for me.

Ron E Vanness

In the Garden

Sitting pretty as a rose,
That's where grandma always goes.
In the garden
She'll be found
Planting flowers in the ground.
In the garden
When the tulips bloom
She's not hiding in some room.
In the garden
Her veggies planted
They taste so good, you can hardly stand it.
In the garden
Spring, summer & fall
That is where she loves them all
In the garden
Where grandma goes
Sitting pretty as a rose.

Jennifer Lynn Corkins

Walking at Midnight

Caressed by the black midnight sky,
I felt the moonlight way up high,
It continued forever, the black through and through,
But only remained 'til the sky became blue,
Day carried on and night fell again,
The bliss returns and leaves now and then.

Rhonda Martinez

Trust in God

I thought my path with God was right
One day the past came into sight
By looking back and not living today
I stumbled blindly and I lost my way
I became bitter and negative, not knowing why
I blamed God, Oh, what a fool was I
I cried out Lord, if you had answered my prayers
I would not have become restless and weakened to snares
I became sick in body and stressed in my mind
Then God healed me provenly and left it behind
The next thing he did was open my eyes
I was not trusting him and that was unwise
Now that I see, I prayed forgiveness my soul
I said Jesus, I love you, please don't let me go
The prayers to be answered in Jesus' time
The trust in Jesus I first had to find

Peggy L. Denney

Last Three Words

My knees start to weaken
at the first site of your face
my heart starts to melt
at the thought of your embrace

Your love flows through me
like a river flows down its path
your kiss lifts me up so high
I could probably fall to my death

I really wished that
when I looked into your eyes I could see
exactly how it is that
you feel about me

I get nervous when your around me
I feel I could cry when your away
I dream about you
every night and day

I want you to know
my last three words will always remain true
regardless of what I may say or do
You'll always know that I love you. . . .

Paolo M. Manicni

The Eternal Bond

Monuments of stone reflecting yet another sunset.
Moonbeams of light cast on them in the night.
Carrying the names of lives once lived before then.
Wisdom now gone with them to an eternal light.
New fallen snow and autumn leaves that blow.
Aroma of flowers laid down upon them.
Candles of white burning ever so bright.
Gifts from the living, so special and giving.
Shadows cast from those left behind,
as we say a prayer that it's peace they will find.
It's a place we hold on, now that they're gone.
A blanket of warmth, a pillow of love,
as we lay them down for their eternal sleep.
A place to be proud, shout a name out loud,
or recall the fondest of memories and weep!
They have touched us in life,
and in death one might say.
The eternal bond, it is yours and it's mine,
and together we face the hands of time. . . .

Susan M. Clark

My Rescuer

You rescued me when I was filled with sorrow
convincing me to live like there's no tomorrow

You gave me new hope I thought didn't exist
turning me on with temptations I couldn't resist

You filled me with love and gave me devotion
making my heart soar with sweet emotions

You made me want to keep living my life
asking me if I would be your wife

You make me feel secure with each little kiss
filling my soul with such tender bliss

L. K. Yost

The Sidewalk Plot

I had forgotten, long ago;
That buried beneath the imposing cement,
Lie acres and acres of frustrated soil.
Were it not for the sidewalk plot,
Trying desperately to sustain a single elm;
I would have forgotten yet.

Sherri Montgomery

Waiting Room

The answer echo is not the one I have waited to hear.
I am sick of all these blaring bright pink and blue happy laughers.
I cannot share in their ecstasy, for it is
ecstasy of my own that has brought me to this agony.
Movie-of-the-week nightmares flash like angel tears in my brain.
But this is no dream.
It is my pathetic soap opera life coming to
a brilliant haze that remains unscripted.

Allison René Thorp

Take a Child by the . . .

Take a child by the hand and show him the way.
Lead a child each morning into a beautiful day.
Take a child by the mind and give him the strength
To fight every challenge and go to great lengths.
Take a child by the soul and let God be known;
It is by his mighty grace that so big they have grown.
Take a child by his sight and show him wonders galore;
Teach him curiosity and the need to explore.
Take a child by his smile, so beautiful and sweet,
And tell him of all the friends he will meet.
Take a child by his wonder of the life all around;
Let him savor each flavor and hear each new sound.
Take a child by his dreams and say it's all right
To follow those dreams as far as he might.
Take a child by the heart and teach them to love,
For there is no greater gift from our Creator above.
And after your child has grown, and alone they now stand,
Watch and enjoy as they take their children by the hand.

Ty W Krotzer

Doubt

Doubt crowds in overcoming what's fighting to win.
It grabs hold and won't let go.
Stealing the life inside of me.
I gasp for air as it pulls me under.
Drowning in my own fear.
Fear, it stabs like a knife.
It rips through your flesh, like scissors cutting paper.
So silent, yet so loud.
A pin drop sounds more of thunder.
Lost in a maze of my own battles.
It's cruel and unfair, but there is no place to seek comfort.
It follows your every move as if it's one step ahead of you.
There is no escaping.
It drags you under, taking your last breath.
It takes control as it consumes you.
Until your dreams no longer exist.

Adrea Martine

Two Percent of the General Population

When you've crawled around as much as I,
Your faith in God seems so quick to die.
And the Emotions followed by a violent attack
Would break the bones of a strong man's back.

Would you see if I were to tell you
Of the sorrow my life holds so true?
Could you comprehend this sadness
Or pass judgment on these tears for madness?

Chronic feelings of emptiness seep through,
Blinding me from seeing what is real, what is true.
My misperception of social cues
Impairs my ability to have trust in you.

I have become a monster unaccepted by man,
Ignorant of what I cannot do and what I can.
When sad I am unable to refer to times of glee,
So dwelling is the only choice this life has given me.

Rebecca Ann Fowler

The Black Hole of Desire

As we enter the doors of the black hole of our soul
We feel the abyss of evil's kiss.
In this hole we reach for the honey falling
Like the wounded just crawling.
We can't seem to stop just got to have another drop.
We scream for help in despair
But desire says don't you dare.
The bottomless pit of desire burning within us like a bonfire.
The lusts will never leave our minds
As desire will never leave our sides.
Our hearts feel like the desolate loner
And always searching for another donor.
We try to follow our hearts' rights and delights
But the black hole causes endless fights.
Only the souls of the Lord's strong can fight the devil's desire
And all its wrong and on their dying day sing their song.
It is all a test to see who's faith is best unlike the rest.
Only in our moment of death will we receive the kéy
To unlock the doors of the black hole of desire and leave.
Only then will God's light set us free.

Vincent Marsh

Reflections

With so much being said and done and many hours past,
Reflections of our lives, our loves, our memories may pass.

Never to be forgotten, just scattered in our minds:
The moments that we cherish that stand the test of time.

As you take these final steps toward becoming man and wife . . .
Reflect on you childhood, your family, and your life.

Know when problems arise and we known they always do
The love that has bound you close will help you see it through.

And when you see your own reflection, in a mirror or a pond,
In the eyes of a child or a Sunny Sunday morn,

In the eyes of a storm or wind howling through the trees,
Know that lives many reflections are filled with times like these.

Keri Ann Delisle

Dark Passion

How bright the night, my love,
as on moonlight's silver beams we dance.
How deep the night, my love,
as we in shadows caress, taking a chance.
How soft the night, my love,
as my name carried on your bated breath.
How hectic the night, my love,
as our passion sings Life, foiling Death.
How warm the night, my love,
as your eyes burn with immortal desire.
How eternal the night, my love,
as in your arms I bask, Light's bright fire.

Gary E. McCray

When I Remember

Sometimes I laugh
At the things we used to do and say
As we played and danced the time away.
The days just flew by, Oh, so fast
Autumn, Winter and Spring at last.

Sometimes I cry
Thinking of that last good bye.
We stood at Heavens door that day in May
With the key in hand and threw it all away.
It's with regrets and bitter tears
Now and then through out the years
When I Remember.

Lola Cotton

When the Sea Is Black

When the sea is black against the night
And the water reflects the moon,
The waves are a well-timed rhythm
That splash o'er the shore like a tune
Were being played to ease the pains
Of all those men there gone to doom.
As if this brine which took these men
Could somehow soothe the wounds
That all have felt who've known the death
Which gave them unalarmed the tomb
Wherein these dead shall spend their time
From flood 'til ebb's eternal June,
When the sea is black against the night
And the water reflects the moon.

Nicholas Kent Williams

I Like Nature, Yes, It's True

I like the trees and the spring breeze.
I like the flowers and the wind's powers,
To soar on my swing, in the middle of spring,
And to smell the smell of sweet grass, as I go pass,
To get my swing in the middle of spring.

Amanda Cronce

Looking for a Love

Looking for a love will always be my destiny
But finding someone to share that love
has always been hard for me
Maybe the problem is that I look too hard,
or maybe it's because I let down my guard
I've tried plenty of times to build bricks around my heart,
but finding the right brick in this world
makes it hard to start
I tell them about the things we can do and the places
we can go, but still it's never enough to let
them know that it's one way to let my feelings show
Time will tell what is up ahead
That my perfect match is married or even dead

Victor Byrd

My Treasure

Now, when I'm growing up,
I found a treasure in my life.
A treasure that is worth more
than a thousands rubies, emeralds, diamonds and gold.
This treasure fills my heart with happiness,
my soul with hope, and my mind with knowledge.
She discovers the shadows of my heart
and fills the emptiness of my soul with mother's care.
With the warmth of her gentle touch
she paints a smile on my face.
She makes my heart sing with delight.
She's my shield from a storm.
When I am lost, I will always
find a light in her eyes to help me find my way out.
She's the one who wipes the tears of my face,
chases away the doubts and fears.
She is proud when I succeed and supportive when I don't
She is my richest treasure
and I never want to lose her!

Magdalena Bartolik

Kindness

Seldom can we justify, words or acts which are unkind;
wounding someone else thereby, and ourselves,
as we will find. Self defense is not unkind, but a duty,
in the main; they aggress whose little minds,
show a need for growth, or gain.

Kerwin Kerr

Untitled

My lady
You are the moon
I am but the sea
So much in between
Could our love ever be
Unworthy am I to look upon your grace
But I do
Yes I do
For I know to be true
Is the love that I have for you

My lady
My lady
My raging waves can be still for no other
I part my waters at its deepest depth
So that my heart may be revealed to thee
Take it with you to paradise
For I feel no rapture without you here with me

Roderick D. Alston

If Only Now the World Could See

If only now the world could see
how peaceful and quiet it used to be.
The leaves on the trees, crimson in autumn,
could fall silently to the forest bottom.
And when the snow of winter came,
Oh, how silent the world would have lain.
When spring came around fresh and green,
with baby animals the forest would teem.
Then when summer came, hot and bland,
hunger and thirst would reign over the land.
Now that forest doesn't exist,
and someday, when we're dying, it will be missed.
But until that one awaited day,
I will always hopefully pray:
If only now the world could see
how peaceful and quiet it used to be.

Sarah Brubaker

Easter

It is Easter Sunday once more
As in the years long before
Jesus trod the lone path by the sea of Galilee
He died upon the cross for you and me
Now all God's things spring anew
And rise up as the morning dew
With God's great power and His grace
And you may find that special place
When Jesus gave his life of love
So we could meet Him high above
Amen

D. W. Sheffy

Ever-Changing

As the darkness changed to a sea of blankness,
Early morning, shining brightness, as a new day explodes.
In life's changing episodes, from happy to sad to pain in sorrow,
Try to find life's meaning. Life is as a blink of an eye.
Once standing in life's pride.
Now stumbling, in an aged old soul ready for relaxation.
To overcome our goal in life's mysteries.
So find nothing in hiding, hide nothing in finding,
Nothing is as it seems.
So be free, hold on tight, don't let the rains fall,
Because the journey you're on
Means nothing at all.
The past is gone;
It's history.

Timothy L. Crain

I Wish I Could

I wish I could see the world around,
And all the things that are abound.
I wish I could see the mountains dear,
And hear all the sounds there are to hear.

I wish I could find a cave unknown,
So I could go there to be alone.
I wish I could think of the past being good,
But it was just like walking through wood.

I wish I could read every book,
But that would take more than a look.
I wish I could know everything there is to learn,
But that would be a long, long turn.

I wish I could feel your hand in mine,
And you asking me out to dine.
I wish my lips will someday touch yours,
But your lips will always touch hers.

I wish I could know my dreams to come true,
Which would mean I'd always be with you.
But those are just wishes
That will never come true.

Jennifer Gill

Her Eyes

Who knows what those eyes see
When they gaze my way
Is he a gentleman
A scholar
A vagabond
Am I handsome in her eyes
Or just another strange man in a restaurant
Staring at me over his drink
Does she wish she could talk to me
Or does she want met to stop looking
People's eyes hide a lot
If only I could see
What existed behind them

Chris Gordon

I Am

I am curious and sweet
I wonder when Jesus is coming back for me
I hear the trumpet sound
I see God smile at me
I want for him to say, "Well Done"
I am curious and sweet

I pretend I see Him sometimes
I feel happy
I touch the clouds
I cry when my mom cries
I am curious and sweet

I understand the Bible is true
I say, "God, are you listening"
I dream I went to Heaven
I try to see his face
I hope He will come back soon
I am curious and sweet

Kristy Fitzgerald

Days

Some days are hot and some days are cold
and some days ya' just feel bold.
But I tell you these days aren't easy.
Nobody kneesy, Portuguese Latin easy,
and some days are cheesy.
Days bad days, good days, that's the ways.
Days . . .

Danielle Smith

The Venom of Life

I see it all around us, disguised in every way;
Lurking in the shadows,
It works to lure in its prey.
It doesn't have a preference with your gender or race.
It sneaks onto your path with pure determination and grace.
Constantly testing your will,
Even the strongest cannot resist.
For the moment that we give in,
The laws of life no longer exist.
It will crush all your values,
Once you give into its course.
It has no sense of feeling. It has no remorse.
With its world of empty promises
And those wicked, devilish ways
It will invite you onto its road,
And leave you stranded in a maze.
So, the next time you meet temptation,
Remember its venomous, toxic stat.
And never, ever forget, my friend,
That curiosity killed the cat.

Monnica Shae Herndon

Waved a Good-bye

I have a picture from some time ago.
    You could not have been much more than three.

All strapped in the baby seat of your mom's car.
    You waved a good-bye to me.

Walter L. Mitchell

Clouds

Clouds are like marshmallows in the sky,
Puffy, fluffy and flying high.
With a whisper of wind,
They float to an endless end.

Some have faces and shapes we know,
Keep a watchful eye they may look like snow.

On a bright and sunny day the sun shines through,
And on cloudy days they fill the sky with gray,
Hoping for a better day.

The clouds will part,
And the sun will shine,
Giving us a day that's Heavenly and divine.

Frances Morrison Brown

Home

I left the land of my birth, many years ago
No choice did I have in the matter
Mom migrated to this new land
And like a bird in migration
She took all seven of us along

Often in my nostalgic mood
I hear the waves splashing against the shore
I watch the orange sunset
As it disappears behind the hills
And I sit on grandad's lap
And listen to his favorite stories

I've been to Europe and Africa
There I dreamt of another home
A home in a land where the mistletoe grows
And the winter cold freezes your toes

Yet in that home how distant it might be
Are the ones dearest to me
They greet me with a kiss and a smile
And say welcome home with a big, big hug

Hepta Deslandes

Death of a Pilot, at Night, over Vietnam

I heard a man die,
    last night—

 Mayday! Mayday! Mayday!

 I've been hit;

I'm
    going
        down! he cried.

That was all;

    then he died.
    Eugene Duff

Words of Wisdom

When I was one in a million . . .

Growing up as a teen people tell me to learn
from other people, People I didn't even know.
Give away all but your heart.
They say don't fall in love,
it isn't worth it.
Maybe not to them,
but it may be worth it to me.
I know what I want
and my mind's made up.

He reminds me of what was said before.
Your love is meant for granite not for hate.
I've been hurt more than once,
but still I love him which is endless.
I am who I am.
Except me!
    Heather M. Brown

Call of the Wild

Resounding echoes of wilderness calls,
Taunts the depths of my heart and soul.
Renewing visions of days long gone by,
With exciting tales still untold.
Enchanting memories of jungle lands,
Across the seas so far from home
And the piercing cry from those yonder hills,
Where untamed coyotes freely roam.
Desert mirages, sagebrush covered hills,
These thoughts come drifting back to me.
Oh, to escape from asphalt jungled streets,
My spirit yearns to be let free.
For on a darkest night stars light my way,
Out in the great big vast somewhere.
Amidst God's perfect untouched creation,
I find my peace and solace there.
    Virginia M. Evans

Life's Battle

Emerge from your mother's womb to the unknown.
After a cold horrible winter, suddenly green grass, green
leaves and warble of bird songs.
Wonderful things to be learned: life, geography, reading,
writing, arithmetic, and history.
There is courtship, passion, love, jealousy, and hate.
Maturing, finishing high school, some college, trade school,
forever learning, trying to determine your fate.
Marriage to a lovely, loving mate.
Your country calls, "I need you!" You answer, "I will and I do!"
Loved ones die in battle, from disease, heart attacks, and
all others linger long waiting death's rattle.
Now you are alone! No loving mate, no mother, no father,
no sister, no brother.
No one to love; no one to be loved.
It is over, for you have lost Life's Battle.
    Ralph N. Vinson

Last Emotions

As I walk through the bright forest,
All I could think of was his face.
Is there a chance in the world that
I'll ever see you again?
As I sat down by the rushing water,
I saw your reflection gazing up at me,
your brown eyes, and all the sadness in them.
It felt as if my whole world had come to an end.
Would there ever be a chance in the world that you could
learn to love me the way you used to?
Could you just hold me one more time
and make me feel like nobody else matters to you?
As you walked away from me,
tears filled my eyes.
I whispered in the wind, I love you and goodbye.
    Rhonda E. Linders

From the Angels

Far from this place but close to the heart,
I can feel the angels gather for the dance.
It's a celebration, it's a time for pause.
It's a time to welcome a long awaited soul.
And as the dance continues,
The breeze blowing so gently.
The angels whisper softly
"She's here and we adore her"

I get my thoughts together and am suddenly at peace.
Because I know my angel is watching over me.
    Elizabeth Britton

I Do Not Understand, My Beautiful Sister

I do not understand, why you keep messing with that man,
when he continues to beat you, with his hands.

I do not understand, why you use drugs
and hang around with thugs

I do not understand,
life has been only bringing you troubles and making you mean,
my beautiful sister you are only sixteen.

I do not understand,
my beautiful sister you say that your life is in check,
while looking around, your house is in a wreck.

I do not understand, why you choose to steal,
instead of being in the kitchen, cooking your two kids a meal

I do not understand, what brought you to this path,
please change your baby's diaper and give him a bath

I do not understand, why a beautiful girl has to deteriorate,
I will help you pray to God, that everything will be okay.
No my sister, no my beautiful sister, it is never too late

Even though you started on the wrong road,
my beautiful sister, God will bring you abroad
I am saying all of these things out of love.
    Dereldia O. Clendening

The Candlelight on the Night of Despair

The Candlelight was so bright that night,
The night of despair,
The night the sun never came
The Candlelight kept half the world warm
The Candlelight was the sun that night
The Candlelight was still lit a year later,
And every one came to see the Candle that
Kept the world alive and warm that night,
And it has its gold plate in front of it,
The Candlelight on the night of despair.
    Holli Ranae Strait

First Birthday

A.J., our beautiful baby boy
You gave to us much love and much joy.
Born September eighteenth, nineteen ninety-eight,
We didn't realize our hearts would break.
You left us for a happier place
Now you have a smiling face.
With Jesus you are now at home,
We've missed you much since you've been gone.
You've played and danced with children above
All nestled in the arms of Jesus love.
As your birthday rolls around.
I see your beautiful golden crown.
So tiny, yet so sparkling bright
You often comfort me in the night.
Taylor sees you as a little tiny light
As the stars shine out at night.
She sees you in the sky above,
"There's my brother," she says with love.
We know you are happy way up there,
One day we will join you and have not a care.

    Louise Steadman

Writer's Fury

Feel the rhythm of the angry black pen.
It bleeds its black ink, again and again.
Constructing revolutions that appear in one's head.
The silence of a pen leaves another one dead.

Deep shallow thoughts spill from our minds.
Releasing cruel intentions that appear satisfying.
Killing the fear by spilling on white.
The bloody black ink takes another bite.

A shadow of darkness searching for anger.
Midnight persuasion falls back on paper.
Fingers of hatred cry out in laughter.
Writing away on an endless chapter.

Creative motivations penetrate the sick.
Injecting lethal words that never want to quit.
Unleashing through your veins the worst feels like a hit.
The words come alive as it drops its black spit.

Shackled to a rock, the end has no meaning.
Addicted to the ink that shows no mercy.
Life without black would sure seem scary.
The bloody black pen survives on misery.

    Gregory J. Hedlund

Philosoetry to Guide Me

Poetry is rhymes of what has been done
Hearing them read, can send a chill for some
In life, there are lessons we learn
Listen to this one, if you are concerned
Often we are told, of all the bad we've done
So we never hear, of what we can become
Only if you could see, there is more to life than regrets
Everyone could believe, their life's not over yet
Try to find something, in your life
Reach for heights, you could not climb
You can change who and what you are
That's what tells me, I can go far
Once in a while, I can take a look back
Glance down and look, see if I lost track
Understanding what got me where I am
I have to be pleased, with where I stand
Dreams can become real, if you have faith
Envision your future, but remember your place
My way of helping me to see what I need
Explains why I use Philosoetry to guide me

    Robert L. Slaughter

In Loving Memories of Our Mother

Fly, Babies, Fly!
Said the mother eagle as she gently
pushed her flock off her tree.
Go on now, babies, she said, go on and be all that you can be!
But remember, she said, just remember
that mommy will always be a part of this old tree!
So don't worry about the storms, she said,
and try not to worry about me, 'cause mommy's
in Heaven now and God is holding on to thee.
So don't you cry too much, she said,
and don't put up a fuss, 'cause
mommy wants you to know that when she left,
she left loving you very much.

    Earleana T. Stewart

The Travelers

They came across lands of barren, hot wasteland;
lands that held no life like the sun.

Travelers of mystery, spirits of enigma.
They came from nowhere, asking for a drink of
cold, glistening water.

Standing by the well they filled their empty
cups with the thing they so asked for.

Their cloth of silk robes fluttering in the warm wind.
Their parched throats quenched with the pure liquid.

They with heavy hearts embraced each other
with the salt tears of sorrow they wept, their
dirty faces cleaned with the tears.

They left as mysteriously as ghosts do, back into
the burning wasteland.

    Lauren Catherina Durbin

Anatomy of Spirit

Death saps life force, vitality, breath,
Death moves in,
Being leaves
And there lies—a shell.
Who was that person who no longer is?
You mourn a prisoner set free?
World-weary traveller tired, soiled,
exhausted from a long journey.
Now changed,
Energized,
Returned to the realm of spirit.
Restored from form to formlessness.
Earthbound to spacelessness,
Finite to infinite.
Now here, now there
Wherever I will to be, never was, always is.
No used to be.
I AM with the night,
I AM with the day,
I AM with all there is,
I AM with you.

    Florence Eulene Norville

Time

Time
the worst enemy of a lover
Time alone
which should be spent holding one another
Time for thought
where doubts and fears arise
Time together
where all my fears subside
Time away
each moment seems a day. . . .

    Jason C. Beaupre

The End

I never thought that I could love like this
I never knew that I could feel this way
All and all our time has past
There won't be any happiness at last
The love we shared ran so deep
I can still feel you in my sleep
All my heart belongs to you
I really can't see myself getting through
I will love you always no matter what
Until it's time for me to depart
Please don't let go of what we share
For I will always hold you near.

Ateka Milledge

Ode to Lea Clayton

I have not known him long. Only a few years, really.
But in that time I witnessed activism supreme.
He was the master.
Not with aggression or hostility, but assertively, with conviction.
Listening to opponent and ally alike.
Weighing options, backing principles.

Risk-taking was natural to him, frequently at his own expense.
The benefactors mostly unaware that he toiled in their behalf.
A man of quiet passion. Compassion playing a louder role.
A paradox to some. A paragon to many.
Model of what is moral.

A lover of nature. Beyond the surface.
Deep into the soul of all God's creatures.
Working tirelessly to protect the innocent.
Defender of creation as it was meant to be.
Believer in future generations.

I did not know him long.
Far too short a time for what he taught,
But long enough to learn the value of the man,
And note the imprint he has made upon the Earth.
With the mandate to carry on.

Rosilee Trotta

My Little Star

Here you are, my little star
Brought to Earth from Heaven afar
You're bright and you twinkle and, Oh, how you shine
I'm thankful to God that He made you mine

Your smile, though little, brightens the day
Your cry, though small, lets you get your way
Your fingers and toes, small as can be
God made you that way for all the world to see

They call you a preemie for being so small
but one of these days you'll grow big and tall
For now I'll take you just as you are
from Heaven to Earth, you're my little star.

Jennifer L. Trexler

Living with MS

My body is weak.
The outlook is bleak.
I'm so tired.
After all this caffeine I should be wired.
I'm so run down I can barely stand.
I can't meet life's daily demands.
My body has gone numb again.
The feeling will come back, but I don't know when.
I'm looking for something I can't find.
I guess my memory has escaped my mind.
I get depressed a lot, I must confess.
That's what it's like living with MS.

Trena Hartman

For My Mother

This is for you my mother
So caring, so smart, so full of advice
Anything for you I would do
Without thinking twice
When I was a child you would tuck me in
And keep me safe in a world of sin
Even though I didn't understand it then
I now know that a mothers love is without end
Stupid things I have done in the past
Some of which have left you aghast
And for this I do apologize
In no way do I ever want to jeopardize
This relationship between mother and son
You are the only lady in my life who is number one
Friends may come and friends may go
But through everything a mother's love will show
After reading this I hope your spirits will rise
So that you get that motherly gleam back in your eyes
These words I say come from the heart
I promise nothing will ever keep us apart

Jason A. Shaw

A Pond I Am

A pond I am a pond I am crystal wetness
clear water the meadow my home a solitude place
your beauty is more than one you are a swarm of prettiness
you are a swarm of butterflies
and you have taken flight I have captured
your reflections you are beautiful
beauty that stains my forever
wetness my forever home beauty.
that stains my forever solitude
my mind my thoughts of you
filtered through golden sunlight
filtered through silver moonlight
filtered through diamond raindrops
tenors tenors of your voice like a song
turns a forever echo song songs of voices
echo echo of echoes on my mind
like a morning mist sits on the surface of the ocean
a swan sits on the surface of a pond.

Junior Anthony Chambers

Fusaichi Pegasus

He pawed with fury in the starting gate
The rider trembled, seconds ticked away
The bell sent horses running down the straight
But Pegasus let others lead the way
He took the turn and thundered side by side
With lesser beasts to make them feel good
The nags beside him matched him stride for stride
Along the backstretch resting while he could.
Around the final turn, the rider felt
A burst of will, a surge, a thunderclap
And Pegasus began the track to melt
And made his lowly comrades will to snap.
He crossed the finish line to roaring cheers.
And Fred and I knew this was Pegasus' year,
To win the run for the roses in the Kentucky Derby.

Lisa Ball

Happiness

Happiness is the color of peach.
It tastes like white chocolate.
It smells like a daisy in a garden.
And reminds me of when I went to Las Vegas.
It sounds like the scream from someone
Who is happy to see someone else.
Happiness makes me feel like a beautiful rose.

Hillary DiMaggio

Grandmama's Words

If grandmama could speak words to us today,
I am sure that she would have plenty to say.
The advice she would so freely offer to you and me,
She would challenge us to be the best we can be.
Of her first priority—make God the head of your life,
You will be a much better husband, parent, or wife.
Your friends, new and old, will see a difference in you,
If Christ and the church are in the center of what you do.
Live your life to the fullest each and every day,
Reaching people, loving people, and showing the way,
To lead a full, productive life that is happy and glad.
She would also tell us that life is sometimes sad,
But if our faith in God is strong, secure, and true,
We can face whatever—God will see us through.
Enjoy your life while here on this great place,
Keep up the good fight, and keep running the race.
God has a definite plan for me and for you,
Keep focused, and He will show us what to do.
Last, but not least, Grandmama would say,
Do not forget others and their needs when you pray.

Sherl W. Lowe

Cure for MS

Multiple Sclerosis
I am a man with multiple sclerosis—do you have a cure?
I awake in the morning with a smile, yet in pain
I sit still and listen to the beauty of nature

I am a talk show personality, yet all the fame and
glamour and glitter doesn't stop the pain.

I take cayenne pepper for the pain, a dash to make life
last, a slice of lemon to tighten up my grin, a bit of sunshine
to put the radiating in my skin.

I go the river to wash the unwanted pain. I let all of
the elements take to my brain.

I let loose of all negative thoughts.
I hold on the gift of life I have left.
I hold onto life as I close my eye with a plight that
when I awake there would be a cure in sight, while I'm still
here on my tour.

Shawqui Echevarria

Summer Serenade

The light from the cigar was a pin point
until he puffed again.
It glowed then, through the smoke.
Ghost grey smoke that just hung there
After all, he didn't blow it away.
He just puffed.
He puffed as we sat in silence
on the creaking front porch swing . . .
Moving ever so slightly—toe-heel, toe-heel.
Thus at dusk we waited for the symphony
in the small town.
Slowly it began, and soft.
Crescendo-decrescendo,
Crescendo-decrescendo,
Momentarily the old, green swing slowed.
Dad looked at me, I at him.
We grinned as though we shared some secret.
Then slowly the creak of the swing picked up the tempo
and became the accompaniment for those cicadas' songs,
Our summer serenade.

Jean Warrick

STRENGTH IN YOURSELF

S—someone who is always there.
T—the ability to regard or disregard.
R—respect yourself mentally and physically.
E—energy from every being and thing.
N—nothing will stop you from your goals.
G—grasping every second of every day.
T—technical skills to survive in this day.
H—helping yourself to build own self esteem.
I—inside you is power to accomplish anything.
N—never deny yourself the ability to fail.
Y—yes life can become good if you let it.
O—only you can improve yourself.
U—understanding your own self and worth.
R—reject negative input from non-believers.
S—strengthen by being positive.
E—every second and day is truly blessed.
L—life will become what you envision it.
F—focusing on what makes you happy and content inside and out.

Daniel Watson

Preparation

Bathed and perfumed,
I slip softly into that sweet night,
As if slipping silently into satin slippers
And a lace-adorned, white silk gown
Shimmering in late evening's candlelight.
Upon my down couch, for gentle dreams
I shall recline and close my eyes;
With a smile and an hour of prayers,
I'll bid a goodnight to the world
And all of its mundane cares.
Then a settling in, a covering of sleep,
Of poemed dreams of infinite bliss.
"Death?" you ask.
"Life." I answer.
"I am prepared for Paradise,
For union with my Master,
My God,
Who is Love."

Frances Crook

A Longing for You

As I go through life with a longing for you.
From a fetus you grew me and then you left me.
I never knew you, but a part of me went with you.
I'll never know why or who I am because you left me again by death.
You tried to protect me by giving me to others,
 but all I ever needed was to have you hold me
and comfort me through life's ups and downs.
Every day I think of you and I still need you to talk to.
But that can never be.
I hug and nurture my own that I have
because I don't want them to feel the hurt and pain
of a longing for a person who,
in the end, hurt you by growing you
and left you without knowing you.

Mary J. McCarty

The Life of Spring

I dedicate this to my wonderful parents!
Look around and see the colors of the trees,
The sweet little birds and the happily buzzing bugs,
See the mommies giving little babies hugs.
Feel the wind, breath the fresh air,
Go outside without a care.
Look at the flowers coming back to life,
Enjoy the stroll with a husband or wife.
Be glad about spring's happiness,
And live your life to its fullest.

Amanda Dame

Moxie Moron

Have you ever pondered what a Moxie Moron serves
Could it be an oxymoron with a lot of nerve
Violent about peace, love to hate, living to die
Dying to live, tears of joy, I'm so happy I could cry

It certainly is fun, an act of playing with words
Don't knock it till you try it, rearranging silly blurbs
I find this very therapeutic, hypnotic to one's soul
This could be the ticket that helps your inner self grow

I was so naughtily nice wearing my wicked Cheshire grin
It felt so good, I had to ask, could this possibly be a sin
Like the good bad guy who was so brutally kind
Even though he's one big a**hole, you still don't mind

Moxie Morons are a form of art, a way of expression
Neither right nor wrong, they give a different impression
Don't ever sell yourself short by being miserably happy
New boots in the sewer could be a clean kind of crappy

Diane Wormington

Violated Angel

Rain can bloom in starlit pastures
Nymphs laughing at dying skies.
Lovers scream in heated passion:
Hands on ears, I'll tell no lies.
Feel my bones and my faces,
Ruby lips and onyx eyes.
Press against my perfect figure:
Hands on ears, I'll tell no lies.
Curving hips accent your senses,
Breasts of gold caress your thighs.
Screaming bliss in virgin sunlight:
Hands on ears, I'll tell no lies.
Claim your love against my lashes,
Raking nails against soft flesh.
Share the heat a little longer:
Hands on ears, I'll tell no lies.
Waste your breath on your sweet nothings;
Destroy my life with diamond rings.
Love was meant to *murder* spirit:
Hands on ears, I'll tell no lies.

Moni'ca Kay Flythe

The Bubble Bath

Water raging, gradually filling
almost to the top . . .but not quite.
Thick liquid poured in,
creating bubbles.
Sweet smells drifting up,
heat rising, fogging up mirrors and windows.
Toes dipped in testing out the waters,
temperatures adjusted if needed.
Finally acceptable, it is time. . . .
Stripping off clothing to total nakedness
a mixture of heat and cold air on the body
hard nipples and goose-pimpled skin
until the naked body steps into and lies down in. . . .
the hot, bubble filled water to finally relax.

Helene Ann Castle (Chesebro)

Kristallnacht

Crashes
The broken glass sounds like cats screeching
It starts out smooth, then jagged and sharp
There are loud, high-pitched sounds all around me
Yelling, screaming
The sounds are so loud it is like my ears are going to explode
Sharp pieces of glass lying on the floor
Glass is everywhere
Horrifying

Stacey Fenton

Mr. Hustler

For the journey into change . . .
From deep within my dreams
An outlaw lives and I am haunted by his memories . . .
Yet I knew it would not be without great pain, I write . . .
Often troubled, kill me quick
Because that's a big-*ss fight, "Mr. Hustler"
They wish we could lie down and die
That's why they have labeled us for genocide
And when one goes to jail another takes his place
Do you have your bail money?
The murder weapon syndrome
An outlaw labeled, sanctioned
But all we're really doing is
Trying to feed our family, "Mr. Hustler"
Gettin' dogged for the rack-up . . .
Stop the crap up, me I cry desperately
For peace and fairness,
Which always seem elusive in "Mr. Hustler"

R. Rollins, Sr.

The Joy of Man and Woman

A man . . . a woman
They come together once again, only in bare skin.
They express their feelings of joy for being with one another
He gently caresses her silky smooth shoulders.
She runs her fingers through his hair.
Then; she cries out . . . not in pain, but in joy.
Barely a few moments later,
he smells sweetly of perspiration and she can feel it,
dripping slowly from his face onto hers.
This miracle has just begun.

He holds her hand. She pants heavily.
Suddenly, she cries out, again in joy.
But wait! . . . it's not just one cry.
It's two. One hers and one . . . a small cry.
One of fear, joy, and hope.
The sight of this miracle, that is the joy of . . .
A man and a woman.

Rebecca Coleman Meyers

Bittersweet

Bittersweet this love may be
that which haunts in waking as well as in dreams
yearning for fingers heated strokes
that do provoke
a fire I'm unable to douse by will alone
a mouth which beckons my lips to taste
and drowns me in pure desire
no earthly words to describe this fever heat
when his body enters mine
moving in perfect harmony seeking out our
ecstasy and grasping at it hungrily
ah, how can I not crave this forbidden fruit
so bittersweet.

Jan I. Birney

The Warriors of Old

What a battle it was, hewing and slicing
through sinew and joint

Hacking, slashing, cracking and mashing
Steel clashing, bodies thrashing

Blood spurting, curdling cries, a quick
moment to say "goodbye"
Of all the battles they had fought before,
this surely was the pinnacle of war

To the warriors of old who had always been so bold

What was the final point?

Robert Foot

Hopeless

All that I see is all I thrive to be.
Nothing in my mind.
But it's all here, in this place where I keep myself confined.
Ran to my heart to see a sunny day.
Keep slackin' off sh*t that causes my pain.
Always . . .
Blind to those many things that they call the right way.
Alone in my soul once more I stray.
Easing all, staying away.
Keeping thoughts of that sunny day.
Now it's gone, and there I lay.
With open arms I feel the pain.
I feel it every day.
So divine it is to hear the words you say.
And still on the cold, damp ground I lay.
Madness consuming all the pain.
Here I go again, here I am with a withering mind.
All I knew is gone, for once again I've gone insane.

Korry Cassidy Hernandez

The Silent Cries of Help

I'm told to hold my emotions and feelings.
Don't say this or that, they might not like it.
F*ck everyone that can't understand me.
I walk like the depressed and emptied shelled person
I am now. I slit my wrist to end my life for good.
For some reason I still live on. What is a person to
Do with their emotions and feelings? When they have
Nowhere to go. I have so many things to say to
Everyone, but ssh we can't talk. We may hurt someone's
Feelings, know what? Who gives a sh*t. I'm hurt
Inside, I kept dying. I believe in no one and I trust no
One either. I'm tired like hell of getting hurt by people.
I have a lot of hurt and pain from it all.
Maybe one day it'll stop, whenever that is.

Traci Jurasin

Dancing Pativrata

Converse with my essence.
Reach deep within and tear out the throbbing
Postulate subsistence and the correlation to internal tranquility.
Far away beneath the crumbling barriers,
Explosions ravish, turmoil proceeds.
Egalitarianism lies to the wayside.

Facetious liberties serenely dancing with sativa,
Mutilating the creative pleasure, dreams, and procreation.
Freudian hysteria floats above this incestuous cloth
That we leave as our legacy.
The pativrata, inherently wicked but teachable, asks,
"What would you like for dinner, dear?"

Lori Kaleka

Mom Said

Mom said,
Patience is a virtue,
Cultivate it with glee.
Well, it may be a virtue,
But it's never been me.

I'm like the old buzzard who surveys and sees nothing,
Saying, "Patience, my *ss, I think I'll kill something."

My mom knew me best,
It's so hard to be me.
I'm just like that buzzard perched high in the tree.

My mom knew me best,
She said, "Try not to worry; ask God to grant patience."
So I did—and said "hurry."

Carol Allen

What Are Friends

Friends are really your enemies
hiding their secret identities.
They talk to you, they get to know you.
They hang around with you from 9:00 to 5:00,
always saying they're happy to be alive.
But when you think you're close enough to be brothers,
they come from behind and stab you in the back!
They b*tch about you, they cuss at you,
and before you know it, they got everyone against you.

Stephan Wehner

I Am African B*tch, Am Not

I am part of you and see part of me.
Why? do you think calling me, African black b*tch will hurt me.
African I am b*tch I am not.
The other part of you
don't have anything to do with you.
That is not a big deal.
Because you have mother Africa.
Do not call her a b*tch no more,
remember Africa I am b*tch I am not says mother Africa.

Bella Tietie Rice

Road Kill

The wind was a needle piercing my leg
a river of blood flowing from veins
head breaking like a cantaloupe hitting the concrete
my wheels popped like a needle piercing a balloon!

Spencer Fujinaga

The Pain

As I gaze into the hollow eyes of darkness
I feel pain creeping up my legs into the deep
pit of my stomach
and churning my soul until it's ready to ditch
my body to find another victim
As I ask why, the pain continues its journey,
up my torso to my chest
twisting my lungs 'til I feel like they are
going to collapse along with the
rest of my organs, boiling until there's nothing left
The agonizing pain once again advances on its path
toward my skull
winding and amplifying in my brain, until my eyes
enlarge and pop out of their sockets, leaving
them hanging there,
swaying back and forth, back and forth
Alas, the pain retreats back down to my toes,
waiting and watching

Lindsey Murphy

Summer

Early morning sunshine, warm, pure and bright starts off a
summer day, much like the way I fell in love with you.
As a summer day reaches to mid-afternoon heat,
the sun in all its glory, erodes my human energy.
I become lazy, cool thoughts of drinking something cold and
tasty, arise in mind, my body craves to be refreshed in cool
inviting waters and thoughts of nakedness pull me into
deeper thought of my secret passions for you.
I close my eyes day dreaming of our bodies rising in heated
lovemaking drenched with sweat, only to cool each other
down with our luscious wet kisses and fresh water dripping
from a cold water cup or champagne glass.
What a mass of thought I endure time after time.

Marie Dominy

In Remembrance of Me

To the one man who made me remember that love was mine for the taking
Can you feel me?
That tantalizing, full-bodied, hands-on caress
That soft wind blowing gently against your cheek
Your neck
Your back
Can you smell me?
That alluring aroma in the air
That beautiful fragrance that surrounds your every breathing moment
Can you taste me?
That liquid core called my Best Friend
That wonderful mouthwatering flava that has you begging for one More
Nibble
Lick and
Swallow . . .
I know you remember.

Shawnta M. Maddox

Casino

Perpetual dreams, so it seems, are often nightmares
Where gamblers chase their losses and sit in high chairs,
And big babies weep 'til they sleep, while wondering "if" blares!

Those casino chicks do their tricks out back in the parking lot,
With the money that they earn, another spin of the wheel's bought,
While the businessman, their counterpart, wonders if he'll get caught.

Through some fluke, a new king of duke is the latest winner to be crowned,
For the one in a hundred who rise above, the other ninety-nine are downed,
Some of those who never will recover are too soon found underground.

Time spins on until money's gone and the sanity slips away,
Tired faces too long at the tables, knowing no night or day,
It's a strange way of life, the casino, where all who enter pay.

Aaron Brenner

The Bomb

Out sphere lies still and seemingly unpossessed. Unguarded and infinitesimal, it streaks along its ritual path through the vastness of space, beyond the eyes of tortured souls who strain to see beyond their own sky.

The shattering quiet . . . a foreboding grips the air tenaciously; and nerves held taut await the flash and man-made cloud of man's most vicious toy.

The sound . . . loud and not, gives birth to something new; an alien fright takes hold and bleeding fingers scratch the earth, but destiny forbids escape. Children, hugging close with fragile arms, hear the pulsating fear from their mother's breasts. Along the skyward path a winged monster casually points its belly to upraised heads; a tiny speck appears against the sun and whistles downward to destroy itself.

Futile prayers are heard amid the throngs of burning flesh; the last amen's cannot be heard above the piercing agony. The cries have stopped . . . and no one sees the death but God.

Paul Tessier

Daddy's Girl

I keep her in a glass box, hair golden and skin so fair.
Only my past knows why I keep her there.
She's not allowed to speak, her secrets I only keep.
Her weakness I bury, her vulnerability is my sin.
Foolish baby put out your candle,
this world's too much for your mind to handle.
Wipe away those tears, where you're going no one will hear.
Do not touch the woman with the little girl inside,
she knows no tenderness, heart's set aside.
I love you can't you see, it hurts me to hurt you but it's what you need.
You're my little girl as long as it suits me, but I don't see you anymore,
you're no longer Daddy's shining star.
I will make all your fears come true, leave alone, cold, and blue . . .
that's just what I'll do.

Heidi Micah Nelson

Sin

I want to blacken you
dress you in ash
you said
spiraling galaxies in my hand
your eyes—amber and musk
my wrists locked
I want to blacken you
like a curse
you said
putting out your cigarette butt
on my endless yards
of canned snow
and I bit
my lip
hard
as blood roses
seeped lovely as sin
along my thigh
blacken you
as you'll blacken your vow

Gabriela M. Debita

A Repository for Rusty Nails

I am a repository for rusty nails,
for some reason, I can never throw
them away. They gather
intertwined, chipped-off
flecks of brittle iron collecting
in my bowels. Plaster adhering
to some, sawdust to others,
some end up jotted down
in journals, but most work
their way toward bone, forgotten
eventually but always present.
Always threatening tetanus,
communing with hemoglobin,
becoming indistinguishable from memory
or reflex, from all the redundant
genetic material intertwined
within every cell of my body,
because I cannot throw them away.

Bradley Earle Hoge

no stone tablets

it wasn't
chisel in stone
writing "i love you"
in cursive
on an etch-a-sketch
was just
hard work
and temporary
like us

Breck Reliford

Grow My Heart Like Hers

Throw her
a thread
of an idea
and she'll adorn it
with wisps
of herbs
and tinsel
and lint from saris,
twist it into
loops of paisley whispers
and give it back,
saying:
"What a wonderful idea!
Look what it made me do!"

Melodie McLellan

Alphabet Lessons, Alphabet Men

A! Art, imitated life, told lies and untruths
with my heart he played loose.

N! Nick, was sly and slick, his game so quick
with two girls, three girls it had to be,
what number girl did he value me?

G! Gary, was big, sexy, macho and hairy
I think I found him . . . Oh, no! A fairy!

U! Uri, refined and sensitive, took care of my needs with flourish and flash . . .
What do you mean . . . no credit . . . just cash

I! Isaac, was sweet, so kind; understood crucial thoughts on my mind.
How was I to know Sara, his wife, a previous find.

S! Sam, was a man who was my greatest fan.
Behold modern medicine: Sam is Samantha a beautiful woman.

H! Harry, punches, smacks kicks and scrapes—he liked it rough.
My heart breaks, tears split, he shouts tough.

7! 7 lessons learned by 7 awful teachers, the lessons taught were great.
Perhaps I'll learn true love with lucky lesson number 8!

    Catherine McKoy

Dragon's Lair

The Dragon's Lair is never bare, its victims strewn the ground.

There's no remorse from this recourse, its deadly work abounds.

Yet drivers tread amongst these dead, oblivious of their demise.

As physical need for deadly speed, they fear not Dragon's eyes.

While unaware their life was spared, returning to seek its path.

Then mortals slip and sometimes trip into the Dragon's wrath.

When caution's thrown and fear's not known of deadly Dragon's sea.

Where tangled metal and strangled flesh, is all that's left to be.

A fingered gesture, a horn molester, a need to get by fast.

A soul regrets all death's sweet bets, amid the broken glass.

When need is greed it will succeed and let the Dragon win.

The final course would be remorse, where caution begets sin.

The Dragon's Lair is never bare . . . you're always welcomed in.

    Mickie Molnar

Premature Escribulation

Ladies ever I try to please, stoke their hunger, foreplay, tease.
Not manhood, tongue, with quill, their mind, not body, thrill.
Procreating child or verse, the climax of all powers.
Premature making love, writing I endure for hours.

To write, to make love, similar! A lady's passion, both ignite.
Turgid, urging, surging, my quill erect excite.
Blue-brained, thick idea, through quill flows my fire.
Her mind and soul to penetrate, my hard words, hot desire.

Quill aquiver, throb and shiver, moan, groan, exciting.
Escribulate! Spurt words! Baby, I'm writing! I'm writing.
Premature not my fault, lost my head, did best.
No cerebral orgasms in poems 20 lines or less.

If this verse comes in first, hide my quill in shame.
On poet's resume a stain, best unknown remain.
To write, to sex, serious! At times delirious, maybe.
Now you've read this ode, was it good for you, too, baby?

    Pat M. Reeves

Boy, You Are Essential

I was soaring
on the
stormy purple
symphony of your finger
screaming
diamond voids next to your arm
as tiny lights incubated
our shadows

Watch me as my garden petals
see moans manipulate puppy girl stares
into delicate heaves of womanly lust
and envision the sweetness of your skin
smelling like
honeyblood

I will eat this raw moment
and fall asleep
lovedrunk and sweaty.

    Rachel Grace Diaz

Unrest

On a path that I have drifted,
on a path we some times choose,
where nothing is gained but you
always seem to lose.
Tortured, am I sore and bruised.
Within deeper than flesh
emotions twisted to nothing,
And my sky is always gray,
pieces of me scattered.
On top were my love faded away,
I search for an answer,
it brings another question.
I found the end.
Can I find where it began?
I lie on a field of razors in a state of unrest.
constantly thinking "was it just of flesh?"
Once full of love,
Now full of regret.
Both apart we know
that we are nothing left.

    Matt Dunkleberger

The Innocent

I think I love you
You've always been my friend,
There since . . . I can't even remember.
You're so good looking.
Sweet surrender, warm melting kisses,
That soft touch on my back,
The scent of ocean air,
That rough hand against my breast,
That cruel fist pressing down—
Roughly shoving fat fingers into my cleft.
Suffocating violation,
Forcing penetration
Pain Horror Helpless
Shoving into my virgin body,
Shredding my self respect,
My naive innocence, my childlike beauty.
That rough hand pushes me up
Tucks my shirt in—drives me home.
The weeping. Alone in the bath,
My dreams betrayed, my love destroyed.

    Kyla Sorensen

American Buddha

The American Buddha was born in South East 'Laska
Out in the woods 'yond Skagway was forged a man from suffering
He tried to let New York go; without he wasn't sh*t though
The American Buddha was much younger than you'd think so
You could tell it by the way he did not let people's thoughts flow
His words flurried like a snowstorm, the drifts already'd been formed
He's in such a goddamned hurry cuz the people'd eat then scurry
Then he was asked a spefic question, his ignorance been paid for
Yet he'd smirk all the while, he thought he'd been beguiled
When all it really was was his lazy mediocrity
But with drink his belief faltered and so had all the others
The one friend he had in civilization he said p*ss on
The man on which he did had his own revelation
Now he watched the town's lamps dim from atop the AB mountain
We stop watching for his grinning when the snows began their blending
In the spring his head was stepped on by a hiker who had faltered
And he must have suffered greatly from the fall that had not killed him
For the trail of blood had dragged on rocks and dripped o'er many ledges
'Til a nurturing black bear mother turned her cubs to opportunists
His remains are in a graveyard made of cold wet metal drawers
        Darrin Jones

Chris's My Name and Wraslin' Will Be My Game

Off the ropes and in the ring, bloodshed,
You will feel my sting.

Future wrestler is what I'll be.
Mess with me, and you'll suffer a DDT.

Ten power bombs and five pile drivers later,
I'm sorry you didn't phase me,
But don't be a hater.
Please wait for the proper date,
So I can show you the Hardy's Twist of Fate.

That's right, baby, I'm electrifying,
And to prove it, I'll do somethin' death-defying,
Like a shiznit move involving Senton high-flying.

So throw in a Stunner,
It's only funner.
Toss me off a cage or hit me with a chair.
Go ahead, try it Jabroni,
Anything you dish out, I can bear.

Lightning quick, I be bookin'.
Did any of you smell what the Rock was cookin'?
Have a Nice Day!
        Chris Ivy

I See

I see this death before me eyes, a silver casket held to my head.
Being asked the question, "Do you believe in God?,"
Animates my emotions and stirs my thoughts.
In the precious seconds that I have to answer, my brain,
instead, ponders the question. The God I know, so kind and sure,
The One who protects, restores, endures,
Watches, leads and loves so pure.
God's love is the answer, the absolute cure.
I see not my life before my eyes, but God's promise of eternal life.
A beautiful land, blessed with grace, is promised to me, a hopeful place.
I see Heaven, bright light in my eyes, my future, my home, before me it lies.
"Yes" I answer with power and love, "Bang" goes the barrel pointed right above.
Out pours the blood, my life giving fluid. Out goes the light, my light of life ruined.
But, I see that beautiful Haven, the place I long to be—a place with no sin.
I see love, the love of God, the love that cost me my life.
I see myself a kind of martyr. The words I spoke with life, with hope,
did not save me from my fate. This evil mind, body, full of hate.
His actions so cruel, harsh and course,
The gun he held with evil force, ended my life with no remorse.
I see now, all truth and love, no pain, no suffering, just God's love.
        Krista Boyd

Nebulous Perpetuity

swimming aimlessly
through the remnants of a Dream
floating in the Afterbirth
silent stalker of Mother Earth
muted Key
Bearded Star
Perfectly Structured
Random Thoughts
stare out
stared at
God's angry eye is watching
Wake up to realize the plane
isn't so simple
every Answer is its own Riddle
rub your own eyes
try to Wake
try to Break
from this
Infinite Prison
        Esteban Calvo

Not Like Mom

She's a cold hearted woman
She's bad if you please
She'll break your heart
Put you on your knees

She'll have your child
Then take it away
If you want to love her
You'll just have to pay

She's got no conscience
She loves no one
She'll push you to suicide
Then hand you the gun

Her children are only
A means to an end
She'll steal your man
But say she's your friend

She looks like the rest
But the difference is there
It's a frightening thing
When her soul is laid bare
        Erick W. Miller

Columbine Reaper

In the morning, dress in black,
Shave my head, fill my pack,
Run into the sun, have fun with my gun.

I will confront my fears,
Free my mind, kill my peers.
I am pain, I am sorrow,
Kill 'em now, forget tomorrow.

I'm an angel, I'm a demon,
Gotta keep 'em screaming.
Gonna bring my load,
Touch me, I'll explode.

Fear in their eyes,
My pain in their cries.
I'm a dead tree on a hill.
Nothing like the thrill of a kill.

Nothing comes to a sleeper but a dream,
Nothing comes to a reaper but a scream.
Hole in my heart I can't fill,
Nothing like the thrill of a kill.
        Robert Tuell

D*mn Alzheimer

Do you remember the laughter?
How I loved you when I was young and life was fresh and easy,
Do you remember the tears?
As we passed through my teenage years,
How I thought I hated you, did we ever understand each other?
But throughout the love stayed strong.
Now you are old and I am grown and the love stays with us,
Strangers see an old man losing himself in the dark maze of his mind,
But I see you!
I know you are still there, don't be afraid,
I'll remember the laughter,
I'll remember the tears,
I'll remember the love!
Good night and God Bless.

    Susan Nye

The Train to Anywhere

From Station of Birth the train of your life
brings you to a fog of dream
Throughout roar of iron wheels of time
nobody hears your scream

The silent captive of minute, your train goes by will of good-luck wind
And the Conductor-Hope has left at previous stop.
Eating on the move a soup of own blood—
Habitual taste . . . and dusty window makes you blind.

Stops of the Childhood, Youth, Old Age flash one after another
Infinite route with rails like two loops of Father.
The Eternity lies on fragile circle,
Where aimlessly rushes The Train to Anywhere . . . circus.

    Anya Ruvinskaya

Venus

My red clay womanhood. Could be.
Pieces of me sliding deep down this spiral carnelian groove.
And I bring forth of myself. Without consort. Still a maiden.
My whole self being stitched up hatched over and over again.
Most perplexing! At least it seems so.
How my ballooning breasts thread down
And fumble the abyss of my groin.
How my hips track down in crescents to prowl my inadequate feet.
How the moonbeams seep through my blood nest
My womb lullabying my bubble eggs.
I'm gownless unaware of the secrecy of my filiations
Totally uncharted weaving the meshes of my otherness.

    Maria V. Rivas

Ambience

Shy moments.
Unable to search each other's faces
because breathing becomes too painful
and the truth of our intimacy, revealed.

Our eyes speak the universal language,

while our bodies move rhythmically like ocean swells,

breaking against the shore,

releasing soft white foam that slides along the sand,

dripping into the grains and the sigh of the waves

as they release and find rest on the shore.

Ah, sweet ambience . . .

    Wataya Roberson

When I Died

I'm lying down, somewhere apart.
My neck is there, on the floor
My blood is cleaning up the door
I just died, I don't know why.
Maybe I should start to cry
I felt no pain, I felt no fear.
Something got me from the rear.
My body is there in the mud,
Entrails ripped, a lot of blood
The Sun has gone; The wind is storming;
The field cries; The crows are tripping.
I'm alone on a big plain.
There's no one to call my name
No friends to cover me with dust,
No enemies to hate my past,
No Heaven for my dirty mind,
No Hell to fit a piece of mine
Only crows for my big flesh,
Grown with pains through years of trash.

    Raul Mihali

Drop of My Blood

I help you whenever you ask
I will do any task
I put a drop of my blood in every favor
Just so you can sit there and savor

Keep in mind anyway
As soon as you drain me that day
My blood will run black
Bleeding from the knives in my back

It will be my turn to live my life
Then I will take out every single knife
It will be your turn to suffer
And under me it will be so much rougher

    Matt Gulbranson

Feelings

I felt your love today
And inhaled the essence of your heart
As we exchanged breath by telephone.

I felt the warmth of your love
As the simple words you spoke
Intertwined, hugged, and wrapped me
In satin sheets and pillow talk

I felt the pulse of your love
As it throbbed a crimson stream of life
Umph! Umph! Umph!
Wow!

    Diane M. Lockett

I'll Tell Ya

I tell ya that night I cried
Saw the moon in its rarest form
Star dipped and kissed the crust of humanity
In all its sanity
I tell you that night I cried
Reaching for her deepest crater
Hide all of my fears for her goodness sake
Lie still at night and for her voice stay awake
I tell you that night I cried
Found her warmth blissful and at peace
With ever angelic touch a warm release
I would have waited forever for this promade
on the wings of dusk
I tell you that night I cried
If only inside

    Adrian Hodges

A Heart in the Right Mind

Dark souls forgotten
black hearts bleeding
a strong feel of absence
a blunt urge for needing

Torturing of one's heart
sheds idealistic pain
Premonitions of watery eyes
while shivering in the rain

Head hung heavy
spirits dragged low
twisting bursts of anger
help my salty tears flow

Another mind to waste
one more life to regret
aching in my body
makes my suspicions sweat

Those who try to make this deceivable world
a place to live, love and learn
are not only putrid to me
but to themselves in return

Kelsie Burns

Chaos

In the midst of battle the cry is heard,
Of a lady not of wealth but of word,
That we do not recognize the sign,
Meaning we shall not die
Of pain—but of terror and murder.

The fang of death be that of gothic,
Marking that which be erotic,
Paying death with an eerie wickedness,
Making all that be seen be an eternal darkness,
Unless that of which we made mythic
Be made Pure.
Silver, a shade of richness,
Shows that which we think to be spiritless,
Telling of evils with a total being,
Knowing in our hearts it's all a fling
Of Pain or Bliss—
Exist as Chaos.

Kristina Gail Painter

Erimako's Pen

Your pen is six inches long and strong.
Its head is big, bald and bold, brainy.
Its nib will write—to right the wrong.
Your pen is it any day, sunny or rainy.
Handled well, it rises to any occasion.
It can trace a concatenation of strokes.
A brainy issue can come out with passion.
It comes alive even with impassive stokes.
Held with fingers of sobriety, propriety;
it will ooze with a lot of rationality.
Fingered with a touch of emotive variety,
it will exude with a cup of seminality.
It is free as the wind is always free,
circumscribed only by a sea of eternity.
It minds not fear nor a proffered fee.
It gets madness into a nest of serenity.
Your pen is six inches long and strong.
It pulses with the beat of a mighty horde.
It is pushed or pulled to right the wrong.
Your pen is mightier than a mighty sword.

Eduardo Jr. Alicias

To Love Is to Live

To love,
to put a gun against your head.
To want to suffer,
to give yourself to hurt and pain,
or to, at last, live and feel the beauty of life.
To love,
to be devoted to the only one.
A wonderful pain you can't wait to suffer.
To be in love with the person you adore.
To feel the warmth of a smile,
or the pain of a turned back.
To love is to feel you can't live.
To love is to live.
Those who cannot love,
I'm sorry for them all,
For although it hurts,
behind that pain, behind that sorrow,
there lies the answer,
To love, is to live . . .

Ivan Morales

Fate

His almighty eyes gleam with fire
His mighty wrath, most feared and dire
His thirst for blood take all men to pyre

His obsidian blade is cloaked in red
With each victim, his power fed
And all men to him are lead

His cloak is ebon, his eyes are gold
He is of ancient ages old
With his presence he brings icy cold

He is the inevitable, the great, the feared
His sword is hot with souls he's seared
With each day your fate is neared

He is the destroyer, the end, the strong
To him, none are right or wrong
By his side, Time has been for long

His name is Death

Michael Pearson

Sibling

Hey I'm your sibling
What ya think of that
No, I'm not your boy
But for LIFE I got your back
To you I'm just a kid
A snot nosed lil' brat
All I ask of you is a lil' time
And a couple of pats on the back
Yeah, I know your older
Things to do and people to see
So, did you ever listen
Or just pretend to hear me
D*mn right I may be annoyin'.
H*ll, that's my job.
But, when you neglect those special moments
It feels like I've been robbed
So keep on seein' your people
Keep on doin' your thing
But just between you and me, I'm your sibling

Dianne Grainger

Gen-X

Hey look at me, I'm a product of society,
Generation X, great drugs,
and hard-core sex.
Never mind the rights and the wrongs,
I'll smoke my weed and hit my bongs.
LSD and I don't care,
AFDC and mother-f***ing welfare.
Generation gap a load of crap,
and I can see Generation X will always
be baby booming with bullets flying.
Every minute someone's dying,
but leave it to Beaver to pick up the cleaver
and finish the job, but what about Bob?
Hey, Bob, generations mean nothing.

Josh Carnes

My Secret Love

I knew a pretty Girl
I knew her Oh, so well
But now I'm not allowed
To have her for my own
The sweetest thing I know
Small and so petite
A body soft and warm
And brown from the sun

To know her is to love her
Not to see her is so sad
But our love is not allowed
They say she is too young

Some day my love my own
I will see you once again
To hold you in my arms
And tell you of my love

Terence Gardiner

Passion

Running my fingers throughout her hair,
Kissing, caressing without a care.
Sensations mounting light and rough,
Our bodies swaying with the touch.

Moans of ecstasy fill the air,
I gaze at her with her body bare.
The dream come true as we lie with no bother,
Passion found in the eyes of each other.

Michael J. Daigle

Nickies Youth

Clinging to my thoughts
of past times for forgiveness
of petty sins
Reminiscing juvenile behaviors
elaborate schemes
to make reality real
life made simple
Through irrational insanity
makes perfect sense
ripping your thoughts apart
from the worlds point of view
pride turned to pity
Waking to find you
constantly unchanging
The seasons on the calendar
flying off the wall
that I climb trying to escape
your never ending attentions
suffocating my fantasies
of a world gone right

Sarah Wixson

Cave of Comfort

It is warm and dark, beckoning with the comfort of a womb.

A haven of softness, where you know that you will be safe.

Music soothes you, and you are surrounded in a cocoon of love and protection.

How long has it been since you have felt safe and warm.

How long has it been since you could feel the core of you begin to come to life.

Now, feelings come back as if they had never been gone.

Strong arms hold you and tender hands caress you,
the dead cave inside of you begins to glow.

Hot hands, mouths, and body's reach and touch, devouring each other,
enjoying and savoring the passion and love.

Eagerly we share and pleasure each other, in this soft dark place
where there is no one but the two of us.

We peak and explode in colors that only we can see, then rest in this dark,
safe place where the world cannot come in.

Cave of comfort, you are my refuge, your dark warmth reminds me that.

I am alive again. I have passion and love in my life again.

I am beginning again and I don't have to be afraid.

I can come out of that safe dark womb and look to the light.

    Catherine Schaumburg

So Hard on Me When We Part

Do you know how much it hurts my heart,
to see you once, then see us part?
To only feel you in my dreams, but never real, unlike I've seen.
When we are alone together, I cherish it to last forever.
Day by day I want you more, my growing heart of that is sure.
If you look at me, you'll understand that all I want is to hold your hand.
To keep you close and keep you near, to make your life far from fear.
Sometimes I find it so hard to talk, 'cause when I do, it is like I'm not.
There is so much I need to say, but without my seeing you, I feel so far away.
I've felt this way for so long but can do nothing, 'cause we don't belong,
Not being with you, I'm falling apart because I cannot have what is in my heart.
But if we end up here together, I'll be content with your smile and laughter,
Going to live my life forever, with my love and only bearer.
Hold on to you and, Oh, so tight, will not let you leave my sight,
I pray to the Lord for his love and yours.
I will never lose faith 'cause our love is pure.

    Kris Cheung

Falling

The way I see it, our relationship has been like a pit of love.
I couldn't help falling in love with you.
I just kept falling deeper and deeper,
desperately grabbing for something to slow me down. Then it hit me.
I struck the ground unexpectedly, thinking it was a much deeper pit.
Now I can neither fall anymore, nor climb to the top.
Now, I guess the only thing for me to do is to stand back up.
I'll get up, and watching my step, so as not to fall so easily,
I will start searching for other people's broken dreams
that they might have dropped down the pit.
I will collect these all together, and build a broken shack.
There, I can try to start again, being a better person for surviving the fall,
and yet still hurting from the impact.

    Kaleb Sanderson

Nothing Fancy

Here I go again trying my luck on something I don't know if I will ever win.
I don't think I'm that unusual or even that talented mind you.
I just know when I write, I write from the heart
and I never know where it will end up from the start.
I don't use fancy words or try to confuse you.
I just say what's on my mind. I don't try to pretty things up.
Maybe I'm not fancy enough.

    Tara Lorensberg

Determination

Far before the sun emerges
A figure stirs in bed.
They push away the sleep and dreams
And start another day.

Now the sleepy sun comes up
And spreads its soft lit rays
As a figure steps into the light
And starts a known routine.

The grass is moist from morning dew
And the fog still hugs the ground
As the figure steps onto the field
With a soccer ball in hand.

The morning goes on longer
And a group forms on the field
All with common goals in mind
To win the game at hand.

    Jenni Ann Rabey

To Van Gogh

What a beautiful gesture
to cut out your chest
one delicate movement
leading to an explosive conclusion
you were a bright flame
with a painted history
that vanished
by
your
calloused
hand.

    Brooke Ashleigh Summers

lip treat

it's strange the way
the honey drips
from the corner of her lip
down to the golden pool
at her feet
and he laps it
feeding on the sweetness
drowning in the light
his hands and knees
in a cradle
the soft grass of God
a bright being
she can't see
her eyes glazed with the sap
she cries thick honey tears
falling on the face of him
molding his features
in the pure state of ecstasy.

    Dezaraye Bagalayos

Blindness of the Heart

Black and white are both the same,
each the other cannot reign.
Close your eyes and you will find
where colors end and love's divine.

    Marcie M. Regenthal

Owner of a Submissive

To Ser2hth, my devoted submissive
Submissive
Devoted, Loyal
Waiting, Serving, Hoping
Obedient
Jan

    Leatrice Sykes

Two Kinds

There was once a beautiful flower that grew so tall
Its blossom was the most fragrant of them all.
Now on the other side of a wall grew a flower not half so tall
It hardly had a fragrance at all.
The fragrant flower grew and grew, but the other flower
stayed quite small it could hardly be seen at all.
The tall flower so brave and bold,
Looked down on the other flower, so I'm told.
It laughed at it and cried each day;
Why don't you grow up someday.
Then something happened as time passed
The little flower grew at last.
Not up, but out and wide it grew
Then suddenly over the wall it flew, with flowers all bright and blue.
The little flower meet the tall flower and last,
And grew around it as time passed.
Now soon the tall flower could hardly be seen
To the fragrant flower it seemed like and awful dream.
The arms of it went around the plant, until at last down it went.
It now cannot be seen at all, the flower that cried, I'm so fragrant.

Don V. Axtell

In a Quiet Voice

With your gentle touch and enlightening smile you have stolen
my heart, your strong will is evident as you slowly say the words, "I love you" . . .

God puts special children like you on Earth for a reason,
I truly believe you are here as an angel to show the world
the determination that exists within you and other children like you . . .

To capitalized on your determination by encouraging and praising
small achievements will fuel the desire that exists within you . . .

I can see potential and want so much to be a part of the process
to ensure you are given every opportunity to succeed and prosper

Johnathan Lee Gusha

Tasmania—Emerald Isle of Australia

Two hundred miles south of Melbourne lies "Tassie," as Tasmania is affectionately known,
Where the east coast soil is a rich red-brown, and the biggest vegies are grown.
From the coastal northeast of Georgetown, through to the southeast village of Swansea,
The water is clear, and the fishing is good, with plenty of variety.
The people are happy and friendly, as they have every good reason to be,
Because, unlike the States on the Mainland, there is no heavy industry,
Which means the air they breathe is much purer, with little pollution at all.
This explains why Taswegians are so happy, and are obviously having a ball!

Tasmania is shaped like a triangle, with its base facing north at Bass Strait,
From east to west, it's two hundred miles long, making it Australia's smallest state.
Close to the southern tip is its capital, Hobart, a really beautiful scene,
Which, seen from the top of Mount Wellington, is like myriads of diamonds, en-
shrouded in emerald green.
With the blue waters of the Derwent, meandering to the south and the west,
It's no wonder they have spacious orchards, and trout fishing is considered the best!
Just sixty miles north in the midlands, is the picturesque village of Ross.
Here you'll think you must be in Heaven, or it's close to winning the toss!
One hundred and twenty miles north of the capital, rests Launceston—
"Lonnie," Jewel of the North,
Half the size of Hobart and as resplendent on the Tamar as Edinburgh, on the Firth of Forth,
With its peacocks, parks and gardens, the unique Gorge is a fabulous sight to behold!
And still there is the rugged west coast, rich in veins of various ores, copper, iron,
tungsten and even precious gold!

Fred P. Place

Spring Time

In the springtime I hear the unforgettable songs
Of the robins playing over in my head,
And feel the cool but soothing breeze sway against my smiling face.
I see the purple, yellow and white flowers
Blooming and buds on the trees bursting with new beautiful green leaves.
Every living thing fills the world with color.

David Rascati

The Current State of Medical Care

Patients beware,
You can no longer get
Quality care.
Insurance companies
Don't want to be a fair
And HMO's just
Want market share
Sensitive doctors
Are extremely rare;
Find where they are
And get yourself there.
Hospitals constantly
Trying to merge;
The nursing profession
In a terrible scourge;
Doctors fearing
Malpractice suits.
The system's against you,
They're all in cahoots!

Barry S. Rich

Three Worlds and Two Lives

There are three worlds
And two lives to live
Where you may go
Depends on what you give.
The first of the three
Everyone goes,
The first life you live
Isn't to be chose.
The second or third
Are different you see
Life or death
They both come free.
Outside the universe
Time stands still
In your first life
Your might makes your will.
Heaven or Hell
Time can't wait
The world is the first
The next is fate.

Shannon West

Love of a Mother

The touch of her hand
A kiss on your cheek,
Her soft stern eyes
Giving you strength when you are weak.

A pat on your bottom
When you did something bad.
A hug around the neck
When you were just feeling sad.

Trips to your room
When you were frightened in the night.
She'd snuggle beside you,
And make everything right.

Talks of your confusion
As you got older.
Still, knowing when you were scared,
You could lean on her shoulder.

There is no love greater
Than that of your mother.
You could search the world over
But, you will never find another.
This was inspired by my mother!

Ruth Ann Chadderdon

Thinking, Wondering, Waiting

Sitting here thinking about the good and bad times.
Wondering that if we'd done things different would things still be the same?
Knowing that we can't go back in time,
we become pleased with all that we've struggled to accomplish.
As the time fades away and the familiar faces come and go,
this time we wonder when the pain and suffering is going to stop
and when we'd again be with those who've gone to the other side.
Listening to people tell us the end is coming soon wondering what it'll be like
and hoping that the ones we leave behind will be okay until it's their turn to pass.
Loved ones all around us.
Each one with their own witty personality. Making a smile come to our faces.
Wondering what they're keeping behind their smiles and long glances of concern.
Wanting to leave, wanting to stay.
Mostly just waiting to say goodbye to everyone.
But still here we sit . . . thinking, wondering and waiting.
Until it is our turn for the last heartbroken goodbye.

Brandi Poulos

A Treasured Piece

A special jewelry.
Rowena Lester.
Oh! What a cute little jewelry.
At the table it glitters, makes some people shiver.
Some stare, even when I am not aware.
Someone is always inquiring about this cute little ring.
Eyes are always looking
On this my most treasured piece, especially when I pick up
My glass to make a toast,
Or even try to sip my wine before I dine.
Oh! This cute little ring certainly speaks
For itself as it sparkles, leaving me with just one question to answer.
Should I take it off or just show it off?

Rowena Lester

Oasis

For Lisha

I've dreamt the dream of dreamers, so lovely and so bare
To glide beneath the waters, to dance in neon air
To touch and hold my heartbeat, so disarming and so real
To wake up from that silent madness with longing that keeps me still.

To sing the song of dreamers, and have it felt by them
Who've never dreamt a single thing, and cannot account for grim
Feelings that make them virgins, to tremble with delight
To plead for shrouded secrecy, and curse the morning's light.

To dance to songs of nothing, that are like abstract art
The painted picture truly lies, in the viewers disheveled heart
To move to beats and voices, and never be alone
With music lies a paradise whose moments you can't disown.

I've dreamt that dream of lovers, a mockery to all that lives
The perfect faceless lover, to everything we will give
I danced my songs and symphonies, around immortal glass
With dreamers lie the paradise, of moments that will not last.

Christopher Sablan

The Rose of Sharon

As I walked through the tall green grasses of the meadows in the Spring,
I saw the Rose of Sharon, which Jesus made for me
the beauty of His creation, which has touched my very heart,
yes, it is such an awesomeness, the love of God,
yes, our Lord gave us beauty for ashes,
oil for gladness, and such peace to calm each and every storm
Oh, how God loves us, and if you take the time to know His beauty,
you will find God is always everywhere.
Our Lord's love is never-ending through each and every day
through someone or something in His very kind, special, loving way.

Deborah Moulster

Right and Wrong

Right and wrong, two five letter words
Fit for a song,
Yet of the utmost importance,
Like two roads
To be traveled all life long.

Throughout our life
We are left to choose.
Right to happiness, wrong to blues,
Right toward harmony and success,
Wrong toward discord and distress.

To know right from wrong
Is a gift not outright given,
Developed from cradle to grave
With the help of role models
Encountered along the way.

The right values laboriously learned,
Is our magic carpet well spun.
Clouds might appear here and there,
But we can fly around them with care,
Avoiding collision and despair.

Angela Allessandrini

Exam!

brief beams stream through my
bamboo shades, a new day dawns,
swarms into my soul . . .

television
laughs at me as I scurry
through bun, coffee—flee!

steadily falling
rain streaming down my lifted
face to taste the wind . . .

slashing winds rip me,
I bow into pure chaos
spring in Chicago . . .

blossom pushes through
broken glass, sad detritus,
ancient glory shines . . .

eyes glued to the screen,
fingers tremble on the board,
my brain must work now . . .

Delphyne Woods

Tongueless Lightning Melting through the Outless Bounds

And the sylph
Screamed
In her symbolic panic
To warn those of lessened power
That one day
He who holds that grand scepter
May fall
And her hair whipped through trees
Extracting leaves like teeth
And the maple's pain
Fell audible as a howl
On the floor of nature
Her voice again sounded
And shook the ground
Forcing fire into the eyes
Of those around, yet with a flash
Then, and only then, can one see her
As she pirouetted
And laughed
At the sun

Vincent Xexaviar

Millennium's Cabins in the Skies

Poppied California's motherlode genteel farm folks walk by ponderosa pine byways.
Giddy little ladies, giggling little sisters, mama mia cries out girls! Boys!

Hear! The mating crickets by the glowing fireflies oak tree, squirrel thickets.
Shimmering harvest moonbeams falling on woodsy woodchuck thickets.

Look, gliding ducks go, gobbling turkeys drinking by Miwuk Indian coon creeks.
Amador lover of motherlode gold mine, Miwuk cowboys fishing delights bluegill school streams.

The jewel of the motherlode Sutter creek's lively little theatre, quaint shops.
Amador county's seat jackson formerly botellias, amodor lake fishing, comanche cruise boats.

Almighty God, bless cow country amador's lyrical lark green meadows.
Homestead farm folks never on the dole, never lost souls.

Praying together, staying together passing warm homemade dinner rolls.
Kind father, kindred mother's chili con carne, sweet corn on the cob.

See! Rose cheeked farm kids milking contented cows, feeding sows.
Light at the end of the tunnel, country pumpkin's line dancing, taking bows.

Come see! Red Mr. Lincoln, queen Elizabeth pink roses, perfumed magnolias.
Fragrant lilacs, sweet pea aromas on blueberry mocking bird hills.

Farm folks finding rainbow's end gold pots, baskets full of kisses, bellies and beaus.
Envision moonlight walks falling, twinkling stars, honey bear hugs, blue birds over rainbows.

Cheerful, joyful little children singing paradise songs, country style rejoicing.
Look! Migrating snow geese, starry celestial greetings, millennium's cabins in the skies.

David Millan Grant

The Golden Can

My hair spray comes in a can of gold, which makes it easy to see.
That's nice 'cause my eyes are getting old, just like the rest of me.
My spray's my trusted friend, since my hair is getting thin.
It makes it behave and not look so much likes a rat's playpen.
I'm going to lunch with a friend today, so I'll do my hair and face.
She always looks so neat and together, with not a hair out of place.
So I'll try my best and hope that I have good luck with my hair.
I'll wear a nice outfit, try to look my best, since going out is rare.
Oh, look! What happened to my hair? It looks like it just died!
I did it the way I always do, but it just lies there on its side!
I guess I'll have to cancel lunch. I wouldn't want anyone to see.
I can't figure it out, I'm all in a tizzy. What can my problem be?
Oh, dear, I think I know what happened to my hair today.
The culprit sits there, where I put it to be out of the way.
Can you guess what happened to my hair and made me feel so blue?
Dear friends, always check the can, or you will be a victim, too.
Have you guessed what made such a mess and ruined my day?
It's really very simple; I didn't check the can, I'm sad to say.
My air freshener comes in a gold can, too, and I'm the one who did it.
I just sprayed my hair with air freshener, and there it sits.

Martha Gresham

Yellow Rose of Flushing

Oh, the Yellow Rose of Flushing,
you've got to stop hurting me.
You may have spent your entire life in Flushing,
but you've spent it hurting me.
I've gazed upon you with longing, from the day I laid eyes on you.

Oh, the Yellow Rose of Flushing,
I did not believe in love at first sight.
But you changed my mind for me, albeit reluctantly.
You changed my mind; as I first laid sight upon you, it was love,
unadulterated love, that swept over me.
Oh, yes, I believe, I now believe in love at first sight,
for you've made a believer out of me.

Oh, the Yellow Rose of Flushing, I now love you totally.
Unsatisfied with longing from afar, I need to hold you in my embrace.
I need to feel your essence, and you need to feel
my hands on your loveliness. So, Yellow Rose of Flushing,
where do you want me to pick you? Perhaps at the stem?

Diamond Phoenix

Mom

I know the Heavens cried for you
Weeping tears like rain
But no amount of tears
Could wash away the pain
You've gone on to better things
Things we pray to one day see
You've become an angel now
I feel you watching over me
If you had a choice
I know you would have stayed
You wouldn't want to hurt me
By going so far away
But God wanted a star
To make the heavens bright
And now your kindness shines
The brightness in the night.

Katy Anne Wilson

Come

Love is a cancer,
the answer from above.
It will feed.
It will breed.
Is this not what we need?

Love is our freedom,
the kingdom of the dove.
It will bleed,
It will heed
the answer to our greed.

Love is our leader.
mediator of Allah.
It will lead, supercede,
hear our plea, and set us free!

John Michael Renyak

Do Not Love too Much

The winter dark comes fast
And shrouds the sun with sudden shade;
The night so soon defeats the day
And speeds the dark without delay.

So death sometimes comes soon,
Before the plot has run its course;
We dare not love too much the day.
The twilight haze so soon turns gray.

So do not love too much
The one who turns your night to day.
The blushing dawn not long can last
And night comes sure when day is past.

John C. Dvorak

Lafayette

Upward throws mine eyes gaze
To the sky, amidst the harrowing haze.
As if no other peak on Earth,
As high as this one lays.
Icy turf throughout we tread,
Icy air, high above our heads.
The world around us screams rebirth
To Mother Nature our souls we wed.
Modern life has well we've shorn,
Has October winter born?
What has made us have this worth
On this early autumnal morn?
Lost our fears, worries, regrets.
Our expectations overly met
In a bout of uninhibited mirth
On the summit of Lafayette!

Colin Hastings True

Distant Tears

I fear the pain of losing you, yet what pain is greater than the truth?
I move with the world, and I step away from your brightness.
I am lost in words, a sea of confusion around me.
I miss you, I need you, I desire you.
But only my tears know the truth of my loneliness.
The despair of my life, the emptiness of my world.
I have lost you, because of my own greed.
I pushed you away. Wanting all and needing no one.
Now in the face of this reality, I see you with another.
Free of our love, and I sit here, crying my tears, in the distance,
Watching and feeling my heart break.
I was a fool. I let you go, and in your happiness, I lose my mind.
My soul. My life. . . .

    Luz Cabrera

Inspiration

Most people come from the past and recreate it with subtle changes in the present.

They allow the past to dominate the present—and thus, destroy their chance for a better future.

But we who excel, who survive the past to thrive in the present, come from the future.

A future we envision. That vision—our mission, pulls us forward so our dreams become reality.

    Frevi Ann Blanes

Alone

To hold strong wind and touch blue sky;

I wonder who that girl may be.

Could I, as definition of mis-grace, catch the eyes of she?

If I ask her name, and she not reply, why;

Then all God's creatures unwinged shall fly.

I glance toward the direction of she, to see blue eyes right back at me;

It fills my heart, and a once bound heart, set free.

Ever ready to meet my love am I;

So I go to, walk to, but find that I walk right past.

For deep inside, I see how by me, her wild love could not be tame;

So I pass on through without her name.

I lost the love I always yearned, quicker than a breath is fast.

For now I will duck tail and make my way to my empty home;

Where I shall always live alone.

    Jason Miller

Is There Hope, in Such a Time as This?

As time ticks away, the Earth has no sound that is pleasant.
Only sound's of horror in the night,
followed by violence, gunfire, and the cry of children
not knowing where they are going or where they have been.
As they look on every side there is hurt and pain,
nothing to make them glad they were born in such a time as this—
A time of horror and grief, pain and sorrow.
Nothing to help them smile or be happy they were born in such a time as this.
Mother's and Father's do not know where they are going,
for all they know is where they have been.
Again I say, in such a time as this
every day babies are being born entering the world crying
as if they know when they arrive that it is a cruel, cruel world.
A world is unloving, unkind, unmerciful, unjust, unholy, unrighteous,
but only if they would believe that there is a Man called Jesus,
who will come to save them, and give them hope, peace, joy, gladness, love,
and most of all a brand new life, in such a time as this.
Amen!

    Laura Ann Holloway

Keep on Truckin'

THERE'S A FEELING THAT YOU FEEL
WHEN YOU GET BEHIND THE WHEEL
when you're truckin'
A CAMARADERIE OF SORTS
FROM THE MOUNTAINS TO THE PORTS
when you're truckin'
MILES AND MILES AND MILES OF ROAD
GOT TO GET THERE WITH THAT LOAD
keep on truckin'
SHIFTING GEARS FROM ONE TO TEN
SLOW IT DOWN THEN START AGAIN
keep on truckin'
THEN FINALLY THE JOB IS DONE
TIME TO MAKE THAT HOMEWARD RUN
keep right on truckin'
FRIENDS AND FAMILY WAITING THERE
HOT MEALS, BEER AND EASY CHAIR
keep right on truckin'

    Joanie M. Dayton

Once Upon a Dream

Come and dance with me,
Come to my dreams and
Dance with me.

Meet me somewhere in dreamland,
Meet me and understand
My dream with me.

I want to know you, as if
We've known each other forever.
I want you to be my best friend.

Once upon a dream, I want you
To come and meet me,
Once upon a dream . . .

    Olivia M. Devine

A Dusty Faded Photograph

A dusty faded photograph
Rests alone inside the drawer
With faces that echo dreams
Forgotten long ago
With simple smiles of last year
Lingering on their blurry lips
And the promise of tomorrow
Flickering softly with their kiss

    Eleanor Bevil Smith

The Old Woman

Within four walls she sits,
living in the past,
time has no meaning,
for her it doesn't go fast.
The days all run together,
seasons change on a daily base,
to want to live in reality,
doesn't seem to be her case.
Someone comes in to cook—clean,
and help with the necessities;
but who the old woman talks to,
no one else with their eyes sees.
She appears to have been forgotten,
her visitors are rare,
letters aren't received in the mail,
no one seems to really care.
The only one she trusts
is her Father up above;
the only things real to her heart
are the Bible and God's love.

    Angela K. Lamb

Dancing with the Angels

Though you're just a memory, lovingly engraved inside my mind
I could search a lifetime, no greater love I'd find
I can still see your smile, feel the warmth of your touch
After all these years, I still miss you so much
I still miss you so much

Now you're dancing with the angels, in a Heavenly place
I hope one sweet day, again I'll see your face
Although I'm all grown up, and you're not of this world
Deep in my heart, I'm still your little girl

I look back and wonder how you found the time to do it all
You wiped away my tear drops, picked me up every fall
Always gentle and wise, now in Heaven above
After all this time, I still miss your love, I still miss your love

Now you're dancing with the angels, in a Heavenly place
I hope one sweet day, again I'll see your face
Although I'm all grown up, and you're not of this world
Deep in my heart, I'm still your little girl

No more sorrow, no more pain, streets paved in gold that never see rain
I promise to watch what I do, so I can walk in that Heavenly place
with you . . . such a precious memory.

Marjorie E. Vizcaya

Sounds

Her mother and father chuckled
the clock ticked
the dog whined
her brother's pencil scratched up and down his paper
she sighed
closing her eyes
absorbing the sound around her and pushing it down deep
down deep to the place where tears went when she was at a dinner party
down deep where desperate shouts went when she was at an endless conference
down deep where feelings went when she was being smothered by friends
the feeling of hatred
betrayal
syntheticness
love? maybe
maybe somewhere underneath the years of bottled and processed
tears, shouts, pain, and feelings
love may be hidden
squished and distorted and mixed with tears, hatred, and pain
maybe it was somewhere underneath those sounds

Diane Ghogomu

Dreams of Magenta

My soul is gone. My time has come.
I search and dig and find no more.
I wish I knew which way to turn,
Which light that flickers through
And yearns more cautiously than 'twas before,
Like oceans never meeting shore.
In lines of dark we hide our lives.
Flowers die. Black birds cry.
In wonders of lust and love unknown,
And signs of power overthrown,
We search for time, a tick, a tock,
But those who know have power unlocked.
In fearful rage I live.
I make my way to the heap of dreams, of magenta warmness,
Fullness never seen. In this land, things of blue, things of green,
Never touched by human hand.
This place of night, of breeze in trees, the birds have flown,
The day to seize. A million voices in my heart, the greatest time,
Flowing towards a hole, apart in wisdom.
A beetle clicks. A husband dies. These never seen by human eyes.
To never again reach the floor, you fly. Just like the birds,
You soar. In a box in the corner, still live your dreams,
Of merciful gunmen and perfectly torn seams.

Valena Arguello

When Nature Talks

I took a walk today
A tender little breeze
Touched me lightly
Trees whispered, nodding
Ever so slightly
Telling me
I am alive.

Gloria Ann Morris

Tell Me

If everything has a time,
When is mine?
If everything has a season,
When do I blossom?
How long will I last,
How much can I take?

Your time is now,
Your season has come,
Go without me.

For you are special,
A swan you are to become.
As for me, I'll wait for you,
Until you do return.

Shokry Dante Eldaly

Fame Fades Fast

when you're up
you cannot drop
you know it all, you're at the top
six feet, strong and tall
fame, you're soaring, all that glory
well-defined, you're on time

friends, money, soaring pride
ego values, dreams that die
positive, negative
X-ray life
grease on the firehouse pole
climb to the top
Fame Fades Fast
and then you drop

Fame Fades Fast
glory dies
aging lives, death decides
that . . . Fame Fades Fast in our lives

Barbara Njeri Scott

1942

A sea of handkerchiefs
hug the shore
little girls blow kisses
to sailors—
little boys,
perhaps just barely men,
puff out the chests,
wearing a country's glorified bravery.
A man with a short cigar
sucks at the juices of Patriotism
and jots down memoirs
that will later be translated
into a headline:
"America Gathers to Wish Her Boys Well"
accompanied by a flash,
so that the moment
is suspended
forever
in black and white.

Joey Lee Nicholls

Michelangelo

Michelangelo, I met in a dream,
Telling me with a proud demeanor
That time could never alter his sculptures.

Co-eternally with him, I was also
Chiseling a mighty block of stone.

In the misty morning when I woke up,
I buried myself winding my still watch,

—Translated from the Pashto original by Aqila Zaman.
   Hasham Baber

Heart Shattered by Irreplaceable Loss

If I see a golden hue, or a streak of blue, is that a sign from you?
Who is wrong? Who is right? Why did you choose the light?
Why did you leave me here so sad?
Where you are now, does it make you glad?
Waiting now at Heaven's door, did God let you in?
Or did you go the other way because of sin?
Life is a game which you must play, if you lose you go the other way.
You have won, you kind man, because you always let out your hand.
To people in need everywhere, you were never stingy, you always shared.
Our Father now has you for His own, all I have is your name in stone.
It is here gathering my tears, you have been gone for so many years.
Why must I wait so long to hear you sing another song?
I miss your warm embrace and your tender kiss upon my face.
I do not understand this pain I feel, all I know is that it is for real.
   Christy Suzanne Savage

Cub Once Loved

You are the boy who steps on me.
Disappointment slowly settles over me like leaves falling in autumn,
slowly gliding from one side to another, gracefully
swaying in the light air, an emptiness gnawing at my gut finding a way to make me more hollow.

I should have known better somehow.
Sadness overcomes me but I cannot find the tears to show it.
My heart turns to a puddle of vanilla ice cream boiling on a sidewalk on a summer's day.

Why am I not used to these letdowns?
You cannot keep your word.
Still I find the hopeless faith to believe this time will be different.

All I want to do is glow,
glow like a Christmas tree with all its lights decorating it.
All I want is to dance,
dance like the other girls,
as beautiful as a shimmer of the setting sun bouncing off the ocean.

But none of this will happen.
I cannot be a lit Christmas tree.
nor a glimmer of sun on a wave.
No, not with you.
   Nicole Nina Rosenloecher

To Love a Fireman

When you love a fireman, you sometimes fall asleep alone.
Or you wake the next morning, to find he is gone.
You spend a lot of time worrying, his life is always on the line.
You pray for his safe return, as you constantly check the time.
When you love a fireman, you rarely feel like number one.
It seems he always has somewhere else to be or something he has to get done
You must take the time you have together and spend it having fun.
In your heart you know he loves you, and you'll always be number one.
When a fireman loves you, he worries about you too.
He wonders if you can handle this, he hopes you know how much he misses you
Firemen have an important job, whether paid or volunteer.
No matter where your fireman is, in your heart he is always near.
When you love a fireman, remember a fireman loves you too.
Though he is helping others, if you need him, he'll be there for you.
To love a fireman, is one of the hardest things I've ever had to do.
When I have to give up time with him, I remember he has to give it up too.
   Wendy L. Hamill

Lifeflight

She lay there clutching hard my hand
Her stone face turning slowly sand
Sweet sugar grains rush the floor
Grain by grain, life flies the door
The hourglass runs too short
As dying wish be spoke
In utter silence tenderly
Ne'er life be revoked
Her eyes look one last look to mine
Leaving all pain far behind
Grinning one last gritty smile
Waiting to walk life's one last mile
The hourglass runs too short
As dying wish be thought
In utter silence tenderly
Ne'er life be retaught
She lay there letting go my hand
Her stone face turns no more to sand
Sugar grains no longer rush the floor
Grain by grain, life's flown the door.
   Ashley Coker

Needing Him

As I lie here
I dream of you
And how it would be to kiss you

Your soft lips pressed against mine
Feeling your arms around me
And our bodies become one

I love you so
You couldn't possibly know
How very much I do

I so hope for you to feel this way, too
And maybe someday soon
You could tell me this saying, too
I love you.
   Danielle Stoa

The Two Attic Doors

The house with two attic doors,
brought happiness to my children Four.
Oh, their side of the old house,
threw their attic door,
they could sneak to grandmas,
threw her attic door.
It was like a secret tunnel,
to a special place,
full of hugs and kisses,
from someone they loved so dear.
It was great to have their
Grand folks near.
Grandpa say, who's that knocking
on my attic door?
He pretend to be surprised,
to find it just those four.
He call down to Grandma,
as they ran right threw.
In the kitchen of the house,
grandma pretend she too was surprised.
   Janet L. Mulligon

Simply Me

If I were a stairway,
I'd tell people to walk the other way,
But since I am a wall,
I do not care at all.
   Kimberly Seeland-Penny

My Dad's Hands

My Dad's Hands tell a story,
A story of strength, just looking at them you can read history.
If you look closely, each line, scar, and thick layer of skin is
distinct, for some aspect of his life.

My Dad's Hands picked America's Cotton,
My Dad's Hands fought in America's Vietnam War,
Oh, yes, My Dad's Hands . . . "They too, Sing America!"
My Dads Hand's.

And like so many country boys, He and His Hands,
migrated North, for a taste of the good life . . .
And of course, some good pay.
And then, My Dad's Hands . . . took on a new challenge!
They began to build America's cars. My Dad's Hands!

And now, His hand's seem to be a little worn and tired,
from years of hard work and dedication . . .
And living his "American Dream."

But today His Hand's . . . can clap for themselves, and give a big, Hurrah,
Because they have made it, they have made it,
Through War, Segregation, Racism, and Years of Hard Work.
And most importantly, My Dad's Hands,
My Dad's Hands, My Dad's Hands . . . Are still Intact!

Dawn A. Johnson-Muhammad

The New Sound of Heaven

On this day a child was born,
Wonderful, marvelous, created by God.
A perfect gift to uplift the sounds of Heaven.
As a little boy you were good with your hands,
You played musical instruments, you hit on pots and pans.
The enemy tried to keep you from knowing the secret of praise is power.
Though God has sent His beloved son to be raised from the grave,
There is power in the praise.
Sometimes you feel lonely, though you are not alone.
God speaks His Heaven best when you're at rest in Him.
Your mouth began to open with new sounds steaming from the grounds.
You look up in the sky, you see two moon eyes.
God's eye is on the sparrow, He watches over thee.
Be aware the secret of, praise is power.
Praise Him with the sound of the trumpet, psaltery and harp.
Praise Him with the tumbrel and dance;
Praise Him with stringed instruments and organ.
Praise Him upon the loud cymbals,
Praise Him upon the high sounding cymbals.
I am the God that answers by fire.

Kim Lawrence Albert

Britannia Rising

The ravens nestled in their tower, hear the wind, a whispering.
They see the past, feel the power, and wait upon the unfolding.
The lady, resting on the lake. The boys, now safe outside the keep.
The drum awaits to recall Drake, and Arthur shifts in restless sleep.
The finest hour, yet to come, is looming in tomorrow's dawn.
Though roses seem to fade to some, tomorrow's lot is not yet drawn.
The goddess smiles and reaches, tests her hand out o'er the waves.
She smiles and she remembers, that we are free men, not slaves.
Past days, there are, still yet to come. The lady, waiting by her lake.
The waiting for the sounding drum; two boys the tower will not take.
The ravens nestled in their tower. Hear the song their voices weave?
"The past, now mingles with the hour, we have now, no plans to leave."

John Hamrick

Who Pushed Back the Darkness

As I lie here in this white room with all the tubes
and hear them say it's a miracle, I wonder who pushed back the darkness.
As they look at charts and confer
and whisper to each other,
I wonder who pushed back the darkness.
God, was it you?

Margaret Schmieder

Strength

Reach inside yourself
What do you feel?
Look in the mirror
Who do you see?
I see your strength
I see your perseverance
I see your failure to succumb
I see your will to live
You must keep fighting
You must never give up
'Til your last breath is taken from you
And when it's time to leave this world
You will know you tried your best!

Cindy Traxson

Too Many Saviors

Too many Saviors
in a world of unsaved souls.
Too much glitter
when the streets are paved with gold.
Too many promises
giving way to empty lies.
Too many smiles
backed by blood shot eyes.
Too many Kings
too many Uncle Sams.
Too many "Trust Me's"
from extended bloody hands.
Too many punishments
spewed forth from preachers' lips.
Too many business men
with power in their grip.
Too many homeless
sleeping all alone.
Too many saviors
in a world of unsaved souls.

Derek Curtiss Morris

Suttee

During intimacy
and despair
Chaos waxes holy
Apparitions, in time's fire
A breeze which sweeps
away the widow
Into her husband's
funeral pyre.

Stacy Edward Meadows

The Spring in You

Mirrored in your thoughts,
And touched by your vernal smile,
I'll glisten in your sunshine
And bathe for awhile.

And roll through velvet hills,
And drink the honey dew drops,
And trip through golden daisies
Where the music never stops.

And frolic in felicity,
And dally in silken groves,
And relish in the thoughts
That friendship never goes.

And so tomorrow's kiss is another kiss
That yesterday's kiss will see.
But tomorrow's kiss and yesterday's kiss
Are both beautiful to me.

Eliza E. Desmarais

We Walk Together

It is by our goal we come together on this eve.
Our hearts are warm our spirits pleased.
For on this night we shall walk as a team.
For all the loved ones who must leave.
They may survive by what we achieve.
By raising money, spirits, and needs.
And by this stand they will know that our hearts of love are true.
Release you all your cares when walking here.
The light of darkness will not come for by our love the path is lit.
The word is read the word is hope, The strongest word ever wrote.
And by the sunlight, The candles die.
That one more life may survive.

Laurie Ann Ebensteiner

Antiquity to Eternity

There was a Lamb slain from the foundation of the world with the healing for a nation.
It was God's plan for eternal salvation, which came down through 42 generations.
He came not to destroy the law, but to fulfill the law with his Grace.
He allowed a sinner like me one more chance.
When Justice said that I should die, He took my place.
As part of the Trinity, He was both God as well as man all in one.
Because of Him, I can hold up the bloodstained banner which the final victory has won.
On this Christian journey, we are bound to encounter a storm.
Just stay under the blood, Jesus' blood, and the world can't do you no harm.
This man prayed in the Garden: Father, remove this cup, but nevertheless, let thy will be done.
This was the beloved of the Father, God's only begotten Son.
My Jesus was about His Father's work and went willingly to the cross for no man took his life.
It was his blood shed on Calvary that paid the price;
He was the ultimate Sacrifice.
Jesus' journey to overcome death and grace began in antiquity,
But as Christians, if we follow his path, for us it will end in eternity.

S. Paul Dixon

Breaking Free from Society

Hearing without listening, words overstuffed with logic and reason.
Words dulled by picturesque illusions crafted for the youth of the season.
Prick me with your stern commands and bind me with your views.
Bomb me with your rights and wrongs and leave me so confused.
But I know you can't reach completion living only
through what's safe and known.
So let me be to wander free and I promise, I'll do it on my own.

Lindsy Allen

Dear Administrator

Dear Administrator, regulator, outside the classroom spectator,
You who get paid more than me, don't forget, where I am you used to be.
Dear Administrator, fellow educator,
didn't you know that education was a helping profession?
Why stick out your hand and put your foot on their head?
Being blind too those who do wrong and punishing those who do right instead
Dear Administrator, my evaluator,
each child you know is unique, Bobby, Samantha and Malik.
None of them learn the same, tell me how can you
say what's best for them if you don't know their name.
Dear Administrator, part human, part alligator,
I do realize you have a master's degree,
but that is no reason to talk down to me.
You've been gone from the classroom for a while,
but you still should know the difference between an adult and a child.
Dear Administrator, understand that I am no hater,
this is just my standpoint on what I see,
You may or may not choose to take advice from me.
You may just be doing your job, and doing it well,
still that is no reason to send me through Hell.
It may have been easy to go up, but it's harder to come down,
think about that when you're doing those things and you think no one is around.
No matter where you go, or what you do,
you're an Administrator, all eyes on you.

TaShauna Adams

Ode to My Room

When I'm feeling stressed up,
And totally messed up,
From tension, anger or gloom,
I leave all my trouble,
And go to my bubble
My place, my space, my room.
There I play my CDs,
And do as I please,
And sort out the things in my mind.
When my door is closed,
don't poke in your nose,
I want to be left alone.
It really perturbs me,
When some disturbs me,
Unless it's for dinner or the phone.
Was that call for me?

Giovanno Elcock

As I Be

Why am I the way I am?
I don't know I just am
I didn't ask to be me
But I be the way I be
God made me as I am
with his hands he molded me
with flaws and faults I be me
So why can't I with thee
Except me as I be
No more no less can I be
For all I am is just me
so whose to say what I
could be if I were not me
But me is who I am
so why can't I accept me as I am
But with his help some day I will see
I can accept me as I be.

Elaine C. Emmons

Goddess

She stood before the moon
In awe of its magnificence
Wishing it could be Hers
The moon told her story
as she glided into
the night sky of cobalt
She knew the moon smiled at her
and would follow her only
when kissing the water-sparkling
Making the flow dance with light
When she made love,
to her favorite lover,
the moon disappeared
leaving the sky to the stars.

Danielle Cary Morrison

Would You?

If I kissed you,
would you kiss me back?
If I loved you,
would you love me, too?
If I hurt you,
would you hurt me back?
If I said I needed you,
would you need me, too?
But of all the things I ask of you,
You need to answer this one Q.
Would you?

Toran K. Muldowney

The Wall

The Wall stands, so very long and dark,
On a grassy knoll, in a setting like a park.
It bears the names of the ones who died in that faraway fight.
It bears the names of those still lost to the night.
It holds within and without the loss and terrible pain
Of those who died in the skies and those who died in the bush of rain.
From a country of luxuries to a jungle, primitive and lost,
They gave their all, but, my God, what was the cost?
Those who returned were treated like trash.
Their hopes, their dreams, came down in a crash.
Some got on their feet, they looked the world in the eye.
They let it know: I fought for this country and, no, I didn't die.
Some lost their sanity, their eyes, their legs, their arms;
Their luck ran out, they lost their lucky charms.
The wall doesn't have a list of these men, I fear.
They spend their time in hospital rooms, year after year.
They left this country, young and eager to serve so well.
Those who returned had grown old and weary, for they served in Hell.
No other war has left such a bitter trail of tears,
A war that still lasts in our hearts and mind after all these years.

Loretta Barlow

Man Vs. Earth

Is there such a thing as a soul mate
Or are we our own soul mates
that we find as we reach our last breath.
As I sit on this tall steep mountain full of strength
And unimaginable power, I stair at the Heavens
That pours the purest of peace amongst the Earth.
Amazing how the Earth and sky coincide in harmony
Providing to each other all of the necessities and yet manages
To stay with illustrious beauty for each other and by itself.
Unconditionally the Heavens provide the Earth with warmth,
Tears, and colors that are undefined. The Earth with its bold
And rich mystery, ready to accept gracefully what the Heavens
Will surprise them with. All of this love without one thing, Thought.
Is it possible for human life to produce this type of beauty?
As long as we have the gift of thought and imagination
That we yet do not know how to master
We will never create what the Heavens and Earth give to each other
It will hide in our souls forever.

Aileen Malave

Reddest Blood

The wind blowing heavily; a furious gust that bends tree branches.
Bright lightning lights up the sky of thick, flowing clouds passing by.
Dead tree branches sway side-to-side,
crumpled, dry leaves scattered on the ground.
Ripples wave through the vast sea, sunset almost lost under the horizon.
The moment is dark blue, moon and stars start to shine.
A pool of red constantly drips upon the dirt path.
Pain shooting up my wrist, my hair flying around my face.
Wetness falls from my eyes; tears splatter beneath me.
Inhaling the clear breeze, closing my eyes to see black darkness.
Letting myself get lost in this moment before my life ends
of my cause and soon regret of my reddest blood.

Star Dalangin

You Are

Angel eyes, my one true best forever friend!
You are the light that shines for me to get home.
You are the sunshine that brightens up my gloomy days.
You are the strength for me when I feel life's weaknesses.
You are the breath I breathe to keep my heart alive!
You are the laughter that dries away all my tears.
You are the rose that blooms in the true garden of friendship!
You are my heart, you are my soul, you are my thoughts
and you are forever felt within my body!
For all that you are, for the way you complete me,
I will forever love you and give you my all!

Donna Popp

Photo Illumiere

Transpose
one click, rapide,
with the speed of light,
shutters, fluttering,
(Neurons, protrons) a movement
electronically—
Transmission
articulated
with the silence of an image.
Brightness
Shadows
Pentimeters_15,30,500 ?
War
Black/White
Color
Cinema
Still Art, one man and Cannes

Diana Z. Mihailovich

Raven and the Turtledove

Friends may come
And friends may go,
I am here to let you know,
I'm here to change, that ebb and flow
Nothing you can say,
Will make me fly away.
Nothing you can do,
Would make me leave you.
Nothing in my heart,
Can tear us apart.
This has surely shown,
Together,
We have truly flown.

Marilyn Jean Vogt

My Magical Place

If I were to live in a magical place,
where everyone has a smiling face,
where flowers bloom until the spring,
and all the church bells go ring-a-ling

where we will run and play all day,
until the clouds all go away,
and when I leave this magical place,
I'll think of it with love and grace

Lynette Rosemary Rodriguez

The Girl and the Trees

there is something
that is solemnly sad
about the girl
that stands amidst the trees
she bends to scratch
her legs
and remembers the lovers
that she once knew
the lover who drove
her to the park
and watched her walk amongst
the trees
there is something
so beautiful about the
trees
and her half-naked
back
as she bends to scratch her
legs and mingle
with the trees

Bridgette Acklin

Finally

Silence is the darkened room that flows with cutting air,
Ponder is the action done to wonder who will care.
You've overcome amazing feats, and death you have defied,
You've grown into your icy shell, where access is denied.

Time pushes on and life resumes, you mustn't take the bait,
You have control, now take it back, forget the hands of fate.
There will be times when life's too much and death can seem a bliss,
But take the strength that you have learned and rid yourself of this.

Head up high and shoulders back, it's time that you are proud,
Find your beauty deep inside, and let it come out loud.
Life's been hard but let's move on, and grow up from your past,
You've fought for years and reached your goal, you've made it here at last.

Lyndsay Mallette

Down

I can't reveal my emotions to you.
I can't tell you how I feel inside.
I can't trust you with my heart.
Simply because you have betrayed me.
You have let me down so many times before.
How can I let you know how I feel without you criticizing every little step I take
towards progress?
Why can't you let me be the way I always wanted to be?
I am so sore and damaged by the way you've brought me down,
down this endless road to nowhere.
After you have lashed me with all of this grief stricken sadness that I can't defeat.
Look at this mess you have conceived.
I will never be okay.

Jennifer Prichard

Lost Love

Lying against the cold wetness that some call earth
Chained in a despair that exists only in the mind
Seeing what some call insignificance of existence
That which grants the ability to snarl and bite
To prove they exist where the heart shuts them out
To bring light to the darkness of betrayal
Reaching up, the chains weighing down your arms
This word love that holds residence in yourself
This word trust that binds down the logic and reasoning
Being born with teeth, to chew one's way out of the pit of heartbreak
The prison of flesh that sent you kicking and screaming into the world
This world that forces us to learn trust, to obey love
Meaningless words that gain meaning through the daylight of the mind
Inside the prison of heartbreak
The sins upon your shoulders
The gates open wide, the light shines through
Outside moonlight from mother sky shines on skin, the cold night of her breath
Chains give way, falling to the Earth, changing with protest
Set free as a new soul as one spirit says to another
The key to absolute freedom . . . I love you

Michael McGee, Jr.

Another Day

Looking for an exit, an end to the misery and depression that plagues my existence
here on this forsaken place called Earth.
Searching for a way to end the pain, cause all of my suffering to cease,
trying to find an escape route out of all this evil destroying my life.
Voyaging through the despair, I see easy ways to end it all,
but does it cease, or does this just keep all the more injustice upon my shoulders?
I seek answers to my questions, not knowing where to turn, lost in depression of darkness.
I decide to end it all, hoping my pain will finally end, although now undecided whether
I should give it another try.
Can I break through my gloom and find a reason to live, proof I have a purpose in this life?
Will I get all better or will the struggle continue?
Is there anyone out there that feels this way?
Let's come together and strive to make an imprint to ease the pain and suffering from our minds.

Roger Schmitz

In the End

If you must love another,
Let me rejoice that I cannot see.
Take her and love her,
As you once loved me.
Make her strong
That she might survive.
Be faithful,
Always by her side.
Take our children
And teach them right.
Remember, my love for you
gave them life.
When you look at her
don't see me.
Where I am was just my destiny.
But when there is an end
to all your nights
come and lie down
by my side.

Brandy J. Anderson

Everything but Nothing's Clear

Striving towards every goal
relentlessness taking its toll
Gone is good and evil's lost
on stormy seas confused and tossed
A ship to shore a plane to land
the comfort of a gentle hand
Before the rise but after the fall
known but once or not at all
Fighting for each breath to take
waiting for the dawn to break
Reaching far but touching near
now everything but nothing's clear

Kimberly S. Beaupre

dragon

oh, dragon with your fiery eyes,
your evil ways i do despise,
with your razor teeth,
shining oh, so bright,
waiting to make the deadly bite,
in the eerie night time sky,
you see the horrid creature fly,
hear his unbearable taunting hiss,
feel the glare pour through the mist,
the dragon's teeth rip through the skin,
and then you know that he will win.

Heather Nicole Hamilton

The Five Seasons of Life

Spring is like life's beginning
Like a baby so tender and sweet.
Summer! We have reached young
Adulthood, we struggle against defeat.

Autumn; we're turning life's corner,
We are older and wiser now.
Our burdens seems less heavy
Our problems, we solve them somehow.

We journey a little farther,
Indian summer approaches at last.
We are entering second childhood,
A season through which we all pass.

Then winter is upon us
Like death, so cold, it seems.
But after we have passed through winter,
There will be another spring!

Maxine B. Hunt

Good Night "Bar Bell"

In answer to the flicker of the stable lantern light,
moving shadows of people in the darkness of the night;
a stormy wind is rising, and the beeches bend and sway,
scudding clouds seem trying to chase the moon away.
I pull my jacket closer, for the air is bitter cold.
The silver moonlight mingles into lantern's gold.
More shadows in the changing lights move faster than before.
The whistling of the wind now rises to a roar . . .
then fades into the distance . . . to be followed by a blast,
of whirling storm, howling, louder than the last . . .
On silent wings a hunting owl now flits across the beam,
vanishing as a wraith might do in some ghostly dream.
My shivers as I make my way are not all due to cold;
on such a night as this, I don't feel very bold.
Every night at half past six, I've one last job to do
that never could I share with any one of you:
to say good night to Bar Bell and to thank him for the way
he shared with me another Oh! so happy day.
A labor when it's a task of love is one we cannot share.
Love will be confounded should other eyes be there.
That's why it is alone I go and never fail to say
a last good night to Bar Bell so as to end our day.
Each night a gentle whinny greets me as I slip through the door;
Bar Bell lies there resting, upon his bed of straw.
His forehand half is sitting up, his quarters lying down,
his silken, sheeny coat is like a velvet gown.
I put my arms around his neck. He nuzzles into me.

 Gayle L. Taxis

My Lonely Prayer

Every time when I stood right here,
I'd gaze at every single star
Amidst the sea of scintillating constellations,
For I only longed to see the moment when a shooting star
Descending down the vast horizon yonder.

I then desolately pleaded to the comet to continue to light up the path of hope
Upon which I'd move.
How meaningful that mere little request was!

I have always wished that someday you would possibly come back to me.
If I would ever be granted such a slim chance again,
I would do anything to keep you from departing.

Since you were gone, no one has ever gotten into my life.
Over the long current of time I have had only you in my heart.

Every time when I stood here I have only those stars as my congenial companions
While I was seeing a faint light in the sky over there,
The picture of you kept wandering around my languid train of thought,
Then entering into my mind.

When a long white faded streak of starlight is appearing and stretching across the faraway sky,
Do you realize someone here is desperately praying
For you to return?

 Suphawut Wathabunditkul

Humanity

We all see the same moon at night, the same stars.
We all feel pain when we lose someone dear.
We all feel afraid when we enter the unknown.
We all long for love.
We all feel joy that lifts us to the heavens,
and we all create and dance and sing.
We come in many colors, shapes, and forms;
I've travelled the world and seen.
We come in all shades of brown, black, yellow, red, and white.
Some with large bodies, some small.
Some with straight hair, some curly.
Eyes of all types and sizes.
Yet underneath this thin packaging we are so much the same.
See the heart inside those eyes that longs for warmth and acceptance,
and let's love one another.

 Bill E. Goldberg

My Love

For Jon K., my best guy bud—
I miss and love you lots, honey!
I watched you from across the room,
Your face soft but sweet.
Wishing I could be with you,
It would make my life complete.
Seeing you all alone,
Wishing you were mine.
Even though we're different,
We can still cross that fine line.
I see you in my dreams,
Every night as I sleep.
And when I wake up,
You're in my heart to keep.

 Stacy Lynn Hahn

Stormy Clouds

Stormy clouds and sinking skies
a flood of rain drops sting my eyes.

To the ground the leaves do fall,
A dark, wet carpet for one and all.

I close my eyes and feel the storm;
the soul and body now have torn.

To the clouds my soul does fly,
looking down I feel a high.

To the ground my soul does drop;
in my body it makes its stop.

My body surges with life refreshed,
a clean pure spirit and tainted flesh.

 Jennifer Lyn Ganther

Breathe

When I breathe I
Think about time and
How we never know when
We will die and
Am glad to
Be alive.

When I breathe I
Think about love and
Hate and how both can
Start a war but
Only one can
Bring peace.

When I breathe I
Think about life and
How if everyone would
Be kind to everyone else our
World would be a
Happy place.

 Laura Bowles

Minor Thirds

It once was you
at the piano,
wearing the ivory thin,
practicing for a concert
in another life.
The cat sat on the strings,
watching the tiny mallets
pounding out the sounds.

I sat on the sofa, watching
the chandelier's teardrops sway,
imagining them, one by one,
falling to the floor.

 H.D. Motyl

New Morning Sun

I'm lying tonight on this cold, damp ground,
thinking of the new love my darling has found.
There's no hope in regaining her love,
I'm left with her memory and the stars above . . .
But wait! What's that in the darkness I see?
A figure of a woman, as fine as can be.
Her silhouette against the full moon's light
is such an exotic and beautiful sight.
She is walking silently, straight toward me . . .
she stops now and leans on a giant oak tree.
I start toward her and break into a run . . .
but my dream is broken by the new morning sun.

Mary Janis

Man Meets Woman

In the morning when I awaken, yours is the face that proclaims my place at your side.
Sometimes the days resemble themselves when thoughts of you involve.
Always the most perfect thoughts of a man and his queen to quench my thirst.
I have learned to love lusting for you. I have learned to love you.
In this judgment I pledge myself to your whims and curious speech.
And if the forgiveness of the hour is not favorable,
then I shall tear out my insides for they are of no use.
Only the soft contentment that is your motion can place my shortcomings out of the way.
I have found the beauty of all I desire in your eyes.
I have found the comfort I seek in your arms.
Though my breath is stolen with but a single touch,
I would gladly hold your hand the whole day through.
It is inevitable that all roads end, but who we travel them with is ours to choose.

Philip Priore, Jr.

Look Up When You Are Down

I drift off, slowly thinking of the days you and I spent together
holding back a tear, each minute thinking of you goes by like hours in slow motion.
I feel you hair brush against my face,
I can hear your whisper in my ear, your smile lights up my world
like nothing else I know, Oh, I long to be together again.
Lord, please let today be like all the yesterdays, please let it be so.

I look up when I am down, up into the sky, looking for the star we found.
No matter where I am, you are close to me, even though you are not around.
I think of the days you and I made love under our star and the moon.
Our focus together was always on us, our hearts beating in tune.

I go to bed each night saying a silent prayer,
whispering your name, I wish these words I could send.
I pray you hear my voice and know you are my one true love
from now until the end; I am lying here staring at the sky
gazing at our star, I wonder where you are,
hoping you are thinking of me the way I am thinking of you,
praying for the day that you and I can say, "I do."

So, look up when you are down, as we, together, long for the day,
hopefully not far away, a time that you and I will lie and gaze at our star.
We'll make love under the moon, knowing all that matters is you and I.
Lost in each other's eyes, each other's touch, never again to say goodbye.

Clark S. Thompson

Magic

People say there are magical things to be told.
Like goblins, unicorns, and leprechauns with pots of gold.
But the most magical things and this is true,
Lives inside of each of you.

Hope, when there is suffering
Is more magical than genies and ruby rings,
To forgive and love, when all you feel is hate,
To have the patience to wait and wait,
And to not get discouraged when you don't get your reward in the end,
That is the most magical thing, my friend.

Marisa Marcus

A Storm

Glistening upon the clouds,
racing through the sky,
the flashes of alarming light
speak beauty as they fly
and cut a path through darkest night,
frightening, yet lovely sight.
As all is thrown about the world
and all is sent awry,
I watch and hear the furious waves
of storm and light go by,
all loud and coming fast in staves
against my window and its panes,
the world beneath the torrid rains.
When all is done, it is as if
a dream has just passed by,
a surreal, strange, enchanting gale,
like nature against sky,
and through the bleak and hazy veil,
damage done will always pale;
the chaotic splendor will prevail.

Kerry Mauck

Unnoticed

To all the loners
I'm like that ant in the grass
working ever so hard and quickly,
but still . . .
I go unnoticed.

I'm the "loner" who's
never chosen for anything.
I ask if I may join, and
reluctantly they let me join,
but still . . .
I go unnoticed.

Dear God, what did I do
to deserve this?
Am I ugly or clumsy,
or annoying, or stupid?
Nobody notices me.
Why am I unnoticed?

And so I live my life
unliked,
unloved,
unnoticed!

Joseph Oates

The Contest

Writing a poem for a contest,
The pressure to create is immense.
Finding the words for the paper,
I feel strained, nervous, and tense.

The poem needs to be clever,
To show what I can write.
This could be my chance at Hallmark;
I must be clever, witty, and bright.

Choosing just the right topic
Is priority on my list.
I would welcome any ideas.
Oh yes, please, I insist.

As many thoughts are swirling about,
It is suddenly becoming clear
That the number of poetic lines
Is quickly drawing near.

So with that knowledge in mind
I see I am at the end.
The only thing left to do
Is to get this out and send.

E. Joyce Bott

Memories of You

The eyes I knew sparkled with laughter,
Joy and untold secrets; beckoning to all.
Eyes now clouded over by years of pain and sorrows.
Looking somberly through lowered lids at a world they
Once embraced, now searching and seeking for what's been lost.
Feet that once moved quick and light to the beat of music
And the pace of life lived at that time.
Now shuffle and stumble to another of music but over the same old ground.
Hands once quick to grasp at life, and all it offered.
Now hesitate and tremble slightly in brief uncertainty.
Shoulders once squared; with all pride, dignity, and self-worth
Sloop now with unseen burdens of time gone by.
Head once held high filled with plans, hopes and dreams of things to come.
Hangs heavy now burdens and unseen regrets of all yesteryears gone by.

Charlotte Allen

Angels in Our Path

Each corner of the world, we sit in different places.
Each one to their own experience and thoughts in their places.
We, who dwell in the higher place, seek forth your thoughts and embraces.
Those that reach to God's plan of life,
know no path of world's devastation.
They are the light and way for all souls' misfortune.
Compassion and love will guide
in the path for those of little understanding.
Oh! Children of Earth, we cry out in truth.
Expression of love to feel each being.
Your needs we hold in our souls so near.
Guiding and lighting each step of the way.
Come forth, my children, for we shall help!
Make that path a ray of light.

Mary L. Clarke

Walk with Me

We walk each step forward into the future we go
Learning from yesterday guided by our past we grow
Gaining strength from our triumphs, confidence is our resource
Enduring mental anguish, climbing our walls, facing our course
Challenging ourselves striving for excellence in a imperfect world
Through insanity we repeat, each time a new lesson is unfurled
The answers we look for cannot be seen only found within
Our souls possess the freedom of will, choose or be destined
There are no limits except the limits one places upon himself
Realizing a man's worth is weighed by his actions, not material wealth
Perseverance is a personal decision,
Blame only what you see in the mirror
Do you believe you're strong?
Is your mind clear or clouded with fear? . . .

Timothy Dornaus

The Woman Master

Tiny, petite and glowing with a humble, sincere beauty—does this lady really know karate?
If she knows karate, can this lady really "do" karate?

Yes—but big men never know until they are wrapped up like Christmas bows
and kneel at the feet of their gorgeous victor: they soon get the clue who is boss.

With a sparkle in her eyes and a shake of her angelic hair,
attackers melt like solid metal in a furnace.

Brawn and badness are no match for the virtuous woman sensei
who treads those with bad attitudes beneath her feet.

Children smile and beam in her presence.
Her husband's friends ask her for manly advice.
The dojo hums with balanced harmony,
like the rolling of a Yin Yang in perfect equilibrium.

The woman master radiates kindness. She smiles and sings her kiais.
But best of all, she fights like a ninja.

Benjamin York

wannabe

i wanted to be you
you wanted to be me
but we did not notice
that we wanted to be a wannabe
because you are who you are
and i am who i am
we should be grateful
for what god has given us
and not worry about
what others think of us
so forget that straight
hair i wanted and that
curly hair you wanted
the brown eyes i wanted
and the blue eyes you wanted
because we should be grateful
for who we are and not what
we wannabe

Tina Miles

So Many Words

I have so many words,
And my voice is still.
Hear me.

I have much to do,
But his grip is hard.
Free me.

I have love to learn
And passion to share.
Teach me.

I have dreams to follow,
But the day is dark.
See me.

I have much to feel,
And my soul is numb.
Touch me.

Maryllew Partlow

This Day, My Way

God is giving me "This Day."
Maybe He will let me live it "My Way."

A Love to love
Always, all ways, to love

To help a friend
A heartache to mend

A sunbeam to see
And all the things God gives to me

A quiet walk
With myself to talk

To thank God for giving me "This Day"
And for letting me live it "My Way."

Florence H. Cottrill

A Friendship Lost

I will not play with you today
Your eyes are blue and mine are gray

And so the war was thus begun
And since that time no one has won

Blue looks at Gray with indignation
And Gray hates Blue in retaliation

Neither stops to count the cost
Thus a true and faithful friend is lost

Beverly D. Harris

Our Heritage

You see the clothes on my back, the beads round' my neck.
Well, when you see the green, *black* and red flag you'd better show some respect.
See, we've pledging allegiance to the American flag just a little too long
When we can sing "Oh, say can you see . . . "
And don't know the words to our own anthem song.
Something's wrong when we can celebrate Christmas, but forget about Kwanzaa
Never even heard of Umoja, Kuumba, Ukima, Kujichagula, Nia, Imani, Ujamaa.
Black people, it's time to unite, we need to a be few steps ahead;
I'll start us off by explaining the green, the *black*, and the red.
Green represents the land, and all of our hopes and dreams,
Black represents our people and all that togetherness means.
Red represents the struggle of the past, present, and those yet to come.
We get our color 'cause we're favored, highly favored of the *Son*,
The groove in our hearts makes us sing, rhythm in our soul makes us dance.
Black women are protected by black men that stand in their soldier like stance.
Kwanzaa is Swahili for first fruits of the harvest, all, yeah, it's time to eat:
Black-eyed peas and neck bones, chitterlings, ham hocks, greens, and pigs feet.
This is a time for our people to come together and don't ever forget that,
'Cause not only are we celebrating Kwanzaa, we're celebrating being *Black*!

Lorenthia Daniel

Child of Two

Amidst the squalor of dirt floors, sat a small child of two
—fingering dung beetles crept through the door, deciding this was not new.
Above the stench of heathen's life, a stream of sunlight came,
to fall upon the father's wife—who lies there in Death's shame.
Of grotesque illness that bulged the eyes, and hurt the stomach so—
not knowing this child of two knelt down—
Her sweet face screwed into a frown
of death, now she will know.
She cried aloud for all she saw,
and ached deep down for her mamma.

Joan M. Croft

Lonely Man

A teardrop runs down my cheek to my toe,
to fill the puddle of sorrows and woes.
A lonely man cries alone to hide
the feeling that he's now alone.

The love of his life has broken his heart
and scattered his dreams, on the wind afar.
A lonely man drifts alone because he has no love left in his bones.
Shy and full of doubt and with no one on his side, he tries to make a
stand, before his secret is known to the land.
A lonely man cries all alone until the day, he finally comes home,
Home to a place where peace is in the land
and the Almighty God is there to bless every man.
So peace to you, Oh, lonely man.

John McDonald

Small Town

They all pretty much look the same
Same stores, same roads, same people
They ask little from life and expect little
They're good people, not perfect, but they can live with that

They're boring, out of touch, and backward
and I'm sure they can live with that
They know what is important to them and
for others, well, they shouldn't worry.

Dust and the heat hang around like unwelcome visitors
But that's okay; they have felt them before.
Winters are worse; the silence is even more quiet in these small old towns.

We passed through these towns without a second glance or
at best a small pause, thinking that we get to go on
We won't pick up any of the boredom or dust or the sameness
We're on our way out of town
And they can live with that

Edward Sphrehe

Pillow Talk

You Promised Me The World
Before We Went To Bed
And When The Morning Came
You Forgot Everything You Said
I Knew Right Then
That You Could Never Be Mine
And To Take You Seriously
Would Be A Waste Of My Time
So I Put On My Clothes
And Took A Very Long Walk
'Cause All You Were Saying
Last Night Was Just Pillow Talk

Danny W. Davis

Therapy

I drown my sorrow deep in sleep
up tomorrow within I weep
begin each day the same old way
wait 'til night my only day
push and shove you make me feel
I whine and scream to fight the real
see the light dull and bright
believe you can and yet I might
to need and want you shall not take
you see and don't because it's fake
visions of mirrors without reflections
the kind of people without connections
before after beginning to end
we all are a chapter in time we'll mend

Jason Check

Realization

I swore to myself
It would never happen again.
I vowed to myself
That this was the end.
The end of this longing,
This yearning so strong.
I said I was over you,
But . . . Oh, I was wrong.
Now here it is
Quite a while later,
My love for you is even greater.
I spend all of my time
Thinking of you.
I am in love with you again.
The rest is left 'til the end.

Christina Mills

Sweet Dreams

Into the darkness
Disguised as visions he comes,
Dancing and bribing us with his bliss.
He calls upon us one by one.

He encircles your reveries,
Enchanting your thoughts.
He induces vivid images
Until you've been bought.

He leads you to sleep,
But keeps your eyes bright.
He elongates your unconsciousness
Then returns you to light.

He stays fresh but for moments.
He'll put a smile on your face.
You forget when your day begins,
As your memories have been erased.

Kelly Speight

The Game

Earth is a minute speck in the universe and we mortals are but amoebas.
Perhaps life is a game and we're losing.
Maybe some higher force is overseeing all of us insignificant atoms,
and we are but chess pieces of the galaxy.
Some of us beings are back line pieces, and the rest are front line pawns.
Unfortunately we are the only mammals of this planet with reasoning powers.
Being of this species, we wish for independence.
Once we have arrived at this imaginary status, we strive for more . . . Alas . . . Power!
The magical word power . . . is our arrogant downfall.
The arrogance of man is the undoing of mankind.
This shallow existence of animal life may have been created for the amusement of the
Grand Chess Master of the universe,
to observe us mortals making our amateurish moves and slowly destroying ourselves.
This destruction is the result of the never-ending obsession
with the imaginary strength of power.
If only our perception was as great as our greed,
then maybe our short existence would be as sweet as the forbidden fruit we seek.
Perhaps we earthlings could then see the magic in the stars,
and enjoy the beauty of an autumn sunset.
Making the fleeting moments of life count, I would rather be a moving Pawn,
than a King in checkmate.

Charles B. Anderson

Remembering Mother's Love

It takes a mother's love to make a house a home.
A place to be remembered and yearn to return.
No matter where you roam.
It takes a loving, caring, patient mother to bring a child up right.
Her understanding, courage, and cheerfulness makes a dark day bright.
It takes a mother's thoughtfulness to mend the heart's deep "hurts"
and her skill and endurance to mend little socks and shirts.
Remembering mother's love, kindness to forgive and forget when we error,
to sympathize in trouble and bow her head in prayer.
Remembering mother's wisdom and knowledge to recognize our needs
and to give us reassurance by her loving words and deeds.
Remembering mother, how she dressed us up each Sunday morning
and walked us up to church, she stayed to hear the preacher preach and pray.
Remember how mother loved Jesus, she cared about our souls,
about us learning God's laws, so we wouldn't be lost.
Remembering mother's love how she went through each day
singing, praying, cleaning, and cooking, doing her chores.
Never complaining, she seemed to have such peace and joy.
Being grateful for the gift she received from God.
Remembering mother's love, her endless faith, confidence, and trust
that guided us through the pitfalls of selfishness and lust.

Mary Ann Jones

Love Scenarios

I'll write and say it as many times it takes,
even sing if you think I should,
Although I don't rule the world, if I had it to give to you, I would.
Cut from cheap cloth, salvaged from a good will my seams continue to fray
Your skin is like the finest linen, more glow than the sunniest day.
Two worlds collide at the turn of the century to fulfill each others needs,
I was alone in the galaxy 'til I found you, no longer does my heart bleed.
Stranded in the forest, had lost my way by falling from my tree,
A wounded creature caged in the wilderness your nature has set me free.
I confess to the courts and testify that what I say is true,
Pass judgement if you will . . . my defense is still . . . I love you.
Lay with me, pray with me, that life won't end too soon,
I don't ever want to leave this Earth, got too much loving to do.
For better for worse, for richer for poorer, 'til death surely do we part,
Picasso himself would shine down upon me, loving you is a beautiful art.
I lay down my pen and fold my paper to take you into my arms,
Forget clovers . . . horse shoes and rabbits feet . . . I'm holding my lucky charm.
From the tops of the peaks to the depths of the ocean,
through skies gray and blue,
In sickness . . . and in health, I love you, I love you, I love you!

Ricardo F. Mills II

First Light

Darkness has faded to light
Tears have dried
I no longer sigh in the night
Smiles I have tried

At last my sorrow has flown
And my Joy has grown

Since you my hand took
And my face held
My life is like a new book
Its pages yet to be spelled

You have taken me in
You have touched my skin

My heart you have seen
Sorrow you've taken
My senses now keen
My joy spoken

For you these words
I have uttered
You hold the cords
Yet my heart unfettered

Scott Alan Farley

Spirit of the Wolf

It is nearly nightfall
Our dance will begin
To let our spirit rise
So in the war we'll win.

The spirit of the wolf
Comes to us in times
Of good, bad, joy and sorrow;
Listens to our cries.

His stature is magnificent,
Shiny black is his fur;
Lightning speed and great strength
With eyes of red that deeply burn.

For I am Shaman!
And I summon him
In special times of need,
His spirit comes to me.

For I am the Shaman!

Tabitha Elise Mancini

If I Could Give . . .

If I could give you WISDOM
I'd give it to you in GOLD
WORDS of such VALUE
It couldn't be bought or sold.
If I could give you HOPE and PEACE,
I would give it to you in SILVER.
The likes you've never seen
Pouring from the RIVER.
If I could give you LOVE
I'd give it to you in SPARKLING JEWELS
For such a LOVE would flow
In WATERFALLS, and POOLS.
If I could give you TOMORROW
It would be in a BEAUTIFUL PEARL.
Never could one person
Hold such RICHES; not in all the WORLD.
If I could give you HEAVEN
And all its HEAVENLY BLISS.
What need would you have for JESUS.
If I could give you All OF THIS!!!

Shirley Ann Shell

Friendship Is Forever and Ever

Getting to know you the way that I do, getting to know how you feel
about a lot of things, being able to help when needed,
being able to talk to someone without worry,
your problems are mine if you want them to be.
Any hour, any day that you need a friend, I'll be there for you
in any capacity, just because we are friends, and that is what
good friends are for, so don't worry (be happy) about life,
just because life throws us a lot of curves and a lot of fast-balls.
Just step up and do your best, but remember I'll be there if you need me.
Tough times, we all endure and grow from them.
We all need help sometimes, even if we say we don't, so when those times come,
just let me know and I'll be here for you.
That's what really good friends are for. Friendship is forever.
Friendship is a love that does not die; friendship is a love
that will always grow, friends through all that is bad and good.
I don't have to be there all the time in person Just look inside and that friendship is there.
I will always be with you in spirit, at least.
That's what friends are for . . .
With love from a Friend . . .

Scott M. Robnett

Who Am I?

Traveling all over the world in a cloud of happiness and tranquility,
teaching you to open your mind to the endless possibility.

Searching for loneliness wherever I can,
hoping to bring together every woman and man.

In a world that is full of hate and despair,
I gave hope to the hopeful and wisdom to the wise.

I evolved from a place deep inside the heart,
with a bond so tight no man can tear it apart.

I'm in your mind every second, every minute, every day,
I'm also with you every time you sleep, think, or pray.

Bringing my wonders in mysterious ways,
I determine the memory that goes and the one that stays.

Because of me you would sacrifice your lives,
but without me there would be no husbands or wives.

I am a force so strong I could only be created in the heaven's above,
What else could I be but love.

Nathalee Bailey

Just Tense

I am presently tense
And going insane.
Though not in my right mind, I need not a new brain.
"I'm sorry," I say, "I won't do it again."
"We've been through this," they say, "Don't try to explain."

One choice meal I eat without complaint,
While pondering the fate that awaits me:
A frenzy, I'll vomit, then faint.
After, there will be what there will be.
Things I'll neither hear nor see.
Rejoicing? Maybe. Crying? Not for me.
Horror? Probably, but I need not worry
For then I'll be free. Finally.

The Walk. The fear. The cords—
That adhere to me and
The chair,
And the soul freeing flick
By, which Justice sends a life changing
Switch.
Now I am past tense.

Elijah Randall

I Am Poem

I am a Christian and an athlete.
I wonder about my future and what
It holds. I hear the sounds of football
In my dreams. I see every hit. I want
To go to Heaven. I am a Christian and
an athlete.

I pretend to be a Ninja. I feel the
Pain I inflict. I touch the birds in
The blue sky. I worry about nothing.
I am a Christian and an athlete.

I understand the Bible. I say I am a
Child of God. I dream about my future
In sports each and every night. I try
And never give up. I hope to meet Him,
Jesus, The Holy Ghost.
I am a Christian and an athlete.

Kenneth Trull

Grandma

She was an angel
sent from above
to nurture and guide us
with her pure love.
She never would judge
and was a good listener;
she was my Gram
and I'll always miss her.
Her faith was her strength,
her smile was so bright,
she met all life's challenges
with pride and delight.
So when you feel weary
and are falling apart,
just remember Grandma
and her amazingly kind heart.

Rae Weakland

Untitled

He tried to catch a butterfuly
Jumped right up to touch the sky
Fell back down to the ground

But he did touch me
Reaching out don't you see
Reached right out and grabbed ahold
A part of me no light beholds

That cat of mine
I want him back
Can't have him now
My soul will lack

Brenda D. Gulliford

Fire

Lord, set me afire
so that my soul may never tire.
Flood me with love
with grace from above.

Lord, set me aflame
and you I'll proclaim;
with a righteous heart
each day I shall start.

Lord, give me a power
that Satan can't devour.

Break my heart,
reconstruct it with steel,
for Lord it is you, and only you,
to whom I shall always kneel.

Jacob Allee

Mirror Complex

Mirror complex
infinity we see.
Curved glass or straight,
all images are to be.
Glance at the time
for you are never alone.
Shadows on your face
may be from a clone.
Light comes from your eyes,
which is a beam of all matter.
But be careful of your lies
for you may shatter.

Thomas S. Roeder

Constant Prayer

I need thee every hour
I seek thee then in prayer.
I yearn to feel thy power
My burdens thus to bear.

I feel thy presence near
Whenever I speak with thee.
I know that thou wilt hear
And right the wrong for me.

Thou art my source of strength
A spring of peace and power.
In thee I am born anew
As I seek thee every hour.

Rose Elaine Schoonmaker

Changes in Love

Darkness covers my face
as everything is displace.
No more happy tears,
no more smiles.
Thoughts of love soon in denial.

Where did those days go
when I was so glee and free?
Maybe in the shadow with
my shining star.

I wish things could be the same,
but time has put out the flame.
I now bow my head in shame.
The memories we had once,
are now being framed.

Kimberly Jane Carl

Them

Whatever it was that they perceived
was distorted,
they're deceived.
They think they're right,
they think I'm wrong,
but don't they know that
life is only so long?
They left me here to feel so cheated,
and now I understand
why it was that I was defeated.
So I feel it is my responsibility
to let them know,
before I decide to take myself and go.
That this is me
and I am this,
the chance of a lifetime,
they made me miss.

Lindsey Nolene Grodzicki

Glimmer of Dawn

Cascading satin
colors broken only
by a few curls of your hair,

Breathing ever slightly
just enough
reminding me you are near,

Mindful of body
my hand drifts forth
waking first being so rare,

Familiar smile greets my touch
your laughter sign enough
you were waiting for it—how unfair!

Lancelot Elarionoff, Jr.

Wonderful Feeling

The birds are singing;
The sun is out,
I feel so good,
I want to shout!

I don't know WHY
I feel this way,
I guess the Lord just said,
"Today is YOUR day."

So join me now;
Put a smile on that face,
And let's thank the Lord
For all his good grace,

Without which we can't go on;
But with which we can grow strong.

Virginia T. Coffee

In 20 Lines or Less

Sometimes I think I'd like to write,
And sure would do my best,
But what you ask is quite a fright—
In 20 lines or less!

To set the mood it takes a while
And this one you must guess,
Can one decide to cry or smile
In 20 lines or less?

Now here my friend, with some chagrin
And hope that you may bless
The thoughts that came from deep within
In 20 lines or Less.

Samuel Vincent Myers, Jr.

The Lighthouse

On a dim lit evening, the lighthouse
whispered to the ships upon the
waves, thy waters are rough, but I
shall guide you to the safe arms of
thy love's tender kisses. Trust
in my wise beacon and I shall not
forsake thee in thy quest for
passion, long missed by the weeks
away. Be not taken by thy Ocean's
fare complexion and let not the
craggy rock, which seeks thy hull,
forsake thee. Listen to my whisper
and I shall covet thy heart like
the beauty of a white dove or a
fast, yet gentle current of
Ocean's breath.

Jimmy Dean Wade

Autumn

Leaves of gold, of red, of brown,
flutter form the boughs above;
by the gentle breezes blown,
here and there they seem to rove.
The bright blue sky with clouds hung,
the flocks of migrating geese,
the garden spider's web slung
between two evergreen trees.
All these are signs of the fall,
of impending winter time,
of the end of summer's all,
inspiring an autumn rhyme.

Richard Askew

My Dad Died

My dad has died, I have cried.
But he will always be in my heart,
We will never be apart.

Cassidy Hartman

I Will Go On

Blackness fills the space
alone in the nothingness
finally at peace
not feeling the carelessness

Then I open my eyes
and emerge from the depths of my mind
I am back to reality
to a world so unkind

All the good feelings
created in my imagination
gone away, for now
I'm back to this crude creation

But still I continue
I must remain strong
I will live my life
I will keep going on

I will not be defeated
and I will not give in
I will struggle on
and I know, somehow I'll win

Ben Plunk

Medication

It was medication, I know.
The bottles stood in a row.
Take one of these, take two of those,
For reasons that nobody knows.

To the MRI I must go
And the bed moves very slow.
Knock, knock, knock here.
Knock, knock, knock there.
It was more than I could bear.

Now they turned on the X-rays;
That put me in a daze.
They showed me my bones
And the joints that gave me moans,
Until I told them to go away.

So right now I must end
Before I offend
The nice nurses and the docs
That put me through all of this
And said I must not resist
If I wanted to continue to exist.

Ted Isaacs

Dreams

Someone told me once
To follow my dreams
I am happy now
But yet falling apart at the seams
I have everything I used to want
Money, a big house
And all that junk
But it turns out
I had the wrong vision
Everything did not
Turn out to precision
I realize now that what I really need
Is trust, love, and a family
So now I must follow
My dreams once more
Only this time
I'll make it through the right door

Kayla Jackson

Justice?   Mercy?

Give us justice! Give us justice!
We continually shout.
Is that what we want?
This I doubt.

What if fate would
Obey our plea?
What would happen to you?
What would happen to me?

Our future
We would bemoan
If, indeed, we were to reap
What we have sown.

Although of justice
We often speak,
In reality, it is mercy
We actually seek.

Willis J. Jones

Once Knew

I once knew a man
who had a crown
who had twelve devoted fans
He was never seen with a frown

He led a life with no sin
He had a Heavenly father
He had a virgin for some kin
He had not many bothers

He hung on a tree
where He paid for our wrong doings
on that tree He died to set us free
and nobody thought once about booing

He died for us that day on a cross
so won't you accept Him, for He's the boss

Meggian Wilhite

The Voice of Life

Never leave dream street.
Never lose control.
Always know the difference between
Pleasure and principle.
Until death do you part from life,
Never stop seeking knowledge.
When love knocks on your door, you'll
Know because your heart will throb.
Always feel the need to feel special.
And no matter what, never leave
The free zone!

Rebecca M. C. Vaughns

Us

You said you loved me
and whooshed me away
to a place in your heart
to forever stay
you touched my soul
and gave me life
you were my love, I was your life
you held me close
in good and bad
we loved each other—it was a fad
I still loved you
but was pushed away
you kissed someone else
my heart had to pay
Now we're not together
We can't be friends
you broke my trust
That's where "Us" ends

Kelsey Knotts

Madrigal

The melody of life
is continuous
and harmonic.
There are certain
minstrels, though,
whose song,
like one uninterrupted,
pure, clear note,
played long,
followed by
silence . . .
continues, playing,
and echoes
endlessly.

Kathleen Romana

Your Diamond

Greg's Diamond
You found your diamond in the dust
shining full of light.
But then you let her slip away
because of what was right.
You asked God if you could keep her
to give you so much joy
but you dropped your diamond in the dust
as though she were a toy.
Your diamond's lost its lustre;
no more will she shine.
Until you come to dig her up
forever she will pine.

Julie McCann

Nightfall

As the sun sets on the horizon
A thick vapor of fog
Begins to fill the pellucid sky
Engulfing
Absorbing
Eventually bleeding it dry
Overwhelming fear
Terror
Start to control your mind
Transmitting goose bumps
Forming shivers down your spine
Nightfall watches over you
Like a lion hunting its prey
Intruders dealt with in a harsh
Merciless way
Nightfall.

Mark Luciew

My Hobby

Writing has become a hobby with me
It seems the only thing that fits
It helps me when I'm down and out
And ready to call it quits
So lift my spirits high, Oh, pen
And write my worries away
For tomorrow I'll be a better person
Than I ever was today

Kathleen Totty

The Eyes of a Child

To everyone who inspires me
I look into the eyes of a man,
and I see nothing,
an endless void,
two black holes,
no emotion,
no joy,
no sorrow,
nothing.

I look into the eyes of a child,
they are filled with wonder,
two gleaming balls,
filled with curiosity,
energy,
hopes,
dreams.

Ian Myers

That Is the God I Have

The God who helped me though my rape.
The God who raised the sun.
The God who helped me to escape.
The God who let me run.
That is the God I have.

The God who helped me cry at night.
The God who loves me so.
The God who helped me cure my fright.
The God who lets me know.
That is the God I have.

The God who helped me see the light.
The God who cured the blind.
The God who helped me calm the fight.
The God who loosened the bind.
That is the God I have.

Amanda Elizabeth Brower

Mother Earth

We just stand and watch
She gets raped around the clock
Every minute every hour
We destroy and devour
In the name of just living
We loot and we plunder
She's getting raped
Our mother
She gets raped every hour
By her sons and her daughters
She gives so much
But we always want more
To satisfy our greed
We are shredding her soul
She's getting raped
Our mother
Can't you feel her pain
Can't you hear her cry
Can't you see her anguish
Don't you know she's dying

Imran Khan Abbas

War

It's me against an army,
One against them all.
The fighting's never ending,
The pain is never gone.
Even when I'm hiding,
I see and hear the troops.
Even though I'm fighting,
I know that they can't lose.
And when this battle finally ends,
I know that I'll be dead.
A war against an army,
Fighting inside my head.

Justine Werfelman

Wedding Day

As you walk through this life
hand in hand,

You're joined together by love
and two wedding bands.

You stood before God and
proclaimed your love,

He sent you his blessings
down from above.

Be good to each other and
always be true,

your days will be happy and
your skies will be blue.

Love each other with
all of your hearts,

for as the vow says
'til death due you part.

Gwendolyn Ann Wolfe

One

One Love,
One Life,
One Glove,
One Knife.

Stacia F. Pryer

Soul Death

I dwell here in my coldest grave
to lie here in my wretched tomb.
I bask in shadows of the cave
to soak in whispers of the moon.
To be so still—to barely breathe
to numb my parting of this rage
I cannot sense to feel—to seethe
let me break this shallow cage.
My heart beats slow and then no more
I'm tasting my last breath.
The raspy creaking of the door,
this is my touch of Death.

Kyra Aleece Fergeson

Alone

I grasp in the night
For things I can't see
I cringe from the light
From things that are free
My world is a cell from which I may cry
If one chances to hear
Won't you come be with me

Shawn White

Saturday in the Park

*Dedicated to my teacher, Hope Alexander,
thanks for having faith in me*
Once on a pretty Saturday,
with the sun high in the sky.
I rode my bike to the park,
and saw my friend there.
We ran and jumped on the swings,
and glided to the sky.
I heard a distant rumble,
and the clouds began to shake.
I hurried to my bike,
and pedaled fast away.
For I knew this was the end,
of a beautiful day!

Melissa Gladys Kelly (Age>10)

Firestarter

Silly aspirations . . .
Constellations
Drifting, shifting
I bare my thoughts of you
In a glued together vessel
Of heart shapes and star shapes
My beautiful apparition
Glowing ablaze
Like a fiery supernova
Racing through my sky
To light up my life
To an existence like no other
(Let's go)!
Escape with me
Into this crimson night
Of kings and queens
From the firefly heavens
Be amazed . . .
Inspired
Mesmerized

Isabel Stephanie Tomas

Better Days

With all the words I say,
you still will go away.
Your heart has gone away
and I remember better days.
Remember the bright sun on the meadow
we were so happy, you and me
Life was made for living,
our love was a realty.
Truer words could not be spoken,
our love was just a token,
of better days.

Rochelle Rodgers

Untitled

Imprisoned like an innocent man.
Chained and hardened.
Cold and alone.
Not able to feel any more
Pain.
Will live on, for
The spirit is there,
But the light has gone.

Time means nothing.
Weeks, years, no matter.
Closed down, rusted shut.
Unable to breath.
Sentenced without a fair trial.
In a prison, chained,
Is were my heart lives.

Joseph La Mattina

Ball of Twine

My mind's a ball of twine
with a center, with a core
throughout the twine
is my interest
throughout the twine
is my goal
it's a twine of emotion
twine of action, twine of pride
twine of memory, twine of life
around me, under me
a present wrapped so tight that
I cannot see it, feel it
shake it for hints
no loopholes, twine is so tight
so new, just wrapped, or has been
I see it now, what unwraps it?
myself? another?   Where is the core?
Where is the twine? What is it?
Why?

Matt Ruscio

Parrot

Parrot repeats,
He hears and speaks.
A student at work,
Patterned speech.

Simon N. C. Petts

When the Wind Blows

To Mom: I love you, Ashley
When the wind blows,
I'll be there to protect you,
When the wind blows,
I'll guide you home through the storm,
When the wind blows,
I'll always love you still,
When the wind gets too strong
And we are separated,
You will always be a part of me forever.

Barbara Uren

Drink

Sipping joyously
Life. Cool, refreshing, quenched.
Ah, knowledge found.

Gloria Louise Guynes

My Little Valentine

We found a kitten in a dark alley,
looking for food and a home,
lost and alone.
Her hair is soft as pure silk.
Her cries feeble but shrill.
Her moans pierce your soul
and penetrate your bones.
Her look wins over your heart
and you wish she's your own.
Gently we took her home.
She jumps and prances,
asking for food.
She sniffs and swallows
all that's in her bowl
'til contented.
She rests in my soft and cozy lap,
purring with delight
and fear of her plight,
dreaming of a place called Home.

Kwai Hing Keung

Sand Castle

You are like a sand castle,
So proud and defiant,
Daring the sea to touch you,

Magnificent in your charm and warmth,
Yet firm in who you were,
But so easily taken away,

Like waves that came,
To claim their prize,
You too, so quickly left my life,

You are like a sand castle,
Beautiful and strong,
But all too soon gone,

Your memory lives on,
Like that of a sand castle,
From a past, long gone.

Leandra Fuller

The Face

I see the face
of the man
who held me down
who held my hands
he touches me
not gently
a violent caress
he could care less
many hands
grabbing me, raping me, holding me
He's too strong,
I'm so weak
and I can't fight
I'm small and meek
I'm part of him
I am his wife
I don't know
or understand
I see the face
of the man

Misty Case

Contentment

Within my soul there lies a place
locked up beyond life's icy grasp
awaiting one unyielding key
to set these strong emotions free

The raging storms that swell within
assault this fortress firm and strong
longing for the soothing peace
that only comes with sweet release

The day will come with gentle touch
to softly turn the bolted door
morning sun will warm my face
while I am held in love's embrace

Aurora Knight

Crystal Ball

A voyage I take to the world
Through your eyes
Every step I take
Found on your mind

You give me the world
Of brilliant, brilliant emptiness
No matter how hard I've tried
I cannot see through
Your unfaithfulness

Jie Cai

Acceptance

Oh, Jesus, I am so sorry
I did not sooner answer Your knock.
To see You standing at my door,
It really was quite a shock.

To think that You would take the time
For a lowly sinner like me.
At first I could not comprehend this,
But true I know it must be.

For there You were, patiently waiting,
'Til I opened my eyes to see
That when I took that outstretched hand,
You would forever walk with me.

Dorothy Kemp

My Father, What a Guy

My father, what a guy
Though he may make me cry
When he disciplines me
He is creating in me what I should be
He teaches me right from wrong
He makes me feel like I belong
Because he sees the good in me
His daughter I will always be

My father, what a guy
He helps me when I'm feeling shy
He will catch us when we fall
He is a family man and he loves us all
He believes in the good Lord above
And He shows it in his love
He is the man who adopted me
Because he saw in me what I could be

Brandi Jerby

Moth

As you hang upon the wall,
Knowing well that you will fall,
Think you need not heed my call,
You stubbornly will make your crawl.

Tremble as you manage to cling,
Cry out though you don't say a thing,
Panic when you can't take wing;
Would do you better listening?

Hang until the day is gone,
Wait for an idea to spawn,
You hold until it is the dawn,
In this race of brains and brawn.

Amy Lehrmitt

Summer's Over

No more summer,
It's a bummer.
Just school,
No more pool.

No more fishing,
No more wishing,
No more birthdays, not even mine,
And I didn't even get a dime.

No more vacations
Or travel to other nations.
Now I can't stay up late.
Isn't that a terrible fate?

Oh, well, I guess I'm stuck.
Maybe next year,
I'll have better luck!

Curtis Peterson

Not Enough Hours

Quicken Pace, Short Embrace
No Time Now, It's Getting Late
I'm so sorry, I have to go,
I have things to do, you know,
The World Around me Moves so fast
I can't be late, I won't be last
So right now I must leave,
There's one more place I have to be,
The daylight is Fading, Slipping Away,
Not enough Hours, not enough Days

Mary Rae

The River

Flow with ease
Without a care,
To the places
Man cannot fare!
The excellence of
The current's flow
will lead to
The places you must go.
Tarry not,
Come to Me,
For this is where
Life must be.
The flow of the winds
Will guide the tide,
To complete the current
For all who abide.
For I Am the River
From whence you flow,
Stay on course,
There is much to show!

Barbara Cady

I Will You Mine

I love you woman
I will you mine
I've been searching for you
Since the dawn of time
From distant stars
Light years away
For eons of time
This heart of mine
Has searched the heavens
For that glorious day
When I will rescue my princess
Far away
You see mine is the love
That will never die
My love is the truth
It will never lie
I love you woman
I will you mine
Our love will endure
Past the end of time

Kevin L Burton

Whittling Man

I came across a little old man,
Whittling by a tree.

Can you see? He said to me.
This is my life, you see.

Life can be so peaceful here,
Whittling under this tree.

I have much time, since she has passed,
To whittle under this tree.

Woody Woodall

The Art of Being Unbaffled

BAFFLED is a distraction
that keeps us fresh and alive
CONFUSION is mysterious in itself
like being there . . . before you arrive
WONDER is just like a song
if you are attentive to the words
CRAZY is my middle name;
being sane is for the birds
DEMENTED is a state of mind;
I've lost mine long ago
CRACKED is when you've lost it
like Larry, Curly, and Moe
MYSTIFIED is a sensation
we try never to forget
CONFOUNDED is a curse word
like . . . when booted off the net
DERANGED is what I call myself;
so there, then, plant this seed
UNBAFFLED is this simple art . . .
and knowing how to read

Margaret Jackson

Deer Hunting

it is the first day of deer season
and you get up before dawn
you gulp down some coffee
then off, you are gone

you get to the woods
and pick up your gun
then climb up your tree stand
in anticipation of fun

at the top of the ridge
you see a big buck
he is coming your way
you cross your fingers for luck

you squeeze the trigger
and all you can hear
is the sound of a click
that rings in your ear

for in all of your haste
in anticipation of fun
you stupid, dumb fool
you never loaded the gun

Les Boutcher

As She Bleeds . . .

The birds started calling
One early morning
The sun peeked over the trees

As I got up roughly
I whispered softly
To my wife as she bleeds

It's not that easy
To tell this story
I tried to give her all she needs

As she walked in the brightness
Someone stole her life
And left the grief with me

She had been shot
I Never once thought
That she wouldn't wake up next to me

Now that she's gone
I try to hold on
To my wife as she bleeds

Mike Looney

Gateway

Alas,
you look upon your life
and think of all you've done,
wondering if angels exist.
Though now you try to understand,
are there trees, then,
clustered with angels?

Thoughts of waving trees
and birds and bees
play a beautiful tune.
Upon your final breath
you think one final thing,
perhaps you will find on
in the trampled meadows.

Even in death you look
through your impossible gateway

Aneela Ayasha Patel

Timeless

The Rose and the Time
a gift are
of the restless Universe
that awaits.

The Rose in the Time
is withered.

The Time without his Rose
is just a path.

JosT Luis Hereyra Collante

For Fear

I see your soul,
Every time I look into your eyes
But I only get a glance
of your inner beauty
Because we are both afraid to stare
For fear that we might fall in love
something we can't have
For fear we'd lose our soul
over a love we can't control
For fear we would lose
all that is dear to us,
over a love fated in the stars
The risks are worth the joy,
But you don't see it that way
So we shall never know
What together we could do

Tiffany Brown

My Broken Heart

There once was a girl
Who made me feel whole
She had all the love I had
In her hand she held my soul
At one point she shared
The feelings I had for her
And to keep her loving me
Was all that mattered in the world
And when our love ended
That didn't matter to me
She still has my love
In her heart it will always be
She no longer loves me
It tears my soul apart
But she is still with me
Deep inside my broken heart

Brandon Holden

I Am a Throwaway Baby

I am a throwaway baby;
you may never know where to find me.

My mother has hidden me secretly,
from anyone to see.

She's not bad, just scared,
thinks no one cares.
Her secret will be my death.
I will cry alone, no one will hear.

Don't turn your back;
I will be lost forever.
Please help us, I need
a home for me and my mother,
to live to see another day.
I don't want to be
A throwaway.

Mary Neal

Invitation to Dance

'Tis a vision splendid
that I have seen
as I look into your eyes
to see where your life has been
and though there has been sorrow
and pain before
I can see that you refuse
to close that door
for there is still life to be lived
and paths to walk down
and with it a share of heartache
as you continue to enter new ground
for if it is joy that you do seek
then you must prepare to take the chance
for to experience what life has to offer
you must first accept the dance

Would you care to dance?

David Easter

Angels

*Dedicated to my precious children,
Tanya and Daniel*
Dream your dreams as night enfolds
A soft caress of sleep.
Your precious brow I kiss with love
May angels safely keep.

No tears nor time shall ever divide
Our hearts that love has so entwined.
Your smile forever lights my day;
The love you gave us guides our way.

Though darkness tears my very mind
'Til shredded soul laid bare.
A voice is found to tell them all
What causes such despair.

At last they know it's not their fault
The reasons why I cry.
I open up my weary heart
And look toward blue skies.

Kim Skinner

Motto!

The Magic of our lives
Are created through experiences
Those experiences we can learn from
Experiences that are substantiated
By our own innate passions
And desires to succeed.

Cristina Sanzano Ferrer

Two Souls

Two Souls dancing in the night
Mine in darkness yours in light
Yours in blindness mine in sight
One Soul dancing shining bright

In your waters feel me steep
Tears like wrinkles I feel you weep
Glass under fire you feel me bend
Love through a wire I feel you send

Vladislav Miransky

Magnetic Island

Some where an island is calling,
Lazing in the green blue sea,
Some where an island is beckoning
Calling to my love and me.

Some where an island magnetic
For this is her name you see,
With enticing Pacific enchantment,
For lovers like you and me.

On white wings sea gulls seem to tease,
Eager spray that reaches for the rocks,
On the beach are coconut trees
Where the kookaburra sits and mocks.

Her sands are so warm and golden,
Lets return to this happy land,
For we can feel that urgent pull.
Of this friendly magnetic land.

Some where an island is calling
Lazing in the green blue sea,
Some where an island is beckoning
Calling to my love and me.

Phyllis Cahill

The Sea

Waves murmur softly
retreating, advancing
along the smooth beach

Strange secrets they tell
in their constant whispering
to the listening sand

Serenity reigns
wave calls ton listening wave
the sea breathes repose

Comes the hurricane
murmurings become roarings
smooth and vanishes

Furious waves boil
all nature is seething
apprehension reigns

Edna H. Kusnirak

Waiting

Under your boot soles,
Trampled.
In the back of your mind,
Forgotten.
Hanging on your every word,
Abused.
Looking into your eyes,
Invisible.
This is where you'll find me,
Waiting.

Sarah Rempp

Surrender

Listen to the voice
When the fear grabs hold
When you don't know what to do next
When you feel powerless and lonely

Listen to the voice
When the blackness creeps in
When you feel hopeless and lost
When the anger takes over

Listen to the voice
When you wake in the dawn
When you hear the birds singing
When you see the sun smiling down

Listen to the voice
Then the answers will come
Your soul will discover harmony
And you will find the treasure

Della Kovach

Left Out

All who cry and all who fall
will over come and beat them all.
My kind were laughed at
and left in the shadows,
but our time will come
when we shine bright on them.
People change and people learn—
that life is a circle
of happiness and sorrow.
We have girlfriends and boyfriends
who come and go.
Families are created
and then destroyed.
These are just changes
that we must put up with.
We must put these changes behind us
and try to move on.
If we don't move on,
everyone else will continue on
and we will all be left out.

Mitch Leslie

On the Tip of Your Tongue

To have something on
the tip of your tongue
and not have it jump off
the cliff of your mouth
is frustrating to the pyre
of your brain
which, by the energy
of a profound spark
results in nothing
but the flicker of the lost light!

Dave Lapointe

The Last Chapter of Life

"You did not choose Me,
but I chose you . . ." John 15:16 NKJ
On the day I will fly away
And the faded look of the Holy Book
Will turn to gold
He'll be quite bold

And with the brightness of the Son
I will shine into the bright light of God

He may keep His deep, sad look
But I will know He loves me so

Freedom Holloway

To Find

To find
My mind
I ask to thee
Why does it have to be?
But to a clue
Not blue
What could it be?
But not a plea
What I ask to thee?

Katie Ruane

Perils

The perils have me fettered
If only my life could be bettered
I'm hating myself
For things I cannot help
I'm trapped inside this box of glass
Watching all of my life go past
I find my confidence
To be the only tool against
The pressures of my existence
And the glass is now a distant
Memory of my troubled time
Hidden behind the grime
Of this society's ideals
No one knows how it feels
Until they experience the fight,
The battles of equal heights
Of frustration, and feelings
Of incompetence and grieving

Kristine Ferrone

Isthmus of Love

Hi, hi, Catalina hi,
Did I tell you you're on my mind?
Try, try, baby try,
Steal my heart with a smile
Cry, cry, Catalina cry,
Open the floodgates of my eyes
My, my, baby mine,
Where have you been all my life?
Crawling with curiosity
Staggering on gravity,
Dignified personality,
Such a baby majesty,
Adorned with a sly smile
You loving, I never tire.

Daniel Har

Essence of Time

It rages.
Sparked by the essence of time.
Groping forbidden skies.

It burns.
Penetrating the sphere of uncertainty.
Lapping the walls of desperation.
It seeks.
Coiling around the unknown.
Leaping to heights unforeseen.

It preys.
Engulfing the unsuspecting.
Empowering in its fortitude.
It rules.
Dictating in its supremacy.
Swallowing all sustenance

It calms.
Tamed by the essence of time.
Lowered to crust the Earth.

Patricia Quarry

Roiling and Boiling

Electric fire
Pouring rain
Life is electric
inebriate drained
sitting and thinking
musing and drinking
the lightning is crackling
the thunder is booming
smell the burning
lightning not cooking
listen to that booming
it's society leaking
all that raw power
alive in the swirl
roiling and rolling
crashing and boiling

Matt Benson

Scared

Mi madre, she has died,
For days and nights I cried
I asked my family why
Did my mommie have to die?
This isn't being written by
A graduate of college,
I'm a six year old boy,
Named Elian Gonzalez.
I've headed out to washington,
With my father I was paired,
But what I haven't really
Mentioned is I, Elian,
am "SCARED."

Daniel Monge, Jr.

Best Friends

You slowly criticize,
you quickly praise.
You're there for tomorrow
and yesterday.

You give me no fear,
you make me feel bold.
You're there to protect me
form dangers untold.

We sing in the sun,
we dance in the rain.
We're there for each other,
no matter the game.

We do this by loving,
we do this by caring.
You are my "BEST FRIEND,"
my friend, 'til the END!

Kelly Aronson

Finding Peace

As you walk in the fields,
or sit under the trees,
Let yourself drift
with each gentle breeze.

Listen to the stream.
How loudly it sings.
Be one with nature,
and all living things.

Savor the beauty of life.
Feel it, watch it slowly unfold.
Look for the rainbows,
not the gold.

Sharon Cullins

Summer Is Coming

Drip, drop, drip, drop,
On my roof top,
I can hear the rain pour in,
As well as my Dad snoring,
While the thunder is roaring
Now that the clouds have gone away,
They have left a bright new day,
And now all the birds are humming,
That summer is coming.

Kara Ann Cosgrove

Now You're Gone

While we were so many miles apart
I had your sweetest memories
But today I got a phone call
That sent it gone upon the breeze

The voice on the line was shaky
As it said something was wrong
And as they burst out crying
They told me he was gone

My eyes filled up with tears
As my heart began to ache
I felt the world spin beneath me
And felt the ground begin to shake

Will I be able to handle this
Knowing you're now gone
I think of all the good times
As I listen to our song

I feel your eyes watching over me
Because in my heart you are alive
And for now we aren't together
But I can't wait 'til the day I die

Whitney Jade Havranek

Nothingness

Nothingness is what dwells inside me
Nothingness is what I feel
Nothingness is all around
Nothingness is always at my heel

Nothingness is what I have
Nothingness surrounds you and me
Nothingness is in the world
Nothingness please let me be

Ashlyee Dalton

Undone

"It's all been undone," I cry
The howling wind's the only eye
I look around the forest floor
And meet my shattered life's front door
A naked man stands before me
His teeth chattering to ancient glory
His gnarled and wrinkled hands and feet
Begin to make their own true beat
I run around in morbid fury
Of all the fireflies dancing near me
Flashing images of ancient light
The purple sky burns just right
Beckoning me to journey on
An old hag begins to sing her song
The trees around all fall down
A crash of thunder the only sound
The hag lies dead at my feet
The man has lost his only beat
A time will come for this dream to end
Then all will be as it was again.

Ben Harnwell

A Tribute to My Homeland

My province is New Brunswick,
Charlotte County is my home.
There's no more beautiful country,
Wherever you may roam.

We have rivers, lakes and mountains,
And the rugged coastal shore.
There's fishing, swimming, hunting,
And ever so much more.

Our industries are booming,
We have seafood galore.
Our food supply is abundant,
How could we ask for more?

It's a wonderful place to live in,
It's great for tourists, too;
No matter who comes to visit,
There's always something to do.

I've travelled to far off places,
And seen many delightful isles,
But nothing compares to our province,
It's the best by a million miles.

Constance L. McGowan

Broken Love

From the very first day we met,
I instantly knew
That I would die
If I couldn't be with you.

Our love was so pure,
So right, and so good,
I would have given you the world,
You knew that I would.

Then you stepped on my heart
And threw it all away;
I think about you while I am in bed
Day after day.

I see you around
With your friends having fun,
And I can't stop thinking
What I could have done.

I want you back so bad,
Please come back to me,
Return into my life,
And set my heart free.

Lukas Brown

Paradise

All the nights in Paradise
I spent alone with you,
The journey of two souls
Through the Rainbow's ebbing hue.
Locked in secret whispers,
We joined hearts and hands,
Sailing through the open skies,
Skimming golden sands.
Turquoise waters drowned us
In an enveloping wave;
We played amidst the froth
And love was all we gave.
Then when we came to rest
On a wave of silver foam,
The blue sky was our beacon
And the sun a golden dome.
Together we were free to go
To anywhere we cared;
Together we entered Paradise,
And this is what we shared.

Michelle Hayward

My Pearl

My pearl, which adorns my tie,
Like a floret from the sea,
Looms greater than its size,
Luminescent with a haze of hues.
I stand in awe of you!

You are universal and unique
Among the world's jewels!
At first glance, you feign modesty,
But one cannot escape your virtues,
Which so impress me!

You are a complement and beautiful,
Enhancing all that touches you.
What remarkable qualities you possess
To charm any woman to a wizard,
My great gift from the sea!

I behold you in reverence,
For you need nothing to improve.
Only remain in single
Exquisite individuality,
The loveliest gem of the sea.

     Benedict Markowski

A Letter from the New Paradise

Marooned in age,
he sits and tends his bees . . .
and in his mind's eyes
the view is not death that encroaches,
but paradise.

There, with rampant verbiage,
his fragrant roses speak . . .
not of death, but a New Heaven
and a new Earth.

Would that the unawakened eye
of youth could be
as keen of heart
and soul and mind
and see as clearly as he.

Uncle Bill, your letter speaks so true:
Paradise on the other side
will not be new for you.

     Flora M. Kosoff

My Heart's Desire

Early will I seek Him,
making Him my heart's desire
For Him a love I feel,
that sets my heart on fire

I kneel at a footstool,
a prayer to hear His voice
He whispers to me of
life's giving choice

My way I commit to Him,
all through the day,
Trusting Him for my best,
delighting in His ways

Devouring His Holy Word,
food for thought I need
He directs my paths, choices,
clearly I can see

A love He's always given,
in abundance to me
Our life, our love, our victories,
these God desires to give to thee!

     Yvonne Lynnheart

Nights

Drops dripping down,
drowning your soles,
my face,
as I watch you melt away
like a snowflake in spring,
into the wetness.
I begin to miss your soul
clinging to mine,
my strength.
Seven hours passed
like five minutes,
too soon.
Alone I start to think
of 19 months,
next time,
as drops continue dripping down
my face.

     Neroli Maharaj

Sixpence

It is the sense of time passing.
I make the programme of the testament
Like the ones who burn, burn, burn

As falling on the floor.
A part of spontaneous melodies
That were hammering in my head.

It felt so surreal.
So the heart be right.
One could go up the hill of St. Lucy.

Looking for a elemental place.
How many people do look at themselves
In vain mirrors?

Botanical curved line, waved desert—
Those are all so alive.
The dew is my usual breakfast.

I do not need visionary things.
I carry all that in myself.
One copper on the tablecloth.

     Yuko Ishii

Color by What Name

What color is the sparkle
in the eyes of a blind child
amazed by the blended beauty
of his first sunrise
after surgery?
What color is the inside of a cocoon
or the interior of a mother's womb—
of an ice cave,
implosion,
or supernova
beyond human visual range?

The universe contains colors
only the imagination
can invent a name for.

     Marieta L. McMillen

Wolf Cubs

Wonderful animals
Overaggresive
Loyal to their mother
Forceful

Cute
Unexplained traits
Beautiful creatures
Skilled

     Adam Smith

An Old Stale Act

The same lines.
The same clothes.
Why do you continue?
Heaven only knows.
Like old bread with moles.
Like a street full of pot holes.
Stale, day-old coffee, wine
left too long in the racks.
I have had enough of you and
your old stale act.

     Yolanda Pope

Wonderful Autumn

The trees lift up their branches
The leaves they all fall down
Wind blows
Tide turns
Altogether a wonderful dawn
Autumn has finally arrived
Apples, damsons and pears
Just ready for the pickers
Yet, when the harvest comes
It is something wonderful
It is a common sight
God behind the glory
Of the autumn leaves
The farmer mows his field
The glory is all his
The autumn sun slowly sinks
Into the night
Into the following day

     Elaine Day

What Am I to Do

The phone will never ring again,
Bringing her sweet voice to me.
Her letter will not come,
Telling how she misses me.

No more to hear the gentle sound
Of her soft laughter
When something pleases her,
Or dry the tears she sheds
When saddened by some sorrow.

To see the wink that said
She was just kidding;
To feel the touch that was so warm,
Caressing both the body
And the soul.

My dearest cherished one,
I miss you so.

What am I to do?
The phone will never ring again.

     Stephen Scrak

The Girl

A little girl sat there alone,
She was an orphan, without a home.
She had sadness on her face,
A sadness deep with eyes of lace.
One day the sadness was not there,
The girl had left on a galloping mare.
The mare of death took her away,
Into a land where children play.
With laughter and music all around,
This little girl had happily found,
Paradise, where angels fly,
A Heaven high up in the sky.

     Francesca Savioli

Red Devil's Gate

If Heaven is up and Hell is down,
What is left in the middle to be found?
Free me of pain, free me of hate,
Drag me down to the Red Devil's Gate,
Make me a coffin in which I'll soon lie,
Of my own free will I shall soon die,
Try to stop me you may,
As my last thread of life is cut,
With the blade of the Red Devil's knife,
Open the latch of the Red Devil's Gate,
And there you will find me,
Free, of all pain and hate . . .

Renay Hayes

The Lost Sock

There he goes again,
Racing into the rain,
A red sock hanging from his jaws,
Then sits with it between his paws.

He chews the top, his eyes on me,
Waits for me to join the fun,
Call him, offer him a bone,
Reach out to him and off he'll run.

After racing 'round the yard,
By this, the sock's in tatters.
I give up and go inside
As if nothing matters.

He drops his prize upon the lawn
And runs to bark at the gate.
The ragged sock, badly torn
Now retrieved, but all too late.

Judy Cooper

Grown Up

Somewhere under my big girl bed
there is a forgotten child
with big brown eyes
and berry-red cheeks
that are feverish from climbing trees.
She plays with my old pink teddy bear
and my puzzles,
with only a few missing pieces,
and my board games
left in favor of Spin the Bottle.
She and my stiff-limbed,
ringlet-curled dolls
enjoy my cracked tea set
and the Easy Bake Oven
that didn't work
like the commercial said it would.

Billie Jo Bales

The World by Way of Wal-Mart

I'm only one of them—
the ones who always stop at Wal-Mart
before a trip around the world.
No matter where we go,
be it Europe, Asia, Africa,
or anywhere else on Earth,
before our flight,
before we call a taxi,
before we leave our hometown,
before we lose our minds,
we stop for something—
anything—
everything we're sure to need—
at Wal-Mart!

Priscilla Garrett Wright

Happy Teacher's Day

Having teachers are great fun
Although not many think so
Putting upon us work in tons
Plus teaching all they know

Yes, I think they are nice
To talk and share with
Every lesson makes us wise
A teacher's special gift
Cherish school moments together
Hoping the best for the future
Every teacher's a second parent
Ready to help with pleasure

Shaping us into good people
Developing us day by day
Always dedicated and capable
Yes, I would just shout out and say

HAPPY TEACHER'S DAY !

Ooi Chiann

Nunnery

"Get thee to a nunnery," someone said
I hastened to obey
Ivied walls surrounded me
Silvered gates enclosed me
In quiet, shady cloisters I walked alone
Walls, gates, my solitude
Built of my fear
And my desire to forget
What I had never known
Then the music swirled around me
And the ivied walls fell down
The silvered gates swung open
I went out and for the first time
I saw the sun
How bright, how warm
You called to me
Laughing, I ran to you
Trusting, I came to you
And you took my hand

Anne Miller

Roses for You!

For you, my love!
Loving you . . . I climb high hills
And in flame . . . I reach the sky!
From up, I scattered around the World
The ashes . . . of my soul.
Touching the ground . . . they become roses
FOR YOU . . . to pick them up!

Mariella Giumale

Peter—Age Five and a Half

Sometimes I'm big and tough
And sometimes I need lots of love
Sometimes I can do it on my own
And sometimes I just need to be alone
Sometimes I need to give it a try
And sometimes I feel I just want to cry
Sometimes I really want a hug
And sometimes I get covered in mud
Sometimes I like to dress up smart
Sometimes I like to do some art
Sometimes I like to sing a song
And sometimes it just all goes wrong
Sometimes I do things you think are bad
And sometimes I make you really mad
But always I love you
And always you'll love me, too

David Lees

Open the Door

The evening shadows fall.
The day is coming to a close for us all.
Night is near,
Of which many, rightfully, have fear.
Evil alert is on,
Especially for those who live alone.
Fear for no one is easy to condone.
Finally day comes and all is well.
Then, when to Earth Jesus comes
with all his might,
There will not be any more night,
No fear, pain, or fright.
But only for those
who have Him in their heart!
Are you one of those
who can take part?
If not, seek Him
Before it is too late to get in.
Then you, too, can Heaven win
if you get forgiveness of your sin.

Clara Gilley

Stroganoff and Strychnine

Prosperity in the ha-ha
Of recognized zero.
Gritty Edens

Rust and rot in the luster.
So many heavy
Skies to stomach.

Daughters of London,
I pass out flowers
That I call remembrance,

But they have no matter.
All these false
Descents have left

Paradise tossed.
I love the autumn,
When her slower

Leaves fall to the ground
Like so many pins—
Dead as Ophelia.

Lindon A. Sjolander

The Gift God Gave Me

*This poem is dedicated to Ryan K.
Headrick—with lots of love, Daddy.*
God gave me
A very special gift
When he gave me
The gift of you

He taught me
How to walk
He taught me
How to talk
When he gave me
The gift of you

He showed me
There was no more to life
Than any material possession
Could ever compare
When he gave me
The very special gift
When he gave me
The gift of you

David Headrick, Jr.

Shattered

I won't give you the satisfaction
To see my pain
What you've done,
Let you know
You have won

I won't let this tear me down
Shatter my heart,
Tear me apart

My will is stronger
I will win,
You must pay
For your sin,

Destroy your mind
Shatter your soul,
Condemn your thoughts
Of control

Jeff Valdivia

Change

To that special someone who misunderstood
What happened today?
You called me someone else's name.
It wasn't Jan, Jella or J.
Where was your mind today?
If only we could take back today
We would find the pleasant thoughts of
Yesterday.

Theodora Roach

The Love of My Life

I live, I breathe, and I die for you.
You've conquered my fears,
you've made them subdue.
If you were to leave,
you would never believe
the pain you would put me through.
You have to understand,
I love you more than
anything in this land.
I know how much you love me
by the little things you do.
It's the little things that show me
that your love is true.
I just wanted to tell you,
in my own special way,
that I love you more and more
each and every day.
So please just let me know
that you will always be mine.
Because by me knowing that,
I will always be fine.

Michelle Guida

The Rise at Day

The sun rises early morning.
I sit in my car and,
Wonder what it will bring.
It's warm, I have my window down
I new the life of crows,
On the mornings frown.

My work will begin,
And to be what I'm not,
I know is a sin,
But I know someday
Success will happen for me
So I cautiously grin.

Brady L. Kennison

My Soul Be Still

Upon this narrow path I go
To what extent I know not.
But in my heart I have hope
Of a better end.
Upon this narrow path I go
Where treacherous dangers abound
And the road is harsh.
My heart holds onto hope.
Upon this narrow path I go
To follow my master into danger,
Redemption, and salvation.
To the end I go
Where all is revealed
And life's riches wait.

Matthew Ward

The Long Wait

Night falls on day
Day must WAIT for night
Yet I don't want to WAIT
Why WAIT for night to break to day

I don't want to WAIT
I want to move on
I can't WAIT
Night lasts forever

Like a child on Christmas morning
I must WAIT for a good thing
It seems too far away
Why must it be tomorrow

I WAIT to see you
It seems so long
I can't WAIT to see you
Day breaks, the long WAIT is over.

Benjamin Martin Anglin

Symphony Notes

Black and white, symphony notes
On ragged tattered pages
Carry weeping willow memories
That were lost
Along with my rain-cloud soul
They rise and fall
Becoming tides
Which ebb and flow
With the waxing and waning
Of the hunter's moon
While oceans of roses
Snow white, pearl pink
Crimson red, golden yellow
Laugh lazily
In the brilliant noon day sun
There will be no silence
As my internal melody and harmony
Go jetting through the Milky Way
And are uplifted
To the Gates of Heaven

Nancy Pawley

My Daughter

After waiting a lifetime for you,
You are filling my life with joy.

After waiting a lifetime for you,
Nothing else can compare.

After waiting a lifetime for you,
My life is now complete.

After waiting a lifetime for you,
My soul is now fulfilled.

Cheryl Lynn Suk

Away

When I'm away,
far away from you.
I can feel the rain,
beating down on you.
I can see your fears,
And I can hear you cry.
All I can wish is that
I'm by your side.

She came to me out of
the darkest night.
And brought with her
the light of day.
She molded me into a
better man
All I could know is
my love for her.

Jeremy Ward

Alone to Love

Wherever we go
there's people around
and the clouds
turn the day into waste.

Whenever we're together
someone drops by
and the storms
turn the night into gloom.

So take me away
where no one can find us.
So take me to a place
where the sun always shines.

Then there will be peace
whenever we're together.
Then there will be brightness
to help our love shine.

Lisa Vaughn

Ariel

Ariel, a rainbow.
A child's day is child's play.
As walking along the parkway,
With water waves insight.
And winds in her hair,
With a smile of delight.
A child's golden hair,
And eyes of glare.
With a smile divine,
None can compare.
Nature and all its waves,
As the ocean blossoms, day by day.
So as sky so high,
And wonderfully bright.
Even the sun is icing,
On this delight.
Ariel, a rainbow well-known.
For a love of this child,
Is mine to behold.
Ariel, my rainbow.

Philip Garci

Another October 7th

My son left us yesterday.
By his own choice, so what can I say.

Today is just another day.
Sometime in May . . .
   I think.
But, it's really just another October 7th.

Marilyn Meyer

Stairs

Life is like stairs
that never end—
you just keep climbing
and finally descend.
You may get to skip
over a stair,
but take it slowly
this chance is rare.
You may have to go down
to get to the top,
but you have to keep going
don't ever stop.
Remember of love
and all of your friends,
life will keep going
even when it ends.

Jodi Newman

Your Love

To my cowboy, Chuck:
I love you with all my heart and soul
Your love for me is kind,
Your love for me is patient,
Your love for me is never jealous.

Your love makes me feel warm inside,
Your love for me isn't selfish,
Your love for me is never in vain.

Your love for me is very supportive,
Your love for me is also understanding,
Your love for me is very trusting.

I hope your love for me never ends,
For my love for you is the same
For now and forever.

Tina Marie Hesse

Stepping Stones and Wishing Wells

Stepping stones and wishing wells
Forests where the faeries dwell
Mossy earth and sunbeam bright
Introduce me to the night
Dress me in your silver gown
Let me wear your starry crown
Walk with me and hold my hand
Guide me through your darkened land
Show me all you have to show
All illuminated by your glow
Silver lady purple skies
We'll part for now and let sun rise

Kelley Pereksta

If

If I was born
in the same time
in the same place
in the same universe
would you love me?
If I was not as I am now
not dull
not ugly
not strange
could you have learned to love me too?
If I was perfection
would you
could you
should you
be in love?

Elvira Licuanan

Dream for Me

Please dream for me of forest glens
Where flowered paths never end
Where babbling brooks seem at play
And wind swept trees gently sway

Where birds sing 'neath skies of blue
In every color, shade or hue
Where rainbows bloom every day
As rain slips silently away

Where softly falls the calm of night
And glowing stars reflect moonlight
Where angels dance beneath the sun
And all the universe is one

This I ask you dream for me
From now through all eternity
That you may know and clearly see
This now is my reality

Elvira Langlois

Youth

Look up, my young American
Stand firmly on the earth
Noble deeds and mental powers
Give title over birth.

Estefania J. Rodriguez

God Speaks

Did I forsake you, when you
Thought you were left alone?
Did I forget you, when you
Just could not take one more step?
Did I not love you, when you
Felt that no one could care?

And, will I let go of your hand,
When your need for my touch,
Is the greatest need you have?

Forsake you? forget you?
Not love you? let go of your hand?
Can I deny the blood that's
Written on your name . . .
Spelled out by Jesus
Before He even left that Cross?

Vera M. Hicks

The Journey's Fallen

I am alone
In a field where all the combatants
Are Lost.

The pain I have caused
To my vanquished,
The sorrow I have made them feel,
Leaves me bound in cords of steel,
The cords that rip into my flesh,
Flesh that tears apart like ribbon,
Red ribbon with blue lace,
As I learn in my slow pace
And with poor execution
Free myself of the mesh
That I am.

I am. Alone to feel my pain,
For others who already gained
The knowledge and the power
To know on that fateful hour:
Life is not wins and losses,
But only tombs and crosses.

Matthew Weiner

My Lancelot

I had a knight in shining armor
So handsome, young and strong,
But now the armor's rusty
And he snores the whole night long.

But I don't care, not really,
He's still a knight to me
And I'm his lady fair;
Through eyes of love we see.

You might say it's a sad thing
That our eyes are growing dim,
But in his heart he sees a princess
And I see a prince in him.

Our little home's a castle
As wondrous as Camelot
Where I'm his Guinevere
And he's my Lancelot.

Dianna Laws

The Lord's Way

The world today
is full of sin.
So open your heart
and let the Lord in.

The Lord's the way,
it's time to pray.
So let's start
a brand-new day.

The day has come,
and the night will end.
If you let the Lord in,
your new life will begin.

The right road
is the way to go.
So open your heart
and let him in.

Dorothy L. Shaw

Me and You

You're so far away
yet close to my heart.
If there was a way
we could make a start.
We could hold each other
and not wait for time.
I'd fly to you
like a bird on the wing,
nestle in your arms
contented to sing.
But 'til that day comes
my faith will stay true,
so strong and so caring
to become one, me and you.

Ross Long

HOLY LIFE

GOD
GIFT
ALL
LIFE
GOD
LOVES ALL
ALL HIS
ALL HEART
ALL LOVE HE
ART.
HEART

Wilhamena ov God

Fresh Snow

That powdery white that falls from the sky
Covering all dark with light,
Giving the feeling that it's time to start fresh.
Blanketing our mistakes for a while,
It leaves us with a white wonderland
To look at for a moment,
To help us to simply
Feel less heavy-hearted,
Less burdened,
And to give us a reason to smile.

Camille Lakhani

No Justice in the Playoffs (a Hockey Poem)

The tension is growing
The game's winding down
The home team is leading
By only one goal
Just over a minute left
The visiting team pulls their goalie
And they score the game tying goal
Looks like the game's going into overtime

About ten minutes left
The visitors score yet again
They win the game
And the series
For there is no love in the playoffs

James Harris

Graduation Blues

It's been five long years
Yet so brief they seem

Choked by this forceful knot
I curse back my tears that fear it not

Who will believe me when I say
This is the saddest of my days?

Graduation is here again
I never thought I'd say goodbye to you
My friend
So I will not!
I will instead call this a Transition Day
That will occur in May

The real world awaits me now
I aim to survive somehow
MSU has given me the best years of my life, yet
I tearfully leave its quarters without any regret!

Rosanna De Robertis

Give Me My Wings

Refuse me the right to live . . .
The privilege to experience
pain, terror, hurt and living death.
Give me the straight jacket
that will morph into my skin,
preventing my tears to cry the blood
that sobs its way into my heart,
making it beat the drums of life.
I do not wish for my face to go pale,
by staring into the ghost-eyes of truth and rejection.
So restrain me as if I was a tortured soul, which I am.
For I fear I might hurt myself by living or reaching my potential.
But then with the vapor of strength,
I realize that those who fear the dare of life and dreams,
never reach a perfect utopia.
So please unwrap my jacket
and give me my wings.

Ava HaberkornHalm

Mirage

I'm sitting here seeing a sunset that is not there,
Imagining a romance that cannot exist,
And feeling the pleasure of what could never be.
I see you so many times a day,
But you are not here.
I hear you, I speak to you; but you are out of reach.
What am I doing? I ask myself.
Falling in Love, I answer myself,
Feeling as beautiful as the sunset that was never there
And was never meant to be.
Is this love or just a mirage?

Maricza Torres

Maw-Maw's Little Girl

I've always been Maw-Maw's little girl,
right from the very start.
With all your hugs and kisses you gave,
they came straight from your heart.

You've made me feel special
by the things that you do:
setting my hair, shopping for clothes,
attending every dance revue.

You always seem to trust in me,
in everything I do.
That always makes me feel so good
and very close to you.

You show my pictures to all your friends
from kindergarten to high school days.
With pride you always speak of me
in the most delightful ways.

Lisa Chatelain

For an Instant

As I lie here
Watching my life go by,
I think of you.
And as I do,
I fight the tears back with an empty smile.
No one shall ever know how much I love you.
Truly,
No one shall understand my emotions or my thoughts.
Then, again, I think of you
And I smile, a true smile,
As I remember your laughter, your love . . .
And how you could make the whole room light up
With just one smile.
And it is then and only then
That I realize I would give up anything and everything
Just to be with you.
If, for an instant, you were here,
I would embrace that instant for all eternity.

Melissa Fong

For My Kids—Your Mommy's Wish

Your first day of school is coming too fast
Where has the time gone? How do you make it last?
From your first breath of life, until long after I'm gone
I have loved you more with each passing dawn
So as you start a new phase and charter the world unknown
Know I am in your heart and I'm proud of how you've grown
Remember on your first day and each day you live
Make friends, learn, share, laugh, and give all that you can give
You may or may not be the best at everything you do
But put forth your all and try things that are new
Never lose sight of who you are; it's more difficult than it seems
You'll be directed to many roads, but always follow your dreams
And if you should see tears roll slowly from my eyes
Sometimes your mommy wishes she can stop the time that flies.

Michelle LaVonne Stoddard

Priority as the Obsidian of Truth

Telling the fortune in a bowl of fish,
watching cold, stumbling, golden animals
reticulated by the fate of watching eyes,
objectively, the woman applied contentment.
Her formulation was programmed by
the tiny mice in an incandescent
arc rising from the presence of the sun,
setting in the craters of the moon,
magnetic, idealistic, empty, and awaiting
a collection of variables.
Dependence creasing defiance, challenges,
insight warbled essentials as they passed between
surfaces and congealed along the edges.
Doubled, tripled, the slightest image
of obscure sensitivity, the right hand,
the black glass reflected, manipulated,
the resource sculpting inevitability to
make a tract, awkward icons swimming.

Baron Joseph A. Uphoff, Jr.

Graffiti

Dear Nation,
I'm the paint pestering your city!
I advertise a coalition in suppression.
It's my intention to beg eyes that you listen!
Trendy derogatory theme, "No Luv" exposition,
Expresses love's humiliation, dominated by civilization.
Through eyes, hearts, and hands,
Graffiti begs society's pity.
Will you listen, you slumbering city?
Could you plot an invention investigating the graffiti conclusion?
Is the pusher man a magician, connected to the politician,
Who blesses the mortician?
The villain seems to be the musician
Who tambourines the public into intimidation!
Gang war ambition's the catalyst in young buds' extinction!
The pollen of hate's a duration of the curse on creation!
Those with an identity don't need your motivation!
Degenerate decomposition appeals to your intervention!
Rehabilitation's the nutrition that ends the deprivation
Of justice in your nation!

Helen Williams

The World Today

All my life I've lived in fright,
all alone and no one in sight

In this world I have no friend
which seems to me it soon will end

Everywhere I go, everyone is angry
Everywhere I look every child is hungry

I wish people would know that it is better to give than to receive

I wish I could make this world a better place to live

There isn't any left of God's creation that hasn't been abused

I don't know why I go on living, Life has made me so confused

All this world's problems had become a disease
and people should know that all the world needs is Love and Peace

The world today is the scariest place
and the things we've destroyed can never be replaced

I prayed sincerely that all of this will soon be over
and people on Earth will someday learn to love one another

I prayed to Him, dearly to the Lord
to help and save me from the world

I prayed that I soon will die and be out of sight
and maybe then I will no longer be in fright

Irene M. Teodoro

Questions and Answers

Have you ever felt lonely, rejected or sad?
Only God can make you glad!
Look in His word, and there you'll find
Treasures untold, for a curious mind.
What is life on this Earth all about?
Where are you headed? Are you filled with doubt?
Is your life filled with worry, loaded with care?
Feeling all miserable, tired and full of despair?
Sometimes you're up, sometimes you're down,
You want to smile, but all you can do is frown?
Turn to Jesus, and then you'll see
How happy and wonderful life can be.
This Earth is filled with beauty for all the world to see:
Oceans, mountains, flowers and trees—
God created this for you and me.
Do not worry about tomorrow,
Enjoy today, forget your sorrow!
Remember the grass—here today and gone tomorrow!

Tina Laughman

Voodoo Fries

Spicy, delicious,
saucy, voodoo fries:
Now they're here, then they're gone!
Imagine that!
Be careful though, the powerful
voodoo magic
can creep up and sting your appetite,
leaving you with an eternal craving for these
amazing and tasty sticks of nourishment.
Who would have thought a potato could stir up
so much trouble?
Gotta go now, the voodoo has cast its spell,
and another appetite has surrendered!

Denise Nodilo

There

Should I dial your phone number,
Would you answer my call?
Deep in your slumber—
A dividing wall.

When I find in people's faces
Features resembling your own,
Could it be that these traces
Are my memories fond that have grown?

Should I need you here beside me,
Could I just call out your name?
The love in your eyes, is it still easy to see?
Please tell me that death hasn't altered your flame!

Wherever you are, I know you can hear,
I am never alone whilst you're there.

Nella van der Weerden

Don't Be Afraid

This is for Dawn.
I know that life is hard sometimes.
I know it might drag and beat you down.
I know people can be cruel sometimes.
I know the past will hang around.

I understand life's roads are winding.
I understand you might lose the way.
I understand things can seem hopeless.
I understand this feeling might stay.

But don't be afraid when sorrow lurks.
Don't be afraid because you're not alone.
I am always here to lend a loving heart.
And to erase the pain you have been shown.

Caleb Short

My Garden

To my favorite gardening partner, my husband, Adam
My garden is a refuge:
The place I feel rest,
I grow in God,
who supplies the best.

My garden is a healer
My hands in soil,
sun bearing down,
I grow in health, new exercise found.

My garden is my palate
I work to bring beauty,
the flowers abound.
I grow in patience waiting for blooms.

My garden is my pantry
I plant the food my family eats,
Water, weed and wait the gardener's creed.
I've grown in love, my bounty to share.

Glenda Shank

How to Love a Woman

When you truly love a woman,
it is not about taking, it is about giving.
I give my woman a house,
she gives back a home. I give her food,
she gives back a meal.
I give her my seed, and she gives
back a miracle, and I stand here
with tears in my eyes and a stupid smile
on my face, holding the fruit of our love.
And all she asks in return is my love.
Not the love easily spoken from the lips, but the
love she can see through my eyes
into the very depths of my soul.
Everything I give her,
she gives back twofold.

Ronald Jackson

Dad

Why does my heart hurt again?
You came into my life,
You loved me as your own,
Now the healing must begin,
But I have my memories that linger on.
The days of football are gone,
The smile that befriends everyone is no more,
But I have my memories that linger on.
You were always there with a helping hand,
And always there with advice to lend,
But I have my memories that linger on.
I didn't get a chance to say goodbye,
Sometimes I still weep, I still cry,
But I have my memories that linger on.
I love you, dad

Laura E. Walker

Grandma's Tree

A daughter may outgrow your lap . . .
A daughter may outgrow your dreams.
A daughter's child may fill your arms.
A daughter's child with all their charms.
Each child's child adds a link,
Of hopes and dreams with just one wink.
With God's own eye and angel's dust.
Each link is filled with love and trust
To shape and mold a chain so strong,
A gift we share, to each belong.
This chain so long, can only be.
From trust and knowledge of Grandma's tree!

Cathy Leammon

Nature Equals You

I feel the winds upon me,
The fish are jumping in the sea,
For the birds are chirping in the oak trees,
Crickets are playing violins,
Butterflies in the air landing on my nose;
When thinking of these I see you.

Maggie B. Pinnick

You

There was a time I searched for love
And could not find my way
I tried to win the game of love
But did not know how to play

I tried to make myself love sick,
But found there was no cure
I tried to hold out for love
But could not seem to endure

So I took the route of making love
And forced it on myself
But that was not my kind of love
Because it had no wealth

I went to God to pray for love
And ask Him what to do
He sent a message from above
Saying patience is a virtue

So I sat back, and I waited for love,
Hoping my destiny was due
And out of no where, came a blessing in disguise
The Heavens sent me you!

Tonya D. Boxley

An Apology

Please forgive me for what I've done,
I should not have hurt you, because you are my number one

I know that I can't change things or put them back in place,
But I will be satisfied as long as I see your beautiful smiling face

You and I know that no one's perfect in this world,
Not even a sweet, little, innocent girl

All I'm asking is for your acceptance of my apology,
If you can't forgive me, I will feel so hurt and empty

I just hope and pray that there is a merciful
Place in your heart that you may find,
And please, don't blame it on my heart, blame it on my mind

Andre Whitaker, Jr.

Why, Sister

I feel so all alone
So far away from home
It seems I have nobody, you see
Even though I have six sisters and me
Why are we so far away, yet so close to
One another, each day
I can't help but ask myself,
Why is it this way.
I love the way we were at home
Before we grew up, and got on our own
As children, it was always togetherness
And love
Now that we're grown, there's not enough of
It seems that each day we grow further apart
and what I see really breaks my heart
But this is something that I ask myself
Why is it this way.

Brenda Branson

Love Deleted

Staring at my windows
I heard the "welcome" voice.
My heart just froze awaiting
the announcement: "You got mail."
I waited, in despair, to get the message frail
when nothing came I clicked to get some help.
The menu showed several options
that troubled my system.
To find the appropriate answer
and calm my anger and distress,
I clicked the support online world wide web
and navigated through the Internet
Searching the tool bar and the explorer bar,
as any expert driver might have done
I found much easier just to browse
favorite place, and then, recycle bin,
and checked for an infections virus
Since I couldn't find the expected letter
before the voice said its sad "good bye"
I click delete and shut love down.

Elena R. Jimenez

To Cross the Bar

"Ganges" mast and Shotley Gate,
Memories ever near!
Where there we drilled and marched to guide our fate;
With mates to share good cheer.

"Ganges" boys and staff as well
Recall those times afar!
And may there be just gladness to foretell,
When we do "Cross the bar."

Oswald Tighe

Slip Tide

The future has not happened,
yet already I've changed it.
For better or for worse—
currently the negativity has rearranged it.

White—
now black . . .

Meaningless times melt by while
the control lapse is keeping me off-track.

Vacated identity:

It's up to me to take my future back.

Matthew Moore

Goodbye

Woman, it's goodbye, and a tear ran down my face
He stood, he looked at me; This is Goodbye
And a tear ran down my face
My boyfriend, my husband, my soul mate in life
Tells me, Woman, this is Goodbye
Twenty five years, with life's ups and downs
And a tear ran down my face
Was he leaving me for a bit of fancy
We took our vows at the altar in the church
'Til death do you part were God's words to us
Is this a dream or is it real
I reached out for your hand, you drew it away
You were saying once again, I cannot stay, I cannot stay
Woman, this is Goodbye
And a tear ran down my face, my visions of love
Torn in two, there is nothing left
What will I do
Place your hands upon your band of gold
This is where your dreams are stored
As in the vows you made and a tear ran down my face.

Mary Morris

Father

Father is the man that started it all
With designated authority and power
from the beginning
Our creator knew the important position
of the Father

Father is your teacher
He is the one you emulate
Father is your chastiser
He is your advisor and protector

Without Father there would be no son
But a son can look into a mirror and see the Father
Thus presenting am image of Father and son

Sometimes the Father desires the son
To be something that was impossible for him
The son understanding this fact
Will make the Father's dream a reality

Leonard Phelps

My Family

You are my blood where no water can thin.
I break sweat and tears for you when you are down
Your calls break the night when things are tight
I love you for you are my family
My mom showed me the truth of bonding,
for you showed me the truth of destroying
My family, My family, why do you bleed me
My family, My family, why are you kicking me
You are my blood where no water can thin
I see your smiles and hear your hellos
we talk and sit when the moons come and go
I come there, you never come by
why do you treat me so badly
My family, My family, why does it have to be
My family, My family, when will we be one
I hear your truths about me, I see your fears
You are my blood where water cannot thin
I am here for you, but you are gone
I stand alone
My family, My family, please just be gone

Lillian Perry

Untitled

On a day like today,
When the rain is falling softly,
Is when I think of you the most,
I find echoes of your kiss in the quiet patter of the drops,
And the memories of your caresses,
In everyone that glides slowly down my windowpane,
I even find your eyes in the color,
Of the storm clouds overhead,
And sometimes I think if I just reach out and touch,
Those silver drops of memory,
I'll really find you there,
But, only a day like today.

Andrea C. Flanagan

River of Love

The river is deep and wide.
The river will not hurt you.
It's full of love from side to side.
Come, all that thirst.
Come and take my hand.
I'll guide you, for I'll be by your side.
Let us go down to the river, where I'll abide with you.
Take a drink and feel my love,
for my love is all around you.

Rebecca N. McDonald

My Words

Thoughts acquired by the mind
Often leave people blind
I write them before it's too late
And as they read I watch them contemplate
My words are my only friend
They'll stick with me 'til the end
AND . . . as I drift away
My words shall make it to another day
In the hands of another being
Watching them see what I've been seeing
Making them feel what I've felt
And feeling their heart slowly melt.

Tracy Lynn Elliott

Introspection

Will these walls be triumphant
And lord it over my stupid ways,
My lazy slovenliness and utter failure
To have done the difficult, the expected?

Or can I, in years to come, return
To this room, kindly, yet victorious,
And love its dumb cracks and flaws,
In each of which is a dear memory?

Rosa Henderson Murray

Oh, Sweet Pea!

Oh, sweet pea
Come along with me
And we will be a happy family!
Oh, sweet pea
Come along with me
You know I love you tenderly!
Oh, sweet pea
You are my cup of tea
And you'll see I'll never leave you!
Oh, sweet pea
Sit upon my knee, and I'll give you love, eternally!
Oh, sweet pea
You made my life complete
And you are so sweet
I'll love you forever!

Patti Glasgow

My Child Is Leaving Home

Lord, my child has come of age and is ready to leave this home
I'm praying, Lord, that you protect, wherever she may roam

She is not longer that little girl with pigtails in her hair
She's grown into a woman, so tall, and straight, and fair

I still remember not so long ago, I bounced her on my knee
With her eyes all shining bright and laughing loud with glee

We shared so many things, of this world to her unknown
Now she wants to discover things, without me on her own

She is the blessing you gave to me, I've done the best I could
She's been protected by your grace because you said you would

My church and I instilled in her the things you told us to
So with you Lord right by her side I know she'll make it through

I've taught her how to trust in God, I've taught her how to pray
And that through prayer her life will be easier, each and every day

I'll miss her running to and fro, that phone stuck to her face
I let her know that in this life, it's to God we run the race

From child to woman she has grown, with you right by her side
That is why you came to Earth, that is why you died

What waits for her out in the world, are the things I do not know
Yet I'm not worried because you'll be with her wherever she may go

Willie A. Smith, Jr.

The Sounds of Heavenly Music

The sounds of music are very near;
Could it be that spring is here?
Birds all singing,
Each one bringing
Its beautiful sound of joyous mirth
To all the lands upon the Earth.
Each creature has its sound of spring,
Each one has its way to sing
That man may enjoy those simple songs,
As each one peals like Heavenly gongs
To waken each man's soul
And forget the deep hole
That winter has left behind.
Now, our God brings out His Heavenly choirs
Of all His creatures who never tire.
It is His way to give Heavenly joy,
Which man must use to employ
To bring all of the Heavenly blessings
When all of His creatures break forth and sing.

Paul Pasewalk

It Hurts Too Much to Remember! and It Hurts Too Much to Forget!

So much has happened . . .
Problems continue as yet
Sins I know could continue
These, Oh, God, I regret!
"Forgive and forget" they tell me
And forgiving grace I will get
So many goals I have tried to set,
Yet many tell me "You must not fret!"
But throughout, I yet have a debt
I must pay and yet not regret,
I pray "Dear God, let me forget
And worship thee 'til my last day is set."
I try dear Lord and I really do regret
Do you hear my plea? Let me pay my debt
But it hurts too much to remember!
And it hurts too much to forget!

Marjorie M. Bartlett

Heaven's Best

My friend, listen well, for what I say is sad.
Someone killed an officer today, it could have been my dad.

Oh, how must he have known, the end was near.
Many a stranger knew, his courage so very clear.

Our hero, there alone so filled with fear,
Quietly he lay, his eyes with tear.

Heaven he went, blessed be his soul.
God has called unto him, so I am told.

Our protector and our friend, from him we did learn.
There goes our hero, our love he did earn.

Now, his badge and gun lay to rest,
For in Heaven, are angels best.

Someone killed an officer today.
Justice be done, for this I pray.

Carolyn Mae Joiner

Grant Us This Day

Give me strength, patience, and understanding
Keep me strong, keep me wise with wisdom
and grace, keep me in good health in mind
and soul so that I may be able to bring my family
through the everyday problems that we have;
help us to go forward together in heart and soul;
to stand by one another and to believe in you so that we may survive.

Geraldine A. Thomas

Writing in the Wind

A piece of paper on the sidewalk.
A wind is blowing, it's a windy day.
People stop for a second,
Reading a paper; what does it say?

A short message,
A wish of happiness,
A broken heart, a lonely tear.
People who touch your heart,
They're always there.

The person who wrote the message,
These feelings are bigger than life.
A word, a deep meaning, with a lot of feelings,
Are glazing, but written in the wind, it's fading.

A wind is blowing again,
The paper flies.
Only a memory is left,
And a whole thing is gone.

Susan Gallen

Sweet Princess

Sweet princess I love thee.
Your love set my heart and spirit forever free.
Sweet princess hold me tight,
while I kiss your cheek my lovely wife.

Shawn Henley

The Romance Race

I'm running last in the romance race,
Met a girl I could love for life,
Introduced her to my best mate,
They fell in love, now she's his wife.

My heart aches for someone true
To love me and say, "I do!"
Someday we'll meet, I'll know she's my mate.
'Til then, I'm running last up the straight.

I'm outpaced in this romance race
Never manage to keep up the pace,
So, now when I spy a beaut new face
My heart says, give up the chase.

I'm still running last in the romance race!

Jean Noel Minogue

Lonely Bird without a Mate

Lonely bird, singing for your mate,
Lonely bird, he seems to be out late;
Is the tremor in your plaintive call,
A fear he won't return at all?

Lonely bird, so proud and true,
Do birds have hearts, like mortals do?
If the love of your life fails to return,
How long will your broken heart yearn?

Can tears flow from your bright eyes,
When, day after day, your sad heart cries?
Do you have a plan of what to do,
If all your dreams fall through?

Can you sing of long, sleepless nights,
Of no tomorrows, or worldly delights?
Can you bear the sadness of no "goodbye,"
And lose part of your life without a sigh?

Lonely bird, your instinct says don't stay,
But spread your wings and fly away;
Your heart's desire is safe, up above,
Forever waiting to share your love.

Gloria L. Counts

This Night

There was one night that just wasn't right,
no one cared, no one was alike
in the same room on the very same night
I had a feeling tonight wasn't right
they talked about me in the same room,
the same room, which is mine
I do pay attention to it but try to pay it
no mind, but what they did wasn't right
I wanted to write a rap this night in this room
but some people around here don't give you enough room
they keep spaces closed and listening ears
but I am very angry right now, so let me get out of here!

Renee Clinkscales

Home

If I don't live to see another day,
May my critics say, "He won't miss tomorrow,"

If I never look into the eyes of what could have been,
If I never hold in my arms what should have been,
May my eulogy read, "Please feel no sorrow,"

On the day of my absence,
May my critics inform anyone that grieves.
What sadly only my critics were able to see.

That loving each person and moment as it happened,
and not taking one breath for granted,
is the true meaning of destiny

Darnell Perry

It's Gonna Be All Right

Sometimes it may seem hopeless.
The blackness keeps closing in.
The road twists and turns,
just to lead you to a dead end.
The tunnel of darkness seems to go and on.
The wind that keeps you down seems to hold you for too long.
You are in the icy cold,
even in the summer sun.
You feel like you've been through so much,
and the end will never come.
But after every tunnel of darkness,
there is an end with light.
After every thunderstorm,
there is a rainbow of color that lights up the sky.
After every long night,
there is a break of dawn.
So keep your faith and hold on tight.
It's gonna be alright.

Tricia Whaley

I Have to Believe

Lord, I have to believe that you care.
I have to believe you are really there.
I have to believe you hear and answer prayer.
I have to believe.

I have to believe when I'm alone
With no one around—Yet I'm still home
No radio—No TV—a quiet telephone
I have to believe.

I have to believe you hear my call.
I have to believe you are over all.
That you are there when I stumble and fall
I have to believe.

I have to believe when I'm in pain.
I have to believe when tears fall like rain.
You whisper softly—"I'm coming again!"
I have to believe.

Jessie G. Plute

The Poem of Rhyming Words

Hum, sum, and come.
Look, book, and cook.
Souls moles, holes.

Words, heard, Bird.
And buffalo herd.
Sheep and sleep and peep.
Don't forget little Bo peep

What's in? What's thin? What's a sin?
Where the hell do I begin? In the beginning,
Middle or end?

Sitting on a hill, staying very still.
I don't care if people think I'm mentally ill.
They ought to chill out and take a pill.

What do you think this poem is a bout?
Bye now you should have figured it out.
If not you will in time. Okay, I'll tell you
It's a poem of utterly meaningless rhymes.

Robert Locke

Strive

What do you strive for?
For fame, fortune, talent, or more?
Are you ready for what the future might hold?
Do you believe your destiny is cast in a mold?

Do you strive to do your very best?
If you do, then God's plan will do the rest.
Are you ready to face the challenges that lie ahead?
It all begins when you first get out of bed.

No matter what, always try to get better . . .
Remember, sometimes a grade is more than just a letter.
Set your goals high and strive to achieve them;
But, if you don't, change them, don't leave them.

Danny Lehane

Tormented Love

He roams the fields of my mind
Although he is never lost.
I am from time to time.

He invades my privacy I cannot escape
He fills my every moment pleasures.
To be not without him is a timely treasure.

When whispers in the night
I hear so freely go on by,
I bend my ear to hear
What you're trying to say, so shy.

A song, a melody, or are you speaking love to me.
I can't seem to make it out
For the sound of wind is rushing,
Rushing all about.

He calls my name, he wakes me
From my slumber just to see
If I will answer,
Or will it all be lost in the thunder.

To own the love I taste from time to time
Is it real, will it ever be mine?

Patty Carpenter Payne

Diana

Noble spirit
Not gone but with us in another form.
Your love, compassion, sincerity and happiness
Inspire us all.
Noble princess
Not gone but with us in another form.

Isobel Macrae

Pawprints

There are paw prints on the counter
That are neatly etched in flour;
There are black prints on the towel,
And some wet ones in the shower.

There are smeared ones on the window pane
Where Tiger stopped to look;
There are paw prints made of catsup
Where he trod across my book.

There are round ones where he stopped a spell
While walking 'cross the bed;
There are light ones on the lamp shade
Where he caught the fly and fled.

There are snagged ones on the curtains
Where he wanted them to part;
But the deepest are the paw prints
He imprinted on my heart.

Doris Clanton

Mother

The music in the world is like the soft delicate dreamer
who sleeps all night
As the beautiful music rocks her to sleep
she dreams about all the wonderful things of the world.
Then, all at once, the music stops.
She lies wide awake, wondering what to do,
while she lies there, the wind whistles and tells her to get up.
All at once she's up and running around like a machine.
Always running, never stopping,
this goes on and on until the music starts all over again,
going faster and faster until one morning the wind is whistling,
but the dreamer can't move 'cause she's weak from running.
All she can do is wait for the weakness to subside.
Now she must stop running.

Deanna Noel

Empty Lullabies

Down long, sterile corridors
I followed silence—stony, cold
To automatic sliding doors
That expelled me into the black void
Of a night gone as lifeless
As the small, frail form
Lying somewhere beyond my reach
In the hospital's chill, foreign halls
The featherlike weight of the clothes he wore
Just hours before
When there was feeling
And warmth . . . and hope
Mocks the crushing emptiness of the void
That is my soul
I go home to piles of clothes
You'll never wear
And hum empty lullabies
While pieces of my shattered soul slide
As soft as you
Across my heart

Betty Sue Taylor

No Other Mom Comes Close

No other mom comes close.
When I came in this world I saw you.
My first sight of my mom, everything perfect.
You know I love my mom, no other mom comes close.
No one else makes me feel like I do except you.
No other mom comes close
You are the number one mom
Because no other mom comes close.

Robert James Jiron, Jr.

That's the Mystery

It can make your heart take a chance
It can make you want to sing
Until you would like to dance

It can be seen in your eyes
It can be felt in that first touch
For the heart does not lie

It can bring to you joy
It can make you laugh
Or it can make you cry

It can steal your heart
With just one glance
There is nothing in the world that it can't beat

It can also bring you sorrow
It can make you want to die
But you can still find it in another tomorrow

It touches the heart's core
When you don't have it
It only makes you want it that much more

And that's the mystery of Love!
        Janet Corriveau

Can You See Me?

Why do I hide behind this mask? Can't you see the pain inside me?
Why do I choose to hide and not allow anyone to see?

I see my reflection in the mirror, but who's that looking back?
Can't you see the hurt I hide when I put on this mask?

I would love to let you see the me deep inside my heart.
But I can't do that, because I'm scared of being hurt.

We fight one day at a time because that's all we can do.
My true self deep inside, I would love to show you.

If I had to explain the way I feel, you wouldn't understand me.
So I just hide it from you so you won't have to see.

You see what I show you, but when you look at me, can you see me?
Can you see through me, my pain inside that I hide, can you see?

My reflection shows what my mind sees and is told to see.
Those hurtful words, can't you see what they do to me?

This thing we call a mirror, the truth—will it ever tell me?
When will I see what's real, when will I see the real me?

When I take this mask off, will you still love me for me?
When I take this mask off, will you be afraid of what you see?

Let me show you who I am—under this mask I no longer hide.
Will the mirror then show the real me deep inside?
        Sandra Welch

Borrowed Time

The artist
is unwilling to admit
to himself or to the world
that he has created his masterpiece
because he embraces a primal superstitious certitude
that once he has done so his continued existence
will no longer be tolerated by God.
This is why an unanswerable anxiety
scratches at the door of his perception
every
single
time
he
looks
at
his
daughter.
        Scott Gardner Merrick

Dreamin'

Long hot summer nights,
I go to sleep and dream of snowball fights
And skiing down a mountain side,
On skis that softly glide
On powder snow that is still pristine,
Unmarked by man or machine.
I glide along with thoughts of wonder
About all the things that lie under
This snow pack that has covered all
The fragile beauty that was fall.
The white powder sings beneath my skis
And snowflakes drift on a gentle breeze.
I awaken with a start
And try to calm my racing heart,
And then I'm glad my dream has shattered
Just as I was being splattered
Up against a huge pine tree,
Which, of course, I didn't see.
I count my blessings it was a dream
And not reality.
        Lorin G. Maxfield

Wooden Ships of Olde

The ships of wood did what they could
to prove the world was round.
The men of iron swabbed the decks,
an fought like heck and drank another round.
Here's to the sea and men like we,
the men would shout and yell,
as the captain stood his ground,
drink hardy men and have good cheer,
for a new world we have found.
We will claim this land we'll make a stand,
for to our country will we be proud,
for upon this ground their our riches bound.
The seeds we plant,
the message we leave here on this virgin land
will stand a long, long time and grow beyond our time.
Our sweat, heartache and tears,
along with our fellow travelers, faith and courage,
will sail your wooden ship and find new lands
like wooden ships of olde.
        Alda R. Powell

Smoke

Embers with a complaint
Halos on a Saint

Burning bush talked to a prophet man
Burning trees and Bambi ran!

Lungs requiring oxygen tank for an aid
Marlboro Man smoked and paid

S M O K E . . . Stealing my air
S M O K E . . . Dulling my hair

Smoke is really charred used-to-be's
Smoke is ashes from dirty deeds

Hitler's Nazis should have learned
Smoke was Jews never to return

Smoke from peace pipes sealing deals that were done
White man's smoking guns—killing just for fun
Dust from painted ponies—Indians on the run!

Smoke is black not white
Smoke . . . like fog . . . clouds my sight

Smoke—dances like demons when the candle's done
Night-Darkness-Nightmares

Where's the LIGHT? I see none.
        Cinda Kathryn Robbins

Carwash

Going to the carwash one fine day
Had a great idea along the way
Time for plan of action to go into effect
Rolling down the windows I chose to select

Just kids and I were together on this trip
For the next hour all we did was drip
Soaked within seconds because we could not go far
As cool water sprayed throughout the entire car

Not much time to think but they sure tried
To find somewhere in the soggy car to hide
Watching my kids have nowhere to run
Was well worth three dollars to have some fun

Laughing with joy and jumping in delight
No way will we ever forget that night
Bet the whole neighborhood could hear us shout
As the car was getting shiny clean inside and out

Let's do it again, I heard someone say
Yet decided to save it for another day
Needless to say, my kids appeared to be in shock
Next time they will be smart and use the window lock
    Deborah A. Miller

Horse on Wings

Montana Star—
I know where you are.
But still I look in the field for you
Then I remember you're not in view.
And the tears start to flow
And my heart feels the blow
Of losing my beautiful bay
On that sad unbearable day.

I still can see your brown eyes
Looking straight into mine
In my heart you'll always shine.

On Heavenly clouds you canter
Where your pain long gone doesn't matter.
You're free as your black mane flies
Up somewhere in yonder skies.

I know you're not far.
I love you Montana Star!
    Lanette Adell Thomas

Let Me Drink from Thine Eyes

Let me drink from thine eyes
For thoust beauty is't so rare
Let me sit you in the centre of
my stage upon a chair

Let one single glow of light
fall softly on your hair
Illuminating your loveliness
for all the world to share

Thoust beauty is a wonderment
a rich and vital stare
It cometh from within you
and lights thine eyes with such great care

Thoust heart is't a small miracle
Thoust soul is't full of love
For though you are with mischief
your gentleness shines out above

No man hath ever tasted love
like yours upon his lips
and 'til I met with you my dear
my life 'twere but an eclipse
    Rosalyn Berg

The Lighthouse

Most gentle, relentless God, ever mine.

True light in my darkness. Ever do shine.

May always I bask in Your light's shining rays.

You, my bright beacon, as all 'round me decays.
    John Francis Missett

Is Anyone Listening?

So tired of all the arguing and bickering
So tired of all the fussing and fighting
The world is racing toward its doom
People have forgotten how to give
Is anyone listening up there

So tired of all life's eternal struggles
So tired of all life's hassles
The world has lost its direction
People are choosing the wrong path
Is anyone listening up there

So tired of all the broken promises
So tired of dreams not coming true
The world is running to nowhere
People evidently care only about themselves
Is anyone listening up there

So tired of being tired
So tired of prayers not being answered
The world is caught up in constant commotion
People no longer embrace each other
Is anyone listening up there
    Larry Testa

On Your Graduation Day

Keith,
You mastered how to sit and crawl
Survived seizures, surgeries, hospital stays, and all
You learned a few words, like "Hi" and
"I'll Be Right Back"
You learned how to walk and
Keep on the right track
You took the challenges everyone gave you
Crossed every bridge that was laid
How hard it was at times to keep going
Yet you made it through every stage.
You accomplished all your IEP goals and
Became quite a social buff
Sharing with others your special smile
Giving us hope when things got so rough
Now it's time for writing new pages as a
Graduate you have become
May God's Blessings Be With You Always
With Each New Dawn and Setting Sun.
    Nancy Rethman

Victory

As the man ranted and raved from the pulpit
and the bishops clowned in their maitres
I travelled to the center of my being and waited for love
Who hears our deepest cry, thanking God
For the victory won and grateful to
John Hines and John Spong
For battles done!
As we seek God's grace.
May the cosmic embrace,
Inspire our vision
Compel our decision,
For justice for all
On Earth and in space!
    Eleanor B. Smith

May God Protect You, Son

I wish that I could hug you, today
The same as I did when you was a boy
Every time I ask you for a hug, you walk away
I wish I knew why you shy boy

No son, your not a boy anymore
You're grown to a wonderful young man
Each time you walk out of the door
I pray for God to protect you, though your a man

Be us young or old, we need God on our side
There are a lot of distractions and harm, on the highway of life
That's why I ask God to send his angels with you abide
To keep you safe from all harm, sin and strife

When you are driving on that busy highway
Remember that little old lady at home praying
God protect my dear son on the busy highway
She will keep on praying, 'til he returns each day

Trust in God, son, he will send his angels to guide you
In this old sinful world, beware of what you say and do
There are a lot of enemies out there, on you would inform
Your dear ole mom, don't want another son to mourn

Annie Saunbers

Politika

High on a hill a cat looked down, and saw the town
Padded feet and pointed ears, whiskers on edge to catch the breeze
Nose softly sniffing—never a sneeze!
And the he saw what no cat should see
That men in a town are mice to eat.
So with a growl he launched his leap—
Claws stretched out on all his feet!
Cat caught a man and had his meal!
Caught another—each one—real
And then a strange event began.
Cat began to look like a Man!
But cat continued to launch his leaps,
Called two companions and so there were three
Cats with claws who looked like men,
Even when enculturation began! And thus are towns run.
Men are the Mice and Cat Men have fun
For to this day men still believe they are men
And that cat stays on hill.
So if you live in a town and think it's a city—
This poem says you're run by a kitty!

William Gray

Diff'rent Language, Diff'rent Choices

Never thought that what we had
Would ever be infinity
But I guess it's true
Nothing lasts forever 'til eternity

Time has changed our lives
What we had was full of lies
I did not want pretenses to set in
For it would only cause prolonged solitude

Amidst our meeting place
Happiness uncontained
Our conversation untamed
Hearing voices like it's from outer space

What has caused it?
I still wonder
I bet it's me
For often I change as I please

But how can I say sorry
If Mr. Webster doesn't know the story?
And such language you speak
Isn't in my vocabulary

Dekka Belle Panilagao

Reverie

I love the vastness of the sea,
its ebb and flow, its constancy.
Yet lure of calm, serenity,
and beacons blinking endlessly,
belie the possibility
of raging storms and tragedy.
Retreating tides lay bare for me
her treasure trove of finery.
Offered only fleetingly
high tide reclaims the mysteries.
It's only she.
She alone, who holds the key.
And yet I walk that distant shore,
forevermore, forevermore,
to find a sunset, nothing more.
And let its arms envelop me,
reflecting lights upon the sea,
creating twilights memories.

Cherie Francis

Nursing

Nursing is my career, caring is what I like to do, start your iv,
make you coffee, what ever it will be.
You want to hold my hand, squeeze my hand,
that's what I'll let you do.
You want to talk to me, cry to me, I'm here for that too.
Nursing is my career, caring is what I like to do.

Lisa Marchlewski

Who Shall Be the Fortunate?

To my brothers whom I love the most
Once upon a time, on a winter night
A whole wretched tribe was rendered blight
And the sky lamented their plight

Men were enslaved and slaughtered
Women were raped and tortured
Children were abused and murdered

Among the women, there she stood
The queen of the captured tribe
Wearing her resplendent hood

Before her, her soul-mate, the king
Next, her very self, the son
And her eyes' solace, her sibling

"One of these three, we shall liberate
And two of them we shall decapitate.
Who shall be the fortunate?"

The queen firmly retorted,
"The son, as long as the womb lasts,
The husband, as many as the stars,
But the brother is the first and the last."

Farid Francois Ghosn

I'll Love You Still

No matter what you shall do
No matter what you shall say
All shall be forgiven
I'll Love you still
Through it all no matter what
No matter what problems shall arise
Through rejection and through break ups
I'll Love you still
I'll stand beside you thick and thin
No matter what it takes
I'll be here for you until my dying day
Always keep this fact in mind
Locked deep within your heart to remember
I'll Love you still.

Joshua Curtis Henry

African Violet

Seems like 100 years has passed
Velvety flesh has evolved into wrinkles
Black and Beautiful . . . as rich as cocoa
Ancestry of our Motherland, but now a native
of The Land of Liberty
Long shimmering locks . . . sparkles with specks of grey
African Violet
Glancing through her looking glass
the windows of the soul reveal years of
intellect . . . abstractions of ethnic unions. . . .
When she walks she strides with grace from
years of performing the Juba dance. . . .
Silk wrappings atop her head balanced with
perfect precision . . . clothed in a luxurious
afghan which holds rich hues of heritage. . . .
Seems like 100 years has passed . . .
African Lady, Black woman, African Violet. . . .

Lutisha Rena Corbin

The Soul's Food

As if your lips were not lips but honey
then I would taste the sweetness
of your breath and kiss
the magic would consume my soul
and it would be rich.
Your words are but food for my soul
that I am filled with every day
and how your words take on taste
that is creamy and thoughtful grace.
My words and thoughts fill your soul
as if they were a meal to eat
and you are so surprised at the taste
of how it melts and blends in your mouth
that you are completely speechless to me.

Cassie Miller

I'm Angry

I'm angry that friends die.
I'm angry that we didn't get the chance to say goodbye.
I'm angry that you died alone.
I'm angry that you got to go home.
I'm angry hearts are breaking,
and it seems
as if all your dreams are forsaken.
I'm angry that you never saw your gift within,
I'm angry that we lost such a dear, dear friend.
I'm angry when I watch
my loved ones' tears falling.
I'm angry that you never realized
your true calling.
So now it is time to say goodbye
and I'm too angry to even cry.

Molly Long

Star Child

I'm a lost girl,
In my very own world.
I don't know who I am,
What I'm doing,
Or where I'm going.
Everybody says this is who I am,
This is what I'm doing,
And this where I'm going.
Even though I don't know anything about myself,
I do know that what they say isn't true, because
I'm not the little girl they can mold like clay,
Or the star child they see every day,
Nor am I perfect, for that matter.
I'm me, that's all I need to know,
Forever to eternity.

Amanda Myhre

Anything Worth Having

Anything worth having melts.
Thunderstorms melt into Heavenly rainbows;
Music melts into us and awakens our souls;
Blue skies melt away into violet twilights;
Lovers melt into each other's arms;
A child's laugh or cry can melt our hearts;
Endings melt into bright new beginnings;
Moments melt into eternal memories;
Goodbyes melt into longings for what was;
Hellos melt into promises of what may be;
Lost loves melt into bittersweet heartache;
Time melts into a kaleidoscope of hopes and dreams;
Life melts away too quickly forr us to appreciate
So you see, my friend, anything worth having melts.

Donna Greci

Dreams

Dreams are stories that you hold onto,
Will lead and guide you.

Dreams are imagination that comes and goes,
Can predict, too.

Dreams make your sleep exciting,
And so interesting.

Dreams are always there,
That last forever.

Dreams of the sleepless nights,
So hard to remember.

Dreams for the whole world dreams,
That people can't wait,
Until our dreams will come true.

Maye L. Conley

The Blue Tea Cup and Saucer

It was large and round and deep blue
The aroma of blueberries filled the room
As I sipped tea from the special cup and saucer
I was reminded of how blessed we are
I am fortunate to be a receiver of this favor from God
He has not given me all the things I may want
But he has given me what I need for salvation
To be blessed in this day is a good thing
God's love and blessings for us is special
Like the blue tea cup and saucer;
Gods blessings are special to me

Jo Ann Thomas

An Ode to Nellie

I once had a dog, her name was Nellie,
when I'd give her a holler, she'd hop on my belly
many a time she'd go tree a coon,
chasin' um through the woods from ten 'til noon.
Well Ole Nellie, she's had her dander up,
ever since that girl was just a wee pup.
Now on the other side of woods the old bears hide,
waitin' and a waitin' 'til you're on their side.
One day ole Nellie took off after a coon,
I waited and waited 'til long after noon.
Finally I took to the woods a prayin'
hopin' she's safe wherever she's stayin'
Farther I walked and darker it became,
knowin' without her I'd never be the same.
When I saw her on the ground there bleedin' I cried!
"Lord ya said she'd always be with me, ya lied!"
But I couldn't blame the Lord who'd brought us together,
as I put her in the ground, I thought of times better.
The good Lord sure made life worth livin',
but ole Nellie was a spice that He'd given.

Wade West

From a Bird's Point of View

Happy Birthday, Charline! From Grandma and Grampy
Up, up, high in the sky
is a place for me and you to fly.

Over the trees, with you at my side,
our speed is like a wild ride.

My wings spread out, gliding through the blue,
I fly toward the sun and so do you.

But then I hear a bang so loud,
it could have hit my favorite cloud.

I flap my wings so very hard
that my wings feel so very scarred.

Starting to fall, you flap away;
I guess that's called an almost perfect day.

A sound squeaks out from my tender beak,
as I struggle to fly among the strong and the weak.

Charline Woods

Making a Wish upon a Star

One, warm, summer, moon, starlit night,
as owls soared into flight,
making a wish upon a star,
wondering where you are.
Are you near? Are you far?
Trying to find you, don't have a clue.
I asked God, the Angels, in Heaven above,
for guidance in finding, my true love.
I feel his presence is near,
as my eyes fill up with tears.
I hear a whisper in my ear,
have faith my Darling, I'll be with you soon.
Making a wish upon a star.
As, I, gaze up at the stars, the moon,
a smile appears on my face.
I hear God's voice say unto me,
have patience, have confidence,
be giving, be honest, be loving,
but most of all believe.
We will guide you to the love of your life,
for all of eternity.

Donna Bennett

Jersey's Pride

New Jersey's pride
Um . . . I see it in your stride.

The praise in your strays
wakes up the town.

Every step wants to "put it down"
New Jersey's pride
with his style and class worldwide.

He's a working man
He's a man's man.

New Jersey's Pride
Um, I see it in your stride.

Check him out girl,
he's got it all.

The man is fierce
Your heart, your soul he could pierce.

He needs no one but his love is his life
He only wants a strong black woman to make his wife.

New Jersey's pride
With strength worldwide you're never
gonna see a man with more pride

Candice Marie Caldwell

What Love Is

Love is the way you touch my heart,
with feelings that cannot be denied.
Love is the way you look into my eyes,
with emotions that cannot be deprived.
Love is the way you caress my body,
with feelings that cannot be defied.

Love is the way you hold me close,
with emotions that cannot be devised.
Love is the feelings and emotions
that rise from the depth of your heart and soul
that develop devotion and devastation.

Pam Gilbert

All Colors

The darkest ones like midnight shadows,
Lighter ones glisten like diamonds,
Yet the in between like hot beach sand;
Each one a human man.
As we stand together on this land
While holding hands,
We make up all the colors of the World.
We are all a color in God's own rainbow,
Each as beautiful and glorious as the next.
We are each a magnificent flower in God's
Own bouquet of human men.

Alexis Sadler

Silenced Thoughts

Footprints in the sand,
Like a story in a book,
Waves wash over them
Without a second look.
Memories, the same,
Tell the story of a life,
Words of good times,
Words of strife.
Pages are the memories,
Details are the words.
Will this book be read
Or never be heard?
When memories are forgotten,
The pages are ripped out.
When words have been silenced,
Pain is not felt.
Why do we not read
Our stories aloud?
Does an unspoken rule
State we're not allowed?
When my book's been closed, its story will live on.
It will be recited like the words of a song.

Tania Curtin

Can You Hear Them??

With Loving Thoughts—JRM
Angels speak ever so gently
the whispers of warmth and love.
They hold our hearts when we shiver
only to realize the peace of doves.
They walk beside us when we drive forward
with uncertainty and fear.
They are there to console us when fraught
with passion and despair.
They realize our path so often not seen,
and guide us through the fires of life unscathed and clean.
They are all around us, day in and out,
be aware of their presence with little doubt.
So my sweet, I ask of you this day . . .
Can you hear what they are trying to say?

Elaine Pappas

Easter

As we observe the day when Jesus arose,
We think of all our sins that only God knows.
He took them away for evermore.
Is He now knocking at your heart's door?

With each tap of the hammer we were being
Set free!
Yes, Jesus was nailed to the cross for
You and me.

Won't you open the door and let Him come in?
He wants to walk with you and take away your sin.

—The Lord's Hoosier Farmer
    Edward Smith

Dream of Dreaming

As I sit here now just thinking of you
I ask myself how I could do this to you
When the words came out I shut down my heart
And without a doubt it tore us apart

Now my dreams don't know where to start
To dream of things that come from my heart
Or to dream of another that may come soon
But they shouldn't matter for I dream to dream of you

The notes and the letters used to be enough
But now I need better, now I need your touch
To hold you in my arms and watch your eyes close
While you sleep safe from harm and dream what your heart knows

But inside my heart I can see
That since we're apart this can never be
I can never dream of you or hold you close to me
I can't dream the things I choose or dream things I wish would be

Why I said what I said that day I'll never comprehend
And when I think out loud I say, "Maybe I'll pretend"
But then it comes to me, I missed the underlying meaning
The only reason that I cry is because I dream of dreaming
    John Smith

Age

When I am old and full of years
I will forget the pain, the tears
Of youth, I will not sigh and reminisce
O'er bygone loves and chances missed
Tho' I may despise my loss
As pages turn and dyes are tossed
I'll struggle through with hope, my dears
When I am old and full of years
    Mike Soldner

Identity

Each of us is unique
We all have our own identities
Some are recognized by physical features
And some by the way they speak

We all have the same assets
Our bodies are all the same
But we all look different
Though it is from God we came

We all have special gifts
The Peacock his beauty, the Lion his strength
Some are powerful, some are meek
We love to point out the proud and weak

By our identity we are known
It is to others what we have shown
That we are Christians by all must be seen
Then God will make our pastures lush & green.
    Anthony Gittens

Portray Ourselves

Why must we portray ourselves to be someone we are not?

Why can't society accept us for who we are?

Some of us have changed our ways of life to
be accepted in this world today.

We have been criticized and we have been put
down so we will feel worthless to those around us.

We are letting this world kill who we really are.

Why can't we talk and walk in the manner
which we know and love?

Why do we let the men in this world take
charge of our lives?

We fought for our rights and now is the time
to show that we are worth more than gold and
without us there is no them.
    Yevette Farrior-Adams

Maureen

My favorite place in life
Listen to the sound of love
It's so soothing and so gentle
Like the simple song of a dove
I smell the love flowing plentiful
Its aroma fills the air with roses
They tickle my nose then whisk away
So Heavenly is this my mind dozes
Dreams are only dreams and don't stay
The love moves and I dream still
It stirs again and then I awake
Paralyzed by love I cannot move by will
Love's touch tingles and feels fake
I open my mouth to speak
It is filled with splendid flavor
I close my mouth so none may leak
I take time to taste and savor
Within a haze of ecstasy I open my eyes and see
The woman I love in my arms next to me
    Colin Tierney

For a Day Shall Not Pass

Friendship found us
Friendship found love.
With that friendship we found a bond that no man can break.
With that friendship and love we will be joined together as one.
For the Lord blessed each of us with each other.
We will go through life together in love and happiness.
For a day shall not pass without the simple words:
"I Love You."
Those words mean so much.
    Jeanette Geary

A Twin Desire

A Gemini-driven lust can only inspire such moments . . .
Diverging and intertwining notes of a symphony,
Seduction of a mind never to compromise,
Exposed passions, once dormant in atrophy
Laid bare—open, an intimate encounter pries
In which colored moods of the soul arise
Disclosing a crimson envelope of desire.
Instant urgency making me realize
The poignant truth, vulnerable by this blind fire
In which raw curiosity entices you still higher;
To where intellectual ardor ceases—to feelings of
That gripping madness meant to inspire
Words, captivating the fervor of this uninvited love;
As words, meditated control of his hand upon my hip
Say more, just as the imploring kiss upon my lip.
    Lisa L. Krahne

The Last Goodbye

Dying at the crest of the desert green,
I only hope for one last wish—
Breathing one last kiss to your lips.
What's next is up to you, not I.
I'm gone, frozen in time and in mind.
What remains? It's up to you,
But for an instant your eyes deceive.
If not your eyes, then what?
My promise safeguards your heart.
We walk hand-in-hand and laugh.
The long journey hasn't been cold at all.
Nor is heat scalding my memory.
Thought after thought dances now.
God, you're an incredible dancer.
With a wink and a word, we embrace.
White-knuckled, wet cheekbones
And clenched teeth wouldn't suggest
The tenderness exchanged between
Our flaring chests and stare.
Yet, it's there. This is soft.
Never parting ways again, we live.

Trevor McMullen

There Is a Reason

God placed us all on this world for a purpose in life
And only for a short stay. Some may be successful,
Some may be failures. Some may be wealthy and healthy.
Some may be poor and sickly.
Some may not. "There is a reason."

Some may be sincere, some may be hypocrites, some may love.
Some may hate, some may share, some may not.
"There is a reason."

Some may live their lives through crime and violence,
Some may be victims of such, some may not.
"There is a reason."
Some may perish through natural disasters,
Some may live to suffer through such.
Some may not.
"There is a reason."

Some may live by the Ten Commandments,
Some may live by the golden rule.
Some may not.
"There is a reason."

Laird H. Munsch

The Gift

There went out a decree
That all the world should be taxed
And Joseph and Mary went up from Galilee
From the City of Nazareth

Mary being great with child
And her labor about to begin
Joseph tried to find a place to rest
But there was no room in the inn

There were shepherds abiding in the field
Keeping watch over their flock that night
When the angel of the Lord appeared
And the glory of the Lord shown bright

He said, "Glory to God in the highest
Peace on Earth, good will to men
For unto you is born this day
The greatest gift ever given"

The greatest gift ever given
Was not wrapped in bright paper and bows
But he was lovingly and gently wrapped
Up in swaddling clothes

Syrethia M. Ellison

The Train to Agatha

Tomorrow I'll meet the train, just a flutter of wings away,
And softly, softly, he'll soothingly say,
To Agatha, to Agatha, Oh, Anna will go to Agatha
To Agatha, to Agatha, to Agatha my dear,
Where your lips won't cry, come rescue me
And your heart no more will fear.
Then up, up, away we'll fly
To the sunset land beyond the sky
To Agatha, where my pain must die
And my prince will never make me cry
And we'll dance all night, just my prince and I.
But as the sun begins to rise, a crystal tear will cloud his eyes
And he must take me back across the skies,
For we have souls the same, but different lives.
And though I'll cry, and though I'll scream,
My precious Agatha will be all a dream.
But maybe someday, he'll come again
And we'll stay together forever then,
In the land beyond the setting sun,
In Agatha, my dreamland home.

Brianna Thiel

The Old Church Organ

There is a old battered organ under the stairs.
It's a refuge and solace from daily cares.
It seems the strains of a hymn I hear,
Played by the church organist, my mother, so dear.
If that organ could talk, what tales it could tell.
As it once stood proudly in a church we knew well.
To its strains we all sang hymns long ago.
No wonder we all now love that organ so.
Although now it's wheezy and it has so yellowed keys,
It suffices the need to be played.

Edith Lorimer Boudrot

Drugs and Alcohol

Drugs and alcohol might seem cool right now
But soon you're gonna sit and ask yourself how
How could you let something so stupid take over your life
They will make you feel funny and want to stab someone with a knife
They'll change the way you talk and the way you see things
You'll want them so bad you'll sell your diamonds and rings
They will make you think differently and change the way you are
People say when you do these things, you can't drive a car
Some do it because they're mad or they have nothing better to do
Once you smoke or drink, you won't have a clue
Drugs and alcohol are something you don't want to try
If your parents find out, you're gonna make them cry
So do me a favor; if you're addicted, please make that call
Or do something better, don't try them at all!

Joshua Waid

Ode to Timmy

Timmie (Ogie) Owen, was only 18 years old
When angels took him to their abode
His love for is family, his love for his friends
Will keep him in their hearts until the very end
Timmy loved his hockey and he loved playing ball
And as a true sportsman, Timmy gave it his all
He laughed with so many and he cried with so few
In his heart he was happy, as everyone knew
A true friend to many, a loyal friend to have
He was the same with his family
His mother, brother, and dad
A kind hearted kid, a little timid, a little shy
Timmy will be remembered as a real special guy
Your spirit will be with us, even though we're apart
And with this poem we'll remember you
Because it comes straight from the heart

Karen Lazzaro

Forgive Me Lord

One night I was sick and all alone
I said dear God, what have I done
To deserve this pain and sickness I have
He said my child, you're a sinner now
Look around, and you can see
Many people worse off than thee
Some are blind, some can't walk
Some are deaf, and some can't talk
Some are dying with a dread disease
Yet some are well, doing as they please
I said, dear God, you are so right
Please forgive me, on this night
I said to Him, I'm so ashamed, for thinking only of me
Dear God, I've suffered little, compared to Jesus and Thee
You gave your Son to die for me
With a crown of thorns on His head
His hands and feet nailed to a cross
To hang there until dead
He was buried, but rose again, to be in Heaven with You
So, dear Lord, please forgive me, so I may be there too

     Alice M. Cazire

Children

C-is for charm, that sometimes show.
H-is for heart, as pure as gold.
I-is for ideals, that are sometimes wise.
L-is for the love, that always shows.
D-is for daring, tasks they may try.
R-is for the many races won.
E-is for energy, by the ton.
N-is for the nicest, things they may say
Put these eight letters together they spell children
The greatest discovery of the day.

     Omega O. Van Landingham

Dream Come True

Plan with me, my love, a feast,
A feast of song and dance.
A celebration of love and happiness.
Dance with me, my love, for I need your touch!
Share with me a future of adventures,
For I do not know what may come after the present.
Stay with me, my love, for time has no boundaries.
For only God knows my path through this life,
And on this path God lead me to you.

     John D. Villamil

Free

The hour is late, and silence surrounds me,
as the peaceful beat of my heart reminds me
I am free.

Alone but content, my life now my own;
A bright star guides my path.
As a soft voice whispers,
"For someone else's sins
you no longer have to atone."

He is gone and his touch I no longer fear.
His cruel face no more before me, seen through my tears.
His voice is now silent, hurtful words I do not have to hear.
I smile at me and like who I see in my mirror.
I am free.

This darkness is warm and gently surrounds me.
At last I feel safe, no longer afraid;
From pain and loneliness a strong woman is made.

As I drift into dreams of angels and song,
my heart keeps repeating, "He is gone."
And I am free.

     Myrna Monnahan

Show Me, Tell Me, Teach Me

My Master Manipulator,
Show me how it works.
Tell me your wonderful secrets
Of what it's all about,
To be bold and boast of
Hidden truths by the unmaskable lies.
Teach me to be like you,
And learn the words of you.
I hear you speak.
Be personal, you say,
But hold back enough to keep them wondering.
I don't understand.
What are you saying?
Let your voice be heard,
Not a voice that belongs to someone else, you say.
I start to comprehend you,
But now my mind is blank.

     Elizabeth Tenney

The Strange Dream

As I hear my mom say good night
I also hear her turn off the light.
As I try to get some sleep
I hear no one make a peep.
As I sleep within my dreams
I'm in a strange place, so it seems.
As walk across the strange valley
I see a woman in the strange valley.
She says, "Nothing is what it seems."
Then I wake up from my dream.
I still ponder on the edge
As if she were trying to tell me a message.

     Angie Aguilar

Fire's Lesson

The fire's put out, the smoke has cleared,
But the effect on my mind, will last for years,
I've never been subject, to the elements of fire,
I guess money and complaining, were my desire.

Our lives were jeopardized by a single spark,
Now the only thing left, is a place to park,
There was no loss of life, with many thanks,
And it's hard to believe, this was just a prank.

As I sift through what's left, of my life's belongings,
I find myself praying and yearning and longing,
For strength and perseverance, that's my new daily grace.
I know as time passes,
I'll display a happier face,
Because I've learned a lesson, from fire, you see,
I know just how fast,
Life can be taken away from me.

     Diana Hoag

The Song of My Heart

Trees everywhere should I run away
Do I dare snow glistening on the bare trees
I stand there listening to the wind
Its own special song whipping my face
Stinging as it rushes by
My hair blowing across my face
I turn to leave but as I do
I suddenly remember what I'm supposed to do
Not to go away and leave my home forever
But to stay and watch the glistening snowflakes
fall to the ground and to listen to the song of the wind
And the song of my heart

     Stephanie M. Burque

Never a Guess

A gasp, a cry, a slap, a sigh—
Get ready, world, here am I.
Ten years, 20 years, 30 years, and more—
Is anyone even going to keep score?
Forty years, 50 years, 60 years, wow—
Is there anyone left that knows me now?
It all seems to happen so fast—
Never a guess that the years won't last.
Stand up, walk straight—
Just not ready for the pearly gate.
Never a guess to be so strong—
Never a guess to last so long.

Dee Gambardella

Love You Blues

Come on honey sing the blues,
I'm feelin' down 'cause I love you.
Listen to me, hear my song,
I'm feelin' lonely all night long.
Cuz I hurt you, you ran away,
I played the game—now it's time to pay.
So come on honey, yes, it's true,
I've got a case of the love you blues.
I promised you I'd be your man,
and then I took another woman's hand.
I was hoping for one last chance,
until I saw you with another romance.
He's got the suave, yes, he's got the moves,
but one thing he don't got is the love you blues.

Jason Burrow

For Philip and Edward

God doesn't make men like you anymore.
Men who had gentle spirits
and sacrificing hearts.
Men who loved deep and
were not ashamed to prove it.
Men who were always there
when we needed them
Men who could do math and
didn't brag about it.
Men who could fix anything broken.
Men whose lives are written on daughters' hearts.
Men whose sons marvel at the mark of the man.
Men who found soul mates in women made of marble and gold.
Men who were gifts from God.

Phyllis Anderson-Wright

I Am

I am an action movie freak!
I wonder how my uncle is doing at work.
I hear my Dad every day and night.
I see my sister every morning.

I am an action movie freak!
I pretend I'm a sheriff.
I feel like I'm a piece of toast.
I touch the grass every day.
I worry about my best friend.
I cry when I get hurt really bad.

I am an action movie freak!
I understand a lot of weird things.
I say stuff I won't do.
I dream and have nightmares at the same time.
I try to get really good grades.
I hope I live for a really long time.
I am an action movie freak!

Jake Liese

Boy

There's that boy down the street,
Living in a crammed house,
Nine little ones and one tired mother,
His hands surfaced with blisters and dirt,
His face brown from too much factory dust,
Except for the streak,
A trail of a lost tear.
If only the neighborhood kids
Could read this lone tear,
Where there's a boy
Who grew up too fast.
He walks home from another day.
The sun sets slowly and
Only the shadow of the boy is seen.
He's only a boy, only 12,
But he opens the door to his house,
Pushing away his own childhood and desires,
Reaching to be a man.
If only the puerile neighborhood kids
Could understand this boy.

Michelle Yoon

Reflections of Reality

I thought of you as I sat in the warmth of the sun.
My mind began to wander and run.
To a time long ago.
When rainbows were bright, shadows were low.

The memories that came,
Were of us playing games.
We talked and we tried,
To have our dreams reach the sky.

So much clearer I see.
How the fears engulfed you and me.
They strangled our love,
And set us both free.

Free to be frightened and run far away,
From the love that we felt on that warm summer's day.
Freer still freer to stay where we were
Stuck, in our pain, knowing no cure.

We drifted apart, time slipping away,
While we grieved our dead souls, kneeling to pray.
That God would come to show us the way,
To rebuild our lives, to live in today.

Mary Catherine Willey

My Luv

You are my luv, you treat me like gold,
We're together like doves,
We'll be together 'til we're old!

We may argue or disagree,
We may cry or feel as we hate,
We sometimes may not even want to be,
But you will always be my date!

We'll stick together 'til the end,
No saying where we will be,
You will always have my hand,
You will be you, and I will be me!

You are my luv, you are my life,
You are the one I will always love,
I hope one day to be your wife!

Last time we were nothing,
Now we're much more than something,
You are my everything, you are my king!

All I want to say is that I love you with all my heart
I hope you feel the same way, because we'll never be apart.
You are my luv, you are my life . . . you are my everything!

Kim Newman

Almost Persuaded

How you tease my fickle feelings with the indulgence
of your innocence—those feelings wounded and scared by:
bitter betrayal, tainted truths, demolished dreams, lost love.

You tempt and tease my vulnerability with your innovations,
and you almost persuade me to subject myself
to a capricious state of exposure and pain once again.
I vacillate in the futility of my fickleness,
almost persuaded—but not.

Judy Thompson

Another Day at the Beach

pain—unrelenting offense, persistent assault,
mind-numbing, synapses-snapping, vortex of
confusion and fear—STOP
insidious fog which barely shrouds
ever-rising successive waves of tide—STOP
How long, Oh, Lord, how long?

Facing the flood's fury,
with no place to dry my feet,
while parched tears fall like grains,
un-noticed except against the darker fabric—
Oh, sweet, seductive numbness . . .
must you tarry? STOP

Still, the tide . . . then, the darkness.
Now the choice, the hope, the reality.
Now the truth that the greater curse is
to not feel.
GO ON

George Buechner

Strange

A blind man saw me walking down the street
I told him I am deaf I can't hear nor speak

Don't you think it is ironic
when you drink the water then
you figure out it is a tonic

It is like climbing the summit of the valley
It is like spending a night or two with Sally

Sometimes you try to get away
Saying things you never meant to say
After all life is a game we play
A game where you only have one credit
A game you can't set up nor edit
You might think I am strange
Well I am just sick of this life and I need a change

I know you won't understand a bit of this rhyme
If you read it again, you will get it by time.

Ziad Marzouka

Happy Birthday, My Love!

Three years ago, on this very day,
I got on my knee and asked you to stay.
We were new together, but I knew one thing,
That I loved you, so I came with the ring.
Three years ago, during the night,
We talked, ate, and loved just right.
We planned our lives, together and apart,
We shared Lo Mein and one another's hearts.
Three years ago, I fell in love,
Imagine! Falling, but landing above.
I'm better with you than I could ever have been,
And to think, you thought me better than most men then!
Three years ago, I am happy to say,
Started thirty-six months that have gone my way.
Though November seventh is your birthday,
Three years ago, this date made my day!

Rufus Tolbert

The World Dies with Us, Unless . . .

This will inspire you . . .
The world Around us falls apart,
As we destroy God's greatest art.
We destroy ourselves and fade away.
We'll never see another day.
Like a sinking ship; like a setting sun,
The world dies, as does everyone.
We fall into the darkest hole.
As we make carnage we pay the toll.
We give our lives to destroy ourselves.
Say good bye to the world; our only wealth.
As the world dies we will too,
Unless our thoughts become anew.
So Make the change. Give peace to the world.
That's the only way for our future to unfurl.
We can succeed if everyone tries.
So save your world; or say your good byes.

Justin Vazquez

Forever

I remember the card games we used to play
I remember the visits we had every day
I remember the tee shirt with the sun
we made together always as one
I remember your smile your gifts you ways
Ill remember them all for the rest of my days
I remember you little house by the beach
I remember the stories of how you used to teach
I remember Kinross place and how we lived there
I remember the gardens which you loved so dear
I remember Michael my favorite doll
I remember them all with my heart and soul
To forget all our good times I swear never
because I will love you forever and ever

Jamie Mora

Venting about Phil

A small piece of my mind
It's all stuck in a different time
The time that you came to me
The time that you waited for me
The good things happen the bad's what I see
You might show me a rose but I know it'll die
I'm given the rules I'm expected to defy
Where did you come from and why should you be here
It's not like I called you to fix all that I fear
You're afraid of the paranormal, me it's all about fire
But you think just by standing there you'll become what I desire.
You try to shield away flames that don't burn
I don't need protection sometimes tables turn
You're still young, and you still can't fool me
One year's an age difference, what do we call almost three.

Janine Kemmerer

For Beth

Gone to a better place, have I,
where I'll never again have need to cry,
where pain and suffering are no more,
the place to which all spirits soar.
My mind is whole, my spirit is healed,
and to my eyes the Lord is revealed!
I'm here in the place where Love is King,
and no one thinks an evil thing.
Here with loved ones from the past,
including Christ, my joy will last.
So please don't cry and be so sad.
Instead, rejoice! Be exceedingly glad!!
Say, "Good-bye!" with a happy sigh,
for gone to a better place, have I!!!

Thomas Hill

When You Take My Hand

Though I've dreamed it many times, I knew
from the moment I first laid my eyes on you
that we were brought together to not part.
When you take my hand you have my heart.

I look up at the sky and wonder where you
might be and if you are thinking of me.
I pray to the sky, to a God I cannot see,
wishing you were with me or I with you.

I kiss you sometimes in my dreams
as though you are inches away, so it seems.
I remember watching you while you slept,
touching you, to wake you from sleepy depths.

Though at the moment an ocean keeps us apart,
I have faith in my fate—I will see you soon.
As days go by swiftly between sun and moon,
I dream of you and I together, to not part,
Knowing in this moment you have my heart.

Maria Gioffri

Tragedy

The word is Love
The Dream turns to a Nightmare
Once almost untouched, now Pregnant
It sets you Free to Cast a Spell
On the Passion now your Ex
The Few pleasures
Become a lifetime of Hell
Previous friends to out-of-touch Aliens
The Green-eyed monster turns to Blue tears
Die Hard
Tragic
Love
Thanks a bunch . . .

Rachael Denton

A Tribute to Life

Some things can never be answered, some things best left alone,
some things are never revealed, some never known.
But to ones who wonder, and to ones who seek,
the discoveries they do find never make them weak.
Only stronger in mind and stronger in soul
'til one day they may be able to say, I've reached my goal.
The closer you get the harder it seems
'til sometimes you seem to never reach your dreams.
And then there's always an obstacle that comes along,
and the position you're in doesn't seem to belong.
But through the ups and downs that do occur,
hope you can look back and see that maybe your wiser than you were.
Sometimes it's not easy remembering life's lessons though,
and some of them you probably didn't even want to know.
But no matter what life brought your way,
try never forgetting to make the best out of every day.
Know you've got to go on and be as happy as you can,
because in this world for each of us there is a demand.

Jeanie Cummings

Until You Break My Heart

Do I sense a drought in my poetic power?
Empty lines where majestic words of heartbreak and confusion
with underlying hope for death
to relieve me of all the pain
you have placed before me
once flowed so freely from black holes of betrayal and bitterness
that you ripped with those same two hands you used to show me love
Has my poetic expression of depression grown pathetic?
Will there be a shortage of my poetic masterpieces
until you break my heart once more?

Raechel Barrios

2 Touch

2 touch would be like the appearance of Gold at 1st.
it seems rare
2 touch is 2 hold
2 touch is 2 share
2 touch is 2 simple, be there
2 touch is 2 listen
2 touch is 2 feed
2 touch is 2 never, ever have greed
2 touch is 2 make some1 warm when it's so, so cold
2 touch is 2 hold a breeze,
2 touch is 2 sometimes tease
2 touch is 2 let 1 look in2 your eye's,
2 touch is 2 give a pretty little surprise.
2 touch is 2 feel me there,
2 touch is 2 always care . . .
I am in Love.

Ursula Washington

I Am

I am caring and I have love,
I wonder why the stars are so high up above,
I hear the sad cry of the weeping bell,
I saw the little green goblin that was there when I fell,
I want to explore the world up above,
I am caring and I have love.
I pretend that I have won the race,
I feel that I can set my own pace,
I touched the fairy that lived under my door,
I worry about the people that are at war,
I cry a joyful tear when I see the morning dove,
I am caring and I have love.
I understand my left from my right,
I say why bother even start a fight,
I dream one day to become well known,
I try not to talk too long on the phone,
I hope that people will not push and shove,
I am caring and I have love.

Kayla Zieske

Wind

Wind, wind, what is wind?
Is it what creeps ups your back when you're cold,
Is it what cools you down when you're hot?
Is it a tornado that brings new life?
Is it a friend or not?
But really what is wind?
Guess we will never know.

Susan Mayberry

In the Bedouin's Tent

I stand to the side, watching you dance
Arms outstretched, hands raised in the air
A smile plays across your face
With a flourish, you move to the music alone

Swaying, twirling
To sounds of a tambourine
I am mesmerized by the sight of you
And the fluid movements of your body

Delicately echoing finger cymbals
Take you in circles around the floor
Rhythmic, sensual, graceful
You provide a visual feast
For my unaccustomed eyes

From a veiled corner of the room
I see you as never before,
Joyful and alive
Pleasure is mine, watching you dance

Theresa Ann Moore

Olde(?) Williamsburg

The metered barricade of years
Becomes an open gateway when
Across the morning's sunlit green
Musicians call militia men.

Aroused, the ghostly regiments,
As in some secret spiral spun,
Quicken to familiar notes
To march again to fife and drum.

From shadowed vaults of days gone past
A phantom breeze unfurls a sigh,
Then stirs the leaves of yielding trees
In hushed memorial lullaby.

Now present scenes and those to come
In soft suffusion intertwine
With muffled hints of memories
In shifting streams of liquid time.

Thus history's longing for itself
Plucks threads from life's unraveled seams
And weaves on looms of yesterday
The fabric of tomorrow's dreams.

Marion Jean Blaney

Modern Messiahs

High in the sky with the moon in pale
"Patriot" and "Scuds" made it all merry !
Out there in my lawn in the icy, windy night,
My eyes burn from those fires in the wild.
Vivid in my head as was on the screen,
Pricking in my mind as was never before.
In the comfort of my room with the warmth of my bed,
Even not a wink, while the TV screen flashed.
Well above the green the mighty eagle swam.
Comes on the screen, the rolling tiny heads,
Sprinkling red across, all over the bridge.
Screech for a second and vanish in the cold
The tiny little metals giving them the fire.
Roar of that B-2 screaming to my head.
Comes the tossing and right the cheers,
For the direct hit on spot and
The head counts on the floor!
How come I am dumb? It is for the peace!
Drop all over the bomb, forget not to mouth
Peace on this Earth and you are the messiah!

Suresh Kodoor

Daddy's Lullaby

Each time Mama goes to bed,
Daddy makes sure a lullaby is said.

CRACK OF A WHIP
HITTING WITH FIST
HIS HATEFUL WORDS RUN THROUGH MAMA'S HEAD.

Mama's tears are quiet.
MUSCLES ACHE
BRUISED SKIN
Mama's lullaby is near the end.

Why can't anyone hear this lullaby song
but Mama and children each night it goes on?

As Daddy turns to go out the door,
he just looks at Mama and says:
"CLEAN UP THIS MESS!
AND GET THE HELL UP OFF THE FLOOR."

Each time Mama goes to bed,
Daddy makes sure a lullaby is said.

Karen Deitering-Wilson

Distortions

Each day equivalent only
to its own.
As uniquely as we grow
to our own
Who can understand how we're living
Projected reality as fantasy;
actually to what do we compare in despair
Hollow stare; I don't care
fate on my plate, tempting the gate
Negotiate, consolidate
to whom do we communicate?
We don't even associate
disassociation needs renegotiation
Alone we die
together we grow,
how much farther
will we go?

Amber Smith

Lonely

All alone I do my time,
So many questions on my mind.

So much pain is in my heart,
I don't know where my aching starts.

Every time I think of home,
I feel that much more alone.

I didn't know what I had until it was gone.
I've been missing you for, Oh, so long.

Without you life is Hell.
So I sit and rot in my cell.

I just don't know where to begin,
but the beginning sounds like the end.

By myself I shall go crazy.
Will it end? I don't know, maybe!

Neal R. Grothe

Just You

I wrote this for my fiancee, Cynthia Kallmeyer.
I'm you're Romeo,
You're my Juliet.
There's one thing I want to know.
Is our love the best it can get?

I want to be with you more every day,
Yet I still sit and contemplate.
Should I go and be with you, or should I stay
And calmly sit and wait?

You know I love you,
I really truly do.
There is no one new
That I want to be with,
Just lovely and beautiful you.

Raymond A. Madigan

Living and Dying to Say No

Journey through this land
Sorrow, grief crying pain.
Dying to say no
Losing dear loved one, even best friends.
Drugs I let take my life to the end.
The end still have life
Living and dying even crying to say no
Praying for change, pay day coming soon,
May this be the day I say no.
Higher power I'm dying to change
Staying sober two years clean.

Charles Townsend, Jr.

Destined

You were my first love, you are my last.
You are my present, you were my past,
You are my forever love.
It was destiny, it was fate,
We are truly soul mates.
We should have been, but will be.

I breathe your breath as if it were mine.
You've always been in the back of my mind.
You've always had a special place in my heart
Even though many years have kept us apart.

At last we are together again
As it should have always been.
The first part of our lives have come to an end,
Only for our second life to begin.

I will always be by your side,
And your love I will never hide.
I will love you forever more,
Because you are the one that I adore.

Trilby L. Hinnant

My One and Only

I think of you, as a dream waiting to come true.
When I see you, my heart starts pounding
It's not my fault I think you are outstanding.
I feel as though you cannot see me
When you're over being
"Mr. Popularity."
But yet when I see you smile at me
I know you're my one and only.

Heather Strickland

A Walk to Remember

Casting a prism of light across the water
splitting itself into a thousand parts.
Reflections on the days as love unfolds
two souls, lives so close in heart.

The sun meeting the horizon in perfect union
its beauty escaping its confines.
True love now joined together as one
a search so few would ever find.

Memories of the days gone by
times of love and heartache, sadness and joy.
A voice in the wind as it carries the message
that I have found my one true north.

Two beings, though separate but yet share the same
passion that sparkles within but which does not tether.
Reminiscent of the vows and the road ahead
an inspiration to the day as a walk to remember.

Gigi DeJesus

Mr. Moon

To: My Father, my forever dream companion
Gaze ascending into the ebony abyss
Distorted crescent grin shimmering down.
Phantasmagorical dream companions are we,
the three of us: Daddy, Me and Mr. Moon.
Futuristic plans absorb the dream-keepers
of our continuously wandering minds. Daddy
captains our voyage, and I, I sit inquisitively
experiencing the most tiny piece of cream cheese.
Cream cheese? Well, that's what Daddy says Mr. Moon
is made of. "It's getting awfully late," my Daddy
tells me. So I give Mr. Moon a hug and kiss
goodbye. Our star voyage is over once again.
A tear-filled voice says, "Goodnight, Daddy."
And whispers, "I'll see you soon, Mr. Moon."

Michelle Rae Brown

If

If you could only see
Beneath my quiet beaming
and my listening ear,
My unassuming manner and low gear,
And seeming countenance of calm
and harmless smile,
My guarded words with careful glances
all the while.

If only you could see,
You'd be surprised to find
unsteady heartbeats and a strong desire
To face you for one moment
with unfettered fire
That now is restrained, for it must not burn
Outside its tightly bound and secret cage
To ignite sparks that uncontrolled,
could end in rage.

If you could only see.

Mary Hobdy

What Is Longing?

A lasting embrace that has not yet begun
Longing is happiness, take away time
Circumstance pending, drowning in tears
A feeling felt by all who dwell on realization
Snowflake falling on your tongue
but melting right away,or better yet
it never fell your way
Because you long, and so do I
for feelings, thoughts, ethereal dreams
Misunderstanding, or not knowing at all
As lucid as water but as thick as honey
this is the path to oblivion
Along the way, shame to be oblivious
A piece of pie in a coffee shop
A shared moment under bed of twinkling stars
These are the things I long for,
But not for these alone
Alone these are nothing

Joshua Bleser

My Heart Belongs to You

As finger tips feel the sensation to weep
As wax melted candles reflect in your sleep
The beauty that forces the pain to retreat
Even though the waves can keep breaking
The power of destiny pulls like a rage
The touch of your lips hides the beast in the cage
As does wine get better with age
My heart is the one you are taking
I hope and pray as the years run away
An hour glass sand stands still as I say
I love you a little bit more every day

Vicky Occhipinti

In a Heart

In a heart there is a fire
that burns with the intensity of the sun.
This fire has many names:
Some call it passion,
some call it lust,
and even some call it love.
Whatever it is called,
it should not be dimmed by hurt.
So the fire can burn with the intensity of the sun
In a heart.

Nathan Strom

Liberation

I swim in a sea of black velvet
Floating on my back
Gazing up at the vastness I have created
I glide around gracefully, magically
Like a creature born to fulfill this destiny
No one knows about this different world, only me
And no one ever will
It's a secret I treasure dearly
Locked up in my heart with a gilded key
My own music box in my soul
The ballerina dancing only for me
And when the music stops and darkness envelopes
She just keeps dancing
The dance of someone not being judged
The dance of someone who has been liberated
It appears the box is closed and the music stopped
But I will never stop dancing
Gliding around in a sea of black velvet
Doing a dance only I can see

Lindsey Nichole Knutson

Diamond to Mercury

Tears collect the life of a face and drop
to oblivion, travelling the rough lines
of a haggard man.
Oh, how water can bend spines of the strong!
or that once was . . . but then again,
Diamond tomorrow Mercury the next . . .
Thoughts of forever condenses the waters
of sadness, or is it waters of madness
that keeps the river flowing?
and a grimace of disgust keeps the hate from showing?
But it's Diamond tomorrow, Mercury the next . . .
Content in a smile after the fall from the nest . . .
but in return a kick in the face, they
spit on my race, a blow to the chest . . .
Is it ice today and water the rest?
No, it's diamond tomorrow and Mercury the next.

Jon Richardson Heredia

The Memory Locket

Somewhere in a far-off place, a girl sits on her bed,
trying to remember when her father was not dead.
He gave her a locket that held, in so many ways,
dreams and hopes and wishes for much happier days,
memories full of grassy fields, meadows full of trees,
somewhere on a sandy beach, a bluish, greenish sea.
A teardrop falls into the locket, for she knows in her head
that, after all, in her heart, her father is not dead.

Nicole Kissel

Never Lose Heart

Computers are rapidly taking command
Of our lives as we gradually feed them more power,
And more and more people feel lost in a land
Where keyboards and printers make everyone cower,
With chips and conductors and circuits galore
That transfer huge volumes of internal bytes,
Causing so many to gravely deplore
How sadly their minds are sinking to low heights.
But there's a quality of life that can't be assigned
To buttons and switches and other devices,
When serious problems encumber one's mind
And something is needed to settle the crisis.
The greatest decisions arise from emotion,
Which sets all computers completely apart,
When loving and caring and sincere devotion
Are needed and only can come from the heart.

James D. Cullen

Ode to Turning 80

Transmission started slipping, oil pressure
dipping (guess I'll take a pill)
Body frame bending, suspension frame ending
(guess I'll take a pill)
Brake system nil, can't hack a hill
(guess I'll take a pill . . .)
Exhaust system excellent, just a bit flatulent
(guess I'll take a pill)
Power steering's squealing 'cause the belt's
peeling (guess I'll take a pill)
Radiator's leaking, whole damn thing is
squeaking (guess I'll take a pill)
Getting kind of sleepy now (guess I'll take
a nap; life is such a snap)

Melba Nance

Don't Let Us Forget

Christmas is the time of year,
When there is spreading of love and cheer.
But don't let us forget,
The real Christmas set.
The wisemen in the field,
And the angel they beheld.
The shepherds watching the flock,
And the miles they had to walk.
A couple looking for a place,
For the birth of the One of grace.
But don't let us forget,
The most important of the set.
The coming of the mighty God,
The beginning of hope,
The ending of a long wait.

Sarah Corney

Wet Afternoons

time to learn, to look through the window
chatting with you under the blanket

the afternoon goes by into my fingers
i see it going away
and taking
with it
another chance to be near you

tears like rain
lonely pond
smashed by mistake

wet afternoons
rainy days
like my own, wet loneliness . . .

Saskia Levy

A Jewelry Box's Secrets

She puts me on every morning:
a silver rope necklace with a small heart shaped pendent,
glistening in the bright light.
Her skin beneath me is always soft and warm.
The memories I give her are only happy ones.
She touches me unconsciously whenever he is near.

I only like to please her,
not to make her sad.
Sometimes tears slide down her face and
I don't understand why.
She takes me off and looks at me,
and sadness fills her face like students fill an empty hall.

She puts me in her jewelry box,
making sure I'm on the bottom.
She looks at me closely, for one final moment,
closes the box and keeps my memories locked inside.

Stephanie Levy

That Star

Remember that star where we would sit,
Way up high; think of it.
Our hearts would sing to the ocean's roar,
Our love would fly like the eagles soar.

Then a breeze would blow away
The thoughts of love that had come our way.
From that star is such a fall,
I was with you, standing tall.
Through the clouds, on my way down,
I caught a glimpse of your white gown.

And now at night, I look above,
All I can do is send a dove.
If only I could have some wings,
To make it way up there,
And a gentle wind to help me, too,
I could be there on that star above,
And be there always, next to you.

Gary Lee Morley

Maturation

The wind blows, and my body is dismembered.
I attempt to run to catch parts
but the wind is too strong.
I maneuver my body through the strong gusts
and remember that I am powerful.
At that moment my body members are reunited
and I am made whole.
I look to the sky in confusion
and attempt to understand the lesson.
I cannot comprehend.
The wind then finds its place in my confusion,
and I am once again disassembled.

Chamika Evette Hawkins

Acceptance

They say you love me
but I must confess
I don't understand why
I'm in this mess
I've lived a life full
of honesty and respect
But it seems my good points
you chose to neglect
So here I am . . . eyes full of tears
After just being told that the coming years
will be less than I hoped for and full of pain
I could feel bitter, but what's to gain
I raise my eyes and don't complain
I give a smile and say a prayer
And hope when the end comes . . . you will be there

Barbara A. Nowack

The Fall of Autumn Love

I have often thought of autumn's falling leaves,
of turned up collars, warm sweaters, long sleeves,
seeing one's breath in the chill of the air,
an endless flow of clouds in deep blue there.
Colors of autumn painted
from God's brush and palette abound
falling softly, slowly
to blanket the cold barren ground.
Trees stand naked now,
their time to dream of spring.
They listen to children's laughter;
by the fireside warmly they sing
songs of their happiness they long to last,
soon to be a whisper like seasons of the past.
For now they share together
the fall of autumn's love . . . forever.

Jeffry Evan Fickling

TO CATCH A FALLING STAR

To catch a falling star caught by afar,
To study dreams paramount; go, envision your wishes about.
To look at you is like watching the glistening stars
In the sky falling into your beautiful eyes.
I wish to hold your hand, as I strive to understand.
The significance of a wish, to give a special kiss.
To catch a falling star, seeking a form of reality
While playing a mere sweet melody. I want to
Hold you so tight, every day, every night, knowing
Where you are. To catch a falling star as I emanate
What I can, intricate; even as bona fide as it may
Seem, we know that we'll always be a team. My
Feelings I will not bar, to catch a falling star.

Quiana Alexander

Joyful

The Way and the wrong—the good and the bad
The truth and the lies—true or false
Life and death—eternal and temporal
One came down and went back up
The other came down and stayed
Jesus Others You Friends Us Love

"I am Alpha and Omega, the beginning and the ending."
Righteous and unrighteous—"No, not one"
Perfect and imperfect—just and unjust
Solid rock or sinking sand—Heaven or Earth
Jesus Others You Friends Use Love

Not black, but white—no in between
Day and night—light or dark
No night, only God's light
Who neither slumbers nor sleeps
Jesus Others You Forever Use Love

JaneAnn Moody

The Day You Left

My hands are shaking on this horrible day,
As I pray to God not to take you away.
He silently shakes His head and places a hand on my face,
Without opening His mouth He says you're going to a Heavenly place.
Tears start to fill my eye,
And slowly I begin to break down and cry.
Suddenly my world is turning from stone to sand,
But this is something no-one else can understand.
It's a problem I have to face on my own,
To turn my world back from sand to stone.
I have to give my heart a bit of time to heal,
Before I begin to know quite what I feel.
They say that time will only tell,
But I'll never forget the day that my world fell.

Katie Douglas

For My Mom Who . . .

For my mom who . . .
Whose face is like an angel.
Who hovers over me like a hawk to keep me safe from harm's way.
Who is my protector from all things bad.
Whose touch is like cotton.
Whose smile is like the sun on a sunny day.
Whose laugh is like music to my ears.

For my mom who . . .
Who makes me feel better when I'm down.
Who tells me to reach for the stars.
Who allows me to be who I am.
Who fills my heart with joy.
Who talks to me when I need someone to talk to.
Who is the greatest mom in the world.

Brent Heiden

Serenity

The storm has finally abated,
The wrathful wind has been placated,
The surf's stopped crashing 'gainst the shore.

The waves roll in more gently now,
They come with greater peace, somehow,
Not tall and angry, as before.

I'd yearned for this serenity,
But dreaded what the loss might be,
If I'd said, "Begone," "No more!"

I feared that if I wished it calm,
I'd wake and find the ocean gone,
And, Oh, I know I'd miss it, sore.

But, look! Although the storm has waned,
A deep and tranquil sea remains,
For me to love, forevermore.

Jack Brown

Old Toy

My pain is easily concealed with a smile.
Getting over you, my heart asks the question "how?"
You're deep in my soul,
penetrating my inner thoughts.
How to be a man and how to love a woman
are some things that I was never taught.
With no blink, no fear, no second thought
I would willing die for you
the pain could not be that much more
than what loneliness can do.
Within your eyes I see my life and everything I need.
This hunger for love without you here
is something I just can't feed.
I feel like an "old toy" in the corner, is where I lay,
wishing, wanting, waiting, but no one comes to play.

Joseph Johnson

What Nobody Knows

Infrared testimonies are high seated in council,
As the frivolous miracles shine onto the rest.
Who, then, will define the majority of the partial,
As the losers try their absolute to be their best?
Accusations and allegations slandering its name,
As the losers can't even bear proceeding intros,
But they stand firm on the shoulder of shame,
Forgetting nothing but what nobody knows!

Chad Powers

I Am

Lord, I am not rich
But I am worthy
I am not poor
But I accept my journey
Lord, I am weak
But I am not tired
I know I am not all I can be
But still I am inspired
Lord, I hold no grudges
But I do hold tight to memories
When I lose a friend
I still thank you for allowing that friendship to be
Lord, I plan my weekend
And accept the plans you have for me
This in the realm of never seeing your face
And still I lift my hands to thee
So Lord, I am rich and I am not weak
I lose no real friends
However I gain a friend in thee
I Am

Stacey Bozeman

Conception

A platform in the sky, constructed by mind's
eye. I anticipate the arrival of beauty.
The force of nature beckons with a breeze.
Lured by the call, I tremble.
A sudden deep breath,
A rumbling from the left,
I exhale and wait for the vision.
A harmony erupts as the dance begins,
The maestro remains unseen.
The wind attacks from every corner,
I sigh, smile, dream. The war cries are heard,
Essence now released.
I waver with anxiety and fear.
An arrow of white light,
An invisible target,
My soul forthcoming is near.
The impact of the blow ignites my awaited form.
Delicate and fragile, I scream.
The former forgotten,
I begin anew and wait for Him to redeem.

Deana Stringer

As One

I wait for the metro train in Paris to celebrate
One hundred years of la Tour Eiffel
A throng of people wait alongside me
More people join the crowd
Pushing, shoving
A train stops with its belly already full of passengers
More pushing, more shoving
I've unwillingly become part of this unstoppable animal
The train lumbers forward
Its crowded contents lurching as one from the movement
For no one can move except as one
Nor can we breathe except as one
And finally, the train groans to a stop
The passengers echo the sound
Waiting for the doors to open
Pushing, shoving
Against the train's clenched mouth
Which reluctantly opens
Spitting its passengers onto the quai
Where I am once again free to be as one, individually

Caryn Ross

The Ex-Wife

She got so old her milk dried up
And she didn't have mother to feed her pup
The puppy drank water and took a nap.
The wife drank beer and got real fat.

I used to take her to the picture show,
But she barked at the people and blew her nose.
I used to take her to the local dogfights,
'Til she foamed at the mouth and tried to bite.

I bought her a car so she could get away,
But she went to her mother's and she wouldn't stay.
So I left her in our tent, and she needed to pee,
And I moved to town and bought a TV.

She called me last night on the telephone.
She'd been driving all day with the blinker on.
She really wanted to go to roff,
But she couldn't get the blinker off.

What more can I say? I don't see her now.
She wrecked the car and rides a cow.
The puppy grew up and moved away.
Now she scratches fleas and barks all day.

Barry Ferguson

I Did, I Will, and I Am

I Did, I Will, and I Am sat in the den,
Having tea with their gentlemen.

I Did talked of her lovely past
And of how the years had gone so fast.
She talked of stories way back when,
As she sipped her tea in the roomy den.

I Will then told of what she'd do
In the future, when things would all be new.
She said, "I will travel the seas and skies,"
But she was just waiting for time to go by.

Then all of a sudden I Am said to them,
"Listen, ladies and gentlemen,
What you have done is good and fine
And what you will do is still in your mind.
But I am doing so much today!
I laugh, I love, I work and play.
I live for today, not the future or past.
Because nothing is promised and nothing will last."

Donna Blakemore

The Seasons of the Garden of Love

Spring:
Walk past the fresh dirt where life will start.
With just the right amount of love the Earth will part.
Place the seed of love in my heart
Water each day with your smile it will build love for me to impart.

Summer:
Feed me with the just the right
amount of support I will flower in turn for your might.

Fall:
Without protection and food my heart is hurt and starts to die.
Cover me with your blanket of love to keep me alive.
For give me when I have become old and worn
It's because my heart is filled with mold and is forlorn.

Winter:
I am cold sad and alone
I reach out for love and find only stone.
The cold harsh world has covered me up
Please take this last moment in time
to reach through to accept my heart this one last time.

Glenn Simmons

Flashlight Images

Tonight the snow is falling,
Perfect crystals, seeming to glow.
—Reflection—
Memories of younger years.
Snowfall late at night,
You and I anxiously glancing out the window,
Awaiting the arrival of guaranteed fun
If time was in our favor.
It came.
You and I in pajamas,
Wide-eyed, excited,
Mom let us venture out the door into the after-bedtime world.
But it didn't seem to be.
All our friends, laughing down the road,
We followed the footsteps to Ryan and Shannon's
Snowball fight already in progress.
We joined, innocently pegging each other,
Flashlight images
Of late-night snowfall.

Colleen Millman

Worried and Hopeful

I'm sitting here trying to think what to write.
My head and my hand are beginning to fight.
My head wants words of wisdom and feeling.
My hand want those it can spell and are appealing.
The aim of this passage, my friend,
Is to comfort and amuse to the end.
But if one cannot agree with the other,
This script will begin to bother.
Perhaps, due to my age, I try too hard
To prove my aspiration to become a bard.
(Apparently it seems my work will always be
More of a sapling than a beautiful oak tree.)
Even so there are those (I dearly hope)
who know this is not the work of a dope,
But the passions of a young, emotive man
Who wants to show his feelings aren't locked in a can.
I'm sure that this, dear reader, you can see
And know that in your hands is part of me.
At last the introduction is complete
And now you can witness my latest feat.

Pete Wallace

The Three Most Powerful Words in the World

Next time someone
Smiles at you and shakes your hand
Says hello and gives you a kiss
Touches you and listens to you
Looks at you and thanks you
Welcomes you and talks to you
And tells you the three most
Powerful words
In the world
"I love you"
Smile at them and shake their hand
Say hello and give them a kiss
Touch them and listen to them
Look at them and thank them
Welcome them and talk to them
And tell them the three most
Powerful words
In the world
"I love you"

Cesar Vargas

My Life

Sometimes when I sleep I have nightmares
And I wake up frightened and alone in the dark . . .
But sometimes I dream.
I dream that you're not sick,
That you're healthy and happy
And that you love me.

I dream that you're holding me
And will never let me go,
But when I wake up and move,
My bruises still hurt.
My bed is still broken.
I hear your voice shouting cruel things in my head,
And you're still gone.
And I know it's very odd;
I miss you so much.
I hurt so much.
Yet as you have left and destroyed my life,
Also, I know, you have set me free.

Darla Jacobson

Alive in Africa

On the edge of Africa
Above me a mountain called Lion's Head.
Clouds billow and roll down to the Atlantic shore
To the north
Mandela's old home
An island, sparse
He was right, no man is an island unto himself
Nor would he want to be
In Africa
This great, fertile continent
Where the poor share more than is fair
Elephant and lion, rhino and wildebeest
They roam
Not in hologram, in the flesh
This place is real—and you can be in Africa

Juno Levy

Wondering Tonight

I'm sitting here wondering Dad, if you're out tonight,
alone on your porch, looking up at the sky.
Aren't the stars lovely and the moon so bright?
Are there a few clouds to shade your eyes from the light?
Is it cold or cloudy or is it clear as glass?
I wish I could be there, having our private chats.
Alone by ourselves except for a splash from a fish.
We talk of our future and of our past.
But for now, it's the present; our future can wait, our past
will remember as we sit by this lake.
Are you happy here Dad? Are you doing just fine?
I sure miss not having you around all the time.
I'm sure you get lonely, as I tend to do,
especially when I'm alone thinking of you.
So soon I shall travel two hundred miles
to sit on your porch, listening to some ole hoot owl.
I think of you often and even worry some but
I know in my heart you are at home.

Ronda Williams

Grams and Gramps

Thanks Grams and Gramps,
for everything you have done for me.
From taking care of my tummy,
to all the money.
From the hats,
to the baseball bats.
From doing my chores,
to cleaning my drawers.
From locking the doors,
to going downtown to eat at El Conquistador.
From the eyes being white,
to the eyes being red, with a blurry sight.
From the calls,
to that tear that always falls.
From the hi's,
to the goodbyes.
I love you very much, Grams and Gramps!
And thanks for everything else.

Craig Louis Cook

Indigenous Vision

I was one of the ordinary,
nothing important in my terms.
Fought for my nations,
every man waited eternally for the score.
Battled in the valley of their sanctuary,
tactics on the front never came into play.
Obey their laws or nature.
Force is forming us into our ancestors.
The revelation captures the Children strayed from Love.
Now to see the life that we missed.

Tetsuya Honda

Friends

You think they're there and then they're not.
You looked at her and then you thought,
is this one really going to be true?
The last one wasn't, was it for you?
They try, they do,
but none so far have been really true.
They listen and look and they're standing there,
reading you like a little book.
They talk, you listen, they yell, you listen,
and then one day
they leave you there right by the bay.
Your soul it sinks, your hopes they drown,
and upon your face appears a frown.
There goes one more in the sea
and never once did she see what she did to me.
So there you stand,
right on the sand,
until one more "friend"
comes to see how far your heart can float.

Diana Naftalyev

Message of Love

As I look into the night, my eye is focused on a star.
It is the brightest one, and closest to my heart.
Metaphorically, it reminds me of you,
And how you made all of my dreams come true.

Because of you, you gave me the chance to love.
It is the best gift, from God above.
I look back in the past, when my heart was in pain;
Because of you, those tears have washed away.

You are the only one for me, as the sun needs the earth,
To shine upon; you have given me self-worth.
I shall love no other, for you are my first,
Thus, for your love, I shall thirst.

As you read, this message is bold.
It prepares you for life's journey, on how to reach your goal.
Our journey is clear, as it was given from above.
You and I have become the Message of Love.

Kendall Byrd

Once Is Enough

Food poisoning is a bitch
The worst kind of sickness
And once you get it, you never
Want whatever gave it to you ever again
No matter how much you loved it
No matter if you wash and cook it yourself
The sight, smell, and taste of it are
Forever
Indelibly
Associated in your mind
With the worst feeling you've ever had
You lose all desire for anything
That could ever have caused you so much pain
Under any circumstances, for whatever reasons
And that, my once and former
Lover,
Is why we cannot be friends.

Marilyn Bowens

A Day at the Zoo

One day at the zoo, I was very happy!
I saw a sea lion named, Slappy!
The zoo keeper's name was, Moppy.
I fell down so much that they named me Floppy!
I got to see the flamingos that were pink!
I have to end this poem, because I'm running out of ink!

Mallory Ashwander

Life

Look around yourself and see
The world is not as it used to be
The rivers are polluted and the sky has turned gray
When Jesus comes everyone will pray
Death and violence and evil games
Innocent people are not the blame
I wish the world was as it was before
But soon paradise will be restored

John Pearson

Save Forest

The trees stand there fresh and green,
Wave with wind making musical notes,
By clapping their leaves against each.
They cannot move even an inch, but the
Influence of them is of a great reach.
Varieties of trees grow there, some straight
Many creep along, many bend a long way.
They together cover a great area of valleys
Giving shelter to many varieties of lives.
Some of which creep, fly, some roar and run.
The leaves with a coat of mist and dew
Between the trees are always streams, flowing
Silently striking the rocks covered green.
The air is wet and freshness rotates around
There is a dreamy magic in the ground
That creates such a wonderful bond.
Never these few words can say it all
It is the thing to be sensed by senses
By saving, and living with them.
Create and save the forest.

Sheetal Patil

The Silent Witnesses of Domestic Violence

They share—
. . . They care
. . . They make aware.

Their story—
. . . Their stories
. . . Of those who cannot speak.

These silent witnesses—
. . . Once they talked
. . . Once they walked
. . . Once they were.

Where are they now—
. . . They wish to impart?

Who will listen
. . . Who will care as they share?
(remembering eleven children who died needlessly)

Judith Brooker

Take My Hand

Take my hand, my gentle love, let's walk this path together
Sharing the joys and wonders of all that we see,
And live our lives and share our love forever,
I'll come for you, our love renew, together we will be.

Let not our hearts be heavy from the trials that we face,
For we are destined for certain things, and control we cannot,
But we can love one another, and this is our saving grace,
Life is short and so, my love, waste it we should not.

This is my dream, my every wish and my every thought,
Oh, sweet gentle man, do not my love refuse,
Instead sweet one say to me, of this my love fear not,
Oh, come to me, Oh, come to me, for your love I cannot lose.

Katherine Noreen Brantley

See You

I saw you again today,
my soul fleeting, my heart racing
the loss of all apparent lies I do cede

I saw you again today,
my mind slipping, my knees shaking,
the moral of my eternity you are so

In yet another time,
away from this empty shrine,
I would kiss you,
I would hold you,
I'd be with you, don't you know
but now I've lost my mind,
sedated am I in this strange little rhyme.

Can I hold you?
May I kiss you?
Can I make you mine?

David Wang

I'm Sorry

I'm sorry for what I have done
Honest, it was just in fun
I'm sorry for causing you pain
My heart feels like it has been slain

I'm sorry for calling you a name
Just now, during the game
I'm sorry for lying to you
I should always be honest and true

I'm sorry for my loss
'Cause without you my heart covers with moss
I'm sorry for even trying
But it really felt like I was flying

I'm sorry it didn't work
My sadness will always lurk
I'm mostly sorry and this is true
I'm sorry for falling in love with you

Jacob Weston

Pain

he lay there still, in the folds of darkness.
his words muffled,
his tears but a glowing candle . . .
what he said no one heard,
as he was covered
by the painful layers that enveloped him
and clouded his thoughts.
his movements slow, each a spasm of pain,
as he lay there crying in the torrent of rain,
washed away, like the night into day
in a burst of flame.
his mind astray, wandering in a dream
venturing untold tales
of wild sparks of imagination,
from the plays of destiny
to the wonders of creation,
and like the fluttering breeze
with wings on air
his heart arose
into nature's care.

Chandni Mehta

Life

Dedicated to my little brother, Kevin
Tears dripping from my face
My whole life is a maze
Trying to figure it is a case
This pain you've caused me will never end

Osiris Viridiana Pastor

Earth Angel

I fall deeper into myself every day
Suffering and drowning in the pain
I search for a reason,
Wait throughout the seasons,
Still nothing good comes my way.

It's a struggle to get myself out of bed,
All the feelings and thoughts running through my head.
I just want to lie alone in the dark
And know what it's like to be dead.

It's like a knife has cut me long and deep
So much on my mind, I can't seem to sleep
I lie awake and I wish and pray
Hoping to find some peace in my dreams.

Lucky for me, she's always there
She just smiles at me, and I have not a care.
My sweet angel, I won't reveal her name,
The angels in Heaven cannot compare.

So I wish I could stay forever in the night
peaceful and resting, not having to fight,
feelings of sorrow and feelings of pain,
Forever in the night, my Earth angel reigns.

Samantha Stansell

Safe in God's Arms

I will never again hold you in my arms,
Because I could not keep you from harm.
I will never get to sing you a lullaby
Or teach you the names of the stars in the sky.

I will never get to see the smile
Of my sweet precious child.
I will never feel the touch of your tiny hand
Or teach you how to build a house in the sand.

I will never see you go off to school
Or be able to tell you how much I love you.
I will never meet your first date
Or the one who would have been your mate.

I am so sorry that you never got to have fun,
To play in the sun or just go out and run.
But for now you are safe in God's arms;
He will keep you from all harm.

I wish I could go back and change that night,
Make it so that you would still have your life.
But I know that in God's arms you will be loved,
Until the day that Mommy can come above.

Mary Haynes

A Father's Love

No greater love can there be
Than a father's love for thee
He loves you when you're good
Like a father truly should
He even loves you when you're bad
Even though it makes him very sad

A father loves you well or ill
And his love can do more than a pill
A father's love is the best
A father's love cannot fail
A father's love will prevail

We all have a father up above
Awaiting us with open arms of love
He loves us so much, he sent his son to die
So we could live with him on high
If in him you will believe
Then you will truly see
No greater love can there be
Than the father's love for thee.

Tommy Byerly

The Hand

The hand is one of many precious gifts,
that was given to us by God.
The hand is connected to the arm,
for which is one of four limbs of our body.

It is not only a gift, it is also a tool,
that can be used in many ways, to do different things.
Its function and possibilities are endless.

The hand can be used for combing your hair,
brushing your teeth and putting makeup on.
For throwing a ball, to swim or playing basketball.
It can used for writing a letter, to speak with,
to shake someone's hand and change the future.

The handshake can be an extremely important gesture.
It is a sign of character.

It can be used to say hello or goodbye,
congratulations or thank you. For friendship or love.
In place of a kiss or a hug. To touch someone's life.

To acknowledge someone's existence, with admiration,
loyalty, respect and devotion of love beyond belief.

C. J. Smith

Breathe of Life

As I stare into the Heavens blue skies,
glorious life descends upon the horizon.
Dusk is approaching, soon night will have fallen,
and all will be silent.

Though darkness will not blanket my thoughts and feelings,
my heart will continue through hurt and pain.
Massive storms at sadness will not make me lower my head,
to its Heavenly fallen tears from above.

I will stand strong with my chin held high,
higher than the clouds of suffering.
With the Lords love I will prevail and these tears of sadness,
that drench me in sorrow shall dry with time.

The gray skies will part and once again,
Heavens glorious light will shine down upon my face.
I will be blessed within,
with the glowing sense of love and hope.

Though my experience,
I learn in the moment,
That there was nothing to be lost, only gained.

John Queen

Cemetery Plot

A small child is taken to a cemetery
to mourn the death of her father, who is being
put in a grave next to his sister, my aunt, who
I never met but whose name is the same as mine
on a tombstone next to my father, who told me
"You're named for my beautiful sister," so I would
remember her who my mother said was a tramp
and it was a mistake to name me the same name
because she died when she was young and it is
bad luck to be named for such a person.
My father, who is young, is being put alongside.
There is room for me where my name is etched in stone.
"No!" my mother cries in widow's disbelief
that she will grow old without him and I will
have no father. Her laments go down in the hole
in the ground that will soon be filled in with earth
over the casket where my father looks asleep.
Although I know he won't wake up and neither will
my aunt whose name's the same as mine, I'm happy that
my father has company in the cemetery.

Fay Bell

Thanks to You

Pouring down comes the rain;
it never ends, just like my pain.
Nothing to do but scream and cry,
thoughts in which I want to die.
That's when you come and say to me,
"Give me your hand, I want you to see,
in your heart, in your soul,
no matter what, you're beautiful."
More than anything, I love you.
I want you to know this because it's true.
So much thanks to you my friend,
because of you, my heart can mend.

Shannon Lee Mckittrick

Bounding Rose

What you thought you wanted . . .
i apologize to the black rose
for its splendor and perfection
come far from comparison . . .
thou tender, pollinated rose,
how thy life could be so short-lived
to be outdone by someone who
does not even try
i pity you, rose . . . all of your beauty
created and maintained for no purpose
i despise thee, black rose;
you desperate thief of attention,
your worthless esteem of false pride
is your own doing
i laugh at thee, dead black rose
your crippled leaves hath fallen,
lying around you in a heap of self-pity
watch them decompose into the soil beneath
now thou art nothing more than that
which thou hast started with.

Christopher Jonathan Ippolito

You Are Your Desk

What is the personality of your desk?
Is it serious with endless paperwork?
Is it childish with small stuffed toys and gadgets?
Or is it filled with framed photos, diaries and memories?

What is the job of your desk?
Is it a library with manuals all over?
Is it a refreshment stand with chocolates, cookies and chips?
Or is it a napping station, assuming you won't get caught?

What is the activity of your desk?
Is it calculating, inputting and analyzing data?
Is it screaming out for tidiness?
Or is it welcoming co-workers, clients and friends for a chat?

Who are you at your desk?
Are you a workaholic, a lazy slowpoke or a busybody?
It doesn't matter as long you realize this:
You are what you do at your desk.

Grace K. Chik

Why Did I Let Myself Fall?

For two years, I had complete trust in you
You were a good friend
Someone to talk to
Why did I let myself fall?
My past hurts, didn't you know?
Or did you even care?
Why did I let myself fall?
A fire was lit between us
But she was the icy water that extinguished it
You seem to have all the answers
So tell me . . . why did I let myself fall?

Meagan Marie Irving

Fairy Tale

I want to live in a fairy tale
Where all my dreams come true.

I want to live in a fairy tale
Where everything is simple and true.

To be a fair madden rescued by a prince.
To fall in love and be happy ever since.

Oh! I want to live in a fairy tale
Where all my dreams come true.

For if I lived, in a fairy tale,
Then I'd forever have you.

I want to live in a fairy tale,
Where all my dreams come true.

I want to live in a fairy tale,
To be held close to you.

I want to live in a fairy tale
I want to be married to you.

I want to live in a fairy tale
A fairy tale with you.

I want to live in a fairy tale.

Karina Foster

No Man Has Hurt Me

Thoughts filled full of emptiness.
All the small things that you miss.

Do you think that you will last?
Where's your star? Catch it fast.

Keep your eyes closed. Life passes you by.
And when you're old you'll wonder why.

Must have cash, no time for laughter.
But are any of you really money's master?

All you feel are hate and rage,
Like a monopoly of our age.

Do you light a torch to see the sun?
Do mind and body live as one?

You never enjoy life. Never take the time,
For fear the group may leave you behind.

You'll believe, realize one day,
It's not if you win, it's how you play.

How blind you are, pitiful fool.
How much longer will you rule?

Kevin Gipson

The First Christmas Night

On that first Christmas night
there came a star so radiantly bright

That led the lowly shepherds there
to that humble manger so dank and bare.

Here too came the wise men three
with rich gifts offered so gladly free,
To that little child who there did lie
only for us and others too soon to die.

Now Nature broke forth in welcome tribute,
little birds sang the song of a flute
While flowers blossomed bright in a hurry
like the holly tree with bright red berry.

But the fir tree stood alone and bare,
but God—He is loving and twice so fair
Showered the little tree with star after star
so it could be seen from the manger afar.

Charles C. Royer

Never Fading Rose

Remembering you
Obviously missing you
Still loving you
Every moment thinking of you

You are the rose that blossomed in my heart
Remembering each moment right from the start
You are the rose where morning dew settles
Obviously watering your soft delicate petals
You are the rose the perfect shade of white
Still flowing with fragrance softly light
You are the rose, such strong thorns & stems
Every leaf attached like green precious gems

Remembering you always,
You are my rose.

Mary Jo Wright

From Russia with Love

Her hair is golden,
like the sun that rises early in the morning.
Her smile so sweet,
my heart so loving for those lips.
When we kissed,
my heart pounded and pounded.
But then she left,
like the summer has ended and fall is resurrecting.
All I can do is weep.
My heart crying to her,
please come back, Anna—
I love you with all of my heart.
We can travel the world together,
once and forever.
Anna, you stole my heart,
from Russia with love.

Ivica Delija

Words

How much weight?
How much punch?
Things we say casually like the spring wind
Which doesn't care how it blows the branches.

It defines us
Tall or short . . .
light or dark eyes.

People hang on them
Fall from them or
Even die in them.
It's hard to distinguish
the lies from the truth,
The jokes from the sermon.

How do we know their meaning?
Who cares besides the people
That are reading.

Albert Di Salvatore

My Grandpa Sam

I had a fretful sleep last night.
Tossed and turned 'til I saw the morning light.
My grandfather came to me shortly past dawn.
I sat up to hear him, and tried not to yawn.
I needed his strength, that is why he came to me.
He's always been there when I needed him to be.
He had to go when I was but seven.
He needed to find his special place in Heaven.
But when I close my eyes and look up at the stars.
There he is, shining brighter than Jupiter and Mars!
"Grandpa Sam" was his name.
"Guardian Angel" is his fame!

Martha Silverman

Celestial Disillusion

I like to believe
that exploring beyond our sphere,
could one day put an end to our problems.
But while people still die—
from hunger, disease, strife,
and the Earth is poisoned and mutilated,
there is not enough to spare for celestial voyage.
As people die, are their lives worth a shovel-full
of rock and sand from a dead world?
Should we be searching for more life
beyond our boundaries while we continue to
discard what we already have?
I scoff at our pathetic space faring sciences,
and dream of the stars we may never reach,
behaving the way we do.

Jonathan Frank Pollnow

Daddy

Daddy, I love him so.
Daddy is the greatest thing that ever happened to me.
Daddy, I know he will go but not soon.

Daddy, no other man could replace him.
Daddy Is in my heart forever.
Daddy, He will be there for my prom.

Daddy has brown sparkling eyes.
Daddy has some frisky whiskers.
Daddy has beautiful black and white hair.

Daddy, he will always be to me.
Daddy, I love him so.
But I know most of all, Daddy,
I will always be your baby girl, no matter what.

Rachel Rebekah Bish

Restraint

He is caged, a man insane
Held against his will, restrained
confined within a shell, contained
pulling against pain the bonds that bind him
crying to those that will not find him
beaten, blistered, bruised and braying
repressed, obsessed, possessed and praying
to release that beast only once at least
for at last the eternal torment to cease
but his torment continues forever endured
his pain is one that will not be cured
Forever entombed within that shell
contained within his living Hell
restrained forever so no one will see
that raving lunatic inside of me

Scott Michael Whistman

Without

Without Wrong, there would be no Right
Without Bad, there would be no Good
Without Sorrow, there would be no Joy
Without Hate, there would be no Love
Without Pain, there would be no Pleasure
Without Laughter, there would only be Tears
Without the poor, there would be no Rich
Without Heart, there is no Soul
Without Hell, there would be no Heaven
Without the Oceans, there would only be Deserts
Without Life, there is no Existence
Without Darkness, could we see the Light?
Without Today, there is no Tomorrow
Without Diversity, there is no Individuality
"Death is but a Furlough for the soul"

Edward Joseph De Torre

Awaking with a Smile

When I opened my eyes this morning,
A thought of you appeared in my mind.
Then I was pondering
What you were doing at the time.
Were you just being bored at school,
Or were you thinking of me, too?
Hoping that I'm on your mind,
Turning your gray skies blue.
I know that your life can be rough at times,
And I'm here to help you through.
Letting you know I'll be by your side,
Always being faithful and true.
Hoping I can see you soon,
To hold you in my arms.
Letting you know I'm for real,
Keeping you safe from harm.
I'm glad that I found you,
And hope that we grow
To be close with each other,
As I hope time will show.

Jason Siegfried

Lake Tahoe's Persistence

Past the Indian merchant who showcases his hand-crafted beads,
calypso music prances around my ears.
Past the petite Baptist church on the outskirts of Carson City,
ribbons of stardust dot the horizon.
Past the shy horse who grazes by herself,
the wind grows Herculean.
Past the questions of restless children on Jefferson Street,
my replies mosaic across my mouth.
Should I recycle my memories for tomorrow
or store them in my walk-in closet for my scrapbook?
Cilantro and oregano decorate the cabarets
and the Two Guys from Italy sign still seems brand-new
after the celebration of their 20th anniversary.
Circuses of pigeons wing their way toward the beach
as I leave the empty bench,
and snips of old-fashioned harmony satisfy my painting.

Lulu J. Yu

Gone

I am looking for you, but you can't be found.
I am waiting for you, but you never come.
I am waiting for your love . . . yet it is lost.
Your voice echoes in my ears . . .
Your eyes are seen in the sky . . .
The wind calls your name.
It whispers where have you gone . . .
Your presence is in my mind . . .
In my dreams I seek you . . . but you're not found.
Where are you, my love?
Where have you gone?

Amanda Nicole DeJarnette

I'll Take the Blame!

Wrong decisions are now facing me;
the process of correcting them is far beyond what the eye can see.

Confusion has formed a cloud of misery and unhappiness;
the smoke has formed a mist of tears and sadness.

Frustration has overtaken the atmosphere;
there is a solution, but I will not weep.

I understand the connections that caused me to be there;
but I'm not ashamed.

I love what's right and acknowledge what's wrong;
through all the heartaches and pain, I will take the blame.

Dorothy Harris Williams

Dusty Road

dusty road
where do you go?
where have you been?
your future is unclear

like mine

you wind and erode from storm after storm

like my heart
like my ambitions

trampled
forgotten?

but you are still there

and so am i

Scott A. Hargis

In the Eye

In the Eye, the anger subsides . . .
Shedding fear and pain.
In the Eye, the clouds disperse . . .
Giving way to light and hope.
Just moments before—utter chaos abounds.
Just moments before—nothing making sense
    in the World.
What was once . . . now gone
    in a swirl.
Things young and old . . .
Things good and bad . . .
Happy and Sad—
Everything jumbled together,
    and flying by.
All is forgot in the wink
    of the Eye.
Giving relief and solitude—
    I sigh.
Precious Life and Love revealed
    In the Eye.

Juan D. Saclolo

The Compass

There are days when we feel especially tried,
When we desire a place where anxiety can subside.
Within this compass find a directional guide;
That will lead you safely to my side.

I vow to you once your way to me you have found;
Warmth and comfort will in quantity abound.

So . . . when you're lost and confused about which road to take;
When you need loving arms into which you can escape,
To provide these for you I have done my part;
Trust and follow the arrows on this compass,
For they will lead you straight to my heart.

Sandra Pryor

Descend into the Flesh

Come into my world,
descend into the flesh,
the last strand of the silver cord,
to me shows the God loving energy,
of your purely made heart.
    Show from within,
the monad of your individuality,
for the child in you knows,
of the memories you will hold and those that will be lost to you.
    In expressing my innermost thoughts,
you have descended into the flesh of my soul,
hearing from within my inner voice,
my uniqueness and expectations grown.

Cassandra Clark

Husband

To my wonderful husband, Zac
He stood with me at the altar, holding my hand
   showing his love with a gold band.
Until death do we part,
   are the words he said from the heart.
Standing there looking so happy and proud,
   no one can believe the love we've found.
Being with your one true love,
   is what's intended from the one above.
All we need is one another,
   our love we will share with no other.
Now and forever we'll be together,
   side by side through what ever.
Down the road of life we're going,
   and through it all, our love will never stop growing.

   Virginia Delcarmen Ryan

If Ever, We'll Remember

My heart is now yours, your heart is now mine.
It has definitely been worth waiting all this time.
As we start on our journey through our lives together,
We must always remember that love is forever.
If ever we are sad and mad enough to cry,
We'll remember that first we must always ask why.
If ever we are so happy, it seems as though the world stands still,
We'll remember that it can, and always it will.
If ever we are angry and feel we need to fight,
We'll remember to resolve it, by the end of the night.
If ever we are glorious of the bringing of something new,
We'll remember that it could not have been done without two.
If ever times get tough, as all relationships do,
We'll remember the power of saying "I Love You."
If ever we forget how much the little things mean,
We'll remember that it only takes a minute to bring back the dream.
I know we will be happy on our journey of joined hearts,
That alone should tell you that we will never part.

   Billie Jo Lawrence

Saying Goodbye

We gather today to say goodbye to a warm and wonderful lady
Though to all of us she's a different relation
She's touched our lives without hesitation
We shall miss her and mourn her so let us look to the sky
Knowing now that God keeps her close by his side
Her suffering is over no more pain to go through
Now let's all pull together like she'd want us to do
And again look up just give her a grin
To let her know today (of all days) just how loved she's been
She lives on in all of us little pieces left behind
We should put them all together so her light will continue to shine

   Melissa Gerke

Yes, I Understand

To Poppy
Yes, I understand the sun will rise each day
And the new dawn will wipe the fears of night away.
Yes, I understand the moon will rise each night
And it will shine in the last of the sun's pink light.
Yes, I understand the stars will replace the sun each night
And they will twinkle with all their might.
Yes, I understand that during the day, the sky may turn gray
And rain drops will fall, each in its own way.
Yes, I understand all this
But then sometimes I wish
The gray clouds would never be,
The sunsets would just freeze,
And the stars would twinkle just a little brighter.
Why I wish this,
I do not understand.

   Emily Ehardt

'Til We Meet Again

You disappear in dreams upon my awakening;
My mind holds the thought of you still.
Though my memory be full of forgetting,
remember you always I will.
Though you're so very far away
it strengthens only my desire
to see you, and your voice to hear
My hope becomes a fire.
So that when once again we meet
my thirst, in satisfaction sweet
is done away with once again
Until I dream of you, 'til then
Upon awakening I'll find you gone,
and then again the feeling's strong;
I'll find I miss you just the same
My Dear, Until We Meet Again.

   Robert Carneal

I Love You

Mysterious eyes, drunk with the rain,
Offering the desert flowers
And whispering tenderness
To the winds of the soul

You
Child's hello
Holding freedom's desires
Slipping in musical fires
Of friendly, immortal, spontaneous innocence

You
Victorious song on army's lips
As a ritual of triumphant days
As a revelation
Of times, reflected

You
Delightful glory
Golden and graceful
Sailing dawn's breeze, over lilies
In the green valleys of Love

   Heloisa Moreira

My Wondrous Room

As I walk across the threshold of my wondrous room,
and gaze across in strife, something tells me, I need all wife.
I beckon a time, a time that will come,
than I may look across the room,
and find there is no slum.
But for now, as my eyes roll over the floor,
I'll brush the dust away, only to find the door.
I have come to realize, there is a time, and a place;
but stare at my room, and you will say what a disgrace,
So, as I ponder over my room, I don't feel grieved,
nor feel the gloom, I just wish I knew,
what had happened to the broom.
Suddenly I took courage and thought it was time,
to write a new poem, and start a new rhythm.

   Alan P. Lichtenberger

Dance Shoes

What? I have to dance every day
Point your toes, that's what they say
It makes no difference if I can dance or not
I have to do it, like it or not
I dance so much my laces hurt
I sweat so much I taste the dirt
Run and leap every day
But I love to dance, what can I say?

   Brandi Hughey

All I Ever Wanted

All I ever wanted was someone to hold me near;
Kiss my lips, and hold my hand, and whisper in my ear
"I love You," just the way you do.
It makes me want to cry,
But all the trust I've lost from you
it makes me want to die.

This poem is not much, but all I want is to hear you say,
"I love you, Hun, and always will, each and every day."
Please kiss my lips, and hold my hand, and whisper in my ear.
'Cause all I ever wanted was someone to hold me near.

Ryan Stinson

True Love

As she looked upon the picture,
Frail hands caressed the face,
Of the love she had lost so long ago,
And she smiled of his warm embrace.
Alone she was, alone she had been,
Since she walked away that dreary day,
Wanting many times to return to him,
But could not find the words to say,
She watched him go through life without her,
And surrounded herself in shame,
Never showing how much she still loved him,
She didn't know he did the same,
To her surprise, his hand reached out . . .
Warm and gentle like before,
Tears filled her eyes, she grasped for breath
As he stepped through a golden door.
"You came back for me!" she whispered to him,
"Why did you wait so long?"
"Because it's time that we forgave, My Love,"
"And realized that we were wrong."

Evie May Voelker

Going on Forever

Memories of her voice and seeing her smile,
I had no choice.
Smelling her sweet scent and dreaming of her to come back,
she was all of life combined in one,
the one who lit up my day when she
said, "Everything will be OK."
Her strength was of a million men,
her heart so full of love,
it was the size of the universe.
Her smile went from ear to ear.
Her life went on for 81 years,
but her soul is going on forever.

Deseree Nichol Clarke

Kiss of Death

Solemnly I leave this world drained
No person's cries can heal another's pain
For the angels' truth lies within you
Some grow old and are fortunate to see
For others the opportunity will never be
But in the ladden end we all meet
At the same corner in the road
A place where a mere morsel of truth
Remains a story of who we were
Do we truly know the petals of our rose

Unveil yourself to thee
With grace we fall to our knees
With the innocence of a child
Is the existence of every soul born
"Rest assured"—each soul has its purpose
And when it leaves
The angels come to comfort
Those left behind, to mourn.

Linda Van Zandt

Pointless Prayer

Can there be a time when we don't know why
living on is right and not is wrong?
Is there a way to tell when not to fall
and when to stumble but still go on?
Is there time in this pointless life
to conquer our wonders and worst fears?
Can we grow strong enough
To still get punished but hide the tears?
May we all discover what we want to know,
May we all see what we want to see.
Lord, let there be time
For our souls to be freed.

James Lowell Polkinghorn

High Heels

Little girl from next door
in your mother's high heels
oceans too big for you,
yet managing somehow
to edge down the sidewalk.
Too soon you'll have
a pair all your own
to show off those legs,
leaving childhood behind
with the kindling shape of them.
Right now I want those small running feet
with the silk hair above,
the face full of wonder.
You'll be old soon enough,
your beauty a trouble
to all those who see you,
your manner self-conscious,
so terribly proud,
little girl going by
with the click-clack-clatter
of your mother's heels . . .

Ghadi Al Jolen

Redolent Emotion

My hands are of brief and subtle endings
Torn by the choice taken entirely within
They caress the air (without absolution)
With wind beating softly against my fingers
With these hands are the epitome of my being
Never have I forsaken this hedonism
(curled up inside me like a ball)
For it has been too precious to throw away
This redolent emotion has contained me
Poured its wine into the blood of my veins
And with this provenance, found and spoken
I can keep my hands in the fold
(from which they keep)

Beth Anna Elderkin

When Away from You

Though I've known you but a short while,
I've come to love your touch, your scent, your smile.
When I'm with you I feel like a king.
Your as pretty as early spring flowers,
When away from you I can do nothing but count the hours.
When you touch me I feel the butterflies
When away from you my lonely heart cries,
Each day I cannot wait until you're on the phone.
When away from you I can't wait to get home.
As a hill billy I must listen to my gut,
And when away from you I feel loves
Door has been slammed shut.
I don't know how you won my love in such a short time.
I miss you so much I don't know what to do,
for I've never been so lonely like when away from you.

Jeffrey Burruss

Sleep My Gentle Lady

Sleep my gentle lady . . .
Stay peaceful and sleep without fret . . .
Because the things you were all about . . .
I never will forget . . .

The smell of spring is now in the air . . .
The sunlight wakes the day . . .
Just the same as you awakened me . . .
The day you went away . . .

I can see your face amongst the clouds . . .
They form an angels face . . .
I can smell your scent amongst the days . . .
It smells like Chantilly's trace . . .

I can see your eyes, so expressive, now . . .
And all they tried to say . . .
You see, Mom, you awakened me . . .
The day you went away . . .

I smell spring in the air . . .
Your roses catch the rays . . .
The memory of your lasting love
Will never go away . . .

Nancy Byrnes

We Will Remember

Dedicated: Colossians 3:23 (VUH)
There is a day we set aside,
It is the Eleventh of November.
For those who fought for our freedom,
We will remember.

The mere children who fought,
Those of any gender,
Men and women of every race,
We will remember.

The heat, rain, dust, and chill,
The most miserable of weather,
Those brave soldiers did not hesitate,
We will remember.

The blasting guns, cannons, bombs,
These did not hinder
Those who fought until death.
We will remember.

That is why we set aside
This day from all others.
For those who fought and died for our freedom,
We will remember!

Kerri-Ann Down

Artist Unseen

So, here I may die unseen, true?
Here in this, a black shroud
Under which no man can notice me.
All too often, the modern artistic gentry
Dilutes my imagination
With paint thinner and writer's block.
I am held in my den by those who would compete,
And trampled by those who judge.
I want to break out
Such as an inner child would in a mid-life crisis
And shock the pants off of unimpressionable idiots.
I want to condone random acts of inspiration
And fuel the fire of understanding.
I want to send imaginations reeling
And provoke people into paying attention.
But will I be let to
Or let myself?

Joseph Ryder

Plundering

Carefully, quietly I creep onto the chair,
hoisting myself to the dresser top,
seizing my grandmother's prized jar of Topaz perfume—
mission accomplished!
Slyly and secretly I slide to my next spot—the bathroom.
Squish! She'll surely think I brushed my teeth nicely
Gliding into the kitchen, I peek my head 'round the corner,
crawl under the chairs for safety,
and sneak to the wooden cabinets, grab vinegar, salt . . .
Swat! Naughty granddaughter!

Melinda Nordan

Train Sounds

Train Train, going on the track,
Going on a trip, not ever looking back.
All the people riding on the train,
Sitting all relaxed, not feeling any pain.
Seat by the window looking out,
little one on the back seat, about to pout.
Looking out the windows as the trees go by,
Look at the dark clouds taking over the sky,
Here comes the rain, it's going to make me cry.
Hear that train whistle loud and clear,
Letting all the people know a stop is near.
The sound of the engine comes to a stop,
A lot of the people going to get a pop.
There is the whistle to board the train.
Come on, people, let's ride the train in the rain.
The sounds of the railroad, click and clack,
I love the sound of the railroad track.

Brad Kimsey

Life in Light

Bright lights will never be
Never bright enough for me
A bright light doesn't show I
It doesn't show where I'll be when I die
A bright light shows no one's heart and soul
Materials are what a bright light shows
When my life ends one day
I will be in God's arms to stay
People see my blue eyes sparkle in the light
They do not see the real me in their sight
People are blinded by the light
Please keep a person's heart and soul in your sight

Whitney Lee Hamlet

Drama's Plays: Comedy vs. Tragedy

Drama's horriphilation . . . debate a la carte
Rhythmic rata plan . . . the faces aflutter
Costumed felicity on one side
Plethora of finicky anguish on the other

Comedy: "Summoning acid in the belly
crafting despair & exasperation,
you circumvent by touching tear ducts,
causing snot excretion & soul ululation.
—Laughter & joy it's the relief into ardor
depicting the essence of life's manifestation
I tickle the plot & inspire fun."

Tragedy: "The Superlative of sad
I am gallantly veracious
up & down the story's climax ladder, I go
Life's fate of death . . . it's efficacious.
—Meandering love & sorrow is a classic
with the flux of emotive currents being sagacious
I caress the theme & plot twists."

The forever endeavor to get a masterpiece . . .
. . . thou shall be continued . . .

Paul A Williams

Shake It Off

If something is bothering you; shake it off.
If life upsets you; shake it off.
If you are in danger; there is a God who will take danger away.

If you live in desperation; God is your helper and saving station.
If something is worrying you; pray for the Lord to help you.
Shake it off.

If an emergency arises, ask the Lord to guide you.
Shake off worry and fear; you have a purpose for being here.
The Lord will make His message clear; to the Lord you are very dear.

Catheryn R. Nance

Did You Know?

It's the small things that change your life forever.
While floods, hurricanes and earthquakes
bring people together,
in everyday living hides the catastrophes
that no one offers to help with.

Behind corporate doors are images
waiting to steal away your hours,
the act of mundane chores
to take your creative talents
down the drain
with comet and potato peels.

There you are
the happy couple
spinning on an axis
that slowly takes your life
while you are waiting for
the flood, the hurricane, and the earthquake.

Becky B. Carlson

Time

Why?
That seems to be the one question on my mind 24/7.
It's been a long time,
Yet I still can't let go.
You always come back to me, so where are you this time?
No words are spoken between us.
The pain is unbearable.
Seeing you with her is unbearable.
Why aren't you here with me?
Do you think about me?
Do you think about us?
I do, all the time.
Why is it so hard to let you go?
We are running out of time.
I am running out of time.

Amber Veaunt

A Prayer for a Newborn Colt

Heavenly Father, hear my prayer,
please keep him in your loving care,
and grant these blessings for which I pray:
May he grow stronger day by day.
May he please his Dam and Sire,
May he be kept safe from fire.
May he kick up his hooves and run,
May he frolic in shade or sun.
May he rest in peaceful slumber.
May his days be without number.
May he eat grass, oats and grain,
May he have shelter from the rain.
May his drink be fresh and clean,
May his eyes be bright, his hearing keen.
May he become a loving friend.
In the name of Jesus Christ, Amen!

Lottie Ann Knox

My Lament

Can you heal my scars, dear God?
Can you heal the ones inside and out?
Forgive me for hiding in darkness, my Lord
Behind my sadness, so devout
Hidden in shadows, my blood is my sword,
Can you hear me so far away?
When I weep in the night, while the stars play
Can you see me, here on Earth?
Stumbling blindly, with all the pain and hurt
Send your angels to catch my tears,
And take away all the sorrows and fears

Nicki Owens

Proud of "Mr. Mom"

Our son has chosen to be "Mr. Mom"
if only for just a short time.
A new set of twins has come into his life,
and he's taken on the role just fine.
(She) wanted someone who would love them completely,
to do nothing for them but the best.
I think this first year he has shown to be
someone who sure passed the test.
Who could love them just as much as mom,
raise them to be fine little boys?
To put his career on the back burner for now
is an unselfish act full of joy.
Who could teach them, comfort them, meet all their needs
while mom is away for the day?
It's their "special" dad—"yes, that is my son"—
as I'm so very proud to say.

Paula Henry

All I Do Is Think of You

Time has drifted us so much apart
That it seems impossible to make
a new start . . .

It kills to have the thought of having to be apart . . .
But I guess time has changed so much,
that it seems like nature's art . . .

Still on top of my head,
all I do is think of you,
'cause I really miss being a part of you.

All I have to say is that . . .
I truly loved and cared for you
and shall always do . . .
because we are one, not two.
I LOVE YOU!

Ayshah Anwar

Tragic

It is tragedy when men die before their time.
It is tragedy when you lose a friend like mine.
It becomes harder with each and every passing day,
Learning to deal with the heartache of dismay,
Knowing what he could have been, and never was, is Hell.
All the moments we have missed make my eyes begin to swell.
An escalade of emotions, a cavalcade of tears,
Misery spawns deep in my soul, I succumb to my fears.
Since he has passed, in the shadows I have thrived,
My existence a silhouette of my brother who should have survived.
Our bonds were as strong as the blood that made us brothers.
When his time came, unable to save him, I wept for both our mothers.
Light did seldom creep into my soul.
Life without him has not been whole.
A part of me has died now that he is gone.
The wrath of my wake that follows is sure to last long.
He was the wax of our candle, our bond the fire, and I the wick.
Every day since that flame expired, life has been Tragic.

Russell Aaron Long

Perfect Peace

This world as we know it,
Is filled with hate and sorrow,
So many people never live to see tomorrow.
But in my mind there is this place,
Full of peace for the human race.
Where everyone is happy, always full of joy.
You'll never see a pain caused by a girl or boy.
Everyone will always smile,
Always go that extra mile.
A perfect peace where children won't be beat,
A place where your lover and you can meet.
A place where there is no harm,
A place of perfect peace, a place of perfect charm.

Amanda Petersen

My Window

Dedicated with love to anyone who feels they are alone or unwanted

Sitting all alone
Is all I ever seem to do,
Unwanted by this world
Rejected and sullen.
I cry tears like rain.
I've cried with the rain,
But all the guilt of things lost
Remains the same.
I filter out the madness.
I'm plotting to escape,
Planning to one day be on the outside
Where the looking out is looking in,
Still seeing a rejected reflection,
Knowing it's there for all to see,
For everyone to know.
I keep it all a secret,
But keeping it a secret
Is like walking on shards of broken glass
From a shattered window.

Amy Lee Smalley

End of an Era

As these days draw near my smile widens
The walk down the halls seem less torturous
Each day goes by so quickly
My new life is soon to begin

The walk down the halls seem less torturous
The educational wall has been shattered
My new life is soon to begin
This voyage should bring me great happiness

The educational wall has been shattered
The agitated zombies were let loose
This voyage should bring me great happiness
But will I make the right choices

The agitated zombies were let loose
Each day goes by so quickly
But will I make the right choices
As these days draw near my smile widens

Eric James Schoenfeld

The Beneficiary

The dying trees sway in the gentle, toxic breeze.
The waters of a once beautiful stream slowly trickle by.
And a young child sits upon the shore and sobs.
An observer to the foul remnants of a land in desperate ruin.
As he looks on, his father takes a final, fatal breath.
So does he cry. A desperate, pleading cry.
Knowledge comes to him.
He sadly, reluctantly accepts his inheritance.
He has become,
The beneficiary.

Laura Lynn Place

The Blessing

You go to your church and I go to mine.
But today, dear friends, lets walk and pray together.
We thank thee, Father, for this food
and for thy gracious loving care.

Help us to honor the Golden Rule and to be in all things
fair and square, and grant our prayer
for lasting peace for every nation everywhere.
And grant our prayer and blessing too,
for our dear Diane and our dear Pascal,
on this their special day.

Let's give them our love, and best wishes too,
to guide them on their way.

You go to your church and I go to mine.
But today, dear friends, lets wine and dine together.

Irene Evans

My Dad

Who is the man, as a baby held me in his arms?
Who is the man, who moved us to the farm?
My Dad.
Who is the man, who taught me to ride my bike?
Who is the man, who broke up our fights?
My Dad.
Who is the man, who patiently decorated our Christmas tree?
Who is the man, who took me over his knee?
My Dad
Who is the man, whose breathing is tough?
Who is the man, whose lungs are so scuffed?
My Dad
Who is the man, who is scared all the time?
Who is the man, who hardly feels fine?
My Dad
Who is the man, we pray for every day?
Who is the man, we ask God to let stay?
MY DAD!

Arleen Strecker

Big Sister

To my big sister who was always there.
To love and watch over me because you cared.
Taking care of me while our mom was away
Made you the woman and mom you are today,
For how I am today I have mostly you to thank
because if anything was missing in my life,
you filled in the blank,
and even in your life you knew some things you would succeed,
and you've succeeded by giving me exactly what I need;
A sister to help me with school and keep me on the right track,
So that if I ever fell off you could put me right back.
And when I graduate you better be in the first row,
because to the family and you I'm gonna show
That thanks for teaching me what you knew and now know.

Adria McGhee

A Poem for the Children

To the memories of those who died in school shootings

As you were sitting, your friends went by,
Never knowing they would die.

Because of hate, they are now gone,
Leaving you to carry on.

When it was over, you said, "Why, Oh, why?
Why were they the ones chosen to die?"

To you, your friends were Oh, so dear,
To your heart, their memories you will always hold dear.

Margaret Ann Lambert

Giving Courage to a Friend . . .

Having me for a special friend
will allow you the courage to overcome . . .
the pain and anger you hold inside . . .
the courage from negative thoughts that arise . . .
the courage to be happy at sad times . . .
the courage to love when hate crosses your mind . . .
the courage to move forward when you're one step behind . . .
the courage to smile when there's a frown . . .
the courage to be up when you're down . . .
the courage to except what life has to give . . .
the courage to live when you feel like giving in . . .
the courage to see the light when things are dim,
but most of all the spirituality you have within
allows you to share it with another friend.
If it does not allow, think of me . . .
"your special friend," and the negative courage will be set free.
A positive courage will come into place . . .
so you can put a smile on another friend's face.

Dixie Diane Johnson

Graduation

The day we've all been waiting for
We'll spread our wings and fly
The whole world is an open door
I hate to say goodbye
We say that we'll stay friends forever
And I hope that this is true
For I always hate the thought of losing you
We've had our good and bad times
And our ups and downs
I look upon the senior class and see so many frowns
Don't fear the future, look for the good
We'll all be together in the end
My final words I'll give you
The meaning of a friend:
A true friend is the real person
That lives inside of you,
Be true to yourself
Don't be someone you do not wish to be
For I have learned that my best friend
Lives inside of me.

Megan Andre'A Frew

The End

When I look all around I can feel it's the end
The end of a imperfect world
All of the racism, crime is what will destroy us
Because all of this, it will soon be the end

James Anderson

Run from Heaven

Fire in the sky and ice down below
Watch the Earth die while you try to grow
Tears that you're crying fall to the grass
They burn like acid erasing the past
The fire in the sky will burn you down
When you run from Heaven
You crash to the ground
And you hope the pain will just fade away
As you run from Heaven, run from yesterday
Leaves in the wind blocking your view
Of the mistakes you've made
Of all you've been through
You want to move on and just get away
But you can't just throw it all away
But your life drifts by
You're sorry to see it gone
Your life has passed you by
But you can't seem to see where it went wrong

Laura Katherine Mishler

Rose of Eden

The rose that I hold
Is not just petals and stamen,
But the millionth decedent
From the garden of Eden.
The droplets of dew alight on its petals
Are now teardrops of pain from kings, queens,
And peasants.
The thorn of the rose,
Resigned to its cause,
Stands poised for the battle against men
Without laws.
How subtle the voice and how hard must we
Listen, before the world we call home,
Becomes an open air prison.

Michele (Mike) Checchia

Somebody's Soul

Somebody's soul is softly crying
Somebody's soul is slowly dying
Somebody's soul is out there lying and . . .
Somebody's soul has just stopped trying

Somebody's soul can no longer cope
Somebody's soul is strung out on dope
Somebody's soul has lost all hope and . . .
Somebody's soul is at the end of their rope

Somebody's soul is hurting bad
Somebody's soul has too long been sad
Somebody's soul stays every day mad and . . .
Somebody's soul has never been glad

Somebody's soul longs to be free
Somebody's soul wants peace and liberty
Somebody needs to tell them that Jesus is the key
He can unlock their soul and end their misery
I guess the somebody they are waiting for is ME!

Poetic Evangelist Juliette Bartley-Warnke

My Proclamation

In shallow traces of memories, from not so long ago.
I caught a glimpse of yesterday and smile at what I know.
I have come this far based on what I have inside my soul.
Good intentions, wishes and love and a heart I feel is whole.
The ability to look blindly forward, gaining what I thought unable.
Allowing what should be to be and becoming more and more stable.
I forget this from time to time, as I think others they do too.
But it comes back to me in reflections of what I do.
Love as I am loved and see what is unseen,
trust without the rope and you'll understand what it is I mean.

Jeffrey Scott Hankins

The Artist

She stands alone,

Alone in her view,

Until the shapes and forms appear before others,

Beautifully completed,

She pounds the rock to form her shape,

She molds the clay until it's magic in her hands,

She brings life to the blank canvas before her,

She sees beauty where others see only flesh,

She ties colors together as only she can,

She squints to see what others miss,

The world is her oyster,

While she creates from its boundless beauty.

Rebecca Erin Scott

A Sunshine, a Star

You are my light when I am feeling down
A Sunshine, A Star
Far but always close within reach of my heart
You give me hope
A reason for my presence here on Earth
Pray I do it will not fade
This light that has guided and showered blessings upon me
Take me into the bosom of your soul
And remain I shall forever to come.

Catherine Moon

My Very Best Friend

She has been there with me through thick and thin,
No matter what kind of mood I'm in.
Even when I'm not feeling great,
She always seems to change my fate.

She knows me better than anyone,
And doesn't judge the things I've done.
She has grown and is pretty tall,
She is kind and cares for all.

I wish that she could only see,
Just how much she means to me.
Until our lives come to an end,
She will always be my very best friend.

Destinee Egan

AIDS vs. the Black Man

The black man is strong
AIDS decreases human strength
The black man has many colors
AIDS has one—Death Gray
The black man has courage
AIDS brings about a weakness

AIDS has invaded the black race
and destroyed many lives, including
the head of the home, "The black man"
The black man needs to be more

AIDS
The more educated the black man
becomes about this dilemma,
the more help can be given to the
black community. Why?
Because then the head of the home

AIDS to the total family.

George McKay

Deluge

The current rises to sea level,
wrenching the buoyant coffer
into the eye of God's wrath.
Torrents of rain beat down against
the condemned Earth, like the arduous
beating of wheat done by the Canaanites.
Assorted arrays of golden rams, bronze goblets
and clay urns sullied by those wayward tributaries!
Useless hoards of aqueous party favors
littered the seas for miles.

Golden hay lies throughout the stalls,
providing a meager bedding for the
cloistered crew. The golden richness
of warmth is a reminder of the
impermanence of the sun.
Minutes fold into hours, days merge with
night and time becomes incalculable!
At least the sea records the sin of man,
the shame has burrowed deep
within the bitter granules of salt.

Christine S. Reid

Quality of Life

Your real riches are in your head and heart.
Real satisfaction comes from appreciating what you have.
Wealth without enjoyment is little consolation.
There are two ways of being happy:
You must either diminish your wants or augment your means.
It's always better to appreciate the things you cannot have
Than to have the things you cannot appreciate.
It is not what you have,
But what you enjoy that constitutes your abundance.
Your riches will always lie within you,
Not in your material possessions.

Angela Dean

Flavors of Life

I want to taste them all—the lip-smacking,
cracker-jacking, midnight-snacking flavors of
life. Some sweet, some sour, others bitter-sweet,
like licorice candy. Suddenly, my
taste buds are alive with the knowing that I
can savor the textures over and over again.
Coarseness. Smoothness. Textures delicately
woven from days of salty seas, honeycombed
sands, nights of clear bottled breezes and
sun-kissed skin, from peppermint holidays
and orange-flavored fires. These are the textures
of my life. I feel challenged to sample them all—
the bitter, the sweet, and the sour,
letting the flavors and the textures
linger, slowly, like a fire that refuses to
die, just long enough to meet my contentment;
then I will begin to taste them once again.

Maureen Ryan

The Silent Soliloquy

She stands, with her back to the door,
Not knowing anyone is watching her,
Dressed in a blue dress, staring out the window.
One can see the life of a refined lady.
Her posture is so noticeable that she
Could have easily been a dancer
With the right mixture of movement and grace.
Picture this . . . a black tie affair, the guests
Patiently awaiting the arrival of their hostess.
She ascends on the crowd from a spiral staircase,
Dressed in a flowing, white chiffon dress,
Her jewelry done to perfection.
When she is near the bottom, she smiles—
Not only from her lips, but
Though eyes that twinkle.
At last, she turns from the window
And I say, "Hello," and I smile—
For rolling down her cheek is a solitary tear—
A lone reminder of her lost youth, The Silent Soliloquy.

William Towey

Loneliness

My heart was full of loneliness,
Until some special person came into my life.
This special person is so hard to describe because
She is perfect in every way.
The way you walked into my door one lonely night—
I won't forget the way your eyes and smile just brightened
Up my night.
Ever since that night my heart has been full of love and
Is open to whoever needs to be brought out of the sorrowful
World of loneliness.
I guess I am trying to say, "Thank You VERY much for
Brightening up my life!"

Ashley Dean Johnson

Lost in the Mist

I feel caught in you
Your lies and your seduction
How can it be that you can make me feel wanted
yet at the same time feel like you never wanted me
like I don't even exist
It's confusing and I'm lost in the mist
The longing I have for you is so deep
yet at the same time (because of time), it's hazy
clouded by the rejection I feel and the need to get away
but the love wants to stay
I don't know left from right, right from wrong
All I know is that I love you & sometimes so
obsessively that it sickens me;
You're like forbidden fruit . . . lusciously sweet to taste
yet poisonous for the soul and I can't resist
I'm just lost in the mist.

Trier LaShun Waites

Tonight

Tonight I stay up late thinking about your name.
Tonight I cook your favorite dinner and play our favorite game.
Tonight I will wash my hair just the way you taught me.
Tonight I will sing a song, the last one that you taught me.
Tonight I'll watch our favorite shows,
and think of our secrets that nobody knows.
Tonight I'll dance and sing a little song for you.
Last night I heard you were gone and couldn't believe it was true.
I love you so much it made me feel very blue.
And no matter who I meet in life, they'll never compare to you.

Bridget Kelly Horadan

A Lesson Learned Too Late

Living life one day at a time
Savoring every sweet breath
Grandpa, your heart used to beat with mine
A love I shall never forget
Knowing your time here is short
You can't deny the sorrow
Waking and wishing to see my face
You think to yourself, maybe tomorrow.
Time has past, I let it slip away.
Right through my fingers your life did stray
Waking and wishing to see your face
I realize now I should have slowed down my pace

Meredith Rae Blackwell

Green Mango and Peppa' Sauce

It is the space between shoulder blade and neck
that is at once home and longing,
for this child whose eyes are like sunlight on the Essequibo
and sugar before it is burnt, black
who at three months has known the taste of her mother's milk
and the sting of her father's tears,
which didn't fall until later, after she was gone
back to the place where their navel strings were all buried
and whose freshness, even with baking soda, would grow stale,
except for moments, like at Christmas and
in death, always, in leaving
We were children for as long as we could be
I have stretched it out much longer than the other four
My sister is a woman now,
her hair is a river whose source is too deep,
too wide, and too thick to mark
She has walked bare foot down tarred street,
but there is never enough to cover the places she has to go
to find the space that is as familiar as the taste
of green mango and peppa' sauce

Mark Anthony Williams

Strangers

The world is full of strangers
Some stranger than others
Curious, interesting strangers with stories to tell
One thousand stories in "the naked city"
How rare to share your nakedness with a stranger
It's strange to be strange
Stranger still to understand the strange
Listen to the stranger, his thoughts and perspectives
Watch his eyes, grasp the tempo of his speech
Take your time, allow his importance to shine
Search his heart and find the beauty that makes you smile
Embrace the stranger, until strange no more.

Scott Hogan

When Does the Magpie Sing?

When does the magpie sing?
Sitting on the stamens of a blown lotus,
Harvesting the seeds of life,
Croaking, its throat filled with dry hulls.

Out of the mire from below
New life buds,
Penetrating through the water,
Freed from the restrictions and binding of past wounds it comes,
But when does the magpie sing?

Evolving, a lotus unfolds into spring dawn
And with joy it carries the fullness and
Unity of limitless love, surrounded by the arms of Kuan Yin.
Her arms envelop both as they fly together in the clouds,
As their spirits ascend into freedom.
Then, and only then, does the magpie sing
When the two are one, calling for nirvana to enter in.

Jane Hendrickson

Time

Time is like the galaxy,
It never ever stops.
It has seen what no man will ever see,
It knows what man forgot.

Time is like a swift river,
It flows on rapidly,
Sometimes it's smooth, sometimes it's rough,
Sometimes it even scares me.

Time is like our parents,
It tries to teach us right.
It's been through wars and everything.
It tells us it doesn't help to fight.

Time is the one that only knows
when this world will die.
It will be the only one left
here to cry.

Todd E. Maple

The Starlight

Your eyes are like the midnight star,
Shining from afar.
As I look to the skies and admire your light,
What a unique and marvellous sight,
Your ray of light is like diamonds
scattered across the sky.
Please tell me the reason why
There are so many questions that don't make sense.
Give me the answers in sequence.
Those two stars that belong to you,
Tell me and many others the history that
is hidden deep within the two.
As the light shines during the night,
Please respect me and my pitiful plight.

Lauralee Washington

The Perfect Life

The old man sits, waiting for the doctor.
His decrepit body forms to the chair
While his exhausted eyes struggle to see.
What could this man possibly be thinking?
Does he think about his first real love,
The love that was flawless and knew no wrong?
Does he remember the time he spent on
The famous beach dodging bullets and bombs?
He defended the country that gave him
The freedom to live and think as he pleased.
His hands are leathered from working so hard
To provide for the family he raised.
He sees them on Christmas and holidays,
But not enough to show him that they care.
They do not realize the pain he has seen,
The sacrifices made, the money spent.
Does this man even care anymore?
Or is he just content to have a seat?

Stuart Gonzalez

Standing on the Promises

Standing on the promises of God my King,
He daily supplies my needs and is everything.
All to Him I owe so now I surrender all,
I love Him and He loves me when I hear His call.

He saved me from the depths of sin by His love,
and now I am safe in His arms far above
all the sin and strife that would hinder me.
By His Holy Spirit my soul reigns eternally free.

I pray to all that would read this poem,
that they would come to know the truth
that Jesus has for everyone, and will know
how a loving Saviour's peace keeps you warm
against the chill of this world, as proof
there is a place where we will be white as snow.

William Russell Stephens

Sonnet #1 (To My Dear Friend, Charlene)

Could this new found friendship transient be?
Or magnificent, joyous embracing?
Advances warp my dear society,
Ready to unite, yet fear of facing.
Into and through her sweet life she beckons.
She, my comrade of character and zest.
This new care blooming a warming lesson,
Of my cheerful fondness I give my best.
Sensed smiles and laughter fill an aged heart,
Such beauty a gift of great magnitude.
Ever to meet, I wish not to depart,
And find myself again in solitude.
Charlene, fresh friend, I do now beseech thee,
Stay my companion, for I do love thee.

Thomas Christopher Hoffmann

The Blank Generation

The Power of Potential
Especially unrealized

Perfectly symmetrical
The unending, unbreakable circle of life, of mind
Constantly scrutinized by those
Who cannot grasp the beauty that is you

But you, you are the circle
You won't bend, won't break
You feel nothing and everything at the same time

Standing up to confront, only to be shut down by yourself
Tools, really
Specifying the similarity and adversity of us all

Lee-Anne Peluk

Most Holy Father, Help Us

Father, why do we, as Your children, always
act as if we are so superior to Your
Heavenly teachings? We seem to always deny
that we are subjected to all of Your wishes.
You have told us all to "help ourselves, You
will take care of us," but all we do is cry
that we don't know who to turn to. Father,
please grant all of us the courage to
continue performing as You wish and demand.
Most of us are not unable to carry out all
Your commands, we are just plain scared.
Could this be why so many of Your children
change from one religious belief to another
so often? We seem to do our best for a very
brief and limited period of time, then
always fall back on our many weaknesses and
all kinds of self pity. Father, we really
want and need Your superior almighty
guidance and Your love. Have mercy on us
O', Lord. Amen.

Agnes Loretta Porche Wyatt

Walking Shadow

To: Dr. Hull, Uchiyama-sensei, Tanaka-sensei & Sato Sensei

There is a shadow of my own,
Walking with me all my life;
Wearing my shape without gown;
How can it be torn by a knife?

I sat down in the wordless sands;
As a silky cloud under the sun;
Cast its shadow upon my hands,
Trying to reach the sky to shun.

Walked the shadow in the Windy City;
Where was the river that used to run?
Where was the water that reflected pity?

Where was the spec I needed to draw?
I sought to define the paragraph below;
Under the drawing of my walking Path;
For I cannot go back and revise my life.

I stood in the darkness and beheld the sky;
The full moon arose at the night of July;
The surface of the moon began to darken;
The Shadow of the Earth, lunar eclipse;
Bestowed the paragraph unspoken.

Naoko I. Kluka

Crystal Tears Fall

Crystal tears fall,
Twinkling like diamonds,
Glittering like stars.
God, how I miss him.
My heart breaks,
Shatters like a piece of dropped glass,
Exposing my hidden feelings.
He's moving,
I don't want him to go!!
My tears fall,
But only he shall see.
Tears forbidden to fall,
Tears I fight when out amongst the world.
Tears Only He Shall See.
Because I only trust him. Him only.
I cry out to him, "Don't leave me!"
It falls on his ears,
But he's being dragged away,
By family.
And I cry tears Only He Shall See.

AshLeigh Michelle Henson

Momma

I sat beside her in church every Sunday morning
It's the only chance we got the time to spend.

How she ever lived with us I'll never know
But one thing's for sure, she let her love show.

In a hug at night, or a kiss on the head
Cleaning up the house, or keeping us fed.

She worked 24 seven with no vacation days
When the world around, stood cold and gray.

In an old farm house with leaky pipes
She never failed to say her prayers every night.

Lord, watch over my boys and give me strength
With a love that know no lengths.

How can I ever say thank you enough
Or say how much I appreciate your love?

No matter what good I am, it's because of you
Making you proud of me is the only thing I'll do.

All my life I stand on a foundation you made
Knowing that, I have known reason to be afraid.

Jonathan Paul Neblett

Friends

It is good to have friends
when you're feeling down
you look at them and give them a frown
but they give you a smile
and a warm feeling that makes you feel right
you go over to them and hug them tight
when you're in a tight spot they cover for you
they know they'll get in trouble but they know
that's what a true friend should do

I like when my friends tell me jokes
I laugh so hard that I choke
We laugh so hard we start to cry
because we know we are Friends 'til we die
If you don't have any friends
and you know the reason why
you will probably start to cry
and if someone comes over and comforts you
I would say that is a true friend and I pick you
If your friends think you're not there friends at all
I would say I love you all

Briana R. Willis

This Is My World

Every day it rains even when the sun shines in my world.
Twenty-seven years old not a woman but still a girl in my world.
A clown with a permanent frown in my world.
My heart is broken and on the ground in my world.
This is it, these are the things of and in my world.

One is my number the lonely number in my world.
My one true love, my real true love left me in my world.
Honeydip has a new bear in the honey pot now in my world.
Spanky is not enough for honeydip anymore in my world.
My world comes to a speeding crash, spinning out of control.

Cold and alone is now what describe me in my world.
I lost something so important to me in my world.
My head is going to explode just like my heart in my world.
Heart now has no home anymore in my world.
Birth the beginning my love the middle but no ending now.

Now the ending is death in my world.
That's what doctors say, but only God knows the end of my world.
Who will cry, will anyone cry when I die in my world?
Who really cares will anyone care if I die or survive in my world?
Will I be missed if I die, Missed by anyone, only God knows.

Ingrid M. Newman

Friends

For everything you stood by me so strong.
Respecting me although I may have been wrong.
Insisting that I work things my way.
Even though you could have something to say.
Never getting upset with me or walking out.
Delivering on promises and leaving no doubt.
Simply stating that we will always be . . .

Richard Haven Sherrill

A Tear That Healed

I traveled inside your heart today
Along the way I came upon an open wound
It was long as well as deep
As I peered closer I saw my name
I stumbled and I screamed as I felt your pain
My tears formed a river of rage
Yet one lonely tear fell down my face into that empty space
Like a surgeon's knife erasing your pain
My tear worked upon your heart as the smooth oils of love
gently repairing and leaving a tenderness to the touch
The sweet fragrance of a rose appeared
It embodied your entire soul
Where there was sadness petals of love began to grow
My tear of love has healed you!
Never to betray and may it forever flow
gently in the rivers of your soul

Jose Antonio Reyes

Is This the Truth?

Is the outside all they really see
By looking at that, do they see me
It seems as though they just look past
Will this feeling of emptiness ever end

I feel as though it just won't
But then a person looks deep into your eyes
And tells you things that make you cry
No one has made me feel like I am special

You look beautiful tonight
Does he really mean what he said
Can it actually be true
Do I really possess the things he compliments

All these years I have felt second best
But when I look into his eyes
I actually see what he sees
And he makes me see my beauty inside and out

How do I repay him
For making me laugh like never before
For widening my smile more and more
And for making me see the Truth

Meredith Leigh Sabosik

A Tribute

Tragedy, fates faithful emissary
seeks and destroys ones soul.
My crushed spirit yearns for relief
as I see my dearest companion cut down,
stripped of dignity and pride.
O', dearest companion of mine,
one that I've loved since the beginning of my time,
be still and be rested 'cause soon thy strength will be tested.
O', dearest companion of mine,
thy dignity and pride will regain.
So you need not feel disdain,
for those who see you love you
And 'cause there's no-one else above you.

Hope Maxwell

Change of Season

Leaves of green turn yellow and red
falling to ground to form a bed.

Falling from tree seeming to glow
falling like a feather to be iced with snow

Flurries from cloud land on trees
long arching limbs capture with ease

White water clings to shapeless tree
sharing each moment until the spring

Change of Season has just begun
lowering its beauty for another one
Douglas S. Bennett

Someone

Somewhere in my heart beyond all
my pride holds a secret desire so intense.
Deep inside imprisoned with all my
passion and love, unknown to anyone
but the Lord up above, a desire
for someone to cherish and hold,
The need for a love to call my own, and . . . I need
Someone who keeps me shining through day and night.
Someone to kiss & make up with after a fight.
Someone who appreciates & respects all I can be.
Someone who's strong enough to commit and love only me.
Someone who will be there to kiss away the tears.
Someone to secure my doubts and release me from my fears.
Someone who I can depend on to be my best friend.
Someone who can restore my faith in love once again.
This love is like a dream that has yet to become true,
Or so I believed until I met you.

Teja Levato

Emotions

P—People—Who share their hopes, dreams,
memories, expression in life as it seems

O—Opening—Your eyes, your thoughts, your mind
Remembering what it's like to be kind

E—Everyone's—Tears, jokes, laughter and pain
What really counts is there is always something to gain

M—Minds—We all have our own ideas in this world we share
Remembering how much we all really do care (about one another)

S—Sharing—A part of ourselves with each other
In God's eyes you all are a sister and brother
The main thing in life is:
People loving people
Brenda Montoya

What You Mean to Me

Through life we all must fall
No matter what the age is
We all must crawl
When you enter into my life I thought
I'd seen it all
Those gorgeous eyes, the soft voice
I knew I couldn't fall for you
You're an inspiration without temptation
You're like a treasure that no one can measure
For me, to talk to you is a pleasure
You're like a one in a million
Even if I had a trillion
For God has sent you to me
I place no one before thee
And that's what you mean to me
Mary Dingle

Unfulfilled Poet

After all, it's just a dream,
Skimming here, and then unseen.
Off to catch that butterfly,
in my hand and there to die.
Drifting on those clouds, away;
Yesteryear, and now today.

Run the fields and high in the hills;
dream of yellow daffodils.
Flowing dreams in soft dresses.
What thoughts flow between those tresses?

Walk a while with me, my friend . . .
there is much left, before this dreaming ends.
Anna Rawlins Arndt

Kids of Columbine High

Our hearts yearn for all that was lost,
No one or anything can replace them at any cost,
Each day passes by, we try to forget,
By putting the pieces back together,
But they seem to never fit,
Others may never be able to endure
All the pain that you feel,
But with prayers and loved ones,
You shall find time to heal,
Let us journey down the road to faith,
And salvation, for we all know death
Is not an end, it's a continuation,
Our Heavenly Father has taken hold of their lives,
Every time rain drops, that's a song in their eyes,
And a smile upon our heads when the sun comes to shine,
And we'll always in our hearts remember the children of
Columbine High.
Lavonne Thomas

Grandpa

I remember my grandfather
He was my mother's father
He passed away just yesterday
I remember one holiday
It was last years Easter Sunday
It was a very fun day
I remember him cutting the turkey
That day he was very perky
I remember his laugh,
His smile everything
I remember the song he used to sing
It was an Italian song called amore
I remember good times and bad
Just thinking about him makes me happy and sad
I remember him so much,
Just one more time I want to feel his touch
Eleanor T. Modugno

On Her Sixteenth Birthday

If I were eighteen, a monumental age,
I would seethe with emotion and my spirit would rage.

I would search you out, you with your quiet demean,
I would enjoy what I see more than what I've seen.

I would search out your hiding places,
Those cloistered spots where transition is imperceptibly sure,
Where innocence is lost though body and spirit remain pure.

I would find how vulnerable are the human virtues,

And my soul would quiver at the beautiful thought
That if I protected this vulnerability in you,
I would become a man.
Willard H. Lariscy, Jr.

The Rescuer

As I was going to school one day
I passed a stream along the way.
Fed by a rainstorm the night before,
Some autumn leaves on its crest it bore.

One beautifully colored leaf I spied
Clinging to the edges as it tried
To escape or defer a horrible fate,
Swept by the waters through the sewer's grate.

I'll rescue you, dear leaf, I thought,
As the beautiful leaf so bravely fought.
Just in time, I snatched it away
To safer ground where it could stay.

Then some other leaves I saw
Drifting toward that gaping maw.
This was clearly a rescue call.
I must be the one to save them all!

I was a benevolent giant who
Rescued each leaf as it came into view.
'Til the ringing of the school's bell
Broke the magic enchanted spell.

S. Evanuik

Sundays

I told her for the third time—
as we hurried onto the hot, grainy cement,
speckled with dips and shapes of little hands and feet
and a crooked I-heart-Jesus—
that my tights were too small.
But she just said, "I know, Sugarfoot,"
and sat me down on the chipped steps
to force and buckle my feet into stiff black shoes.
People were clapping and singing already
about fallin' into God's arms.
It was only nine
and the August sun was cooking my scalp
right down the center
where my pigtails parted.
Even my elbow and knee creases were moist.
Mom said, "Remember to be extra quiet
when Reverend Hill speaks."
I yanked at my tights.

Ashley M. Seitz

The Sacred Dog

The sun had barely shown any light over the eastern ground
An animal so magnificent, no one could believe it had been found
Crickets didn't chirp, coyotes didn't howl
No one made a sound, the dogs didn't even growl

No beast so majestic had ever been seen
Was this creature kind-hearted or mean?
The sun had come up just a little bit more
It glistened on the water, it gleamed on its fur, Oh!
What in the world was this animal for?

So grand, so regal, it showed in its eye
Just the way it stood on four legs, with its head cocked high
This creature was outstanding, without a doubt
But could it do labor? It seemed strong and was unmistakably stout

A gift from the gods, it had to be
An animal fit for a chief, definitely
Then a curious child stepped forward for a better view
Then the creature bolted so fast hardly anyone new

The Kiowas watched in awe as the creature ran so swiftly
The way it galloped, then sped up most gracefully
As it ran into the setting sun, it jumped over a rotting log
And there went the sacred dog.

Paige Neely

Sleep

Sleep is nothing but death taking its toll on the living

Systematically taking away from your life

Some humans sleep 14-16 hours a day

Trying to sleep

Wanting to sleep

Sleep is addictive in its own way

When you sleep too long you are tired

And when you are tired you want to sleep

It is a vicious cycle

Sucking you in every which way you go

Trying to avoid sleep

You only end up having to

Sleep more than you normally would

Therefore you can't avoid sleep

Only except it as it comes

Your death awaits you . . .

Ryan Matthew Spencer

Paradise

I picture God's face as strong and sweet
I often think about sitting at His gracious feet
Listening to His thunderous but mellow voice
Knowing a long time ago I made the right choice

Sitting around with all the redeemed
White as snow our garments gleam
Everyone smiling and humming a praising tune
In a place where there is light and even night needs no moon

Many mansions on Heaven's wondrous hills
Sitting on a window couch overlooking the thrills
Seeing the streets all paved in gold
I'm so glad I was smart and didn't sell my soul

I am a Christian, yes, a daughter of God
I just can't wait 'til Heaven's streets and grass I trod
It will be so different being in Heaven with Him
It sure makes life down here seem unattractive and dim

Sherry L. Duffey-Baker

True Friends and Lovers

Seeing that special smile in your lover's eyes,
Sharing your lives without any lies
And giving into feelings you cannot deny;
Some will make you laugh,
And some will make you cry.

When two people decide they are
Right for one another, knowing
That they can forsake all others;
Living with what is in our past,
Climbing the fences and staying on a true path,
Making the love strong so it will last,
If you take your time and don't push too fast.

Taking time to understand your partner's wants and needs,
Their dreams and desires,
Keeping the flames of passion alive
That stir each other's inner fires;

Being thankful and appreciating one another,
Not taking things for granted or using the other—
These are the things we need to discover
To be true friends and lovers.

John Atkins

Thanks

I wanna give thanks to the girl who broke my heart
for it took this to help me realize,
she was ungrateful, unappreciative, and unloving
I wanna give thanks for the friend who betrayed me
as I see it now, he really wasn't my friend,
he just played me
I wanna give thanks to my incredible mother
for it is her unmatchable courage
that makes her like no other
Always pushing me to follow my dream,
never give up, keep heading up stream
I wanna give thanks to those who've caused suffering and pain
for it is these people who've allowed
me to obtain the knowledge I've come to gain
I wanna give thanks, for it is these saddening, depressing,
life-altering experiences
that I have found the essence of life
It has made all the difference
and has made me who I am

Kenny Griffin

Never Let a Good Thing Pass You By

It seems I am always thinking about you and me,
I feel inside we are meant to be.
At one time I know you felt the same,
But I am the one who deserves the blame.
What I did was keep you waiting,
But I was so nervous I kept hesitating.
Then I found out it was too late;
My heart shattered like a broken plate.
I couldn't believe what I had heard,
I didn't understand what had occurred.
Someone else had told you the words that lovers do,
And those simple words are I love you.
Now I sit here all sad and blue,
Still wishing that I could be with you.

Dan Brymer

Of Flag

The Flag represents the freedoms we have,
Understand, never to take for granted them
For men, sacrificed and set to them, their lives.
Of Flag, meant to protect its future of free men.

The Flag represents the freedoms we have,
Representing, all natives and immigrants alike,
Together standing for all freedoms, flag, liberty,
Where everyone shares equally in them.

The Flag represents our freedoms, but be of caution,
To separate, to abuse, to try to take one way,
Is to deprive the ancestors its heritage,
And will enslave the descendants of honorable men.

The Flag represents the freedoms of all under it,
And the best of any freedom is in its ideals,
Let there not be an end to passing them on intact.
So as it is, to be Of Flag, protecting its future.

David E. Clemetson

The Wrath of the Owls

Have you ever wondered about owls?
And their mysterious sounding howls?
270 degrees their heads turn.
All the hatred in their souls burn.
You can see in their eyes,
All the prey that they despise.
Their bodies, sleek and stealth,
Birds (their food) give them their health.
Their iron-like talons and grasping beaks,
Is what makes these creatures quite unique!

Jimmy Bouchard

Untitled

When I look into your eyes, I see the rest of my life,
I see the person, the spirit, the soul, all in one,
I see where I'm going and where I've been,
I see my dream playing over and over again,
With each blink is the start of a new day to come,
This feeling so special I've never had for anyone,
It's all happened so fast, to my surprise;
I see the rest of my life in your eyes.

Raeshale Young

We've Never Met

We've never met but I can feel your touch
I hear your voice and the love is too much
You always make me feel warm and calm
Like I hold the world in my palm
I can only imagine the taste of your kiss
To touch your sweet lips with my fingertips
Sometimes it seems, life is not worthwhile
But I'll always be there to make you smile
I will love you without ever knowing why
I won't give up, I would rather die
Though not in person I'll be here
I'll love you without knowing the reason
Or rhyme, and I won't stop
Because love knows nothing of time
When your world is cold, I'm always here
When you lose control, I'll help you steer
We've never met, but I can see your eyes
Every day we're apart, a part of me dies

Danielle Nichole Perkins

I'll Never Love Again

I promised that I'd never fall
Ever again in love.
My heart in two will never break,
At least I planned to prove.
I've said goodbye much too often;
There's nothing left to lose.
But then one day, your gaze was caught.
Again I had to choose.
The promise to me I then broke,
Head over heels I fell.
A spark had flown with every touch.
It seemed I'd chosen well.
But with someone else your passions you shared;
Caught in the act you were.
Crushed I was when I first found out,
Over me you had chosen her.
I vow today and ever forth,
My heart no one will get.
I can live without any other,
My tears are better kept.

Danielle Elizabeth Frieda Kaminski

Sunshine Snow

All around behold the beauty of it all
Spread out far and wide for all to see
How mighty the work of God can be

I can't believe my eyes, they wink;
The brightness of the day, no green, no gray,
Just white, pure white, white stuff

And so the hours pass by to night
Up, up the temperature must go
To glide down back to where no one knows
The sun has given up its fight.
Darkness falls, the snow lies still
We started the day at five below
Keep still, he says to us again
No one can tell me what to do

Hazel McShane

The Story Behind the Tree

What's the story behind the tree?
A tale of which could make men free.
Symbolizing eternal life for all creation,
Let me tell you of this, for your salvation.

King of all men was born to man,
Preaching the gospel throughout the land
Jesus was his name, savior for all mankind.
Teaching of Heaven, healing the sick and blind.

Now jealous were the rulers on that historic day,
We'll crucify Jesus, get him out of our way.
Let's tell the soldiers to cut down one big tree,
Nail it into a cross, for all man to see.

A dogwood tree was then cut down,
Nailed into a cross, stood straight into the ground.
Jesus hands and feet were nailed to this cross,
The rulers now happy, for his life they thought he'd lost.

The dogwood tree grows big no more,
Its flowers when bloomed now do adore.
A cross to symbolize Jesus' sacrifice for man,
For three days later he arose, eternal life began.

Terry Lynn Crocker

It's Spring, They Say

A siren breaks the calmness of the dawn.
I'm awakened, yet not ready.
I let my feet touch the soft carpet as
I rise from my warm bed.
The room is cool as I look out from my window.
The sprawling grass, budding trees, and the streets
are yet wet from last night's rain.
It's spring, they say.

It's chilly out there, the sky, yet gray,
shows no sign of sunshine today.
Cars whiz by on wet pavement.
A neighbor dressed in a hooded jacket
carries his bundled up child to the car.
It's spring, they say.

I glance back at my warm puppy still curled
in sleep on my bed, Sir Radames.
He is serene and undisturbed by this new day drama.
I smile and slip back to bed for a few meditative moments.
The blanket is pulled around my body for warmth.
I sigh and close my eyes. It's really spring, they say.

Alma Simmons

Soul Mate

What tongue could boast your true worth, companion of my soul?
When our spirits mesh like fingers intertwined
My every weakness will find a buckler in your stronghold
And your faults a staunch defender in mine.
Beyond sincere camaraderie lies something more,
A faithfulness of old when duty's spent,
Forgiveness lingers near love's open door
Where consistency and change do compliment
No stranger to your dreams should you reveal,
With careful aim your hope shall find its mark.
In vain do I my deepest thoughts conceal,
For you often speak the very secrets of my heart.
In your seasons of laughter I know joy beyond compare
And with unwelcome loss or sorrow feel your pain,
For in each success or trial as one we bear
And in the fruit of each completion lies our gain.
Should separation come through godly call,
Though a part of me be lacking should you go,
Sweet Jonathan, where ever the arrows fall,
Naught will rescind the mating of our soul.

Beverly C. Reither

Places of My Heart

I can travel lots of places
See many different things

But variety of my senses,
is what your love did bring
You took me to those places
Every time you held my hand
Guiding me through places
that just now I understand

Every time you held me close to you
I traveled many lands
You taught me to love unconditionally
with one touch of you hand

I can travel many places
although I've never been away
I can feel the ocean
and a mountain breeze even tropical array

I can travel many places
and when I want to start
I remember my dear mother
through all the places of my heart.

Sally Ann Commisso

I Am a Head Injured Person with Dreams

I am a head injured person with dreams.
I search for a world lost and one to come
I see things yet to be
I cry for abilities lost
I hear of things that I once did
I am a head injured person with dreams.

I look for a bright new world
I hope for a joyful future
I work hard to make it happen
I feel joy when things go right
I understand things will be hard and take time
I am a head inured person with dreams.

I pretend there is nothing wrong
I worry when things go bad
I want things to be happy again
I dream of things that are good to come
I wonder what the future will be like
I am a head injured person with dreams.

Dwaine Miller

Family

I ran into a stranger as he passed by.
"Oh, excuse me, please" was my reply.

He said, "Please excuse me, too—
wasn't even watching for you."

We were very polite, this stranger and I,
we went on our ways and we said goodbye.

But at home a different story is told,
how we treat our loved ones, young and old.

Later that day, cooking the evening meal,
my daughter stood beside me very still.

When I turned, I nearly knocked her down.
"Move out of the way," I said with a frown.

She walked away, her little heart broken.
I didn't realize how harshly I'd spoken.

While I lay awake in bed,
God's still small voice came to me and said,
"While dealing with a stranger, common courtesy you use,
but the children you love, you seem to abuse.

Look on the kitchen floor.
You'll find some flowers by the door."

Paricia Baugh

Crying

Screaming in silence, with no compassion, no one hears
Crying without tears
Haunted by memory, no vision fans a heart's despair
Crying, no one cares

Tremble in anger; rage removes itself in love
Anxious in danger; desperate desires, dreaming of
Silence is just a state of mind, screaming to be heard
Laughter, just a face we wear, hiding what disturbs

Full of feelings without words
Crying, no one's there
Crying, no one hears
When I'm crying without tears

Happiness a memory, a memory of such sorrow
Past of empty yesterdays, left denying hope for tomorrow

Silence is just a state of mind, screaming to be heard
Laughter, just a face we wear, hiding what disturbs
Full of feelings without words . . . crying.

William M. McDonald

I Didn't Mean to Tell You This

I didn't mean to tell you this,
And now I'm full of emptiness,
I thought of you as just a friend,
And our broken hearts I cannot mend.

I know sometimes it really hurts,
Believe me I've been there,
It feels like your under a curse,
And you feel, Oh, so alone, like no one really cares.

It takes two hearts to make one love,
That lasts so very long,
I thought I found it once before,
But I guess that I was wrong.

Sometimes I stay awake all night,
And only think of you.
I'd wish and hope with all my might,
That you could be here too.

I don't think we'll ever know.
Just which way our hearts will go,
But for you I wish the very best,
I didn't mean to tell you this.

Kayla Henry

In Memory Of

I feel myself being ripped apart
Frightened, doubtful, disbelieving,
Not wanting to believe; My mind is numb

Fighting to erase the memories:
The twisted metal, the sirens' screams
Fighting to blot out the images
Imprinted in my brain of that tragic day

The mourners came
Cloaked in shadows as dark as the velvet sky
I, myself, struggling not to cry
But not succeeding; Blinded by tears

Dark clouds overhead
And those who came to pay their respects Have gone
And I am alone
Wet and cold, surrounded by ghostly shadows

Turning to leave, wishing I could stay
Choking on bitter tears
I glance back quickly,
And find I am comforted as my eyes gaze upon
Rest In Peace forever set in stone

Melissa Lynn Saviano

First Love

I see the look that's on your face,
And know our love has been replaced.
I'll search and look so I can see,
Just why you're going away from me.
I thought we had that special love,
That got its blessing from above.
It seems that we have lost the touch,
That made our love mean, Oh, so much.
Our times together sure were fun,
The things we did, we did as one.
But now those dreams that we both had,
Have turned from good to really bad.
We fight and scream, and say bad things,
As though our love was just a fling.
I know that this was not the case,
For I saw those looks upon your face.
Those looks of love, are gone I see,
The looks of love, that you gave me.
I'll always think, of the dreams we loved,
And remember their part, in our first love.

Ronald S. Leonard

Wake Up!

Wake up! Young people,
Because times are so tough,
The road to success is extremely rough.
Your sense of knowledge, of where you should be,
Will never be found with no identity.
Set yourself goals and use what you've learned.
Education is important, it's what your forefathers earned.
For you, young people,
You're put to the test.
Don't fail but try to be the best.
Your forefathers died to put you here,
Don't let their dreams disappear.
So wake up! Wake up! Have pride in yourself,
When you don't learn you're a closed book on a shelf
That no one reads or cares to possess.
You must look at yourself, it's time to confess
That you can do more to help yourself.
Only you! Only you! And no one else.
So wake up!

Lee A. Russell

Evaluation Time

This is the time of year I dread most of all,
Where you sit in the hot seat, with your back against the wall.

Evaluation time is a stressful time, at best
A time for hyperventilation, perspiration, and pain in your chest

Your boss is in the office with pen in hand
I'm sitting here wondering if it will go as I planned.

A million thoughts go racing through my head
I just know my future is hanging by a thread

I enter the office feeling nothing but fear
Knowing I really could have done better last year

Of course I know there's room for improvement
I just hope there's no plan for my removement!

I pray that the "wrongs" don't outweigh the "rights"
I pray that the "praises" outnumber the "gripes"

Please don't be to critical, and give me some praise
Maybe you could consider just a "little" raise?

And when you're tallying the final score,
Remember, you've walked in my shoes before

I know you remember the "golden rule"
So be wise, be fair and don't be cruel

Carol Brunick

The Transparent Pond

Beneath the surface bubbles of light.
Glimpses of color deep, mercy and bright.
Filled with illusions that dance in our head,
Tranquil waters over a pebble bed.
Fish swimming calmly or insects in flight,
Mosses of green hiding from sight.
A journey of water coloring your head,
As plant life emerges like golden thread.
Gentle breezes causing rippling effects.
Ducks swimming proudly,
With no expectations for less.
This transparent pond,
By day or by night,
Witness how it consumes you,
Experience the delight!

Susan Marie Clark

The Damage Is Already Done

The damage is already done
Please don't try to fix it
I am doing what is best for you
I am letting you go
The damage is already done
Don't worry everything is going to be okay
You'll be moving on to a better life,
Not having me
The damage is already done
I am sorry it had to be this way
but you deserve someone better
Someone who will love you and provide
For you whenever you need
Just remember I never did this to hurt you
And don't forget that I love you
and I always will

Tolika LaShae Wilson

Happiness

So, I'm 80 years old; so what?
I'm not complaining about my lot
I'm among friends and have good care
Even someone to shampoo my hair

I have my moments when I'm depressed
But in retrospect I really am blessed
I have a built in "positive," I'm happy to note
Which explains when in poor health I'm able to cope

So give me laughter, music, and a really good book
An occasional comment: "How well you look"
So I'm 80 years old with advantages galore
I look forward to another 20 years or more.

Marjorie L. Waggoner

Sleeping Beauty

The days goes on without you,
It ages and grows old around you.
The slumber keeps one's self a gem,
To sleep without a care about them.
My darling lives in a world that easily fades.
This is a curse that has been handmade.
You wait for her death to wake,
But I fear that it may be too late.
Why is the beauty still asleep?
Prince Charming does wander while he weeps.
Centuries continue to flow.
Will you wake up? If I kiss you? I hope so.
This beauty has a grace that cannot change,
This grace is shielded in a glass vase.
We came from different worlds, yet we are the same.
I never wanted to wake-up; it's changed.
All is different since I woke up—it's changed.

Veronica Torres

The Dove

The ivory light, in this unlit night,
The speck of hope, when we cannot cope.

When all seems lost and forsaken,
Under its wings we can seek haven

Asks nothing in return, only that its peace, we earn
Full of rapture and love, that is The Dove.

Mgo Mike Talarian

Dervish Whirl

like folk dance circles,
all the friends, lovers, and kin
have been spun around.
now tired and with sweat beads,
they've sat down.
it's fun to be
the only one
tap dancing (for a while),
then it's the number one etiology
of bunions.
it serves an atheist right
not to have any friends
to pray with.
o the music: an inspiration to my plight!
i can slap my knees
with two able hands
and leap to dizziness.
there's substance to this loneliness,
to this unconditional bravery,
to the magnets in my fragmented soul.

Annie Kether

Loss the Death of the Soul

Mournful death of the soul,
When only the memories remain.
Painted scenes in color, now drip
down the endless canvas of the mind.
Leaving drips of color, on the plain black floor.
Streaming down to the coffin that lays closed.

The stench of sadness surrounds the air
and everything turns pitch black and grey.
The sense of loss grows,
and only the width of time makes it stronger.
Anger rises, it only gets paler.

Hands of time reach to open the coffin,
a mirror of the past lays there shattered.
Only reflecting the mirror pieces of yourself, now broken.
Ashes surrounds the broken pieces,
the ash, the frame, the soul.

Sara Herrera

Lonely Canvas

If you were told to close your eyes and just
pour your heart out on paper, what would it
say? Would there be thoughts of me, of our
times we talked, the times we spent alone?
Would your words paint great landscapes, the
good times painted in great blues topping
mountainous peaks, and the hard times we
faced together, canyons of red? Would there
be a river of emotion as clear as a mountain
stream? Would it empty into a lake of love, filled
with every aspect of the canvas. The whole
beautiful picture painted from the colors of
our souls, and our passion for one another,
like the sunset in all its glorious hues
of pink and magenta. I know that is what I
would hope for you to see.

John Christopher Shields

Image of Imagination

Between the sun-kissed daylight and the mysterious moonlit night.
Beyond the endless seas of serpents, creatures, and delight.
Flights of fancy, venture once upon a time through
Heaven's depths and lands sublime.
Enchanting thoughts eagerly endured,
Serenity, and tranquility for all to be ensured.
To be or not to be, will no longer be in question,
but what's real and what's divine will attract all attention.
Childish imagination not expressed but locked away,
will always linger solemnly,
all disheveled and astray; so dream the dreams
that touch the soul for a world of wonder
on one's life can take its toll.
Reach out and touch the things which one could have barely felt.
And stand before the entirety of majesty
and show respect, on one knee, knelt.

Emily Lucas

The Tiny Bird

In the wind, a tiny bird was riding on a weed
So hungry, it was trying to eat some seed
It held on tightly so it could take more bites
While leaves flew by like tiny kites
The tiny bird stretched out its wing
And feeling better, started to sing
Once again as the wind blew by
This tiny bird tried to fly
He flapped his wings and flew towards the sky
Suddenly, this tiny bird was very high
Now it was continuing on its way
And truly was having a good day

Patricia K. Imbelloni

Spots on the Wall

I count the spots on the wall as I lie there,
Waiting for Daddy to call.
Every day he is away, I miss him, as I kiss
The pillow where he used to lie.
I want to keep the hope, but it is hard not to sigh.
I have dreams and ambitions in life I want
To come true, but it does not feel complete
Without a pat on the back from you.
Finally one day I see him walking up to the door.
I yell, "Daddy," and he gives me a hug.
We play, we talk, we eat, and sing songs.
The next day I woke up, ran to his room, and he was gone.
Now I lie on his bed, counting the spots on the wall,
wishing I never yelled Daddy's name at all.

Toya Lyn Pattschull

Ice Cream

Well, Boy, I'll tell you:
Life for me ain't been no Ice Cream Sundae.
It's had freezer burn,
And the sprinkles were sometimes stale
And places with no hot fudge,
Melted.
And drip down the side of the cup,
But all the time
I'se been digging down
Layer by layer
Down to the bottom
Until
I reached that big luscious Cherry.
So, boy, don't you give up
Don't you stop now
Until you reach that cherry
I'se been digging down deep
Layer by layer
And Life for me ain't been no Ice Cream Sundae.

Tory Silvers

Conflicting Realities

Aimlessly, in circles, repeating without end,
each moment is a blow, too vicious to tend.
When words cease to live as hearts do intend,
with the stress's weight, reality may bend.
Set upon ideals whose flavors lost all spice
are fluctuating stings: white fire, blue ice.
Lukewarm, a fond memory, and never to suffice.
Thus, the sorrow of instability's dear price.
Death is reprieve to the ever-bleeding heart,
for ever is it torment to love and be apart.
Much safer are we all to never, ever start,
but foolish, too, to reject the greatest art.
Trapped are we all in the winding world maze
confined within its dull, translucent haze,
and, here we will spend all our final days
restricted to the world's heartless ways.
But, in sleep, eyes are opened to the beyond:
sweet, pleasant love, a crystal clear pond.
Fantastical dreams: unbreakable bond.
As cosmic lovers, eternally fond.

Jim Robert Ciccolini

In the Eyes of a Child

In the eyes of a child

When things go wrong and don't work out,
A hug, a kiss, a smile so bright
Can make the bad things turn out right.

The heart of a child is overflowing
With happiness and bursting with love.
The heart of child does not care if you're shy,
Or artistic or athletic or like things that fly.
It doesn't make a difference if you're red, green, or blue,
If you're a girl or a boy, if you're 50 or 2.
It wouldn't matter if you're from America, China or Spain,
In the heart of a child we're still all the same.

The spirit of a child is what makes them unique,
Let your child spirit free,
So you can enjoy the magic only a child's eyes can see.
Become that child you once were
And for just a moment, or even a minute,
The magic once lost will surely return
You'll see the world in a different way . . .
The way it's seen through the eyes of a child.

Marcella K. Fernandez

It's OK

It's OK to be a dreamer
It's OK to sing
It's OK to laugh out loud at anything

It's OK to wonder why
It's OK to be sad when saying goodbye

It's OK to sleep in late
It's OK to hesitate

It's OK to walk without shoes
It's OK to take a late afternoon snooze

It's OK to go without a coat
It's OK to sometimes gloat

It's OK to be who you are
It's OK to wish upon every single shooting star

It's OK to wonder why
It's OK to just say hi

It's OK to be yourself
And no matter how bad things seem to be
Read this poem and remember me

Everything will be OK

Kathleen L. Paternostro

Engraved Fantasies

The cloud-scattered spirit
Lay deep in the silent new world
The eyes of all the moonlit stars
And the weak one in the rain
Leave him misty, that muted spirit
Tremble the hope of fear
Bless the frosted love of night
So that day light can reappear
Tremble the candlelight, pay the bitter chill
Use the lost soul passion
Eyes of day shall ring tonight
So night do not ring dead
Silent the passionate, moonlit sky
The sun shall glitter with love
The fountain shrine rains with dreams
The thunder lost its boom
To catch the shattered sunlit day
Love the undying souls, deny what hasn't come yet
Then take in all the lightning's gold

Sara Jenkins

Our Gift

It's not how we act but how we feel,
And it's not our looks that give us zeal.
With many it's being rich and strong,
While with others, it turns them wrong.

Too soon for what we want, we're too old.
Things we could have done, we weren't bold.
Our gift we sought, too late we're smart
And are so feeble and have no heart.

The gift I have, it can't be beat.
The gift of God, it is so sweet.
I conquered not a foreign land,
I killed no giant with my hand,

For when I thought my life was at end
I took my pen. I then began
Amidst my trials and my woes.
You see, the gift, to me, came slow. Amen.

Gilbert Johnson

The Golden Kiss

Last night I slept in Heavenly bliss.
Along came an angel with one Golden Kiss.
We stayed up all night and talked about you.
A favor I asked her she said she would do.
With the wink of an eye she was gone in the night.
She said she would return before it was daylight.
She said you were laying so peaceful in bed.
With the light of the moon resting upon your head.

She whispered, "I love you" into your ear.
From the corner of your eye, came one sparkling tear.
So when you awake be sure not to miss
for the love on your lips is my golden kiss.

Wytonna Crider

Who . . . Why Murdered?

Moon Glow Flesh, pale and smooth scarlet
beams of light pouring down to a crimson lake
Dark hallways echoing cries from the hungry mirrors
Swallowing the intense eyes and trembling mouth—
Cold fingers plucking salty drops from
Marble cheeks
Slowly tracing her blue lips
With his thumb
Cheeks cupped delicately in Glass palms
She will have no tomorrow
Because he needed today.

Sarah Emory

My Choice

Silver streaks dance and swirl as the shiny
Blackness slithers by below.
What am I doing here?
So peaceful and calm, yet violent and
Foreboding, the silver swirls beckon to be
Disturbed.
Why am I here?
Soft, lapping waves caress the shore on either
Side, causing a sensation of relaxation.
Where am I going?
Sleep, long-lasting sleep, is promised by
The lustful lapping on the shores.
Who is controlling my mind?
Silently, silkily, the blackness becomes ever so inviting.
When will it stop?
Slowly, I slide over toward the edge, the
Final ledge.
How will things end?
Stopping short, I step back and realize,
"Not now, not yet. It's too soon."

Brandy Scott Donley

You Are My Angel

You are my angel with wings of shimmering gold,
You are my angel, let the truth be told.
This pain in my heart you have taken,
The fears I once felt you have shaken.

Angel, Oh, my sweet, sweet angel sent from Heaven up above,
You are the one who taught me how to love.
You carried me when times were harsh
And you always guided me through the dark.

Who sent you here to me,
Oh, angel so dear to me?
Was it the Lord so proud and so great,
Or was it the one whom we call "Fate?"

Angel, you are so beautiful,
Standing right here in front of me is a miracle.
I'll never be able to thank you enough,
Oh, dear, sweet angel, with the gentlest touch.

Angel, Oh, angel hear my call.

Tonya Leffew

The World

To Alice
This is the world we live in,
The sick, sad, oppressed world.
The world that is cruel and dangerous,
The world in which we live.
The world which we hate,
The world which we love.
The world that revolves around you,
or around me.
The world that seems to torment me.
The world which has so much pain.
The world that tortures me seems so hard,
seems to bind me in.
This world where I can't bring myself to
the easy way out.
The hard way is only evident.
The world that hates me,
and me who hates the world.

Jonathan Markle

The Essence of Friendship

The essence of friendship—a fragrance quite rare,
Like the scent of a candle—fills the air.
It begins with a flicker, a small gentle flame,
Burning quite slowly, friendship its aim.
Fueled by loyalty, compassion and care,
The flame grows brighter; camaraderie flares.

Yet quarrels and strife waft all about.
The candle of friendship almost blows out.
Undaunted by trials, a spark still remains,
Enkindled by love, forgiving the pain.
The flame burns more brilliantly, a glow it imparts;
The warmth of friendship is connecting two hearts.

Like David and Jonathan, long, long ago,
Hearts bask in the warmth of friendship's glow.
Soul to soul, heart to heart, a covenant sealed,
The essence of friendship now is revealed.
To love and respect, cherish and trust,
True friendship is given by Jesus to us.

Brenda Kaye Lambert

Who Am I

I am a woman!
I know a man who is so big.
I know a man who is so tall.
I know a man, whom I thought was no foe.
I know a man who tried to show me his card of serenity,
when I already had my own.
I know a man who hurt me and used no wisdom to know the difference.
I know a man who was really no friend at all.
I know a man that never used wisdom or courage to try and take mine,
is to know the difference.
Oh, God help me please!
I know a man I really never knew at all.

I have been wounded.

Amen

Reta Clayton

Hey God, Thanks!

Thank you God for animals big and small,
And even for the ones I don't like at all.
Thank you God for people so sweet,
And even the ones who make me stomp my feet.
Thank you God for the world so grand,
And even the places that need your helping hand.
Thank you God for feelings glad and sad,
For there are lessons learned in the good and the bad.
Thank you God for angels that sing,
They're always there getting mud out of my wings.
And thank you God for my life that I see,
It makes me feel good knowing your fingerprints are all over me!

Colleen Mary McEldowney

Life

Does life lend itself to your breath the way
you wish? Or does it all seem like a
jumbled washed up mess in your mind? I think
that most people do not realize their
potential and spend time doing things that
add nothingness to their souls. Do you love
to sing? Then sing. Do you love to write?
Then write. Do you love the way your mom
cooks? Then tell her. Don't do wasteful
things. They won't mean anything in the
end. Don't spend your time at college if it
won't help you. Live for what you are, not
what everyone else wants you to be. Then
you'll feel life in your breath.

Kristen Elizabeth Ayres

Life

The winter wind cries
as the snow dances along the ground.
Like the howling of a banshee,
the breath of December whistles through the trees.
The sound of creaking and moaning
coming from the rafters in the attic.
The intense, heavy, dark clouds
bringing the blankets of snow.
The old man on the street,
hungry and almost numb from the cold,
is shivering and begging for food,
but no one seems to notice.
And then there's the baby,
so innocent and trusting,
yawning and preparing for sleep,
as she breathes a contented sigh.
The seasons of time and of life,
the baby awaking refreshed,
the old man not waking at all.
The endless circle of life.

Patti Reaver

Resurgence

I take in hand a piece of stone
And ask what can it tell to a fellow man?
That it has seen and felt the joy of day's start and end,
Has endured the pressure of foe and friend.

This gift from God beneath this mask,
Now nameless and in obscurity, awaits resurgence into life's damask
By someone passing, who can see that this with love can be
A sculpture of what man sees of life and love, longevity.

Frances Zagari Sokul

Alarm Clock and Deadlines

School, Work, Eat, Sleep, Mingle with peers.
Two of you are funny-looking and don't belong here,
And don't give me that look, Work, you know you're a freak.
During sleep I had a vision (dream):
Steal necessary supplies and nutrients,
Build raft and float down a river, attempt to breathe again.
If all goes well, others will come.
Curiosity brings us to good, strange new places.
One of the others (a girl)
Makes me feel all weird,
(Like when we used to climb the rope in gym class). We court.
As our lips touch softly . . .
Alarm clock ends sleep and dream.
I think, in time, I surely find,
I want to leave the deadlines behind,
To wake up after the good part.

Jason McConnell

Royal Memory

Small hands patiently etch,
plotting a course of tradition.
Little feet stir gravels,
searching for rocks in perfect condition.

Tiny fingers testing texture, weight, and grip
slide two prime candidates into front pocket.
Tongue licks rosebud of upper and lower lip,
as arm slowly draws back, then tosses.

A smooth, flat stone lands in square number one.
Broad smiles break across faces of innocence.
Feet take turns jumping, first two then one.
A single leap clears a moon of no consequence.

Triumphant shouts carried indoors on the wings of the wind,
draw a crowd to my side at the window
—where watching brought flashes of a childhood friend.

B. D. Hensley

To an Owl

Wise old owl up in the tree,
What makes you look that way at me?

Is it the wisdom of the world
That makes you look so sad and stern?

Eyes surrounded by radiant feathers,
Plumage so fluffy, in all kinds of weather.

The tree you've chosen for your perch
Is beginning to wilt
As if singing a dirge.
The verdant needles are turning color,
And branches show a silvery pallor.

Oh, you nocturnal bird of prey,
You're causing me dismay.
You sit in regal splendor,
And yet your feathers are so tender
That you can fly without a noise!

Inge Thewman

Where the Shadows Play

Looking over the swell of the forgotten and forgetting sea,
watching the waves work paths by the tides,
they roll and rock and ride back to me,
as every home in the evening hides

as the sunset glints and stabs the eyes
by water shed, by weary eyes,
as the sand cools and dampens in the night,
as rises the moon on silver waters and silver light,

we dance in the moment and know our bliss,
passing quietly in the tunnels of time
over our shoulder we watch what we miss,
and again we await the cascade of sunshine

only in the echoes of the final song,
as our last twilight grows so ever long,
do we realize all that has been undone
we turn in time to glimpse
the setting sun.

Lorenzo Donini

Conversation

Conversations stir your emotions,
From small talk to talk as deep as the ocean.
Analyzing my conversations as a whole,
The most interesting one is with my own soul.
There are conflicts, sadness, and laughter within.
One side tells me to love, the other says to sin.
Everyone, everywhere, in every nation
Participates in conversation.
Some make us stronger, others make us weak,
some make us silent, others make us speak.
It's something history has taught us all:
Conversations are the reasons we rise and fall.

Tyson Welchlin

Event

About last night,
my strength on the bedside table
like a slow clock,
a car hitting me without the slightest
indication of ruining its attractiveness—
by its taillights
it had robbed me of every
self-consciousness for making anger.
How can I hate myself
in being involved in such a cause-and-effect
revealing the beautiful machinery of the city?

Brian Fontanilla Brotarlo

primate blurb

atheist dreams, silent screams, abortion in
a muddy stream. cool aqua inhale. coffee
stains resident pains, seek to find spring
in a bottle (still). the primate i hate,
propagate apostasy. neglected and swollen
like sudden swift abandon, calling out from
bleeding pores and what's in store, the masses
implore. contortionist volition, singing
redolent prose. albumen ready for consumption
asinine leisure, legionary lesion and
corrupt masturbation

David Clark

Of Breaking Gently

Cool and slippery, the white porcelain flew
from my fingers, slid free from my grasp
(wet hands, damp towel)—
and crashed like glass rain to the floor.
My feet bare, cold, and white,
shattered pieces showered, spread like
dangerous confetti around them.
My mother's voices, sweetened by time and
memory, echo wise reassurances
(pulse lightly in my chest, through threatening tears),
"We don't cry over broken dishes. . . ."
Her anniversary plate, my baby cup, no
matter the treasure, she tells me to stop
wishing the pieces upward softly, together
again in one swift motion of redemption.
But to open my hands, palms up—let it
all fly freely out and away, accepting
life's crash of finality with a spirit of grace.

Briana Ellen McDonough

Shadows

Looking at the grey-haired man across the table
and his paunchy, balding friend talking,
thinking they are both eight years younger than I am.
Feeling as though I were pretending to get old
and wondering at the kindness everyone has shown me.
About how the woman pulled out a chair
and I sat down, feeling faintly foolish.
Noticing the smell of arms as they put plates
in front of me, perfectly, as I thanked them.
As though being served were part of the process
of becoming invisible.

Bill Mayer

In His Love

We will fly in the twinkling of his eye.
Put your fears aside and rest, in so much as you know
Along with all the rest, in His love we hide,
As we abide at His side.

Every knee shall bow and every tongue confess,
On that day we are reconciled by the twinkling of His eye.
So put your fears aside and abide;
Trust and prove to all the rest that in His love we hide,
As we abide at His side.

Come and go with me, do not be left behind.
Would you like to fly in the twinkling of His eye?
Fight the troubles in your mind by putting your fears aside.
Keep a hold on the time that is to come,
By the twinkling of His eye. We will fly and
Be ever at His side because we learned to hide.
Lay your fears aside and abide,
For the time will come when we are one with the Son,
In the twinkling of His eye.
Trust in His Love, hide and abide ever at His side.

Donna Maas

I'm Tired

From the sun rising that brightens up the night
While the moon glows and reveal
Our stars show would he or she please go.
Set aside madness and laughter took its tough
I'm tired with a huff then puff.
Say child of our flowers, get out of here!
I'm tired from being picked every hour
maple grass and blow air brain aire
Be pin on a garment mankind fashioned
while peared, glory be alone
Soul sister with a pair of dice thrown
Until Hilltop blues reveals or should
We say end the shown
Reaching higher then the plain
Hand muscle tightly squeezed its frame
I'm tired of building in vain.

Jacqueline Logan Anderson

Roses

She thinks of love as she pours hot coffee
And adds nutrasweet,
Masking the bitterness,
An artificial sweetness
White woven in the black atomic lattice.
With his wine tinted roses by her bedside,
Once brimming with the vigor of life,
But now cracked and pale at the edges,
Spilling its life energy over the table top.
She drinks, cupping both hands around the mug,
As if the heat would be transferred,
Letting the steaming solution,
Travel down her throat,
Scalding the taste buds
'Til taste is reduced to the dull throb
Of liquid running over solid.

Lu Zheng

When Can I Be Me?

The other night I laid in bed,
and thought about who I was.
The memories of yesterdays,
and the thoughts of broken love.
With those thoughts came many tears,
and smiles forever parted.
And when I thought of all in past,
the pain again had started.
From these years I've built a wall,
of stones you cannot see.
From pains and sorrows this wall was built
to protect the real true me.
For every day I hide the pain,
and every time I hide my tears,
Adds bigger, and tougher stones;
hiding what's inside, and leaving me alone.
There's tons that you don't feel,
and much that you don't see,
and every day I wonder when,
when I can I just be me?

Breanne Rochelle Abbott

Time

One day I return home and find
The place of my childhood diminished by time
The roof of my house which used to touch the sky
seems so low now as I pass by
I count the steps 1, 2, 3, 4
The grand staircase is no more
I thought my house would stand on a mountain still
I realize now it is just a hill

Christina M. Nelson

Guts

I met a young lady once on a trolley,
on a brewery tour with my father.
I asked about her necklace.
She asked about my Bad Religion shirt.
I was amazed by her knowledge
of a music genre most girls don't dig.
She was beautiful,
brown, curly, shoulder-length hair,
and a Budweiser shirt.
She was a guide on the barley-hopped tour.
I learned several things on that trolley:
take a chance, sometimes it works;
never judge one's musical interests
by their gender;
always get a name and phone number;
and 2 free beers at a brewery
just isn't enough.

Sean Michael Ritter

True

It's born untouched, clean, and naive,
It grows leaving behind scents of churlish experiences.
It waits to linger yet flees when you want it the most.
It is everyone's happiness and everyone's despair.
It is created without work and sticks to fawn all over you
It is the deceiving way which draws you so
Near to see its many pretty colors and shapes
It is true it speaks in soft whispers and lies
Awake to watch you suffer.
It is true it shapes your freedom
yet you may not ever be able to choose its destination!
It will talk in eulogies and leave
You with fresh new seeds to grow.
It will appear as magical and then
disgust you like an old worn hat.
It will toss you around and then
Leave you unable to reason.
With just one sight it will force
you to become and then grieve
when it hasn't spoken . . . Love.

Melanie James

Love Song to My Savior

Lord, your mercies are endless.
Your compassion abounds.
Your creativity cannot be fathomed.
Your creation resounds!
How beautiful you are, Lord.
Your reflection is in the cool water,
In the lush forest, and barren desert.
The flowers of the field sing your praises;
They know their creator.
The fish of the sea jump for joy,
Praising you, Almighty God.
I stand in awe of your creation, Lord.
Its beauty takes my breath away
And leaves no words in my heart,
Except to praise your Holy Name.
Lord, your mercies are endless.
Your compassion abounds.
Your creativity cannot be fathomed.
Your creation resounds!

Jessica Rose Amos

Heather

I am left speechless now when I look back,
I cannot describe her beauty or my feelings,
Only the experience of that time does it justice.
For the thought of the memory is worth the life time of pain.

Andrew Farrington

The Jewel

I have grown cold
In the palm of your hand
My dreams stir me away
From the dance floor
Across to Bavnaghar garden

Dream against dream
I hear the sea call
In the empty seashell

In red silk, the pearls of the silence
Drop one by one, in the far away
Memory of The Maharajah

Seashell against seashell
Death against death. It is high tide . . .
And my eyes are moist
With the intent to cry
But not a tear care to fall on the ashes
And so, you will never know . . .

Esogurl Rahman Brigitte

Silver Drops of the Sky

In the distance I hear
The roar of the mighty thunder,
With lightning flashing by,
Shooting shiver to my soul.

I look up to see,
The silver drops slicing the clouds;
Thick black ones shadowing the ball of fire,
Droplets of silver showering the meadows,
Splattering in drops,
Turning dry, hard clay into mud.

I saw tiny little green leaves unfolding
And dew on the grass.
There were children splashing the puddles,
Making me realize the beautiful gift
of mother Earth.
I solemnly promise I will take good care of it,
All because of the silver drops of the sky.

Haanusia Raj

Some Might Call It Dancing

Some might call it dancing
I call it stumbling closer to God,
the unrehearsed falling forward into love
as if the world was tipped.
Stuck dumb by ecstasy,
I have arrived by already being there,
lifted by my own breath
like a child in the arms of his mother.
It is here in this place of revival
that something in me moves, turns, reaches,
my body merely residue, a puff of smoke,
an awkward prayer whispered Heavenward.
Operatic in my cells, I arrive again and again,
mute to the moment, mute to the pain,
where dancing becomes infinitely less about
movement than being moved;
for when the world is tipped and we,
drunk to our eyes in love's ballet, are willing,
there is nothing not dance, no one not dancer,
no place not stage, no breath not a standing ovation before God

Mitchell Lewis Ditkoff

The Memories You Gave Me

The memories you gave me will last forever,
The times we shared I will always remember,
The memories you gave me help me remember you,
The memories you gave me, and the ones I gave you.

Jennifer Smaagaard

A Beautiful Person

Is it a certain height or weight?
No, because then God would have told us.
Is it the color of your hair or eyes?
No, because then God would have told us.
Is it your physical strength or body shape?
No, because then God would have told us.

A beautiful person seeks out the lonely
and becomes a friend.
A beautiful person can shed a tear and not
worry what others may think.
A beautiful person is kind, compassionate,
caring and understanding to all.
A beautiful person always tries to see
the inner beauty of others.
Above all a beautiful person puts God before
everyone and everyone before themselves

Lord, help me to be a beautiful person.

Cheryl L. Kroll

I Fell Asleep at Your Funeral

It's snowing phosphorus late afternoonish.
An essence snifter,
nice relaxer:
Bloody Mary and Klonopin
for my petite mal problem.
Curb your tired thoughts.
I need your wakefulness
(although I have crossed)
from the belly of this black shark of a car.

In a game begun
by a dead man on wheels
the headlights play a customary
follow the leader.
Were you here,
(and able)
you would sack the churchy creep delivering your eulogy.
Stir me when he has finished.

Max A. Friedenberg

Doozle

You always called me kid
and said you wanted me
until you went to jail.
(Drugs are bad, Brian.)
And I accepted 30 dollars' worth
of collect calls
from the correctional facility
and I waited and cried for you.
I would have bailed you out
and now you're back with HER
(DIE, BRANDY!).
I thought you hated her.
I know it's illegal,
but because of you
I started singing Jessica Simpson songs—
"I think that I'm in love with you . . ."
Maybe you WERE too old, even though you could
buy me beer.

Beth Bagley

My Best Friend

Into my dark and dreary world you came,
You changed me and I will never be the same.
You gave to me a love that is pure,
Your heart, your soul and a friendship that will endure.
You found a me, I never was before,
You gave me wings and taught me how to soar.

Cheryl Shampoe

Dimschor Street

There are no prophets reading scriptures
And the sidewalks are silver clean
As piles of glamour magazines intercept the sky

The nomads are throwing a party outside
Their cigarettes glow like a thousand small lights
Reflecting the stars above Dimschor Street tonight

Merchants sell photographs of other peoples lives
And there's a full garbage eclipse on the fourteenth floor
As old drunkards laugh and sharpen their knives
Outside the sickly liquor shop door

Late at night the curtains shut
And rain showers silence on Dimschor Street
Leaving behind no trace of any pain

I look back through the crystal window
As the bus fades away from a hidden land of sin
And sitting here I realize
Dimschor Street will never look the same to me again

    Daniel Levine

Dust

This poem is dedicated to the greatest of all healers, time itself.
I sweep dust streaks on the tiles,
shapes remind me of hands held,
time spent in a wistful world,
unlike those of Huxley and Bradbury.
Swept away,
it is a burden I still carry.

A light wind blows gently on the marble,
dusty images of memories mold,
the harder hours held onto fold,
into a dark day where you are no more.
Whisked away,
it is a burden that keeps me raw.

Rain, a quiet shower begins to fall,
dust-filled drops soon disappear
as the torrent trickle becomes quite clear,
past love and its leaving start to thin.
Washed away,
it is a burden that no longer keeps me in.

    Grant Daniel Muir

Guinevere in Geometry I

With majestic grace
the demure maiden enters yet another squalid chamber,
heedless of her fawning blue-jeaned ladies-in-waiting
who bustle and giggle
and encompass her.

Suspended from a pallid throat on a silver chain
she wears the gilded crest
by which her first Lancelot has pledged himself.

With a lily-like hand
the golden band she nestles to her breast,
sighs, and dreams of misty cloistered trysts
and a gallant paramour . . .

Until the clattering of a brazen alarum
rudely awakens her to a stark present,
to endure alone the onslaught of unemotional logic
and chalk-forged angle edges,
honed for cleaving perfect dreams.

    Manuel Mello

Here's a Story I Never Told You

Here's a story I never told you:
Four months from the day that
your chest went still,
I cried so hard that my
house of silence was broken forever.
I wept for an hour, twisted
in the fetal position,
as you did when the disease
was paralyzing you.
The doctors sent thoughts of false prophecy,
but I saw the dreams you cried,
I knew how you longed to dance
with the angels . . .
and although I loved you,
I longed for your isolation to end.
I wanted you to sit among the clouds.

    Brandie Kopsas

Blue in Green

Staring at the world through a windshield
darkened by droplets of jazz . . .

The first full notes won't resound at all
unless you love that piano
the way you love a favorite yellow dog,
the keys licking your fingers, notes that know every
groove and ridge of your fingertips
the way you know myriad eights and shades of touch
and force to coax cannonballs and ice or velvet smiles
from ivory for every note to lope and amble
in the tame and collaring sway of melody and empathy
for every chord of barrel-chested bass and piano
to dance in slow, casual gravity until the gentle
measured release arrives—trumpets unseaming
the heart's crimson curtain to coax dry the wet white
feathers of the uncaged soul, a brass, breathy angel
unballing itself, darting out past the hood ornament,
taking wing and fluttering. . . .

    Michael Pacholski

Careful Gwendolyn

The fire of the world burning
onto the pages of your journal,
your letters to lost lovers
who knelt to your written wealth,
mad from your distance and
direct assault on history and
human artifice and myth.
How wise you were at twenty-two,
how you knew that commitment was
criminal, that the artist must suffer
in arms of many.
Now, Osiris sits on a sphinx at the foot of
her bed, drawing out your magic,
a phone pressed to her chest.
Could Glenn be conducting his breath
or maybe the cries of Milt?
You listen and absorb and lie still
because your lips suck dry the bottle
of our undoing.

    Brandon Flowers

My Heaven on Earth

Where the wind blows
   and the mist is heavy,
Where streams ring
   like Christmas bells,
Where the birds sing happily
   and the deer leap through the forest,
That is where you will find me!

    Brianna Jeffers

The Old Photo

I thought I was invisible in a way that dogs
would not bark or even lift an ear—this was
when I got back from India.
I thought birds would not be afraid and would land on my shoulders.
I was wrong about a lot of things. The rest is private.
At this point my only concern is the
seemingly endless rehearsal of Joy,
the mortal perfumed combat and the same
eternal story over and over
and over the way it was when we were seventeen.
They say it is a life wasted,
and maybe they're partly right,
but we all die soon enough.
So now we will again look at each other
in that shyly desperate trance,
and in the end it will be part of the same eternal Smile
written on the faded photo
lying on the kitchen table
taken just before the accident.

Mark Rudolph

Paradise

Mediterranean sea breeze
Flutters my soul within.
Ember sparks of lightening clash,
While wild horses run free at daybreak.
Thousands of mahogany butterflies
Course passionately throughout my veins.
Moonlight kisses smother me
In a faceless sky of rose petals.
Endless dragonflies
Whispering wordlessly in my ear.
Fervent rainbows endelved within
Each grain of sand I touch.
White, line bed sheets
Passionately waiting on a blood-red moonbeam.
Sweet surrenders of English-tea
Tempt me in my uncarpeted hallway.
Torrents of billowing smoke
Rage within each breath I intake.
A dying thistle pierces my every thought
Effortlessly consuming paradise.

Nicole Andrea Pusateri

Poem on the Fly #1

So I'm on the train and there's this
kid who started talking about Jesus to
a woman sitting down, him standing,
she kept saying "Excuse me?"
Because she couldn't quite hear his soft crazy voice
Above the noise of the train his skin so black
so smooth, silken. This beautiful black man
He was a child once I kept thinking
She was a child once.
This guy sitting next to her avoiding the cadence of their
Nutty conversation he was a child once.
So there I am swaying and holding
on dreaming, dreaming,
holding on swaying
Listening to this crazy, crazy
Speak and feeling the rhythm of the
Train and all of a sudden,
I am flying above them looking down on them.
Free, not part of them, but rising outside of the
Metal confines of the train car.

Lisa Walsh-Miller

alone

half-dead in silence at two a.m.,
maybe earlier, summer heat touches skin
like thorn-pricks a hundred or more.
sliding doors half-closed, four corners
and empty walls, clock ticks in a dying rhythm
with a ten-ton mind slipping seven years back.
among shadows behind bushes, among sunsets
behind crimson lines, where the streets are
warm to wary feet passing by, waves breaking
from afar. but here, where stillness is
lullaby, letters reincarnate into colored
butterflies, among books and crumpled papers,
and an ink-less pen in a fevered hand.
verses stream through ceilings, sweat soaks
sleeves and rugged hairlines, on a bed,
chocolate-scented and purple-brown,
like the earth seven feet down.
solitude is a bliss tonight
and i cry, for god is gone.

Zenon Baquiran Batang

Untitled

I sometimes nail myself to the walls of my room
because it temporarily knocks the world off its axis
and in effect changes time for awhile.
However, eventually the nails fall out of place,
and the Earth returns to its uniform revolving motions.
You see, I have this hang-up with time—
it's always moving at undesirable speeds,
but it only spins that way in my mind,
because time is a constant that never changes pace.
So I sit and continually explode in my room,
leaving pieces of me on the floor,
and my thoughts on the walls,
until the sun goes down.
I'm tired as I pick up the pieces
and pull down the thoughts,
and attempt to reassemble myself once again.

Breniman Green

Tropical Torrent

The rain fell slant-ways that day
Sending poisoned arrows down
Deep under my umbrella.
And lost in its onslaught, my heart
Was searching . . . searching
For a face in which to shelter.

All around in the dismal streets
The gathering pools of grey
Were reflecting their sadness upwards . . .
And the cold disdain of the wind . . .
The cold disdain of the wind

Left me to wonder:
What else is there in the world
But days that are too wet . . . too dry?
Days spoilt by love's sweet overflow?
Days spent without love's joy?

Emery A Cournand

Biographies
of
Poets

ABRAMS, RENEE
[a.] Middle Island, NY [title] "Grandmother's Eternal Love" [pers.] I am 20 years old. When I was 18, something that I thought would not happen in a long time did: My grandmother, "Mom-Mom," passed away from lung cancer. This disease took her three days after we found out she had it—no time to prepare or adjust. Mom-Mom was a very strong person; she worked hard all her life for everything she had. She was a good friend and the best grandma. She was loving, sweet, and gentle. She was there when anyone needed her. I loved her so much, and I hope she knew that I wrote this poem the day before she died; I was going to read it to her but I never got to. I read this poem at her services, and then I knew she was listening because I felt her warm embrace over me. I write poems to let out my feelings, and I knew this was the best thing for me to do. Mom-Mom will always be in my heart for eternity. I dedicate my poem in loving memory of Jeanne Shaber.

ACTON, MICHELLE
[pers.] This was the first poem I ever wrote, when I was 15 years old. I am now 30, and it is as real to me today as it was then. My teenage years were a very difficult time for me, and poetry allowed me an outlet to express my inner turmoil. I feel it is imperative that everyone find an avenue to express themselves; otherwise, we simply shrivel up and die inside. It is my deepest hope that my poem touch just one person—to enable him or her to see beyond pain, sorrow, and loneliness . . . to reach out not only to be heard, but also to hear.

ADKINS, DAVID
[a.] Lorain, OH [title] "Just Riding" [pers.] As a child, I had a love for writing stories and poems, but my childhood was an abusive and violent world. It was difficult to do what I loved back then. After growing up, I found God's peace in my life. Through His mercy and grace, he didn't allow that love for writing to die. Just recently, through the loving support of my wife, Ronna, and my son, Justin, I started writing again. I can't thank the International Library of Poetry enough for making my dream come true. This is something I will cherish for a lifetime!

AGUILAR, ANGIE
[pers.] A way to become a good poet is to tell about your feelings and dreams. They can give you the inspiration to become a good poet. This poem is a picture of a dream that did occur to me. By the way, I am a third grade student at John Muir Elementary School in Glendale, California, and I like to write poetry.

AGYEMAN-DUAH, FREDERICK
[pers.] Poetry, to me, has always been a form of escape from the harsh realities of life. Growing up without both parents resulted in some painful moments, but whenever I write poetry, I am able to live in a world based on my imagination. I have been writing since the age of ten. I was born and raised in Ghana, West Africa, and moved to the U.S. about five years ago. I now attend Manchester College in Indiana.

AHMED, IMAN
[a.] Orlando, FL [title] "Mother, My Perfect Companion" [pers.] I have written this poem for my mother and for all the mothers in the world, no matter who they are or where they come from. This poem is about how much mothers are to us and how much they mean to us, because in this world, we would not be able to live without them. So it is our responsibility and our duty to keep them shining like rubies and to make them twinkle like the stars above.

AKUTAGAWA, DAIJO
[title] "Myopia" [pers.] I'm an artist by trade. I'm sure I got the worst of that exchange. I paint.

It's been said a painting is "worth a thousand words;" it hasn't been stated that you can barely make one coherent sentence out of all those words. So I write. Futility tells me to relax. Guilt tells me to produce. Hate fuels the fire. Love channels the energy. Procrastination orders another round. I get stuck with the bar tab . . . again. Painting describes the indescribable. Writing defines it. Poetry exists in-between.

AL-NACHAR, WAFA
[title] "Mother, I Love You" [pers.] This poem is the translation of one of my poems written in French for my friend's mother. So I would like to dedicate it to Evelyne Pierre, who is this great mother I loved before even knowing her. I also would like to dedicate this poem to my mother, Odette Al-Nachar, who is my best friend, and to all the mothers in the world. Thank you for everything!

ALCORN, TABITHA
[title] "Without You" [pers.] When I wrote this poem, I wrote about a love I couldn't have. Life has its pain and losses, which only shows that we're human. I try to find ways to organize and put things into words that describe how I feel. This helps me cope with life's daily problems so I can feel at ease. I hope everyone finds the peace I do when I write.

ALI, ANGEL
[title] "Spectrum" [pers.] Poetry has most often been the expression of my deepest, most inner, and complex thoughts. "Spectrum" is just such a poem, written while I examined a work of art. I became intrigued with the picture, which I realized was uniquely different from the imperfect world of which we are a part. Poetry itself is a work of art, allowing us to create in words, pictures which form in the minds of our readers. I am proud to claim "Spectrum" as my first published work of art, an accomplishment I owe in large part to my family—particularly my father, who has always pressed me to further develop my writing.

ALICIAS, EDUARDO, JR.
[title] "Erimako's Pen" [pers.] I was born on August 10, 1945 in Vigan, Ilocos Sur, Philippines. I am married to Teresita and have three children—Lilian, Irma, and Eugene. I obtained my doctorate in education at the University of the Philippines, where currently I am an Associate Professor. I did postdoctoral studies at the University of London as a British Council Fellow. The preface of my book, *Humor and Madness,* holds the Guinness World Record as the longest in the world. Social reality is splattered with mud and madness, mainly because of the perversion of self-aggrandizing government officials. "Erimako's Pen" was penned against them.

ALLEE, JACOB
[title] "Fire" [pers.] I only write poetry when under extreme emotion. Whatever emotion it may be—love, hate, sadness, or joy or so on—I write in the climax of it; that way it is pure and real. Anything else does no justice to words. I write because it's a God-given talent, and I will use it without wasting a word. One thing about poetry is that you can only write what you know, you only know what you've experienced, and every experience evokes an emotion. I hope you enjoyed my poem, and I encourage you to write your own!

ALLEN, CAROL
[title] "Mom Said" [pers.] My mother was truly "the wind beneath my wings." This poem came to me at a time when I needed her most, and I believe she again came through for me, even though she had to reach down from Heaven to do so.

ALLEN, JOHNSIE
[a.] Baird, TX [title] "The Old Water Tower" [pers.] As my poem says, the water tower stood as a symbol of yesteryear. When I wrote the poem in early April 2000, I had no idea that it would be

demolished soon. On May 17, the very day before I received your letter and release form, it was cut down. The reason given was that children had been playing and climbing the ladder to the tower, and city fathers feared an accident. Many of us natives have been saddened to see it go. A landmark it was for this area of Texas from the 1880's. It was for so many years—the spirit board for the high school's athletic teams. High schoolers climbed the tower to paint "Beat So-&-So" or "SRS '49" or such on its side, and many times the opposing team, in the dark of night, climbed the tower to paint over the message and leave one of its own.

ALLEN, KARA
[a.] Washington Terrace, UT [title] "You and Love" [pers.] I love poetry, and I use it as my way of expressing love for the people and things in my life. I wrote this poem for my husband, James. We have been together for nine years and have three beautiful children. We displayed this poem at our wedding. He constantly inspires me to write poetry to express my everlasting love for him. He is my light and my life!

ALLEN, MARY
[title] "Eye of Life's Storm" [pers.] I was born in Davidson County. I lived there for nearly 13 years and moved with my family to Williamson County. I graduated from Franklin High in 1960, then attended David Lispcomb College (now University). I started writing about five years ago. I have received awards from World of Poetry and the International Society of Poets. I've published four books of poetry, plus I've had numerous poems published by Great Lakes Poetry Press, Hauldens Press, World of Poetry, International Society of Poets, Sparrowgrass Poetry, and others. I am a member of Plytonsville Church of Christ. I am a volunteer at Williamson Medical Center in Franklin, TN. I live in Waffe House in Franklin, TN. I'm also a member of the Williamson County Arts Council.

ALLEN, ROBERT
[a.] El Paso, TX [title] "They Bleed Red, Also" [pers.] I would like to dedicate this poem first and foremost to my Lord and Saviour Jesus Christ. I would also like to thank my wife Maria for believing in me and encouraging me. I want to thank the rest of my family and my teachers, who have supported me and taught me what is right and wrong as well as that reading and writing are gifts from the Lord. I hope someday my children, Robert Jr., Dallana, Giovanna, and Luis will read this poem and be proud of their dad. With this poem, I hope whoever reads it will realize we are all God's children.

ALLESSANDRINI, ANGELA
[title] "Right and Wrong" [pers.] I enjoy writing poetry—a short way to express my philosophy of life. The poem "Right and Wrong" was inspired by a young adult asking me, "What is right or what's wrong?" Later, I mailed her a long poem of what I thought was right and wrong, from which I excerpted the 20-line limit for publication.

ALLEY, ANN
[title] "Yoswimitee Pam" [pers.] This poem is dedicated to my seven-year-old granddaughter, Hannah. We were sitting in the doctor's office waiting room, gazing at all the beautiful and funny fish in their aquarium. We spotted a bright red one and decided she was our favorite. Then her story began to unfold . . . !

ALOZIE, THEOPHILUS
[title] "Multiple Sclerosis" [pers.] This poem is the fruit of my visions on prayer, technology, and healing in relation to all those afflicted by any form of mental or physical disability, especially victims of MS, who frequently languish in multiple relapses and despair. It's my way of telling them that all will be well, even in the midst of discomfort. Jesus loves

them, and hope, which smiles on them, increases by leaps and bounds. By and large, I'm privileged to transmit this message through poetry, since "silver or gold is not mine to give."

ALSTON, RODERICK
[a.] Queens, NY [title] "Untitled" [pers.] I am a U.S. Naval Veteran, educated at North Carolina University in Durham, NC. The poem was inspired by my college sweetheart, Deranda, and now by my wife, who never noticed my attraction towards her.

ALVEY, GALE
[title] "When Death Comes Knocking" [pers.] I have always enjoyed writing poems. I wrote "When Death Comes Knocking" for my dad. He died a little over a year ago. He said my poem made him feel better inside about letting go. That's what this poem is all about—not being afraid to die. Thanks so much for the publication of my poem. I still can't believe it. Also thanks to my family and friends for their encouragement.

AMONETTE, MARCIA
[a.] Hazel Green, AL [title] "Celebrate" [pers.] I wrote this poem as a gift to my dear friends, Sam and Dorothy Goldman, as they celebrated their 50th wedding anniversary. I do not write poetry on a regular basis, only when I am motivated, and I feel my motivation is always from God. If this or any other of my poems receives any recognition, I would want everyone to understand that the glory all belongs to God. I am only an instrument. Thank you for your interest and the kind words of encouragement; I will continue to write as God continues to inspire me.

ANDERSEN, KATHERINE
[title] "Imagination in a Maple Tree" [pers.] I wrote this poem in a creative writing class I took. It's a memory poem from childhood, when I used to wear my pink tutu every chance I got. It was also a time when I thought hiding in a tree meant no one could see me even when I could see them. This is a poem of every fond memories that I hope everyone shares.

ANDERSON, ANTHONY
[title] "Never in Her Presence" [pers.] This poem's meaning extends out to all who've lost but were afraid to show the pain attached to losing a lover. Every word I have written and will write has a special meaning to me and is my life's experiences. These words and the gift I share are dedicated to my parents, James and Ollie Anderson, but also to my light and soul-mate, who also pushed my emotions to speak loudly—Tina L. Turner. I've never written a poem before in my entire life, and for this new gift given, I truly thank my Creator.

ANDERSON, BRENDA
[title] "Left Behind (But Not Alone)" [pers.] I have written poetry for most of my life. It's a very fulfilling way of expressing my feelings and thoughts. I wrote this poem as a Mother's Day dedication for someone very important in my life and my upbringing—my Aunt Nintha Clayton, who took my two sisters and myself in after the death of our parents. I will always love her and be grateful for her. She has been a real mother to us all.

ANDERSON, CHARLES
[a.] Glendora, CA [title] "The Game" [pers.] Earth is a minute speck in the universe, and we mortals are but amoebas. Perhaps life is a game and we're losing. Maybe some higher force is overseeing all of us insignificant atoms, and we are but chess pieces of the Galaxy. Some of us are back-line pieces, and the rest are front-line pawns. Unfortunately we are the only mammals of this planet with reasoning powers. Being of this species, we wish for independence. Once we have arrived at this imaginary status, we strive for more. Alas . . . Power! The magical word "Power" is our arrogant

downfall. The arrogance of man is the undoing of mankind. This sallow existence of animal life may have been created for the amusement of the Grand Chess Master of the universe to observe us mortals making our amateur moves and slowly destroying ourselves. This destruction is the result of the never-ending obsession with the imaginary strength of power. If only our perception were as great as our greed, then maybe our short existence would be as sweet as the forbidden fruit we seek. Perhaps we Earthlings could then see the magic in the stars and enjoy the beauty of an autumn sunset, making the fleeting moments of life count. I would rather be a moving pawn than a King in checkmate.

ANDERSON, VANESSA
[pers.] Poetry is the soul's voice spoken with appeal and conviction. It rides on the tip of emotion's radical wave seeking freedom's acceptance to rest by the shore. Poetry is my horn blowing realism and passions from the heart. Poetry is my drum tapping melodic rhythm, words of the mind's corner so the soul may exhale.

ANDERSON-WRIGHT, PHYLLIS
[a.] Philadelphia, NJ [title] "For Philip and Edward" [pers.] This poem is a tribute to the memory of my father and father-in-law. These men were members of the "greatest generation," and two of the many gifts God gives to His beloved children.

ANNESS, KATE
[pers.] I'm 17 and I love to write. I write in my spare time and easily get swept up in the process. Poetry is my way to express my feelings, and it helps me to understand myself. It is my way to cope with my world.

ANWAR, AYSHAH
[a.] Sheffield, United Kingdom [title] "All I Do Is Think of You" [pers.] This poem is very special to me, as it commemorates someone who plays a very important role in my life, my Joan, the person who I love very much. Life consists of many chapters, but the best chapter of my life is the chapter in which I spent time with my one and only Joan, though luck and fate were not in our love's favour, and made us go apart. But the presence of my true love still remains within me and shall always remain there, and the fact of how much I love my Joan can never be changed. I shall survive with the help of the sweet, cherished memories. I'm sure people out there that have ever loved someone truly, know exactly how I feel. "Wish all the true lovers all the luck!"

ARANTON, JOHN-RUBEN, JR.
[a.] Wilmington, DE [title] "Love" [pers.] The poem "Love" is dedicated to the love of my life, Tetet. I did not begin to actually write poems that expressed my personal feelings about someone until I met her. She has inspired me to be a better person as well as a better writer. So, to Tetet I would like to say, "Thank you for being who you are and making me the person I am today. Every day is a blessing for me, knowing that you are with me every step of the way. Without you, my life would have No Rhyme! I Love You!"

ARITA, AMY
[a.] La Mesa, CA [title] "Life" [pers.] For the inspiration influencing my poetry and the pursuit of developing the art of English, I am forever in debt to Mrs. Aleen Jendian, who taught me the joy of writing during my freshman year at Helix High School. Now as a junior at Helix, involved in various clubs, sports, and orchestra, I am honored that my poetry is being published. My poem, "Life," came to me while sitting on a rocky shoreline at La Jolla shores, observing all the creatures God, in His majesty, created.

ARMSTRONG, LAURA
[a.] Santa Rita, Gu AE [title] "God Is" [pers.] I

love to write poems about God. I have written seventy-seven poems and ten songs over time. I have three poems published. I thank God for giving me the gift of poetry. I dedicate this poem to my husband, Art Armstrong, who is helpful in every way. God is all around us, we just need to slow down to see Him in His beauty.

ARNDT, ANNA
[a.] Deltona, FL [title] "Unfulfilled Poet" [pers.] Poetry has acted as an outlet for most of my life, starting with the uncertainty of adolescence, and through all the ups and downs that life brings our way. Sometimes I hear one word and it becomes the focal point of a new poem. Other times a dream wakes me from my sleep and I hear a phase repeating its self, and that is when I must get up and start writing. I liken it to a stirring in my soul that bubbles up in my spirit, then manifest itself onto a legible paper. Hopefully, the written word will become the truth someone else comprehends.

ARNETT, TERESA
[title] "For Matt" [pers.] I feel our children are our gift to the future. This poem is about my son, Matthew. He is my gift. He is smart and sensitive and artistic. My dream is that he grows into the man I see in him, with all of his gifts. We live in Springfield, Oregon with our dog and cats.

ARNOLD, MELVIN
[title] "Remember" [pers.] This poem was inspired when two close friends became separated, with each promising the other that there would never be replacements. They soon married and had five children.

ASAMOA-KRODUA, AKUA
[title] "Silent Tears" [pers.] I believe every individual has a gift or talent. I am grateful to God that I have discovered mine and I am able to write poetry. "Silent Tears" was written at a time when I went through each day feeling emptiness and no hope for the future. Writing poems has let me express a lot of feelings. I hope anyone who reads "Silent Tears" will know there is hope at the end of that dark road.

ASHBROOK, JENNIFER
[title] "My Expression of You" [pers.] Getting a poem published is a great reward of accomplishment. I would like to dedicate this poem to my husband, Lawrence Roy Ashbrook, Jr. He is the greatest thing that has happened to me in my life; he's my inspiration, and I would like to thank him for being such a wonderful and caring husband. Thank you, Roy! I Love You.

ASKEW, RICHARD
[a.] Hampton, VA [title] "Autumn" [pers.] Poetry is very dear to me, especially that of the renaissance, baroque, and romantic periods. I am a great admirer of John Donne, George Herbert, Keats, and also Poe. My hobbies include reading, historical research, and collecting antiques, as well as music. I simply wrote the poem "Autumn" one evening while I was alone. Most of my poetry is religious in nature. I go through long periods of writing none, then, suddenly, I feel a certain inspiration.

ATKINS, JOHN
[title] "True Friends and Lovers" [pers.] Life holds many challenges. Poetry, to me, is a way to show the feelings we all need to face these challenges and to overcome them, to find the beauty in all things. This poem is for my wife, Stephanie, and how I feel for her. Inspiration is what you find without looking for it.

AUSTIN, LARE
[a.] El Segundo, CA [title] "I See You" [pers.] It seems like yesterday when I realized I had fallen out of love with the fast, pressure-paced world of the television advertising industry and into love with the calming, sleepy pace of Monterey, California,

which, 'til then, had already been my home for two years. Oh, how I enjoyed daily doses of my breezy, cool, coastal town. I enjoyed taking daily walks on my shoreline bike trail, walking the beach at low tide, watching the seal pups nap, sea otters playing, and couples and families vacationing and wandering through the quaint, scenic streets. No matter where I am, or finally end up, nineteen years of coastal living experience, I believe, has helped shape much of my literary style into what it is today: much like the sea, always in motion, never fully predictable and somewhat mysterious.

AUTUCHIEWICZ, LISA
[title] "Mother, on Mother's Day" [pers.] This poem chronicles my growing up, and how my stay-at-home mom influenced my life. She taught me not to be afraid of trying new things, to be myself, and most important, to make time for myself. My family has always been important to me and a good support system in my life. I have always enjoyed writing poems and I love the thought of giving a true gift of the heart through poetry. I am happily married to Chris, my husband of five years, and we're expecting our first child in early December. I enjoy reading, crafts (painting), and music.

B., GINA
[a.] Moonachie, NJ [title] "My Husband" [pers.] There was a man that I saw that I would cherish, love, and adore. Through the years he has changed: his appearance, his ways. Does he still have the same name? This is a man that I thought I knew. We have changed, we both grew. Now we went through fifteen years of marriage, four cribs and four baby carriages. He is not the same man I fell in love with once. He is the same man I fell in love with once more.

BABER, HASHAM
[title] "Michelangelo" [pers.] Hasham Baber was born on February 18, 1941 in his hometown, Peshawar, an ancient town of the Pathans in Pakistan. He has published three collections of Pashto poetry since 1966, two of which have received national awards. He studied contemporary English literature, since his academic years have left a deep imprint on his poetry, particularly in his choice of forms and rhythms. While evoking his own heritage, he realizes that his poetic experience is, in fact, part of the universal contemporary ethos where newer realities transcend cultural boundaries, where culture is left to be merely the language itself.

BACHAR, BRIAN
[a.] Gibsonia, PA [title] "I Am With You" [pers.] Poetry is a way to say things that are normally hard to tell someone. It is words written by the heart, rather than the hand. I have written poetry all my life to say the things I cannot say aloud. Love is beautiful, love never fades, and poetry is the form of love that expresses it best. It can be interpreted anyway the reader sees fit. It means different things to everyone. Eternity lies in the point of a pen. This poem is for Karen, my light and love. She makes me the man I am. She's my one love.

BADORE, BEVERLY
[title] "My Journey" [pers.] My poetry is a build-up and pouring out of feelings, emotions, and life. I wrote my first poem in 1978, one year after my oldest brother died. I have written twelve poems since then about grief, including the loss of my husband in 1995; I call this collection "Expressions of Grief." The other poems I have written were inspired by a significant person, event, or circumstance that brought me to the point of expression. I refer to my faith often; that is ultimately what guides me. It's a feeling of contentment that has carried me through life's ups and downs.

BAGNERIS, MONET
[a.] Los Angeles, CA [title] "Late" [pers.] I am

in the seventh grade and I am 12 years old. I am also the oldest of three children. I have a ten-year-old brother, Jules IV, and a six-year-old sister, Mariana. Wherever I go or whenever my parents take me somewhere, it turns out that we are almost always "fashionably late." This is what inspired me to write this poem.

BAILEY, ERIN
[title] "Feelings of Rain" [pers.] My poems are usually inspired by nature, but sometimes they are funny or strange. It was raining gently on my roof when I wrote this poem. I love to write poetry. I try to write in all different styles, such as limericks, haikus, and even music.

BAILEY, WILLIAM
[title] "Moment of Truth" [pers.] For all of my life poems have appeared to me while in the mountains, driving home, etc. I can't explain them . . . the words came out. I am not the originator; I give that to a higher power. The poems seem to touch many people's lives as I share them. "Moment of Truth" is something we all can relate to . . . all of us each day have our own Moment of Truth . . . What now? What will you do? Your choice! My hope is your choice is a time of sunshine, joy, and power.

BAILEY, WILLIAM
[a.] Medford, OR [title] "Moment of Truth" [pers.] William E. Bailey was born in the village of Caney in Kentucky in 1930. One of 11 children, he spent his first seventeen years on his family's small hillside farm. Upon graduating from high school, Mr. Bailey left for Chicago, Illinois, to seek employment. At the age of nineteen, he joined the United States Navy, where he served for four full years. He then returned to earn a Bachelors degree in Marketing at the University of Illinois. Mr. Bailey became an American Entrepreneur in the truest sense. He first co-founded a marketing company whose products were manufactured and sold in ten countries. For his accomplishment he received many awards and honors, including the prestigious Horatio Alger Award in 1972. Eleven American Heroes were honored that year as exemplary "Strive and Succeed" role models harnessing the American free enterprise system, which included amongst other, Ross Perot and Ray Kroc. Since its inception in 1947, recipients of the Horatio Alger award include Norman Vincent Peale, Dwight Eisenhower Bob Hope, Art Linkletter, Carol Burnett, Don Shula, Roland Reagan and Oprah Winphrey to name but a few. Mr. Bailey retired at the age of 43. His work with orphans in San Hose resulted in a semi private audience with Pope Paul VI in 1968 even though he is not of Catholic denomination. Mr. Bailey, who thrives on the hectic pace of the business world, has mentored and inspired many of today's most successful and sought after speakers and authors

BAIN, JENNIFER
[a.] Pembroke Pines, FL [title] "The Broken Heart" [pers.] I feel that poetry writing is a gift, one that I found deep within me to help me with letting out my emotions. No one in my family writes poetry, but I hope to pass it on to my children. I feel as if poetry is a link to you and your feelings that run wildly throughout your body and soul. I write poetry all the time when I feel like remembering something in my life that either has taught me something or has a special meaning about it. Everything that I write about has happened throughout my life.

BAKER, ALMA
[a.] Fort Payne, AL [title] "Things I Am Thankful For" [pers.] This poem is very special to me because of my three sons, who have to travel all over the U.S. on their jobs. I am in an assisted living facility because I am not allowed to live alone after having several hemorrhages and having brain sur-

gery and a shunt inserted in my brain. That is the story leading to my writing this poem. I love my family very much and want them to know it.

BAKER, BEN
[title] "Cornerstone" [pers.] I find that poetry is a great release for me. When emotions builds up inside me, sometimes the only way I can release it is by writing poetry or a song. It's a great release that brings me to better understanding of things in life.

BAKER, SHERRY
[title] "Paradise" [pers.] I am a forty-one-year-old that is disabled from fibromyalgia and severe depression. My family, my faith in God's love, compassion, and grace, and a very special husband that has been by my side through thick and thin for twenty-three years and his amazing and loving family have been my inspiration to write poetry. I believe that poetry is a gift and a window into the soul of one who writes it. I also believe it's a very special gift from God, my Lord and Savior, whom I love and worship, and will forever be an inspiration for me throughout my life.

BALES, LISA
[title] "Tears of Sickness" [pers.] Writing, for me, was an outlet. I started a journal when I was 12 and, being confused most of the time, my poetry has helped me be expressive about myself and my inner-most feelings. It has helped me work through things. Reading my poetry is like looking through a window of my soul. I would like to dedicate this poem to my husband, who never stops encouraging me to keep writing. I love you, Rick. Thanks honey!

BALL, BRIAN
[title] "Inspired by Desired Thought" [pers.] I sincerely believe that my talent is given to me by God, and is meant to be used only for Him, so as to reach others for Him through the use of my writing. As for the praise that I get for the writing, which I so much enjoy, that must go to my Lord. I owe the Lord my life because of what He has done for me and what He has saved me from. He has saved me from Hell, and this is why the Glory for my writing must go to Him. My writing must glorify. My inspiration is Jesus.

BALL, LISA
[title] "Fusaichi Pegasus" [pers.] I enjoy horseback riding on Nuketa, so I decided to write about horse racing. My mother used to write poetry when she was alive, now I feel that I need to continue the tradition. Poetry expresses my innermost thoughts about nature and my surroundings. My family members are my parents, Allen and the late Nancy Ball, my sisters, Jo Lankard, Gwen Stalcup, Lela Beam, and my brothers, Jack and Robert Ball. I live northwest of Welda, Kansas. I graduated from Ottawa University in 1996 and Fort Scott Community College truck driving school in 1998. I work in company jobs. My hobbies are writing poetry, reading, horseback riding, jogging, bicycling, and watching movies.

BALOG, KATY
[title] "The Friend" [pers.] In school, for my English class, we had to write a sense poem using the five senses. The background of "The Friend" is based on a book entitled, *A Ring of Endless Light*, written by Madeleine L'Engle. This year I wrote poems for my dad and my grandmother for Father's Day. I wrote four other poems for my English class as well. I enjoy writing poetry, swimming, reading, and shopping. I also enjoy listening to music and traveling.

BANKS, CHARLES
[title] "Autumn" [pers.] My humble talent for writing poems is a gift from God. Poetry heals my heart when it needs healing. I love to write and I write to glorify the name of God. My poem, "Autumn," expresses how I feel about my favor-

ite time of year. I love the four seasons, but I love the fall season most. Praise God for His creation of us and all the seasons.

BANNON, MARIA
[a.] Brookston, IN [title] "Time" [pers.] Poetry is a way to express your love, joy, happiness, and fears, your sorrow and tears. This poem is dedicated to Heather Mitchell, 1981-2000, a wonderful young woman whose life ended much too soon! Special thanks to my grandmother, Mary, for sharing her love of literature. Loving thanks to my family and friends for being my inspirations. Eternal loving thoughts to my husband, Don, my son, Colton, and my stepsons, Travis, Kyle, and Chad.

BANTOS, CHARLES
[a.] Davie, FL [title] "The Wall" [pers.] This poem is dedicated to Michael Savenlli and the 58,317 men and women who died or never returned from Vietnam. We fought in a country so many Americans knew so little about, bound by a Code of Honor taught to us as children: "Love of God, Country, and Freedom." To this day, our loyalty, pride, and honor lives on. May the wall live through eternity, till we meet again, my brothers.

BARBATO, LAURAJEAN
[title] "Earth Gifts Surround Us" [pers.] This poem is dedicated to Jay Szabo for his dedication to his work and his love for the lake and boats, as well as for his caring for people less fortunate than himself. May the Lord bless him in all that he does. His gifts cometh from the Lord.

BARBER, ASHANTI
[title] "Race of Life" [pers.] What inspired me to write this poem was when I saw a poor man walking down the street. This touched me, knowing that opportunity nowadays is hard to come by. So when I wrote it I felt like I was letting people know that by perseverance and hard work the door of opportunity will open. Poetry is a very important part of my life. It is an emotional outlet and helps me to deal with certain situations. I feel my talent is a gift from God and I thank Him for it. I will continue to write as long as I have inspiration and devotion.

BARKLEY, WAYNE
[a.] Washington, DC [title] "We Are One" [pers.] My name is Wayne K. Barkley. I am a native of Washington, DC. I am 40 years of age and a former alcoholic. I came to know God at an early age. I didn't even accept Him into my life because my addictions had me bound. My victory over this darkness in my life started when I came to believe that a power greater than myself could restore my spiritual beliefs, and that power is my Lord and Savior, Christ Jesus. My faith is stronger now that I'm living a cleansed life, filled with the spirit of the Lord. God instilled in me a gift, and now I'm using my gift for the Lord. Be ye transformed by the renewing of your mind. On July 21, 1999, at Gospel Rescue Ministries in Washington, DC, in the Transforming Lives spiritual rehabilitation program, I decided to transform my life. We may all be different on the outside, but on the inside we are one in spirit.

BARNES, FLORENCE
[title] "Four Little Angels" [pers.] My poem was inspired a year after my husband, Roy, and I were married in 1995. I had a daughter, Linda, by a previous marriage, a son David, and a daughter, Sharon. Roy and I were blessed with another son, Bobby. Children are indeed precious gifts from God.

BARNETT, JUDITH ANNE
[a.] Nenoro, PA [title] "When There's No One Else, There's You" [pers.] This poem is important to me because in it I talk about the one person who means more to me than anything or anyone in this world, Jesus. Jesus is the only thing that keeps me sane at times, and He died for me long before the Father brought me into this world; that is reason enough for me to want to love Him the way I do. My poetry is a gift from Him, and I thank Him. Now I can only hope that someone else will come to love Him as much as I do because of it.

BARRETT, EDWARD
[title] "Song of the Unknown Soldier" [pers.] The words to my poem are actually the lyrics to an, as yet, unpublished song that I have written with the same title. My service in the U.S. Army Air Corps. in Guam in World War II inspired this deeply felt tribute to all those who gave their lives for our country.

BARRIENTES, ANTONIO
[title] "The Lifetime Kid" [pers.] I feel good knowing that what I did will be read by some people at least. Maybe I wrote about youth, maybe about a different view of life, but I know that I wrote what I felt was good, even if it's my first and only. Nonetheless, I feel good to be part of something I didn't know I had, and that it will live till the end of my days.

BARTLEY-WARNKE, JULIETTE
[a.] St. Petersburg, FL [title] "Somebody's Soul" [pers.] "Somebody's Soul" was written as a reflection of my own past pain and deliverance. I'm a Born Again Christian, delivered at the altar in 1987 from a $300-a-day crack cocaine addiction, while I was nine weeks pregnant. The spirit of the Lord, through Pastor Linda Sesler's preaching, stirred the writing gifts in me. I have written a book entitled, *Catch On Fire*, about urban evangelism. This book contains this poem and my other evangelical poetry, as well as a mini autobiography, which recounts my path of destruction and God's path of Deliverance and Restoration!

BARTOLIK, MAGDALENA
[a.] Waukegan, IL [title] "My Treasure" [pers.] "My Treasure" is a very special poem. It is about a person who is very important in my life—my mother. Two years ago, my family and I moved from Poland to the United States. It was really hard at the beginning, but my mom was very supportive. Now I am a top honor student at Lake Shore Catholic Academy. I have two sisters, Justine and Aleksandra, and great parents. Poetry is very important in my life, because through my poems I can share my feelings with others.

BARTSCHER, TARYN
[a.] Daytona Beach, FL [title] "Be Together Live Forever" [pers.] I am 12 years old. I have always enjoyed writing little poems, songs, and stories. Every time it's a holiday or birthday I always make a poem or card that rhymes. I enjoy reading poems. I am so into poetry.

BARUSCH, ARIANA
[title] "Milk" [pers.] To me, writing is like another life. I can be anything I want to be. I can be funny or serious, sad or happy, poor or rich. I write about things that make me laugh. I try to make other people laugh when they read my stories and poems. When other people are laughing I am inspired and I take it out in my writing. I am not gifted. I only reached down into myself and grabbed that extra little bit of creativity that everyone has in them and used it in my own way to create my own art.

BATES, KATHLEEN
[title] "Real Love" [pers.] My wonderful husband, Don, inspired these feelings. As a lung transplant recipient, he has shown me love is life. Without him I would never have known real love.

BATTIN, REBECCA
[a.] Taylor, MI [title] "In the Darkness" [pers.] Poetry has always been my emotional outlet. My poems have been inspired by many things: love, heartbreaks, and many also inspired by the light of my life, my three-year-old son, Paul. This poem is inspiredby both love and heartbreak, and I hold this poem very dear to me.

BAYER, EDWARD
[title] "You Are Very Special and I Love You" [pers.] Poetry is a God-given-gift. My advice to anyone is that when you have any gift or any tool, use it. If you do not use it, you'll lose it. That is plain and simple. I would like to thank everyone who has associated with me in the past and present for being an influence in my life and in my lifetime. Many of you may or may not know that I am in the International Poetry Hall of Fame (elected December 22, 1997). When you are in any hall of fame, whether it be music, sports, etc., you are one of the very, very best.

BEACH, STEPHANIE
[a.] Kennesaw, GA [title] "My Family Is a Roller Coaster" [pers.] To me, this poem is one of those that only I would understand. My parents got divorced when I was very young and it tore me up completely. This poem was one of those that came naturally to me. It gave me the opportunity to express my true feelings in a couple sentences. Although I'm not much of a writer, I think poetry is a great motivator for a person like me to express myself.

BEALL, CHAD
[title] "Love by: Crazy" [pers.] My name is Chad Beall and I'm 19 years old. I've had a passion for poetry since I was 13. I love to write and read poetry, and I hope you enjoy my work. The poem is from a pact of my feelings and heart. "All Well."

BEARDSLEY, KIMBERLY
[title] "Through the Eyes of Love" [pers.] Being able to express myself through words is gratifying and rewarding and is a major part of who I am. I find myself creating a poem, rather than writing in a journal, at times when I'm feeling happy, sad, funny, or emotional—whenever I need to let go of feelings. Two very important women in my life, my grandmother, Grace Marshall Smith (1903-1993), and my mother, Audrey Del Tour, passed along to me their spirit of independence, creativity, and compassion, and, therefore, to them I will be forever proud and grateful to have inherited even a small portion of their qualities.

BEATY, GUY
[title] "On Wives" [pers.] I lost a wife, Mary Grady, on May 20, 1997, who I am proud to say was a great woman. As honestly as I can confess, God has given me another great wife, Carol Shaw. Carol's inspiration is responsible for "On Wives." The strength of any endeavor is its inspiration; without it, the endeavor is harder. Lines 9, 10, 11, and 12 from no obstacle will be about, just because he knows she's there with her loving, caring support.

BEBAR, JANE
[title] "Love Well Read" [pers.] For me, poetry has been a way to express what is virtually indescribable. My poem, "Love Well Read," summarizes the impression characters in literature have had on me and, I believe, on others. Although it's simple to become truly mesmerized by one of these personalities, the sincere emotion stirred up can be quite unbelievable. Poetry has been a cherished way for me to communicate my hidden thoughts and I'm ever so grateful for such a beautiful way to do so.

BECKLEY, SUZANNE K.
[a.] St. Francisville, LA [title] "The Mist Ball" [pers.] I live in south central Louisiana, and there are not many cold mornings. When I saw the mist dancing, it was a real treat. I was on my way to work in Baton Rouge, and as I approached the mist, it turned to gold. By the time I should

have been even with it, it was gone. Why do I write poetry? I write because I have to. It is like breathing, and it comes as naturally.

BEDDOES, MISTY
[title] "Down Deep" [pers.] When my grandfather was diagnosed with stage Four-B Hodgkin's I was devastated. When I started my Junior year at Lyman High, a friend of mine told me her dad was diagnosed with the same disease, only in stage A-1. This poem was written during that time. Poetry has had a great impact on my life. It has allowed me to express my thoughts, feelings, and emotions throughout my life. I use my family as inspiration and have received hope and encouragement from them so that I will continue writing. I discovered I could write when I was about 12, and have continued to develop my own views and techniques. I would like to say thanks to my mother, father, cousin, brother, and sister—they have all given me encouragement and inspiration.

BEHRENDT, VAN
[title] "Rose" [pers.] On different occasions I come across something extraordinarily beautiful, or feel an emotion that gets my heart racing feverishly. I try to take its often short lived existence and extend it within the mind to defy time. I hope that by meditating on this short poem, the reader's mind will be stimulated enough to the point where they are able to see and feel without having the actual occurrence before them. Thank you to the great artist who is beyond infinity!

BEISLER, ALEX
[a.] Sarasota, FL [title] "You May" [pers.] In this poem I am expressing how I feel about each one of us being responsible for our actions. There are consequences to everything we do as individuals and a society. All should be held accountable so that our world will be a safer and happier place, not only for our generation, but also for our future generations. This responsibility is not only toward our fellow man, but to all creatures, great and small.

BEITZEL, MARA
[a.] Hilliard, OH [title] "My Poem" [pers.] Regretfully, I am unable to share loving sentimental poetry, for I have lived most of my life without such luxuries. However, I am proud to say that I am the first lady in my family to have graduated successfully from college and to acquire a happy, loving family of my own. So perhaps, after I express my pain through this dynamic genre, I can share with those of you my rebirth and new life!

BELCHER, DUANE
[title] "Love at Second Sight" [pers.] I wrote this poem about my first true love. Poetry is my life; it is my every thought expressed in writing. "Poetry depicts your heart, mind, soul, and intellect."

BENFIELD, CINDY
[title] "Today I Pray . . ."[pers.] I don't sit around trying to write poems, they just come to me. This one came to me one day when I was trying to sleep. "Today I Pray . . . " is talking about the past, the present, and the future. I'm reminding God that I don't ask for much, just to feel His touch. I also thank Him for showing me the way in life. Also, the person inside is who you are; we only live in these bodies. I want to thank my mother for the encouragement she gave me all my life to do something with my poems.

BENNETT, DONNA
[title] "Making a Wish Upon a Star" [pers.] This poem represents, to me, finding an everlasting love, my soul mate. Through a lot of trials, tribulations, tears, and heartache I have yet to find him. Thus, my search continues. I do believe with all of my heart, body, and soul he is out there!

BENNETT, DOUGLAS
[a.] Sunrise, FL [title] "Change of Season" [pers.] This poem is very special to me because it expresses my fondness for the change of the New England seasons. I feel that nature and all its beauty is a reflection of our Creator's handiwork. As the cycle of seasons bring forth new life, it shows me the magical and endless creativity of our renewing Lord. After all, it is His canvas. I thank you all for the opportunity to share this poem with you. God bless all!

BENNETT, LAFRANZA
[a.] Brooklyn, NY [title] "I Am Your Child" [pers.] This poem is very special to me because it expresses an unconditional love for someone in one's life. It doesn't matter if you are a parent, grandparent, a guardian, or care giver of children, no matter what age you are, or the color of your skin, even between friends, unconditional love will always be the same. I love writing poetry and hope to someday write my own book. I am grateful for my writing talent and writing abilities. I dedicate this poem to my daughter, Briana Michele, with all my love. "You Are My Child."

BENNETT, MARK
[title] "My Partner in Life" [pers.] Poetry has a special eloquence not found in any other form. It touches you in a very appealing way. It is forceful in that it makes you think and grasp reality. It searches for your fantasies. Poetry seeks your inner being and outward emotion. Poetry is an advanced form of creative writing, and takes its place like no other form of thought. Poetry is special in a way that touches your inner most feelings. I hope it does the same for you! Search your soul—do it through poetry!

BENOIT, MARGIE
[title] "My Sister's Face" [pers.] My sister was my very best friend. We shared all our thoughts on life, family, and her deadly monster, cancer. I sat with her all those scary days of chemo and radiation. When we knew the end was near, we were together, as always, sharing our time and thoughts. She used to say, "Sit where I can see you, or move your chair where I can see hers." I miss her more than anyone can ever think possible. I miss seeing "Her Face."

BENSON, MATT
[title] "Roiling and Boiling" [pers.] I am a young artist living in Western Australia, about a ten minute drive from everywhere. Poetry is a way for me to release everything that builds up inside me. I'm a pacifist, an animal lover, and a pagan. I operate mostly under the pseudongm Draegath.

BENSON, RHONDA
[title] "Church Women after the Funeral" [pers.] Because I consider myself a religious person, this poem was not one that I particularly wanted to write. Nevertheless, I wrote it as a gift to truth. It reflects on the way in which people who are supposed to be sincere, may not have sincere intentions. It also reflects on the hurt the woman feels, not only because of the funeral, but by the turning of suffering and grief into a source of entertainment. Hopefully, the reader will feel he or she is right there in the poem when reading it.

BENUSIC, VERA
[title] "Children's Lessons" [pers.] I was born 12/02/43, one of the Dalley's ten children. I have two sons, Peter and Michael, and one lovely daughter, Christine Reir. I am a happy grandma of little girls, Brittany, eleven, Nicole, nine, Avalon, eight, Xanth, six, Alora, eight, and Kira, six—each one individual and pretty as a picture. Poetry was my individuality. I wrote in secret for 20 years to have my say about life. I felt entitled to my own opinions and ideas, but then, and now, I still often don't believe others wish to hear the same. I am learning to open up more and share my poetry. I

submitted my first contest entry on December 16, 1995. Since then I have thirteen poems published in eight books. I feel I am doing well. I received word that I was nominated for Poet of the Year again—wow, twice in a row! I feel much happier about being me.

BERDEN, KATHY
[title] "Moving On" [pers.] It's amazing how deeply people can touch our hearts . . . This particular poem is filled with the wounds and scars etched into my heart by a past relationship. Now that my heart has the strength to move on, I am looking forward to my future endeavors. I have a dream of publishing a book about my life and I hope one day it will come true. I hope I have touched the hearts and lives of others with my poem. I hope it gives them the strength to move on, as I do.

BERENTZ, JOYCE
[title] "Freedom" [pers.] I feel poetry is a way to share thoughts that are inspiring, giving meaning to many lessons in life, or to show your love for others. I've written poems to family and friends, trying to convey how special they are to me, as gifts on special occasions. I find it uplifting to me, as much as I'd hoped it did for them. I find, when I am writing, it takes me to a higher level of consciousness, one of greater wisdom and love for our fellowman. Thank you!

BERG, PHYLLIS
[a.] Bismark, ND [title] "As One in the Skies" [pers.] This poem is in memory of my late husband, who believed in the freedom of the eagle. He felt that all life should be as free, graceful, and strong as that eagle. So I tried to put his feelings into words so that others are able to see that beauty he saw in that bird at the sky.

BERG, ROSALYN
[title] "Let Me Drink From Thine Eyes" [pers.] I have taken a section from a much longer poem that I have written to create this one. I feel that it captures the essence of what one feels when in love. Love is such a special treasure that I wish everyone on Earth could experience. I hope that it happens to you, even if it is fleeting. You should keep the memories alive forever.

BERNAL, KATHERINE
[a.] Brooklyn, NY [title] "Betrayer" [pers.] This poem has a meaning in my life. It reminds me of the time my best friend betrayed me. She tripped me and made fun of me. I cried so much that our parents and teacher got involved. This girl tried to turn everyone against her. She made it seem as if I were the bad person. I did nothing to her. I treated her well, but I guess it was only a one-sided thing. I guess she was jealous. That was a while ago. We haven't spoken since. Let this remind people to be careful when choosing friends.

BERNSTEIN, SALLY
[title] "The Broken Pieces of My Heart" [pers.] I would like to send a loving tribute to my husband, Joe, from his family: son Marvin, daughter Sherri, son-in-law Morris, and grandchildren, Ashley, Crystal, and Marc. We'll love you always.

BESERK, JUSTIN
[title] "Street Walker" [pers.] My pen name is Justin McCauley. I believe in the power of a poem. Its tantalizing couplets, the way it draws people in—the way a person can identify with it. The written word is the legacy of man. When sculpted and transformed, words provide a footprint to our time, an indelible mark which says, "I am human, I feel, I am here."

BHANUCHANDRAN, REKHA
[title] "Reflections" [pers.] My poem, "Reflections," has always been very special to me. I guess it has been so because it reflects my past, from my

elementary education in London to my high school and graduation in India. I wrote this poem remembering my past experiences with people in different places and friends who shared special moments in my life. Capturing all these moments in a poem so close to my heart has been a wonderful experience. Personally, I feel poetry can change a person's life entirely and bring a new meaning to it. Poetry is something that is very dear to me and has brought out my deepest feelings.

BHATIA, SUSHIL
[title] "Crazy Mind! (A Haiku)" [pers.] This haiku represents my struggle in moving from being a head-oriented type of person to a heart-oriented type of person. It playfully shows us the soft, female side of the heart and the hard, male side of the head. It symbolizes the conflict created by the usual machinations of the mind, which pull us away from our meditative glimpses of the divine.

BIALER, EREZ
[title] "streets" [pers.] This song was written as a sort of release to questions that were bothering me at the time that I wrote it. I think these questions bother us all in one phase of our lives or another. I wrote a lot of poems during the last year. I write as a way to release my emotions. For example, if I'm sad or angry with a subject, I would write about it. It is a way of therapy for me. I write not only poems, but short stories too. Most of my material is in Hebrew because it is my birth language, but this time it was an exception. I would like to thank and dedicate this poem to my family for helping me and encouraging me to develop this talent.

BIDDLE, ANGELA
[title] "God's Child" [pers.] I wrote this poem for my brother-in-law. He is very special and has touched many people. His name is Rocky and he has struggled through many hardships in the last few years, but has overcome them with his strength and faith. He is an inspiration to all that know him.

BILGER, JEANINE
[title] "The Night Magic" [pers.] I love music and play some instruments. I like all the colors of the rainbow and artwork by children. I like rhyming poems that are funny too. My goal is to write music for a recording company someday. I am inspired by 60's music.

BILLINGS, MELISA
[a.] Lewiston, ME [title] "Never Again" [pers.] Usually my thoughts and happenings go into my paintings, but I found myself writing more often than ever. I hope everyone can enjoy and even learn from my poetry. I feel my poetry is a gift given to me in order to educate and entertain, so I hope you enjoy them.

BIRCHMIRE, LOUISE
[title] "The Wind Surfer" [pers.] I was born in Key West, Florida and am a descendant of a pioneer Florida family. I am married to a career navy man, and we had two sons, both avid wind surfers. The day I saw a beautiful snapshot of my son wind surfing I was inspired to write my poem, "The Wind Surfer." I have been writing since I was a child, but until I attended the University of Miami's senior citizen creative writing class, I did not do serious writing. After five semesters, I had some success in seeing some of my children's stories published.

BIRNEY, JAN
[title] "Bittersweet" [pers.] The gift of poetry is not only a blessing bestowed upon the poet, but upon the reader as well. Each unites as one, as words created from the heart reach out and touch the heart of another and the beauty is shared by both.

BISH, RACHEL
[a.] Wall, SD [title] "Daddy" [pers.] I am the daughter of two loving parents, Shirley and Ed

Bish. I have two brothers, Jamie, and Micheal Hensley, and one sister, April Hensley, and all three of them are older than me. I was born in Olympia Fields, Illinois. I moved to MS, when I was a baby, I lived there for 14 years and then we moved up here to South Dakota. The poem "Daddy" means a lot to me because all through my life he has taught me right from wrong. I decided to write something special about my father because I know he must go sometime, but not soon.

BISHOP, RYAN
[title] "Amaze (The Addict's Lie)" [pers.] I collaborate that which I see and that which I hear into a small, digestible medium. I try to convey life with my poetry. As a 17 years old, I see the intertwining of peace in this sometimes vile, yet sometimes calm, world of the present. I propose only that the misjudgments of man will bring to light the true nature of man, which is that of a Singular Mindspan, the chemical span of peace of love towards one another.

BISKEBORN, EVELYN
[title] "I Cannot Let You Go" [pers.] This poem represents the loss of fulfilling, wondrous love. Poetry is a way of expressing our life's experiences, our gains and losses. "I Cannot Let You Go" takes a slice of mankind's most sensitive, private emotions and presents it is a scene most of society can relate to. It is also a poem about the beauty of eternal love.

BLAN, HENRY
[title] "With Only You" [pers.] This poem is about a man who is trying to save a relationship that has not fallen apart. When I wrote this poem my wife, Heather, was in mind; she is a gift from God and the reason I go on.

BLANCETT, JEFFREY
[a.] Tampa, FL [title] "Bah Hum Bug" [pers.] It is both an honor and a blessing to be published in this poetry book. All of my writing inspirations come from life itself, my family, my friends, and my wonderful daughter, Trisha Shea Blancett, who is also a good poet in her own right. I am French, Indian, and Irish and was born in Sikeston, Missouri on Valentines Day 1956. I have also written several poems, songs, and a children's book, all, as of yet, unpublished. I have always written as a fun hobby and hope that everyone enjoys my poem in the humorist context that it was written in. Thank you and God bless one and all.

BLAND, JASON
[title] "Sonnet No. 5" [pers.] "Sonnet No. 5" is a poem that I wrote for a girl that I met my ninth grade year. It is about the pain I felt to know she despised me. It is included in my unpublished book of sonnets. I am currently writing a book called *Gothic Poetry*. I invented "gothic poetry" a year ago. Gothic poetry is a type of poetry about the dark side of life, such as death, revenge, the living dead, and ghost encounters. Poets that I am inspired by are: Jim Morrison, Bruce Wayne Sullivan, Edgar Allan Poe, and William Shakespeare. My personal philosophical point of view is: "And it harm none, do as ye may." I am strictly against all forms of racism, hate groups, and the death penalty, because taking another person's life is still murder.

BLASUCCI, DAVID
[title] "the godless god" [pers.] When I wrote this poem, I was struggling mentally with many things in my life. As a result, I questioned the existence of my Christian God. However, I have recently rediscovered Him in all His glory. And though my attitude has greatly changed for the better, this poem is still a part of me and warrants due attention.

BOKHARI, SYEDA
[a.] Rawalpindi, Pakistan [title] "Broken Wings"

[pers.] I am a 15-year-old student of senior Cambridge. I am very sensitive and only write when I am filled with emotions. Poetry for me is such an expression of feelings that it is a source of catharsis. This poem is dedicated to my best friend, whose companionship taught me how to tackle hardships in life. She is young and energetic and has faced many troubles at such a tender age and is still determined to face everything courageously.

BOLWELL, SALLY
[title] "Oh, How I Wish" [pers.] Poetry is something that I have always loved and it is something that I have always been able to write. Such a gift should be shared with others, and I hope that you enjoyed "Oh, How I Wish." Thank you to those around me who inspired me to write, especially to my darling Brett, who has brightened my inner world.

BOND, JESSICA
[a.] Stettler, AB [title] "What Does Love Mean to You?" [pers.] My name is Jessica Bond. I'm 15 years of age, going into the tenth grade. I am from Stettler, Alberta. I love all sports, but enjoy figure skating the best. I also love to read and write poetry, and hanging out with my friends.

BONDESEN, CHRISTINA
[title] "Our Wedding Day" [pers.] I wrote, framed, and presented this poem to my husband on our wedding day in 1997. Never in my wildest dreams did I think it would be published in a national book of poetry. Although I have always liked writing, I am not a writer and have never before submitted anything in competition. It is an honor to be recognized in this way, and knowing how much love was put into this work makes the honor even greater. I hope this poem brings joy to others and becomes a marriage statement for all new couples.

BOOTY, ANNE
[title] "Split Pink Blusher" [pers.] In 1977, I came into being, an Aries child, and in 1997, twenty years on, I graduated with an arts degree from the university of Queensland, with majors in Literature and Philosophy. For the past two years I have been living in London, and now, recently married, am returning to England with my husband to make it our home.

BOTT, ART
[a.] San Antonio, TX [title] "Fate" [pers.] The first poem I wrote was on board ship in Okinawa at the end of World War II. It would be fifty years before I tried again. I wrote the words and music to a Christmas cantata for our church choir in 1996. Since then, I have written 172 poems and, God willing, may write a few more in this, my 80th year. I am married with three children and live in San Antonio, Texas.

BOUCHARD, JESSICA
[title] "Some Stairs" [pers.] Some years ago I desired a transformation in my life, so I spun a cocoon. As I began to emerge from this holding place, I wrote "Some Stairs" with the inspiration of my father and my friend, Darlene. I feel that this poem is a treasure, and I am truly pleased to share its contents with the world, with those who appreciate and admire the writing and the reading of the romance life has to offer us. Without the encouragement of my mother and my family, I fear that my imagination would have been contained in a wooden box forever. Thank you.

BOUCHARD, JIMMY
[a.] Enfield, CT [title] "The Wrath of the Owls" [pers.] I think poetry is a great artistic hobby to have. I always write poems around holidays. In Enfield, Connecticut there is not much inspiration. When I saw I could enter this I jumped on the chance to enter. I knew I wanted to write a poem on animals; owls came to mind. So, I described

artistically what I thought of owls. Poetry is a good way to learn from yourself.

BOURNE, MYRA
[title] "Four Letter Words" [pers.] Myra Bourne will celebrate her thirty-fifth wedding anniversary this year of 2000. She is the mother of three grown children and grandmother to fourteen grandchildren and counting. She was born and raised in Montana, but moved to Las Vegas ten years ago to expand her career in real estate. In addition to a life filled with family and activity, she has had to contend with a head filled with words, words that insist on being written no matter how painful or inconvenient the process.

BOWENS, MARILYN
[title] "Once is Enough" [pers.] I have written poetry since I was a child. For me, it has always been a natural way of clarifying, processing, and expressing my feelings. I am a law professor in North Carolina, where I live with my two sons, J.T. and Trey, and my life partner. The three of them, and writing, are God's great gifts to me.

BOXLEY, TONYA
[a.] Galveston, TX [title] "You" [pers.] Tonya Boxley is a native of Galveston Island, Galveston, Texas. Tonya attended Galveston Ball High School where she graduated in 1985. She attended Lamar University in Beaumont, Texas where she received her B.S. in social work. Tonya currently works as a parole officer in Galveston. She has three beautiful daughters, Endia, Armani, and Zoe. Tonya is very active in church activities, especially with the youth at the First Union Baptist Church in Galveston. Tonya has been writing poetry since she was ten years old. Her poems are usually based on life situations, mostly about herself or friends. Tonya believes that a poem should come from the soul. All readers should be able to relate some life experience on poetry. Poetry should inspire the reader to reflect on pleasant memories, or move forward towards a goal.

BOYDEN, DOROTHY
[title] "I Hope" [pers.] I wrote this poem for one of my best friends who was struggling with a great deal of personal change and stress. He is a wonderful man of great depth and compassion, but like many of us, seldom takes enough time to allow himself to just be. Our long distance, e-mail relationship has grown since we've met face to face. He is a forever friend. This is for Bill.

BOZEMAN, STACEY
[a.] Charlotte, NC [title] "I Am" [pers.] This poem depicts the rhythm of my life at this day and time, right down to the wires of every hour. Every thought I've ever thought, every dream I've ever dreamed, and every person I've ever befriended or distanced myself from is represented in these lines. Possessing the gift of touching someone's heart or bringing a tear to someone eye is rewarding enough in itself. I hope that everyone can relate. I also hope that all that they have left unspoken I am saying for them.

BRABAZON, SUNSHINE
[title] "How Do I Forget?" [pers.] Having one of my poems published at nineteen is a dream come true. For as long as I can remember, I've enjoyed writing. It started with short stories, then even a novel. All I've ever wanted was to become a published author. My first poem was a homework assignment and I soon found poetry came naturally to me. Thanks to all who helped make this possible. Now I turn to my poetry for all events in my life, from my first love to breakups with boyfriends.

BRADY, KATHLEEN
[title] "On Hearing Beautiful Music" [pers.] I am very pleased that you have included my poem about music for publication in *Rainstorms and Rainbows*. As a violinist, I love music, art, and poetry. I have had a very busy career as an art teacher, an occupation therapist, a high school counselor, a school psychologist, and a special education administrator with the Bureau of Indian Affairs. I continued writing poetry, and only recently have I been able to get my poems together to be published this year. I am now busy volunteering at the James A. Haley Veterans Hospital in Tampa, Florida. I have a doctorate degree from the University of Florida and have been included in Who's Who of American Women. I have three grown-up children and am a widow—my husband died last year. All I can say now is that I have had a very happy and challenging career and a wonderful husband that I now miss very much.

BRAGEWITZ, KAY
[title] "Thoughts of Youth" [pers.] "Hindsight," as we know, can be a great teacher. Most of us, at one time or another in our lives, have regretted something we have done. We would like to turn back the clock and retrieve the action we regret. Poetry is a vehicle through which a person can express themselves in a beautiful manner. It can elicit a full range of emotions from each of us: tears of joy and sorrow, excitement, fear, disdain, and anger; all can be a kaleidoscope in a poem.

BRANSON, ALANA
[title] "Abrasion of the Heart" [pers.] I state from my adolescence: Take a stand for your beliefs and let not bigotry taint your compassion. Only through your own individuality can you derive the strength to free your mind, and in doing so, yourself in its entirety. To my loved ones: in your absence I'd find myself lost within my own emptiness. Je vous aime profondement. As for the subject matter of this poem, all I can say is: How narrowing it is when one loses herself in the wake of the not-so-hetero.

BRANSON, BRENDA
[a.] Jackson, MS [title] "Why Sister" [pers.] Poetry is a pastime hobby for me. I love writing and expressing myself in so many ways, and I can do it through poetry. I am from a family of 13. Annie Mae Branson, a wonderful mother of seven girls and six boys, has always inspired me to be a strong person. I live in Jackson, Mississippi, went to Jackson State University, and am working at Delphi Packard Electric System's in Clinton. My poem, "Why, Sister," sends a special message to loved ones, and that was my intent. My sisters are: Angie, Margaret, Othella, Linda, Shirley, and Barbara.

BRANTLEY, CONNIE
[title] "The Blessing of a Child" [pers.] Children are very precious to me, as I have two daughters, Amber, eleven, and Ansley, seven. As well as my own, I work with other children every day. I am the media specialist at Johnson Co. Elementary. I enjoy writing poetry and the rewards that the finished product offers. I have written several poems, but it seems that the ones about children are the best.

BRANTLEY, KATHERINE
[a.] Grand Coulee, WA [title] "Take My Hand" [pers.] "Take My Hand," from the collection, *Hidden Heart*, is poetry from my heart. It is inspired by family and friends. I am the mother of seven and grandmother of 18. I started writing as a way to express years of hidden feelings. I owe a big Thank You to my dear friend, Tiziano, who encouraged me and who has always been here for me.

BRENNER, AARON
[a.] San Diego, CA [title] "Casino" [pers.] Like much of my poetry, "Casino" is an introspection of my own experiences, and observations of life in general. I've never been formally trained in writing poetry, so there's probably room for improvement in my work. I feel proud when my poetry conveys my thoughts fluently. "Casino" will be my first published work, but I think it's not my best work. I'm looking forward to it's inclusion into *Rainstorms and Rainbows*. Thanks to my sister, Renee, for always providing me with encouragement.

BRENNER, AARON
[a.] Spring Valley, CA [title] "Casino" [pers.] Like much of my poetry, "Casino" is an introspection of my own experiences, and observations of life in general. I have been writing poetry for over 25 years. I've never been formally trained in writing poetry, so there's probably room for improvement in my work. I feel proud when my poetry conveys my thoughts fluently. "Casino" will be my first published work, but I think it's not my best work. I'm looking forward to its inclusion into The Falling Rain. Thanks to my sister Renee for always providing me with encouragement

BREWER, ROBBIN
[title] "My Child" [pers.] I dedicate my work in this book to my son, Steven. May he live long and healthy. May the Lord be with us. With much love—Mom.

BRIDGES, LINDA
[title] "Night Waves" [pers.] My inspiration to write poetry comes when I am at peace with myself or in nature's wonderful surroundings. I have always felt that God is the greatest artist ever, and that we only re-create what He has already done.

BRIDGET, KARINA
[title] "Melt the Walls" [pers.] Originally written as an exercise in clustering, "Melt the Walls" was much more lyrical than poetic. I read it to five of my friends, all of whom were moved greatly by it. However, my creative writing teacher felt it wasn't poetry, but he did agree with my musician friends, that, as lyrics, it was very good. The poem published here is a modification from lyrics to poetry. Enjoy.

BRIGGS, SARAH
[title] "Free" [pers.] Even when I was a little girl, I loved poetry with all my heart. Each day, as the sun greeted my bedroom window, I would write a new poem. Changing it a million times, I would run downstairs to show it to my man and pray it was good enough. Poetry has made my dreams come true. All my poetry comes from my deepest thoughts my heart can give me. I hope it can touch your life as it did mine. Always remember, never give up on your dreams.

BRITTON, ELIZABETH
[title] "From the Angels" [pers.] I lost a very close friend after a long illness. On the night she died, but before she died, I cried myself to sleep. I awoke suddenly from a dream about angels gathered in a room and felt peaceful. I noted the time and went back to sleep. A half hour later her family phoned to let me know she had passed on. I asked about the time; it was the same time I woke up from the dream. Her family had been trying to decide whether they should call. A week later I woke up with this poem in my head.

BRITTON, MARY
[title] "Name Your Poison" [pers.] I have a daughter, Tammi Britton, and two grandsons, Drake Abraham Britton and William Nicholas Ingram. I have a Bachelor of Science degree in business management. My occupation is travel assistant at Naval Hospital, in Charleston, South Carolina. I am also a member of the All Aboard Toast Master's Club. I write poems for relaxation and enjoyment. My goal is to publish a book of poetry in the near future.

BROBST, SHELLY
[a.] Delmar, DE [title] "Lost in My Thoughts" [pers.] I was inspired to write this poem after my father-in-law, Ronald David Brobst, passed away

on March second. I had hoped that it would give comfort to his wife and children. This poem has given me strength and it has enriched my spirit. This poem was written for my husband, David, my children, Bryan and Ashley, Ronald's wife, Patricia, and his children, Kathy, Ronald, Tammy, Donna, Ernie, Robert, and the rest of the family. This poem is also for his granddaughter, Faye, whom he raised.

BROCK-HINES, JOHN-ISAAC
[title] "Reality" [pers.] At the time of this poem I was faced with a lot of different problems, but no desire to find the solutions. At times like that I just stop everything and sit, wait, and listen. You see, my life is a gift from above. When I think I'm in the driver's seat, God slows me down. He's always calling, but I'm not always listening. This poem, "Reality," is the outcome of me allowing God to move through me. It is also an example of what good comes of listening . . . even when you don't want to.

BROOKER, JUDITH
[a.] Perth, WA [title] "The Silent Witnesses of Domestic Violence" [pers.] This poem was a spontaneous response while I was in an audience listening to women express their grief for children murdered as a result of domestic violence in Western Australia during 1999/2000. One mother, in particular, touched me deeply as she had had her two children shot in front of her.

BROWER, AMANDA
[title] "That Is the God I Have" [pers.] My life is kind a weird because I'm in C.P.S. care (Child Protected Services). I live in a foster home with loving parents. To get my work published is extremely excellent. I hope people will read and understand what God is doing for them. My poetry is about my childhood life. It's scary, but thank God I lived through it.

BROWN, FRANCES
[a.] Sandston, VA [title] "Clouds" [pers.] Poetry to me is fun and exciting. I must write a poem immediately when the thought and feeling overwhelms me. The words have to escape right away on paper, backs of receipts, or whatever is available wherever I am. The poem "Clouds" was inspired by the feelings I get when looking at a beautiful sky of blue and the clouds. I enjoy writing poems and have written for family members for birthdays, Halloween, births, and teachers farewells from their students. Expressing myself in a poem is very satisfying.

BROWN, HEATHER
[a.] Plainwell, MI [title] "Words of Wisdom" [pers.] This poem is for teens and also parents to read. Even though parents have experienced the same situation when they were younger, we teens still want to experienced life for ourselves. So don't yell and be mad. Sit down and talk with us and let us know you still care. I talk of the man I love, Bryan Wall.

BROWN, JACK
[title] "Serenity" [pers.] Although I have written many poems, this one, "Serenity," has a special place in my heart. It was written about six months after the death of my beloved of 45 years.

BROWN, MICHELLE
[a.] Dearborn, MI [title] "Mr. Moon" [pers.] As a poet and songwriter, the legend of the man on the moon is one of great mystery to me. When I was a child I sat for many hours wishing and singing to the moon, and dreaming he would grant my every wish. My father, a stargazer himself, encouraged my nightly voyages to far off galaxies, always describing in detail where we had been, where we were, and where we were going. As I enter a new creative stage in my life,

I thank all my inspirations from the past and anticipate embracing those of the future.

BROZOVICH, ALICIA
[title] "Abortion Kills Children!" [pers.] This poem is dedicated to one of my best friends, Jackie Carl. She inspired me to write it. "Abortion Kills Children" is written in memory of Sarah Brown, a child who lived five years without half of a brain, due to attempted abortion. My wishes are for pregnant women to read this poem and to think twice before attempting the wrongful act of abortion. A special thanks to my parents for letting me live. I have learned to never take life for granted again.

BRUNICK, CAROL
[title] "Evaluation Time" [pers.] This poem, as well as others, is based on life's occurences. I take ordinary words, mix them with ordinary circumstances, add a little philosophy, a touch of experience, and blend with humor. I attempt to touch on everyday life without judgement or contradiction in a playful manner that readers can relate. I find pleasure in writing my "Little Quips." I hope you enjoy the reading.

BRYMER, DAN
[a.] Levittown, NY [title] "Never Let a Good Thing Pass You By" [pers.] The reason I wrote the poem is simple—a girl. I was in love with her or, at the time, I thought I did, but at my age I don't know what love is. Also, never keep feelings inside because it comes back to hurt you. Always be open with those you like because keeping feelings inside doesn't help. At 16 I don't know what love is, but this girl sure gave me a clue of how great love is. It turns out that a few months after I wrote the poem she began to like me again and we went out. Sadly, we broke up, but now we are best friends.

BUECHNER, GEORGE
[a.] Harrisburg, AL [title] "Another Day at the Beach" [pers.] Preoccupation with our own burdens tempts us to label another's problem "just a day at the beach." My poem uses wave and tide images for symbols of both relentless onslaught and for healing. "Another Day at the Beach" is a hope-filled poem. I am a 59-year-old disability-retired clergyman with MS.

BULLCOMING, JOHNATHAN
[title] "Faded Glory" [pers.] Poetry is a form of expressing one's self and I have taken advantage of it, as my mother has. She has given this gift to me. My poem is about a never ending struggle with time; it has no mercy and you have to make the best of it by doing what is in your powers. It also teaches that time should not be taken for granted.

BURAZIN, ANASTAZIA
[title] "She Wants You to Know" [pers.] This poem is something that come from my heart. It is about things that have happened to me and that I felt needed to come out. When I read this poem it helped me through my problems and I actually say it every night to myself and it makes me feel better. I just hope that other people can read this poem and that it helps them through problems, like it did for me.

BURCH, MARY
[title] "Precious Life" [pers.] This poem is very special to me, as it expresses my appreciation of life and all its gifts. I am a care giver and have spent a total of 20 years caring for my mother and mother in-law. After they had a stroke, I was truly given the gift of empathy and love. Watching them struggle with all the everyday things we take for granted has influenced many poems that I've written; this one is my favorite. It came to me in the early morn when I was half asleep. I wrote the words as they came and didn't need to change a thing.

BURLEY, PATRICIA
[a.] Belleville, ON [title] "Remembrance Day Prayer"

BURNS, KELSIE
[title] "A Heart in the Right Mind" [pers.] Poetry is held in a very special place in my heart. It provides me with the opportunity to express so many things in the way I want to express them. In my wildest dreams I never thought I would be sharing something I put my heart and soul into with so many people. I am grateful, as well as overwhelmedm that my poem has been chosen, and that maybe someone else will feel and understand "A Heart in the Right Mind." Mom, Dad, family, close friends, and a special other—this one's for you!

BURROW, JASON
[a.] Spokane, WA [title] "Love You Blues" [pers.] If you have ever made the mistake of a lifetime, didn't know what you had when you had it, and are now suffering the consequences, then you can relate to my poem. I love you Shawna. I'd also like to put a word out to my family: my mom, my dad, my brothers, Josh, Evan, Ethan, and Dakota, and especially to my daughter, Allie—I love you all!

BURTON, BRENDA
[title] "Shadows Dusk" [pers.] Poetry and writing play a great role in my life. For me, poetry is a way of self expression. I've been writing since I was very young. Sometimes after reading what I've written today, I often laugh while reading some of my teenage writings. Through poetry and writing I've grown as an individual, as a sister, as a friend, and even as a daughter. This particular poem is for all the children in the world that suffer each day at the hands of evil. I've touched on a subject that everyone is aware of, but often chooses to overlook.

BURTON, DEBRA
[a.] Wasilla, AK [title] "You Take My Breath Away" [pers.] I live in Alaska. The person I love best lives in England. This was written to him.

BURTON, KEVIN
[a.] Magna, UT [title] "I Will You Mine" [pers.] If I were God this poem would be given to all the women that have walked the face of the Earth. It would be held in a cup of mercy and forgiveness.

BUTCH, ANGELA
[title] "Dear Lord" [pers.] "Dear Lord" was written when so much of my heart was broken with the loss of loved ones. Poetry became my escape during this confusing, sad time. Much like my passion for dancing, poetry allows me to express myself and release so many emotions that are bottled inside. It leaves me emotionally relieved and ready to face the world again. In a world that can make little sense, I believe every individual needs a healthy escape. I hope others can relate to my poem and feel comfort that they are not alone. Thanks for allowing me to share my work.

BYRD, VICTOR
[a.] Gaffney, SC [title] "Looking for a Love" [pers.] "Looking for a Love" will always be my destiny, but finding someone to share that love has always been hard for me. Maybe the problem is that I look too hard, or maybe it is because I let down my guard. I've tried plenty of times to build bricks around my heart, but to find the right brick in this world makes it hard to start. I tell them about the things we can do, the places we can go, but still it is never enough to let them know. There are one or two ways to let my feelings show. Time will tell what is up ahead— that my perfect match is married or even dead.

BYRLEY, JAMI
[pers.] I began at the age of twelve, and now, at fourteen, I am amazed to be published for the

second time this year. To me, writing has been, and always will, be an art form. You carefully paint the background, mold your characters, and find the perfect tune and flow with the words you use in your story or poem, whether it be rough, like a bull rider, or graceful, like a ballerina. This particular poem was inspired by a storm and has qualities like the storm: loud and hard, yet low and soft.

BYRNES, NANCY
[a.] Weymouth, MA [title] "Sleep My Gentle Lady" [pers.] I have always expressed my deepest most innermost thoughts in verse. "Sleep My Gentle Lady" was written to my mother after her untimely death. This poem not only commemorates the simplicity of her life, but also tries to articulate the awakening I felt after she had passed. My hope is that all that read this poem will stop and reflect upon the living. Through the unconditional love and support of the man I love, the words "I love you" will never be left unspoken again.

CABAÑES, JASON VINCENT
[title] "Little Butterfly" [pers.] For me, one of the most magical moments in poetry is when a piece begins to have a life of its own. Of course, I paint my poems with the palette of my thoughts and emotions, but after the final stroke, I no longer have control over it. I created "Little Butterfly" as an ode to my muse, my enigmatic angel. I hope the poem will take flight within you and render you a personal meaning as well. That would be sheer joy for a poet like me.

CADY, BARBARA
[a.] New Iberia, LA [title] "The River" [pers.] I would like to express my heart-felt appreciation for the encouragement and support that my family has expressed about having my poetry published. The Lord has blessed me with the ability to express my inner-most thoughts in poetry. This poem has a special place in my heart. It signifies the ever-flowing "River of Life" of the Lord. By staying in the currents flow, all things are attainable in God. This poem is dedicated to Pastor Sandra Moss, who is the personification of flowing in "The River."

CAGLE, JUDY
[title] "My Tribute to My Children and Grandchildren" [pers.] I enjoy writing poetry about my family. My first poem was for my mother, while this one is for my two children and three grandchildren. My husband, Bill, our children, Bill and Tracey, and grandchildren, Heather, Jonathan, and Anthony, have always been good subjects and good supporters for my work.

CAI, JIE
[a.] Canton, PRC [title] "Crystal Ball" [pers.] This poem is about love, about fortune, about life itself. It is not necessarily a betrayal, but about the pain of growing up. I would love to dedicated it to Jonathan Bannister, who remembers me as Gigi.

CAIL, BOB
[title] "Friends" [pers.] I am a paramedic in British Columbia and I started writing poetry in 1996. I wrote my first poem as a tribute to my father-in law after his death. At the age of 40, I became a father again to my son, Joshua. He is now 22 months old. His best friend is Winnie the Pooh. He takes his friend everywhere. They are always together, exploring. I see innocence when I watch Joshua and Pooh exploring. Through my job I am bombarded by reality. I am fortunate to be able to see life through my son's eyes.

CALDWELL, CANDICE MARIE
[a.] Long Beach, CA [title] "Jersey's Pride" [pers.] Writing poetry has always been an outlet for me for good things or bad, and when it comes to people that have made a certain impression upon me. I went from listing weekend activities in my diary to two poems in my competition

books. With encouragement from my grandmother, Mayme Bone, and family members I kept writing. I've kept a journal of poetry ever since. I never knew there were other people that would see something in my writing. Thank you, Grandma. Thank you International Library of Poetry. You have assisted my dream.

CALVO, ESTEBAN
[title] "Nebulous Perpetuity" [pers.] Why are we here, and why do we feel so compelled to ask this question? Are we alone, waiting in vain for a destined crossing with a distant neighbor? Looking out, perhaps by chance, to stumble upon long lost relatives? We long for the moment. Maybe we are accompanied by some latent being who is watching over us, holding back the answers we seek to find, and the ones we think we think we know. This poem is dedicated to anyone who has ever passed between dimensions to discover that reality and truth change when looked at from different points of view.

CAMACHO, JUSTINE
[title] "What Must Be Written" [pers.] This poem is for my future self, when I have a family of my own. My own mother couldn't say these things to me because she died when I was three. She left me, however, a legacy of books and poetry and art. I take after her. Poetry is my way of making my life a gift to others. I was born January 23, 1975 in Cebu City, AB. I studied communication arts at Ateneo de Manila University. I received the Rian's Award for the Arts for creative writing. I was anthologized in *A Habit of Shores*, a book of Filipino poetry and verse in English, from the 60's to the 90's, edited by Gemino H. Abad and published by the University of the Philippines Press. I am currently working for Globe Telecom, Inc.

CAMPBELL, AMANDA
[a.] Philadelphia, PA [title] "Heaven Has My Father" [pers.] I want to dedicate this poem to my father, who was murdered in 1996 when I was 11 years old. The significance of this poem is that since my father passed away I am living each and every day and learning to become much stronger, facing learning to live without his guidance. It also means that just because my father was killed doesn't mean that I can't continue on with my life, because I know he would want me to proceed with my dreams. The memories my father and I shared together will always remain in a special place in my heart.

CAMPBELL, DEON
[a.] Houston, TX [title] "On Losing the Love of My Life." [pers.] My poem was written at a very crucial time during my teenage years. They were my unspoken words to my boyfriend, who left me to pursue a vocation which couldn't include me, the priesthood! I would like to dedicate this poem to my present boyfriend, Ekong Uffort, who persuaded me to send this piece in. He has been such an inspiration. I am totally grateful for this opportunity to let others view my poem. I would also like to encourage others to write. Whatever your mood may be, put your thoughts to paper.

CAMPBELL, MICHELLE
[a.] Charleston, WV [title] "Perfect Love" [pers.] I am a college student at West Virginia University Institute of Technology. I will be graduating in December with a degree in Business Management. I started writing poems while I was in high school. Writing poetry made me feel better when life got hard. This poem is about my husband-to-be. It describes all the joy and love he has brought to my life. By writing poems I can express myself in a way I never could in person. As long as I can use poetry to express myself my life is complete.

CAMPBELL, SHAREKA
[title] "My Invisible Soul Mate" [pers.] When I first started writing poetry it was just a means to

letting out my emotions. I didn't feel comfortable discussing my problems or adventures with anyone, so I wrote them down in the form of poetry. Then, after a couple years, writing poems became a way of life for me, a way to let it all out without hearing opinions from others. I also truly feel that writing is a gift that God blessed me with, and now I am proud to claim it. My family members that contribute to events that inspire me to write are: my mom, Lillie Skinner, my stepfather, Paul Skinner, Keiran Larkin, and my dad's brothers, Trayon and Keiron Larkin, and my dad, Mark Campbell. I live in Missouri, in a color-filled town called Bridgeton. I am the eleventh grader at Pattonville High School, and enjoy writing every chance I get. I believe everyone that is born on this Earth is blessed with some type of talent. Mine so happens to be writing poetry, and I want to thank God for such a great talent and gift. Thanks.

CANTATORE, ANDREW
[a.] Jupiter, FL [title] "Mystery" [pers.] This poem is one of many inspired by my visions of life and love. Each of my poems has a personal inspiration and I will continue to draw from that as long as the fire burns within. It started when I was young and now I see no end in sight. Thank you, Princess.

CARLSON, BECKY
[a.] Chapel Hill, NC [title] "Did You Know?" [pers.] I feel poetry evokes emotion. Each individuals emotions may vary, but feeling the emotion is what matters. I hope my poem makes you stop and connect with some emotion in your life.

CARNEAL, ROBERT
[a.] Los Angeles, CA [title] "Till We Meet Again" [pers.] If ever in life you have loved someone whose image is all that remains, though nevertheless painful, their absence returns like an unwanted friend. The love in those memories you cherish are something like sweet revenge.

CARPENTER, MARY
[title] "Valley View" [pers.] "Valley View" was written about Freemont Peak, San Benito, California. The breathtaking view inspired this poem. I have enjoyed writing poetry for a number of years. My mother's family in Rhode Island has lots of artistic talent. My Uncle John always sent me poetry books. My father was raised in East Texas. New Boston, Texas is my hometown and is where most of my family and friends live. My daughter, Sarena, is 20, and my son, Christopher, is 13. Jean, my best friend, always believed in me. My fiancee, Danny, always gave me space to write! Thank you all!

CARROLL, SUSAN
[title] "Your Power" [pers.] I wish to again thank the International Library of Poetry for giving me a chance to share my poetry with everyone. It really means a lot. This poem has to be one of my favorites. I hope you like it.

CARTER, JACQUELINE
[a.] Nashville, TN [title] "Sisters" [pers.]The crisis intervention center introduced me to the sister program. I made a phone call to them following the death of my mother. I was overwhelmed with depression, and that one phone call changed my life. Since that time, my life has been very uplifting and God has blessed me to be clean and sober for five years. The inspiration for my poem came from the sister program. This program helps African American women who are addicted to drugs and reside in public housing. They are a supportive group which stands for Supported Intensive System or Treatment Empowerment and Recovery.

CARTER, OSCAR
[a.] Avondale, AR [pers.] I write poetry that allows me to stretch my soul and flex my spiritual muscles. Coming from the small town of Avondale, Ari-

zona, it seems I was always fighting with the evil king called poverty. Writing poetry allows me to be the one who rescues the princess from the burning building and strike down my evil enemy, known as king poverty. My finest hour came on January 1, 1999 when I married my soul mate, Terrie, and became a father to Nikes and Joshua. Now I wake up to wonderful words of poetry every day. The evil king poverty has finally been slain.

CARTER, R.
[a.] Detroit, MI [title] "Life's Strength"[pers.] This is my first venture in all the years I have been writing—submitting a piece of my work for publishing. It turned out to be an adventure. I always felt I had something to say and it needed to be heard. Thanks to the International Library of Poetry, I am being heard.

CASE, MISTY
[a.] Union, MO [title] "The Face" [pers.] My name is Misty and I'm only 17. I recently graduated from Union High. I want to extend a special thanks to Kristin, Alishia, and my mom. Also, I blow a kiss to Phil Hardin, my husband-to-be. He holds me up and lets me fly. Also, a special thanks to Thomas.

CASTLE, HELENE
[a.] Wyoming, MI [title] "The Bubble Bath" [pers.] I have been writing poetry since I was approximately. 14 years old. My mother passed away when I was 13 of breast cancer, so poetry was one of my ways to get through the loss. I also enjoy painting and drawing, as well, to help express myself and my feelings. I am a 28-year-old wife and mother of two children (one boy and one girl) with another baby girl due November 2000. I love animals, children, the arts, sports (especially hockey and the Detroit Red Wings #60 Steve Yzermanx), computers, camping, fishing, the outdoors, studying law, and many other things. I'm really excited to see one of my poems get published in your book and hope to see more of my poetry included once submitted. Thank you for giving me the opportunity to express myself!

CASTRO, ANNA
[title] "Breaking" [pers.] Poetry is in everyone's souls and I am grateful that I learned to awaken that gift in me. It's a medium of expressing the very things that dwell in our happiness and sadness. This poem celebrates the joy in crying, of having no fear in letting go of emotions without boudaries. See, sadness is not just for the meek, but it is a source of strength for the brave. To touch just one soul with this poem is enough for me.

CAVENDER, HELGA
[title] "I Remember When" [pers.] This poem is about a relationship between Whip and myself that lasted on and off many years, from 1982-1998, until he finally broke my heart. Whip was very special. I am very passionate about my hobbies, which include poetry, photography, and painting. All my work is one of a kind. I love doing it all when I have the time away from my job as an auto assembler. I am single, love life, time with my friends, my Rottie Damien, and working on my 1971 Chevelle 55 and beachin' as much as possible. Life is short—relationships never last forever.

CAZIRE, ALICE
[title] "Forgive Me Lord" [pers.] My husband died of cancer in 1969 at the age of 32. With a lot of help from God, I raised my six children. They are all grown now, and I have five grandchildren and one great grandchild. My family and my wonderful fiance help me so much. They are truly blessings from God. They are always bringing food, flowers, fun., etc. I became disabled two years ago and have a lot of pain. I'm up a lot at night, praying and writing poetry. I have been writing poetry since 1968.

CEBALLOS, PABLO
[title] "Lost Rose" [pers.] If reading "Lost Rose" reminded you of that special person that is not next to you now, you know what this poem "means" to you. If that person is still there, you know what you haven't said. Many times we take for granted what we have until we feel the pangs of being famished. My advice is to never let a sun set without saying the words we need to say to keep that rose from being snatched from our very hands.

CEBULA, SUSAN
[title] "What Dream Are Made Of" [pers.] I would like to dedicate this poem to God for His beautiful creation and all my loved ones, especially my most loving grandmother (Baba). Through all my years of growing she has shown me unconditional love, for everyone and everything. Because of this special gift to love, care, feel, and dream I am inspired to write about such things that bring feeling and beauty to one's life. Thank you to all who have touched my life, without you I would not have been blessed with the gift to dream with my eyes open wide.

CEDRONE, AMANDA
[title] "Summer" [pers.] My name is Amanda Noel Cedrone. I'm 10 years old. I go to St. Mary's St. Alphonsus Regional Catholic School. I'm in fifth grade, going into sixth. I first started to like poetry in my English class, thanks to my teacher, Mrs. Fowler, in fifth grade. Ever since then I've loved poetry. I also like to write short stories and I like to read books, especially Harry Potter. I have been taking karate for three years now, and I am a second degree brown belt. I love to compete in regional karate tournaments. I just competed nationally and came home with two bronze medals and one fourth place ribbon.

CEDRONE, AMANDA
[a.] Warrensburg, NY [title] "Summer" [pers.] My name is Amanda Cedrone, I'm 10 years old. I go to St. Mary's St. Alphonsus Regional Catholic School. I'm in fifth grade, going into sixth. I first started to like poetry in my English class, thanks to my teacher Mrs. Fowler in fifth grade. Ever since then I've loved poetry. I also like to write short stories, and I like to read books especially Harry Potter. I have been taking karate for three years now, and I am a 2nd degree brown belt, and I love to compete in Regional Karate tournaments. I just competed Nationally and came home with two bronze medals and one fourth place ribbon

CHADDERDON WALL, RUTH
[a.] Williamsport, PA [title] "Love of a Mother" [pers.] I began writing poetry when I was quite young. As I became older it became a way to express my inner most feelings. All of my work comes from life's experiences through strangers, friends, and most of all, my parents. Many friends and family members have encouraged me for years to follow my dreams. I never felt I had the talent. Through changes I had to make in my life and good friends I decided to enter your contest, and to my surprise I was elected to have my work published. I love writing and hope that I can continue to pursue my dream. Thank you to all for giving me this start.

CHAMBERS, JUNIOR
[title] "A Pond I Am" [pers.] Writing for me started at an early age. At 12 years old I was writing poetry to this girl I had a crush on. She was 14 and she was mean. She was mean to me, but I wrote her nice words. I told her how pretty she was. I would tell her I am like a bowl of white milk and she is that single red rose that sits in the middle of me, afloat like an Island in the middle of the ocean. Imagine an ocean made of pure white milk and all the islands are a just a big bunch of red roses. That's how pretty I let her know she was. I told her in writing each

and every beat of my heart rhymes with each and every letter that spells her name. And she became my girlfriend. I had spoken to her soul and a door opened. A door shut; something had to go or something had to enter her life. My poetry had opened a door or it had closed a door.

CHAMP, ZELIA
[title] "Say Peace" [pers.] I give thanks to God for sending this special poem to me. I believe God gave it to me to share with the people of the world. Our brothers and sisters in every part of the world need peace. It is a therapeutic word that will truly bring about peace, if it is used. So, "Say Peace." God is peace.

CHAPMAN, JUDITH
[title] "Respect" [pers.] Respect was written for mother nature and all small creatures and is sometimes not thought about. Our lives are not that different. We work hard each day for our families, our shelter, our food, and in one quick instant it could all be taken away. My friend is a spider; the alien is you.

CHECCHIA, MICHELE
[a.] Mississauga, ON [title] "Rose of Eden" [pers.] If every action has an opposite and equal reaction, then we should all tread lightly with our senses as witness to our brief moment in the sun. And if for every cause there is an effect, and if the cause is inspiration, then inspiration should be the catalyst for humanity.

CHECK, JASON
[a.] Whitehall, PA [title] "Therapy" [pers.] The poem "Therapy" is about losing myself in an altered state of reality, and how I begin to take a liking to it. But when this reality is threatened it shows how I fought to keep it, and in the process, find myself drawn out of the shadows of fear and into the reflections of life. The poem is also the basis for a short film.

CHEUNG, KRIS
[title] "So Hard on Me When We Part" [pers.] I love writing poems and rhymes because it allows me to express myself in a very unique fashion. Each poem or rhyme that I've written relates to my experience or how I feel about a specific topic. This is a very exceptional poem because the majority of my other works deal with either my suffering and hardships in life, or my spiritual connection with the Lord. Thus, I really value this poem and hope that you will enjoy it as I had writing it.

CHEW, WENG
[a.] Singapore, Singapore [title] "Elegy: the Bed (the Day Mom Died)" [pers.] Chinese customs require that my mother's bed be dismantled upon her death. I shared this bed with my mother after my father's death, so did my younger sister after me. Much to the consternation of my family members, I did not perform this ritual until several days later. As I held the rafters and wooden beams in my hands, I felt a wave of memories intermixed with my pent-up grief, but the emotional release I sought, and for which this ritual is supposed to bestow, was not there, at least not immediately. This poem was my release valve.

CHILCOTT, SHERRYL
[title] "Be Your Own Strength" [pers.] I enjoy the freedom, expression, and passion of the written word. I am greatly honored that the skill of my great grandfather has been passed to me. I hope that readers of this poem and other poems that I have written gain and grow from the experience. The most thrilling thing about writing my picture words is the emotional ride the reader can be taken on.

CHINN, JOHN
[a.] Pasadena, TX [title] "Faith" [pers.] The poetry that I'm doing is very important to me

because through my poetry God is speaking His love. My wish for everyone in this world who reads my poems, is to have their spirit lifted up. There are many hurting people in the world and I believe that through this poem God is speaking to them, as well as to the rest of the people in their everyday lives. Finally, with out the encouragement of Pastor Phillip Morris and my personal pastor, Blake McKenzie, and last, but not least, two of my best friends in Christ, Ed and Christina Shelton, and God, my poetry would never have developed into what it has become.

CHONG, JEREMY
[title] "Depth" [pers.] Poetry is perhaps the most emotionally communicative of all forms of writing. Poetry, in its myriad styles, can convey essential truths or even the most complex feelings in subtle, often sublime ways. My poem is about the bittersweet aspect of love, a whole-hearted pain that I find almost twistedly intoxicating. I hope other people will be able to identify with my poem and realize that life and love are beautiful, despite being hurtful at times; it is all the joy and all the sadness and everything else that makes it so weirdly wonderful to be fully, truly, and passionately human.

CHRISTENSEN, BILLIE
[a.] Anchorage, AK [title] "Day In, Day Out" [pers.] I believe that poetry should be read, not studied. The meaning that an individual derives from a poem is its real meaning, the truth, even if it differs from the author's original idea. I feel that once you break down the poem to study, the essence is gone. "Day In, Day Out" was written while I lived in Alaska. During this time, I enjoyed many outdoor activities, which inspired many poems. I hope you enjoy reading this poem as much as I have enjoyed writing it.

CLARK, CASSANDRA
[title] "Decent into the Flesh" [pers.] Madeline, I dedicate this poem to you, a wonderful friend, who makes me feel like a whole person. I love you. Poetry is my passion; being a published poet has always been my dream. Amy, Max, and Madeline, you became important to me in December and have become good friends of mine through a man we all love. With the support of my family, friends, my belief and love for God, and everyone that is important to me, I find the beautiful words I need to express my feelings and show the true love of my soul to others.

CLARK, LISA
[title] "Kisses" [pers.] This poem was written about a man who is very close and special to me, even though he and I never had the chance to have that first kiss. This poem is how I feel our first kiss would be. I hope that others out there know and understand the feeling in which this poem was written. He is still, and always will be, close to my heart.

CLARK, RONALD W., JR.
[a.] Starke, FL [title] "Clouded Views" [pers.] This poem is about my life and the bad decisions I made while on drugs. I dropped out of school in 1983 at 15 years of age. I was selling drugs, as well as using drugs to the point where my views where clouded. So, at 22 years old I was sitting on death row for armed robbery and murder. I wrote "Clouded Views" in a 9x7 foot cell, hoping to open other's eyes to my mistakes. Life is never as bad as it seems and drugs will not solve your problems, they just cover them up. The only real solution is God.

CLARK, SUSAN
[a.] New Windsor, NY [title] "The Transparent Pond" [pers.] I love to write poetry. With poetry I can travel, have a fantasy, release emotions, heal, and so many other things. It is good for my spirit and it gives me such satisfaction. I also think that poetry is a gift you share with others, as with each

reader it may say something different to them individually. It is my form of painting, and so I paint. I have written poetry since I was a child and it will be something I can leave behind for my seven children to cherish, as one of Mom's very own paintings. "The Transparent Pond" is my reflection of days at the pond with the children.

CLARK, SUSAN M.
[a.] New Windsor, NY [title] "The Eternal Bond" [pers.] As I experience life, especially being the mother of seven children, poetry has become a lift for the heart, my unique expression. I recently lost both of my parents and wrote both their eulogies. At that time, the priest announced my words were a special gift that I should continue to share. I have found poetry to be a gift that has enabled me to heal, to explore, and to satisfy my deepest thoughts. I feel it is possible to paint a picture with words that may be a different picture for anyone that reads it!

CLARK, V.
[title] "Location Is Everything" [pers.] In retrospect, that phrase itself would have probably been a more appropriate title for my poem, since it's theme actually centers around timing rather than location. Too late, we discover that the task we pre-judged as being simple should have been given careful preparation. Conversely, the event that appears ominous may result in little or no bad effects. Apparent problems are often opportunities in disguise. So, this teacher's daughter, who is also a teacher, is saying, "Don't jump to conclusions; get the full picture and all the facts before you act; learn as you go, and enjoy it."

CLARKE, ANNETTE
[title] "Spirit Bound" [pers.] Everyone who puts pen to paper does so to please their own ego, not to please others. Sometimes we can do both. When you read others' thoughts, they can become your own, they can adapt to your brain, and if only a line remains in your memory then we are poets. My father, mother, and grandmother's love of poetry lives in me, making their memories so much sweeter.

CLARKE, MARY
[a.] Cherokee Village, AR [title] "Angels in Our Path" [pers.] My poems are all inspirational, given to me from a higher source. I believe we are lead by spirit angels, if we only listen to our inner thoughts (source) to guide us. Take the time to stop and listen. I do pray this poem will be an inspiration in the realization that we are not alone with love and light.

CLAYTON, BRENDA
[title] "To My Friend" [pers.] He helped save me from a six-year-long abusive relationship. When I had no strength to pack and move he was there. When I would loss faith in myself every 15 minutes, he gave me some of it back. He treats me like an angel, but he was my angel and I thank God for him. I hope I never have to be without him in my life. This poem was written for him, dedicated to him, engraved, and given to him. I love you, Scott!

CLAYTON, RETA
[a.] Big Spring, TX [title] "Who Am I" [pers.] This poem is about a woman who is a victim of a crime. Men, women, children, and babies of all ages become victims to crimes every day in society, and not always by choice. Some are committed by people they know, others are not. "Who Am I" is about a survivor that prays to a higher power for help and healing in her time of pain and suffering.

CLAYTON, RETA
[a.] Big Spring, TX [title] "Who Am I" [pers.] This poem is about a woman victim of a crime. Men, women, children and babies If all ages lay victims to crimes everyday in society, not always by choice. Some or committed by people they know

other or not. "Who Am I", is about a survivor that prays to a higher power for help and healing, in her time of pain and suffering

CLEMENTS, CHRISTINA
[title] "The Shadows of the Night" [pers.] To me, a love poem is the most heart felt way to tell a special person how you feel about them. This poem was written for Mark, a man who is my inspiration of love, hope, and happiness. He will always have a special place in my heart and soul. It wasn't until I met Mark that I felt so inspired to write. This poem and all of the other poems are for you, Mark. Thank you for being there for me. Now I can write as I have always wanted, with love.

CLEMETSON, DAVID
[a.] Akron, OH [title] "Of Flag" [pers.] The century changed and in me stirred a patriotic feeling to write a poem about the flag and our freedoms. I had the first line in mind, partly because I fought for them and fly them by the side of my home. I sensed by comparing the flag and freedom together it would inspire me with a good poem. As Flag Day approached, I came up with the title, helping me to finish the poem. I wrote it to raise the conscience and the imagination of any reader. I dedicate the poem to the comprised wisdom of man.

CLENDENING, DERELDIA
[title] "I Do Not Understand, My Beautiful Sister" [pers.] I pray that this poem reaches many young people and allows them to think twice before making decisions and helps them to realize that irrational decisions may result in negative consequences. I thank God that He has worked through my parents to guide me and instill in me the strength to not become vulnerable to peer pressure. Being 12 years old, it is sometimes hard to avoid peer pressure. Therefore, I always keep God first, because He will always guide me in the right direction.

CLISSOLD, KARA
[title] "Falcons" [pers.] I believe this poem to be a metaphor for our life. We may see only the bad and evil, but when we step back, we can see the whole picture; there still is hope. To me, animals are more capable of understanding than most people, as they have not always had the luxury of safety. Originally, this poem was for a journal we had to do in school. Since I write a lot anyway, it wasn't much of a challenge. Writing has been, for me, a gift.

CLOUGH, CHESTER
[title] "Mother" [pers.] Poetry is a gift I was given and is the best way I know of expressing my true feelings in just a few verses or phrases. I would like to give special thanks to those who added to and supported my creativity: God, for refining me through life's experiences; Jesus, for carrying me through my troubled times; Kacy MacDonald, for true friendship and stimulating creativity within me; and all others whose paths I have crossed— may peace be with you.

COBURN, STEFANIE
[title] "Girlish Dreams" [pers.] Poetry is a unique way of talking about a topic to get people to listen. Most of my poetry talks about daily living and our hopes and dreams. Hopefully, my poetry will uplift and inspire people's spirits. I'm sure that every women would like to be married to a man as described in my poem.

COCHET, T.
[a.] Kamloops, BC [title] "Life in a Shoe" [pers.] When I wrote this poem, I was going through hard times, trying to fit into the crowd and be accepted. Born with a handicap, I felt like an outcast for sometime. It took my loving husband of 27 years and my best friend, Carolyn, to

help me see the light at end of the tunnel. I always looked down at my feet, not straight ahead at life. Then one day I woke up and found the courage to share my love of wisdom, through my poems, with others like myself, in order to give them incentive to carry on as I did.

COFFEE, VIRGINIA
[title] "Wonderful Feeling" [pers.] To me, poetry is my way of expression. It is through poetry that I can really express my innermost feelings, happy or sad. Possessing the ability to write, having someone read my writing, and for this writing to really enlighten them or give them a wonderful feeling through their reading of my poems, makes me want to keep writing poetry as long as I possibly can. It is a small way to relieve a lot of large inner feelings honestly.

COKER, ASHLEY
[title] "Lifelight" [pers.] Inspired by "Because I could not stop for Death," written by Emily Dickenson, and "The Traveller," written by Walter de la Mare, my poem signifies the beauty of fear and death. Although I have been experimenting with poetry for some years, Mr. Balsai, my English teacher, has opened my eyes to a new angle of this art. I would like to thank him for his enthusiasm and encouragement, which has fueled my desire for self expression through poetry. I am sixteen years old and from Pocatello, Idaho. I attend Century High School and am going to be a junior next year. I have an overwhelming passion for poetry. I also enjoy zoology and other life science classes. My love for poetry and philosophy has taken my writing to a whole new phase. I hope that maybe, one day, more of my poems and other literature may be published, as I hope it may inspire others.

COLE, JAMES
[title] "The Paradox of Ascension" [pers.] Artistic creativity is a perplexing occurrence. We call them gifts because we feel we don't own them. We're humbled to be given a means to express and find ourselves with. Sometimes we don't know where it comes from, but when it does come to us we use words like "epiphany." and "inspiration." Where exactly these gifts come from and why, I will not pretend to understand. Perhaps it's not our place to understand, but to learn how to feel. I cannot imagine who I'd be without writing, but I suppose because of writing I am allowed to imagine.

COLE, SUZANNE
[title] "Waking" [pers.] Poetry, a life long hobby, is like hunting for garnets in schist. A poet seizes upon a rough idea, a granule of inspiration, and recognizes its potential. My joy is in chipping away the coating of ordinary perception, hoping to uncover a gleaming heart-red truth. Occasionally I may have found one. This gem is for your appraisal.

COLLIER, RACHEL
[title] "Quest of the Eons" [pers.] We all, at one time or another, reach a turning point in our lives. A simple fork in the road, a junction in "Life's Roller Coaster." This poem represents one of these junctions. These "Questions" which we will encounter are necessary for our growth and understanding. Although painful at times, and joyous at others, we will continue to learn about all of life's "Questions," a very symbolic "Quest of Eons." I found my quest and my path. We are all on an eternal path back. May this poem help each one of you realize that we are never alone.

COLLUM, HARRY
[title] "My Special Companion" [pers.] After 41 years, I lost my wife and my special friend. We had so many plans together for retirement, but those dreams were shattered nine years ago. I wrote this poem hoping to honor the special person that my wife was! I am grateful that you selected my first

try at writing. As I and our three children can attest to, she was the greatest wife and mother ever. I sincerely hope she will see this poem in the publication *Rainstorms and Rainbows.*

COLONNA, ADAM
[a.] Hoboken, NJ [title] "Prayer" [pers.] This poem is very special to me, significant in its rhymes and depth, which reflect some of my life experience. The life of faith can truly be a struggle, but with faith and belief we can overcome any situation or obstacle. We must learn from our mistakes and strive not to repeat them continuously. With faith and self acceptance we all have potential to climb or even move mountains. Life is a challenge, a precious gift, and a blessing that we live by our own free will.

COMBOW, NORMA
[title] "Runaway" [pers.] I enjoy writing poetry about "real life" experiences. At one time, my husband and I were houseparetns for troubled youth. Many of the boys we cared for had been in trouble with the law because of running away from home. Homelife was not so pleasant for many of them. We, as children, may have even considered leaving home because we thought our parents were too strict or that we had disappointed them. Maybe someone older and wiser was able to help us understand that love could still be found in a place called "home."

COMMISSO, SALLY
[a.] Lindenhurst, NY [title] "Places of My Heart" [pers.] Although it has been quite a few years since my mother passed away, a lot of my adult years so far, as a woman, have been structured by the guide lines my mother taught me. I'm just now understanding the meaning of her outlooks and views. The meaning of her life was always in putting her children first. As a mother, I adhere to her doings. My words only partially tell of the depth of her teachings. She was my best friend, confidant, and advisor. I will be a better person because of her, always.

COMSTOCK, LORI
[a.] Orlando, FL [title] "When I Think of My Mother" [pers.] This poem was written for my mother, Judith Ann Aultman, and I would like to thank you publishing this poem and letting me truly honor her for the many years of dedication and love she has brought into my life. She has always been my inspiration through all of life's challenges and my bond with her it has kept me filled with the desire to write. My mother is, and always will be my "Everything." Poetry, for me, is expressing how my spirit sings! I hope those who are reading my poem in this book have received the same "Unconditional Love" that my mother has always given to me.

CONIGLIO, JOSEPH
[title] "I Wonder" [pers.] This poem is dedicated to my wife, Kathleen, who is my heart and soul and best friend. Without her I would be nothing. All my love to her forever!

CONLEY, GRACE
[a.] Fenton, MI [title] "Wonders of the Sea" [pers.] Hello. I'm proud to be the author of "Wonders of the Sea." I love the sea; I like to watch the water waves and listen to the splashes. Oh, it's beautiful. I enjoy the breeze. Different colors and varieties of creatures are so wonderful. There are dolphins, seahorses, fish, and lots more to see. Writing poems is a great way to express your likes and desires, feelings, dreams, and life. I'm 11 years old and the middle child between two sisters, Claire and Maye. We write poems in our spare time; it's a good hobby and interesting. Our mom and dad inspired us to be who we are.

CONLEY, MAYE
[title] "Dreams" [pers.] Hi everyone. My poem is

special; it's real and true. With all my dreams every day, every night, and every time, I enjoy and have fun. I feel great, so excited. I like thinking, I like rhyming, and most of all, I love dreaming. This is why my poem is called "Dreams." I'm full of imagination, which is both good and interesting. I'm ten years old and a fourth grader and happy to have a loving family. My mom, Emelita, and dad, Patrick, are my ideals, including my sisters, Claire and Grace. Grandpa Gaudencio, grandmas, teachers, and friends are all my inspirations.

CONNELLY, MARK
[title] "Life Is . . . " [pers.] As a child, I used poetry as a vehicle for expressing virtually everything. More recently, writing poetry has yielded to the pressures of pursuing a doctoral degree in clinical psychology and other life activities. This poetry contest offered an opportunity to "return to my roots." The poem "Life Is . . . " was written in reaction to the series of adverse world events that have caused many to questions the essence of life. I have been extremely blessed to have already discovered the answer in my fiancee, Wendy, who has shown me how the power of love can conquer all and whose beauty, kindness, compassion, and sensitivity have been the foundations of happiness and meaning in my life. My wish is for others to find the same answer to "What is life" as I have.

CONNORS, JESS
[title] "Dream" [pers.] My grade four teacher, Mr. Kane, inspired me to write a lot. Not only did we do lots of creative writing in his class, but he was also always encouraging me to continue writing. Now I have a published poem. I wrote this poem because I enjoy writing poems, especially about fantasy and fairy tale. I hope everyone enjoys reading my poem as much as I enjoyed writing it. I would like to dedicate this poem to my Mom, Dad, and best friend, Sarah Visser. I love you guys!

CONTI, BRENDAN
[a.] Co. Tipperary, Ireland [title] "Do You Believe in Miracles" [pers.] This poem is dedicated to a very special person in my life: my mother. Growing up as a child, I recognized the severe pressures and hardships with which she was faced. Her courage and strength have been inspirational to me. I have learned so much due to her perseverance and determination to survive in this world, and she has taught me that having a little faith in something is not such a bad thing. She has given me something very precious—a solid foundation and a positive perspective in which to build a life of my own.

COOK, CRAIG
[a.] Chandler, AZ [title] "Grams and Gramps" [pers.] At a very early age, my grandparents were an important part of my life. My father was a single parent of four children. I am the youngest boy. Because my father worked long hours, my grandparents were there to help with the daily chores. I remember all of the times when I was sick, my grandpa or grandma would take off from their job to care for me. I wrote this poem at the age of 13 to show how much I appreciate their love and help throughout the years. Because of their influence I have tried to do my best in everything I do.

COOK, DOLLIE
[title] "Tree" [pers.] I enjoy writing poems about nature and humanity and I'm convinced that God, in His great wisdom, created the two to live in harmony so that each would be of service one to the other. I hope others who read my poem, "Tree," share my view point. I also enjoy writing poems on other subjects, which I give to my children or keep in my humble collection.

COOPER, ELISHA
[title] "Untrue Love" [pers.] I never had such inspiration to write poetry until I lost my first

"Untrue Love." It opened up something inside of me, something creative, and I have been writing poems and lyrics with a deep passion for the past year. I also love singing and recording and hope to pursue a career with that in the future. I love reading poetry and finding myself able to relate to it, and I hope that people can relate to my poem in that way.

COOPER, JUDY
[a.] Wangaratta, VIC [title] "The Lost Sock" [pers.] This poem, "The Lost Sock," is a pen picture of my border collie dog, "Snowy," when, as a pup, he often stole our socks. I am a retired teacher/librarian who loves reading and writing poetry and prose. My other loves are music, painting, and embroidery.

COOPER, SUSAN
[title] "Earth" [pers.] I am in my mid-fifties now and the world has changed a lot since I was a child. Despite wars and pollution, the beautiful Earth continues to supply our needs: water, air, and food. I look at the children of today and wonder if they will have a future. We need to remember we have only one Earth. Hopefully, my poem explains this.

CORKINS, JENNIFER
[title] "In the Garden" [pers.] This poem was written for my maternal grandmother, Margreth Riemer. She always has such lovely gardens every summer. She also worries a lot about me and I love her very much.

CORNETT, MICHAEL
[title] "My Heart Finds Rest" [pers.] This poem expresses the human nature of my heart and, I believe, of many others. There is hope and change within my heart, as the poem expresses God's heart to us. He shared His love on a cross through His son, Jesus Christ, in whom my sins were forgiven, my fears turned to courage, and what seemed the death of me was then given life eternal. Healing unbreakable, love unconditional—all by the blood of Jesus. My heart found rest in His arms. I pray your hearts finds rest as you are moved by the spirit of God, placing your trust in the Savior.

CORNEY, SARAH
[a.] Durango, CO [title] "Don't Let Us Forget" [pers.] Poetry! The words are written by the hand, but the thought comes from the heart. Poetry can take something of little worth and turn it into the desire of your heart. Poetry is that unique window to the world, and no matter if you're a poet or not, you see the world, known or unknown, through that one unique window. God gave the gift, this wonderful gift, to show us beauty in the midst of the storm. Few receive this wonderful gift and I am blessed to be one of those few. Thank you, God!

CORSON, PETER
[title] "This Night" [pers.] Have you ever been in along distance relationship? The poem, "This Night," was my attempt to explain my thoughts and emotions to someone half a world away—between England and the New Zealand forests, where I work as a park ranger. These forests and parks are important for the moods and images I write about. It was a night in one of those forests, thinking about my "friend," when I searched for my pen and scratched out "This Night."

CORTINA, LISETTE DESIREE'
[title] "'Til the End" [pers.] My poetry shows my true thoughts and feelings about people who have inspired my life. Positive and negative experiences have enabled me to grow in a way that I can substitute my inner most feelings with words on paper. I feel very fortunate to have been given the gift to express my personal experiences through my poetry.

COSENTINO, STEPHANIE
[title] "Beach Death" [pers.] To me, poetry is an art; it's not something to be forced on someone. My inspiration and motivation don't exist. When I feel something, I write it. I shared this poem with the people that I know and love because this is how I feel. My poetry is my feelings at that moment on paper. I'm just extremely pleased that my poem is being published. I accomplished that goal at only eighteen years old. I thank my parents for always believing me, my aunt for always being there, and the rest of my family and friends. I love you all.

COSTA, TIM
[title] "Along the Coast" [pers.] Tim Costa is a native of the Monterey Peninsula, located along California's Central Coast. It is world renowned for its rugged coast and sandy beaches: a true paradise. It is here that Tim's love and respect for nature flourished. His favorite activities include back packing and camping. He is a former firefighter and emergency medical technician for State Forestry and now works as a painter. He enjoys being with family and friends.

COTTON, LOLA
[title] "When I Remember" [pers.] I am a retired R.N. in my eighties. I wrote many poems in my youth; some were published in local papers, and one was published in *The World's Fair Anthology of Verse* in 1939. One poem was published in *The Caravan of Verse*. When World War II started, I put my poetry away and gave all my time to nursing. Sometimes, in recent years, I would write a few lines, but when I wrote "When I Remember" I sent it off to you.

COUNTS, GLORIA
[a.] North Little Rock, AR [title] "Lonely Bird Without a Mate" [pers.] My poem, "Lonely Bird Without a Mate," was inspired by a tragic Civil War era mystery/love story. A clue, found in an old Bible, contain the heart-breaking words of my maternal great-grandmother, Martha Harvey Smith, wife of Andrew Jackson Smith, of Opelika, Alabama. Tradition states that she brought her three children to Calhoun Co., Arkansas in 1856, never to see her husband again. She said, "I cannot love but only one." The secret went to the grave with her July 31, 1865.

COWAN, PETER
[title] "One Moment in Time" [pers.] My name is Peter Cowan. I am a 48-year-old water turbine engineer. I am married with two children, Rosemary, 20 years, and Samuel, 18 years, and, of course, my wife, Linda. I was born and still live in a small mining village in central Scotland. My hobbies include surfing the net, P.T.O, and chatting to friends and acquaintances on line. I also like gardening, walking the dog, and writing poetry. My poems were inspired by friends and family while undergoing intensive chemotherapy treatment for terminal cancer, which is still in remission five years later.

COX, JOHN
[title] "Love Sonnet 23 (To Vala)" [pers.] This poem was written for someone who became very special to me, and it explores the risks and depths of love. It is written in traditional Shakespearean sonnet form, which I have found extraordinary well-suited to the purpose. The poem seeks to describe love as a perilous journey into the depths, wherein the lover is lured deeper and deeper. As in true love, there comes a critial moment in which the love is grasped or abandoned. Here, beyond the point of no return, it is grasped, making it a happy ending.

CRAFT, CATHERINE
[title] "No One to Turn To" [pers.] The reason for this poem was because, at the time, things didn't go very well. Now things are better and I can read back to see how it used to be. I believe my grandfather gave me the gift to express, because I can write from personal experience. I hope others will be enjoying it as well. I would like to thank my husband, Troy, for his love and encouragement.

CRAIN, TIMOTHY
[title] "Ever-Changing" [pers.] My talents are dedicated to my mother, who is the greatest, Mrs. Ruby May Green Setzer. Also to George, David, Karen, and Anita. I've written many poems, but only one's been appreciated. Thank you.

CRAMER, BETHANY
[title] "Ode to a Lover Not Yet Seen" [pers.] I haven't written in a long time. For me, poetry was an expression. It was intense and personal. For some reason, I'd abandoned it, until a dear friend wrote a poem for me. It moved me, and I was again inspired do express myself in verse. I'd forgotten how much I loved it . . . I will never abandon it again! Thank you, Brian! My heart is complete again. Thank you for reminding me.

CRANDELL, DANNY
[title] "Home" [pers.] My family and close friends inspired me to write this poem, "Home." It was their love of family that this poem reflects. I therefore dedicate "Home" to my parents, Mel and Martha. My sisters, Rita, Shirley, and my brother, Gary; my friends. Sione, and Sam Smith; their daughter, Donna; and my best friend, Cynthia are truly the kind of family that dreams are made of.

CRANFIELD, PHYLIS
[title] "Thank You, Daddy" [pers.] This poem was written for my father on Father's Day to, in some way, tell him how I feel about him. I am proud of my father and what he stands for. He has never failed me. I have written several other poems, and I also write short stories, but with poetry you can express your feelings without uttering a word.

CROASDELL, JUDE
[a.] Cambridgeshire, UK [title] "Time-The Eternal Peneplain" [pers.] This poem was inspired by the fifteenth Darwin College Lecture Series, held at The Lady Mitchell Hall, Cambridge University in 2000. The theme of the series was "Time" and included an exciting range of lectures from, "Time in Modern Physics," to "The Genetics of Time," "Time Travel," and "Time and Religion." This poem is dedicated to my son, Alex (25 years old), with input from Professor P. Simpson-Housley, geographer. The complexity of the subject was such that I wanted to present something original, a thought provoking celebration of time. Peneplain refers to "the final stage of erosion."

CROCKER, TERRY
[title] "The Story Behind the Tree" [pers.] I began writing poetry in 1997 after the untimely death of a loved one. "The Story Behind the Tree" was one of many I've written for my book, *Visions of Southern Poetry, A Story Book of Poems.* All of my poetry is true and includes accounts of my religious beliefs and of my youth and present life. Also, I'm currently working on my first novel and negotiating with publishers about my work. I'm very honored to have "The Story Behind The Tree" published in this book. I give my Heavenly Father the glory, and this is the story behind me.

CROFT, JOAN M.
[a.] Round Rock, TX [title] "Child of Two" [pers.] I was born and raised in the South by two parents who chose civil service as their lifetime work. I am moved by the human condition and motivated by all its aspects through valves instilled by my parents.

CROOK, FRANCES
[title] "Preparation" [pers.] My grandmother's reading to me and my memorization of Scripture instilled a love for literature and influenced my thirty-three-year career as an English teacher. At three, I memorized my first scripture, "God is love." The purpose of "Preparation" is two-fold:

to state "God is love" and to depict a submissive viewpoint toward "death." Life is a spiritual journey, and poetry a reflection of life. It captures mankind's moments on that journey. My husband and I have two children: Crede, a teacher, and Trey, an architecture student. An avid reader at ninety, my mother lives with us in Richardson, Texas.

CROOKS, ROBERT

[title] "Ajean Smile" [pers.] Robert Crooks is a Montreal born actor who began his career on the stage, appearing in such roles as Cysander in *A Midsummer's Night Dream*. He is an aspiring actor that has worked in film and television, and he writes poetry. Writing is my release and I would like to thank the pure Vermont soil for which this poem was born upon. I would also like to thank Jean for being Jean and for inspiring this and other pieces with her beauty, and to Fred Ward for his belief and friendship.

CROTEAU, VANESSA

[title] "How We Died" [pers.] The things I cannot express in everyday speech, I express through poetry. The raw emotions and bare thoughts . . . what wouldn't make sense to everyday minds are understood and embraced in the world of poetry. For as long as I can remember, this is how it's been. At only eighteen years, I am quite confident in my gift of spinning words into art.

CROW, KAY

[title] "To the Gods" [pers.] When I found the craft fifteen years ago it felt like "coming home." Witchcraft is a gentle and peaceful religion based on nature, and I like to celebrate it in poetry.

CRUSOE, OZELLA

[title] "O' Sea Shore" [pers.] I thank God, who gave me the vision in my writing. I would like to dedicate this poem to my parents, sisters, brothers, children, and husband, and to Mike, who is going to his career in the Marine Corps. I have a master in English and a diploma in fitness nutrition. I love to write. I feel that I can express myself in poetry and communicate with others who write.

CRUZ, CHONA

[title] "Journey" [pers.] God has inspired me to write poetry. Through the physical illness I experience, I have received most of my ideas. The beauty of nature surrounds me as an inspiration to write about sunsets and mountains. And, of course, my poetry finds inspiration in my dad, "Ace," brother "Eddy," and the entire family of Pattons and Cruzs. Poetry expresses itself through one's "Journey in Life." Thank you, Poetry.com, for acknowledging my poem. Thanks to all my friends also. I was very surprised and happy to be chosen to have my poem in your anthology book. It means a lot to me; it has encouraged and motivated me in my pain of the illness I endure daily. Again, thank you for your time.

CRUZ, YVETTE

[title] "A Little Secret I Have" [pers.] My name is Yvette Cruz. I am a 22-year-old Hispanic female in New York. To many, my words may mean nothing, but as an American given the right, having freedom of speech and a talent given to me from the Lord above, I can voice or share with you, through poetry, any opinion, theory, or feeling that may dwell or linger in my heart, my mind, and my soul. I am thankful time after time for an opportunity I thought I would never be given.

CULLENS, BONNIE

[title] "Lifetime" [pers.] As you may surmise by the words in my poem, "Lifetime," I was born in 1919 and have always been filled with the need to create. I am an artist of sorts and publish the newsletter at my place or residence. I love to write and have written a story about my early relations, who were Scotch and Cherokee. I find

words fascinating and love seeing my original thoughts appear on paper.

CUMMINGS, JEANIE

[title] "A Tribute to Life" [pers.] I wrote this poem years ago as I was going through a difficult time in my life, trying to come to grips in coping with the loss of loved ones in my family. I feel honored in having the opportunity to now share my poem with the world. I hope my poem will be an inspiration to others who are going through, or have gone through trials and tribulations themselves, struggling as I have and still do, to try to remain positively focused in the journey of life, no matter what comes our way. God bless you.

CUNNINGHAM, BRANDI

[title] "Mother Night" [pers.] Nothing's impossible. Improbable, maybe: I'm a 16-year-old poet. So reach for your goals, no matter who you are. About the poem: the key-note is "family." You've heard of mother night? Well, I just put a father day in the picture, and a child also. That's the hidden truth to it. The child was imagining, in this poem, that he or she was human (personification), having thoughts and feelings like a person, and by the end, had to leave with mother night. Simple as that. Thanks to everyone that has helped me accomplish this! Love to all!

CURRIER, CLAIRE

[title] "Memories" [pers.] I began writing poetry a little over two years ago. Actually, it started with a poem I wrote for my mother. A few days later, after going to bed, I began seeing words float about my head. Sounds strange, even to me. I must say, the most beautiful, inspirational words appeared the next morning on my kitchen table, while drinking my early morning coffee. Since then I have written over 160 poems and have published an arrangement called "Never Alone." My poetry is a collection of poems about love, life, and the healing of the soul. Many are reflections attributed to pain felt from others, joyful times shared, children, and most important, a walk with the Lord Jesus. I am married and have three grown children and three grandchildren. I am a paralegal, enjoy crafts, gardening, and I have a dog and a few chickens. Living in the country has many advantages and I love them all. God bless.

DABHOIWALA, MERYAM

[title] "Betrayal" [pers.] Poetry is a divine gift, for the writer as well as the reader. It can be nothing less when the writer is inspired to let words flow and the reader's soul dances to their rhythm. I use this gift to express myself, whether in joy, confusion, love, or sorrow. This gift is to be treasured, as are those who understand it.

DALANGIN, STAR

[a.] Colorado Springs, CO [title] "Reddest Blood" [pers.] "Reddest Blood" is obviously a suicidal poem. Yes, as a teenage girl I have thought of committing such a crime to myself several times. I was at the age of 14 when I wrote this (I'm 15 now), and at that time I let so many negative thoughts get the best of me. I see now that, even though life is hard sometimes, I can always think of the positive things to live for. I sincerely hope that whoever reads this poem will have a clearer view of the joy of living. Please don't take death as the last option.

DANIEL, LORENTHIA

[a.] Kansas City, MO [title] "Our Heritage" [pers.] All praise go to God Almighty. Without Him, this gift would not be a reality. I thank Him for the new life which He has given me, and the ability to lead others to find a new life in Christ Jesus. "Our Heritage" was inspired as I observed my origin of people and our lack of knowledge. I felt it was my duty to remind folks were they came from. 2 Peter 3:18: "But grow in grace, and in the knowledge of

our Lord and Saviour Jesus Christ. To Him be the glory, both now and forever." Amen.

DANIELS, PAUL

[title] "A Friend Like You" [pers.] This poem represents a special friendship that holds a large place in my heart, one so special and complex that this poem's contents don't even come close to describing it. Friendship means a lot to me, sometimes it's even the most important thing in my universe. Also, this poem is a way of saying "thank you" to Daphne, the most special friendship I have ever experienced. Between us exists a close connection of some kind, and nothing in this world can ever change that. Daphne has had quite an inspirational impact in my life. She has helped me to understand the values of friendship, also to understand the different kinds, and completeness of love. In honor of all that she's done for me, I would like her to know that even though she doesn't believe the word "perfect" exists, she's still the perfect friend, and I will always be there for her, no matter what the cost. She has always been there for me. For that, the world means everything to me. For that, she is the world.

DANSBY, JO

[title] "To My Husband" [pers.] This poem was written for my husband on our 20th anniversary. To me, poetry has become a way of expressing myself. The highs and lows of my life are reflected in my poetry. This poem reflects the gratifying and welcomed maturity that 20 years together has produced.

DARRISAW, GERRI

[a.] Fort Lauderdale, FL [title] "Branded" [pers.] I was born in the deep South and I did pick cotton for a living. I think every person God created is a poem to be reached down into and analyzed. I tried to represent what people are and, at times, what they are not. I hope my poem will shed light on the miscalculation of people of color.

DAVIS, DANNY

[a.] Harvest, IL [title] "Pillow Talk" [pers.] As a Christian and BMI songwriter, I believe that poetry or songwriting is a gift from Almighty God. I especially want female readers to know that I, an African American man, have feelings too, and writing poems and songs is a good way for me to express my innermost feelings. I write poems and songs because written words will not change when repeated. I believe we are here on Earth to serve God and to love one another, and writing a poem or a song is a beautiful way for me to express my love to God or someone special.

DAVIS, DEIDRE

[a.] Clinton Twp. MI [title] "She is Still a Slave" [pers.] I am an artist. In high school I was very surprised to learn that poetry, as well as art, provides an emotional outlet for me. "She is Still a Slave" is one of a series of poems which focuses upon domestic violence. It was written during a period in which I became poignantly aware of domestic violence against women in this nation and around the world.

DAVIS, JOHN

[a.] Ft. Stewart, GA [title] "Christmas Time" [pers.] To me, poetry is experiences that we have throughout our lives. I have been writing since the age of 12. I am proud to have this gift that God gave me and I will use it to my full advantage and always strive for excellence in my poetry. I would like to first thank God, second, my mother, Mrs. Jewel D. Davis, and my four siblings for their everlasting support. You all are truly an inspiration to me. I love you all.

DAVIS, LILLIAN

[title] "The Unemployed Dragon" [pers.] Other poems, stories, and sketches by this author include:

Dream Dragons, Book number one, Shake Dragon, Lonely Dragon, "Pat" Lacy Dragon, Mother Dragon, Book number two, Pasely Dragon, Multi-Colored Dragon, Nervous Dragon, Rattle Dragon, Book number three, Fire Dragon, Hair Dragon, Dirty Dragon, and Patchwork Dragon.

DAY, MIRIAM
[title] "Love Story Eight Thousand Miles Away" [pers.] I graduated from Liceo de Cagayan, Cagayan de Oro City Philippines with a Bachelor of Arts degree in English in 1973. That same year I was airborne to Connecticut with my soul mate and husband, George H. Day. This poem was originally written in December 1972 for my, then Connecticut Yankee, penpal. I was inspired to write this after I received his letter bemoaning the distance between us and yearning to be near, to touch, to hug, or share laughter together. Our "airborne love letter relationship" resulted into a lifelong commitment and three beautiful girls: April-Joy, Kara-Elena, and Gemma-Mae. Our family relocated to Oceanside, California from Waterbury, Connecticut in March 1979 to follow the sun. George is now retired, while I still work for the Superior Court as an Independent calendar clerk. My hobbies are reading, writing, fishing, and gardening. Lately, I have discovered the pc (personal computer) to be a good playmate too!

DAYE, SHANO
[title] "Rainy Night" [pers.] This poem reflects being free and happy to enjoy the peaceful sights, sounds and smells of falling rain. It was written on a rainy night at the request of my mother. I have been writing poetry since I was 12 years old; I am now 15. Writing is something I truly enjoy and hope to do professionally someday. My first love, however, is performing arts.

de la CRUZ, MAYURI
[title] "Tomorrow's Dream" [pers.] I have always found inspiration in life's situations. This poem was written for my best friend when she lost someone very special to her. I truly believe that one can only do two things with life's situations, and they are: solve it or forget it. My way of "forgetting" is writing it down. Hence, my mind is cleared to solve.

De TORRE, EDWARD
[a.] North Bergen, NJ [title] "Without" [pers.] With every word I write, and/or speak for that matter, reflects my philosophy on life. Every event, every person I meet adds to it, and will do so forevermore. If not for it all, negative and positive, there would be nothing.

De YOUNG, JOLENE
[title] "A Father's Love" [pers.] Performing was always a great source of joy to me. I was inspired by Shakespeare at the age of 11. I began writing at 15 to express my feelings. I was even more inspired after seeing a one woman play about Emily Dickinson. I have always felt bad for children of split parents. So many times, innocent children become victims of arguing parents. One such instance tore my heart up when the father of friend of my son and I was falsely accused of child abuse by his ex. "A Father's Love" is dedicated to Dan and Eric Brown.

DEAN, ANGELA
[a.] Obetz, OH [title] "Quality of Life" [pers.] This poem is dedicated and inspired by the values my father and mother taught me, and also to my husband, Bill, for reminding me of the "Quality of Life." I truly love them with all my heart. Every morning I tell myself that every day, every minute, every breath is a gift from God, and these things are truly what make the quality of our lives.

DEAN, JERROLD
[title] "Beer" [pers.] "Beer" was born in remembrance of my brother, Carlos Dean Jr. He was killed in an auto crash in 1974. He was my only brother. He also loved to drink beer, as I do. "Beer" is dedicated to my mom, Juanita, and my dad, Carlos Sr. I am a Vietnam veteran and am married to Angela with two children, Carly and Vanessa. I also have one granddaughter, Madison, and a sister, Judy. Here's a special toast to my drinking buddies, "The pond gang": Eddie, Bobby Gary, Ray, Jimmy, Glendale, Ralph, Rick, Jig eye, Doug, Joey, David, Roscoe, Rodney, Roy, Mike, Bill, etc.

DECK, SARAH
[title] "She" [pers.] This poem is how I feel about a terrible event in my life. The poem states how I felt at the time and has given me great insight into myself and many others. I hope when others read this they can relate to my pain in a terrible situation.

DeJARNETTE, AMANDA
[a.] Burliston, TN [title] "Gone" [pers.] I am 15 years old and have a love for writing. I feel that I can express my feelings and thoughts through my poetry. This specification poem is about my boyfriend, Jacob, who is a big inspiration in my poetry. I would like to say thank you to my family and especially Jacob for supporting me and giving me the courage to follow through with my dream. I love you all.

DEKAJLO, DIANA
[a.] East Meadow, NY [title] "Silence" [pers.] Being an only child, I experience silence often, so I thought it would be an interesting topic. I love to write all kinds of literature and am glad that I can share my gift with the rest of the world.

DELAMAR, JOHN
[title] "Your King Has Come" [pers.] Poetry is a precious treasure and very significant to me because it allows me to know my heart. It is also a release from a world that can often be stressful and burdensome. God has blessed me with this very special gift and I only hope to bless others with it. I want to thank Jason Davis, the man who encouraged to me to begin writing poetry, and my mother, Jeri, for never giving up on me.

DELIJA, IVICA
[title] "From Russia with Love" [pers.] The poem that I wrote was created using feelings hidden in my heart for a woman that had made a huge difference in my life. Poetry was never a really strong point in my life, so I guess it is a hidden talent. But I think that poetry is a great form of art to express feelings that are trapped inside themselves.

DELISLE, KERI
[title] "Reflections" [pers.] Initially, "Reflections" was a gift to my cousin and his wife-to-be, a compilation of what I have learned and found to be sound advice, since the birth of our daughter, Alivia Jane. I realize this poem has much greater meaning. Holding my daughter in my arms, I am moved that this is the first of many reflections in her life. Although she will not remember, I will forever hold the memory in my heart. I love you Alivia and I'll always be here for you.

DENIKEN, ABBY
[a.] Cherry Hill, NJ [title] "Homework" [pers.] I wrote this poem when I was ten years old. I love poetry and love reading poems. My favorite author is Shel Silverstein. I have all his books and have read them all. I will always love poems. Being selected to have my poem in this book has been a thrill to me. My family, friends, and teacher are very proud and happy for me.

DENMAN, DAVID
[a.] New Albany, IN [title] "Man in Red" [pers.] This poem just came to me and everything else clicked. His birthday is on Christmas, the man in red that comes once a year—maybe it's God's way of to help us remember His birth. I want to dedicate this to Sherri Whelan for all Christmases to come, and to God, for allowing me to believe in miracles.

DENNEY, PEGGY
[title] "Trust in God" [pers.] This poem was written as a result of a true life experience in my Christian walk with Jesus. I dedicate this poem to the Lord, as I know in my heart that He inspired it, that I could see truth in my relationship with Him, and hope that it would be a ministry to help others as well.

DENNIS, RUBY
[a.] Sherman Oaks, CA [title] "At Last It's Twilight"

DENSLEY, SIOBHAN
[title] "In the Heat of the Night" [pers.] I wrote this poem around mid 1999, a few months after my 15th birthday. Most of my poetry has some meaning, but it's not usually clear to me until well after it's written. When I'm writing, the words just happen! This poem was influenced by my breakup with my boyfriend not long beforehand.

DESLANDES, HEPTA
[title] "Home" [pers.] When I was 18 years old my family migrated from Jamaica to Canada. I've been to the U.S., Europe, and Africa. However, Canada remained my base. I've had to ponder the meaning of "home" many times. Still poignant in my mind are the cherished memories of each home. "Home" is a soul searching, spirit-filled and heart warming poem. I hope it will conjure images of home for the readers. I am a teacher of English and a homestay host for foreign students. In addition, I share my home with my son, Yannick, and my golden retriever, Visa.

DEW, ANGELA
[a.] Fayetteville, NC [title] "Have You Been Through the Process" [pers.] This poem has such a special meaning in my life because, as I continue to face certain obstacles from day to day, it stands as a constant reminder of just how wonderful the Lord is and how the Lord continually strengthens me with each passing day in the essence of adversity. My poem also serves as a memoir for those who have impacted my life in such an untouchable way. These wonderful people are my mom, dad, sister, bishop, and my best friend. All of these special people have been spiritual mentors and loving friends. Thank you and God bless.

Di SALVATORE, ALBERT
[a.] Philadelphia, PA [title] "Words" [pers.] I'm nineteen years old and I live in Philadelphia. All my life I lived in the same house, growing up in a black neighborhood. It was hard when I was younger, but looking back it was really great because I was able to grow up well-rounded and diversified. I have a long Italian family who has always been there for me. I was also raised a Christian, and some of my spiritual themes come through in my poetry. I wrote the poem "Words" when I was a freshman in college; it's all about how what people say define who you are, eventhough words are just words and you decide whether they have meaning or not. I want my poetry to reflect what I go through so that people can relate and not feel they are the only ones feeling these emotions. I hope as well, that people can see through my poetry that Christians are not self-righteous, but people that go through the same things that we all go through. It's all about being real.

DIMARTINO, PHILIP
[title] "The Bench" [pers.] I began writing poetry at the age of 40, inspired by a lost love regained after 20 years. It unlocked words that could not be spoken, only written. This poem tells the story of our secret meeting place. It also memorializes all lovers who have ever etched in

stone, bark, or bench slat their expression of love for each other.

DIMOPOULOS, PETER
[title] "Inspiration" [pers.] In life's highway we walk alone, sometimes above, at times below. Freedom and love create all, and inspiration turns us on, to smile and fly above and beyond. "Inspiration" was written at three a.m. with plant leaves on a beach wall of a hotel, during the below times of my life, like all of humans go through. I was inspired by a small white bird playing by itself with the waves. I hope all people find inspiration during the below times of their lives. As for the leaves, I forgot to bring my Montblanc.

DINGLE, MARY
[a.] Philadelphia, PA [title] "What You Mean to Me" [pers.] I'm a mom of two, Angela and Jason. I've been in management for 18 years. I love to express my feelings on paper. I live in Philadelphia. This poem was written for Melvin Richardson because he's just like my inspiration when I'm sad or happy, and as you read the poem it describes itself.

DIOGO, JENNIFER
[title] "Strawberry Blossoms" [pers.] I have always loved expressing myself through writing and discovered my talent for poetry when I was 13. My work is based on emotions, ranging from happiness to grief, betrayal to true love. At 17, I haven't experienced every situation my poetry describes, so when I'm inspired by others I try to put myself in their shoes and write about how I think people are feeling. Nothing brings me greater joy than hearing that my work has touched someone, bringing complete strangers together with a common bond.

DIRAZAR, AMALIA
[title] "The World" [pers.] I am ann Argentinean born American, married with one child. I have been in Africa and the Caribbean for many years. I am a teacher and interior decorator. I also have a Master's Degree in business administration. I like to travel, plays sports, and read. I believe God has inspired this poem. He can be a constant inspiration in our lives if we let Him come into our heart.

DOLAS, EVELYN
[title] "Eternity" [pers.] I would like to thank the International Library of Poetry, the Selection Committee and the Managing Editor, Howard Ely, for publishing my work. Moreover, I would like to acknowledge my induction into the International Society of Poets and for receiving two award-winning plaques. I also extend my best wishes to everyone that has viewed my work in this edition, along with my poetry in *Echoes of Yesteryear* and *America at the Millennium: The Best Poems and Poets of the 20th Century*.

DOLORES, MARY
[a.] Brooklyn, NY [title] "Remember"

DOMINY, MARIE
[title] "Summer" [pers.] Poetry is the outspoken soul of an individual bellowing from deep and conscious thought of how life is viewed from one person's eyes. If only I could be in his shoes for one moment, I may be in his mind. Words, rather harsh or sweet, can create a violent storm or a calm sea. Words of love can show moments of insanity or of happiness that can stretch far into infinity.

DONINI, LORENZO
[a.] Sherwood Park, AB [title] "Where the Shadows Play" [pers.] Recently I lost my mother to bone cancer, but previously she had asked me to write her a poem, knowing it was the best way I dealt with great loss, especially after the sudden death of my father about a year earlier. It is difficult to appreciate the present without ignoring the future, and difficult to prepare for the future without wasting the present moment. It is equally difficult to love and appreciate the caring people in your life enough, as their importance is perhaps only realized when they are gone. This poem is dedicated to my mother, Ingrid Donini, with undying love.

DORAN, PENNI
[title] "Brayden" [pers.] This poem was written for my beautiful grandson, Brayden, who was born with a vascular tumor of the liver and was taken from us at three days. This is dedicated to his loving parents, Greg and Dawn Jones, and his sister, Adrianna.

DORNAUS, TIMOTHY
[a.] San Gabriel, CA [title] "Walk with Me" [pers.] "The cards you are dealt in life are exposed through time; you can accept or refuse, but chance favors the prepared mind." Adversity affects us all in one form or another, but I believe it is how we deal that sets us apart. Poetry is my therapy for life. It helps me consolidate my feelings on a sheet of paper so I am able to see clearly, without the confusion of scattering thoughts. I feel that if poetry did not run through my veins, society would have sucked me dry a long time ago.

DOSS, PENNEY
[title] "You!" [pers.] This poem is very special to me. It was written about someone very special in my life, someone who had faith in me and my talents, someone who gives me the self esteem boost I need: my very best friend and my inspiration for a lot of my poetry, Kim Manuel. Thank you and I love you. I would also like to say thank you to my parents, Bobby and Gail Herrington, my grandmother, Dianna Herrington, and my brother, Bobby Joe Herrington. Without all of you I would have never been able to follow my dream. I love you all. I also want to say thank you and I love you to my family in Texarkana, Texas and to all my friends and family in my hometown of Knoxville, Tennessee. Being 21 years old and having a poem published is a dream come true. Thank you everyone at the International Library of Poetry.

DOUGLAS, C.
[title] "A Journey from Nowhere" [pers.] I've never had a positive or optimistic way of looking at life, but through writing poetry, I am able to express my feelings of joy or pain. This poem is for all men and women who look for joy/happiness in all the wrong places. It took for me to find myself to know that the journey was right in me—poetry.

DREWRY, KATHERINE
[title] "Quaint or Modern" [pers.] I'd like to dedicate my poem to my parents, James and Annie Drewry. The spiritual upbringing I received from them inspired and enabled me to write this poem at the early age of 16 in 1958. Their strong teaching regarding morals and scruples were very much a must during those years. I was fortunate to have been reared in that era.

DUFF, EUGENE
[title] "Death of a Pilot, at Night, over Vietnam" [pers.] I was born 1942 in Portland Maine and raised in Rhode Island. I attended Hillsdale College, in Hillsdale, MI, and the University of Rhode Island in Kingston, RI, where I received a B.A. in Psychology. At the University of Southern California I received my M.S. in Education. I served as an United States military officer, with 13 months in Vietnam, where wideout recorded actually occured in 1970. I retired from the Texas Dept. of Human Services in 1999 in San Antonio, Texas. I am a divorced father of three daughters; Desiree Marie, Dawn Michelle, and Hope Elaire. I have written poetry extensively, and tend to emphasize singular events with significance to all.

DUKES, JENNIFER
[title] "Visionary" [pers.] Poetry is the essence of my soul that communicates the true meditations of my heart.

DUNCAN, MARILYN
[title] "Love Me Not" [pers.] Writing is one of my passions. I feel all good poetry comes from deep within the heart. High and low points in my life seem to always show up in my poems. This poem I dedicate to my husband, Larry.

DUNKLEBERGER, MATT
[title] "Unrest" [pers.] This poem represents a lonely time in a person's life, when there's no understanding and no emotion but that of hurt and sadness of being alone. It is also about having no way to vent these emotions. Poetry is one of the ways I vent my emotions. I consider poetry to be a sort of therapy to get out feeling instead of keeping them inside. Poetry is a releasing of yourself in an artistic vision.

DUPREE, ELIZABETH
[title] "Hand in Hand" [pers.] I wrote this poem as extra credit for my English class. It has become so much more to me. It represents the core of many dreams and reveries, a true example of a fairy tale ending . . . and they lived happily ever after.

DWIGGINS, SHEILA
[title] "My Little Man" [pers.] First, I would like to say, "To God be the Glory," because nothing is possible without Him. This poem was written over 20 years ago and is my first poem. My son, Ray, was four years old at that time. Poetry has always been a hobby for me and a gift from God. I am extremely proud to have this opportunity to share my poems with everyone. A special thank you to my husband, Roy, and Roy Jr., our son. Thank you both for giving me the confidence, determination, and will to not give up. I appreciate your encouragement to follow my dreams. I love you.

DYCK, ANITA
[title] "Winds of Change" [pers.] I'm from Herbert, SK, Canada, and, for me, poetry isn't just a forum to convey my innermost thoughts and feelings, it's also an exercise in mental dexterity. To slave tirelessly on a single piece for just the right phrase or word, while keeping your original concept intact can be challenging. It's the successful combination of emotion and syntax I find most rewarding of all. So it was with "Winds of Change," my contribution to nature's echoes. And if that feeling of accomplishment wasn't enough, having it published in such a prestigious anthology is satisfaction indeed.

DYER, JENNIFER
[a.] Windham, ME [title] "The Golden Sea" [pers.] I have always loved writing poetry. I feel that I inherited this talent from my Nana. I love to give poetry as gifts. A gift from the heart means much more than a gift from the store. I live with my Nana, papa, great grandmother, and my little brother, Anthony. I am eleven years old and will attend Windham Middle School in the fall as a sixth grader. Besides writing poetry, my hobbies are listening to music, bike riding, talking, visiting with my friends, and debating with anyone who dares to debate with me. My papa says that I am the world's best debater. That's debatable!

EDMO, UMIOKALANI
[title] "Translation of Aloha No Aina" [pers.] Born in Los Angeles, California of European and Hawaiian parents, let's say I'm American all the way through! I live in a growing town, near Vancouver, Washington, on the Columbia River, nearby. My education is in commercial art school in San Francisco, California, at the Academy of Art. So I do landscape, oil painting, non fiction, and fictional short stories on Hawaii and Japan, San Francisco and the experiences I have in travelling to Japan, Hawaii, Europe, and Mexico. My hobbies are the garden, walking the Aussie shepherd, reading, and playing with my cats. Enjoying my adopted grandchildren, I try to be as positive as possible, and to forgive, laugh, and enjoy each day

a little or a lot. I also try to be thankful to the Heavenly Father for all that we can do and have! Breathe in the Earth, the air, the nature of things! Stop to take time for everyone! Love all the people around us! Love life!

EDWARDS, KYLIE
[title] "Mask" [pers.] I feel that poetry allows me to be myself in my own corner of the world. My poetry describes my life and the different paths, that for many reasons, have been a challenge. All of my challenges have been supported by my husband, Jason, my Aunt Karen, and my wonderful grandmother. They have all supported and inspired my poetry. By being able to express my love to them through my poetry, I feel it is my way of showing them that they are the true reason behind who I am today and all that I have accomplished in life.

EDWARDS, PATRICK
[title] "Last Call" [pers.] The process of attaining what it is that one desires is something that has always fascinated me. The increases in the physical, mental, and the emotional energies are part of the process, part of the struggle to achievement. This gives way to the solidification of a direction that in turn leads to an explosion, then calm. Then we begin anew. Inspirational souls: my mother, Christine; my father, Bobby; my brothers, Gary, Michael, Kenny, and Doug (one of my biggest supporters); my sister, Beverly (who helped Doug and I through many a Saturday); and my brother-in-law, Jerry.

EL, KWESI
[a.] Hattiesburg, MS [title] "Divine Blessings" [pers.] As a writer and Moorish scientist that is interested in the uplifting of fallen humanity, my intention was not to cause any confusion, but to try to enhance those who are of an open-mind to capture my expressions of the beauty of being in my writing. And as for those that are one-dimensional minded, I tried to enhance their thought ability to acknowledge the beauty of becoming. So, peace and love to all those who are becoming and who have became. Peace and positive energy activates constant elevation.

ELARIONOFF, LANCELOT, JR.
[a.] Norfolk, VA [title] "Glimmer of Dawn" [pers.] As an aspiring writer, I often use poetry as a means of finding my creative focus when hampered by writer's block. Every one of my poems is a snapshot of emotion, a glimpse into the journey I have undertaken as a writer. I do not believe in endless revisions, for I feel a poem loses strength when you begin to edit originality. Every writer, from struggling poet to established novelist, requires some source of inspiration. Mine are my father, the first to believe in my ability to write, and my wife, Brooke, who makes it so easy to dream.

ELDER, BRANDON
[title] "Nature in the Sky" [pers.] A poem is one of my many ways to express myself. A poem can truly reach other people and tell them things about you and about things you care about. It can also give a message to the reader. Poems play an important part in everyone's life. They are in songs, television, Internet, school, and many, many other events of everyday life. I try to think of poems in my life everywhere I go because of all the inspirational events I encounter. I would like to say that I hope poets will inspire more people.

ELIO, RALPH
[title] "Too Many Butterflies" [pers.] I write a poem down as I feel things or when someone does something good or unusual. I am a chef and have been for over 20 years. I see and hear life and write it down in a poem.

ELLISON, SYRETHIA
[a.] Parma, OH [title] "The Gift" [pers.] I was inspired to write "The Gift" by my son, Brian. He wrote and directed a Christmas play for our church in 1999. I want to dedicate my poem to my husband, Clark, and our three blessings from God, Brian, Lisa, and Joshua. Thank you for the privilege to share a part of my heart with everyone who reads my poem. May the true meaning of Christmas take root in their hearts. I thank God for the talent He has given me and look forward to the opportunities to continue to use it.

ELTERMAN, MICHAEL
[a.] Redding, CA [title] "Plastic People" [pers.] In 1977 I was exiting a therapy group where I had been working out my trauma about Vietnam. I was feeling good about myself again and feeling again for the first time in almost ten years. As I was leaving, I listened to a lady in the group who had a sister in the back wards of some state mental hospital. This lady was in deep pain and said to me, "I wish I were plastic so nothing mattered." I wrote this poem in celebration of my healing and in hopes the message would help her along the way.

EMMONS, ELAINE
[a.] Lynn, MA [title] "As I Be" [pers.] I was writing during my struggles to get sober and clean, to accept myself as God made me, and also to believe others could accept me the way God made me. It was worth the journey. I am also a veteran, who served three years in the U.S. Navy (1963-66). I have since returned to my home town of Lynn, Massachusetts, where I am currently employed as matron at the Lynn Police Station and also employed at the Salem Mission, a shelter for homeless men and women in Salem, Massachusetts.

ENGELHARDT, ELIZABETH
[title] "Every Other Night" [pers.] I am a 16-year-old girl, who was diagnosed with Multiple Sclerosis (MS) in November 1999. I will be entering my senior year of high school in September 2000. My poem is how I feel deep down inside, in that corner of my self no one sees. It represents the feelings I face when I stop and I really think about my life. This is for every person who has ever been scared to face reality in the mirror.

ENOCHS, TINA
[a.] Dyersburg, TN [title] "The Ocean" [pers.] I am 16 years old, a sophomore in high school, and live in Dyersburg, Tennessee. I was inspired to write this poem as a school assignment, although I have never been able to see the ocean. I imagined the different things I might see and gave vivid descriptions of each.

EPCHOOK, BRIAN
[a.] New Stuyahok, AK [title] "Love" [pers.] I started writing poetry to express my feelings to my family, the one I love, and friends. To me, poetry is a gift, one talent I will treasure. I'm glad I'm blessed with this talent. It helps me express my feeling's to the one I love very much.

EPPS, THOMAS
[title] "Angel Kiss" [pers.] I write what is in my heart and mind, of broken love, a child's cry, about a news report, or a beautiful sunset. And I have to thank my parents, for giving me a sense of wonder and beauty, as well as my English teachers for encouragement and good criticism.

ERIZ, SAMUEL
[a.] Goleta, CA [title] "When I Dream" [pers.] Sam Eriz is an artist of words, who has found that as the eyes are the windows to the soul, art, in its various forms, expresses its essence. He has discovered his light of God and enjoys reflecting it in verse. He is convinced that, through dreams, we are able to see one's own God, who lives both within and beyond ourselves.

ESCOBAR, WILFREDO
[title] "Wishing . . ." [pers.] Poetry, like few others, has the ability to effectively communicate the thoughts and emotions of its creator. In a poem, ideas are conveyed both through what is said among the lines, and that which remains unsaid between. The poem "Wishing . . ." was my attempt to express what I had been thinking and feeling, but had never been able to in any other way. It truly means much to me, for not only was it written to someone I deeply cared about, but also because, it's the poem that reignited my interest in writing. May those who read it enjoy.

ESTABROOKS, SABRA
[title] "In the Winter" [pers.] I wrote this poem in grade three and then rewrote it this year. My grade six teacher was very encouraging and helpful. I will always remember her. My family has been a great help also. I am overjoyed to have this poem published.

ESTILL, CINDY
[a.] Lima, OH [title] "Life Is a Continuous Struggle" [pers.] In life, we try to correct our mistakes and sometimes, no matter what we do, it doesn't work out. This poem is about the past and then the future. Even in the bleakest moments in one's life there is always a light, someone or something that will make all your efforts worthwhile. The people I love inspire me, as do nature and life itself. Poetry is from the heart!

EVANS, IRENE
[a.] Somerset, NJ [title] "The Blessing" [pers.] I was born July 6, 1909 in New Brunswick, New Jersey. I owned The Dress Bar, instructed long distance operators, for ten years was part owner and general manager of the Offsett Printing Co., and have spent the last 20 years in retirement. I wrote "The One Hundred Year History" of her family, the grandmother of three. "The Blessing" was composed for my granddaughter Diane's marriage to Pascal-Pinoie of France.

EVANS, RICHARD
[title] "Happy" [pers.] The poem recalls memories of carefree holidays spent in the south of England, when days were endless and sunny, and everything around me was so secure. I have written poetry, either as poems or as lyrics for music, and it plays an important part in my life. My parents and younger brother live in Norfolk, England. After a year studying at the University of California in San Diego, I shall return to Birmingham University in England to complete my studies. I play the guitar and enjoy blues music and sports.

EVANS, VIRGINIA
[title] "Call of the Wild" [pers.] I reap the harvest of intrinsic wealth by giving gifts of framed poetry to people for their comfort and joy. In so doing, I am also giving them a part of myself. The poem "Call of the Wild" is my perception of a free-spirited young man, Phil Spano, Jr., whose life is drawn to the call of the great outdoors.

EVANS, WILLIAM
[title] "This Much I Know" [pers.] This poem was inspired by a young lady named Brigitte G. It was written to let her and the world know that my feelings will remain forever unchanged.

EVANUIK, S.
[title] "The Rescuer" [pers.] Whenever I see colorful autumn leaves, I remember a day, when I was a child, rescuing the leaves. One beautiful leaf seemed almost alive as it caught on pebbles and twigs in its struggle to prevent being swept along by the rushing water. I had been reading about leprechauns and fairies and I imagined the leaf was a fairy in a colorful gown, who had been transformed by a wicked witch into a leaf and sent adrift on the water. I was absorbed with "Rescuing" the leaves, until the ringing school bell brought me back to reality.

EWANIUK, DEBORA
[title] "The Angel" [pers.] The appearance of the little old man I wrote about really happened. I hope this poem helps anyone and everyone who may need a word of kindness, realize that someone, be it a friend or stranger, does care.

FALESHOCK, ANDREA
[title] "Strings" [pers.] I am a native of Pennsylvania and am the daughter of Andrew Faleshock and Theresa Padora-Faleshock. My poem, "Strings," is a time capsule of the life and times of my wonderful mother, who I love dearly. This poem is very special to me, as it is my first venture into the art of poetry and also because my family, especially my mother, can share this unique and quite unexpected experience.

FARAR, CAROL
[a.] Cedar Rapids, Iowa [title] "The Love in My Heart" [pers.] Having a serious illness has made me slow down and appreciate the time we are given. This poem is dedicated to my husband, Larry, who reminds me daily he loves and encourages me. It is also for my sons, Kreg, Toby, Johnny, and Jeremy, but especially my daughter, Jennifer, who has such talent—I hope you learn the art of forgiveness and love. As well as to all my friends and family—I want to say, "Thank you and I love you all."

FEEGER, VIVIEN
[title] "Self-Inflicted Injuries" [pers.] Poetry is the voice of the void, that third reality forever outside subjective and objective, where words refract colors that only the soul knows exist. When grief's echo bled "Self-Inflicted Injuries," I was unaware that I am schizophrenic; I was merely "Alone-in-the-Void," marriage failed, sons alienated, judged guilty by all and sundry for a love that remains beyond rationality, above morality, transcending marriage. Alone, because my beautiful Sun Lion Man remains a rational man, moral and married. Alone, because I could not bear the pain in his eyes when he said, "I can't". . . so neither could I.

FEENEY, JOHN
[title] "Beyond" [pers.] Each poet has to reach so far within to express that which haunts the human soul. To share the inexpressible—this is how I reach out to life.

FEHL, SHAWN
[title] "Wandering" [pers.] Most of my writings stem from deep thoughts. I was feeling hopeful about a newfound love between a woman, who was my best friend, and I, but when the feelings weren't returned I began to write down what I was thinking to help sort out the confusion I was feeling. While writing it down, I started to daydream of the things we did together, and this poem emerged from that. That is how a true poem should be written . . . not through conscious thought, but though a natural flow of the deepest feelings and experiences.

FEILER, PEG
[a.] Holly, MI [title] "Rippling River" [pers.] We are given a talent, a special gift from God, and I have been blessed to be able to express myself in writing. Most of what I write is about nature and the peacefulness we can feel if we take time out of our busy lives to experience it. I have written since I was young and am in awe every time something new starts forming. Many times the words come so quickly I can hardly get them down. I am a wife, mom of six, and grandma of twelve, with another little blessing joining us around Thanksgiving. Feel life around you.

FERGESON, KYRA
[a.] Grand Junction, CO [title] "Soul Death" [pers.] This poem is very much a part of my soul. I am dedicating it to the one I love for the one I'd lost long ago. "Soul Death" was written when I had blindly let go of the most precious gift of true beauty I have ever known. Since then, a part of me has died, leaving me forever changed. From this heartbreak I wrote this ode, for the pleasures and for the pain, the tears and all our memories . . . Thank you for being a part of my life. I'll never forget you. This one's for you, Chris.

FERGUSON, SALLY
[title] "My Mother Died" [pers.] I sit down and listen, and my hand begins to move. When I am finished, I look back and part of me is in black and white. Writing has always been a part of my thought process, a reflection of who I am. I have just recently found the idea of sharing my thoughts with other people exciting, and hope that somewhere, someone, will be touched by what I have written. I also express myself through photography, sculpting, and painting.

FERNANDEZ, WILBERTO
[a.] Brooklyn, NY [title] "Declaration of Love" [pers.] Through my poems I express beauty; it is the feel of my self. When I write poetry, it's impossible hell, as poetry of myself is in the library of poetry.

FERREIRA, MARY
[title] "Love of God" [pers.] This poem relates me to my beautiful sister, Lorraine, who passed away at age 56. Every word in this poem is Lorraine. I was born in Fall River, Massachusetts, and attended Durfee High School. I worked as a switchboard operator at a curtain factory. My hobbies are sewing and art, and I trust in God.

FERRER, CRISTINA
[a.] Naples, FL [title] "Motto" [pers.] At 26 years old, I cannot recall the exact place or time in which I began to write poetry. However, I can tell you that it has always been a part of my soul. Poetry is like the air I breathe, a necessary component for my existence. Poetry has helped me pay reverence to humanity, to develop a sort of insight into the essence of our lives. The poet is the voice of his time and if you read closely and wholeheartedly, you might learn something about yourself and, moreover, about the world we all inhabit.

FINLAYSON, KAILA
[title] "Beauty" [pers.] "Beauty" is my first published work. At age 12, I am honored at the chance to share my thoughts with the world. I hope that my poem will move people to pause and see the wonder and beauty surrounding them.

FITZGERALD, INA
[title] "On My Husband's Death" [pers.] I grew up in Indianapolis, where my parents had greenhouses and a flower shop. After graduating from Butter University as a botany major, I went to the University of Iowa graduate school for my MSC. There I met Lawrence, a zoologist, who accepted a job in Memphis teaching anatomy. This is the first poem that I have submitted anywhere. It speaks for itself.

FITZGERALD, KRISTY
[a.] Mesquite, TX [title] "I Am" [pers.] I am 13 years old and I've been writing since I was ten. I love to write poems. I believe it's a gift from God and I love Him for that. I also love my mom, Brenda, and my brother, Don, for always loving and supporting me. Writing poems makes me feel good. Sometimes it may be hard to think of the right words to say, but it's totally worth it in the end.

FLAVE, RECHELLE
[a.] Cleveland, OH [title] "Inside the Sea of Me" [pers.] "Inside the Sea of Me" is a rhythmical expression that captures the woes in all of us. Since I was a child, I have always expressed my life through poetic form. It became a natural way to document my life. I am very excited to share this poem with all of you and I hope it brings you closer to understanding the sea inside of you. Thank you, Samantha, Aaron, my mother, Sheila, and Michael for helping to create a life worth writing down.

FLYNN, DONNA
[title] "Horse" [pers.] My poem, "Horse," is about the horse I owned. I like horses and riding them. Poetry brings words to life. I have a husband named Roger Flynn, and a son, Cody Flynn. We live in Rock Springs, Wyoming. My hobbies are cooking and outdoor activities. I am interested in writing and photography as well. I would like to work for an outdoor or wildlife magazine sometime. I am very excited to be included in this beautiful book. It was great to get my work recognized. Thank you for publishing my poem.

FONG, MELISSA
[title] "For an Instant" [pers.] This poem is something that I am extremely proud of. I wrote "For an Instant" to express my longing to be with my brother, Michael, when he went to boot camp to become a United States Marine. When he left, I did not know what to feel or how to act. Hence the part, "I fight the tears back with an empty smile." I tried to hide my emotions. I am only 12 years old and it means so much to me that my poem is being recognized. In addition, it is an honor to have my poem included in this wonderful collection of verse.

FORD, KELLY
[title] "Civil Star" [pers.] Whether wars be fought in our own backyards or thousands of miles away, this poem is dedicated to all who fell in its wake. Their blood cries up from the ground for mercy and recognition. My many years in God's word, experiences in teaching, and an astronomical physics class led me to write my first book, *Ancient Signs of Deception*, dispelling several errors in our calendar. I graduated with a B.S. in education at SWTSU in San Marcos, Texas in 1988. My wife, Charlene, and I are celebrating almost 30 years of married bliss in Dallas.

FORDYCE, STEVEN
[title] "The Bond of Our Love" [pers.] This poem is very special to me, as it celebrates the love that I have for my wife. This is one of the very first poems that I wrote for her before we were married and it is still the only one that truly expresses how I feel about her. I am dedicating this poem to my one True Love, my wife, Tracy Fordyce. I love you, Tweety!

FORSTER, HILARY
[title] "Scripted" [pers.] Sometimes emotions are elusive. They can consume our souls, and yet our minds can't quite classify them. This becomes the ignition for my poetry. I seek to externally define what I cannot internally decipher. I let the words and rhythm pantomime my singular vision of experiences and their personal effects. "Scripted" reflects a period of my life when poetry evolved into such an outlet. The poem provided a tangible documentation of present feelings, serving as a springboard into deeper exploration of myself. It proved a faithful companion through that trying life phase. I am confident poetry will continue to lend such kinship now and into the future.

FORSTER, JILLIAN
[title] "Before I Rise I Must Fall" [pers.] I have been able to write since I was a little girl. It was, and has always been a way I can express myself, especially in situations when I was not able to tell people how I felt. So I would write a poem. In life, we fall a lot in many ways, whether it's physically, mentally, or in our spirit. "Before I Rise I Must Fall" was written for us to realize there is a rise after a fall; sometimes we need to look for it. Even the sun has to fall at night before it rises in the morning for a new day. This

poem also represents new beginnings, the same as when the sun rises and we begin a new day.

FOSTER, LORI
[title] "Roger" [pers.] In memory of my big brother who left his family on August 12, 1997, at only 30 years old. But most of all, this is for Adrian and Cora, to maybe help them understand. And for all who think life's come to an end—lots of people have it worse; you just need a friend.

FOUTCH, DORIS
[title] "Children" [pers.] I live in the small town of Campbellsburg, Indiana. I am the mother of one daughter and two sons. Writing poetry is my way of relating my feelings. This poem, in particular, is how I feel about children. I own and operate a day care out of my home. In what little free time I have, I like to read, listen to music, watch movies, crochet, and just be with my family. I come from a very loving family, who are important to me. I live a simple, yet fulfilling life and would not have it any other way.

FOWLER, REBECCA
[title] "Two Percent of the General Population" [pers.] Poetry is an expression of the soul. It's, in a way, like painting a portrait, but with the construction of a thousand words. To me, it's a way of releasing that perpetual sting I hold so deep inside.

FRALEY, TONY
[title] "Something's Missing" [pers.] This poem was written after one of my best friends told me how much I had changed in about four months. He told me that my soul lost something that once made me a person others enjoyed to be around. I have about 400 other original poems expressing my views on life, death, love, happiness, and the world. One day I'd like to have an entire book of my poetry published, but I have other dreams to pursue first. Beside that, I have to find what is missing from my soul.

FRANCIS, CHERIE
[a.] Barefoot Bay, FL [title] "Reverie" [pers.] We have the unique opportunity to publicly share our innermost thoughts and feelings through language, through pictures created by words. Poetry is my personal window, the access to life's joy and life's pain. To see and feel my poetry is to know me.

FRANCISCO, MONIQUE
[title] "The Vigil" [pers.] When people read my writings, they say it's mysterious and morbid. "The Vigil" is just one of my poems about death. I like writing about the mysterious, the unknown, and subjects that most people fear, like death. Death is a fascinating phenomenon that happens every day, yet when it does, it catches us by surprise. On the other hand, I Love Life! I am a cheerful, happy, positive person. My friends are the jolly, noisy type, typical of 15 year olds. Writing is a passion that makes me express my inner thoughts when I want to get a break from it all!

FRAZIER, SHIRLEY
[title] "The Wall" [pers.] I have always loved poetry. "The Wall" is a combination of memories that are precious to me. I hope it will be a blessing to my five children and their children, and to anyone who reads my poem.

FREDETTE, DIANE
[title] "Joys of Spring" [pers.] I was born and raised on the Canadian prairies and developed an appreciation for nature. I have written several song lyrics, but decided to try poetry. My poems come from my heart and are usually about my life experiences and nature.

FREEMAN, ROBBIE
[title] "Funny It Seems" [pers.] Poetry is a way of expressing myself. I started writing when in high school and have continued through college, marriage, having children, and now grandchildren. My cousin told me that she likes to read my poems "because they have bite to them; they go beneath the surface and touch feelings we often keep hidden and protected." I like that appraisal of them and hope others get something from them too. "Funny It Seems" and "The Question" are examples of the "bite" found in my poems.

FREY, JANET
[title] "Kitchen Memories" [pers.] This poem was written for my mother, Daisy Pevoto, who will always be remembered for the love she expressed to her family through her cooking. She grew up during the Depression and being in a large family of eleven gave her plenty of opportunity to be in the kitchen, as she was the bread maker for the family. As a child, I loved to watch my mother rolling out biscuit dough, her floured hands deftly cutting the dough with a tuna fish can. To this day, when I visit my mother I anticipate the aroma from her kitchen as I enter her house. If I am quiet as I enter, I may catch her singing. I am grateful to my mother for learning the pleasure of simple things.

FULLER, LEANDRA
[a.] Washougal, WA [title] "Sand Castle" [pers.] Leandra Dawn Fuller, 16, lives in Washougal, Washington, where she attends a college preparatory high school. She spends her leisure time successfully competing on horseback and writing. "Sand Castle" is one of a book of poems she is writing in the memory of her late uncle, Clint Daly-Walker. As the collection nears completion, she will be seeking a publisher.

FULLER, VICKY
[a.] Holland, MI [title] "Life Isn't Easy" [pers.] I have enjoyed poetry all my life. I started writing poems at a very young age. I believe that poetry is one of the best ways to release your innermost thoughts about life's situations. I would like to thank my family for their support and encouragement throughout life, especially my husband and children, who encouraged me to enter "Life isn't Easy" into the contest that placed it into this book. My parents' names are Harold and Viola Downing, and my husband's name is John Fuller. My children are: Veda, John, Angela, Kelly, and Bridgette. My grandchildren are: Vendela, Alicia, Stephanie, Zachariah, siblings, Sheila, Rodney, Alta, Dale, Dennis, Shelley, and many foster brothers and sisters.

FURMAGE, EDYTHE
[title] "Trapped Emotions" [pers.] I use writing as an outlet for my feelings and emotions. Feelings can sometimes get trapped because people feel alone. They feel like no one cares and that no one wants to listen to their problems. That is what this poem is about. I wrote this so that people don't get discouraged and think that they are the only one to feel this way. Hopefully, one day everybody will have a friend, no matter what race or gender.

GAL, VANESSA
[title] "Can You Hear the Footsteps" [pers.] There exists neither adequate nor enough words to illustrate the impact of poetry within my life; it has taken on a life of it's own that transcends all boundaries of experience. It began as a simple tool that assigned my understanding of an ever-elusive world. It is, at present, a cherished gift that, occasionally, I can offer humbly to those willing to listen. And I hope it will be, in the future, something that I can incessantly improve upon. Sometimes a few words can make a world of difference. If I could offer my advice to those about to write poetry: Be wild! Be calm! Go far! I know no limits! The world needs you to alter its perspective.

GALINDO, OTILIA
[a.] Los Angeles, CA [title] "Alive and Died" [pers.] My poetry is very special to me. It reminds me of someone who was very important in my life, Ms. Allen, my sixth grade teacher. She always believed that I could do anything I put my mind to. She taught me that there was no end to what I could do. She taught me that poetry was a journal of a person's life, a journal for everyone to enjoy, but without them knowing that it's my journal. The poem "Alive and Died" is a part of me. It speaks of a question that I tend to ask myself every time I am lost or just confused.

GALIZIA, RHONDA
[title] "Wish You Well" [pers.] As the Lord's Scribe (MT.13:52) and founder of "He Writes the Words on My Heart," I use my anointing to reach and uplift the hurt and hurting, so I may teach them to see through the eyes of God. One of life's most vital lessons is the awareness of harvesting from one's own seed. Planting is essential, balance, the crucial key to unlocking wellsprings of "living-water," which will "irrigate" every corner of one's existence. One must choose to labor, providing abundant deposits before making desired withdrawals. Jesus stretched out both arms before He died. Choose balance.

GANGULY, NIRMALYA
[title] "A Plea to the Ignorant Multitude" [pers.] Truly, poetry is the most artistic way of expressing one's innermost thoughts. Being a tenth standard student, I do have a lot to learn and experience yet, but it is never too early to make a beginning. We have but one life, which is meant to be utilized beneficially. It is too precious a gift to let wither away. Material possessions only bring transitory happiness, which is fleeting. Inner happiness comes from devotion; a feeling of complete mental satisfaction, in my opinion, beats ephemeral joy hands down. Therefore, while it is fine to dream of wealth and fame, let us not become slaves to our desires.

GARCIA, LARA MIA VERONICA
[title] "Dry My Tears" [pers.] I have been writing my deepest emotions since I was a little girl. This poem was written during one of my emotional loves. Problem after problem, death after death, yet I still believe there is hope.

GARCIA, MICHELLE
[title] "Reflections" [pers.] This poem is about women and the many hats we wear. Poetry is one way to express our complexity and inner beauty. I also use my poetry to express joy, sadness, anger, and beauty. Poetry is a gift that can be shared with everyone.

GARDINER, TERENCE
[title] "My Secret Love" [pers.] I am a retired army officer living in Hobart Tasmania, a state of Australia. I had never written poetry 'til this poem taught at school. We had poetry lessons and I like reading bush ballads by Australian authors. To me, poetry is nice to read, especially action poems. The story behind this poem: I lost a girl I had known since birth and whom I adored with all my heart and soul. When I was told I could no longer see her, I cried for days. Then one night, I found Poetry.com on the Internet and entered the poem for fun. I have several others in the same vein, all about Samantha. Someday she will read the book—I hope.

GARDNER, KATHERINE
[a.] Houston, TX [title] "Equus Rex" [pers.] This poem was inspired by a very rare and special breed of horse, the Spanish Barb. More specifically, I wrote this for a stallion of trust, breed named Castillo, whose strength and beauty captured my heart.

GARNO, AMY
[title] "Have You Ever?" [pers.] I feel that poetry is the best way to express how I feel inside. I hope that readers will be able to ask themselves these

questions and maybe relate to them as I do. Poetry is like a part of me, and without it I have no true way to show how I feel inside. Hopefully, after reading my poem, others can open up and let poetry be a part of them as well.

GEARY, JEANETTE
[title] "For a Day Shall Not Pass" [pers.] This poem is my husband's and my wedding poem. We really do not let a day pass without saying, "I love you." I wrote this poem at three a.m., before we were married in 1994. This was a special way that our wedding could really live each day and not be just a faded memory. My husband and I are still very much in love because of our foundation of friendship, but mainly because of the true blessing of the Lord.

GEDDES, CHARLES
[a.] West Hollywood, CA [title] "How Wonderful It Might Be" [pers.] I am a pastor of a teaching (Religious Science) that seeks to build bridges of understanding, instead of walls of separation. If we are one humanity in God, then it's time we live as such, appreciating the uniqueness of each soul and the unity we share in spirit.

GEETING, CAROLYN
[title] "One Lovely Rose" [pers.] This poem was inspired by my granddaughter, Ashley, whom I lost to adoption when she was two years old, and by my friend's grand-daughter who was brutally murdered after being raped by her baby-sitter. She was four years old. This poem was written in memory of them and extends to everyone who has lost someone they dearly loved.

GEORGE, VICKI
[a.] Newport, AR [title] "The Frame" [pers.] I am 47 and live in Newport, Arkansas. I have been married to Jimmy D. George for 25 years and am a mother to 23-year-old twins, a son, Sean George and a daughter, Shelley George. One of the greatest joys in my present life is my granddaughter, Skyla, who is 18 months old. I have been writing and creating poems and song lyrics since childhood, with music and song-writing being my main passion. Thousands of lines that I've written over the years have been inspired by my own personal experiences with love, joy, heartache, pain, sadness, and the basic human emotions that come with daily life and living and loving. I hope to continue writing for the remainder of my lifetime, with the knowledge that my writing touches a part of my being that no other thing in life can.

GERKE, MELISSA
[title] "Saying Goodbye" [pers.] This poem was very special. It was for my grandmother, referred to as "Mommom." She had passed away and my family, knowing I wrote poetry, asked if I would put something together for her funeral to be read to everyone. I felt it could have said more, yet everyone said it was great. Upon hearing of Poetry.com, my mother sent the poem in for me, and, to my surprise, it is even further appreciated. Thank you. I've been writing for 20 years and never published anything or yet tried. Needless to say, I am extremely thrilled and grateful.

GETTS, MARIE
[title] "A Poem for My Husband" [pers.] When I met my husband, we were parents of two sons each. I was divorced and he was widowed. We were lonely. We met and spent the next three weeks talking. But more than that, we communicated so well that we fell in love. The first time we kissed I felt so alive, and I knew we were meant to be together. We were married, had another son (to make five), and had 31 memorable years together. I have missed him since he passed away, but I feel he is near me still.

GIANNI, SAL
[title] "Pure Love" [pers.] I wrote this to my wife, Denise, for our 18th wedding anniversary! Flowers don't last forever and knick-knacks collect dust! I didn't know what to give her, so I wrote this poem in my truck, while at work. When I gave this poem to her she cried! I knew it was right! I am a father of two children, a nine-year-old son and a three-year-old daughter. They are life! To my wife, Denise, and Sal and Rebecca: life is short, fulfill your dreams! Love, husband and father, Sal Gianni.

GIBSON, KATIE
[a.] Sydney, Australia [title] "Fairy Tales" [pers.] My grandfather passed his love of poetry and reading on to me at an early age. I was encourage by both him, Nanna, and my parents to express my feelings through poetry. This has not only aided my creativity, but also helps me to sort through my feelings and put them into perspective. To Nanna and pop (Joyce and Dave Gibson)—I hope you're resting in peace. Mum and Dad (Carolyn and Peter Gibson), hopefully all the bad times are behind us. Andy, where's the Dragon Army? My fiance, John Siapis—we've had our ups and downs over the years, but we always pull through; you truly are my soul mate. Thank you all for your ongoing encouragement, enthusiasm and love. Love to you all always.

GIBSON, SCOTT
[title] "My Wife's Balance" [pers.] I have a wonderful wife. At the time of publication we have four beautiful sons, ages one to seven. We live in Boise, Idaho, where I work as a life insurance salesman. I have always enjoyed poetry. Many poets have helped me to laugh and cry, as they expressed themselves. I have only recently allowed myself to express what I feel through this medium. I hope to be able to do so for a long time to come. My heartfelt thanks to those at the International Library of Poetry. Keep spreading the fun!

GIFFORD, CHUCK
[title] "Glee" [pers.] When I write these things I'm not sure what they mean. An urge comes over me I write, don't care about anything around me, I just write. It's only when I go back and read them, I have to admit, I'm amazed. I hope that people enjoy reading "Glee" and find a meaning for their selves. That's what I try to do. Reminds me of a line from a song I like by Roxette, "listen to your heart and there are voices that want to be heard so much to mention, but you can't find the words."

GIFFORD, MARTHA
[a.] Hendersonville, NC [title] "Heartwoe" [pers.] Poetry is not just words, it is therapy for the soul, a friend when there is no other, a guide when life passes us by. This poem is dedicated to Diana, Robbie, Brandi, Chelsea, and Dakota, with love special thoughts of Ricky, Donna, Debbie, Justin, Russell, Emily and Kayla. Thank you for your love and support.

GILBERT, DOROTHY
[title] "Skyward" [pers.] When my son was 18 months old, he became enamored with the sky and planes. He said he would fly, and never wavered from his fascination of planes. He is now a captain for a large airline, and still, after 40 years, is ongoing with his love of the sky. Sometimes I feel he is the third person who stood beside Orville and Wilbur!

GILL, JENNIFER
[title] "I Wish I Could" [pers.] Well, I wrote the poem quite a few years ago, when my "first love" broke-up with me. I guess one good thing came out of my broken heart. Writing stories and poems is how I express myself. I can really write what I'm feeling without making anyone mad or upset. I feel really at home with a pen in my hand. I am the middle child of a family of five: my dad, Donald Earlenbaugh, and my mom, Kay Earlenbaugh, my sister Kay Hughes, and my brother, Don Earlenbaugh. My husband is Dale Gill, and my son is Steven Gill. I am a college graduate. I am a licensed practical nurse at Woodlawn Nursing Home in Mansfield, Ohio. I love writing, and, hopefully, in the future I will be able to publish more of my poetry or some of my stories. I am an avid Pittsburgh Steeler fan, and, yes, I am a 38-years-old woman with a huge crush on Donny Osmond! I also love to sing and act. My philosophy in life is: "Life is just what you make it. You have control of your own destiny." Thank you!

GILLILAND, BETSY
[title] "The Clone and I" [pers.] In order for me to write poetry, a significant event or emotional moment must occur. I like to share and write poetry with my fifth grade students, and for many of them poetry becomes a vehicle to express what is in their hearts, or to show what they have learned. I believe that writing poetry requires one to convey a message in as few words as possible. I tell everyone that if you write freely, choose powerful words, and speak from your heart, thenyour poetry will reach out to others.

GIOFFRI, MARIA
[title] "When You Take My Hand" [pers.] I have been writing poetry since I was a little girl looking out the window at the rain, fascinated by sun-showers and butterflies and the world around me in general. As a woman I feel things deeply. My poetry reflects my thoughts and emotions, tied into whatever life-experiences I am having at the time. "When You Take My Hand" is a poem I wrote after being separated from someone I love very much. He, in fact, wrote to me once about finding something that inspired me, and poetry does, words do. I only wish he was here.

GIOLA, FRANCESCA
[title] "Waiting for You" [pers.] I've always enjoyed writing poems. Somehow, it was my way of escaping from everything, forgetting about troubles, and mostly expressing myself. This poem, "Waiting For You," is about a guy that I truly loved. But as we know, life doesn't go quite the way we would like it to go. I hope it will be a good source of inspiration for a lot of people. I live in Haiti in a town named CAP-Haitien, a really beautiful and peaceful town. I'm in 12th grade at Externat St. Francois Xavier. I like to write, read, have fun, go out shopping, the beach, music, friends, and a lot more. This poem is dedicated to all my loved ones.

GIPSON, KEVIN
[title] "No Man Has Hurt Me" [pers.] I was born in Los Angeles, Califronia on February 27, 1962. I am an artist, poet, and writer who believes that art is an expression of the mind. Poetry is a wonderful, sometimes fleeting gift that opens the soul and uncovers our deepest feelings. It is my sincere hope that I can share my experiences in life with others through my artistry and honesty.

GIUMALE, MARIELLA
[a.] United Arab Emirates [title] "Roses For You!" [pers.] I am truly a citizen of the world. I lived in different countries, and in the last 20 years, I worked and lived in Dubai, U.A.E. I have no family left except for my beloved daughter, Maria, who studies in NYC Cinematography. The only way I could express my innermost feelings in this part of the world was through writing. So I started! These verses are the story of my life! I "lived" this poem! "He" did not pick up the roses and I left them around the world . . . for you . . . the reader . . . to pick them up!

GIVIDEN, SANDY
[title] "Soul Mates" [pers.] A few people you know in life affect you deeply. Some affect you mildly, and still many do not affect you at all. The man I knew in this poem gave me far more than anyone I have known. He was able to touch my soul with

his love, yet our love was pure and untouched, so too, he was a great friend. As with most poetry, this too is very personal. I dedicate this poem to Art, my friend, my love.

GLASGOW, PATTI
[a.] Ft. Walton Beach., FL [title] "Oh, Sweetpea!" [pers.] This poem is about my darling, white toy poodle named Sweetpea. He got Pet of the Week in our local paper! I saved him from the pound! He was an abused dog, the vet said. He is gentle. My husband, Bill, named him, and I am going to put his poem to music. He is a gentle poodle and sleeps with me on the couch or underneath the bed. I already have a CD out,"The Keys to Key West." He has traveled to the Keys with my husband, Bill, and me in our camper. He is a joy! We love him so! Oh, Sweetpea!

GOLDBERG, BILL
[a.] Santa Monica, CA [title] "Humanity" [pers.] Bill E. Goldberg is a marriage and family therapist and writer. He writes poems about nature, wonderment, love, parenting, and spirituality. He has dedicated much of his professional life to helping parents provide an emotionally healthy environment for their children. He is the author of two poetry books, *Catch the Current, Poems from the Rhythms of Life* and *Be Like the River, Poems from Around the Bend*. "Humanity" was inspired by world travel and seeing the diversity and commonality that exists in people.

GOMEZ, MARGARET
[a.] Tucson, AZ [pers.] Writing poems is my "quiet time." I find it to be very relaxing. My two children are my top critics. "Too Late" is a poem I wrote in hopes that anyone out drinking will not get behind the wheel and drive.

GONZALEZ, KRISTINA
[title] "Is It Worth It?" [pers.] This poem is very special because it explains how I feel. I had lots of things on my mind at that time and this explained everything. It explained how I thought and how I wanted to react.

GONZALEZ, STUART
[title] "The Perfect Life" [pers.] This poem is very close to me. It is also very representative of how I try to live my life: simple and hardworking. The stranger who was the focus of this poem has no idea that I wrote about him, but I hope he knows that his life has not gone unappreciated. Share this poem with your children to show them what came before them.

GOOCH, LAURA
[title] "You Will Be There" [pers.] I would like to dedicate this poem to my mom, Jill Gooch. She has always been there for me through thick and thin. Thank you, Mom, for being you! I love you very much.

GOODNIGHT, DONA
[title] "Our Country's Heroes" [pers.] As a teacher at Hillcrest Elementary School in Jonesboro, Arkansas, I was asked to write a poem for our Veterans' Day Program. This poem was easy to write since many veterans are special to me. It is truly my belief that our lives were greatly enhanced because of our veterans. We should think very highly of them since they served and fought for our country. I want my sons, Michael Goodnight and Shawn Goodnight, to admire, respect, and understand the importance of our veterans. I believe this poem, written by me, their Mother, will help instill this belief in them.

GOODWIN, DANIELLE
[title] "Disguised" [pers.] This poem is about how I feel when my family seems to not give enough attention to me, when friends disappeared, school failed me, and when my counselors ignored my cries

for help. I have been through more serious problems than most teenagers have at my age, which forced me to mature and grow quicker than most. These experiences have made me a stronger person and have given me more of a realistic outlook towards the world.

GORDON, CHRIS
[title] "Her Eyes" [pers.] You can find breathtaking beauty in the world wherever you look. And poetry has always been the best way of remembering that beauty. It's truly difficult to feel lost in the world with a book of your most beautiful memories by your side. I'm 21 years old, and I think I'm in for a beautiful life.

GORDON, JACK
[title] "He Is, but He Is Not" [pers.] My poem is dedicated to and about my brother-in-law, a sweet, respected, and talented man whose mind has left this world in the dense forest of Alzheimer's. He is alive and is missed by our family. Poetry has been an important and essential part of my life for many years. In my retirement years it has become an indispensable and urgent labor of love almost everyday . . . creating another purpose and challenge to each day.

GRAF, ROBERT, JR.
[title] "My Mother's Love at 70" [pers.] As the years pass, we come to appreciate the contributions and sacrifices that many people have made on our behalf. This is most true of my parents and, as I am now a parent, I appreciate them more each year. This poem takes the opportunity of a birthday to say thank you in a special way to my mother. The picture of a rose and all its attributes seems the best way to represent this wonderful woman. As children are a gift from God, so too are loving parents.

GRAHAM, KIMBERLY
[title] "Remembering You" [pers.] This poem was written about a doctor that I was in love with years ago. He had to spend most of his time working. As a nurse, I was also busy. I have a BSN from UNC, Chapel Hill. My three children use most of my time. I have to be inspired to write poetry. A thought blossoms, then I write it immediately. Poetry expresses how I feel about God's beauty and love.

GRAINGER, DIANNE
[title] "Sibling" [pers.] This particular poem was written for my older brother in order for me to express my feelings on our relationship as he went off to college. "Sibling" was specifically inspired by Martial Artisan, who often felt and thought the same way I did. Poetry is the thoughts and feelings that you're able to write about. I'm blessed by the grace of God to be raised by such wonderful parents like Joyce and Greg Grainger, as well as an appreciating and loving family. Much love to my cousin, Aaron—keep writing.

GRAY, WILLIAM
[a.] Newton Center, MA [title] "Politika" [pers.] I was born in Omaha, Nebraska, and I work as a psychiatrist. My hobbies include poetry and reading scientific articles. I am a member of the American Association for the Advancement of Science and the American Psychiatric Association. I am married to Lucille R. Gray, and we have three children and two grandchildren. I have been the editor of two books on general systems theory and psychiatry, as well as the author of articles on the same subject and on the system precursor/system forming theory of personality. Now retired, at age 83, I have long been interested in people's relationships and in how they form systems, internally and interpersonally.

GRECI, DONNA
[title] "Anything Worth Having" [pers.] Poetry has always been a catharsis for me, a way to mark

my journey. I once had about 50 notebooks filled with stories and poems. In a very difficult time in my life, the box of notebooks was lost. It took me a long time to write anything. This poem was my first in about ten years. It reflects how I feel about the value of life and the people who I meet along the way. It's a resurrection of a creative muse. When I tell my kids to be persistent, I can be an example. After 20 years, I can see one of my dreams realized.

GREEN, BERRYMAN
[title] "Glouster Point Pilot" [pers.] Alfred Gary Lambert, retired as a USAF Col. He served in the RAF from 1938 to 1940, believing, as Winston Churchill did, that Hitler was nothing to ignore. When America joined the growing cause, he joined the Army Air Corps. He was shot down and put to work in a Rocket Lab "sabotaging as much as we could" in Nazi Germany. Liberated in 1945, he served as Commandant at Langley Field in Virginia. He also was a bomber/pilot in Korea, lead engineer on Mercury, Gemini, and Apollo teams, and was head man on the B-S2 maintenance schedule project.

GREEN, CANDACE
[title] "Anger" [pers.] I was born in Elizabeth, New Jersey and grew up in Washington D.C. I have always loved to sing, and, most of the time, I sing what I write. The reason for writing this poem was that I was sad and I could only write what I felt— so that's what I did. It has won me two publishings, and I'm going to win more with some more of my work. I currently work at the National Geographic Society, and I enjoy it very much. I want to become a veterinarian. I plan on going to Tuskegee University in the year of 2002. My life is going very well, and I thank God.

GREEN, FRED
[title] "Chess Game" [pers.] This excerpt from a song I wrote, reflects my philosophy that life is a battle of choices between good and evil, and then about living with the consequences. I've experienced the pain and hardships of bad or wrong choices, which has made me smarter and stronger. Waiting helps me vent my feelings and thoughts, and makes me feel happy. Through my vigorous pursuit of music, I hope to have a positive impact on my audience.

GREST, JENNY
[pers.] Poetry is something I like to read and write, and I like to write about things that I like. In this poem I combined some things I like to express my view of a fairy's world. The colored blossoms and rainbowy skies are colors of the world that I love so much, as well as the sun, the moon, and the stars being part of the sky that I am intrigued by. Finally, the fairies are like the butterflies and angels, which I think of as guardians over animals and people.

GRIFFIN, KENNY
[title] "Thanks" [pers.] This poem is very close to my heart. It represents a time in my life when I was hurt really bad by people I held very close. The poem is thanking them for making me a stronger person.

GRIFFIN, REA
[title] "He Weeps" [pers.] A shooting star at just the right moment, a twinkle in a child's eyes, a blade of grass that is longer than the others around it: Life is my inspiration. My poetry is a piece of me, of who I am. It is my deepest passion. And now that I've finally gathered the courage to share this most intimate part of myself, I hope that "He Weeps" will touch you in some small way. This poem, I dedicate to you, the reader, for believing enough in me to read this.

GROTHE, NEAL
[title] "Lonely" [pers.] I started writing poems when my friend, Kasey, suggested that I write my feelings down on paper. I dedicate this to Kasey Busch.

GUALA, AMY
[title] "Sight Unseen" [pers.] When I originally wrote this poem when I was much younger and was referencing an encounter in a coffee shop with a prospective date. I have since discovered the true weight of this poem and am glad to share this insight. Poetry has been a release for me since childhood. I have never written anything with a specific intent. I hope I never do either.

GUIDA, MICHELLE
[a.] Budd Lake, NJ [title] "The Love of My Life" [pers.] I wrote this poem for my husband, Mike. He is a wonderful husband and a wonderful father to our son, Alex. I feel poetry is a beautiful way to express your feelings about someone or something.

GUTIERREZ, GABRIEL
[a.] San Marcos, TX [title] "Paradise" [pers.] This poem is one of many of my favorites. It is not easy for me to write down a lot of things that I feel. I'm not a professional poem writer. I take this poem and apply it to my life, truly searching for paradise. I feel, in the future, you, the reader, will see a lot of my work in print! I'm yearning for success. So watch out, 'cause here I come. I got a story to tell—peace!

GUTTMAN, LOU
[title] "Julie" [pers.] The poems I have submitted in the past were written before I was 41 years old, although I did submit them when I was much older. Almost 40 year have passed since I wrote the poem "Julie" for my wife's birthday. It could be my own song.

GUZMAN, TANIA
[title] "My Heat Longs for You" [pers.] This, being my first work of poetry, makes me proud to have "My Heart Longs for You" published. I've never considered myself a poet, but writing is in my soul. I'm a single mother of a beautiful daughter and work for a prominent university in New York City. Inspirations for me are easy because my family surrounds me with love and understanding. I dedicate this piece to them, to the someone "my heart longs for," your memory is forever embedded in my soul.

HAASE, CATRINA
[a.] Latrobe, PA [title] "He's Gone" [pers.] I would like to mention my family: my mom, Beverly, my step dad, John, my sisters, Jenny and Wendy, Abbey the family dog, my brother, Ralphie, my sister-in-law, Chrissy, my niece, Bobbi Jo, my grandma Betty, my grandpa Bill, and most of all, my dad. I wrote this poem about my dad, who passed away a year ago. I love you all very much. Thank you.

HACKING, BARBARA
[title] "Our Shining Star" [pers.] "Our Shining Star" was written for my husband, Mark, as a Father's Day gift from our son, Ryan, age nine, and our daughter, Rachel, age six in the year 2000. It emphasizes the importance a parent plays in the lives of his/her children. This poem is dedicated to Mark for always being there for our children and showing them the way. As we guide our children we find that they are the true "teachers" in our lives.

HACKING, BARBARA
[a.] Stratford, ON [title] "Our Shining Star" [pers.] This poem was written for my life's partner Mark as a Father's Day gift form our son, Ryan (age nine) and our daughter Rachel (age six) in the year 2000. It emphasizes the importance a parent plays in the lives of his or her children. I dedicate "Our Shining Star" to Mark for always being there for our children and showing them the way through life. As we guide our children each day we find that they are the true teachers in our lives

HAHN, STACY
[title] "My Love" [pers.] This is one of my many love poems and means a great deal to me. I wrote this when I was in eighth grade about a guy that I liked. He was the most popular and I wasn't . . . that's the fine line. I've gotten over him and moved on, but the poem still relates and reminds me of a time period in my life . . . just like all my poems. I hope you enjoy this poem and look forward to other ones . . . and there will be others! Thanks a bunch!

HALEY, JEREMY
[a.] San Jose, CA [title] "Neglect" [pers.] The world can move fast and cause some people to neglect things they love, including people. I will never neglect my passion for writing; it has become an important part of my life. "Neglect" is my first published poem, and I think it is a good first. It truly portrays what a person feeling neglected would be pleading for: to be noticed. I was born in Los Gatos, California. I was raised by an ever-loving mother and grandparents, who helped me to become the intelligent and talented person that I am today.

HALL, BEATRICE
[title] "Notorious You" [pers.] This is my favorite poem because it was my first one, at the tender age of fifteen. I've been intrigued with poetry since then. "Notorious You" relates to life's experiences: my spirituality, my intimacies, and my written expressions. It is synonymous with my whole being'sevolution, past and present. I really hope that you also enjoy my poem, "Poetic Justice," and that it strengthens your future aspirations.

HALLING, MIGUEL
[title] "Appreciate the Colors" [pers.] I always believed that we should take the time to appreciate the simple things in life. You never know—one day it could all be gone.

HAMMAN, JO
[a.] Sulphur, OK [title] "Jeanne" [pers.] This poem was inspired from a dream about a beautiful, little daughter, and a dress I made her for her fifth birthday. She was 22 when she was taken from us as the result of an ice covered highway in New Mexico. She grew up to be a beautiful lady, so very caring. Her sudden departure from this Earth has been such a tragic loss to all who knew her. I want my poems to immortalize her memory. I have been writing poetry about, and for my four beautiful daughters, and all family members since I was a child. It is a way for me to show my love for them. I will soon be 79 years old and I will never stop writing until the end of my earthly journey.

HAMMEL, JUDY
[a.] Des Moines, IA [title] "A Friend Like You" [pers.] I wrote this when I was a Bible College student on a missionary trip to Brazil in the summer of 1992. I wrote it in English and Portuguese for my new friends to remember our time together. However, I dedicated it to my husband, Lynn as I gave it to him when we got engaged in 1994. He is my dearest friend, now and in all our years to come. When I have the time as a servant of God, homemaker, and mother, I write poems for family, friends, special occasions, and as an encouragement to others.

HAMMES, RAMONA
[title] "Anamallovr" [pers.] Poetry is a gift I cherish. It is the means by which I can pay special tribute to all of the animals and critters God has created for all of us. So much can be given and so much can be received by the emotions only poetry can reveal. My love of the simple and beautiful things in life can only be expressed fully in my writings. I also believe that it is a gift that is given to be shared among many, or it will be lost or taken away. This poem is a tribute to a bird, "Singapore."

HAMMOND, CAROL
[title] "Epitaph for Scattering Ashes" [pers.] This poem was written because I have never heard of a remembrance or "marker" for scattered ashes. It should help to fill a need for some families and friends. I acquired a love of poetry at an early age, and began writing it in high school in New Jersey, where I won poetry awards. At the University of Michigan I won two Avery Hopwood poetry prizes. About 12 and 10 years ago, two of my poems were published in World of Poetry books. I hope to publish my own collection in the near future.

HANCOCK, SHIRLEY
[title] "Wishing" [pers.] This poem is one of my favorites. I dedicate it to Cathy, his daughter, who recently lost her father. I wrote this years ago, and am so happy it is in this beautiful book to be viewed by millions. I have been expressing my feelings in verse for years and am glad when I am inspired to do it again, to share with others. Poems are beautiful and a very nice way of expressing your feelings.

HANDLETON, JANET
[title] "Rag Doll with No Eyes" [pers.] This poem was written many years ago, when I was a teenager. As an adult, re-reading this poem, I see the human struggles that we all experience: separation, identity development, rebellion, individualization, many of us as teenagers, many of us adults, struggling with our own identities and perceptions. Human emotions and the human experience can be confusing. Poetry is a wonderful avenue for self-expression and self-exploration, as we try to see ourselves and our lives more clearly. This poem is in memory of my mother and dedicated to my husband, Bob, and to our extraordinary children, Taylor and Lauren.

HANING, TINA
[title] "If I Could" [pers.] If any of us have ever loved, we've known the pain of watching the person we love hurt. And, "if we could," we'd move any mountain to bring peace back into that loved one's life. This poem express that desire, but also shouts my personal belief in the power of prayer. Prayer—the only weapon we have that guarantees victory! This poem becoming published serves as an encouragement to my own personal hopes and dreams, for I've written an amazing book that's inspiring and heart-warming. And as "If I Could" has been selected for publication, my prayer is that the first of many books to come will find the same fate.

HANKINS, JEFFREY
[a.] Manlius, NY [title] "My Proclamation" [pers.] I feel that my ability to manipulate words is a residue of what I'm really about. I see "My Proclamation" as the child inside me telling the adult that I am that it's OK to be who I've become. When personalized, poetry is the ultimate gift to others. I currently live in Mancius, New York, where I continue my efforts in pen. Customizing words for the people in my life has become a secret passion, one I know will never die.

HAR, DANIEL
[a.] North Hollywood, CA [title] "Catalina" [pers.] A pregnant mother guided my hands over her womb to feel the baby's movements. Then she gave birth to adorable Catalina. Weeks crawled by, months staggered away, and thousand of little hugs later, I became irresistibly drawn to her. Tears streaked down my cheeks, overcome with adoration at the cutest little thing reposing in my arms and tugging my hair gently. Is it possible we bonded early on, while still in her mother's womb? Had our fingers reached and touched, she is her world and me in mine, as had E.T. and Elliot's? Had I communicated with Catalina about life on Earth and expressed a desire to welcome her? Sure hope I had.

HARBIN, JUDY
[title] "Missing You" [pers.] "Missing You" was written 25 years ago, after my dearest friend died

in a car crash. I dedicate this poem to him. We laughed with each other and helped each other through hard times. I miss him dearly.

HARDING, SUSAN K.
[a.] Minneapolis, MN [title] "Hand Prints" [pers.] "Hand Prints" portrays a young child's discovery of his own hand prints. Will his mother joyfully share in the uniqueness of his hand prints or get upset about a messy wall? "Hand Prints" commemorates Mother's Day, encouraging mothers to treasure "discovery moments" with their children. Soon, their children will be grown! Life is full of special moments, if only we recognize and savor them, rather than let irritations, daily schedules, or wrong values snatch them away. Savor the uniqueness of each person in your family. I have been a teacher for thirty years. Larry, my husband, and I have three teenagers, Jonathan, Robin, and Rachelle.

HARGETT, BETHANY
[a.] Redmond, WA [title] "Twisted Agony" [pers.] I don't believe there's anyone in this world that hasn't once felt as if they didn't fit in. My poem is about the agony of rejection. Words hurt as much as physical pain and words spoken are never forgotten, only put aside. Violence all comes down to how people treat each other. What people say influences how we view ourselves. I hope that others reading this poem will be touched by the pain in this young girls' life. It's so important to think about what we say to one another, to put our differences aside and remember what an impact love and compassion can have on a life.

HARIANTO, NOVITA
[a.] Surabaya, Indonesia [title] "Silent Night" [pers.] This poem is about life, how days go on and on. They leave us memories of the one we love and are sometimes filled with tears and laughter when the bitter side has come. But we just spit it out and let the good things stay. In life, many things happen. Many things we could feel: falling in love, a broken heart, feeling speechless when we lose guts to show our love. But after all, all those feeling are great. It's great to love and to live, have fun and create a good memory. I am 16. That's a little story behind my poem. I live in Surabaya, Indonesia. I love poems and music. I love singing and I love my doggie, Zendo. I study at a private high school and sometimes I write my poem during my classes. "Silent Night" was written when I was having a boring day and boring lesson in class. A friend of mine has copied my poem. She said it was good and she wanted to have it on her notebook. After all, poetry is just a way for me to express what I feel or what I think that maybe people do not understand.

HARNWELL, BEN
[title] "Undone" [pers.] Currently, I am a writer who writes for the sheer joy of telling a story—to give people the escape they may need in the life. I am trying to experiment with many stories and lyrics for my hand. I wish to be given the medium one day to show the world my world.

HARRALD, KYLIE
[title] "A Dolphin's World" [pers.] This time I was a dolphin. I imagined what it would be like to live in the sea. I wanted to express how wonderful it would be to have the freedom of a dolphin. This poem is dedicated to my dear friend, Colin Blacket, for all the times he has taken me fishing in his boat and the times we have seen the dolphins play. It is also for Liesa Phillips, for her love of dolphins and her encouragement of my poetry.

HARRANEK, WHITNEY
[a.] Yutan, NE [title] "Now You're Gone" [pers.] This poem was written in loving memory of Jeff Welsh. Jeff was my close friends who was killed

in a horrible car crash, which still haunts my heart with pain. This poem is a sacred piece of art to me and my heart is given to him each day I have to live without him. As the poem states, I feel Jeff is still with me. Maybe Jeff is not here physically, but in my heart he will always be. I dedicate this poem to Jeff, and I hope everyone will realize how much people mean to you, and to never take a friend for granted.

HARRINGTON, FAYLA
[[pers.] This poem is especially close to my heart because I have opened myself to you, the outside world. This boy will always have my heart, even if I never get the chance to met him.

HARRIS, CINNAMONE
[title] "Missing You" [pers.] I like to write. Last year was when I first started writing poetry. This poem was written for my grandpa, who died three years ago. He suffered a massive heartattack. I live in Lockport, New York with my mom and dad, younger sister, my three foster sisters and my foster brother. In my free time I write, draw, play basketball or softball, and hang with my friends. In the past year I have written many poems, but I only save some of them. The ones that I save I keep in a binder. Some of them are typed, but are mostly hand written. In addition to poetry, I also write stories, which I do not save.

HARRISON, JANET
[title] "Ultrasound Vision" [pers.] I wrote this poem after my daughter, Jennifer, sent me an ultrasound of my grandson, Mathias Hamen. Jennifer, her husband, John, and their daughter, Rebekka were stationed in Germany at the time, as John is serving in the United States Army. I had been searching into my family's genealogy when Jennifer sent the ultrasound. I was frustrated with the distance between she and I, and in this melancholy mood I was inspired to write "Ultrasound Vision."

HART, SEAN
[title] "The Shadows Grow Longer" [pers.] This poem was inspired by my most recent relationship. These adventures can bring out the best or worst of someone, but something beautiful is always created. People or possessions, once discarded, will never be what they once were, but art and poetry exude that moment, that indescribable feeling, better than any amount of coffee-house dialogue or contrived chit-chat. I am a born and raised Iowan, lived in Des Moines all my life, but people, no matter where there native habitat, are my drive. They'll never stop making me better understand myself. I presently attend Iowa State and major in art education.

HARTGERS, NATALIE
[a.] Almelo, Netherlands [title] "Revision" [pers.] Like many others, I've been looking for the meaning of life. There were always more questions than answers. I've had health problems all my life, so I questioned everything. But by looking at things differently (positively) I turned my own life around. Believing that life is more than just chance, I now express this opportunity through writing. I describe my work as reflections, suggestions in rhyme. Speaking about love, compassion, and spiritually, I hope people find comfort in my words.

HARTMAN, CASSIDY
[a.] Marietta, OK [title] "My Dad Died" [pers.] I am eight years old. The poems that I write are from my heart. This poem is to my dad, who I love and miss. I live in Marietta, Oklahoma. Poetry is a gift from God. I love writing poems, swimming, arts and crafts, playing with my four dogs. I have been a honor student, at Marietta Elementary School, and I'm going to be in the fourth grade this fall. I had not missed any days of school. I've been a member of Christ Tabernacle Church for six years

and I love the Lord. I've got the greatest mom on Earth. This will be my second poem published.

HARVEY, ELAINE
[title] "On My Visits to Grandma's Place" [pers.] My grandparents hold a special place in my heart. Though many years have passed since they have gone to their home in Heaven, they are still very much a part of my life. Lessons they taught and love they shared are legacies I have carried with me all my life. As a child, I loved to play and explore at grandma's house. As a young woman, I loved her for her wisdom and loving kindness. Now a woman in my twilight years, I see reflections of her in myself and am thankful for these wonderful gifts she gave to me.

HATCH, CHERYL
[a.] Salem, OR [title] "My Heart's Desire" [pers.] It is my desire as an inspirational writer to passionately share the sweet love of Jesus as I reach out to others in my writing! I wish to dedicate my poem to Jesus; He loves you and me!

HAWLEY, GENE
[title] "For God and Country" [pers.] I have always loved to write poetry. It will be an exciting thrill to see my poem, "For God and Country," included in an anthology, *Rainstorms and Rainbows*. This poem expresses my love for my country and my Creator. I feel the saving grace of our lovely Lord Jesus Christ to be so very special. America is so very unique; to live here is a great privilege. Writing poetry is an outlet for me, just like playing the piano used to be.

HAYES, KATIE
[title] "Do You Remember When?" [pers.] I have always loved writing poetry. I wrote this poem to remind myself and others of just how precious our childhood years are and to always cherish those years.

HECKATHORN, RHONDA
[title] "A Friend You Are" [pers.] This poem was written for Alice. She ran the food court in the main building at college. This is where many students would visit or study. She was always there. I do not remember a day when she wasn't. She smiled and cheered-up everyone. Her present just helped people get through their day, finals, and even lunch.

HEDGES, JOHN
[title] "A Broken Mirror" [pers.] This poem is about coming to terms with one's self, or lack thereof. It is about love that I know will never be requited. Being gay, one learns quickly that not all love will be returned. I use poetry to show how I feel, what my life is like, and how I hope it will be, all of which are in this poem. It is also a way to tell the people you care about that you love them. I hope that my poem is loved by you all as much as I love it.

HEDLUND, GREGORY
[a.] Barrington, RI [title] "Writer's Fury" [pers.] It's been a few years since my mind has been able to release some good poetic cravings. I always knew there was something brewing in my eyes. As a package handler and route runner at FedEx Ground, you tend to see the world in one shift. I can read a shipper's attitude by the way he or she ships their packages. The words that were used to sculpt "Writers Fury" came from the daily focus of you.

HEIDEN, BRENT
[title] "For My Mom Who . . ." [pers.] Brent is a very bright and talented young man. This last school year Brent was on the academic team, enrichment, vocal music choir, and in honors classes, which gave him high school credit in 8th grade. Brent also enjoys video and computer games and sports. He is a very loving and caring young man. When Brent was in 7th grade he was chosen by Duke University to take either the SAT or the ACT; he took his ACT and scored 19

on it. He has won many awards, medals, and trophies. As his mother, this poem was just one more of the many accomplishments that has made me very proud of my son.

HELFERICH, MEGAN
[title] "Look at Me" [pers.] My name is Megan Helferich and I am ten years old. I live in Cincinnati, Ohio with my mom, Michelle, and my dad, Charlie. I have a snow white cat named Baby. What inspired me to write this poem was the children in my school. All the kids would point and laugh at all the other kids with mental disabilities or in a wheelchair. This poem is a message that we are all equal. It's not right to do that because how would you like it if you were pointed and laughed at? In closing, I hope you and other people enjoy my poem.

HELLSTROM, VALERIE
[a.] Newark, DE [title] "No Boundaries" [pers.] I am an amateur poet with a great love of the arts. I am a fifty-two-year-old mother of two: Daneyeil Potts and Readeanna Williams. I am also the grandmother of three: Austin, Cortni, and Paige. I am an international English language home stay mother for the University of Delaware as well.

HENDERSON, AMANDA
[title] "Sorry" [pers.] The meaning behind this poem is that my cousin died; he was 29 when it happened. This poem was dedicated to his parents. I want to thank my 4th grade teacher for getting me into poetry. I also want thank my mom and dad, my brothers, Joey, Larry, and Matthew, and my sister, Jillian, and all of my friends for inspiring me to continue writing poetry. I would like to thank my band/music teacher, Mrs. Joy Wegner, for being understanding, and my art teacher, Ms. Marta "arta" Langowski, for always making me laugh.

HENDRICKSON, JANE
[title] "When Does the Magpie Sing?" [pers.] This is for to Dr. Kathleen Jenks, my husband, Bob, and children, Christine and Robert. This poem is dedicated to those undiscovered poets who have become separated from their own voices. As a teacher of the arts, I have always stressed the importance of inner voice through writing, thereby combining the word and the image with song and play. Now involved in a doctoral dissertation that combines mythopoetics and the visual arts, I am currently working with Pacifica Graduate Institute to develop new curriculums for high school students. Sometimes in our lives we become chained and unable to sing, imprisoned in our own sorrow. Thus, we are unable to get in touch with that voice that lies hidden deep within our true selves. An ancient tale from China, Japan, and Korea is the basis my words. It is a story about lost love between two lovers placed in the night sky. Theirs is the story of the star Altair and the star Vega, who reside on opposite sides of the Milky Way.

HENRY, FRANCE
[a.] Quincy, FL [title] "I Am Special" [pers.] The poem was written in conjunction with a sermon preached to a youth group. It is very important for us to recognize and know that we are all special in the sight of God, especially our youth, who face even more moral issues than we did. One's self-esteem can be easily damaged, which could, and does cause detrimental and lasting effects. Therefore, my focus in life is to be a light upon someone's pathway in times of darkness and to be a touch of self to put some seasoning into a dying soul.

HENRY, KAYLA
[title] "I Didn't Mean to Tell You This" [pers.] Most of my poetry is from real life experiences, others are my thoughts on a subject. I wrote this poem in regard to my friend, after I felt I had really hurt him. Poetry means a lot to me. It helps me organize my thoughts. Basically, it is a form of release. I believe that

everyone has a calling in life. You learn everything you do, so shoot for the moon! Even if you miss, you'll land among the stars.

HENRY, PAULA
[a.] Wilmington, NC [title] "Proud of 'Mr. Mom'" [pers.] As an adoptive mother, I feel that I have been blessed in a unique way. The conception and development of a child is God's greatest miracle, and the value of each child's life is unquestionable. The intense love I feel for my children is deep within my heart and soul. As they were the most precious gifts to "my life," there was never a question as to where "my best efforts" belonged, so I chose to be a stay-home mom. When my son and daughter-in-law became parents of twin boys a year ago, they decided one would be the "stay-home mom" for the first few years. I was so pleased! After all, who cares (or should care) more about the love a child receives then the parents themselves. I hope my son realizes, and feels within, the "good" of his sacrifices now, and what it will mean to all of them in the years to come.

HENRY, RICHARD
[title] "Pieces of Rain" [pers.] I live in a small, rural area in Central New York state with my family. I have always loved writing and seem to have a knack for poetry that I never really realized. When I started seriously pursuing my writing, I thought I'd try publication submission to see if my poetry was appealing to the general public. I am pleased that it is. Many of my poems are about nature; living where I do, I'm surrounded by it, although I do write about other things also. Sometimes they may have an underlying meaning and sometimes they are just what they are.

HENSON, ASHLEIGH
[a.] Shelton, WA [title] "Crystal Tears Fall" [pers.] This poem is special to me because it is about my boyfriend, Nathan Henderson. I wrote this before he moved. I also wanted to let hone my poetry skills. My last English teacher recommended your site to me. I grabbed at the chance. My personal quote that I go by is: "I'm me and you can't stop me or break me. I have the spirit of a poet and artist, the soul of a warrior." All in all, this year I have written a total of 71 poems, and still going. One last word: I love Nathan Henderson. That is all.

HENSON, FRIEDA
[title] "January Weather" [pers.] Haiku poetry is known as "Visual Poetry," written in a three line technique. The reader can picture the message or scene in his "Minds Eye" and then has the option of filling in his own details. My love and fascination of haiku goes back 30 years and continues to grow. Being a canvas painter also, pictures seem to be my objective, be they with pen or brush.

HERNANDEZ, KORRY
[title] "Hopeless" [pers.] I would like to thank everyone who has helped me along the way: my sisters, Karlin and Nicole, my mom, and my girlfriend, Gina. Without them, I wouldn't have been able to do this.

HERNDON, MONNICA
[a.] Arlington, TX [title] "The Venom of Life" [pers.] Poetry is such a precious gift. I feel truly blessed to have been given the ability to express my thoughts, feelings, and life experiences through my poems. I am grateful to two English teachers I had in high school, Ms. Norton and Ms. Sanders, as their belief in me and my writing has become a constant inspiration. This particular poem has tremendous meaning to me because it stems from my own personal battles throughout my life. I can only hope that the readers remember my words when they are faced with temptation.

HERRERA, SARA
[a.] Salinas, CA [title] "Loss, the Death of the

Soul" [pers.] It has always been important to me to be able to know what I am feeling and to express it. I believe poems express our inner nature and how it reacts to certain things in life. Poetry aids in the building of our inner sense of comprehension of what we feel.

HESSE, TINA MARIE
[a.] Riverhead, NY [title] "Your Love" [pers.] I have been writing poetry ever since high school. It is a source of enjoyment and a way to express my feelings. My boyfriend, Chuck, was the inspiration behind this poem, as well as several others. This will be my fourth poem to be published. Poetry runs in the family, as my sister has also written poems.

HEUER, LORI
[title] "Addicted to Familiarity" [pers.] My life has been filled with many blessings. The most powerful, thus far, was the birth of my son, Jordan, when I was 17. He has blessed by life greatly! Thank you, Jordan! Life is infinite, and though we choose different paths, I believe the ultimate goal is the same. Through lifetimes we go, sometimes toward the light and sometimes toward the night. Without judgement, it is soul evolution through human embodiments. The ultimate goal: unconditional love through forgiveness and acceptance. Thank you mother earth, father sky and the universal pulse-creator of light. May we humbly honor this.

HICKS, VERA M.
[a.] Springfield, MO [pers.] "God Speaks" [pers.] Writing is a special portion of my own being. . . . The ability to put down my deepest, innermost thoughts and/or feelings, as well as my perspective upon them is a gift from the Divine Creator. As long as I can remember, I have used His gift in a personal manner, as I walked down path after path life set before me. This year is the first time to submit my work to anyone for consideration. My desire is to use God's gift in such a way that others maybe able to read my words, and at the same time, feel "their" feelings.

HILL, THOMAS
[a.] Omaha, NE [title] "For Beth" [pers.] One Monday at work, Beth didn't seem herself. I asked what was wrong. She told me her grandmother had died over the weekend. In the course of the conversation, she said, "She's gone to a better place." That stuck in my brain. A few nights later, I got out of bed and sat at the computer. God poured the poem through me. When I presented it to Beth she read it, and headed for the copier. I have since presented the poem to several people. I always request that they pass it on. I hope you share it too.

HILLE, KATHERN
[a.] Phoenix, AZ [title] "Oh, My Precious Tiny First Born Girl" [pers.] This poem is about my daughter. She was born August 1986. She was a still born. I put all my heart into this poem. I enjoy writing poems straight from my heart. I also enjoy reading poems. Poetry is an inspiration to me.

HINDS, SUSAN
[title] "My Brother" [pers.] My inspiration for writing this poem came when my twin brother, Theodore, was subject to a major mishap. He is now comatose. The love I have for him motivated me to such loving and inspiring thoughts. This poem will always be treasured in my heart. I hope that others will read it and find it to be very unique. My family and I, along with God's grace and mercy, pray that one day my brother will wake up and be able to read, for himself, this inspirational poem.

HINNANT, CAROL
[title] "When the Time Comes" [pers.] I write in the spirit. I hope to share a message that will help someone. I write as my mother wrote. My writing symbolizes transformation, healing, and restoration. It reflects a new birth, or renewal of the true

self. Experiencing levels of change, we are refined and molded into perfection. As heroes, we take the journey with great expectation and faith. I am a teacher of small children, and I often use my work in the form of poetry therapy. I hope that the readers will be inspired to connect, reconnect, or create. As we elevate to the Divine Dimension, let us rekindle family ties.

HINNANT, TRILBY
[a.] Newport News, VA [title] "Destined" [pers.] When I was 16 years old, I fell in love for the first time. Despite my youthfulness, I knew it was the real thing. We dated for two years and I decided that I needed to "experience the world" before settling down. Experiencing the world meant that, eventually, we both married other people, and that we were to lose those people, either to divorce or cancer. He always held a special place in my heart. Twenty-three years passed and life brought us back together again, which seemed just like yesterday. It had to be fate.

HOAG, DIANA
[a.] Toledo, OH [title] "Fire's Lesson" [pers.] I've always used poetry as a way to express my feelings, good or bad, on paper. My poem, "Fire's Lesson," represents a trying time for me. On April 1, 2000 there was a fire where I work, and just hours later, I was able to walk through the building. What I saw and smelled from the remains of the fire are still with me, and probably always will be. It made me realize how precious life really is.

HOBDY, MARY
[a.] Grambling, LA [title] "If" [pers.] Poetry has always been my mode of expression since I was an elementary school student. Reluctant to reveal the intensity of my emotions, I have unconsciously kept them hidden in a modest countenance. Poetry is a medium that permits bare honesty in emotional release; what an expressible joy! Your publication affords an unusual opportunity for one to use a God-given talent for sharing with kindred hearts and spirits. Thanks!

HOCHMAN, GREGORY
[title] "34 Children in 7" [pers.] This composition is for thirty-four school children I instructed. Briefly, the poem expresses: that these children are a gift from God "blessings through providence;" my nostalgic memories of them "sang the song of childhood with . . . frolicking together, contagiously happy;" a declaration that virtues "goodness" and talent "skills" are best achieved through Christ "godliness;" a prayer to God for them "a spectrum of blessings to shine upon their souls;" hope for all children to grow in truth "each young mind explodes into awareness;" and the observation that being childlike "God's Spirit is youthful" is characteristic within loving people "hearts that care."

HODGES, ADRIAN
[title] "I'll Tell Ya" [pers.] Savor life and take the time to sip the wonderfully sweet nectar that oozes from its essence. As I witness my own ambiance, I share it's likeness with the Earth. Share with me this surreal dream. I am a freelance writer, photographer, and urban professional from Norfolk, Virginia.

HOFFMANN, ALEXANDER
[title] "Visions of Love" [pers.] My actual artistic field is singing. I am a tenor and I am still waiting for my breakthrough. One evening, I decided to find out whether I could write songs. What happened then was an incredible experience; to notice how the words just started flowing out of my hands was unbelievable for me. If "Visions of Love" makes me known throughout the world I will be very happy.

HOFFMANN, THOMAS
[a.] Melbourne, VIC [title] "Sonnet #1" [pers.] This sonnet is a reflection on the dawning of a beautiful friendship and the mixed emotions it brings. It commemorates Charlene, a wonderful person who captures the hearts of all she speaks to. Through words, I hope to give life to feelings of joy, contentment, and love that can be felt through a new and exciting relationship, or even just the thought of it.

HOGAN, SCOTT
[title] "Strangers" [pers.] I was inspired to write poetry four years ago while visiting Savanna, Georgia. One morning I sat quietly on an old park bench and began to write about the beauty of this peaceful town. The following day I had a wonderful conversation with two homeless men who were buddies, and I wrote the poem "Strangers." Today I write about a great many subjects, about love, humor, and inspiration. My perspective is one of appreciating the beauty and enjoyment of life. Poetry is a blessing to me. I enjoy the writing process. It has great mystery; I often find that it takes on a life of it's own.

HOLDEN, BRANDON
[title] "My Broken Heart" [pers.] Poetry, for me, started when I met Chis Grossman. He doesn't look like the type of guy who would write poetry, but yet, he writes some of the best poetry I've ever read. He got me interested in poetry, however, a girl named Cero Wald inspired me to start writing poetry. My first poem, "The Girl," along with many more, including my most recent poem, "Awakening," were written for her.

HOLDER, DIANE
[title] "Growing" [pers.] I have a wonderful family of five boys and a husband. I also have grandchildren. I am the only child in my family. I am also 55 years old and teach Deliverance Ministry to help people make the right choices in life to keep them safe. I have had a nurse's background for 35 years. I have lived in Copingue Long Island, for all of my married life, of 35 years. I was born in Brooklyn. Poetry, to me, means to express to the world what life is about. A hope of a choice that can really be done, if you believe. I wanted to see how my poems can become reality to share with the world and other's who believe as well.

HOLLEY, RUTH
[a.] Meritt Island, FL [title] "Little Miss Mariah (Mon Petite Fille)" [pers.] "Mon petite fille" is French for "my granddaughter." I was studying the language when Mariah was born, and this poem was written for her first birthday. Mariah was born prematurely. From the time of her birth she has shown a love of light. She exhibits a passion for and radiates a glow of brightness unlike any I've known. It is my hope that all who read this poem be inspired to embrace the change babies bring into our lives and delight in the joys therein. Children are our hope for a future. Blessed may each one be.

HOLLIS, WAYNE
[title] "Bridge in Winter" [pers.] In writing the poem "A Bridge in Winter," I was reminded again of something one of my college professors once told me: "Open up your sensibilities and allow the poet inside you to see." As a result of the advice, I am now more aware of the poetic quality surrounding those items in my environment, and I now have the ability to see things and events with some degree of passion and intensity. In my opinion, poetry is not necessarily a "pursuit" one engages in, but a special "awareness," a unique way of seeing things, not only with the eyes, but with the heart and mind as well. I believe that poets often use the soul as the primary instrument of recording, in order to make the ordinary and mundane into something extraordinary and exceptional. In keeping with this philosophy, I provide "A Bridge in Winter."

HOLLOWAY, FREEDOM
[a.] Oklahoma City, OK [title] "The Last Chapter of Life" [pers.] Writing poetry is a way people can deal with overwhelming emotions dwelling within them. Sometimes, writing is the only way we can handle the horrific realities life has dealt us. "The Last Chapter of Life," written when I was eight years old, tells how a young girl looks at Jesus Christ and knows, without a doubt, that even if she fails, God loves her just the same. Many times in my life, I had to overcome difficulties and extreme obstacles, but my Lord has always been there. Read John 15:16.—"You did not choose Me, but I chose you."

HOLMES, BRANDI
[title] "letter to my savior" [pers.] This poem was inspired by my true feelings. There was a point in my life when I felt disconnected from my Savior. I realized this separation was the source of my unhappiness. At that point, I decided to reconnect by writing this letter. As a result, my life is much happier and the light of my Saviour is burning brightly within me. I hope this light touches many people's hearts because it shines directly from mine.

HONDA, TETSUYA
[title] "Indigenous Vision" [pers.] This poem was originally a prologue to my graphic novel. "Indigenous Vision" was an abandoned project of mine that I wanted to develop as an epic. My relationship with poetry started from song writing that expressed my isolation concerning the present world. I learned the value of creative writing (including poetry) when I was attending an art school in New York. By any means, an artist must attempt to write their own dreams and visions down in words. I feel comfortable with poetry because I am able to meticulously form the essence of Life.

HONEY, VALERIE
[title] "Don't Grieve for Me" [pers.] This poem commemorates the death of my father, Terrence Honey, a writer himself, who shared his gift with many throughout his life. It is also for my mother, Joan, who passed away a year and a half before him. I wrote this poem from what I perceived they would want to say to those they left behind. I hope it gives other people who have lost a loved one the same comfort it gives to me.

HOUSTON, JANICE
[title] "God's Greatest Creation—'The Black Woman'" [pers.] This poem is very inspirational to my growth and maturity. I didn't realize until it was completed that I had discovered my innerself. The woman I was truly born to be. But mostly, it commemorates my mothers, the late Wilma Adams Turner, along with my sisters, Yolanda, Angie, and Robin. I admire and respect these four women as they are my role models. To my daughter, Jannise Nicole Houston, may you follow in our footsteps and always remember that this poem is also a mirror of your image.

HOWELL, ALLY
[title] "The Cold" [pers.] I received a B.A. from Huntington College in 1971 and a J.D. from Jones Law School in 1974. I am the author of four books, two single volumes and two sets of two volumes on Alabama law. I like drawing and painting and poetry. I am transgendered.

HOXEY, TERAH
[title] "You and Me" [pers.] My poetry is a reflection of who I am and how I feel towards life. Most of my poems are written from events that have occurred, whether it deals with love, hate, emptiness, friendship, or dreams. I write when I feel strongly about something. "You and Me" was written because of a dream I had. It was written for someone I care for deeply. I have written many poems throughout the last couple of years and I hope to one day to be a famous writer. Writing is something I hope to do forever.

HUBBARD, RAYMOND
[a.] Herriman, UT [title] "Simple Pleasures" [pers.] I just started writing poetry about a year ago. This was my 7th poem. I enjoy writing poetry on a fairly regular basis. I find it very satisfying to be able to express feelings, which most of us share, in a way that I never dreamed possible.

HUGHES, DION
[a.] Douglasville, GA [title] "Desert Rain, Here I Am" [pers.] My biggest fear in life has been dying before I could share the vivid image of desert rain that stirs my heart, soul, and mind. We are so close to everything around us, but many take for granted this special place we call "Earth." I hope others will find the poem as timeless for them as it is to me. Images and words inspire, which eventually lead to an natural happiness. I don't have to hope I'll reach the desert and feel the rain, for it's found deep within me.

HUGHEY, BRANDI
[title] "Dance Shoes" [pers.] Poetry means a great deal to me. I think that is one of the best ways to express feelings and emotions. I was inspired to write this poem because I also love to dance, but hated practicing every day. Then I thought of what my shoes would say if they could talk. That is what gave me the inspiration to write this poem. I enjoyed writing "Dance Shoes," and I hope you enjoy reading it just as much. Thank You

HULIT, AARON
[a.] Buxton, ME [title] "Constitutionalized" [pers.] I entered college in August of 1999, and that is when I started writing poetry in my free time. Since that time, I have written over fifty poems. Poetry has now become my main way to specially express my ideals and morals on life. Many of my poems are established through the emotional state of mind I'm in when writing them. My poem, "Constitutionalized," concentrates on how society is somewhat brainwashed by the government's contradictory laws. My poems is also my view on how conformity and "norms" have affected my life. Poetry is the essence of all that is true.

HUMELLE, ARIANNE
[title] "A Night to Remember" [pers.] I feel that poetry is a good way to express my feelings and my thoughts. My poem, "A Night to Remember," may have been inspired by tragedies that have occurred in my life, as well as the lives of others. I'm glad that I can be able to write things down in this way because I feel it creates a better picture. Both of my grandmothers have been able to recite poems to me as a small child and I have always enjoyed the rhyme and rhythm that these poems hold. Interests that I have other than poetry include: participating in various sports, reading, drawing, playing the piano, and enjoying the company of my friends. I enjoy the fact that I can share my poems with others and the fact that they always encourage me in what I do! Lizz "34" Cunningham, thanks for always listening to what I have to say. I want to thank mom and dad, friends and family for being there to encourage, help, and strengthen me through the years. I hope my poem is read by others and inspires them in some aspect of their lives!

HUNSBERGER, SIDONA
[title] "Quintessence (butterfly)"[pers.] My poetry is very private and personal to me. It is a means of emotional expression, through which I work out much frustration. This poem expresses my need to do my best to accomplish day-to-day tasks; even though they do not seem grand, those tasks have purpose in the long run. We are all part of a natural progression and must do our parts, no matter how mundane it all seems at times. We (I) must be there, doing.

HUNTER, EVELYN
[title] "My Diamond Necklace" [pers.] I composed this poem to let all my children know how much I love them. This last year has been hard on all of us. The work they have accomplished together is all the reward their father and I could ever wish for. It shows that no matter what is in store for each and everyone of them, they will be able to cope, and each is there for the other. You may find my literary efforts feeble, but my love for them is powerful.

HUSDAJA, KANTIKARN
[title] "Awaiting" [pers.] The word "waiting" tears my heart apart. It gives an image of an unknown, endless time. The poem "Awaiting" is a scene not in my past, nor my present, but predicts my future in which, sooner or later, my waiting time will come to an end. I believe poems are abstruse pieces of an art that perfectly describes feelings.

HUTTON, DAVY
[title] "Maid of Mullaghmore" [pers.] This poem recalls a day trip to Mullaghmore, outside Sligo. The harbor looks across the sea to the Donegal hills. The poem is an attempt to put into words the beauty all around me.

HUXLEY, FANNY
[title] "The Thought of Losing You" [pers.] I was born in the Philippines and came to London in 1973. I have one son, and I used to be a teacher here and abroad. I have an M.A. in home economics. I love poetry, reading, singing, and dancing. My motto in life is: "Always follow your instinct and endure whatever comes." This is my first attempt to write poetry. My poem has a significance to my life. It is a true feeling to a special person who has touched my love, my dreams, and my life. Since I can't tell him personally, I decided to write it in poetry. He gives me an inspiration and I was able to develop a talent. I can't believe that I can compose such verses just by merely thinking about him. I do believe it is the will of God.

IACOPI, DIANE
[title] "Life's Garden" [pers.] This poem was inspired by the life essence of Beverly Genetti and her affinity with the pink rose. Beverly was an interior designer who passed away in January 2000. Her friendship with Marcelyn Ratner of Chicago was the inspiration for "the dance," as their lives connected and intertwined over the years. Marcelyn is my cousin.

IMBELLONI, PATRICIA
[title] "The Tiny Bird" [pers.] This poem was inspired by a beautiful little bird, about the size of a canary. In the spring, as I was drinking my coffee and looking out my window, I watched this tiny bird trying to eat while it was so windy outside. Since retiring and not having to rush out in the morning, it's such a pleasure to watch the birds, rabbits, and quail running around in the mornings, getting their breakfasts. I live in a rural area and truly enjoy watching the little animals and birds.

IMLAYS, JASON
[title] "Pretend" [pers.] This poem is about a girl who can't decide whether or not she wants to get to know me better. I want her to ask me anything she wants to know because I have nothing to hide. I want to make a commitment, but I need to know how she feels about me before I give myself to her without anyone getting hurt. This is one of several poems that I've written, all about love, friendship, loneliness, or having your heart broken. "Pretend" is my favorite one because I think everyone can relate to the situation I was facing. I hope this poem inspires everyone who reads it in some way.

INMAN, AMBER
[a.] Loveland, CO [title] "The Struggle" [pers.] Writing poetry, for me, is a great way to express my feelings. Being able to express my feelings through poetry, I feel, is a great gift. It relaxes me and it lets me show others how I feel. I am very proud to be able to write poetry, and have read poetry by many other people. Sharing my poetry with others is like sharing a personal part of myself. It gives me great pleasure for you to be able to read my poem, "The Struggle."

IQTIDAR, ASIF
[a.] Union, NJ [title] "Emotional Decisions" [pers.] Reading the poems of the mystical poet and saint "Sultan Bahoo (RA)" and contemplating the verses, my thoughts became poetic. Whenever I am inspired from an event, I start transcribing it into lyrics and rhymes. In this poem, I tried to describe the affliction that came from the story of an innocent and affectionate girl whose life was spoiled by a selfish, vicious guy.

ISAACS, TED
[title] "Medication" [pers.] I am an engineer and throughout my long career have written many technical articles and advertising copy on engineering products. Two years ago I wrote a short novel, now published under the title *Executive Sweets*. Taking a mouthful of pills morning and evening led to this, my first poem.

ISABELL, PHILLIP
[a.] Dearborn, MI [title] "A Poet's Lament" [pers.] This poem was, more or less, a spur of the moment idea. My sister, Cindy (Isabell) Adam, e-mailed her siblings, including me, about a place on the web where she had submitted some of her poetry. I like reading poetry and lots of other things too. After some thought on the idea of trying to think of a poem to submit, I realized what poets and writers may experience while trying to think of what to write. Voila! There you have it. This poem is dedicated to my wife, Patricia Jean Isabell. My philosophy? Have fun!

ISHINO, CHASON
[a.] Santa Ana, CA [title] "Whenever" [pers.] Change is hard for me. Writing has been my way to work through the moments when I was too tired to deal with change. So, this poem is dedicated to my constant companion, my partner in crime, my best friend. I know our friendship must someday become secondary to another, but the times we've endured are golden and precious to me. "Whenever" expresses this sentiment.

ISLAM, SCOTT, JR.
[a.] Danville, IL [title] "The Many Lessons of Life" [pers.] My poem, "The Many Lessons of Life," represents my outlook on life in general. See, I'm only 19 years old and currently reside in prison, due to some wrong choices that I've made. Now I'm learning from my past mistakes to make myself a better person. Life is the most precious thing there is, and there's a lot of responsibilities that come along with it. By that I mean that there are lessons to be learned everywhere. Hope you enjoy.

ISRANEY, NAREN
[title] "Golden Drops of Dew" [pers.] Life is a bundle of memories, sweet memories and not so sweet memories. The sweet ones are those that we cherish. These memories give us enormous strength and confidence. These also give us motivation and inspiration in everything we do. The extent of such sweet memories may be small, but their quality is so very spell-binding that they easily lift us up from the depths of depression and loneliness. Such powerful, sweet memories we must always keep fresh in our hearts. Their magical effects would then keep us enthusiastic and full of zest throughout our lives.

IVY, CHRIS
[a.] Evansville, IN [title] "Chris's My Name and Wraslin' Will Be My Game" [pers.] Who or what can we rely on in a world filled with skeptics? Ourselves! True power can only exist in those

who possess the ability to follow their hearts and embrace their instincts. That's what I've learned the most about, and will never forget in my lifetime. In a sense, deep beneath the power and attitude, that's the theme of my poem. It's a bold statement of what I hold true and dear to me: my everlasting dream to become a professional wrestler and the extreme limits I'll go to satisfy that dream. If I had but one request to make, it would be this: don't let anybody tear you away from the dreams that are locked in the depths of your heart. It will be a regret that you live with the rest of your life.

JACKMAN, DEANN
[title] "Behind Those Loving Eyes" [pers.] I live in a small town in Colorado. I began writing poems when I was fourteen, as a way to express feelings that I couldn't say out loud. Poetry became a way for me to speak without opening my mouth; an escape from the pain of a first love, who broke my heart; to helping friends with their troubles. I am now attending college to become a veterinarian. In seeing more of the world, poetry has become a much greater gift than I ever thought possible. I would like to thank my grandmother for always believing in me.

JACKSON, FLORENCE
[title] "Dolls" [pers.] "Dolls," with over 1,000 other poems, has special meaning. Married at 15, and widowed by hate crimes at 19 in 1967, I started the hard road to success. Recently married, now I press toward poetic freedom. I attended John J. Wright Consolidated School in Snell, Virginia. Now I am federally employed. Inspired by poetry, I give glory to God, gratitude to my parents, children, and present husband. Poems are being published while saying "Reach out to the mountain of hope" that awaits your enthusiasm.

JACKSON, KAYLA
[a.] Quincy, IL [title] "Dreams"

JACKSON, LAURA
[title] "Time" [pers.] This poem is a reality check for me. I am impatient, and reflecting on this helps me put life in perspective.

JACKSON, NIKLAS
[a.] Wasilla, AK [title] "If to Say" [pers.] I chose to write this poem because I felt a need to express the beauty I saw in nature, more specifically, in God's creations. I wrote it in order to thank Him, as well as to show others the beauty and purity we take for granted.

JACKSON, RONALD
[title] "How to Love a Woman" [pers.] I wrote this some years ago, while in a reflective mood. It is my way of allowing my daughter to understand the love that she was a product of. She, in turn, has surrounded her son and the twins she will have soon in a continuation of that love. With the publication of these words of love, she is able to pass this love on for generation after generation.

JAGUST, ERICA
[title] "I Keep Walking" [pers.] I believe that most poetry is written when the writer's emotions are at their highest. The artist is so happy or sad that the words just explode from the pen. That is the way it is for me when I write my poetry. When I wrote "I Keep Walking," I was at a turning point in my life. I had a few decisions that I had to make and they affected me deeply. Writing this piece was a type of therapy for me. I am extremely happy that I can share the end results with the world.

JANSON, JESSIE ANN
[a.] Waterloo, IL [title] "My Apology" [pers.] I was born on January 21, 1980 at St. Clement's Hospital in Red Bud, Illinois. My home town is Waterloo, Illinois. My parents are Mark and Winnie Janson. I also have a stepfather, a brother, and two sisters. I graduated from Park Hills Central High in May of 1998. I work at a grocery store in Waterloo. "My Apology" is about a disagreement I had with my boyfriend, Gerald Nungesser. This poem was my way of saying I was sorry. Since then, we have settled our disagreement. We are still together and doing well.

JENKINS, SARA
[title] "Engraved Fantasies" [pers.] I'm a 14-year-old poet from Iowa. My free time consist of baby-sitting, volleyball, and writing. I'm recently taking voice lessons and piano. I intend to be a singer. This poem was written because I always dreamed of a world to escape to, and now I believe I found my way.

JENNINGS, ERICKA
[title] "Buster" [pers.] I am twelve years old. I live in Saint Petersburg, Florida with my mom, Brigitte, and my dad, Jerome. We own one dog, who is the subject of my poem, one fish, named Puff Daddy, and one cat, named Spike. I love to read, write, dance, shop, play a variety of sports, hang out with my friends, sing, and play the drums and the guitar. I am involved in the magnet program at school. I usually make A's and B's. If it wasn't for my English teacher, Ms. Torre, I would not have thought of this poem and entered this contest. Thanks, Ms. Torre.

JENNINGS, RUBY
[title] "Mothers of the Next Generation" [pers.] I became a single mother at a young age, which changed my life for the better. As a young mother, I did indeed deal with people who were in doubt, but that only drove me to succeed. This poem is dedicated to all the young mothers. It was inspired by my daughter, LeAnne. I give my thanks to my mother and my grandmother, who have supported me through "good times, as well as the bad."

JENSEN, ANNE
[title] "Unit Number Nine" [pers.] In a world that's forever growing and changing, the search for individuality is one that becomes increasingly difficult by the day. This poem is about trying to give in to the opposing force of society; about the difficulty in denying your human instincts and bowing down to the fact that, although we think we are different and unique, we are only being protected. It's about wanting to let it all go, but not being able to, and the fear of actually not being like everyone else. I hope this poem can communicate to others that they aren't alone with that fear. If we stand together, there's nothing to ever be afraid of, even in this oppressive Western society.

JENSEN, JANE
[title] "To the One I Love" [pers.] "Never Fade Away" goes out to my 9th grade teacher, Ole Aagaard, Skals Skole, of Denmark. You gave me the word, and you taught me how to use it. For that, I will be forever grateful. Thanks for believing in me.

JEWETT, PATRICIA
[title] "Love Is . . ." [pers.] This poem means a lot to me. I feel as though this poem is an explanation of true love. So often, a person thinks they have found a broken heart. Love is something that takes time and effort. Like I said, the more you tend to it, the more it will grow.

JOHN, THERESA
[a.] Chicago, IL [title] "Pragmatist" [pers.] Born in Washington, DC to Nigerian parents, I have lived few years of my life in the U.S. Raised in Britain and Nigeria, and having been given the opportunity to visit other countries, I have been able to appreciate various cultures and ideologies. Having seen the easygoing, carefree, holistic attitudes of Africans, as well as the stiff, expressionless propriety of British culture, I arrived at the harsh reality of modern day U.S.A.—pragmatism! While I am a pragmatist myself (by African standards), I have come to realize that pragmatism, beyond holistic realism, is vivid deception.

JOHNSON, CARLTON
[title] "The World" [pers.] This poem was written at a time in my life when there were great trials and tribulations. At this time, I experienced fear and had to learn I couldn't run from it. God had to show me to fear no one but Him. I give special thanks to my sister, Ms. Jennifer White, who introduced me to mediation, which brought me back to God; my mother, Mrs. Fongie Johnson, who raised five children by herself, giving us all the love she could give us until her death (God bless you mother); and to Bronica Barber, through whose eyes I see innocence.

JOHNSON, CRAIG
[title] "Ave Vita" [pers.] The poem was born of a four-year journey and a lifetime of conversation. Just me and the two of them. Rafael and Camilo. My pupils and my athletes. The country was Brazil, the road taken was soccer, and the language was world literature. The company we had along the way (in order of appearance in the poem) was Camus, Eliot, Shakespeare, Kipling, Cervantes, Hesse, Conrad, Hemingway, Marquez, and Miller. The message we took from it all (and put down here in words) is how to live.

JOHNSON, JOSEPH
[a.] Philadelphia, PA [title] "Old Toy" [pers.] "Old Toy" explains a point in my life when I was in love with a woman that I would die for. Unfortunatelym she didn't feel the same way. My poetry is an extension of my deep love for art. I have been an artist for most of my life. Now I have tried to paint with words to create mental pictures.

JOHNSON, MARION
[title] "To Be Manic" [pers.] This work is an endeavor to more effectively demonstrate to those around me what living with bi-polar disorder (a.k.a. manic depression) is like for me. I have repeatedly found that describing its characteristics: the mood swings, the highs, the depression, and often, the fear that I experience to those people who have had no prior encounters with mental disorder, can be quite difficult. Yet, while it has been a ravaging, disabling, and constant presence in my life, it has also opened the vessels of creativity within, from which many wonderful things have poured out.

JOHNSON, NAOMI
[title] "I Will Be There" [pers.] This poem was written by Sherry while she was stationed in Germany with the U.S. Army. It was written to her sister back home. Unfortunately, she did not receive it until after Sherry's death on May 10, 2000, at the young age of 27. Sherry loved life and was always concerned about others.

JOHNSON, RACHEL
[a.] Geneva, OH [title] "Just A Friend" [pers.] This poem is extremely special to me. It concerns someone that I had hoped loved me, but that was a blinded hope. We're nothing more than friends. We almost did, but it never worked out. Poetry is something that I think everyone should try. If you say you are not good at it, but you have never tried, how would you know? Poetry only needs to show feelings, not so much to rhyme. Sometimes, when I am really depressed, I write my best poetry. It helps take my mind off my troubles. I suppose that is what they are suppose to do.

JOHNSON, REBECCA
[pers.] Poetry has been a part of my life for as long as I can remember. I feel that it's a gift from God and I'm blessed to have received it. I'm a 22-year-old registered nurse, full time student, and foster sister from Roanoke, Virginia. I live with my mom, Nancy Wood, who has always encouraged me to write and to believe in my dreams. Through my

poetry, I try to express to others to never stop dreaming, for one day those dreams may become reality. I believe, through poetry, our dreams, hopes, and loves can be shared with all.

JOHNSON, RICH
[title] "Caged Beauty" [pers.] I'd like to say "hi" to my parents and the rest of my family, as well as my brothers of Alpha Tau Omega, Epsilon Nu Chapter: Craig, Kyle, Chilvers, Big Mike, Jay Poogie, Bays, Ben, Joe Fun, Cort, Di Branchio, Justin, Clark, BJ, Drew, Chad and Chad. Eli, thanks for picking me up in Alabama after spring break. Special thanks to the beautiful inspiration for this poem, Rebecca Joan Stachnik.

JOHNSON-MUHAMMAD, DAWN A.
[a.] Detroit, MI [title] "My Dad's Hands" [pers.] "My Dad's Hands" is a story of my father's life in poetry formation. My dad is an African-American, Detroit auto worker, who moved north during the great migration to escape Jim Crow. My father, now in his older years, has lived a full and complex life, picking cotton, fighting in Vietnam, and working so,so hard! He has contributed fully to American society. Nevertheless, throughout his life he has been a victim of racism and discrimination. Therefore, as a birthday gift to my father, I composed "My Dad's Hands" to honor him for his strength and courage!

JOHNSTON, AMBER
[title] "With All My Heart" [pers.] This poem was written for my cousin, Shirley, who was taken from us, suddenly, in a car wreck. I wrote this poem to let her know that, no matter what, I will always love her. I hope that when people read this poem it will remind them of someone special in their lives.

JOHNSTON, S. VINCENT
[title] "Is There?" [pers.] This poem is, I believe, is a thought that runs through everyone's mind sometime in life: is there life after death? I thought I could bring it out and let others think about it. I write a lot of poetry, of all types, about everything. It helps the thoughts to be able to let loose on paper.

JOHNSTON, VIKI-JO
[title] "To Sierra" [pers.] I am the mother of three beautiful children, and when each was born, I felt that it was important to try to capture the wonder and joy that they brought to us. As the years pass, and they grow older and more independent, we'll still be able to look back and remember that feeling. And if, as often happens, there are times when we don't see eye to eye, I can always remind them how much they mean to me.

JONES, BETTY
[title] "Blood and Tears" [pers.] I was a single parent in Alabama. I did not have many ways to express my feelings, the time to do so, or many understanding people in my life to converse with. I thank God for the experience of raising my daughter, for Abbey, my new granddaughter, and for the ability to express through words the feelings that might otherwise be kept inside and alone. It is nice to know that there are others out there that have shared these same feelings and that they might find comfort in reading them.

JONES, BRIDGET
[title] "Untitled" [pers.] Many of us feel we work hard trying to make things better for ourselves and close ones around us. You start getting a lonely feeling. This is a reminder that through tough times we still need to remember to love yourself, then everything else falls into place.

JONES, CAROL
[a.] Valparaiso, IN [title] "The Man I Love" [pers.] I am honored that you have chosen my poem to put in your book. I wrote the poem for the one true love of my life, Dan, who was taken away from us too early!

JONES, JENNIFER
[title] "The Note He Left" [pers.] This is a poem for Michael Louis Giovannini, whom I loved so much, and always will forever, for eternity. It comes from my heart and my soul. I hope readers will enjoy it. Thank you.

JONES, MARY
[title] "Remembering Mother's Love" [pers.] This poem is a tribute to my mother, Alice Bracley, who is now resting with the Lord. We loved her so much. Mother certainly was a God-fearing, virtuous woman. She loved God and trusted in Him. I am happy today because my parents instilled God in my life.

JONES, STEPHANIE RAE
[a.] Durham, NC [title] "Separated" [pers.] "Separated" was the escape door to express the way I was feeling during the turning point of my life. My parents were in the process of separating after 16 years of marriage. I kept quiet and never let anyone know my true feelings about the developing situation. Writing "Separated" gave me the opportunity to express myself instead of harboring the feelings inside. Even though it may seem to some that it is just a teenager's thought on paper, to me, it is an expression of relief, as well as the need to cope with the agony of this new transition. I hope you enjoy reading "Separated" as much as I enjoyed writing it.

JONSSON, MAGNUS S.
[a.] Keflavfk, AL Iceland [title] "Regret" [pers.] Hi! I'm Magnus Sveinn, born in 1982 in Iceland. I'm a swimmer, and my future goal is a career in computers or engineering. When I wrote my poem, "Regret," I was 17 years old. I think it's very important for everybody to express themselves in some kind of artistic form, and poetry is my favorite way. My poems are very easy to understand, and are, therefore, for everybody to enjoy. Poetry doesn't always have to be complicated, and anyone can make great poems if they're not afraid to try. Best wishes from Iceland!

JORDAN, ERRYN
[a.] Signal Hill, CA [title] "Fate's Betrayal" [pers.] This poem was inspired by an argument my fiancee and I had about our outlook on our future, at that time. We're totally different. However, because of our strong love for one another, we swallowed our pride and compromised our ideals to make things work between us. In actuality, fate hadn't deceived us, but rather, gave the maturation time to realize what we ultimately wanted, which is to be together. We're getting married Saturday, July 21, 2001.

JORDAN, ROSLYN
[title] "Sing" [pers.] It is my desire to encourage others to "sing" with their lives, as I am endeavoring to do. When we "sing," we are moving in harmony with the plan, the purpose, and the will of God for our lives. We all are different and we have all been given a sound that is uniquely our own. When we recognize that sound and move in a way that makes our sound grow louder and stronger, then our very lives become the songs of praise God created them to be and the ones that He delights in hearing.

JOSEPH, DENISE
[a.] Queens, NY [title] "Separated" [pers.] Poetry has always been my outlet of deepest emotion. Through my shattered moments and my tears of joy, my poems take true moments in my life and verbally photograph them. Thus, each time I reflect on one, I vividly recall that moment in time in which it was written and all that enveloped me. And so, I dedicate this poem to my dearest Roy. You are the reason my life lives. May God lead our paths so that we are never "Separated." There is no journey in life that we cannot travel together.

JOSHI, AIDA
[a.] El Cerrito, CA [title] "My World of Fantasy" [pers.] She is currently a professor of international and multicultural education at the University of San Francisco, and has been for the last 25 years. She started writing poetry more than thirty years ago when she was still in her home country, the Philippines. She earned her M.A. and Ph.D. degrees from U.C., Berkeley, on two scholarship awards. She married to another scholar, Sudhakar "Arvind" B. Joshi, but was widowed in 1996. She turned to poetry as an avenue for healing over her great loss. She has a poetry exhibit on the Internet, put up by the ISP Hall of Fame. Other poems can be viewed at www.poetry.com.

JURADO, FRANCES
[a.] San Antonio, TX [title] "Reflection" [pers.] Frances Jurado received a Bachelor of Arts Degree from Our Lady of the Lake University. She also received an Administrators Certificate from the Archdiocese of San Antonio. She was a teacher and administrator, and has conducted numerous lectures and workshops in which she has communicated her educational philosophy. Frances lives in San Antonio, Texas with her husband, Gene A. Sturchio III. Frances now devotes her time to the care of her mother.

JURASIN, TRACI
[a.] Rancho Mirage, CA [title] "The Silent Cries of Help" [pers.] I write poems, songs, and short stories. My dad's side is very artistic in every way (music, art, etc.). That's where my writing talent comes from. I've been writing poems and short stories for at least three or four years. My poem is about a person who has a lot to say to people, yet is told not to. She is being forced to hold her emotions back. So in turn, she feels like dying. She tries to slit her wrists, but instead of dying, she lives. Maybe her will to live is stronger than her will to die.

KALBAUGH, RANDALL
[a.] Kansas City, MO [title] "My Heart Talks to You" [pers.] My poetry is about my "first" love. After our break-up, I went through a time of depression, during which time I wrote numerous pages of love poems. This girl I loved taught me so much, yet I know so little.

KAMALI, MITRA
[title] "meditation" [pers.] This poem formed in my mind as I was analyzing a gas well production curve at my reservoir engineering position in the office. I am an artist/painter by nature, and I tend to look at life as a whole. As human beings, we study things, we dissect, categorize, classify, and label everything. In doing so, we are distancing from the wholeness. Keeping my heart open as a way of life brings me closer to my origins as pure consciousness and as part of a whole. This is where I feel grounded with universal love and security, where possibility has no boundary. In here, music, art, science, philosophy, religion, and all other categories harmonically merge and melt together into One.

KAMALICK, JOSEPH
[a.] Peoria, IL [title] "Shamrock" [pers.] This poem, a symbol of my faith, is the embodiment of the valued events that have occurred and remain prominent in my mind since the age of reason developed within me.

KAPLAN, DONIEL
[title] "Dash's Time Out" [pers.] I dedicate my poem to my twin brother, Nathan, who is very special, and to my grandma, Sibyl, who wrote poems all the time, for all occasions. I am eight years old and I started writing poems when I was three. I plan on being an author when I am older. I usually write poems that are funny. My mom and dad always read to me, so that gave me the idea to write poems.

KARUNAKARAN, SURESH
[title] "Mindscape" [pers.] Poetry is a gift that I treasure, and I need to thank my sister for it. Being a poet herself, she inspired me from a very early age to put thoughts on paper. To me, writing poetry is a very moving experience. It has helped me reach out to people and light a smile where none existed. "Mindscape" is a reflection of the tangible and intangible price we ultimately pay when we lose the ability to think objectively and desire becomes the sole yardstick of measure.

KAVANAUGH, NAN
[title] "Question Is" [pers.] This poem was inspired by the novel, *Ishmael*, by Daniel Quinn. As members of this great "civilization," we seem to have forgotten what it means to be members of the delicate ecosystem on this planet. As a species, we have put ourselves above all other life in this world, forgetting that our very existence has and always will depend on that life. We evolved over millions of years with the balance of nature. Only within the past ten thousand years have we taken the world into our own hands. It is time we give it back.

KEENER, JENNIFER
[title] "Goodbye to a Friend" [pers.] Throughout my life I've learned that some friends come and go, but the best ones are with you always. My mother has always told me that no matter how far away your friends are, they will always be with you in everything you do, and in all that you go through. So always remember, you're never alone when you have friends, no matter where in the world they are. After all, what are friends for?

KELLEMS, ANGELA
[title] "When You Look at Me" [pers.] Writing has always been a vital part of my life. I write from my heart about my own experiences and what I see around me. I hope every person who reads my poetry will see a little bit of themselves in my writing and will be provoked to view themselves and others with compassion and love. I believe we can all make a difference in the world if we could just love ourselves and each other. I give credit to God for my abilities and want to thank Him for the opportunity to touch the lives of others.

KELLY, BRIAN
[title] "Great Poetry" [pers.] As a secondary school teacher of English literature since 1968, I came to find that although my students appreciated the themes and construction of the "great poems," they found true enjoyment in reading poets that immediately "touched them." I have found that simplicity is the best approach in all walks of life, be it championship, spent tears, sweet music, or impressive poetry. This is the philosophy that inspired my poem, "Great Poetry."

KELLY, CHARLENE
[a.] Port Jervis, NY [title] "Santa's Heaven" [pers.] Child abuse is very real. I try to make people aware. By writing this poem I hope to somehow help those children out there become noticed and to stop their abuse. With the grace of God and help we can protect our children. My poetry allows me to express feeling that my otherwise be locked inside. I, being an abused child myself, hope that some abusive parent may read these words and stop. God protect our children.

KEMMERER, JANINE
[a.] Hopatcong, NJ [title] "Venting About Phil" [pers.] I wrote this poem simply because I was angry. I was interested in a guy three years younger than I am. After hearing from people that it would never work, I started to believe it. Everything I found appealing about Phil, I was starting to despise. That only lasted about a week. This is the first of three poems concerning that period of time. Phil, you're a great guy and you've given me a lot of material to write about.

For that, I thank you. Thanks for being a really great friend. Rock on!

KENDRICKS, JOHNNY
[title] "Forever and a Day" [pers.] I was inspired to write this poem, by the woman I love so dearly, Nancy. It's just one of many ways to remind her that I love her and that I will continue to love her forever. I enjoy writing poetry because it's a special way to tell someone how you really feel inside.

KENEALY, LUCY
[title] "Solid Light" [pers.] When I was in school doing an assignment, I was just putting words on a piece of paper about how Jesus died. Then it all just clicked. I started thinking about what He put up with to save people like me. This poem is very special to me. Every day I think back to when I was just writing, and now I'm like, "wow, I wrote that." Then I thank God for sending His son to die on the cross. He is the most important thing that is in my life and He will always be Solid Light in my life.

KENNEDY, LISA
[title] "Clover Lake" [pers.] Driving the Mississippi highways in the spring can be a spiritual experience. Many of the highways are surrounded by fields of crimson clover, which, when stirred by the breeze, look like waves upon a lake. The day I began writing "Clover Lake" I was driving to Louisiana to be present for the birth of my nephew. This poem is his. I am thrilled to have my poetry published. I write fiction, magazine articles, and poetry. Now I can say that I have been published in each genre. I am a graduate of Northeast Louisiana University. I live in Yazon City, Mississippi, home of the late, great Willie Morris.

KENNER, MICHELLE T.
[a.] Barberton, OH [title] "The Clothed Servant" [pers.] This poem is dedicated to my daughters, Tayloria, Allison and Brooke, that they too may live out God's purpose for their lives. This is also for my mentor, Pastor Jim Roberts, for helping me find that purpose. We have only to step out on faith to walk into the light. This poem reflects that victory. To God be the glory!

KENNISON, BRADY
[a.] Eucrett, WA [title] "The Rise at Day" [pers.] When I was eight, I place third in a color crayon art contest. My mom took my talent to heart; she enrolled me in private drawing lessons. Since then, I took art as an elective through school. In 1991 I enrolled at North West College of Art in Poulsbo, Washington. I enjoyed learning that creative talent comes from the same curiosity a child has. I hope the same curiosity allows me to become a known artist. I have to say thank you to all those who believed in me: my instructors, my parents, my brothers, and my long-term girlfriend, Kim.

KERR, KERWIN
[title] "Kindness" [pers.] I was born on June 28, 1921, weighing 14 3/4 lbs. in Dayton, Oregon. I'm the sixth of eight children of Henry A. Kerr and Sylva Hewitt Kerr. I graduated from high school in McMinnville, went through Navy Flight School, and took commission in the Marines, serving as a fighter pilot in World War II and Korea. I graduated from Oregon State University in 1954 with a Bachelor of Science in Civil Engineering and worked 17 years as civil engineer for the Corps. of Engineers, U.S. Army. I retired to my home in Boston, Kentucky in 1972.

KESSLER, DIANA
[a.] York, PA [title] "What You Do" [pers.] This poem of mine was written about someone very special in my life who inspires many of my writings. I hope that everyone who reads this poem is as emotionally effected as I was at the time of writing and, still to this day, reading it. Poetry is the only way to express the

deep feelings that are hidden within. Poetry is a gift that is given by the Lord and we need to use that gift to show others the love that is not easily expressed in actions, but in poetry.

KEUNG, KWAI HING
[title] "My Little Valentine" [pers.] I fell in love with poetry and wrote my first poem when I was in secondary school. My love for writing is like a fire that warms my heart, a fire that can never be extinguished. I wrote "My Little Valentine" on the evening of Valentine's Day in 1994, and that is how the poem got its title. I was walking along the road with my nephew when we heard an animal's feeble cry. We found a kitten abandoned in a dark alley and decided to take it home.

KIM, JOHN
[title] "Moments" [pers.] I never much cared for the term "poet" because it seemed so exclusionary to me. I believe there is poetry in everything, from a pair of worn shoes to an empty glance. Our impressions of these things, as fleeting as they might be, make us all poets. I'm no bohemian, nor am I an aspiring artist, I just like to write because it helps me find balance in my life. I am humbled that you see something in my need to express that would compel you to recognize my writing. I am grateful to have shared my thoughts with others.

KIRNON, SHARON
[title] "you're loved" [pers.] This is for my family, for two people, and for my son, the young adult. I'm waiting for Mr. Right, and so this is my poem for him as well. I have always had within me the love of poetry. I write poems when I feel the words within me, as simple as they may be.

KISSEL, NICOLE
[title] "The Memory Locket" [pers.] This poem was written to children who lost their parents. I have three friends who have lost a parent; it is heartbreaking to see them cry. The only time I have seen stories of this is in the movie "Annie," and that was a comedy. I wanted to see it taken seriously, so I wrote what I felt.

KLANN, CHRISTINA
[title] "I Loved You!" [pers.] I love poetry. It is very special to me. This is the second time one of my poems has been recognized. The first time I was in the fourth grade. My poem, "I Loved You," represents my first heartbreak in the seventh grade. I would like to thank my family and friends for everything they have done for me, especially my mom, for helping me through my first heart break.

KLUKA, NAOKO
[a.] Arlington Heights, IL [title] "Walking Shadow" [pers.] I wrote this poem in July, 1981, when I was taking English composition class. I was struggling with my English, my second language, in a 1000-word-essay. The original title was "Revision" and was 29 lines long. I would like to dedicate this poem to Dr. Hull (Harper College) and the three teachers who encouraged me to write in my teen-age years in Yame, Japan.

KNIGHT, AURORA
[a.] Poulsbo, WA [title] "Contentment" [pers.] I dedicate this poem to God and to my children: Heather, Joshua, DJ, Seth, and Clayton. Without you, my life would not be complete.

KNOX, LOTTIE
[title] "A Prayer for a New Born Colt" [pers.] Writing poetry is a God-given gift. I've written many poems and short stories since I was a child. My mother received many homemade cards during the years I lived at home. Being part of a family that included nine children, money was hard to come by. I learned to read and write by age four. I thank God for my talent. Being able to express my feelings through poetry or stories is also a great

emotional outlet. My love for all living things will never fade with time.

KOGEL, SYLVIA
[a.] Pembroke Pines, FL [title] "Octogenarian" [pers.] I am an octogenarian, born in 1920. I am blessed with two daughters, Iris and Randy, and four grandchildren: Matthew, Michael, David, and Gabrielle. I am a retired interior designer, ASID and ISID. I am also a past president of the Long Island Cultural Center and the founder of "Decision for Women in Commerce and Professions." My interests are "women's rights" in the political sector and artistic venues. At age 79 I decided to learn and use a computer (lap-top) and now have two domain names. I hope to develop a web site in the near future. I look forward to writing lyrical verses; two of my poems having been set to music. I started writing poetry at age 60 and am now poetizing from an octogenaric point of view.

KOLSOVSKY, DEBORAH
[title] "Where Is Love" [pers.] Poetry to me is a way to open up and express my feelings, good or bad. Take it from the heart and put it into words. It helps me cope with the bad times and helps glorify the good.

KOSHINSKY, SANDRA L.
[a.] Luxor, PA [title] "A Family Is Love" [pers.] This poem is to everyone who finds family by the way they are loved, not be the way they are related. It is also to anyone who feels alone, because everyone deserves to be loved.

KOTOWSKI, MIKE
[a.] Biloxi, MS [title] "Poor Little Moon" [pers.] Fear had cast a pall over the population with the uncertainty of the new millennium on the horizon. The poem itself was (originally) based upon a short story about the end of the millennium, the now infamous Y2K, and the end of the mankind. These factors were attributed to doomsday: the end of the world! Therefore, I wanted the audience to experience an apocalyptic feeling, and "Poor Little Moon" was created! The title came at the very end. Creating short stories has been an interest of mine for quite sometime. The opportunities to have my material published and shared with other readers would be a personal reward. I look forward to the publication of "Poor Little Moon," and for others to enjoy. Thank you.

KOVACH, DELLA
[title] "Surrender" [pers.] I simply cannot describe how overwhelmed and astonished about being published makes you feel. Writing has always been of special importance to me and I would like to dedicate my very first poem to my late father, James Kovach, who passed away ten years ago. My poem expresses all of the feelings and emotions I have felt over the past years. I hope this poem will give hope and inspiration to many other people who have lost loved ones.

KOWALSKI, KEVIN
[title] "The Loss of a Daughter" [pers.] "The Loss of a Daughter" is dedicated to a beautiful little girl named Shahiyena (Cheyenne), who was in our care for two and a half years, until the tender age of three. In that time, she legally became our foster daughter. The love we shared was . . . indescribable. Then, out of nowhere, Children's Services gave us 37 days to transition her to being reunited with her biological mother, to whom she shared no bond. We would lose her forever. This year she will be five years old, and I miss her more and more with each passing day. Now we have only our memories.

KRAHN, EMILY
[title] "Ode to the Violets" [pers.] I am 15 years old and have been writing poetry since I was nine. I hope that this poem helps to show how poetry can be found in many different forms, even in the simpler things of life. Poetry is one of my favorite ways to express myself. I hope that people will enjoy reading my poem as much as I enjoyed writing it.

KROL, JOHN
[a.] Milford, CT [title] "But, a Messenger" [pers.] The son of Polish immigrants, I was raised in Connecticut. Most of my adult life was spent in the Coast Guard, and later, the postal service, where I met my true love and soul mate. Meeting her led to heartbreak, a spiritual experience, and inspired me into poetry. The aftermath was my resignation from the U.S. postal service and my relocation back to Connecticut to reside with family. "But, a Messenger," though inspired by my "True Love," was written for my dying friend, co-worker, and fishing partner. Although I could not face him in his last days, he is forever remembered at his humorous best!

KROTZER, TY
[title] "Take a Child by The . . ." [pers.] This poem was inspired by the two most wonderful teachers in the world—my parents. These words were written through their actions and from their teaching. I would like to thank them for their gentleness, love, and support. I pray that every parent lives by these words and that every child will smile as a result of that love.

KUJAT, DAVID
[title] "Blind to Love" [pers.] "Blind to Love" was inspired by a long-term relationship with my first love, who is no longer a part of my life because of some mistakes I've made in the past. This poem was an outlet for me to sort out my feelings about our relationship. "Blind to Love" is dedicated to M.R.K.

KUMBERGER, CATHLEEN
[title] "Everlasting Love" [pers.] The Poem "Everlasting Love" was written for my mother, who passed away in 1991 when I was just 13. My mother also wrote poetry and I think that she lives on through my writing. I am more than pleased to share my poetry with the world and I will continue to do so. Thank you, Poetry.com, for believing in me and letting me express my thoughts to the world!

KUNG, JULIANA
[a.] Macao, China [title] "Shouldn't Have Loved You" [pers.] Poetry has special meaning for me. I think that it is a special way of communication and we can always express our feelings through a poem. When it is done, then we will be satisfied. I am a fifteen-year-old girl from Macao, China. I am studying in an English school, that is why I can write poetry in English. I like writing, reading, and anything related to music. My inspiration for writing this poem was not from my own experience. In fact, it was my friend's experience. I think it is a special way to express our own feelings through poetry, and to let that special someone know how we feel inside.

KUSNIRAK, EDNA
[a.] Lakeland, FL [title] "The Sea" [pers.] I was born 93 years ago in Otejo, New York. I was an elementary school librarian. I received my B.A. from American University in Washington, DC. My library license was obtained at St. Lawrence University, in Canton, New York. I have been retired since 1967.

La MATTINA, JOSEPH
[title] "Untitled" [pers.] The poem was about someone who I thought I was in love with, someone who eventually broke my heart. I wrote it and put it away until someone came into my life and inspired me to show my poem to the world. Now I think I have found love.

LaBARGE, WILLIAM, JR.
[title] "Unity" [pers.] Poetry is a gift for some, a blessing for others; for me, it is a release. To be able to put my emotions onto paper so they don't cloud my mind, in a way, is a gift. When I write poetry, I lose sight of everything. When the poem is finished I can't remember a word I wrote. Sometimes a few words can release my feelings and sometimes it takes a couple of pages. When I read the finished poem though, I am always amazed at what I have done.

LaFLOWER, VICKIE
[title] "Lifeline" [pers.] This poem was written after deciding to make the best of a bad situation, instead of becoming a victim of depression. I dedicate this poem to my children, Keith and Andrew, and to my family, who continues to encourage and support me. I also thank God for this strength.

LAMB, ANGELA
[title] "The Old Woman" [pers.] All my poems have special meaning to me because they are inspired by God about people and things that touch my life. My ability to write poetry was a gift from God at a low point in my life when I needed something to help me through some very hard times. I thank God every day for this special gift.

LAMBERT, MARGARET
[title] "A Poem for the Children" [pers.] This poem came to me one day as I was watching the news about the Columbine shooting. It is dedicated to the children who died in all of the school shootings, hence the name of the poem. It is especially important to me because the first shooting, at Pearl, happened not too far from my hometown of Meridian. I originally wrote this poem during eighth grade year for my school newspaper.

LANDRAM, BRENDA
[title] "Mom" [pers.] Mom was left to shoulder the burden of raising us. Although we had little, the values she taught us were worth more than all the money we didn't have. Mom went to be with the Lord a few months ago. She never knew I had entered this poem. So when I got the letter that it would be published, I cried. My sister wanted it read at Mom's funeral. I changed the last line to: "We'll never forget, we'll miss you every day!" Maybe now, others can see just how special my mom was, and always will be to me.

LANGDON, LISA
[a.] Ontario, Canada [title] "Dad" [pers.] I am very proud of this poem. The poem has deep personal meaning because I wrote it for my dad, Robert E. Langdon, when he was diagnosed with cancer. I had the poem framed and I gave it to him for Christmas in 1997. He had tears in his eyes when he finished reading the poem. On December 19, 1998, my Dad passed away, and that poem went with him. This publication is dedicated to you, Dad, because I will love and miss you always.

LANGLOIS, ELVIRA
[a.] Chicopee, MA [title] "Dream for Me" [pers.] This poem was written in memory of our beloved grandson, Nathaniel, who passed away at two years of age in October 1999, following a bone marrow transplant. I am sure both God and Nathaniel were the inspiration for this poem, which then, as now, is helping heal the many wounded hearts this very special child left behind. It is my sincere hope that others who may have lost a loved one will also find solace and healing in this poem.

LANGSTON, LOU
[a.] Tempe, AZ [title] "Life" [pers.] Writing enables me to transfer a perception of my soul to my family. It allows me to be understanding and lends a new meaning to my life. Special thanks to my husband, Dave, and our children: Christi, Roy, Sandra, and Brad.

LANIE, BETTY
[title] "Myself" [pers.] Being in touch with how we feel about ourselves is always a constant challenge throughout our life, but the bottom line is that we always go on!

LAPEKAS, JEN
[title] "Would You Love Me If I Sent You Violets?" [pers.] I live in Bangor, Pennsylvania with my parents and brother. I began writing/reading poetry about two years ago. Poetry has been a guide to me, enabling me to express myself to the fullest extent. I read Shakespeare, Dickinson, Whitman, Frost, and Poe. Poe is, by far, my favorite poet. I believe that true poetry comes from the heart. It loses its purpose if it becomes too artificial; poetry is meant to inspire and renew. I am wiccan and have been practicing for about seven years. I am currently putting together a story about a heretic who returns after death.

LARISCY, WILLARD, JR.
[title] "On Her Sixteenth Birthday" [pers.] I wrote this poem after having attended a birthday party honoring the daughter of close family friends. This is a Briar Creek poem. Briar Creek poetry is written and/or read by the banks of that fabled stream that winds through Screen County, Georgia. The primary purpose of Briar Creek poetry is to elevate the human spirit. The Briar Creek Poets Society meets annually. Each member reads a poem that had been written for, and read at an activity that the member attended during the trailing twelve months. We welcome poets as special guests.

LAUGHMAN, TINA
[a.] Gettysburg, PA [title] "Questions and Answers" [pers.] I thank God for His inspiration of the words to my poem. Before giving my life to Christ, I went through life with questions that were unanswered, just like in my poem. I love poetry because, while there can be thoughts you can't express, things in your heart you have no words for, poets can express exactly how you are feeling or what you want to say. It's like looking through a window of another person's heart. They touch the soul of every person regardless of age. You can learn from poems, and they can maybe make you laugh, or even cry.

LAWRENCE, BILLIE
[title] "If Ever, We'll Remember" [pers.] I am a 20-year-old woman with a degree in early child education. I wrote this poem to my fiance when we first moved in together. I have been writing since I was 12 years old, but this is the first piece I ever submitted for publication.

LAWSON, ANNIE
[title] "Love Is" [pers.] This poem was inspired by my daughter, Charisse, who is very dear to my heart. It is also for my best friend, Emma Jean, who gave me the strength and courage to write this. You always hear about the bad things in this world; now it's time to hear some positive insight. This is my own personal thought about what I think love is all about. This is through the eyes and what I feel inside. I think there's a poem in everyone's heart and this is how I choose to express mine.

LAZZARO, KAREN
[a.] Keswick, Canada [title] "Ode to Timmy" [pers.] I have always enjoyed writing my thoughts and feelings to poetry. Whenever a special occasion arises, I love to relate my feelings in a poem. Although this topic was difficult to express, I wrote this poem as a tribute to my son, who lost a close and loyal friend. If Timmy's family and friends have taken comfort from my heartfelt poem, then I have accomplished my goal. So, for me, if writing poetry can enlighten one's spirits with laughter, or sometimes a little tear, it is only then that I feel truly fulfilled.

LEACH, CHERYL
[a.] Castine, ME [title] "Mommy" [pers.] I felt inspired to write this poem by my two daughters, who always gave me encouragement, and my granddaughter, who is my inspiration. This is my gift to them.

LECLAIR, TIFFANY
[a.] Hampshire, IL [title] "Talking to God" [pers.] This poem was written for a friend of mine who died in a car crash in April 1999. Her memory gave me strength to move on and to live life to its fullest. This just captures her memory, so that I will never forget her. Tragedies impact people for the rest of their lives. I just took a tragedy and turned it into something positive.

LEE, CATHERINE
[a.] Seattle, Washington [title] "My Father" [pers.] I grew up in Seattle, Washington. My family was just that—my family! We did activities together, but when I was alone, my words were my way of escaping some of life's realities. When I grew up and had children of my own, poetry was my way of expressing myself. Words kind of flow to the paper and swell my heart. This poem was written for my father; he'll always be "Daddy" to me. To Shawnita, Rhoda, Marcus, Caressa and Kiante: Keep your heads up high; he's always with you.

LEE, KIN
[title] "As Clear as Water" [pers.] Poetry is very important to me. It's one of the few ways that I can express myself. This poem is written for two people: my girlfriend and my God sister, who I both love deeply. As a guy, I feel that poetry is as important to any guy as his life. I hope that poetry will have a greater appeal towards other guys, as it did towards me.

LEE, NINA
[title] "Since You've Been Gone" [pers.] This poem is dedicated to my father, Vang Chong Lee. I love you, I miss you dearly, and you'll always be in my heart. I wrote this poem as a closure and a way of saying goodbye to my father, who was ill for sometime and has passed away. Because we were distant, there were words left unspoken, which I regret very much to this day. For anyone who has loved ones, please, don't hesitate to tell them how much they mean to you. You never know what will happen tomorrow. Don't wait until it's too late!

LEE, STEPHANIE
[title] "These Are Times" [pers.] This poem has extreme sentimental value. It reminds me of the times I had with a love that was lost to me. I would like to also share with the world that, without the love of my brother, mother, and father, I would never have developed into the unique person I am today. Mom, Dad, Zach, I love you.

LEFFEW, TONYA
[a.]Wyandotte, MI [title] "You Are My Angel" [pers.] "You Are My Angel" was written and dedicated to a person whose generosity and kindness continually inspires me: Frank LaPeue. I figured that this would be the most justified way to thank him for everything he has given me and everything I have accomplished due to his consistent encouragement. I thank everyone who has inspired and encouraged me in my life, like my mother and father, who always believed I had a special talent.

LEHRMITT, AMY
[title] "Moth" [pers.] Poetry is one way to express opinions on a topic close to one's self, and on a subject that a person feels strongly for or against. My poem, "Moth," symbolizes my attitude toward children ad their actions. Basically, it states that children don't listen to their superiors warnings, which gets them into trouble and situations they assume their parents will resolve. This is my opinion: I have trouble with children because of their lack of inhibitions, their egotistical ways of

living, and their overall extemporaneous behavior. I know some people will oppose my opinions, but I wanted to have it expressed.

LEMMON, JOANN
[title] "The Image in the Mirror" [pers.] This poem is dedicated to my three grandson's, Michael, Dobber, and Dusty, who wanted to know who the man was in the picture with me on the fire place. I looked at the picture: it was my dad, and the woman was my mother. Yes, my dear grandsons, she does look a lot like me.

LEON, NIRJA
[title] "The Bug" [pers.] My hunger for love led me to a special man who I have come to know. Yet I know him not. I know not what he looks like, nor do I know what he sounds like, but, for some unknown reason, that seems to have no bearings on my feelings for him. I try to control it, but eventually it resurfaces and takes control over my head, so in the end my heart always wins. In his absence, I am desperate for his companionship, warmth, and harmoniousness. This hunger and longing for his love inspired me to write this poem.

LEONARD, KELLY
[title] "The Summer I Grew Up" [pers.] This poem is very special to me, as it reflects an important time in my family life. M y mother had serious surgery and we all shared in her experience; we truly became a family. I enjoyed sharing this tribute with other people.

LEONARD, RONALD
[title] "First Love" [pers.] This poem was written, along with some others, in the hope that someday it could be put to music. I have been writing since I was very young, and I love it. All of my poems have special meanings for me.

LESNER, JOHN
[title] "Soul Mate" [pers.] This poem is meant to show that there's always hope, and that no matter how bad things may seem, you can always count on a loved one. This poem is dedicated to my wonderful girlfriend. Words couldn't express how I feel about her, but maybe this poem will.

LESTER, ROSA
[title] "Thoughts on Space" [pers.] Poetry is the release from stresses of a high tech DSL management job as a national help desk manager. I've enjoyed poetry since early childhood, and feel privileged to have a second poem chosen for publication in the ILP collections (*Days of Future Past*, 1989). Who says poetry and technology are separate entities?

LESTER, ROWENA
[a.] Jamaica, NY [title] "A Treasured Piece" [pers.] White or blue collar worker, all classes will read and get whatever message the poem is sending. In my childhood days, I used to recite, act, and dance, growing into an adult, touring the world as a Christian Ambassador. The things I saw gave me a clear view of how to paint a picture in my mind and how to write. I encourage all ghetto children to do their best in order to become artistic.

LEVATO, TEJA
[a.] Dulce, NM [title] "Someone" [pers.] I enjoy reading, writing, taking, walks, and I love writing poems. It is because of this that I have inspired myself to write my poem entitled "Someone."

LEVRIER, TRUDY
[title] "A Look at the Bible" [pers.] This poem is special to me as it will help a person to look through the Bible to understand and receive salvation through Jesus Christ. Most of my poetry teaches the word of God. Gleaning from sermons, I write in poetic form almost every Sunday. It is a blessing to me and, I hope, to others.

LEVY, JUNO
[title] "Alive in Africa" [pers.] Sir Francis Drake called Capetown, "The fairest cape in all the world." I consider myself lucky to live here—the southern-most tip of Africa. I am a writer and an artist who works with oils, nudes, and landscapes. Poetry and song writing keep my mind alive. My body loves to box, eat ice-cream, and ride naked on a motorbike when the moon is full! I adore America and I am waiting for my husband and sons to take time out so that we can drive through that country at leisure, and explore, learn, and discover.

LEWIS, JAMIE
[title] "Love" [pers.] I am 19 years old. Poetry is an escape for me. It helps me express what I'm feeling. It is a special gift I have that I like to share with others.

LEWIS, SHAUN
[title] "Try, Try, Try" [pers.] I was born Shaun L. Lewis to the proud parents of Mrs. Gloria Tuggle and Bennie Nicholson. I have one child, a very beautiful daughter, Ms. Alexis Lewis, as well as five sisters and one brother. I was educated in the Davidson County, Nashville, Tennessee public schools, a graduate of Hunters Lane High School, class of 1991. Currently, I am employed at M. Lee Smith Pub, where I've worked five and a half years. I am also serving in the U.S. Naval Reserve, with eight years of current service. The poem "Try, Try, Try," as well as all of my other work, is a very personal experience that happened to me. Poetry, as I write it in my artistic vision, is a combination of experiences and what's going on in the world today in order to help give my readers a visual as they read my work of art. Hopefully, they can relate and enjoy reading my poems as much as I enjoy writing them, as more are sure to come!

LICHTENBERGER, ALAN
[a.] Las Vegas, NV [title] "My Wondrous Room" [pers.] My philosophy—my faith: observe the true God, keeping His commandments. Living in a violent, hate-filled world, we've become depressed, turning towards temptations. Turning towards God, we are strengthened and given hope. Turning towards humor, comic relief, and reproofs is madness. Comedy is not pretty; it is fine line between pleasure and pain. A common rhythmic thread runs through poetry and music; they are gifts from above, from God. Few know what eyes have not seen, what ears have not heard, nor conceived in their minds the things God has prepared for those who love Him.

LICUANAN, ELVIRA
[a.] Makati, Philippines [title] "If" [pers.] I had never realized that I could write a poem, much less a good one, until Miss Perez, my English teacher, encountered me. And since then, I've been writing poems, stories, essays, and others in an almost unconscious effort, on my part. I want to make this opportunity given by Miss Perez worth it. Perhaps I'm good at what I do. Despite being a Filipino high school student, my primary language is English, having been raised in a fluently English-speaking family. It is with their constant encouragement that I am able to write poems, and for that, I thank them.

LIEBERT, DANA
[title] "Lemon-Aid" [pers.] God has blessed me with a gift of writing. It's my way of expressing my feelings with what life brings my way. Since I was a child, I have dealt with many illnesses and spent a lot of time in hospitals and doctors' offices. I have taken many medications. As I grew older, my faith through this became stronger. Joking, my dad would call me a "lemon," and say I was born from lemon tree. My mother was my aid in faithfully taking care of me through all my illness. Thanks, Mom, for all of your devoted love, care, and encouragement.

LIESE, JAKE
[title] "I Am" [pers.] I was eight years old when I wrote "I Am." Now I'm almost eleven. I live in Stanton, California with my mom and two younger sisters. I am now starting the sixth grade at Phyles Elementary School. In my poem, "I Am," I'm simply explaining what I am; what I wonder, hear, and see; what I pretend, feel, and touch; what I worry about when I cry; what I understand, say, and dream; and what I try and what I hope for. The answers to these questions makes up what "I Am."

LIFORD, BRITTANY
[title] "Summer" [pers.] I'm a ten-year-old girl who really likes to write poetry. "Summer" is a poem I came up with because it talks about all the things I like to do in the summertime. I hope you enjoy this poem as much as I do.

LIKOMITROS, CHRISTINA
[a.] Port Richey, FL [title] "The Path" [pers.] This was written for the one I love. Our love has endured all, and yet still shines bright, with as much passion as when we first met. Love has no boundaries, nor does it have any limits. To experience love is truly a blessing, for love is the ultimate reward in a life full of obstacles. To my love, this is my vow to you, for all to see: I will love you until the end of my days, and then some.

LILBURN, GAVIN
[title] "Reflections of You" [pers.] Poetry was something I played with during my teen years as a form of self discovery. Now and again I will still write a poem. "Reflections of You" was written for a best man's speech at a wedding. The inspiration for the poem was my wife, Vivienne. The poem tries to touch on something I feel that even words can't truly capture. I enjoy poetry, as it allows me to explore my emotional dexterity a little bit more with every poem I write. Also, with every poem I write, I learn a little bit more about myself.

LIM, MARIANNE
[title] "Not My Religion" [pers.] As a student enrolled in a university science course, I find that indulging in the arts is a great way to escape logic and reality. Poetry is one of the ways I do this. "Not My Religion" was written after I had been to church and was questioning my religion and its values. Believing in something gives you something to fall back on, but you should never believe simply because you were told to. Question it, examine it, turn it inside-out until you are sure that you are the one who thinks it, and that you are not reciting someone else's thoughts for them.

LINDER, DEVON
[title] "Death in My Heart" [pers.] The only reason I started writing poetry was to express my feelings to a lovely young lady. Her name is Jackie, and she is the most perfect female in existence. Not only is she drop-dead gorgeous, but her mind is fascinating. She drives me crazy—not always in a good way, but still, but still, I love her with all my heart.

LINDERS, RHONDA
[title] "Last Emotions" [pers.] "Last Emotions" came to mind when I broke up with one of my boyfriends. I can express myself best in words, but I wouldn't be able to do this without the support of my parents, Al and Beckie. My parents had faith in me and gave me faith. I do not know what I'd do without them. I'm just a young girl in Fort Worth, Texas trying to make it in the world. My inspiration comes from life itself. That's also where most of my poems come from. Life is beautiful, so why not write about it?

LINDGREN, LAURIE
[title] "My Life Is in the Hands of Destiny" [pers.] My poem is a reflection on a future perspective. I enjoy an opportunity to share my ideas and thoughts with the world. This poem has

inspired me and it has recaptured my creative side. I now dream of turning the poem into a painting, song, or perhaps a story. I love being creative and have forgotten the artistic skills I've known since childhood. My poem is a reminder to me of how much I miss working with art, and I hope to rebuild more of it in my life.

LINGENFELTER, ADAM
[title] "Sitting by the River" [pers.] This poem is special because it was written in my hometown of Jacksonville, Florida, while sitting by the St. Johns River. It is about hoping to one day find that one true love, and about waiting forever for him or her.

LITTLEDEER, PAULINE
[title] "My Enemy" [pers.] My name is Pauline Littledeer, of the Littledeer Clan. I currently live in Wunnumin Lake First Nation, located in Northwestern Ontario. I am a Native American Indian and I speak two languages: oji-cree being my first, and English being my second. I enjoy travelling, writing, having pen pals, going on the Internet, broomball, swimming, and spending time with family and friends. My poetry is like a window to my soul, allowing people, like yourself, a little peek at the real me.

LIVINGSTON, JASMINE
[title] "Mom" [pers.] I was inspired to write this poem in the eighth grade because my mom was my hero and I thought she deserved to know how I really felt. I am so thankful she sacrificed in order to raise me in a way that was pleasing to God. I am now married with two kids, and I just hope I can be the mother to my kids that she was to me.

LLOYD, HASTINGS
[a.] Ingersoll, ON [title] "Seeking the Answer" [pers.] I believe that expression is a part of being human. There was a point in time when I needed to speak, but I couldn't find the words to be spoken, so, instead, I wrote. I entered into poetry as a hip-hop MC. "Seeking the Answer" is an excerpt from a song I composed. I divided what was originally three verses into three poems. One day I woke up and realized that music isn't just to be listened to; spoken lyrics are poetry in motion.

LOCKETT, DIANE M.
[a.] New York, NY [pers.] A native New Yorker, Diane M. Lockett is an educator, vocalist, prolific writer, and performing artist who makes poetry and story-telling come alive! She has been affectionately named "Big Mama" for her moving performance in *Big Mama's Watching You!* Professor Lockett received the Golden Apple Award of Merit for Outstanding Teacher of the Year (1995, Michigan). She has also done voice overs for radio and TV commercials. A member of the Detroit Writer's Guild, Diane loves to perform for all ages and has been featured in venues throughout the nation.

LOESCHER, ANDREA
[title] "Anticipation of Your Arrival" [pers.] I was inspired to write this poem while waiting for my beautiful daughter, Sabreena Suzanna, to be born. Waiting for the birth of a child is a very exciting time. It seems like an eternity before one is born. Now that the anticipation of her arrival has been fulfilled, her father, Dan, and I get to enjoy each day caring for her and watching her grow. I hope one day she too will experience the beauty of childbirth, because children bring so much joy to life. I love you, Sabreena.

LOGAN, JAMAR
[a.] Fair Oaks, CA [title] "Why Did You?" [pers.] Poetry is my expression to the world. I write what I feel and feel what I write. However, this particular poem is for my uncle. He committed suicide and I'll never know why he did it.

LONG, MOLLY
[title] "I'm Angry" [pers.] I dedicate this poem to Robert Cooper. He was a great soul and soldier in the war on poverty, injustice, and alcoholism. His presence will be forever with me and my loved ones. We love you, "Cooper." See ya in Heaven.

LONG, PAT
[title] "It's OK" [pers.] This poem is dedicated to the people living with multiple sclerosis. The "hug" is the best medicine you will ever need.

LONG, ROSS
[title] "Me and You" [pers.] This poem is my first poem. It was inspired by my love for Deanna, a lady from California, who is a brilliant poet herself. We met on the Net. For her, pain of being apart an my love materializes in the form of a poem. She encouraged me to try my hand at poetry, and entered my poem in the contest for me. She is also entering poems in the contest. We will meet in person next year. Poetry has become an outlet for my emotions, and that is when the best poems are written, from the heart.

LONG, RUSSELL
[title] "Tragic" [pers.] Tragic is a melancholy passage composed to commemorate the passing of Joshua, a friend lost in November of 1994. My inspiration for poetry stems from the tragedies I have encountered. Losing close friends at an early time opened my eyes to how precious life is. Every time I feel my worth in life has become non-existent, I remember Josh, my brother, who would trade every minute of my "wasted" life for just one more moment in time. So you could say "Tragic" is a reminder to myself that life has worth; its what we make of it before our death.

LONSDALE, ELISSA
[title] "The Little Angel" [pers.] Poetry is a way to express thoughts or feelings you may not want to express in words. This poem is dedicated to a foster parent I once had as a child. I was lost and an emotional wreck. She came, scooped me up, and showed me life and love, as an angel would.

LORENTZEN, NAN
[a.] Scottsdale, AZ [title] "On Parenthood" [pers.] I have been writing poetry for the better part of my 84 years. "On Parenthood" was written in 1967 in order to help one of my four daughters cope with being a stay-at-home mother of two bright, active toddlers (both boys). She kept the poem on the front of her refrigerator for years. Those two bright, active toddlers are now bright, active young men.

LOVE, RICHARD
[a.] Orlando, FL [title] "Photographs" [pers.] I started writing poetry in September of 1998. I use it to help me through difficult times in life. "Photographs" was written in memory of my mother, who I lost to death two years earlier—a fact I could never seem to accept. I have written several other poems in her memory, which somehow have allowed me to accept her passing. I hope that anyone who reads my poem and may be grieving for a loved one, will find comfort through it, like I have.

LOVEGROVE, ANDREW
[a.] Indianapolis, IN [title] "Life" [pers.] My poem offers many questions. It also answers many more questions than you might think possible. Just keep going and living your life to a soulful standard, and you can expect expression at every event encountered. That alone will keep tomorrow alive and keep you searching. Words to live by, indeed.

LOVELADY, CORY
[title] "Being Alone" [pers.] I don't want to be forgotten. So the best thing I can do is pass my thoughts from me down to you. Hopefully, I'll be remembered for what I did, and what I'm going to

do. So I ask you to pass this on, whether it's by rhythm, rhyme, or song.

LOVING, EDNA
[a.] Meridan, MS [title] "The Wonder of It All" [pers.] The love God has for us is shown in everything He created. We take so much for granted. If this poem inspires people to realize that all we have comes from God, then the purpose in writing it will have been achieved. I am a life-long resident of Meridian, Mississippi, the mother of two sons, Bill and Michael Moffett, the grandmother of four, as well as the great-grandmother of four. I retired from Puckett Machinery, a Caterpillar dealer, in 1995.

LOVITCH, SUSAN
[title] "Remember Me?" [pers.] As I reach middle age, I realize that I have many talents. I enjoy painting, writing, and crafts. This is the first poem I have ever written and hope there will be more to come. Women can do anything they set their mind to, no matter what age! Set your mind to do something you have never done and maybe your results will be as rewarding as mine! Thanks to my children and parents, who have given me support on my projects.

LOVITCH, SUSAN
[a.] Pompano Beach, FL [title] "Remember Me" [pers.] As I reach middleage, I realize that I have many talents. I enjoy painting, writing and crafts. This is my first poem I have ever written and hope there will be more to come. Women can do anything they set there mind to no matter what age! Set your mind to do something you have never done before and maybe your results will be as rewarding as mine! Thanks to my children and parents who have given me support on my projects

LUCAS, EMILY
[title] "Image of Imagination" [pers.] I think personal expression is very important. Reading my poem allows someone see the world through the eyes of younger children. Watching my five-year-old sister play and pretend inspired me to write my piece. Being only thirteen, I haven't really had much life experience to motivate my writing, but still enjoy it and I hope other's will as well.

LUDWIG, NANCY
[title] "You" [pers.] I have a hole in my heart for my brothers, who died within two years of each other. It's the hardest thing, losing someone you love. They were the best. In their memory, I wrote this. This dedicated to: my parents, Bill and Carole; my oldest brother, Bill; my husband, Gary; my children, Chris, Jenny, and Stephanie; my grandparents; nieces, nephews, and in-laws; and my friends, —I cherish every moment I have with you. I love you all.

LUNSFORD, CHARLES, JR.
[title] "Fireflies" [pers.] Sometimes there is someone in your life that becomes a beacon to guide you, to inspire you. This poem is for April, someone very special and most unique, whose light will shine a thousand times brighter than mine ever will. She always reminds me, "What you do for yourself is selfish, and dies with you. What you do for others is immortal, and lives forever."

LUNSFORD, STEVEN
[a.] Connersville, IN [title] "Lady in Chains" [pers.] I believe freedom comes from God. This poem represents where I think we are headed as a nation. I firmly believe that if we think of freedom as the sole faculty of making money, the shackles we will wear will not be broken off for a long time. Then, our freedom will be taken until we unite to regain it, or we let freedom expire in a convulsion. The changing of a free nation must be done from within, not simply by changing our minds, but by the changing of our hearts.

LUPTON, CONSTANCE
[title] "Beating Hearts" [pers.] Constance, known as Conny to friends and family, seems to have always had a passion for writing. It began 12 years ago, when her teacher at the time encouraged her to pursue her thoughts on paper. So she began using her writing as therapy throughout her adolescence, and she finally became comfortable enough to share her work with others after she felt it had healed her wounds. Since then, poetry has always been a way for her to express her thoughts and feelings when her voice did not seem to work. "It enables me to empty that which seems locked up inside myself." Her poetry reflects her memories, her life experiences thus far, and her fascinations of that which surrounds her day to day living in Austin, Texas.

LUZHAK, ROB
[a.] Caldwell, NJ [title] "Out of Fate's Hands" [pers.] Poetry was really my only way of expressing myself and I'm glad that this one got the recognition it did. Thank you: Grandma, Mom, Dave, Mike, Matt, Tom, George, Steve, Chris, Frank, Matt, Tedd, and Amir.

MACDONALD, B.
[title] "Restaurant (Dinner at Eight)" [pers.] This poem was written as the author struggled to survive the ravages of AIDS. When taken in the context of lonely a struggle to live, it is heartbreaking. I submitted this to honor Byron MacDonald's life and art. Submitted by his brother Bruce, with love.

MACDONALD, SCOTT
[a.] Boonton, NJ [title] "Omnipotence" [pers.] I started writing before the age of 12 as a release from whatever I was feeling at the time. Whenever my life had become so fragmented that even simple decisions may have seemed life-changing, I found poetry to be able to piece the puzzle back together and find reason.

MACKO, TONY
[title] "A Cold Day" [pers.] I serve on board a naval vessel as an electronics technician. In the Navy, we all live a structured life. Individuality and self-expression are things that are not taken kindly to. However, I believe that true individuality resides in our own hearts and minds. Morals, thoughts, and beliefs are what truly make us who we are. I have found the ultimate freedom in poetry. It gives me the ability to express myself freely, despite my strict lifestyle. I proudly sacrifice my freedom every day so that you and the rest of the free world may experience self-expression.

MACMULLEN, JB
[title] "Un-Known" [pers.] I usually write when something is on my mind. If I feel upset, then I write till I feel better. Sometimes what I write might not describe my situation, but more how I feel. I was feeling depressed when I wrote this poem. A lot of times, I keep my poems to myself; people ask to read them, but to me, a lot of them are just too personal. My life is my inspiration to write, and I usually do it listening to music. I'd also like to say thank you to a special person who told me about the talent I have.

MAGINNIS, KELLEY
[title] "Stars" [pers.] I have been a writer all of my life. I feel that poetry is the music of the soul, and I just love music! The inspiration for "Stars" came while I was standing outside in my backyard one night. I just find stars to be fascinating. Words were coming to me as I was watching. But I still haven't a clue as to where the Big Dipper is! Writing has been there for me and has comforted me when no one else could. Writing was my solace when my parents died. I was able to write something about them as a tribute. Writing puts my thoughts and feelings into perspective. I come from a very creative family. My brother Michael is also a poet; he is also a very talented guitar player and songwriter.

My other brother, Patrick, is a social studies teacher, a profession he enjoys. My sister, Kristine, works for Bell Atlantic in directory assistance; she really enjoys helping people. Each one of us chose something in which we could express ourselves and connect with people at the same time. Writing is my form of expression , allowing a brief glimpse into my soul.

MAKAR, HEATHER
[a.] Corapolis, PA [title] "Ethereal" [pers.] Every word I write, every line I draw, every note I play, is an expression of the higher self, which I share with every other person on Earth. This particular poem was written in wonder and awe at the ability to learn and grow and observe beauty. I enjoy being able to share my creativity with those who can appreciate it, and also enjoy sharing in the creativity of others. Life, love, and joy are timeless and eternal, so I feel that through the pursuit of these, anyone, myself included, can live forever. Be intelligent, be alive, and most importantly be free, for all else is dust and air.

MAKAR, HEATHER
[pers] I would also like the commemorative plaque, for $38 and also a compact disc with my poem and others being read aloud, for $29.95. The enclosed page has the statement I want to use as my profile. Thank you very much

MALAVE, AILEEN
[a.] Bronx, NY [title] "Man Vs. Earth" [pers.] I consider this poem to be a stepping stone to future writing. Due to the publishing of this piece, I have been inspired to create other poems. My occupation is a teacher's assistant at an alternative H.S. in New York City. I thank two important people in my life that motivated me to pour my heart and soul out on paper; my mother, Margarita Malave, and my son, Michael A. Sanchez Jr. This poem represents my interpretation of beauty in all things and how they interact. It also allows you, as the reader, to have your own vision as to what a soul mate symbolizes.

MALLETTE, LYNDSAY
[title] "Finally" [pers.] As far back as I can remember, I have always been a writer, but poetry was my gift. I would write poems about anything; butterflies, rainbows, you name it. But as I grew older, my topics became deeper. Pretty soon I was a teenager, and I was writing about real issues. Then at one time I was faced with my own obstacle, and after a long difficult fight, overcame it. I wrote "Finally" as a form of encouragement to other battling teens. Not only is there a light at the end of that tunnel, but you will reach it!

MALONE, JEANNINE
[title] "Light" [pers.] My talent and compassion comes first from God, then my parents, for giving me life. I would like to thank: my ex-husband, Roy, for always being there as friend; my daughters, Janie and Jami, who gave me the confidence in myself; Jeremy, Mica, Brandon, Steve, Brian, Joshua, Geven and Brittany; my girlfriend Carolyn, of 53 years, who never let me down; Doretta, who encourages me; Alice, who is deceased and who the poem was written about; and my son, Jim, who found me after 41 years and brought my life full circle. I am blessed by everyone.

MALOY, MARIE
[title] "Without" [pers.] I was inspired to write this poem viewing the beauty that surrounds us—breathtaking scenery, love of family, friends and respect for one another. In our daily lives we seem to have lost track of the simple pleasures our Heavenly Father lovingly bestowed upon us.

MANCINI, TABITHA
[a.] Boonton, NJ [title] "Spirit of the Wolf" [pers.] She is so motivated to write poetry about life, nature and love because of the impact it has on people. Her poem, "Spirit of the Wolf," has moved many people including herself, upon reading it, the idea came from a short story. Tabitha wrote in fifth grade. Now in grade seven, she continues to write about spirituality and nature. Tabitha enjoys traveling to NYC and Europe. She attends Glen Meadow Middle School in Vernon, NJ. She lives with her mom and sister and also has two brothers in Tennessee. Tabitha is becoming an accomplished pianist and is grateful to her mom, grandmother and Dad for their support. She thanks the Poetry.com staff for publishing her poem.

MANICNI, PAOLO
[title] "Last Three Words" [pers.] My poem was inspired by my girlfriend. She had asked me to write one and I agreed. I really appreciate the fact that you have published my poem in a book of other selected poems. The poem states the feelings I have when I'm around her. My family has also inspired me to do the best I could, and once you have an opportunity in life, you should go for it.

MANLEY, LILA
[title] "Music—That's the Thing" [pers.] I've always been able to come up with something clever on the spur of the moment, maybe in an off-hand comment, or a quick note. There was always an immediate reaction. It never occurred to me to put things down in a way that lots of people would read. Until one of my co-workers saw this poem and insisted I submit it. Now I wonder why I haven't been writing (and saving) more of my "silly stuff."

MANN, BETTY
[a.] Muncie, IN [title] "Like the Snowflakes in the Winter" [pers.] My mother and some of her brothers and sisters wrote poetry; so does one of my sisters, so I might have inherited some desire to write. I wrote "Like the Snowflakes in the Winter" during the first year I became a Christian. I was so happy with my Christian life, this poem just flowed into my mind and I believe the Lord gave it to me.

MAPLE, TODD
[a.] Memphis, TN [title] "Time" [pers.] I can't help that Dr. King died in Memphis in 1968 and that I was born in Memphis in 1969. I can't help that Dr. King's birthday is on January 15th and my birthday is the same. Didn't you know the dreamer never dies? God is blessing me tremendously.

MARCH, RANDI
[title] "Persistence of Friendship" [pers.] I wrote this poem because my best friend had moved away and my mom, Donna March, helped me realize we could still be friends and do things together. If it weren't for my family and friends, I'd be lost. I'm glad that I'm allowed to dodge the obstacles that stand between my friendships. Sometimes I need a little push.

MARKOWSKI, BENEDICT
[title] "My Pearl" [pers.] I am a retired archivist, who has pursued the writing of poetry since age eleven. In college, I was honored the title of "Poet Laureate" for three years at the annual convocations. My press, The Poet's Mark, published my lyric drama, *Carissima* in 1980 (written in 1964), as a libretto for an opera in free verse. I am a distinguished and lifetime member of the International Society of Poets, The Iliad Press and the American Academy of Poets. The first two organizations have recognized my poetry with awards and various publications, including two cassettes of Visions (400 lines) and in several anthologies of Best Poems. Most of my poetry describes the creative process, aspects of all art, my philosophy of art and life, its wonders and varieties and man's noble and heroic aspirations. I believe we must insist on the best audible language for poetry, which should be profound and uncommon. We must recover its former merits for the future. I employ free verse and invented the Free Sonnet.

MARKS, ALICE
[title] "Seasons" [pers.] I have loved poetry since my mother held me on her lap and read *A Child's Garden of Verses*. My husband, Murray, and I were high-school sweethearts and over the years we've found, written and read poetry to one another. Verses were in letters to the South Pacific when he was a B24 pilot in WW II. Poetry was scarcer during career days (he's a chemical engineer and I'm a speech therapist) and while we raised five children. It is good to look back over the years and defy the cynics and divorce statistics—good and happy marriages due last and Murray has always been my "Man for all Seasons."

MARLOW, TRISTA
[title] "The Flock" [pers.] My name is Trista Marie Marlow. I was born in Edmonton, Alberta and when I was five, I moved to Lougheed, Alberta. Lougheed is a very small village where everybody knows everybody. Over the years, you become close to most of the people in the town and in your family. The poem "The Flock" is a metaphor comparing birds to family and friends. The poem describes how going through life, you go through everything, like hardships and happy times, but the "V" or family will always be there and even on that day when you leave home and start your own life, the original "V" will be there. This poem is my look into life, maybe not everyone's life, but definitely my life.

MARLOWE, PAUL
[title] "Nurani" [pers.] I want to thank my brother, Wayne D. Marlowe, who without his help I could not live in this world; my mom, Thea Okla Marlowe, who I love very much, but most of all my wife, Nurani Marlowe, who came from halfway around the world to be my wife knowing I was a poor man and handicapped! I dedicate this poem to her. Also, I want to thank my father, Fred, and my sister June (deceased), and to God in Heaven, who caused all this to be. I am disabled an unemployed, I don't know what life has in store for me, but maybe somewhere, someone will have mercy on a poor boy.

MAROUF, MAYSAN
[pers.] I'm a 20 year old Syrian girl studying environmental health in the American University of Beirut. I have lived in Italy, England, Syria and now I live in Lebanon. As a result, I am in touch with several cultures and speak Arabic, English, french, Spanish and Italian. I find in poetry the expression of the different shades of moods and feelings that we walk through in life. It is a wonderful tool I cannot do without. I thank all my friends that encouraged me to enter, but most of all I thank my family for believing in me at all times. In this poem, I use the image of the sea, which I cherish. This image is often found in my other poems; it is versatile.

MARSH, VINCENT
[a.] Olive Branch, MS [title] "The Black Hole of Desire" [pers.] Before I wrote this poem, I sat down with a pen in hand and paper. I didn't think about what to write. I began feeling what to write. The words then just flowed onto the paper with overwhelming emotion. This poem represents all of us human beings. Our daily battles of the flesh the heart, and the soul between good and evil. In the end, we all long to be with God.

MARSHALL, ASHLEY
[title] "Falling for You" [pers.] The poem I have written is about a very special man in my life, who I have been in love with for about two years. To me, the poem portrays a situation of unrequited love, because in my case, I have fallen for an older person who I cannot be with. This poem was written at a time in my life when I kept all feelings and thoughts to myself, and no one ever knew what

was going inside my head or my life. But, now through my poems I have begun to open up and express myself more freely. I have also learned to accept the fact that me and this guy may never have mutual feelings for each other, but we can be friends, and I now share almost everything with him, as if he were an older brother.

MARTIN, MICHAEL
[title] "A Crack in My Armor" [pers.] Some people reading my poem might think or believe that I wrote it for someone in particular. That simply is not the case. I wrote this poem in the belief that if I ever fell in love, that is what would happen.

MARZOUKA, ZIAD
[title] "Strange" [pers.] My name is Ziad Marzouka. I am from the Hashemite Kingdom of Jordan. I am only 17 years old. I never took poetry seriously, so publishing my poem was an unexpected surprise.

MASON, SANDRALEE
[title] "Suicide" [pers.] "Suicide" was written at a very difficult time in my life when I was diagnosed with a life-threatening disease, and plagued with unbearable pain day and night. My spirit, as well as my flesh, were battling for existence, while my mind was contemplating suicide. My spirit rose above my flesh, and God's grace healed my body, mind and soul. Poetry to me is a pouring out of the inner spirit into an art form; the mind is the canvas and words flow to create the picture. My hope is that "Suicide" is not an alternative for anyone.

MATHEWS, ALICE
[a.] Lodi, CA [title] "God's Plan" [pers.] Our family is very important to my wonderful husband of 47 years and myself. For fifteen years, we have lived two thousand miles from all of them. All of our lives, we knew God had a plan for us, but how He brought us all back together again left no doubt in our minds we had been living that plan unconsciously to prepare us for retirement. Our dream for many years was to live near our four children, four grandchildren and a precious great-granddaughter. This poem depicts my feelings after having our dream fulfilled.

MAULDIN, JOHNNY C.
[a.] Tyler, TX [title] "Mother Nature's Medicine" [pers.] This poem was inspired by actual childhood experience. I spent eight years in the state orphan's home in Corsicana, TX. The time spent there was 1946 to 1954. The talent I have in writing poetry, songs and now a book is God's gift to me. Words cannot explain the peace and joy that God's gift has brought me over the many years that I have been writing. I have written some 130 poems, over 600 songs and now have a finished manuscript of a book filled with laughter, sadness, peace and spiritual content. I am finding extreme depth in my senior years that lay somewhat dormant inside me until recently. I thank God for turning the key and releasing me from the chains of a life of continuous circles. I yet have so much to write about. Watch me

McARTHUR, JACK
[title] "This Love" [pers.] Poetry is a valuable asset to my life. I first started writing poetry to vent all my frustration, rage, anger, etc. Now I use poetry to express all my feelings. I feel poetry is one of the best ways to explain the feelings inside your heart. My poem, "This Love," was written to express my love for my girlfriend at the time.

McCALL, BRANDY
[title] "Listen All!" [pers.] I'm just a girl from Belleville, Illinois who wanted to tell it like it is. Everyone knows the world is crumbling around them, but no one wants to take responsibility for it. I wrote this poem to let people know that if they want a planet for their kids to grow up on, then things need to change. I'm glad I had this chance

to express the way I feel, and I hope people enjoy reading my poem as much as I enjoyed writing it.

McCOY, ARTHUR
[title] "Life" [pers.] I wrote this poem in 1971. It was a time of awakening for me. I was influenced by the murder of Dr. Martin L. King, the death and destruction in Vietnam and the liberation movements in my own country and community - Black Power, women's liberation, Gray Power and all the others. Two years later, I shared this poem with Gwendolyn Brooks, who signed a copy of it for me which I still cherish. Although we have progressed, there are still too many examples of how much we seem to disregard life.

McCRAY, DEIRDRE
[title] "My Eyes See" [pers.] This is an answer to an old lover who warned me that he didn't deserve my love and affection and surprisingly, I was hurt and saddened by his words. Everyone deserves to know how to love and feel loved by someone. Jesus loves us all—all the time. I want to thank a very special person in my life for giving me the courage to be creative, my Aunt Carol. Through her undying love and her strength, she taught me the importance of expressing myself creatively, emotionally and spiritually. I hope this poem can do for others what having an aunt like C. Dawn Mac has done for me.

McCRAY, GARY
[a.] Nashu, NH [title] "Dark Passion" [pers.] A poem is simply a collection of words given structure, the poet is the source of life to the poem. He or she supplies the fire, the spark that brings the verse to a higher existence. Poetry is not just written, it is a product of the heart.

McDONALD, JOHN
[title] "Lonely Man" [pers.] There's not much to say about myself except; I'm very outgoing and easy to get along with. As for my poem, it speaks for itself. I also like to say thank you for taking time to read my poem and I hope I can share more with you in the near future. Thanks again.

McDONALD, PATRICE
[title] "The Image" [pers.] I see poetry as a gift given to me, where I can express my thoughts, feelings, opinions, and etc. It takes up a part of my life and also my heart. I feel that anytime I cannot voice myself, I can take out a piece of paper and pencil and release everything on my mind. This poem was actually written for Halloween, although my household doesn't celebrate or believe in witches and goblins. I was still inspired by the fall colors, the turtlenecks and the unimaginable costumes. I'm glad that my inspiration will be shared with many others.

McDONALD, WILLIAM
[title] "Crying" [pers.] I write poetry simply to convey, express, or release whatever emotion is within me. Writing seems to balance things in my life. My chosen occupation as a police officer in New York City could be perceived as a poetic contrast all by itself. Putting a pen to paper can sometimes soothe the day's events. I hope to someday write for a living. Ten years into a profession that I cannot call a love of mine, I finally realize what I want to do for the rest of my life. I'm writing my first book and am driven by its challenges. I hope dreams truly can come true.

McELHANEY, STACY
[a.] Niles, OH [title] "Angel" [pers.] I have just graduated from Youngstown State University and received my degree in Medical Assisting. I am getting married next summer. I have had a passion for writing poetry since about 7th grade, when my grandmother passed away. I wrote this poem for my mom in memory of my step dad. He was a wonderful man and loved everyone he touched. I

hope my poem will help others who have lost someone very close to them.

McGHEE, ADRIA
[a.] Omaha, NE [title] "Big Sister" [pers.] I wrote the poem "Big Sister" for my oldest sister, Aisha for her 21st birthday because she has given me her support in everything I have chosen to do. My parents, Adrian and Cathy Murphy, have also given me support and are always telling me how proud they are of me. They always frame my awards I get from school. I go to Central High School in Omaha, Nebraska. I am 17 years old and I will graduate in the year 2002. I believe I have a gift because I write poems based on feelings. I love to draw and design clothes when I'm not working and I want to be a fashion designer when I grow up. I think that's great, coming from a person that is the youngest of four, besides having three halfsisters and three half brothers and a great supporting cousin named Nikki.

McGHEE, TERRIE A.
[a.] Newark, NJ [title] "Giving" [pers.] This poem is very special to me. It commemorates and describes a unique woman's attitude about giving, Mother Theresa. She gave her priceless time, faith, and courage to combat the adversity of poverty in the lives of many nationalities of people suffering. With her love and kindness, she should never be forgotten. She demonstrated all her strength with a focused mind to reach the lost at any cost, while operating under direct orders of her commander-in-chief. In fact, her character spoke for all humanity. I believe if we are digest the seeds she planted in our hearts, the world would reap a harvest of giving and caring people, therefore, leaving no room for poverty and racism to grow. Only then will we find ourselves living to live again.

McGOWAN, CONSTANCE
[a.] Maces Bay, NB [title] "A Tribute to My Homeland" [pers.] I was chosen to be an ambassador for Charlotte, Co., N.B. in 1991 as an asset to encourage tourism. I visited every school and nursing home in the county on a regular basis and attended and spoke at meetings for various organizations. I attended parades and visited tourist bureaus informing people of all the wonderful things we have here in New Brunswick. I live on the Atlantic coast, where fishing is the main industry. Lobster, herring, scallops and clams among the most common catch. We have raised three children and now have six grandchildren and four great- grandchildren—all are healthy and strong. God has been very good to us. This year we will celebrate our 59th wedding anniversary! This poem was written to remember our heritage and to remind us that wherever we live, we have only to look around us to see and appreciate God's glory.

McGRATH, DANIEL
[title] "Softly, As in Summer Morning" [pers.] I started to write poetry about twenty years ago. I hadn't written for about fifteen years. I began to write again about a year ago when a very special person came into my life and inspired me to once again write. I write mainly as a way of releasing what I feel inside at the time, whether it be happy, sad, or indifferent. I feel that if I touch someone with my poetry, that is the most rewarding thing a writer can hope to achieve. "Softly, As in Summer Morning" was written for someone who is very close to my heart, who, at the time it was written, I thought had gone from my life forever.

McKAY, BRAEDY
[title] "Fat Cat" [pers.] This poem was written about my cat, which I found near a barn close to our house. His name is Boogers. I myself am from Ligonier, PA I live with my mom, dad, brother and sister. I really enjoy skiing, playing hockey, and building model rockets. I go to school at Ligonier

Valley Middle school and hope to got to college at the University of Toronto. It was just this year that I really got into poetry. My writing teacher is the one that inspired me to write "Fat Cat." I am glad I can share my poetry with other people.

McKAY, GEORGE
[a.] Ocala, FL[title] "AIDS vs. the Black Man" [pers.] Poetry is a gift that was imparted into the very essence of my spirit by God. I cherish this poetic gift with my total being. The purpose of my Poem "Aids vs. The Black Man" is that I want the black man to wake up and realize that this disease is real. I pray that this poem will reach many people and make them aware that this disease is destroying the human race body, spirit and soul.

McKOY, CATHERINE
[title] "Alphabet Men" [pers.] I've always enjoyed reading the written word! It was like a man from Heaven. It thrills me to think that my written words, my thoughts, are meaningful to someone. If just one person says "Yeah, I know what that feels like," then it's worth it to me!

McMENEMY, REBECCA
[title] "Heaven in His Eyes" [pers.] What my poem is about is that a girl is dancing with this guy she likes. But when she looks into his eyes, she sees something peaceful. She thinks and thinks for the whole dance. When the dance is over she says aloud "It's heaven" and every time she sees him in the school halls, she's reminded about that place. My name is Rebecca McMenemy and I'm only twelve years old. I love poetry and I want to study it someday, and I think that poetry is the best way to get a message through to some people today. Well, I want to say that I love all my family and my best friend in the whole world, Amanda Harvel, and all of my friends for this inspiration.

McNEILL, KIMBERLY
[a.] Jonesboro, GA [pers.] I think poetry is a gift, one that was given to me by God. The fact that I didn't write about God was surprising to me. I usually write, or base my topic of poetry on God, because I love Him so, but I was inspired to write about an everyday event. I was inspired by the fact that I'm always leaving my shoes somewhere. I never put them where I can find them, so I never can. I didn't expect my poetry to be published, but I give God all the glory that it was.

McNELIS, CECILIA
[title] "Demands of Death" [pers.] My writing began in 1969, when the history-literature teacher, Mr. Dennis Hastert (now Speaker of the House), made writing a journal class assignment. I have continued to write over the years. In 1980, I was accepted at Women's Writers Center in Cazenovia, New York, but did not attend. Writing is one of my lifetime loves!

MEAD, SARA
[title] "Taken Away" [pers.] To me poetry is a gift every one has, but most are unable to express it. I am 16 years old and have been writing poems since I was eight. I began to put my sadness on paper when my grandfather died and have moved on to writing about everything. Life is not easy for me and I expect it to just get harder, but writing takes the pain out of life. I am happy that my poems are finally getting published. I thank the people who wouldn't let me stop writing and the people at Poetry.com for everything they have done for me.

MEDRANO, JOSE
[a.] El Paso, TX [title] "Wind" [pers.] As a young adult attending Americas High School, I enjoy many things, poetry being one, but I also love to draw. This poem, which I entitled "Wind," is one I think many people can possibly relate to. It's about feeling alone inside, even when you think you have everything in the world, as if something

is missing, a part of yourself you can't seem to grab on to. I selected this poem out of a few I had written, because I felt this poem had a lot more feeling to it and also that it was coming from deep within myself.

MEHTA, CHANDNI
[title] "Pain" [pers.] I will be 16 on July 29th. Though I have a comfortable home and am encircled by family and friends, I feel an ever-present sense of alienation. "Pain" relates to the way I see myself in life. The way I have shut out my feelings from the people around me, and the way no one understands what I'm really trying to say. The poem also expresses my fear of dying the way the man in the poem does . . .alone!

MEISKEY, RENEE
[title] "This Place" [pers.] All of my poetry is based on true experiences in my life. My special poem, "This Place," was written from a dream of owning the house two doors down from where we rented. After my husband and I rented for eighteen years, ownership seemed impossible until now. I would walk or drive by the shaded backyard with so many flowers; not a special house to anyone else, just to me. I'm happily married twenty years with two grown children. I love God, my family, our semi-detached home in Ephrata, PA. I also enjoy reading, writing, anticipating quiet walks, coffee with friends, gardening, and decorating.

MELONG, MAUREEN
[title] "The Queen of Broken Hearts" [pers.] Poetry is good for the soul. I have been writing for many years and have dedicated this particular poem to a lady who has always been close to my heart, the First Lady of Country Music, Tammy Wynette.

MELROSE, MELANIE
[title] "Once upon a Time" [pers.] Poetry to me is an expression of emotions. This particular poem reflects that everything around us—people, places, nature. The things we take for granted will not always be here. Things diminish, yet stories and books in general seem to last forever. Take fairy tales; the characters live forever—Snow White, Cinderella and Prince Charming. They all have entered our lives and the will be part of the lives of generations to come. Reading and writing are what make history and well, I'm just glad to know that one of my poems will be part of it all.

MELTON, VALERIE
[title] "Sea's Song" [a.] Fountain Valley, CA [title] "Seas Song" [pers.] Poetry and art are important aspects of my life. I strive to express the beauty that surrounds me, whether it be found in my poems, paintings or photography. I see beauty in all things, such as the setting sun or pattern of a single leaf. God has blessed me, and I am thankful for this gift. I hope others enjoy this verse. I wish to dedicate this to my family who encourages me, gives me continual inspiration, and devoted love, and to God, for allowing me to find beauty in each new day, and the ability to express it!

MENDEZ, MARINA
[a.] Valparaiso, IN [title] "Untitled" [pers.] I would like to give thanks to my friends and family, and I thank God for making this possible. I would like people to know that my poems come from my mind and heart. This poem was written because it just came to me. Everyone has a rough time in life and want to do something foolish like end their life. The () marks are where I vision those objects. I think people sometimes fall in love too fast and don't think before they take that journey. Then, they end up doing foolish things, like my poem states. Thank you, everyone, for just listening to what I have to say in words and poetry.

MERRILL, BETTE
[a.] Naples, FL [title] "Life" [pers.] I was southern

born and bred in Mobile, Alabama. I now live in Naples, FL with my naval Officer husband. I was educated at Trinity College, San Diego State, Tufts University, and abroad. My travels ignited my emotions to translate visuals and the culture of the people into words. I am a retired educator, floral designer and realtor. My hobby is life itself. I love all sports and literature. My passion is poetry and ballroom dancing. Dancing is poetry in motion. My philosophical basis stems from my southern roots and Catholic traditions. It doesn't matter which stone of life one steps upon, as long as the stone is headed in the right direction. This poem I leave as a legacy for children and grandchildren. My poem, "Love," was published in 1985.

MEYER, MARIE D.
[a.] Clovis, CA [title] "A Haiku Offering" [pers.] I chose the genre of haiku because it is through this form that many of my students have found their poetic voices and launched into new layers of seeing. It's secure structure, and at first notice, seeming simplicity guides their passage into the line breaks and white spaces of thought. And nature's realm, so intrinsically connected to this form, is capacious enough to welcome, inspire, and include all my students' efforts, regardless of academic prowess or language proficiency. The haiku invites varied levels of expression, only requiring as requisite a receptivity to the delicate, a readiness to perceive, and a desire to express.

MEYER, MAY
[a.] St. Louis, MO [title] "My Aunt's Spiritual Legacy to Us" [pers.] I minister as a chaplain in a large hospital. As I reflect on my patients' visits, I have begun to express my and their feelings and insights on poetry. I want to continue to develop this gift to promote healing and wholeness. "My Aunt's Legacy to Us" is dedicated to my eighty-two year old aunt, Sister Duchesne Herold, FSM, who has been a mentor to me and a valiant sufferer with Parkinson's Disease for many years.

MEYERS, REBECCA
[a.] Rockton, IL [title] "The Joy of Man and Woman" [pers.] I started writing poetry when my mother passed away. I was thirteen. I used my writing as an outlet for my feelings because I felt I had no one to talk to. I continue to use writing today. When I find something difficult to verbalize, I write it down. This process has served me well throughout my young marriage. My husband, Matthew, and I are both twenty-six and together we have four daughters. Our family and relationship can sometimes be quite a challenge. When our communications suffer a temporary breakdown, I use my writing to help build them up again.

MICK, VALERIE
[title] "Flight" [pers.] The poem "Flight" is a journey through darkness, and a major choice to stay and fight. This poem is a walk through a person's solitary pain into the light of humanity that works together for the common good of all people. I attend Portland State University. I am a returning student of the year 2000, after twenty years of work and motherhood. I am working toward my masters degree in writing. I have two wonderful sons, James and Abraham. I am pleased to have two beams of sunshine, my grandchildren, Taya and James.

MIEROR, YAFFA
[title] "No Means to an End" [pers.] I feel honored and privileged that my poem was chosen for this book. I honestly did not think it would be picked with the issue of God being such touchy subject. I felt my poem would be looked upon as too opinionated and controversial, but I am happily corrected to see more people believe in divine intervention then I gave credit for. I, simply believe that when all else fails and everyone you thought

you loved is gone, God will still be there, smiling down on you, rain or shine.

MIHALI, RAUL
[a.] Fairfield, CT [title] "When I Died" [pers.] Sometimes unique marginal circumstances and moods can make me sit down and write. I write very little, with myself as a present reader and an audience in mind and with the relaxed understanding that anyone else in the future could discover the words of any particular emotional interest. I would definitely not mind a one-way mission in space if given the opportunity and scope.

MILAZZO, SHERRILL
[title] "Memories" [pers.] I started writing poetry after my husband passed away two years ago. My poems help me express all my feelings. Thanks to my family and sister for always being there.

MILLEDGE, ATEKA
[title] "The End" [pers.] Poetry is the one aspect of my life that I can always know my place. This poem is for all of those who lost someone in their life that they can't get out of their systems. I hope whenever you read it, you will see that you are not the only one who feels that way.

MILLER, ANNE
[title] "Nunnery" [pers.] "Nunnery" and "Irrational Love" reflect the many conflicting emotions of sexuality and romantic love experienced for the first time. The act of writing or reading such poetry helps the young person to work through these exciting and challenging life changes.

MILLER, DEBORAH
[title] "Be Strong Knowing Love" [pers.] This poem is for my boyfriend. I love him, so he must be strong, knowing what love is. My poem serves as a definition of love and what he can expect from me. There should be no fear from past relationships if he trusts these words. We will grow as a couple and conquer new challenges. Our foundation now is solid.

MILLER, DWAINE
[a.] Garland, TX [title] "I Am A Head Injured Person With Dreams" [pers.] In 1985, when I was 24 years old, I suffered a severe closed head injury in a motorcycle accident. I am now a 40 year-old male who lives in Texas. Since my injury, I have obtained an associate degree and graduated valedictorian from ITT Technical Institute in 1996. My interests include going to church, movies, and restoring old cars, of which I own two (a '69 Grand Prix and a '73 Corvette). I do volunteer work and tutor in math when I get the chance. Every line of my poem is heartfelt, for I know what it is to have suffered a head injury.

MILLER, ERICK
[a.] Salem, WI [title] "Not Like Mom" [pers.] Erick Miller is a father of four and a grandfather of three. He has written a three-part novel and over one hundred short stories dealing with horror and police work. He served as a foot soldier in the 101st Airborne in Vietnam during the latter part of '69 and most of '70. Some of Mr. Miller's military stories may be published in *Chicken Soup for the Veteran's Soul* in November of 2000. He is hoping to make a movie of his novel titled "Quiet Neighbors."

MILLER, MEGAN
[title] "The Art of Imagination" [pers.] I believe poetry allows people to express themselves in way they would otherwise keep hidden inside. I was inspired to write this poem by my niece, Colby, and I also wanted to remind people that imagination is an important aspect of any person, old and young alike. It can take you anywhere you want to go and it allows you to continue to hope and dream, despite what may happen in your life. This is one of many things I have learned in my 18 years on

Earth and I will hopefully continue to learn much more in the future.

MILLER, TRAVIS
[title] "Take Time Out to Pray" [pers.] It has been said that every man carries within him the world in which he lives. For me, poetry is my way of sharing my world with the rest of the world it is my way of sharing the wisdom of my years my hindsight, insights and my way of expressing my innermost feelings and my love for Almighty God. I hope the verses of this poem will be an inspiration to all who read it and may God bless.

MILLIGAN, PAM
[title] "Heartbreak" [pers.] "Heartbreak" came from my very own broken heart. As I sat on the beach gazing far out into the ocean, I began writing the feelings from my heart. It's a tough thing to go through, but as time passed and healing began, I found a tremendous inner strength that led to self-development, improvement, growth, and change. So despite the sadness of this poem, things have worked out in a very positive way, and I never even imagined myself writing a poem. I have moved on and I'm no longer blue..

MILLS, CHRISTINA
[title] "Realization" [pers.] This poem I treasure. I wrote this poem shortly after my boyfriend of seven months broke up with me. It was the first serious relationship I was in, which broke my heart once it ended. I had fooled myself into thinking I wasn't in love with him and denied it to everyone, yet I woke up one morning to realize that I still loved him, and always will. Yet again, it was impossible to have another relationship with him as I had come to discover from a close friend that he was not the man I thought he was. So after our break up I had started writing mainly just in journals, then I gave poetry a try and it is now a part of my life. Writing poetry to me is very relaxing and it helps when things don't go the righteous, but I think a lot of people are like that. Poetry will forever be a part of my life, the same as my ex . . . whom I will never forget as long as I live.

MILLS, REBECCA
[title] "Revelation" [pers.] My poem represents an awakening inside one's soul. I am a recent member of Alcoholics Anonymous and I have recently dedicated my life to a new set of ideas and principals. By examining my life before the program, I could see the sadness and despair my life had become. I dedicate this poem to the millions of alcoholics or addicts who still suffer and may one day see the light of recovery.

MISHLER, LAURA
[title] "Run From Heaven" [pers.] Writing to me is an escape and one of the greatest joys in my life. I have the muscle disease Fibromyalgia and with missing school, I often found myself alone. I embarked upon writing. I wrote this poem one night when I could not sleep because of being ill. I am now only seventeen and starting college. This is my first piece of work to be published, and at least I can say something good came out of the pain.

MISSETT, JOHN
[a.] Liverpool, UK [title] "The Lighthouse" [pers.] I wrote this after praying to God for the ability to write something as beautiful as the German Christmas carol "Silent Night." It's not quite that good, but closer than I have ever been to fine. I wish to thank Mr. Howard Ely and Poetry.com for all their encouraging help and support.

MITCHELL, WALTER
[a.] Mesa, AZ [title] "Waved a Good-bye" [pers.] Some say poetry is an art, but I say it comes from the heart, so I will write what I feel and mean what I write; from that I will never part.

MODDERMAN, WIM-JAAP
[title] "Holy Oak, the Druid's Path" [pers.] Some time ago, I started my journey on a druid's path. This poem describes my feelings about the druid order that I have joined: the order of boards, ovates and druids, or for short, the obod. This poem came to me when I was reading the study material of the obod. I hope you will enjoy this poem.

MOHR, MARIS
[title] "Night's Companion" [pers.] Since I can remember, I have had to express my feelings and opinions about the world around me: people, politics, the weather, seasons, changes, relationships, friends, lovers. After 30 years of writing, I finally published my first book, *Memo Book of My Mind*, here in Israel. Since then, I have written enough new poems for a second volume. In addition to writing poetry, I have been teaching high school English in Israel for the last 15 years and trying to pass on my love of poetry and my respect for those who have created art from the English language to my students.

MOLNAR, MICKIE
[title] "Dragon's Lair" [pers.] Inspiration . . . worlds and thoughts that flow from my fingertips like an artist portrays a vision through colors and brush strokes on canvas. It calls to me; it invades my mind and captures my soul. It is pure happiness and obsession at the same time. My poetry repertoire usually covers subjects of a loving and spiritual nature. "Dragon's Lair" is an exceptional diversion from that path in that the inspiration came from daily commute via Southern California's notorious freeway system. Need I say more?!

MONCRIEFF, MAUREEN
[title] "My Father's Gift" [pers.] I wish to dedicate this poem to the best journalist I know, Tom S. Sloan (my father), who, if it wasn't for all of his funny verses in my kids' and my own birthday cards, this poem would not exist.

MONNAHAN, MYRNA
[title] "Free" [pers.] This poem speaks of my past and my fight to find the woman I really am. Writing has helped me to see life as it really is and get past the pain and be who God intended. My family has been some of my biggest inspiration and support, and the man in my life, Wally Rogers, has been my guiding light. His love has shown me how to be all I can and love each new day. To abused women, there is help and there is life. Reach for it, fight for who you are, because life is wonderful.

MONNENS, JENNIFER
[title] "The Fire I Seek" [pers.] The night I wrote this, a full moon hung over a Minnesota lake and a moth perished in the molten wax of my candle. We all seek love in our lives, but I also seek the romantic possibilities of our beautiful globe, and therefore ourselves. A life drunk deeply of a long highway travelled into our spirits, and full moons that never come often enough in our hearts, this is what I seek.

MONTGOMERY, SHERRI
[title] "The Sidewalk Plot" [pers.] After teaching elementary and junior high school, raising three children, and pursuing art and literature on the side for thirty years, I "retired" to pursue my passions: literature, art, history, and traveling. I design and weave wearable art, which includes hand-woven clothes and hand-woven bead jewelry. My reflective time is spent writing. This particular poem was inspired by a grey summer day in San Francisco. Everything was grey: the sky, the buildings, the street, even the people. The only sign of life was that single, struggling elm. Seeing that surviving within the grey, to me meant life itself. I considered it a sign of hope; I still do.

MONTOYA, BRENDA
[a.] Barstow, CA [title] "Poets As We Know It" [pers.] This poem is special. It talks about God, my family, my friends, and even people I've met who has inspired me and touched my life. I hope it finds a way to touch people's hearts the way people have touched my heart in so many ways.

MOON, CATHERINE
[title] "A Sunshine, A Star" [pers.] Dedicated to all those who have shown me the true meaning of friendship and love, and especially to Soon, for always believing in me.

MOORE, LAQUITA
[title] "The Promised Land" [pers.] The Promised Land is an eternal place. It is the ultimate dream destination, and yet it represents much more than a physical location. The Promised Land is a divine state of being. It symbolized the sense of triumph and sheer joy that accompanies personal growth. It is the achievement of an intended transition. The Promised Land, therefore, is the manifestation of heart-centered desires. For these gifts, I thank God Almighty.

MOORE, WAYNE
[a.] North Vernon, IN [title] "The Ole Cowboy Prayer" [pers.] I wrote this poem in the Comechire Mountain in Oklahoma in April of 1999 at the request of some cowboys in Oklahoma. All of my poems are special to me. I feel especially thankful for the fact I have been given this special gift, as I have written poetry for over fifty-five years of my life.

MORA, JAMIE
[a.] North Island, New Zealand [title] "Forever" [pers.] Poetry is very important to me, and having a poem published is a dream come true. This poem is for my grandma who died May 8th, 2000. She was a great woman and I love her so much. I live in Te Aroha, North Island, New Zealand and I'd like to thank my cousin, Daniel and my Dad, for making this dream come true. Writing is such a great way to say things you could never say up front. I love you Grandma—this one's for you. I'll never forget you.

MORALES, CARLOS
[a.] Van Nuys, CA [title] "Theater of Life" [pers.] This poem reflects, in part, how I passed through life without being somebody defined. It expresses my volubility, the passion of doing something new every time, keeping the love for everything, and still I would finish the moment in a deep, sad emptiness. At the same time, I try to express how loneliness taught me that wonders are everywhere. After all, when I wrote this poem, I was just trying to play my part.

MORALES, IVAN
[title] "To Love is to Live" [pers.] Some things are true, whether you like them or not . . . I've always thought there's something more to what we see, to what we feel. This, I believe, is the true nature of what we are and why we're here; to make ourselves happy. There are three things in life I'm passionate about: poetry, love and film. There's nothing more spectacular than portraying your innermost feelings on paper or on film. Touching people, that's what it's all about. Thank you CR, for the inspiration. "The fear of becoming a 'has been' keeps some people from becoming anything"—Eric Hoffer. "Life is what happens while you're busy making other plans"—John Lennon. "Spending life, questioning life, is a waste of life"—Fred Durst. Peace, Love and Lemon Snow—Ivan Morales

MOREIRA, HELOISA
[title] "I Love You" [pers.] "I Love You" depicts hallmarks in my journey. It symbolizes life cycles, growth, and transition. This poem is dedicated to my Lord and Savior, Jesus Christ; to a brilliant and skilled writer who initiated me on poetry's path, Dr. Arlindo Pires Moreira, my father; and to the memory of Helena Sousa, an inspiring Portuguese poet and ancestor, my great-grandmother. Stanza III of "I Love You" was omitted due to contest limitations.

MORENO, MICHAEL
[a.] Fresno, CA [title] "Dear Mom" [pers.] This poem was written and is dedicated to my mother, Dolores. She stood by me through some very tough times and encouraged me in my decision to go back to school at the age of 41. With only 11 months left before I earn my B.A. in English Literature, I'm glad I followed through and listened to her. Thanks, Mom! There are two additional people who have been very inspirational to me in the pursuit of my degree and they are Mr. Vicki Martineau and Professor Don Cleave of National University, Fresno, CA.

MORGAN, HENRY, JR.
[title] "Fools in Black and White" [pers.] In my life, my marriage to Edie, my wonderful wife, and the blessed fatherhood of my three children, Anthony, Kimberly and Damon, I have tried to live my life according to the teachings of our Father's son, Jesus. My poems have helped me to live in a world of unthinkable contradictions as to race, gender, religion, wealth and politics that have permeated our society since Adam and Eve in the Garden of Eden. I dedicate this poem to my pastor, Bishop Dennis Leonard, and to my inspirational church family of Heritage Christian Center for making me a witness to the universal love of all people.

MORLEY, GARY
[a.] [title] "That Star" Sarasota, FL [pers.] A sensitive and feeling soul can be crushed by a broken heart, and that is what inspired me to write. It is an outlet for my thoughts and feelings. I will continue to write poetry, songs, and lyrics and hope to share them with the world. I would like to find a market for my work. I would also like to thank my best friend, who I love dearly, Mr. Lori Jean O'Berry, for her friendship, love, and inspiration.

MORRIS, GAYLA
[title] "Life" [pers.] I am 12 years old. I live in Metamora, IL, with my mom. I have one cat and one dog. I would like to thank my student teacher, Mrs. Carol Bally. She inspired me to write my poem. I would also like to thank my aunt and my mom. I would like to say to my cousin Debbie, that I think that she will become a good, creative writer. Thanks to all of my friends and family. "Life" is a poem about how life works. Life is something we all should treasure!

MORRIS, JACKIE
[a.] Alton, IL [title] "Love" [pers.] As someone with has suffered and recovered from mental illness, I feel happy that my poetry will be published. One of my goals in life is to be the first mentally ill person to fly into space on one of the space shuttles. In fact, I believe my love for space fueled my recovery.

MORRIS, JOSH
[title] "Two Tiny Souls" [pers.] My favorite subject to write abut is my pets. My family owns two stray cats, one bichon feise, and two labs. One of these is Maggie, my little puppy. I wrote this poem shortly after I discovered our two cats (kittens at the time) cuddling on top of the clothes in our laundry hamper.

MORRIS, LINDA
[title] "We Are One" [peers.] Poetry, words from within. No other genre of writing reveals one's soul as quickly as a poem. My earliest experience with writing poetry was in elementary school a rhyme about my dog. My peers' reaction was laughter, not my intent, which left me hating poetry, until my eyes were opened through the teaching of the late Marjorie Sharp, during my high school years. Peer reaction changed and was more than favorable and my soul took flight through a medium I now cherish.

MORRIS, LOU
[title] "A Vision to See" [pers.] The version of this inspired description came to me like a rushing wind upon a sea. The thoughts and words run rapidly. Not a dream I had to show my position because the words and thoughts came from my heart. A vision to see; it pours out love, and cries. It blurred the tears within my eyes. A special dedication to my parents and loved ones in sharing in poetry for family, obituary, children's and etc. I feel very appreciative for this special little gift, even for a moment or always, that was given to me

MORRIS, MARY
[title] "Goodbye" [pers.] I was born in Aspull Wigan in Lancashire. I believed when I came into this world, I must care for all God's beauty, which is free, peaceful, and full of love. I believe poetry to be a source of healing. The poems and I write come from the heart. I hope the people who read my poetry enjoy them. My poetry is part of my life, and a gift from God to have the ability to write a poem. I have found much healing in my life with nature, with many birds eating from my hand. My garden is a sanctuary for birds. I am a member of the RSPB and the RSPCA. Take His hand, and trust.

MORTON, ANDRE
[title] "Music" [pers.] My poetry represents who I am as a person. It also represents the major influence jazz, rock-n-roll, rhythm and blues, and hip-hop, have had in my life. Music transcends all boundaries (race, color, culture, economic status, etc.) and is the most popular form of expression, next to the spoken word. My poem expresses the beauty of music and how people relate to its vibe. This poem is a step in my long journey to fulfill my insatiable appetite for musical nourishment.

MOSHER, LEANNE
[a.] Alice Springs, Australia [title] "Death [pers.] This poem was written on the death of a friend. It helped me deal with the pain and made me remember, despite the hurt, my heart knew he was in a better place. I feel poetry is very personal; like music, it's from the soul, and few have seen mine. My parents, Anna and Bill, husband Damion, daughter Bailey and soon to be born baby are the most important people in my life. I dedicate this to them with love. Please remember that even when it hurts the most, a smile, a happy memory, is not far away; just search with your heart.

MOULSTER, DEBORAH
[a.] Phoenix, AZ [title] "The Rose of Sharon" [pers.] I've always known I had a gift. One day I sat down and started writing. What a surprise—poetry came forth! I call them love letters from Our Lord. The poems I write have been a blessing to so many people. I am thankful for such a special and beautiful gift.

MOYER, SUSANNE
[a.] San Antonio, TX [title] "Arks" [pers.] The first of my poems to be published was a rhymed verse about birds. I was then eight years old. Since then, I have continued to revere the manifestations of nature and to write poetry whenever the spirit moves me. "Arks" is for Laura, who loves all animals, except fire ants.

MUHIA, ANTHONY NJOROGE
[a.] Atlanta, GA [title] "Last Words" [pers.] Anthony Muhia is a student at Kennesaw State University, Kennesaw, GA. He was born in 1979 in Nairobi, Kenya, and attended Muthaiga Primary

School. He then proceeded to Nairobi School, where he graduated with the class of '97. His hobbies include chess, theater and soccer. He is very interested in finance, economics and writing poetry as a means of rendering the moments of life.

MUHR, CHERYL
[title] "Ill Dream" [pers.] Everyone seems to have someone who has been their inspiration to reach for their dreams. My family has always challenged me to reach for the goal that is just out of reach. Encouragement started from my parents and has continued from my husband. One of my dreams was to write and I am following that dream now. My poem, "I'll Dream," is my way of thanking those who have encouraged me to follow my dreams. I hope that this poem will encourage others to follow their dreams as well.

MULLICAN, KARA
[title] "A Meadow of Thoughts" [pers.] This poem expresses my thoughts about the way people molded me into the young woman I am. The many flowers in the meadow represent the number of people that made a difference in my life. In this poem, I mention two particular people—my grandmother and grandfather. Although they both have passed on, they continue to mold me each and every day by the examples that they left behind for me to follow. I wanted people to realize the conciseness of life and the importance of knowing that we all, as humans, help mold someone's life through our example.

MULLIGON, JANET
[a.] Frenchtown, NJ [title] "The Two Attic Doors" [pers.] I raised my family of four. The old Stryker duplex home. God bless Grandma and Grandpa Stryker for the blessed memories. We all miss you.

MURPHY, EDNA
[a.] Richlands, NC [title] "Daddy's Little Girl" [pers.] "Daddy's Little Girl" was written in tribute to fathers who love their children and want to take care of them. It was also written for the greatest love a father can show for his children—the sacrifice of "His only begotten Son." I've never had anything published before. I'm excited about this. Please don't disappoint me!

MUSICH, LAURA
[title] "X-Country" [pers.] This poem is about cross-country running. It's not the same as running laps around a track with everyone's eyes on you. You don't have that pride factor so much. That makes cross-country so much harder—if you give up, who's going to know? It's very tempting and half of cross-country's appeal to me is to try to finish without stopping.

MUTCH, MEGAN
[title] "Imagination" [pers.] I like to write, not only poetry, but short stories and essays as well. I am sixteen years of age, and I feel that society today only sees people they feel are important. Everyone is the same, not in physical appearance or soul, but in general. We all have hearts and a mind of our own. Don't be afraid to be yourself.

MYERS, AUBREY
[title] "Seasons" [pers.] This poem was written to explain how I feel about the seasons and the way they change. I am very fortunate to live in a place where I get to experience all four of seasons. I enjoy the outdoors and look forward to the change of every seasons. This was my way of expressing those feelings.

MYERS, SAMUEL, JR.
[a.] Coeur d'Alene, ID [title] "In 20 Lines or Less" [pers.] Upon learning that each poetic entry should be of 20 lines or less, the writer decided to speak his thoughts, all in truth and some in jest.

NADEAU, HELEN
[a.] Southbridge, MA [title] "A Special Silhouette" [pers.] This composition is about everyone seen through the eyes of themselves. Its hidden message and meaning is to honestly get to know yourself. Know who you are deep inside and above all . . .like yourself. Only then can you find your true gift in life. But also, my poem has a greater meaning . . . a life lesson. Before you judge others, take an honest look at yourself. Don't expect anyone to be you . . .everyone is different! And through that contrast, they're special and deserve respect for who they really are! Who knows, maybe you'll make a new friend. My poem is universal and was created for everyone in my lifetime.

NADGRODKIEWICZ, ANNA
[title] "The Hour of Amber" [pers.] I look at life as a string of ambers—those special moments extricated from the mundane and carefully bound together on the thread of memory. This is my version of carpe diem. As an international student at the Robert E. Cook Honors College at Indiana University of Pennsylvania, I constantly cherish gem-like images of my native Poland and all the dear ones there. Simultaneously, however, every day spent in America shines with new friendships and unforgettable times. Thank you all who have given my heart the reason to glow like precious amber at the recollection of your names. I remember.

NAHLE, RANDY
[title] "Memories" [pers.] I believe that writing and poetry are tools to change the world. While most boys my age consider aggressive force as the supreme power, I have acknowledged that the pen is mightier than the sword. The poem "Memories" is dear to me because I feel that our reminiscences are priceless, for they can condole us in our time of sorrow and motivate us to achieve remarkable things in our lives. I hope that everyone who reads my poem will be inspired by it and that it will evoke some of their sweetest memories.

NARVADEZ, DULCE
[title] "Longing" [pers.] This poem is about love and friendship unreturned. It speaks of the person's willingness to love the other person although how painful it is hoping that someday the person will love him in return. I sincerely dedicate my work to my Mama and Papa, my siblings Dennise and Gerard James, to Ninong Romy and Ninang Lela, the Sormela and Narvadez Clan, my friends, especially Bernadeth, to Gabrielle and Portia, to JVM III and to God the Almighty, who had given me this gift of writing and the opportunity to share it with others for His greater glory.

NEAL, MARY
[title] "I Am a Throwaway Baby" [pers.] Countless babies die, some before their time because of ridicule and shame society has placed on them. We must give them encouragement and hope, instead of damming her! Her desperation, too overwhelming, controls the situations, brings forth the fear and "The Throw Away Baby!" Ask if there is help; save your life and your precious baby.

NEBLETT, JONATHAN
[a.] Waverly, VA [title] "Momma" [pers.] My name is Jonathan Neblett. I wrote "Momma" about Shelby Gene Neblett, my mom. I have written over two hundred poems; this is the first of which I have sent to be published. I want my mother to know that she was the first person to inspire me to become a writer. At twenty-one years old I know the value of family. In my writing, I want to show appreciation to my family, my God and search for love. While building a following of interested readers, I hope I can build this passion into a career.

NEELY, PAIGE
[a.] Justin, TX [title] "The Sacred Dog" [pers.] All

my life I have loved to write. It has always been a favorite hobby. I wrote this poem while studying native Americans. I imagine that's how the Kiowas felt seeing a horse for the first time. I don't remember the first time I saw a horse, but I don't see how anyone could look at one for the first time and not be in awe.

NEIMEJER, HOLLY
[title] "Like an Old Ragdoll" [pers.] My poem, "Like an Old Ragdoll," symbolizes how I felt when my dad left. I am 13, and I was 10 when this happened. I am in the 7th grade at Nimitz Academy in San Antonio, Texas. To me, poetry is a way to get my feelings out. I wrote this poem for an English assignment. I got a 73 on the project, but on all (66) of my original poems, I got max points. When I entered any poem, I didn't expect to win anything. But to say the least, when I got this letter, I was in complete shock for all hours. I feel very gifted and honored to be chosen. I enjoy watching baseball, and I used to play with 14 and 15 year-old boys. I love the shows "Ally McBeal" and "E. R." My ambitions are to become a lawyer or a doctor or maybe both. I also plan to join the Navy.

NEIMEJER, HOLLY
[a.] San Antonio, TX [title] "Like an Old Ragdoll" [pers.] My poem "Like an Old Ragdoll" symbolizes the pain I felt when my dad left. I am 13 now, but was only 11 when it happened. I am going to 8th grade at Nimitz Academy. For me, poetry is a way to get my feelings out. I wrote this poem originally for an English assignment. When I entered your contest, I didn't expect to win anything. But to say the least, when I got your letter was in complete shock for 24 hours! I feel very gifted and honored to be chosen. I enjoy watching baseball and used to play with 14 and 15 year old boys. I love the TV shows Ally McBeal and E.R. My ambitions are to become a lawyer or a doctor, and maybe both! I also plan to join the Navy

NELSON, HEIDI
[title] "Daddy's Girl" [pers.] My poetry is an extension of what makes me who I am today. This poem in particular reflects he relationship I had with my father. To write it was therapeutic; to be able to share it with others is profound.

NELSON, ROSALIE
[a.] Atherton, CA [title] "The House" [pers.] This is one of several nostalgic poems written recalling memories of life on a southern Wisconsin farm, far from my present California home. My writing life began after mid-life, at a point where I began looking backward as well as forward. In addition to poetry, I write memoirs and short stories.

NEWBRAUGH, CAROL
[title] "Life's Storms" [pers.] During our lifetime we all experience "storms." This poem came out of a particularly difficult time in my life, but I discovered that God is always close and will shoulder our burdens as we turn to Him. My prayer is that as others face their "storms" they will remember to turn to God and find the comfort and help that only He can give.

NEWCOM, DEBORAH
[title] "Sense of Love" [pers.] My poem has great meaning and feelings for someone whom I love more than life itself—my fiancee, Michael. Each day, my love for him grows greater than the day before. We've known each other for a year now and plan to be one in each other soon. I know many people can relate to this poem, for they have felt this way at least once in their lives. Poetry can express your feelings for someone from deep within your heart. Everyone has a poem within their heart, but most prefer not to share.

NEWMAN, KIM
[a.] Regina, Canada [title] "My Luv" [pers.] Poetry, I feel, is a time to relax and write your innermost thoughts down on paper. It's a time to express yourself in any way you wish. I wrote this poem "My Luv" basically because it just came to me and also because I like to write poetry. I was also inspired to write this poem from one of my closest friends. He is always there for me, and we are very close friends. I have three older brothers, and my mom and dad. I am the youngest at 14. I enjoy playing sports, spending time with my friends and family and much more. I am going into ninth grade this year.

NG, MICHELLE
[title] "I Am [pers.] "I Am," is a reflection of my inner self. I believe that everyone has to get in touch with their own spirituality. We are unique in our very own way, and who knows better than that "you" in you? A word is just a word. It is what that is hidden inside that gives it its unique expression. Let us not judge, nor be judged by our cover, but let this holistic flame in us shine through. I wish to dedicate this poem to my darling bunny, Marcus, who touched my life and inspired me so with the love and wisdom so often shared that is known as the essence of life.

NICHOLSON, RHONDA
[title] "Shattered Dreams" [pers.] I am a full-time college student majoring in social work. In my free time, I like to read, hang out with friends and family, watch my favorite sport, track and field (my dream is to one day meet my idol, Michael Johnson) and write poetry. At 10 years old, the art of poetry entered my soul. Now 13 years later, poetry still runs deep within me. This poem is dedicated to those, like myself, who have lost loved ones to an act of violence. We, as human beings, need to love each other and not kill each other.

NIELSON, CHERYL
[title] "Life" [pers.] I wrote this poem as a guide for myself to show if you work hard enough, life will bring truth and happiness. While I wrote this, I kept one specific individual in my mind—my best friend. This one person is the one that gives me hope to keep going. I believe some of the most beautiful things in life are words. If you really look behind my words, there's always a story told. Thank you.

NIERMANN, CHRISTI
[title] "Darkness" [pers.] This poem was written while I was in the psychiatric ward of a hospital, following a suicide attempt. I felt as though the ground had dropped out from under me. My poem, "Darkness," is how I felt at the time. I felt lost and extremely hopeless at the end of the poem. I simply have realized that my depression is hereditary, and is not my fault. Along with this, I want to thank those that stood by me throughout this ordeal. Mom, Dad, Ryan, you mean the world to me. Dr. D'Oleire, thank you. Johna, you are so helpful and finally, Jenny and Mandy, I love you guys! Thanks!

NIETO, AUDREY
[a.] Edison, NJ [title] "Sweet Blue" [pers.] I don't remember the time and place of when I wrote this poem. I don't remember a lot about it, actually. It mostly informs the reader that if you wait through all these beautiful things, the sky, the sun, and a perfect day, you'll soon have someone to sit with you and share it all with. "Sweet blue" was neither my first poem nor my last; it doesn't have any significance to me, but I'm happy to share it. Thanks to Rainstorms and Rainbows, this poem now has significance. It is my first published poem ever. Thanks, Mom and Dad.

NIEWINSKI, LISA
[title] "Prelude" [pers.] We had only been dating a few months when we decided on that rainy afternoon in May to take shelter from the storm. We were both tired from the day's events and agreed to rest for a while. Sometime later in the evening, I woke to the sound of falling rain and his gentle breathing. As I gazed upon him, I suddenly realized that he was the love, the one I had been waiting for. And so, not only was "Prelude" inspired by you, Lou, but I dedicate it to you as well, for you truly are the love of my life.

NISHIDA, KOREN
[a.] Kahului, HI [title] "Koren Nishida" [pers.] This poem is very special to me. It is about how I feel about the love of my life when we were apart. My true feelings are expressed for this very special person.

NODILO, DENISE
[title] "Voodoo Fries" [pers.] This poem is very significant as it is one of the first I've ever written. It commemorates a fun evening out with friends who challenged me to write it after not coming up with an idea themselves to describe this unusual snack and the way in which it was presented. It has inspired me to develop and become involved with writing poetry on a regular basis for an art group. I'm pleased to be able to share this with the public and hope it in inspires many others to explore their talents.

NOEL, DEANNA
[a.] San Pablo, CA [title] "Mother" [pers.] I believe my poetic ability is both a heavenly gift and a maternal one. The meaning behind this poem "Mother" is a metaphor for the duties of a mother who has a home and family to take care of. I'm disabled, currently living in a suburb of the Bay Area. I was born and raised in this area. I'm both a high school and college graduate with an AA Degree in Dramatic Arts. I am currently studying for my BS in Psychology at California State University, Hayward. I am honored to have this poem included in this Special Anthology.

NOOR, DORA
[a.] Charlotte, NC [title] "Weeping Heart" [pers.] Poetry is mystery of life. Its unique, creative imagination, with eloquence and versatility, reveals the secret of lust/pain, desire/deception and grief/passion. The intrigue melody of a poem mesmerizes the lushingly romantic hearts, sending ripples into the bloodstream. "Weeping Heart" is a lyric of my devastating feelings for the loss of a caring and thoughtful friend. Last Valentine's day, the news of his death shattered me tremendously. I didn't even say goodbye to him. It pains me to think life is so unpredictable. My unrelenting quest for the mystery of life reached its term the day I hold my baby Sarah in my arms. My beautiful little angel, my hope and inspiration, made me a vigilant innovator for survival in this mysterious world.

NORD, JULIE
[title] "Waiting to an End" [pers.] My thoughts are put together between a flowing of mind and my soul, written by my own experiences and memories. I feel worn out at times by the past and how I grew from it, yet I still show tears and scars from life's stones hitting me, years after from those wounds.

NORDAN, MELINDA
[a.] Clinton, NC [title] "Plundering" [pers.] Childhood memories of a loving grandma inspired this poem. When visiting her I oftentimes concocted "scientific" formulas by mixing "a little bit of this" with "a little bit of that" while Momma and Grandma talked in another room. Although Grandma never actually swatted me for scooping from that jar of perfumed cream, I'm sure I well deserved it. As a teacher of trainable mentally disabled children, I strive to reflect that same patience and Christian values my grandma showed me so many years ago.

NORDLAND, LYNN
[title] "My Dad" [pers.] My dad was one of the most influential people in my life. His love for his family, friends and his country could not be compared. When he died last year, he left many people behind with broken hearts. He was given full military honors and he is buried at the Ft. Richardson National Cemetery in Alaska. Although he is gone now, his memory lives on and continues to grow. We talk of him often so we do not dull his remembrance. His hugs can still be felt when the wind blows and his laughter still echoes off the mountains.

NOVELLO, TINA
[title] "A Mother's Nest" [pers.] I am grateful to have poetry in my life. It gives me the freedom to express my thoughts in a creative and intelligent manner.

NOWAK, SUZANNE
[title] "Soulmate in Time" [pers.] I've been writing poetry on and off over the years. Raising two sons, Josh and Zach, has kept me pretty busy. A couple of years ago I started going through a lot of personal changes and spiritual growth, which led me to focus more on my writing. This poem is very personal to me, as it exposes of my own heart's desire to find that right person, that soul mate, asking yourself if you ever will. But, being the hopeless romantic and optimist I am, I believe, at least most of the time, that I will find him. Or him me.

NTUMBA, IVETTE
[pers.] I wrote this poem at a time in my life when I thought I wasn't going to make it through. I was just learning to make God my strength, but I hadn't learned everything yet. I had to learn how to get on my knees and ask God for the strength to move forward. I'll admit that there was pride there, but only God can humble the proudest heart. I've had to endure things in my life that not every 17 year-old has to go through. At first, I thought that since I was know for being a "strong" person, I would be fine. I was wrong—finding my own strength was what made my life even harder. Although God was always there, I sometimes refused to let him hold my hand or carry me. Once I did, however, the peace was overwhelming.

NUNLEY, NICK
[a.] McMinnville, TN [title] "Arrows and Hearts" [pers.] Since I was a child, I have better expressed myself with poetry than by any other way. Poetry has always been a convenient outlet for my emotions. People have been searching for love from the beginning of time. When creating "Arrows and Hearts," I wanted to reflect on the pursuit of love in a unique way.

OATES, JOSEPH
[a.] St. George, UT [title] "Unnoticed" [pers.] I was not very popular in high school, which for me was just last year. So, with that in mind, I dedicate this poem to all the "loners" out there, and would encourage them to write about their feelings. Most of all I would like to thank my 12th grade poetry teacher, Mrs. Wenzel, for all the time she spend on me and for not giving up on me, and for giving me the support and confidence that has brought this poem this far. Thank you so very much

OBERREICH, RENEE
[a.] Plymouth, WI [title] "Who Findeth Me" [pers.] My mother wrote poetry, and so do I. I wrote the story first and then the poem. In the curves life has given me, raising four children alone, and then four grandchildren, I have had one companion. He is in the Bible, and when you think you cannot go on he is always there, one step ahead of you. As I write my stories and poems, it is in grateful praise of the one who has guided me well. It is my hope that through my poems, others will come to know Him as I do.

OBILLE, ELENITA
[title] "A Baby . . ."[pers.] Poetry enables me to be in touch with my spirit. Every word gives depth and meaning to what I do. My inspiration for this poem are my first born daughter, Kristine and husband, Bryon. I graduated college with a degree in Bachelor of Science in Commerce at St. Scholastica's College. I was born on Oct. 26, 1962 in Manila, Philippines. I'm presently residing in Las Vegas, Nevada. I'm in administrative and accounting positions. My hobbies are playing the guitar and piano/organ. We must see God in all things so that there will be peace.

OCCHIPINTI, VICKY
[title] "My Heart Belongs to You" [pers.] Vicky Occhipinti, born October 5, 1974 in California. I attended Parkridge Private School. I am currently attending Pepperdine University in Malibu, CA. I'm looking forward to making a difference when I become a doctor. I enjoy writing and putting poetry together. If you allow discouragement and doubt to blur your vision and wash away your dreams, then you will be left with nothing. Today you must pause, rest, catch your breath and then look ahead. Each step brings you closer to your dream. This poem is dedicated to my true love . . . because I love you.

OLDEWURTEL, KATHRYN
[title] "Loneliness" [pers.] Late each night, a soft light escapes from my bedroom window into the woods around my home in Grand Rapids, Michigan. That's because no matter how late, you'll usually find me at my desk, writing stories and poems. I love to write and feel that it is one of the most expressive ways to show yourself to the world. It is both my escape and inspiration. My poem, "Loneliness," reflects a personal experience that I endured. Writing the poem helped me get through the experience and realize that in any difficult situation, moving on is the best thing.

OLOULA, DAVID
[title] "i believe i can die" [pers.] This poem started off as a joke with my cousin. These words came straight out of my head. My cousin laughed and said it sounded like a good poem and I should write it down. The funny thing is, I prefer MacDonals to Burger King!

OLSEN, ERIC
[title] "Where Do You Go" [pers.] My best friend, Charles A. Nadeau, whose work is also published in this volume, was my inspiration to start writing. We would be hanging out when he would decide to write a song. It always amazed me as within a half hour or so he would have a song written. To sit there and watch a song come to life truly amazed me. My poem was my first attempt at writing a song and my first poem. I wrote this poem for my mother, who has been at a state mental health facility for over thirty years. I love you.

OTTO, ROBERT
[title] "The Grave" [pers.] This poem is about four years old, but this is the first time it has been published. The poem came to me in a dream. I know that sounds made up, but it's true. I dedicate this poem to my family and friends, for they helped me see the way.

OWENS, JILLIAN
[a.] Rogers, TX [title] "If I Had One Wish" [pers.] I am 11 years old and love to read. I always liked the *Chicken Soup for the Soul* books because they inspired me to write this poem. I love my dad, but he died when I was three. My dad was someone I never knew, and I hope this never happens to you.

OWENS, NICKI
[a.] El Dorado, AR [title] "My Lament" [pers.] Throughout life, we all have our ups and downs. At one point in time of my life, I am sorry to say I had more downs than ups. I was very excited when I was notified that my poem had been chosen for publication in *Rainstorms and Rainbows*. I hope my poem will help others, especially teenagers, see that they are not alone in their problems.

OWINGS, KAREN
[title] "Missing You" [pers.] I wrote this poem in memory of one of my best friends: Kelli Ann Krpata. She passed away at the age of thirteen. I was so confused and in shock that I did not know how to deal with all of my emotions. I found in this poem that poetry can be a sanctuary for your emotions.

OZUMERZIFON, TARIK
[title] "Morse Mail" [pers.] My name is Tarik Ozumerzifon and I think that poetry is a great gift in life. The way I like to write poetry is in quiet places. I wrote this poem alongside a lake. I usually write poems in a chair looking at the water, then I just get it in my head and I write it down. One of my favorite hobbies is poetry writing while I am in quiet places, and while I am in not-so-quiet places. I say them to myself to help me relax. While I am saying them to myself, I try to write them, too.

P., PRABHATH
[title] "What I Love" [pers.] The poem, "What I Love," is special to me because I believe it is in what we love that we find the true meaning of life. I dedicate this poem to my dear mother for showing me the path of love. I'm 29, from Kollam (Quilon) City, Kerala State, South India. I did my M.A. in English Language and Literature with First Class and Third Rank from the University of Kerala. Now I am into journalism and web content writing. I am also engaged in writing novels, short stories, science fiction and non-fiction.

PACE, CINDY
[title] "The Cowboy" [pers.] This poem is dedicated to my husband, John Pace, who from high school until 1994, rode bulls in every rodeo around. He retired from the rodeo life before I had our daughter, Cassie. He is a very loving and thoughtful husband and dad. John, this one is for you.

PAL, KRISTOPHER
[title] "Paper, Pencils and Ideas" [pers.] To be creative is a gift from God. My comments on "Paper, Pencils and Ideas:" This world has many creative talents in it. Just take a look in book stores, music stores, movie stores, or your mail you get throughout the week. "Paper, Pencils and Ideas" salutes the creative people of this world.

PALMORE, MALCOLM
[title] "Hope Restored" [pers.] Poetry has given me a means to express who I am and what I'm about. Through writing, I've grown as a person and expressed my creativity in countless ways. The ability to inspire, encourage, teach and motivate people through the written word is a great gift to have. I feel blessed to have such an inspirational and therapeutic gift. I hope my poem can make your load a little lighter.

PARKS, DREW
[title] "Interior Fantasies" [pers.] Poetry is wonderful in that it can convey so many different emotions to its reader. Wonder, mystery, sadness, and joy are only a few. My poem, "Interior Fantasies," is about a vivid imagination and the disappointment that this unrealistic vision brings. The poem expresses different forms of frustration and self-questioning. It is by no means joyful. Most of my poetry isn't. It expresses a want for simple pleasures and outlandish dreams that could never unfold realistically, dreams that are oppressed by every single being about. Poetry then, I suppose, gives me a means to express my own disgust.

PARRISH, JAMES
[a.] Kennard, TX [title] "Forbidden Lovers" [pers.]

I wrote this poem for a special person in my life, which has helped make my current tour of duty a pleasant one. I am currently serving in the U.S. Air Force, and poetry has followed me all over the world. Many of my works were inspired by events around me and those that have involved me.

PASEWALK, PAUL
[title] "The Sounds of Heavenly Music" [pers.] I started writing poetry after I was retired from my job as a highway engineer. I had helped build roads and bridges in my work as an engineer and also as an inspector. I never ever failed to stand in awe of nature's handiwork and the seasons. I realized that only the Almighty God can create all of nature's beauty and rocks and mountains shapes and sizes. So, when I retired, I decided to write about what I had seen and felt; in that, I kept my mind active in creating words and descriptions and also giving God thanks for allowing me to see so much of His creations. This also gave me the chance for others to read my words and enjoy what I had seen, and to thank the good Lord for giving me the ability to write about it all.

PASMORE, JAMES
[title] "The Building Blocks of an Inmate's Life" [pers.] I am currently a prisoner of war in Texas. Just one among the ever-increasing numbers in America caught by the war on drugs. While here, I have almost completed a degree in business. I like to write poems in my spare time. I am 25 years old.

PASSEY, MARTYN
[title] "Merry Christmas?" [pers.] "Merry Christmas?" is a simplified poem that expresses my feelings with regard to the Lockerbie disaster. The devastation and tragic waste of life touched the majority of us, but for all our wonderful advances in science and technology, we still haven't learnt the most simple lesson, which is communication. Violence is an acceptable substitute. I still with my poetry to make easy for others to understand. No flowery words say what you feel. People understand truth, whether they agree with you or not. They respected it in the past. I've done a performance on poverty, voice overs, and song lyrics, but to date, no lasting work has come along. This poem is dedicated to the memory of my mother, Jure, who taught me to enjoy life and love people.

PASSMORE, LOURIE
[a.] Edmonton, AB [title] "Can't Stop a Storm" [pers.] I've written over 200 titles. I've had one poem already published in *The Sounds of Silence*. I was born on April 27, 1960

PASTIER, ANITA
[title] "Debbie" [pers.] This poem is a special tribute for a special girl who was lonely and took her life. A note to those trouble young people out there—hope is but a phone call away. Do not be afraid to ask for help.

PASTOR, ANTONIA
[a.] Harvard, MA [title] "Your Embrace" [pers.] Poetry is not something you do, it's something that happens. It's when you're most yourself because you're not trying to be something. I was twelve when I wrote "Your Embrace." I'm now thirteen, yet every time I read a poem, I shed a tear. That's what poetry does to you. It makes you lose all the people you've pretended to be, and brings out your innermost feelings. All I'd really like to say is this: Mr. S. and Auntie Angela, I miss you.

PATRICK, STACY
[title] "What is Your Imagination?" [pers.] I live in Commack, N.Y. with my parents and two Pomeranians. My poem "Imagination" teaches people to open up their minds and see what wonderful things you have hidden in your imagination. The person who taught me to think with my heart was my sixth grade reading language arts

teacher, Mrs. Ettinger, who works in Commack Middle School. She did such a wonderful thing for me, so I think I should pass it on to all you writers out there. Even if you don't write a lot, when you decide to, think with your heart and don't let anyone stop you.

PAYNE, PATTY
[a.] Cross Lanes, WV [title] "Tormented Love" [pers.] My poem is very important to me. It speaks of a one-sided love and the pain and sorrow of loving someone who doesn't return your love, and that is what most of us want—to be loved. I believe poetry is a beautiful love song of the soul, waiting to tell the world its innermost thoughts and feelings—all you have to do is open its door. I have try to do that. I hope those who read my poem will be touched in some way.

PEARSON, JOHN
[title] "Life" [pers.] I feel that since I was a kid, that life has changed so much. I was inspired by John Lennon, my mother, and my older brother Sonny Elvis P. My hobbies are martial arts (I am a first degree Black Belt), guitar playing and rollerblading. My interests are computers, the Internet and writing songs and poems.

PEARSON, MICHAEL
[title] "Fate" [pers.] This poem commemorates my belief that life is a limited privilege and that one's time is set. Although this poem is viewed as "dark" by some, I see it as one of my better writings. Poetry is more of a hobby for me and I look forward to a career as a writer. I will be entering the 8th grade in the fall and look toward to another year of poetry.

PECHMANN, DENNIS
[title] "What We Are" [pers.] A chapter of my life is what a poem represents to me. I feel the need to express new experiences or world issues that touch my heart on paper. Not in an article or a book, but in a mosaic of words. In the poem "What We Are," I decided to try and expresses what I felt about us, humanity. In it I hoped to capture both the good and bad about us, showing the two different sides that exist in all things. I do believe that words can move mountains, but I also believe that we must listen to those words first.

PEDERSEN, ANN MARIE
[a.] Stuart, FL [title] "A Day in June" [pers.] Ann Marie Pedersen is a youthful grandmother with an artistic sense and a creative enthusiasm. First and foremost a loving wife, mother and grandmother, she is also a retired social services counselor and administrator, and holds both bachelor's and master's degrees. For years, she has comprised poems and stories depicting events in her daily life.

PEDERSEN, KJELL
[title] "The Eagle" [pers.] I'm 28 years old and I live in Sweden. The poem "The Eagle" was originally written as a song for a band I used to sing with. This poem took form when I was reading a book about native Americans, which indeed is my main interest besides singing and writing poems.

PEDERSEN TRUAX, DORINDA
[a.] Canaan, CT [title] "The Storm" [pers.] I love thunderstorms and I wrote this one late spring afternoon while waiting for predicted storms to arrive in our area. To all others who enjoy thunderstorms, I hope you enjoy my poem.

PEEL, MARIA
[title] "Commitment" [pers.] I believe that poetry has a lot of meaning. Poetry it allows me to express the way I feel. This poem is very special to me, as it is based on the love for a dear friend, David Johnson. Being only twenty years old and growing up in a small town (Chipley, Florida), this gives me a chance to share with others my opinion on life. I hope that others

who reach out for that one special person's love will be able to identify with my poem.

PEFFERMAN, RAY
[a.] Allison Park, PA [title] "Here in Prison: For Now and Forever" [pers.] When this poem was published in my high school's anthology, *Contrast*, my friends said that they were worried that I was depressed. Actually, the ideas for this poem came from a picture of a man in prison, not from my own feelings. I began to think of how it must feel to be imprisoned, and described those feelings in my poem. Is a prison life worth living? You decide.

PENNELL, SHEENA
[a.] London, OH [title] "Musty Old Attic" [pers.] I like to write about things like "what if this could talk," or about people who have traits both similar and opposite of my own. I also like a put historical backdrop into my stories. Most of my inspirations are spur of the moment ("Musty Old Attic" was first written in the margin of a spelling test!) I think writers should write what is in them instead of changing their style so their friends will like it. I rarely win writing contests in school, but out of school, I'm writing left and right! I am 12 years old.

PEREZ, VICTORIA
[title] "Life's Unkind Infliction" celebrates eternity after one passes from life to death, meeting God—the Creator and life itself. This poem was inspired by a very special person, Mother Concepcion of the Order of the Discalced Carmelites, who was so full of life, even until death consumed her. May we all experience the fullness of life as she did.

PERKINS, YVONNE
[title] "My Love for You" [pers.] This poem is dedicated to my children. It represents the bond between a mother and her child. It expresses the everlasting love that a mother holds for her child without ending. With this, I feel there is no other way to express to a child the meaning of a mother's love for them.

PETERSEN, CHRISTY
[title] "Have You Ever?" [pers.] I am twenty-one years old, been married four years, and have a beautiful daughter. I have been blessed with much love, more than I could ever put on paper. Most of the poetry I have written comes from the love that's been planted deep within my soul. I would like to thank my sister, Bethany Rose Hobson, (age 11) who encouraged me to enter my poems. She has already had a poem published; "We the People," in the book *In Between Days.*

PETERSON, HAROLD
[title] "Her Love it Leads Me" [pers.] Growing up in the interior of Alaska, in the city of Fairbanks, I have learned to use poetry as a means of sharing the wondrous beauty of the state. Although this poem is not specifically about Alaska, it was inspired by a special person in my life who shared a similar respect and admiration for its many natural wonders.

PETTWAY, CHANNIE
[a.] Camden, AL [title] "Hear My Cry" [pers.] I am from a family of 16 children, eight boys and eight girls born to Evan and Ruby Matthews. I am married and I have three children, wonders Walter Jr. and Annette. I have six grandchildren. I lived in Miami for thirty-five years. We both retired and moved back to our home town. We have a wayward son; hopefully, he will change his lifestyle. Me being a Christian inspired me to writer this poem.

PFLAUMER, LINDSAY
[a.] Tracy, CA [title] "Grandma" [pers.] My grandmother was one of my best friends. She was very dear to my heart and I will never forget her. I love

writing poetry because it helps me to put my feelings on paper. I want to say I love you to my family my friends and to my boyfriend, Jerimee. You are all very supportive of me. Uncle Chris, Myron, Mom, Dad, Nana, grandpa, Aunt Tracy, Uncle Joe, Gramps, Carol, Joshua, Joseph, Christa, Bill Curtis, Jessica, Mike, Monique, Chris, Karen, Matt, Robyn, Crystle, and Sara, you all are very important people to me. God bless.

PHILLIPS, JANE
[a.] Keon Park, VIC [title] "I Am Rage" [pers.] Mothers and daughters—go figure. I wrote my poem in the aftermath of a massive fight with my mother. We've always had a somewhat strained relationship for as long as I can remember. It's a problem that continues to linger now that I'm a grown woman. I do love her very much and I wish things could be different, but when I speak, she does not hear. My writing, therefore, has always been my sanity and my most valued form of self-expression. Words are the window to my soul and my soul is my gift to the world.

PHILLIPS, JILL
[title] "Starlight Tears" [pers.] I wrote this poem after my best friend asked me to help her write a poem for homework. I showed it to many of my friends and all said it was an outstanding poem. I based it on how I felt about someone I love very much, but at the time didn't love me. Although what I wrote at the time was true, it is now nothing. My heart and his both chose not to forget and I am now engaged to him.

PHILLIPS, JULIA
[title]"Reflections on a Spring Morning" [pers.] This is my favorite poem, although I have saved it for several years. I wrote it one spring morning, as I stood on the bank of a saltwater creek and admired my growth of marsh reeds. Most of my neighbors had cut theirs back, and planted grass, Their banks have eroded! Mine stood firm! I'll celebrate my 83rd birthday in October. It is time to share my parents' poem, Enjoy!

PIERSON, MISTY
[title] "Warm My Heart" [pers.] It is a great honor to know that my love of writing can be shared with others. My interest in poetry is something I shared with my grandmother, who passed away when I was very young. This poem is special to me, and I dedicate it to the person who inspires me and gives me so much love and encouragement, my husband.

PIERSON, TERI
[title] "Sister to Brother" [pers.] In 1996 my brother was leaving for college, so I wrote this poem for him as a going away gift. I was 15 years old, living in Miami, Florida. I think that your siblings are important in your life. I have learned a lot from my older brother, who I love dearly. His name is William Pierson.

PILEGGI, MARGUERITE
[title] "Opposites Attract" [pers.] This poem was written in 1974, when I was young enough to believe that "Opposites Attract." Maturity has taught me that love is more passionate between those who agree. My present contentment has led me to begin a series of short stories based on my ancestors. Their hard-to-find-records have led me to imagine their lives and maybe to make them more interesting.

PIRAK, TRISTAN
[a.] Edmonds, WA [title] "Streaks of Red" [pers.] I'm not sure how or why I got started, all I know is that I sat down, started typing, and enjoyed the result. However, I have always been a writer of prose, authoring 20 skeletons all standing a row and collaborating with three friends on *Sad . . . But True.* A junior in high school, my current project is "The Mirror," a film that I wrote and will be

directing this summer. In closing, I'd like to thank The International Library of Poetry for deeming "Streaks of Red" worthy of publication.

PIVEC, ROBERT
[title] "Claire Marie" [pers.] I'm a big mean gorilla—and gorillas don't cry and they certainly don't write poems! However, this big gorilla, who only had one daughter, loved her, admired her and was so proud of her that he wrote poems about her all the time. This poem was the beginning, the middle and the end of a once in a lifetime adventure.

PLAZA, ANTONIO
[title] "The Homeless" [pers.] I have to admit that I'm delighted for having my poems published, despite the fact that I'm a junior high school dropout and not intellectually educated. The "Homeless Rhymes" came to me after an experience I had in my neighborhood. I'm hoping other people will be touched and inspired by my poem. It was a delightful experience which led me to these "Homeless Rhymes" after having a conversation with this homeless man in my neighborhood. I contacted the visiting sister in my parish, and after taking him downtown to Manhattan to a shelter from the Bronx in my van, under unsanitary conditions and taking all the foul odors and foul language I had to put up with, he walked out of that place the next day to go back to the same corner we picked him up from. But that was the result of the vision I got the following day on the "Homeless Rhymes."

POLLARD, LYNSEY
[title] "You" [pers.] Poetry is a very powerful tool. When used properly, it can uncover feelings that have been long ago forgotten and persuade thoughts otherwise unheard of. The poem "You" describes the emotions that go along with feelings never returned. Emotions, I find, are very common while attending high school.

POLLNOW, JONATHAN
[a.] Tulsa, OK [title] "Untitled" [pers.] I love writing poetry became of its ability to embody abstract thoughts through beauty and creativity. In my poem "Celestial Disillusion," I am on one hand fascinated with the prospect of space travel, but on the other hand, disgusted with the pursuit of said technology because of its seeming ignorance of Earth's real problems.

POPE, YOLANDA
[title] "An Old Stale Act" [pers.] Yolanda Pope is a freelance artist writer, banker and poet. I have been writing poetry most of my life but this is only the second time I have shared my work with others. I also publish a quarterly newsletter publication called "The Third Eye, Inc." "The Third Eye Inc." features poetry and writings of other artists. Furthermore, I am a single person (native Houstonian), who is inspired by people who stand up for themselves and others by being proactive, positive and helpful. Love to you all.

POPP, DONNA
[a.] Aurora, IL [title] "You Are" [pers.] This poem was written is honor of the truest friend I have ever had! She has opened up my heart and enriched my life with the true meaning of "Best Friend." She has shoved me what true friendship is all about. So, with much appreciation, I dedicate this poem to her!

PORCHE WYATT, AGNES LORETTA
[a.] Lake Charles, LA [title] "Most Holy Father, Help Us" [pers.] I was born January 21, 1938 in Lake Charles, LA, to very loving and caring parents. I have been married 44 years to Armond Joseph Wyatt, retired USAF. We have lived in Japan, Bermuda, several northeastern and western states. We have three children and four grandchildren. I arbitrate much praise for my education and knowledge to my beloved parents and nuns who taught me for twelve years. I feel God Almighty blessed me with an unusual ability to write words others accept as genuine interpretations of their basic Christian or religious beliefs learned from the Bible or other writings.

POULOS, BRANDI
[title] "Thinking, Wondering, Waiting" [pers.] This poem was written as a dedication and in loving memory of my grandmother, Martha Slater.

POWELL, JOEL
[a.] Concord, NC [title] "The Wardrobe" [pers.] This poem illustrates my vivid imagination as a young child growing up in an old country house in South Carolina. An actual antique wardrobe, it was quite ominous and eerie. However, as in life, once investigated, things aren't as they first appeared. Instead, it became my "thinking place" and hideout, and further fostered my imagination and creativity. In retrospect, opening its doors seems symbolic of facing new challenges and opportunities for me in life and gives me the strength and courage to not just wonder, "What's behind those doors?"

POWERS, CHAD
[title] "What Nobody Knows" [pers.] This poem states that everybody is a loser to somebody, and to pay no attention to judgements of man. I believe God writes through me, for the expanding, of some mortal's souls. Life should be approached with the realization that God is everything. He's not really even a He. He's the universal consciousness. The energy ribbon of life wants you to stay in it's stream. All the temptations are lures to pull you into a facade of your inert love. Brace the moment of now, for the present is what is always happening. The world is twisted, because we as individuals are twisted. We must learn the value of perfection. Also, I would like to thank my wife, Janelle, and my son Noah, and my friends and family.

POWERS, JAMIE
[title] "Wings" [pers.] I have a master's degree in counseling psychology and I am working toward my marriage and family therapy license. Writing has been healing and comforting, especially in difficult times. I enjoy letting the words flow as my muse brings me these things of pleasure.

POWERS, JYLLIAN
[title] "Frozen Spring" [pers.] I would like to praise God for this blessing and thank you for this opportunity. I attend Bishop Hogan, where I am Captain of the varsity volleyball team. I'm also in *Who's Who Among American High School Students*. I'd like to thank my family especially Anthony (father), Linda (mother), and Brandi (sister), for always encouraging me and supporting me. When I'm writing poetry, my heart and soul are flowing through the pen directly onto the paper. It pulled me through the hardest times of my life and no words can express how it feels when someone else appreciates it!

PRATT-ELLIOTT, CAROLYN
[title] "My Hiding Place" [pers.] I wrote this poem because I have a busy life and often need to sit back and relax. I am a middle-aged married woman with two wonderful teenage boys. The pace at my job as a registered nurse has become very hectic. Spending time with nature and writing is much more conducive to my peace of mind. I have a diploma in creative writing and intend to spend more time nourishing my creative soul.

PRESNELL, MARLENE
[title] "Blossom and Grow" [pers.] This poem was written at a time in my life when I wanted to be myself. I left my husband and drove cross country from Oregon to Michigan with my children. I had always been somebody's something—daughter, wife, mother; I just wanted to be me and true to myself. Poetry has always been a way for me to express my feelings. I am very proud of my poems and especially this poem. It took a while, but I finally, was able to blossom and grow!

PRINCE, A. GEORGE
[title] "Kris Kringle" [pers.] I began my creative writing in high school. It was Christmas. My friend and I were joking as it snowed. We made up these verses: "Jingle, Jangle, Jingle, Rock it with Kris Kringle, Rock around the Christmas tree." We could not figure out anything after that. He did not assist me in finishing the song. I continued and finished the song after a few days. That's how I started my poetry.

PRIORE JR., PHILIP
[a.] New Haven, CT [title] "Man Meets Woman" [pers.] Poetry for me has always been a means of escape. I've often times felt the only way to find relief is to write my way out of a particular feeling or situation. This particular poem has really nothing at all to do with men or women. I always thought of my writing as being a separate being, one that I can talk to or through. This poem is written directly on my ability to write. The title was written for the readers' benefit, since the actual meaning is observe, but I do think the title leads itself well to the poem.

PRYCE, ENID
[title] "Take Time" [pers.] This poem tells a lot because as individuals, we take the simple things for granted. Life is precious . . .we have to cherish today and live for the moment because this life gives no guarantees. Denzel, you are the apple of my eye.

PRYER, STACIA
[a.] Phoenix, AZ [title] "One" [pers.] One love, one life (in my life), one glove (fits like a glove), one knife (killed, like with a knife). I have enjoyed writing poetry from grade school, and would like to publish my own book.

PRYOR, SANDRA
[a.] Bellingham, WA [title] "The Compass" [pers.] The sentiment within this poem is very special to me because it was borne of feelings for the most phenomenal person I have ever met. The refuge-like love described within the words, this friend has shown me without condition. His courage, strength, ambition and moral fortitude have been inspirational for me; his words, insight and spirituality have enlightened and enriched my life. He has helped me, like a butterfly, shed the safety of my cocoon and live. What more wonderful way to be told thank you than to read it in the words of a poem!

PULLEN, CHRISTOPHER
[title] "I Can . . .[pers.] I was born in Kennesaw, GA, but I was practically raised in Virginia Beach, VA. I am 17 years old and I was born on April 20, 1983 in Kennesaw Hospital. I am a senior in high school and I will graduate in the year of 2001. From there, I will join the Navy and work my way to becoming a commercial airline pilot, which is my main goal in life.

PYTLIK, JACOB
[title] "An Answered Prayer" [pers.] God has answered my prayers by blessing me with my beautiful wife, Jessica, and precious son, Cyrus. For this, I thank Him every day.

QUAH, SHAWN
[title] "Traits of a Family" [pers.] I am honored that my poem has been selected for publication, as it was written to commemorate the closeness of my family and relatives here in Singapore and therefore has a very special meaning to me. It was this unity that inspired me to write "Traits of a Family" and I am proud to share this with others around the world. I enjoy writing poetry and have written

many for special occasions. Poems are often a vehicle of the writer's innermost thoughts about life, and so I hope my poem conveys to you the message of being a close-knit family.

QUARRY, PATRICIA
[title] "Essence of Time" [pers.] Poetry and songwriting gives me a diary I would otherwise not have. I thank my mum, husband and children all for giving me their support in my many hours of solitude. I love them all. My only wish is that my dad could have read this poem, so I dedicate it to him. Poetry and songwriting are the two things I probably do more than anything else these days. If I can make one person smile or feel they can relate to my writing then I have achieved my goal to bring people words that can express their feelings, needs, happiness, and pain. For that, I am genuinely thankful. Always smile— it suits you!

QUINN, DARLENE
[title] "The Cross," [pers.] My poem, "The Cross," was born at 4:00 A.M. one morning. I have Parkinson's disease and do not sleep well at night. When sleep evades me, I boot up my computer and put down my thoughts and feelings. The house is silent and still, just the right atmosphere for deep thinking. Having a chronic disease has made me very introspective. I examine my life, my goals, my reason for being. It has made me closer to God. Darlene Rae Quinn—wife, mother, grandmother, retired, and loving it!

RABORN, KATHERINE
[title] "Half Past" [pers.] I am American Native Indian, Cherokee and Shawnee. Though I write the words from my heart, it is the gift of the ancestor grandmothers that place them there. It is my wish that I will walk Mother Earth, in light of all I have been taught, and I will never leave behind a bare trail.

RADDALGODA, YEHARA
[title] "Senses of My Heart" [pers.] This poem is dedicated to my love, my life, my inspiration and my husband. Sanjeewa, I love you more than words can truly express. This is to my most treasured friend.

RAHAT, YUSUF
[title] "War Souvenirs" [pers.] War, which is a problem in itself, cannot solve the problems of mankind. Peace is the ultimate solution. It is only in an environment of peace that the human mind can function constructively. For the attainment of peace, however, human beings the world over would have to rise above the petty differences of caste, color and creed, and with "charity towards all, and malice towards none," launch a combined crusade against whatever it is that plants the seeds of hatred in our midst and succeeds in dividing us amongst ourselves so as to be able to rule over us.

RAI, GEORGINA
[a.] Del Mar, CA [title] "Ocean" [pers.] I am eleven year-old who lives by the ocean. I love the ocean and poetry, so I decided to combine the two things. I love to write a poem that I would truly be proud of. I've always thought of the ocean as a living, nurturing, being. When I am not writing poetry, I love to swim, surf and walk along the beach. At home, I like to play with my friends and my sister, Pippa. I also like to spend time with my two cats and rabbit

RAJ, HAANUSIA
[title] "The Silver Drops of the Sky" [pers.] Poetry is very meaningful to me. It helps me to understand and to see the best in everything. My poem, "The Silver Drops of the Sky," helps me to mesmerize the beautiful gift from Mother Earth to us. I am grateful to God for bestowing me this talent. I would like to thank my parents and sisters for encouraging me not forgetting my best friends for inspiring and supporting me. Lastly, I would like to share this quote, which is very special to me

with everybody; "Talent is a special gift from God, and our duty is to polish it and give it back as a sacrifice for His glory."

RAJSKI, V.
[title] "I Seem to Be" [pers.] I am very honored that my poem was chosen to be included in *Rainstorms and Rainbows*. I didn't expect such appreciation for my young age and lack of publishing experience. Now I am aware of endless possibilities. Being awarded as "poet" at the age of 12 is something I can be proud of, and whenever I feel like giving up, there is always something to remind me that I can succeed. My poems are pieces of myself; every word is a door to my soul. I welcome you readers, to my world.

RAMASUBRAMANIAN, AMARNATH
[title] "Lost People" [pers.] This poem is about Indian Americans who come as immigrants. It describes their mental state as life goes by. I dedicate this poem to my elder brother, SR Sankara Narayanan, who is so inspirational to me.

RAMIREZ, JO MARIE
[title] "On Pondering" [pers.] I wrote this poem when I was in junior high school, during the crest of those tumultuous years. It remained untitled until this epoch year "2000." I'll become a "49er" this week (in years old, that is) and I continue "on pondering" these questions.

RANDALL, ELIJAH
[a.] Oakhurst, CA [title] "Just Tense" [pers.] Can a person on death row become a Christian? I say yes. In fact, I like to think of the speaker in "Just Tense" as one who found the forgiver. A freed soul that will spend eternity with God in Heaven, though it first was trapped in consequence through the choice of disobedience.

RASCATI, DAVID
[title] "Spring Time" [pers.] I feel that poetry comes right from the heart and soul. If you put love and open your imagination into poetry, you will get something beautiful.

REATH, DIANA
[title] "Rose Petals" [pers.] I was born in Montreal, Quebec. I'm married with three children and one grandchild. I am also an artist (oil paintings), and hope to publish a book someday. I sing in a choir and do lots of volunteer work for Palliative Care. I am a speaker and care giver. My poetry tells of life, and I hope people take the time to digest the true meaning; it is from my heart with love. I have some other works of poetry which I think are excellent about life's traumas we endure and the facade we project so people will not see our pain, and what we do to hide it.

REESE, JENNY
[title] "I Love You" [pers.] Poetry, to me, is something more than rhyming words on paper. Everything that goes down in my poems comes from deep within my soul and my heart. I love to write poetry and I love it even more when I inspire others to write what's in their soul.

REEVES, GINGER
[title] "The Name of Jesus" [pers.] I never thought this poem would get any farther than my heart, but thanks to Sister Nancy, I got the courage to submit it for your reading. I would also like to say "Hi!" and a great big thanks to my best friend Hannah (Hanners) for encouraging me to write poetry. I love ya, girl! To all of my family, you all are the greatest! I love you very, very much! Smile always!

REEVES, PAT
[title] "Premature Escribulation"[pers.] An auto collision resulted in a near fatal head injury, exploration brain surgery (parietal, temporal lobectomies and removal of subdural hematomas), a bi-

polar disorder, emotional problems, two suicide attempts, a visit to mental institution, and baldness! My final suicide note was a poem; "The Pencil and the Bullet." I became so mesmerized in creating this poem, I forgot to self-destruct. As long as I wrote, I lived, and wrote a volume called "Bi-Polar Poetry," two novels and essays. I have regained my sanity and hair!

REGENTHAL, MARCIE
[title] "Blindness of the Heart" [pers.] Written at the tender age of nineteen (amidst at the interracial unrest of the 70's), my poem "Blindness of the Heart" strives to implant a powerful message into the hearts of all people—unfeigned love transcends the human eye to dwell in the heart, which is oblivious to color. The innocence of young children (like my own David and Lyndsey) reflects this truth. Perhaps we should become more like them, instead of them like us.

REID, CHRISTINE S.
[a.] Los Angeles, CA [title] "Deluge" [pers.] I am an UCLA graduate with a B.A. in English Literature. I'm currently teaching in the L.A.U.S.D. My goal is to express my writings in the genre of poetry. The impetus of this poem derives from the events surrounding "The Great Flood" (Deluge) as depicted in the Old Testament. It further emphasizes the anxiety experienced by the faithful survivors.

REILLY, VICKIE
[title] "I Finally Found You" [pers.] I've been writing poetry for as long as I can remember. The true meaning of my poetry didn't come forth until a few friends of mine helped me to see that my poetry isn't just a hobby, it's a Heaven-sent gift. I would like to thank Rich, Tammy, Sara, Stephanie, and Shelby; they helped me find myself and Jesus. A great big thanks and I love you goes to my parents and my family for always encouraging me. Most of all, I would like to thank God, for giving me the power of poetry and the wisdom of words.

REIMER, KATIE
[title] "Grandma" [pers.] My poem is very special to me for a few reasons. This was a poem that I wrote in 8th grade as an assignment and it was the first poem that I've written. It is also about my grandmother and it describes the feelings I felt when she died while I was still young and feelings I still feel now at age 14. My grandmother cared a lot about others and me. Whenever my family or I read my poem, it brings back many good memories and reminds us of what a wonderful person she was.

REINERT, JULIE
[a.] Philadelphia, PA [title] "Nature's Goodnight" [pers.] I am twelve years old. My family has been vacationing in North Carolina for seven years. This poem, "Nature's Goodnight," describes the scenes I love so much. I enjoy writing about things that mean a lot to me. Poetry is a way of expressing feelings close to my heart. I believe God has given me this talent of writing and am excited about continuing this family tradition of poetry writing.

REITHER, BEVERLY
[title] "Soul Mate" [pers.] While the relationship and thoughts in "Soul Mate" are my own, I chose to use the example of David and Jonathan as the subjects of my poem. Little was said about their friendship in the Bible, yet they were described as soul mates, kept apart physically, but closer than brothers spiritually. Poetry is my way of meditating on subjects or experiences that move me. Expressing myself in verse has become more than a pastime, it's really a journal of what means the most to me!

RESONARI, CRYSTAL
[title] "She Is . . ." [pers.] Poetry is the language of the soul. This poem has the energy of life itself

for me. When I wrote this poem, I was searching for life. Poetry expresses my very essence. It comes from my core, totally uninhibited and honestly. Sharing this expression and vision with others is a true joy to me. Sparking interest and planting seeds in the minds and hearts through my writings fulfills my desire to touch humankind and ignites more passion for expression in our world.

REYES, JOSE
[title] "A Tear That Healed" [pers.] I was born Jose Antonio Reyes, in a small town in Puerto Rico. I was raised in New York City, where I lived until age 19 when I enlisted in the United States Air Force. I served my country for 24 years during the years of my life. I have seen and felt the joys and sorrows of life, which I express in my poetry

RIBERDY, ROSEMARY
[title] "The Desert" [pers.] When moving to the desert five years ago, my youngest son, who is always positive in his efforts to do a fine job for his company, transferred from SFO to Phoenix. Because he is always there for me, I felt it necessary to keep up his morale until his family could join him six months later. It was on one evening when I spoken with him via telephone. I felt his loneliness, which inspired me to write "The Desert." And so, in appreciation for his support for so many years, I dedicate this writing to my beautiful son, who will always remain my best source of inspiration and love.

RICE, BELLA TIETIE
[a.] Riverdale, MD [title] "I Am African Btch, Am Not" [pers.]"I am African Btch Am Not" is about an African who married an African-American that is partly white and partly black. Whenever he get mad about some things his wife did, he will call her the A.B.B. word, which is" African Black Btch." The wife then reminded him that the part of him that loves him the most is the Black family members. Why, then doesn't call her African black btch? All his life the Africans loved him. She then put all those words of this to write this poem. This woman is Belen Rice

RICH, BARRY
[a.] "Gibbsboro, NJ [title] "The Current State of Medical Care" [pers.] Since the concept of "managed care" burst on the scene, I have been very concerned about its adverse impact on health care. The only people I want to manage my care are my doctors and I. A contentious atmosphere has been created amongst all facets of the system and the patient suffers. As I sat in a hotel room in Boston, with my significant other on the phone trying, in frustration, to set up meaningful doctor appointments, this poem was written within minutes on a scrap of paper. Like most of my poems, it really wrote itself.

RICH, CATHERINE
[title] "Fusion or Fission" [pers.] This is part of an ongoing work in progress. I have continually worked on this piece for three years and hope to acquire an agent to contract for the entire body of work to be published. Realizing that goal would be sweetness in the perspective of the integral parts of my life, as one has lived, loved and developed into this personality expressed in poetic faceting of diamonds given to me as a gift—my life.

RICH, MICHAEL
[title] "Shepherd's Bond" [pers.] The people in my life are of immense importance to me. The most important task for me is finding ways in which to help them grow and learn. In writing "Shepherd's Bond," I attempted to express the sense of reward felt in guiding those of my "flock." I love writing, and try to convey a sense of beauty in all that I write. I believe beauty is sharing of yourself in a way that can benefit others. I look forward to sharing my dreams and

ideals with the world, one person—and perhaps one poem—at a time.

RICHARDS, BRENDA
[a.] Birmingham, AL [title] "My Love for Thee" [pers.] I am a real emotional person. When I write, I am drawing from deep within myself. I thank you, Lord, for giving me the gift to be able to put down on paper what is inside of me so others can feel it.

RICHARDSON, BETH
[a.] Baltimore, MD [title] "Not to Have You" [pers.] It's really amazing seeing my own work in print. It's something I have always wanted since I started writing. I love writing poems. It's how I express my feelings and even if I never make any money for my writing, seeing it in print is the greatest thing.

RICHARDSON, BONITA
[title] "Search for the Undying Love" [pers.] This poem was inspired by a longing in my heart that I feel will be forever there because of my missing soul mate. I think the ability take what you feel, express it in words and touch so many lives is a God-given talent that I was fortunate enough to receive. My only wish is that my poem gives you hope and inspires you to search for your own true soul mate, or thank the good Lord for allowing you to find yours in the short time that we grace this Earth.

RISNER, ALBERTA
[title] "Imbedded" [pers.] My poem is a statement of my view of me at a special time in my life. Perhaps it speaks to many women at a precipice in their lives also. Memories of the past, trepidation of the future.

RITZ, EARLA
[a.] Waterbury, CT[title] "Runaway" [pers.] In the poetry world of love, hope and dreams, there is also harsh reality. "Runaway" depicts desperate youths seeking an escape from their homes and families, only to find other means of escaping the harsh reality of the streets.

RIVERS, JACKIE
[title] "So Much Pain and Poverty" [pers.] I found out in 1972 that God had given me the ability to express what I experience and feel through the gift he gave me to write poems to share with others. I'm also very grateful to my husband, William, for pushing me to use it. When I looked around me and saw all the homeless, crime, drug abuse, and the deaths of so many young people, I was inspired to write about it by writing "So Much Pain and Poverty."

ROBERSON, WATAYA
[a.] New York, NY [title] "Ambience" [pers.] For me, poetry is one of the ways I've been able to passionately express myself. Poetry is my soul's dialogue with God and pen and paper my close companion. I've loved writing ever since I was a young child. When I feel emotionally stuck or incredibly inspired, this is one of the ways my spirit chooses to release nine A.M. I'm grateful for this gift, which has been handed down through my heritage.

ROBERTS, SHERON
[title] "Forecast" [pers.] Growing up in the south, I worked in the fields, rain or shine. I loved the smell of the earth on hot days and the cool damp of rainy day. I watched my grandparents "read" the weather, weather that was and is critical to farmers, making or breaking them. Grandparents, nature, everything made an impression on my young mind, filling me with ideas that found their life in poetry and art. As an adult, poetry and pottery continue as outlets for the wonderful images and ideas that continue to crowd my head and cry for creation.

ROBINSON, DONALD
[title] "Of Thee I Love" [pers.] I have been writing poems of love and romance for many years. I have

hundreds! I know them to be true, for I live them. I have lived by the ocean all my life, so most of my poems are about the sea and the nearby lands. Almost everyone of us has memories of our past loves and romances. My poems include a little bit about all of us; sadness, happiness the ocean, love, the fields, a part of all of us.

ROBINSON, SUE
[title] "New Beginning" [pers.] I am just a little lady, living by faith. My birthday records say I'm 78. I am just a humble Christian soul; I chose salvation instead of gold. I thank the Lord for my childhood features today. I am a new creature because today, I know the Lord holds my future in His hands. On His word I have agreed to stand. My God-given gospel ministry keeps me free today. I claim the victory because all of God's chosen people have been a blessing to me, the great to the small. By the grace of God today, I can say, may God forever bless you all.

ROBLEDO, LINDA
[a.] Kearn, UT [title] "I Saw You" [pers.] I am a single female struggling to survive in very difficult times. A few years back, I was literally forced into joining a prayer circle called "The Healing Circle." The circle was conducted by my sister, Connie I Deuel, who knew that I needed spiritual guidance in my life. This was a time in my life when I was definitely tripping over life's rocky road. Since that day, many blessings and miracles have come my way. Not only has the circle inspired me with words, it has brought many wonderful friends into my life, including one special friend with whom I share many spiritual adventures. I dedicate this poem to those friends from "The Healing Circle." The Circle members hold hands, left hand up and right hand down, to form a circle of energy. Each person prays in his or her own way. I am the Silent One. I never pray aloud. My prayers are silent, only meant for Yahweh to hear. It was during this prayer circle one evening when the words to "I Saw You" popped into my head. I immediately wrote the words down on paper when the circle broke. The poem has not been edited or rewritten. The way you read it is the way the words came into my head during the Healing Circle of Prayer. Throughout my life, I have written other things, but this is the first one I have entered in a contest. I am thrilled and I thank you for the opportunity.

RODGERS, ROCHELLE
[a.] Brooklyn, NY [title] "Better Days" [pers.] This poem was written as a teenager's lament for the end of a relationship. I wrote "Better Days" over twenty years ago! Anyone who has ever loved someone and then lost them will understand the significance of the poem's words. Hopefully, anyone who can relate to the poem will experience "better days" ahead. I did!

RODRIGUEZ, ALBERTO
[a.] El Paso, TX [title] "Angel" [pers.] To the love of my life, Lynnda Diane "Baybe." She inspired me to write these words. When I leave this world, I will be her protector, her guide, her guardian angel. Never, ever will I leave her side. To my children, Elaine Frances and Albert Michael—the world awaits you, give them your best!

RODRIGUEZ, ESTEFANIA
[title] "Youth" [pers.] I dedicate this poem titled "Youth" to my mother, Muggie Belva Adams, who came out of the south. Her grandparents were slaves. My mother would always say how important it is in one's life to display noble deeds. She always said, "Look up—we are Americans." My mother was my inspiration, as well as my brothers' and sisters', to enhance our "mental powers" in love and whatever our goals and accomplishments to make a new "birth."

RODRIGUEZ-AVILES, LISA
[title] "My Sister" [pers.] I have been writing poetry all my life. I am fortunate to have had this talent passed down to me by my father, Santos, and my grandmother, Margarita. They both have been so inspirational in my life. My mother, Maria, and my husband, Anthony, have been so supportive in encouraging me to refine my talents. This poem, "My Sister," describes my sister, Emely. My strength and will to succeed stems from her devoted love. She is my role model, my second mother, and my best friend. She genuinely is my hero. I dedicate this poem to her and my entire family.

RODRIGUEZ-AVILES, LISA
[a.] Elizabeth, NJ [title] "My Sister" [pers.] I have been writing poetry all my life. I am fortunate to have had this talent passed down to me by my father, Santos and my grandmother, Margarita. They both have been so inspirational in my life. My mother Maria and my husband Anthony have been so supportive in encouraging me to refine my talents. This poem "My Sister", describes my sister Emely. My strength and will to succeed stems from her devote love. She is my role model, my second mother, my best friend. She genuinely is, my hero. I dedicate this poem to her and my entire family

ROESSAAK, STEIN
[title] "Twisted Mind" [pers.] Love is what it's all about. Finding "the one." That's also what my poetry and songs are all about. They're my way to be free from my frustration in certain situations. This is a tribute to my best friend, Line Madsen.

ROGERS, INA
[title] "Rule of Law" [pers.] As Dependants of the USAF Strategic Air Command, my family's very sinew was forged in the furnace of the Cold War. From a childhood dominated by the horrors of WWII, I very early became aware of "The Powers That Be," but have just recently been apprised of the extent of dangers facing our precious freedoms. The future facing one little alien, so karmically named, causes tears of horror to spring from the depths of this mother's soul. God, help him. God, please save us all from our own comfortable complacency.

ROGERS, JO
[title] "Angel Boy" [pers.] "Angel Boy" is written for Bryon, my oldest grandson. The poem depicts adventures that he, his grandfather and I have shared together. His quick wit, vivid imagination and zest for life inspired me to write about him. We truly have always called him Angel Boy. The greatest gift of my only child, my daughter, has been giving me my three grandsons. I hope that every parent or grandparent that reads my poem will see something that reminds them of their own child or grandchild. Bryon is one of the greatest blessings that God has given me.

ROGERS, SHIRLEY
[title] "Temptation" [pers.] This poem was written with a special person in mind. Without him, I would not have been inspired. I greatly appreciate his persistence and love—Inspector Smith. I also appreciate all the support from my children, sister, family and friends from the bottom of my heart.

ROHLOFF, LARRY
[title] "O. C. and Me" [pers.] O. C. stands for Outagamie County Highway Department in Northeast Wisconsin. I wrote this poem while plowing snow and grading roads. You have a lot of time to think on those jobs. I retired from the highway department this year, after working for them for forty years. I would like to dedicate this poem in memory and honor of those I worked with throughout those forty years, and to my wife Janet, and our three sons, Jeffrey, David and Michael, and their families.

ROLAND, RUTH
[title] "Yes, I Am Eighty" [pers.] I'm a retired college professor, a specialist in Asian politics and government. I have always read poetry for relaxation, although two prose books (non-fiction) of mine have been published. "Yes, I Am Eighty" is my first attempt at poetry. I was inspired by my ever increasing anger at the age prejudice in American culture. The incident depicted in the poem did happen to me.

ROLLO, JAMES
[title] "Children" [pers.] Poems are all written from the heart, and this one is no exception. It is about the love a daughter and father share and signifies the future to all of us: our children. I am especially grateful to my mother, a woman who has forever shaped my morals and provides me all the contentment a son could ask for. I also thank a special group of people who feed my inspiration—keep climbing our "beanstalk."

ROLSTON, CHRISTINE
[title] "Never Again" [pers.] I started writing poetry this year after separating from my husband as a way of expressing my hurt and heartache. I have three sons, William, fifteen; David, six; and Charlie, seventeen months. I am now a single mom. There is someone special in my life. His name is David. He lives in the UK and I live in Australia. He has acute Myleloid Leukemia. When he goes into remission, he is coming here to meet me. We met through the Internet. I pray for him every day.

ROSARIO, MILAGROS
[title] "Deep Silence" [pers.] I'm Milagros Rosario, a single, strong-willed, beautiful, intelligent, sexy Latina residing in Ridgewood, NY. I'm the second oldest sibling of a family of four. I've earned my living working with the law and presently continuing my education with same. I have always felt I was born to serve a greater purpose in this world, and my poetry reflects those passions and experiences I welcomed into my life that I would like to share this world and future generations.

ROSENBERG, ELISE
[a.] Fort Lee, NJ [title] "Pages" [pers.] Since I have only just begun to write, this was quite an honor that my poem made it this far. I really feel that I summarized the meaning of life, as I used the metaphor in a book. It shows how every day is new and different things can be done and learned. Basically what I'm saying is to live life like every day is a new page of a book. Thanks to my family, G. and L. K

ROSINE, CATHERINE
[title] "Full-filled" [pers.] As a mother of four children, it is difficult to set aside time for myself, so poetry and other writings are an escape for me. I usually try to find humor in most common (and might I add repetitive) situations, and in my household, it is unceasing.

ROSS, AARON
[a.] Laramie, WY [title] "Alone" [pers.] I'm adopted, so that is the reason why I wrote "Alone." I'm originally from Torrington, Wyoming. I am the oldest of two in my immediate family, and the middle child in my biological aim family. The real story started with many of my closest friends dying. I really felt alone then. I felt all alone with no one to talk to that I could really trust that was close to my age. I just finished up my junior year in high school. My ambitions are to finish high school and join us the U.S. Marine Corps. I just want do to something that I can serve my country and to live up to the U.S.M. motto; "Semper Fi". That is Latin for "always faithful." That is what I want to be to both my family and country.

ROSS, CAROL
[title] "In Love" [pers.] My grandmother taught me at a very early age of God's true unconditional

love for me. My mom is in her sixties and she is writing poetry again. God has given our family the gift of poetry, each unique. God gives me different poetry to help me through the phases or difficulties in life, death murder, hurts, family, even though some came from anger, etc. They all end with God's love. Yes, God's given me a special gift of unique poetry. Believe me, it's extremely appreciated! Can't you tell I love the Lord with all my heart soul and being?!

ROSS, WILLIAM
[a.] Elk, OK [title] "Love of a Song" [pers.] My words I write in memory of my father. His life was full of many things he loved. He had a loving family, who he gave all to provide for. He had a passion for country music that outlived his life. He sang his songs from the heart and he never complained about not becoming a star. To me, he became that star in the life of his wife and all his children. He shines bright in all our lives and still shines bright today. This is for you Dad—I love you!

ROXLAU, DARA
[title] "Always and Forever" [pers.] I dedicate this poem to the person who inspired me to write it, and also to my friends and family, who have been there for me through everything. Love you all.

ROYER, CHARLES
[a.] Catonsville, MD [title] "The First Christmas Night" [pers.] I had written many stories and poems as a youth, but had not written anything for years. The Christmas after losing my wife of forty-five years, I felt inspired to jot down the lines to this poem. I remembered the joy of all the Christmas seasons with our children, grandchildren and friends, and I remembered the great love of nature we shared all our years together. The result was this little poem dedicated to the wife I miss so much.

RUDY, KATI
[title] "It's Great to Be Me" [pers.] My name is Kati Rudy. I'm nine years old. I have three sisters: Tiffany, Jill, and Julie. I have one niece, Alexis and one niece on the way. My cat's name is Socks. I'm going into the fourth grade. My teacher's name is Mrs. Mathews. My favorite color is blue. The poem I wrote was a homework assignment. My third grade teacher, Mrs. Fisler, entered it in a contest at school and I won third place. My dad and mom helped me enter this contest. We were happy to find out it was going to be published. I would like to say thank you to all my teachers, Mrs. Eyers, Mrs. Burnheimer, Mr. H. and Mrs. Fisler.

RUSCIO, MATT
[title] "Ball of Twine" [pers.] I would like to thank everybody that has ever touched my life because, good or bad, you've contributed to the person I am today. Special thanks to my parents and close family members who taught me many life lessons just when I needed to hear them. I wrote "Ball of Twine" when I was in the middle of a philosophy overload. It describes my search for answers to questions I had about life. Ultimately, the true answer is always that the search continues.

RUSSELL, BETTY MCCANN
[a.] Pearland, TX [title] "Doing it My Way" [pers.] My poetry is usually prompted by an event in my life. "Doing It My Way" was inspired by a revelation that I could have life after lost love.

RUSSELL, LEE
[a.] San Antonio, TX [title] "Wake Up! [pers.] This poem came about as a revelation to my perspective of this society. Although if focuses on young people, my heart is telling the world to wake up. I honestly feel that one must understand where one came from, who one is, and where one is going in life. This is a cruel world, and one must protect oneself by using one of God's greatest gift to man— the ability to reason. This will not remove any

problems, but hopefully choices in dealing with life's problems. I thank my family, spiritual leaders and friends for helping me to wake up.

RUSSELL, MISTY
[title] "Contemplations" [pers.] Life. Question everything and never forget what matters the most. Look deep inside yourself and constantly see the changing individual you are. People are just like life; they can change in a flash of light without knowing where they are heading. People are afraid of the unknown, but what they do not realize is that they, themselves are the unknown. People are the greatest mysteries of the world. Dedicated to the people who have taught me what life is.
Never forget "awaiting destiny's moment." I was born 24th June 1984.

RUSSELL, NASNAGA
[title] "Native Sun" [pers.] I am very pleased that "Native Sun" meets the standards you have set for you new book. Being a mixed blood Shawnee, I've written mostly on the American Indian for the past 30 years. I hope I've written well enough to please those who went before. I'm sure this will please them.

RYAN, MATT
[title] "Week" [pers.] I am white, male, not quite 50, a left-handed computer type who was once told by a college lecturer to write "elegant" code. I use the production of poetry as a form of stress relief although, in my past, the only poems I really read were my mother's. "Week," triggered by reports in the news and a certain amount of window-watching, is typical of me. I tend not to write about dreaming spires or unrequited love, but prefer to comment on current events. When I can, I try to insert a little humor into my poetry.

RYAN, VIRGINIA
[a.] Port St. Lucie, FL [title] "Husband" [pers.] I dedicate this poem to my one true love. We have always loved one another and will continue to love each other. Zac, you have always been there for me and for that and many other reasons, I love you!

RYDER, JOSEPH
[title] "Artist Unseen" [pers.] My motivation for this poem stems from the struggle I went through as an artist in my youth. My artistic focus was not honed in on one art form, but all of them (videography, theatre, visual art, music, literary arts, etc.). Though I was angry at society for lack of recognition as an artist, I realize now that I actually held myself back, not realizing I was letting my focus drift from one art form to the next. I am now taking care of that problem. I am studying artistic multimedia design for the Internet.

RYKERS, LAURA
[title] "My Love" [pers.] This poem I wrote for my husband, Tony, for our wedding day. He has given me so much joy and happiness. Tony is truly a light in my life. I love him with all my heart and soul. Without him, my life would be incomplete, boring and unhappy. For "My Love" Tony, you inspired me and made me the person that I am today.

SAAR, S.
[a.] Carrollton, TX [title] "The Old House" [pers.] This poem commemorates the house of my aunt and two uncles. They lived on a farm and I spent holidays and summers with them as a child. The house was the extended family home, which had been in the family for about a hundred years.

SAAVEDRA, CARLO
[title] "While" [pers.] There is only one reason why I write poems—inspiration. Without it, poetry would have never existed in me. My poem, "While," was created because of a special person, Kathlyn Louise G. Ong. She is the sole reason why these words paint the universal images of love and hope. Kathlyn once said that she would like to be

remembered "as someone who saw the world through my kaleidoscope." Now, this is for the world to see and remember her as a woman who inspired me to conceive a vision . . .a vision of a love like hers worth hoping for.

SABLAN, CHRISTOPHER
[a.] Apia, Samoa [title] "Oasis" [pers.] Oasis is longing. Oasis is one's need for love, and the hollow life one leads without it. It is man's sanctuary and his prison, the comforting but sad vision of a dreamer whose eye turns inwardly towards himself to hide from the desert that is his desertion. That was her desertion. Dreams are deepest felt when they serve to define the dreamer. Poetry for me is an outlet for emotion. Felt with happiness or not, poetry to me is as grey as the very feelings that it arose from. Poetry is release. This is for Lisha.

SACLOLO, JUAN
[title] "In the Eye" [pers.] In dedication to Colleen Erin Lewis. My girlfriend and a bad day at work were my inspiration. This poem describes how I can be swallowed up by everything happening to and around me and how it can cause me to lose sight of what is most important to me. However, once I gaze into the eyes of my love, I can separate from the chaos and return to what is truly important in my life. Colleen, I love you! Special thanks to Mr. Farmer, my junior and senior year English teacher.

SALEEM, ANOSHA
[title] "The Grandfather Clock" [pers.] Poetry is very important to me because through writing poetry, you can share your innermost feelings with anyone or anything, which is exactly what I've tried to do with the grandfather clock. I've tried to show how the grandfather and his clock understood each other and because of that, when the grandfather died, the clock "died" as well. That's what poetry is about— understanding different people through their poems and considering the efforts that have gone into it.

SALINAS, JACQUELINE
[a.] Los Angeles, CA [title] "Beware" [pers.] I am seventeen and ward of the court. When I was seven, my mother went insane. My dad left her. When I was eleven, I was in juvenile hall for a very wrong mistake. I ended up in probation and was sent to a group home. I got off probation on December 7, 1999. I started writing poetry before the age of thirteen. This poem, "Beware," I wrote while in the group home. I wrote it in the middle of the night when I thought clearly about things. My main influence for this poem would be Ernesto Grajeda, a very good person with heart. He reminds me to smile.

SALVATORE, ANDREW
[title] "Without You" [pers.] This poem tells about the person that means the most to me in life, my soul mate. She is what makes my day to day life worthwhile and my biggest inspiration when I write. I wish everybody could feel the love in their life as I feel the love for her.

SANDE, BOB
[a.] Amsterdam, Netherlands [title] "What's" [pers.] What's life, what's cyber? Which is right, which is wrong? My poems are flashes (maybe) by Maureen and Justin, the best mother and son a man can wish for. Friends and a brother and all other family, blood or not, thank you all around me to make me think. What's faith? What's believe who is religion. The triangle of morals to sting our hearts a lifetime, makes a good person. To give true cyber, life and goodness.

SARKISSIAN, KAREN
[title] "I Love You" [pers.] I live in Yerevan, Armenia. I'm 16. This year I finished school and will be entering university in August to study

geography and languages for a career in hosting and tourism. I enjoy reading poetry and from time to time also enjoy writing poems. This poem was written to a girl in my class. Her name is Seda. When I told her that I loved her, she didn't answer. A couple of weeks later, she said that she didn't love me. Today we remain very good friends, and I hope we always will.

SAUER, CHRIS
[title] "The Lamentations of a Student" [pers.] My poem originated from my perspective on school in general. Public schools are filled with those who fail simply because an ignorant teacher failed to recognize their problem immediately. In my opinion, more people should be home-schooled for the individual attention. I hope those who read this are convinced to take the time to home-school their children, because not everyone fits right in the mold the school demands, but let them fill another that allows them to excel beyond anyone's expectations.

SAVAGE, CHRISTY
[a.] Stow, OH [title] "Heart Shattered by Irreplaceable Loss" [pers.] I wrote this poem six years ago, immediately after my father died. I was only thirteen at the time and his death has had an incredible impact on my life. The words bombarded me, flowing like liquid onto the page. I am currently a student of Kent State University, studying psychology and art. I hope to help people with their problems by showing them how to express their thoughts, feelings, and dreams through art. Writing is one of the most powerful techniques for creative expression. Writing and drawing have been effective ways for me to cope with my heartache. I want to help people find their inner voice and show them how to freely translate their deepest secrets into a beautiful piece of art.

SAVIOLI, FRANCESCA
[title] "The Girl" [pers.] I am the only person in my family, (except for my grandmother) to have the "gift of poetry." This poem was partly based on the very sad story of "The Little Match Girl," by Hans Christian Andersen, and partly on the children of my home country, Tanzania. The only difference between my poem and the story is that in my poem she is an orphan, and in the real story, she isn't. I hope that this poem will make the children (and adults!) that read it aware of the Third World and what the children may feel in these circumstances.

SAWIN, MAE-ELLEN
[a.] Newton, IA [title] "Voices of the Past" [pers.] We are all a part of past generations and future descendants. What a person does and believes affects generations we will never know. We will make a better world believing the best in all people, regardless of race or creed.

SAXENIAN, HRAND
[title] "Silver Against Deep Blue" [pers.] High on a cliff on war-scarred Saipan, then the "Japanese Jewel of the Pacific," I looked out and asked, "What next in this mad world?" In 1952 I left physics, computers and outer space to explore inner worlds of personal effectiveness and psychological freedom. I proposed hypothesis two. "One effectiveness under pressure increases with the expression of one's own feelings and convictions, with consideration for the thoughts and feelings of others." Macroscopic statistical testing supports this as a foundation for popular cross-cultural awareness of "what really works," and for constructive leadership in our lives.

SCHARF, NANCY
[title] "Reflections and Hope" [pers.] My poem is dedicated to my parents, who enabled me to have a childhood to be treasured forever. My hope is that my children will someday reflect

these same feelings. It is my wish that everybody would recognize that when human nature and Mother Nature are properly balanced, life becomes a glorious experience. Watching a robin build its nest, planting a seed and watching it grow, a child's smile accompanied with a giggle are some of life's free experiences that money can't buy. When we learn to dine on nature's beauty, material things become unappetizing.

SCHEUERS, T.
[a.] Chilton, WI [title] "Life's Sugarplums" [pers.] Born in Fondulac, WI. Occupation: Nursing. My hobbies include outdoors, gardening, crafts, writing, caretaking, enjoying children, life. I am divorced with five children. I graduated from Lowell P. Goodrich High School of Fondulac and completed two years of college at UWGB and Bellin College of Nursing. I'm currently writing a book about life experiences, especially about parenting a child with special needs.

SCHEUERS, T.
[title] "Life's Sugarplums" [pers.] Born in FonduLac, WI. Occupation: nursing. My hobbies include outdoors, gardening, crafts, writing, caretaking, enjoying children, life. I am divorced with five children. Graduated from Lowell P. Goodrich High School of FonduLac, completed two years of college at VWGB and Bellin College of Nursing. I'm currently writing book about life experiences, especially about parenting a child with special needs.

SCHEUERS, TRACEY
[title] "In the Aftermath of Disease" [pers.] Born in Fond duLac, WI. Occupation: nursing. My hobbies include outdoors, gardening, crafts, writing, caretaking, enjoying children life. I am divorced with five children. I graduated from Lowell P. Goodrich High School of Fondulac and completed two years of college at UWGB and Bellin College of Nursing. I'm currently writing book about life experiences, especially about parenting a child with special needs. This poem was written for those with severe life- threatening diseases, as well as those patients with whom I spent their last few breaths. Just have a wonderful, meaningful and unforgettable birthday.

SCHOENFELD, ERIC
[a.] Naperville, IL [title] "End of an Era" [pers.] This poem was written in celebration of my high school graduation and the new challenge of college. The original draft was titled "School's Out." As I read the poem, I realized this could be applied to more than school; for example, marriage, career change, retirement, and death. I want to thank some people that inspired me to write—my parents. Without their hard work and kind hearts, I wouldn't have been presented such opportunities. I would like to thank my high school poetry teacher. She opened my mind to a whole new way of expression.

SCHUH, ERIKA
[a.] Rochester, NY [title] "Lost in Time" [pers.] Poetry is very special to me. I enjoy writing poems for school and for pleasure. If something has a deep impact on my life, I write a poem about it. My poem "Lost in Time" is about the point in my life when my great-grandmother passed away. She meant a lot to me and I loved her very much. In the poem I express how I am lost without her and that I miss her very much.

SCHULLER, DOLLY
[title] "Come Follow Me" [pers.] Poetry has always been an excellent way to express my innermost feelings, whether it's a time of joy, an expression of love, sympathy or even a fantasy. I am truly blessed to have the love and support of my husband, who makes all my writings even more heartfelt and sincere. "Come Follow Me" is a

musical journey to a perfect place with that special love, a somewhat magical fantasy one may tend to daydream after reading. Should any of my verses cause one to smile, find comfort or inspiration, I will have accomplished sharing my gift of poetry.

SCHWARTZ, RICHARD
[title] "Who's Who in Education" [pers.] One day in spring 2000, I was walking home from student teaching at Flushing High School in NYC. Life as a student teacher has its moments, and that was one of them. I started thinking of metaphors for teachers I had in the past, and for what I hoped to be as a teacher. I hope to be that "air" to my students. I don't mind so much if I'm unappreciated if I know I am giving life to my students through what I teach, whether it's English, the Bible, or biology.

SCROGGS, JULIE
[title] "My Angel" [pers.] To me, poetry is a special gift from God sent to warm the heart. My poem is dedicated to my family, especially my brother. He is a true miracle and the light in my life that keeps me smiling. I love to write poetry and I love to read it, especially the poems that bring a tear to your eye and a smile to your face.

SEDORE, FAY
[title] "Where'd You Go" [pers.] Brother by marriage, friend by choice, staff Sgt. Stephen F. Sedore was brutally murdered by a friend of 20 years (he was in the wrong place at the wrong time). He was a 15- year army career man, served in the Gulf War, aided in the liberation of Kuwait, and was loved by those who served with him and under him, as well as family and friends. Having had no children of his own, he made nieces and nephews his special children. Bright, warm, and fun-loving, he's a candle in our family's life that will shine no more. For you, mother—Margie J. Sedore.

SELLERS, MELINDA
[a.] Monterey, CA [title] "Introspection" [pers.] I have often felt the brush of death's finger against the back of my neck in my work as a medical transcriptionist, frequently manifested in patients whose history I had come to recognize along with their illness, most recently that of my son. It would have made him very happy to see something of mine published; he had read and typed many of my scribbled notes from the notebooks I always carry with me. My poem reflects the soul-searching I underwent relative to his early and untimely demise. So young; such a waste of genuine goodness and character.

SELLERS, NATHON
[title] "I Am" [pers.] I was born in 1987 as a premature baby, so I have always been very small. I had a lot of health problems. I was told I may never play sports. I told myself that was not true. Now, at 13, I play every sport. I can do without overlapping. I play basketball, baseball, and my favorite, football. I was born on Super Bowl Sunday in 1987, so my dream is to someday be in the Super Bowl.

SELLMEYER, KATIE
[title] "Loved by All" [pers.] The story behind the poem is really sad to my family and I. My sister and I had two friends who, unexpectedly, were killed in a car crash. They lost control of the car and hit a stone and concrete wall. Lacey, my sister, went to school with both of them for a little over two years, up until the time of the accident. They were both loving, caring, and funny young men. I'm 13 years and was born on December 31, 1986. I'm going into the eight grade for the upcoming 2000-2001 school year. My sister, Lacey, is going into the 12th grade. She's 17 years old. My mother, Sherry, works at the Hostess Baking Company. She's 45 years old. My mother and I love to read.

SERRANO, RICHARD
[title] "Who Am I" [pers.] My motivation for my poetry is my recent and unexpected divorce. Painfully being separated from my children forced me to become what I call a "Weekend Dad." I drew strength from this pain and gained trust in myself to love again. I feel that my poetry allows people to catch a glimpse of how most experience such deep pain feel, although they may not express it. It is my wish that my poetry may in some way help someone to express him or herself to another.

SESSIONS, RONDAL
[a.] Grandview, MO [title] "While You're Away" [pers.] I was inspired to create this poem on a lonely day at home while my love was away on vacation. It had been six days since we seen each other and I expressed how much I missed her care and compassion. Writing poetry is a part of my life; it's a way that I can bring my feelings to life. I can show how my true meaning of life could be addressed through such words that could bring tears of joy. To share my love for poetry, as well as for my true love, is a gift I will cherish. Brenna Nicole Mead, you have brought me happiness, and shown me a way of life I could have never found with out you. I will love you forever. Thank you. Thank you.

SETHI, RUBY
[a.] Richmond, BC [title] "Reason Not to Give Up" [pers.] To me, poetry is not just words on paper; poetry is a method of expressing one's self. I wrote this poem during a very stressful period of my life and I feel that it has helped me to overcome many obstacles. Life is not easy, which is why it is so important to believe in yourself.

SHARPE, SAMUEL
[a.] Seattle, WA [title] "Dreams"

SHAW, BERNICE
[title] "Of Trying Times" [pers.] As life progressed throughout the years, loved ones and friends departed, filling my heart with emptiness. Speechless, deep within my soul, emotions scattered in all directions as if bewildered of knowing what to say. One shimmering morning, I picked up my pen started writing, amending my inner-most feelings, which was so profound.

SHEFFY, D.
[title] "Easter" [pers.] My 6th grade teacher, Margaret New, asked me to write a poem. I did "Spring Day." She thought it was pretty good and had me recite it to five other classrooms. This was in Ballinger, Texas. I graduated Ballinger High School 1939. I have written about a dozen poems since then; poems concerning my church members, pastor, my mother-in-law, ("Somebody's Mother,") my wife ("Ella Mae"); sure glad you came along! "No Stranger Here" is on my business men's Bible class. I am a past president. This class is 72 years old and is in San Angel, Texas. My church is St. Paul Presbyterian. My great-grandfather was a circuit riding Baptist minister. He started a church in 1872 in Mt. Veron, Arkansas. I love the Lord! He has been looking after me for 82 years.

SHELL, SHIRLEY
[a.] Hopkins, SC [title] "If I Could Give" [pers.] I have been writing since my teenage years. My inspiration was a troubled and sad childhood. Writing was an escape because I had no one to talk to. As I entered into adulthood, my children and Christ made it into a beautiful gift of words and the expression of them. If I can help others through troubled and hard times by uplifting their spirit with my gift of words, then my troubled past was not in vain. God has given me a way to bless him through my poetry and turned an ugly past into a beautiful future.

SHERLOCK, DEREK
[title] "Best Friends" (Pets) [pers.] The idea for

this poem came to me as I stroked my cat and tried to deal with the death of my mother. Whiskers definitely helped me to relax. The inspiration to write any of my poems came from my family and their love. Now, the reason for this poem being published is solely my sisters Sharon's responsibility, since I didn't know she had submitted it. For that, I will always be thankful to her. I am excited and proud to have my poem in print. This will always be a treasured memory and would have been for my mother also. I love you, Mom.

SHERRILL, RICHARD
[title] "Friends" [pers.] It's hard to believe how far I have come with a talent I discovered when I was a sophomore in high school. I can remember writing about family, friends, and matters from the heart. Fast forward to today, and I still write about the same things, but from a more experienced and mature perspective. I also write about the memories I had. Thanks to my son, as he goes through his life much like I did. I have drawn inspiration from all my family, whom I thank for always supporting me. Thank you, God, for them all. They're such wonderful gift.

SILVERMAN, MARTHA
[a.] Hillsborough, NJ [title] "My Grandpa Sam" [pers.] I live in New Jersey with my wonderful husband, Steve. We have two beautiful children, Hope and Marc. To me, poetry is magical! I am thrilled beyond words to be included in this book! About a year ago, I was inspired by my aunt, Anne Marion, to write poetry. She is a very talented lady who creates her own poetry and art. Her unconditional love and support have enabled me to express myself poetically. This support has enabled me to express myself poetically. With Aunt Anne for inspiration and Grandpa Sam as guardian angel, how could I miss? I thank them both for the gift of creativity.

SIRAVO, JOANN
[a.] Mar Vista, CA [title] "Ocean" [pers.] Life's beauty and pain are the real poetry. I open my heart to it and it comes through me in the form of creative expression. My husband and I live the writer's life in beautiful California, where the ocean often inspires me. I have just started my own business, Purple Rose Publications, through which I publish a magazine called *Promise*, featuring verse, short prose, photography and artwork. My dream is that all artistic publications find joy and success in providing safe spaces for people to share the echo of the artist's heart.

SJOLANDER, LINDON
[a.] Hayward, CA [title] "Stroganoff and Strychnine" [pers.] The poets who have influenced me the most are Charles Simic, Fernando Pessoa (with all his various poetic personas), Jane Miller, Anne Sexton and especially Sylvia Plath. Other authors would include afa, Shakespeare (Hamlet), Sartre (Nausea), and Camus. I don't identify myself with any particular philosophy or religion. I am simply a skeptic, one who is free to suspend conclusions and concentrate on art. I don't create poetry to prove anything—I create poetry to open doors that lead to wherever one wants them to. For me, it is an archeological adventure of the mind.

SKENE, HEATHER
[title] "The Thoughts that Come with Silence" [pers.] I wrote this poem in thoughts of the first love of my life, Adam. I wanted to be able to express the love I still felt for him, even though he didn't have the same feelings for me. We had gone through so much and spent most of our time together. Then I could tell his love began to fade away. So I knew we couldn't be together much longer. This was one of the saddest times of my life and I wish I could have changed the way it ended.

Lastly, to the first love of my life, I will always have feelings for you, even though we are not together

SKINNER, KIM
[a.] Albion, Brisbane, QLD, Australia [title] Angels [pers.] As so often happens with the death of a child, SIDS strikes tragically, leaving no answers . . . only questions and a great emptiness. Parents enter a time of darkness and despair; siblings become lost in the confusion. I found myself writing short lines of emotion, memories of my son, and the effect of his death came out in the form of poetry. I prefer to think not of his death but of the joy his short life gave us. His life had meaning for all of us. He lives on in our hearts forever. He gave me the courage to publicly acknowledge something very private. This poem is for all of us who share sadness and joy in the lives of our children.

SLAUGHTER, ANNETTE MARIE
[a.] Broadview Heights, OH [title] "Color of Words" [pers.] I appreciate the talent I was given to write. I adore the whole creative process. I've reflected upon this idea in my poem, "Color of Words." I am currently working on an extensive work called "A Window to the Heart." It is a collection of my personal poetry. In this work, I reflect on such issues as infertility, the beauty of love, and the endurance of the human spirit. I currently need a publisher to complete this work. In addition to becoming more recognized as an author, I aspire to continue my college education and become a teacher. It is within education that I believe my creativity can also contribute beauty to society. I thank God for giving me the gift of writing.

SLAUGHTER, ROBERT
[title] "Philosoetry to Guide Me" [pers.] My poem, for me, is a personal motto that I try to live by. My good and bad experiences in life have to be remembered, so I won't repeat my past, or pass up my future. Poetry is an outlet that lets me keep in touch with my past, live for the day, and reach out for my future. I combined philosophy and poetry into one word because it suits my style of writing. I could only hope that my work would someday help someone with their struggles in life, as well as their triumphs. God bless all.

SLOTA, DORI
[a.] Mt. Kisco, NY [title] "Home Again" [pers.] This poem reflects my deep, spiritual feeling that there is a Heaven and a peaceful place where we all come together. We all are here on Earth for a specific purpose, and when we complete that, there is a wonderful place just waiting out there, beyond our wildest dreams.

SMALL, MEGAN
[title] "Relationships" [pers.] I write poems simultaneously; often I am full of ideas throughout a day and I am not calm nor satisfied unless I write my thoughts down and elaborate upon them. In "Relationships," I respond to a situation most have had to endure—unrequited love. My hope is for others to identify with this poem and realize they are not alone with this issue.

SMITH, ADAM
[a.] Odessa, ON [title] "Wolf Cubs" [pers.] I am twelve years old and I attend Odessa Public School in Odessa. Nature has been a love of mine since I was very young but wolves in particular are such unique animals that have developed a bad name. They really aren't mean. They are just very strong, beautiful, wild animals.

SMITH, CANDICE
[a.] Tampa, FL [title] "The Poet" [pers.] I wrote this poem for "The Poet," Jim Morrison.

SMITH, CHARLES
[title] "Nobody Knows" [pers.] Our receptionist at

work lost her husband, and "Nobody Knows" what do I do? What to say? Driving home that night, "Nobody Knows" started hopping out of my head. I pulled off the road and wrote it on my lunch bag. I bought a sympathy card, and typed an insert to put in place of the original insert. The receptionist told me one day a calm comes over her whenever she reads it. When my writings come to me, I must stop and write it or I fear I'll forget it. To God be the glory.

SMITH, EDWARD
[title] "Easter" [pers.] This poem tells us what was done for us 2000 years ago. Through much pain and suffering, I came to trust Jesus as my savior. I write poetry about many subjects. My father told me many years ago I should get my poetry published, but I only write for relaxation.

SMITH, G. E.
[title] "Mist of Our Dreams" [pers.] G. E. Smith authors a poem dealing with abstracts, giving voice to intangible feelings or a visual perspective from inanimate objects' point of view. Residing in Indiana, Smith also pens short stories of various venues, crediting a private on-line literary group known as "The Nook" for a recently rediscovered muse.

SMITH, LISA
[title] "Flowers" [pers.] When I see a blossom or delicate flower, I think of my late mother. Losing her was such a tremendous loss. This sparked my need to be around something growing, green and beautiful. To put it simply, life. I think of the beautiful flower I lost at only 48 years of age and realize she was truly a gift from God. My life is much better and much sweeter, having known such a blossom as she. My mother, my flower. I love you and miss you with all my heart.

SMITH, MATT
[title.] "A Virus for the Mind" [pers.] I was inspired to write "A Virus For The Mind" after I saw that, at all levels, people were being held back by "Nanny States." It just expressed the power that thought can have and the fear that the establishment has when the populous makes its own decisions. I hope it empowers those who read it to direct their own futures and not to be held back by the petty thoughts of small-minded bigots we see every day monopolizing the media.

SMITH, TRAVIS
[a.] Atlanta, GA [title] "The Next Level" [pers.] Greetings! My name is Travis Smith and I am originally an Atlanta native who has been writing poetry since the age of 10. I currently am in the Air Force (about two and a half years), where I have been abroad in Europe. I wrote this poem in response to a conversation I had with a very special lady dealing with me being overseas and how it affects our relationship. It was this conversation that inspired me to write this poem, and I dedicate it to her.

SNYDER, ED
[title] "Valentine's Last Stand" [pers.] This poem basically means I love women, but I'm not stupid. Also, what wasn't rectified on my home streets, will be done in the books. To all the women I was ignorant to, especially Amanda Durkin, I'm so sorry. To Tupac (RIP) and all other West Coast rappers, may my poetry ride for your cause.

SOBODAS, TARAH
[a.] Shorewood, IL [title] "The Gift" [pers.] I have been running cross country and track for six years. I am a junior in high school and throughout my running career, I have had both success and failure. I have crossed the finish line with both smiles of pride and tears of sorrow. But through the years, I have learned that running a race itself is an accomplishment. Running is tough, it is a gift, not just God-given, but self-created. This gift is determination, courage,

strength, and passion. I am more of a person because of this and I would be less if I did not know both the pain and joy of being a runner.

SOKUL, FRANCES Z.
[title] "Resurgence" [pers.] I am a store sculptor. This hobby has given me much gratification and pleasure in establishing a legacy for my family. I believe you must look at the past in order to appreciate the present. In 1994, I exhibited my collection at the Plantation Historical Museum for five months, and again in 1997. I was awarded the President's Choice and First Prize from the Greater Federation of Women's Clubs-Florida for "Cleopatra's Asp," and First Prize for "Retrospect from GFWCF." Through the mediums of sculpture and poetry, I have tried to incorporate my feelings regarding God's greatest gift—life.

SOLDNER, MIKE
[a.] Jakarta, Indonesia [title] "Age" [pers.] Having been raised under very rigid near cult-like circumstances, poetry has for me always provided a reprieve from the pressures of reality. Life is filled with disappointment, heartbreak and lost opportunity. It is, however, these dark experiences that often bring out in us a depth of creativity often unmatched by more favorable conditions.

SOLIS, DESERAY
[a.] La Puente, CA [title] "Your Dream" [pers.] "Your Dream" has taught me many things, and through poetry, I have learned to express myself. In this piece, I wanted to let my special someone know how I feel. I wanted to let him know that dreams can come true. I would like to thank "My Chiller" and my best friend, "Roo." Without you guys, I don't know where I would be. I hope you have all enjoyed my poem and the many others in this wonderful book. God bless you all.

SOLOMON, BRITTANY
[title] "The U.S. Today" [pers.] I'm a 13 year-old in the 8th grade and I like to write poetry. Some of my hobbies are reading African and African-American historical fiction books, and playing a variety of sports. My poem came about when my teacher assigned a poetry project. I wrote an extra poem, assigned as a poetry project. I wrote an extra poem and my mom read it. She encouraged me to send it in, and basically, what the poem is meant for is to confront issues we deal with in everyday life.

SPINELLI, JENNY
[title] "Graduation" [pers.] This poem is very memorable to me. I wrote it close to the conclusion of my senior year in high school. I had hopes of contributing a piece that could be shared by many people. Graduation is a time when you realize your life has just begun and it is solely up to you to take the right path. The past thirteen years of your life have just been stepping stones to what is about to begin. I have learned from writing this poem how inspirational it is for myself and for those who read my poem. I was never aware of my poetic ability until recently, but as a result, I will continue to write more. I believe that if people try to explore themselves, they can find hidden talents that touch the heart and soul of those around them.

SPINK, HELEN
[title] "Love" [pers.] I have enjoyed writing and reading poetry all my life, and feel that it is one of the most beautiful expressions of emotion that we have as people. Words are very important. Poetry is something that everyone can enjoy. I hope people will enjoy reading my poem and that at least one person will be able to relate to it as I can with so many poet's works.

STADEY, SHANNON
[title] "Father of the Bride" [pers.] The poem I wrote portrays the feelings I have for my own father. I hope when my poem "Father of the Bride" is read, people can reflect on their relationship with their own fathers and cherish that special bond between them. I also hope my poem is heard with your heart and shared with your hero, whoever he may be.

STANSEL, BRANDI
[title] "The Storm" [pers.] Poetry is nothing but your own thoughts and feelings written on paper. Everyone is capable of being a poet in some way. Fortunately enough for me, I have someone special to write about—my father. He is a great inspiration for me. After the death of my father, I discovered the wonderful world of poetry. "The Storm," along with many other poems, is my way of speaking to my father in Heaven. I believe that deep down, everyone has his talent, yet some of us go through a dramatic event to realize it.

STEADMAN, LOUISE
[title] "First Birthday" [pers.] This poem is very special to me, as are all the others I have written for A. J. (Adrian Duane Hill, Jr.). He was my first great-grandson. He weighed two pounds, six ounces. He struggled with life for forty-nine days, then went to his heavenly home. I feel that poetry is a gift given by inspiration to express my deepest thoughts. I enjoy writing for family and friends in hopes that it will be a blessing in a special way. I hope my poem "First Birthday" will be a comfort to others who have lost a loved one. I have no special training. Writing and painting are my hobbies.

STENNETT, PAMELA
[title] "To the One I Will Always Love" [pers.] The death of my beloved friend had taken its toll. If not for another, this death would have claimed my soul. Dedicated to Barbara Jean Daniels, whose kindness, understanding, and love saved me and in memory of Zinnie Marie Boose, whose dreams were to write poems and one day have them published.

STEPHENS, WILLIAM
[title] "Standing on the Promises" [pers.] God gave me a talent for writing poetry, not only to minister to myself, but to others around me and around the world. All my thanks and praise for this poem and with each one He allows me to write goes to Him. Expressing Christ on paper in verse is a way of life for me, and I would trade nothing in the world for it. So if you have a talent from God, you better use it or it will be taken away and given to someone else who will. So use what you have to minister to souls!

STERNBERG, ROBERT
[title] "My Many Collective Friends" [pers.] This poem addresses the terrifying anti-creative tendencies of collectivist philosophies. I believe the principles behind such ideas are outwardly attractive for their apparent compassion, but their logical conclusion is destructive and sickening. As an aristocrat, the great thinker Voltaire was subject to execution during the French Revolution. When someone protested he should be spared for his brilliance, the judge responded with the quote I use, and carried out the beheading. Any ideology that will sacrifice unwilling individuals for its cause is a menace, whether it be a theocracy's inquisition, a communist purge, or anything in between.

STEWARDSON, KAREN
[title] "The Only One" [pers.] This poem is a part of my life. So many of my family members have served in this country's armed forces, proudly defending, remembering and honoring the love and life God has freely given to us. My parents made sure we knew about our country's legacy that was left to us, how blood was shed and lives were given to make sure I could grow up and have children and pass this legacy on to my child. I pray my child honors her God, country and family by remembering the stories of our lives. Their courage and strength has been an inspiration to me all my life.

STEWART, ALISON
[a.] Sydney, NSW [title] "Dear Friend" [pers.] Poetry is one of my strongest passions, and I write to express all of my feelings at any time. This poem is about a dear friend of mine. He has done a lot for me, and is always willing to give support and encouragement. I will always remember him, and especially all we have shared. I often try to express my love and appreciation toward my friend through poetry and songs, but this is the poem I find expresses it the best.

STEWART, EARLEANA
[title] "In Loving Memories of Our Mother" [pers.] This poem was originally written in memory of my grandmother, Elnora Garrett, who passed on in 1998, the matriarch, the glue that held us together. I compared her to an eagle, because of its strength and powerful wings. Both, protecting their young, perched on their trees. I revised it this year (2000) while going through a transitional period. Still struggling with my mother's death after 22 years, I needed her blessing to get on with my life and become that creative person. Then I heard a voice—"Fly, Baby Fly . . . Be All That You Can Be."

STILES, AMY
[title] "Inspiration" [pers.] This poem has brought my spirits up so high when I felt I couldn't go on anymore. I hope that when you read it, it'll give you hope as well.

STOCKNER, ALICE
[title] "The Man That Stole My Heart: [pers.] This man is all that and more than I ever imagine. Poetry is deep thoughts and expressing feelings for me. I have a son, Lewis and a daughter, Robyn, also a daughter-in-law, P. J. and have five grandchildren live in Whiteville, N.C. I have a G.E.D. I do everything I can set my mind to. Love writing, singing, and dancing. This poem is powerful to my heart. And it shows dreams can come true, so don't give up. It can happen for others like it did for me. Say you can do it and you can do it. Reach for the stars.

STODDARD, MICHELLE
[title] "For My Kids—Your Mommy's Wish" [pers.] This poem is dedicated to my children, who never cease to make me proud of them. Jordan, Sierra, Kayla and any other Stoddard baby that may come along, I love you with all my heart. Glenn, you and the kids compete me. All my love.

STOLOW, DOMINIQUE
[title] "Angels" [pers.] Through the words, I adorn my visions; through rhythm, I create a world where soul and body bond! Poetry is a link to the above images, thus formed by melting the spirit into matter into spirit in an endless dance! As a painter, I color my feelings and shape them so that you can see what I see, and as a poet, I transcend distance and differences. I draw emotions and share inner sight, so you can feel what I feel! I dedicate this poem to all of you who understand about changes and inspiration, about trust and faith!

STRACK, LIZBETH
[title] Observations in a Laundromat" [pers.] I feel truly blessed when I repeatedly discover the beauty, value, and diversity in even the most seemingly mundane life experiences. This poem not only reflects one of the most important lessons I've learned, it also literally marks the moment when I felt over- whelmingly inspired to express myself in verse. My hope is that this poem will encourage on their life's journey. My life, like my love of poetry, is richly enhanced, and made more beautiful and meaningful by the people and experiences that shape it.

STRANGEMORE, LOIS
[title] "Song Writer"[pers.] I have a good friend who is a really great singer/songwriter. Even

after all the years I've known him and listened to him play, he never fails to amaze me. Hearing him play always makes me want to play; listening to his words, makes me want to write. If I did not know him, this poem would never have been written. He is often an inspiration and truly my favorite songwriter.

STRICKLAND, HEATHER
[title] "My One and Only" [pers.] To me, poetry is a way to express feelings. I love to write poetry. Poetry is a gift only so many people have. If I did not have any poems in my life, it would be absolutely boring. My hobbies are, of course, poem writing and singing. I also love to sing and some day, I hope to be a singer. But poems are just like music—it expresses words from the heart. I hope my poem has touched other people's hearts like it did mine.

STRICKLAND, JULIA
[title] "No One Even Cares" [pers.] This poem is for all the veterans who made it possible to have the freedom to be able to write and to say what I feel. I'm a single mother of two with one grandson. I'm from Crystal River, FL. My hobbies are writing poetry and lyrics. I work in wire craft and lapidary. I have three brothers, and my mother lives in Florida also, and is an accountant. This is mostly dedicated to my deceased father, Herschel R. Baker, Jr. who taught me to appreciate all the veterans who fought for my freedom, and to appreciate music and poetry.

STROM, NATHAN
[title] "In A Heart" [pers.] This poem means a lot to me. It was written at a time in my life when there was a lot of change and hurt going on. After writing down what I felt in my heart, I used it to define my life. I think that this is a very powerful poem because it is the only one I have written and kept. There are three people to whom the poem is dedicated: Sarah K., Amy and Amanda. I love you, and I wish you the best in love and life.

SULLIVAN, APRIL
[title] "Lovers" [pers.] For me, writing has always been a joy, no matter if I'm writing short stories or poetry. Of course, I would have to say that writing poetry is my favorite, as it comes to me so easily. When I write a poem, it never has a title until the whole thing is finished. My inspirations for writing come to me from my four beautiful children, plus the experiences I've had in my life. I have always wanted to make a career out of writing and who knows? Maybe it will finally come true, as writing for others is a beauty all of its own.

SUMBI, JOSEPH
[title] "Ghetto Girl" [pers.] I appreciate the honor of having my poetry featured in this compilation of poetry. I live with my mother, Annette in Vallejo, California and I am a junior at Jesse Bethel High School. The inspiration for the poem "Ghetto Girl" was a young woman by the name of Mikelle, with whom I attend high school.

SYKES, LEATRICE
[title] "Owner of a Submissive" [pers.] This poem was created based on an experience I had with a new form of communication, via cyberslave. I used this communication to obtain new submissives. One particular submission has left a lasting impression upon me. I wrote this poem to describe how I view this submissive. This verse is how I choose to share relationships with the rest of the world. I have received an associates in mental health and I am currently working on my bachelor's degree in behavioral sciences and employed as a mental health counselor. My hobbies include reading, spending time with my nine grandchildren and a part-time cyber-mistress.

TACANG, BRIAN
[title] "Novella" [pers.] Artists, regardless of medium, have a responsibility to tell the truth about the human experience—about longing, exultation, love, rage, ennui—the truth about what it means to be alive. And we must be diligent in expressing, even if it brings us to uncomfortable places. I have endeavored to convey some of my humanity in "Novella" and I hope it mirrors, for the reader, those abstruse moments he or she feels stagnation is less dangerous than potential or more comforting than defeat.

TANGUAY, KAREN
[title] "Verse for a Halloween Night" [pers.] I began writing Halloween poems for my children when they were quite young. In the days preceding Halloween, they would often wake up to find a verse, hastily written on a torn piece of paper. Most of these poems were saved over the years, and I eventually formed a collection which I call "Poems for a Halloween Night." I hope that one day it will be enjoyed by my children's children, and theirs—and all those who remain young in their Halloween spirit.

TATE, ENID
[title] "The Rose" [pers.] Love is such a strong emotion that everyone feels in their lifetime. The euphoria of love realized is unsurpassable. The pain one experiences with love is unequal to any other pain. The loss of a loved one, the disappointments, the distance while a loved one is away are examples of the times we hurt, as well as love. However, we still love because there is no sweeter feeling in the world and a little bit of pain is worth it to experience the euphoria of true love. I love you with all my heart, Tabitha, Britney, and Adam!

TAXIS, GAYLE
[title] "Good Night Bar Bell" [pers.] Bar Bell was my horse. It took six years of learning about horses and how to ride before my parents let me get a horse of my own. After one year of owning him, he got used to my routine of feeding him and I was extremely happy to have my own horse. In school, we had a poetry assignments of your favorite pet.

TAYLOR, SARAH
[title] "Love Has No Boundaries" [pers.] If there is any emotion that finally forces our minds beyond and below the innermost extremities of sanity itself, it is love. To explain or justify this energy in terms acceptable by modern societies standards is virtually impossible. The reasons appear to lie in the underlying workings of the universe itself. If love's initial blindness and various disguises of fear transform into paralyzing sadness, we ask why and search the universe from the inside of our minds outwards, for answers that almost seem to arrive from nowhere. I love you David . . .forever.

TEBIB, TERESA
[title] "Fragile Yet Strong" [pers.] Daniella, Daisy and Audrey are my three daughters. Daniella, my newborn, inspired this poem of truth, but it has my older daughters, Daisy and Audrey's souls in it, also. "Fragile Yet Strong" holds an essence that only parents can understand.

TEHRANI, SAYEH
[title] "Standing Alone" [pers.] This poem is based on a picture that come out of the feelings inside my heart. The picture, alone, made me sad because it made me face something I never realized I felt and when I decided to base a poem on the girl, I did not realize that the girl was me, not until I finished and read the final effort to myself. I do not know where the words came from, but I do know that it came from somewhere inside of me, because if they didn't, it would not hurt so much when I read it.

TEIXEIRA, LAURA
[title] "Rainstorms" [pers.] This poem is most important to me because it symbolizes everyday life in my eyes. It also symbolizes the different things that I go through as a young teenage girl. I'm struggling to survive in a society that doesn't want to accept me as a person of different views on how life should go for me in my eyes. It also symbolizes the things of the past that I had to go through and discover in order to move onto the future. I mainly owe my success in writing poetry to my family. They have encouraged me to write poems and have inspired me to strive to achieve my goals in life. My grandfather also had a major part in this because he tells me to write poems from different aspects of my life and what I go through day to day with my friends at Brighten High. They also tell me that my poems are good, and that they can relate and my extended family, which is my church family, always tells me that when you have faith, nothing is impossible to achieve and accomplish.

TENNEY, ELIZABETH
[title] "Show Me, Tell Me, Teach Me" [pers.] Writing poetry has been my passion since I was eleven years old (I'm currently 19). I have now written over two hundred poems. My dream is to be famous for my writing, "the next Robert Frost." To help pursue my dreams, I moved thirteen hours from home, Northfield, Vermont, to go to a woman's private college, Mary Baldwin College, in Staunton, Virginia. I want to thank The International Library of Poetry for helping pursue my dreams of publication. Also, I want to thank all those who inspired my poetry, especially James Covey, to whom most of my poems are dedicated.

TENNIHAN, DIANE
[title] "I Had A Dream" [pers.] God gave me abundant gifts of compassion and love. I feel both happiness of sorrow at a heightened level. I have used poetry most of my life as a means of expressing my feelings, in hopes that it will evoke an awareness of feelings that others share. I also love writing fun, sometimes silly poems that will make children (and the child in each of us) laugh. As this poem indicates, I have recently suffered a great loss. By writing this poem, I wish to honor my children, my mother and my friends who have encouraged me through this time.

TERHUNE, JENNY
[title] "The Storm" [pers.] I thought of writing this poem one day in winter when I saw storm clouds gathered over the mountains around where I live. I have always enjoyed reading and writing, and I spend time every day reading the King James Bible, God's only true word. As a Christian, I believe a piece of literature is truly successful only if it glorifies God or is a witness of Him. I try to accomplish this in all my writing, and the success I have I owe to God and His Grace.

TERRIEN, PAGGY
[title] "A Better Day" [pers.] I am inspired by many people and things—deep emotions, a lover's kiss, a child's smile of innocence, sun sparkling on calm water, leaves dancing in a summer breeze. I have loved the texture, sound, and color of words my whole life. If I touch just one person with something I have written, to see or feel emotion, then my writing is truly a gift. After all, not everyone sees the same view through the winds of your soul. I like sharing my view with others; it is exciting to find kindred spirits.

TESSIER, PAUL
[title] "The Bomb" [pers.] In 1945, when the war ended, I was 11 years old. This poem was written many years later, but the memory of the war and its aftermath was, and is, very fresh in my mind to this day. I know that my words will evoke a terrible sadness in those who chance to read my poem, but

I also know that the compassion which will fill their hearts will also move them to reject the idea that war serves any useful purpose.

THATCHER, DWAN
[title] "What a Father Means to Me" [pers.] I discovered my talent for poetry at the age of fourteen when I thought I wanted to be a singer and I began to write "songs." My first serious poem was for a fourth cousin who died at the young age of six. My poetry since then has been written about whatever I am thinking or feeling when I decide to write it. This poem is one of four that I have written for my father since his death on November 7, 1999. He died for a heart attack at age 43. He was a beautiful person and now is a beautiful soul. He deserves to have something special to his memory and who better to provide that for him than his own daughter.

THIEL, BRIANNA
[title] "The Train to Agatha" [a.] Grand Rapids, MI [title] "The Train to Agatha" [pers.] Some people think that dreams come when you close your eyes, but the truth is that they come when you open your eyes. All day we talk, worry, rush and work, and we are robbed of the joys of fantasy. But at night, new worlds dance before our eyes. They mesmerize us, enchant us, and sprinkle our lives with fairy dust. So I hope that when people read my poem, they will fall asleep with open eyes, and wake up with memories of that wonderful sunset land. And maybe someday, we'll find the key to the door of Agatha.

THOMAS, DOUGLAS
[title] "Heaven Sent"[pers.] At night I have dreams, yet there are times I feel that this must be a dream, even though it is not. Thanks to my God-given talent, my dreams have come true. I dedicate this poem to the love of my life, Patricia Thomas, now my wife.

THOMAS, JOHN
[title] "If I Could See Behind Your Eyes" [pers.] Love is the strongest, most powerful emotion (to me), and that is the basis of all my writing. There's joyous love, painful love, love apart. Love has many forms, and I write about love with the love that I feel. Poetry and songs go hand in hand, and I write both.

THOMAS, LANETTE
[a.] Roseburg, OR [title] "Horse on Wings" [pers.] I live in the beautiful state of Oregon, on a farm surrounded by scenery that truly inspires me to write poetry. I was quite sad recently upon the loss of my equine friend, Montana Star. Thus, I was inspired to write the poem to help me deal with my emotional healing. I have five wonderful children—Jason, Robin, Chelsie, Cody, and Colton, and my husband, Danny.

THOMAS, LAVONNE
[title] "Kids of Columbine High" [pers.] I wrote this poem in remembrance of those children, and as a consolation to their families. I now know what it's like to lose a loved one. My grandmother passed away in 1999 and just recently I lost my sister July 6, 2000. I express my deepest and most passionate words in poetry. It is a gift I have and I'm proud of. I love writing all kinds of poems, even children's storybook poems. I hope one day that my poems will become an inspiration to many.

THOMAS, STEPHEN
[title] "Heaven" [pers.] A poem is just a collection of ordinary words, arranged in a certain way to portray a particular thought, feeling, or emotion. This poem has a special meaning for me and possibly for a lot of other readers also. We are individuals and we view the same things in life in different ways. I hope that whatever you discover in my poetry, about yourself or your life, helps you.

THOMPSON, CLARK S.
[a.] Ring Gold, GA [title] "Look Up When You Are Down" [pers.] Some people go through life and never experience "true love!" The kind of love that is earth-shaking. The "can't eat, can't sleep" kind of love. The "all I think about is you" kind of love. The "I want to be your everything" kind of love! Those out there that have felt this, know what I'm talking about. I am 37 years old and for the first time in my life, I am head over heels in love with someone that I cannot live without. She is on my mind 24 hours a day. All my poems that I had written are inspired by the greatest of all emotions. One that God said will endure above all else. Love never gives up, it never fails. With this assurance, I know we will always be together. I know when she reads this poem in this book, she will, in another small way, know that I love her with all my heart and soul, forevermore.

THORNHILL, JUDY
[title] "A Moment" [pers.] I wrote this poem after coming out of an illness. I was celebrating life and the wonder of creation. This poem also represents those of us with fibromygia who, in our illness, still have the strength to hold on and support each other. It's to remember that we are held in God's hands and his care until he releases us and our spirits are carried on the breeze. We are never alone.

THORNTON, LISA
[title] "The Leaf Falling off the Tree" [pers.] I was inspired by my loving grandmother to write this poem. I love to read and write poetry, especially when it's about someone I love. I hope people read my poem and realize that life is short and need to enjoy every minute while you can.

THORP, ALLISON
[title] "Waiting Room" [pers.] I have been inspired to write on many occasions following memorable experiences, and "Waiting Room" evolved from time I spent with a friend going through a hard time. It was such a relief to get out on paper what I was feeling for my friend.

THURLING, CRISTIE
[a.] Kambah, NSW [title] "Numb" [pers.] Poetry is how I have always expressed myself, something I found at a young age which grew into a passion. I love being able to touch other people with my words and allow them a glimpse into "my world." Poetry allows me to explore emotion and feelings otherwise left buried and encourages the reader to do the same. I enjoy the satisfaction of watching the face of someone who has read my work and found their own meaning within it that they relate to. I find inspiration in the beauty of other artists' forms of self expression. "Within Creativity and expression, lays peace; and within peace, lays our future, so indulge and be happy."

TIDWELL, PATRICE
[title] "Love Anew" [pers.] I began writing poetry while in high school. My poems were shared with friends and family. Through poetry, I could relate to the world around me. "Love Anew" was written after I found myself in love the second time around. One day, I was reflecting on just how happy I was and out of those reflections, "Love Anew" was born. At that moment, my heart took flight as my spirit soared. Poetry can be very therapeutic for the soul, especially when used as a tool to express your deepest feelings to that special someone.

TIDWELL, POLLISA
[title] "The Wall" [pers.] At the point in time in my life in which I wrote this piece, I was in a lot of pain. Writing helped get some of my feelings out in the open to my friends and family. I'd like to thank all the people in my life who told me I could do something great and believed in me. I would also like to thank all the other people who told me I could never be a writer. You've chal-

lenged me the most, because I did something even though you told me I could not. Thank you

TIERNEY, COLIN
[a.] Saint James, NY [title] "Maureen" [pers.] I know of worlds beyond. I have heard fantastic stories of fate. I have witnessed miracles of life. I have knowledge of death; I have seen it, I have heard about it, and I know I will experience it, yet none of this impressed me or frightens me anymore. I am now within the shell of our hearts, secure within the essence of our minds. The perpetual connection of our bodies we'll share; a fear of the eternal force of love that keeps life going, that makes it worth loving. Maureen is what I write of. She is love to me.

TILLOTSON, BELINDA
[title] "Passion, Desire, Forever" [pers.] I have been told that I have a gift and to share it. Friends and family have been my greatest inspiration. I live in a small country town in beautiful Wisconsin. I enjoy writing poems as a way of expressing myself, as well as making my own occasion cards. Having a chance to share my innermost feelings with others is a dream come true. Poetry to me is a gift of one's inner beauty, placed on paper to touch the hearts of others to share, enjoy and grow from.

TILREM, SYNN'VE
[title] "Missing" [pers.] Although I am Norwegian, I've always felt more comfortable expressing myself in English. Composing poems is a wonderful way to express both sensations and moods in one action. I've always been fascinated by words and I love to play with them. The poem "Missing" is a very personal poem, describing the loss of a dear friend.

TINGLE, BARRY
[title] "Heavenly Agenda" [pers.] I'd like to thank my mom for nurturing my sensitivity, my late teacher Audle, for providing a definition of life, and I can sink my teeth into and my sweetheart, Linda for spicing up the flavor of life with her inspiration. It was her tenderness that caused this poem to leak through my pen. I'd also like to thank the IL for validating my childhood hours of isolation spent reading comic books, mythologies and science fiction while the other children ran amok in the background thinking, along with most of the adults, that I was off of my rocker.

TINK, WAYNE
[a.] Cunderlin, WA [title] "Give it Time" [pers.] This poem was inspired by a very special person who will always be a part of me, and I hope everyone who reads it can identify someone they know within it. The special ones know who they are.

TODD, RICHARD
[title] "Lonely Without You" [pers.] Words from the heart for a special lady special a world away. When we met, I knew she was special the very first day. To leave her was more painful than being cut with a knife. The joyous thing is, she will soon be my wife!

TOLBERT, RUFUS
[a.] Lancaster, PA [title] "Happy Birthday, My Love!" [pers.] Despite his many flaws, my father was a hopeless romantic. So whenever I was rifling through his music collection, I could find plenty of beautiful ballads that have since become timeless classics such as "Three Times A Lady" or "Still" by the Commodores or Peaches and Herb's "Reunited." My father also kept romantic poetry clippings wedged into the vanity mirror. So as a child, I always hoped, and I just knew that those love songs and those poems were for my mother. So while waiting for my parents to get back together, I inherited my father's romanticism and developed a talent for poetry. My wife and my father never met. However, they are connected

through me in a way that neither of them knew. My father instilled in me a sense of hoping for the best, regardless of circumstances. My wife has given me a reason to strive for my best. Just as my father's love for my mother seemed to me to be the driving force for his romanticism, I've only given real life to my verbal creativity in times of heightened emotion for my wife. I am forever thankful to God for them both.

TORKINGTON, AIMEE
[a.] South Wales, UK [title] "My Wishes for the World 2000" [pers.] I live in a small seaside town called Porthcawl in South Wales U.K. I wrote this poem for the millennium when I was eight years old. I feel proud that my poem is going to be published for all my family to read and people in other countries. I hope it sends a message to keep the world clean and tidy.

TORRES, DIANA
[title] "My Dream" [pers.] My poem has a special meaning to my life. Ever since I wrote it, I want to share my unique poem to the whole world. I cannot take all the credit for the poem that inspirationally I admire. I would only be selfish, for my heavenly Father, pure in heart and faith, helped me write my poem by surrounding me with his beauteous of nature. He is the one and only who divinely inspired me through his beautiful works of art, and I adore him for that. My Love for God is deeper than the crystal blue ocean.

TORRES, JUAN
[title] "In Your Eyes" [pers.] Through my journey through life, struggling to survive, my mentor and saviour Jesus Christ has guided me through all my transgressions and has blessed me with an earthly angel who has helped in inspiring me to look for a better tomorrow, Mr. Christopher M. Barnett. Also, to all my friends who stuck by me through the good times, the bad times and the hard times, I love you all. Thanks for everything.

TORRES, MARGARITA
[a.] Shirley, NY [title] "Thinking of You" [pers.] The meaning to this poem would only define the person, who is Guiseppe Chariamonte, the man I will love to my dying day. Even though we could not stay together forever, this is dedicated to my best friend and once my lover.

TORRES, MARICZA
[title] "Mirage" [pers.] This poem was the second poem of hundred years after. I learned of the power of words at 12 years old. I felt strength, love and escape in opening my heart and expressing my deepest thoughts. I dedicate this poem to my mother, who always encourages me to pursue what is in my heart and my passion. She is our family's strength. Thank you for your support and love. I love you.

TORRES, VERONICA
[title] "Sleeping Beauty" [pers.] My poetry is my voice. I was never truly able to express myself vocally; writing was my outlet. It pleases me just knowing that my poetry is being read by other people. So I dedicate this poem, to all other the "Sleeping Beauties" of the world who refuse to wake up, my Prince Charming, who inspired me to write such beautiful words—thank you Dave, and the fairy godmother of poetry and song, Stevie Nicks, my motivation for wanting to write.

TOWER, ELIZABETH
[title] "It's Time to Say Goodbye" [pers.] This poem is a special tribute to Bob, my husband and best friend who passed away on August 21, 1999, after a sudden illness. I didn't have an opportunity to say goodbye to him. It was eight months before I could clean out his personal belongings, which was a very traumatic experience. I wrote this poem as an expression of my love for him, as well as a form

of closure for me. Poetry is my way of expressing my heartfelt thoughts and feelings.

TOWEY, WILLIAM
[a.] Norristown, PA [title] "The Silent Soliloquy" [pers.] The inspiration for this poem came from Sarah, a patient at a nursing home. While delivering dinner meal one evening, I saw Sarah standing staring out the window, contemplating. She was to get married the next day. Having spoken with her on numerous occasions, I could actually picture her dressed this way. When she turned around, I noticed that she had been crying. Thus, I thought a speech without words, or a silent soliloquy.

TREMBLAY, DAWN
[title] "Cancer" [pers.] I wrote this poem about a very special person in my life, my grandmother. When I first found out she had cancer and it had spread through her body, I was upset, but with that, I also thought that she would be fine. She got worse as the days went by. Seeing her suffer and how my family was dealing with it, I wrote this poem. Not even a week later, my grandmother passed away. Before closing her casket, I read my poem. Grandma this is for you. I love you and I will always will.

TREXLER, JENNIFER
[a.] Tully, NY [title] "My Little Star" [pers.] This poem is dedicated to all the preemies and their parents. My son, Joshua, was one pound, six ounces when he was born, and he, like other preemies, are tiny little stars that twinkle in our eyes. There are many obstacles to overcome as a preemie and as a preemie parent, and I hope this poem can give each of you the confidence, strength, faith and love to shine as bright as the brightest star in the sky.

TRIPKOVIC, BILJANA
[title] "Farewell to the Friend" [pers.] I wrote this poem on the day my very best friend should be buried. The poem was read a few minutes before they put her beloved body into the grave. Before, I read so many poems, expecting them to tell me something meaningful. But poetry is personally telling me now secrets of living, because the gift of art was given to me. Poetry is my big love. For fifteen years, I have been in a wheelchair. I live now with my husband, Dragan, in Ljubljana, Slovenia. I am absolved of Natural and Mathematics University, without a degree. My occupation is ceramic artist, but now I am retired. For the last five years, poetry (writing in reading) are my occupation and my only friend during the day.
I write about my searching for happiness. Luckily, I found her. The essence of my poetry is that love and truth reside inside in heart of every human being. My hobbies are traveling and listening to music (jazz and rock). I want to enjoy this life and existence to the fullest. The way how to do it, I discovered, thanks to my teacher and master Maharaji. He shows me something beyond and far ahead philosophy.

TRUDELLE, SARAH
[a.] Chateauguay, QC [pers.] I was chosen to join a Creative Writing Club at school, which I really enjoyed. Our teacher, Mr. Naidoo, was impressed with my Mother's Day poem. He suggested that I enter it in your poetry contest. I really appreciate Mr. Naidoo's encouragement. My parents also give me a lot of encouragement. Now I have you to thank for your encouragement. I am so thrilled that you liked my Mother's Day poem. My mom is thrilled that I appreciate her so much. She gets goose bumps when she reads it. Thanks for a great opportunity!

TRULL, KENNETH
[a.] Lobelville, TN [title] "I Am Poem" [pers.] "I Am Poem" is a statement about my belief in Christ. All of my athletic ability is due to Christ. If and when I fail, I will be made stronger through his victory.

TSOUTSOURIS, SILVIA
[a.] Western Springs, IL [title] "Old Fashion Curfew" [pers.] Sharing my experience in verse in a special way of remembering the past. Growing up during the '40's and '50's was a wonderful time in America. Family was not important. We had close family ties. "Old Fashion Curfew" clearly indicates that Daddy was the head of the household and we followed his rules. Times have changed, and these rules border on the ludicrous. Still, those were the "Good Old Days" that we love to hear about today. I am truly pleased to share my experience in verse.

TUCKER, GEORGE
[a.] San Diego, CA [title] "Forever Waiting" [pers.] For my first poem, I would like to dedicate it to my very special friend, Lolita, who I think is the greatest. She brings so much happiness to my life. There's always be a place in my heart for you.

TUCKER, ROBERT
[title] "Autumn" [pers.] This is the one season I truly wish could go unchanged forever. It is like a Renoir or a Botticelli—priceless.

TUCKER, SHANE
[a.] Wichita, KS [title] "A Walk On The Beach" [pers.] I wrote this poem after reading a verse in the Bible about Jesus telling a man to give up all His possessions and follow Him, and the man decided not to do so. After reading that, it dawned on me that most people are more concerned with everything around them except the one thing they should be concentrating on—what God can give you and not what man can give you. So remember, in life it is not what you gain, but what you sacrifice. And that, my friend, is the meaning of life.

TUELL, ROBERT
[a.] St. Petersburg, FL [title] "Columbine Reaper" [pers.] For me, poetry is a release—a way to express my feelings, and often outrage at life's events, both public and private. Much of the subject matter for my poetry or lyrics is not chosen, but rather comes from something that has evoked a strong reaction within me. I like to think of my work as social commentary that takes on a different form. When I'm not spending time with my wife and three year-old daughter, I enjoy reading, playing the bass and singing.

TURNER, JACQUI
[a.] Christchurch, New Zealand [title] "Unicorn" [pers.] My poem, like all my poetry, is very special to me, as it is a means to express my inner feelings and thoughts. Poetry for me is about expressing what is in my heart, not my mind. In "Unicorn," I am conveying the innocence, beauty, love and hope that the unicorn holds for me.

TURNER, KATHERINE
[a.] Hygiene, CO [title] "Forever Will I Be Yours" [pers.] I am 15 years old and I wrote this sonnet for my boyfriend, Bill. He means the world to me, no matter what my parents say about teenagers not being able to experience true love. He's my inspiration and what makes every day bright and warm. To Bill—I mean everything I say. I love you! You make me feel beautiful. You give me the power to make my dreams come true!

TURNER, ROMYA
[title] "the woman who birthed me" [pers.] No young child looks at her mother and says, "One day we won't understand each other." Unfortunately, for many women, this is exactly what happens. "the woman who birthed me" is a cry for reconciliation. This poem is about understanding misunderstandings, and reaching out to the woman who loves you more than anyone else . . .because you love her.

UDLER, LEA
[title]"What Seems Is Not" [pers.] This poem means very much to me for various reasons. First of all, it

is my sister's favorite one. This is of great value to me, because she is the one who encourages me the most. As one begins to read it, one gets the impression that the poet writes about a lost love, which is untrue. I wrote this poem because many times people encounter the loss of those they love due to death. This is an awful feeling, making everything seem unfair. So, I suppose this poem deals more with my feelings towards the unfairness of death.

UNG, DARA
[title] "The Arrival of Spring" [pers.] I wrote this poem for my first baby daughter, Adelene who was born on April 21, 2000. She made me realized how joyful and fulfilling is to be a father. Suddenly, she's become the priority in life. It is a challenge to find time to make a living and share love among Adelene, her mother and others.

UNIKEL, VIOLET
[a.] Los Angeles, CA [title] "The Children" [pers.] This is just one of the many poems I wrote about my brothers and my parents, who perished in the concentration camp of Auschwitz in 1944. I feel what I have lost money cannot replace and time cannot erase.

UPLINGER, ADAM
[a.] Oakdale, CA [title] "Love" [pers.] Like everyone else in this world, I have views on everything that happens. This poem happened to be my view on true love. This poem is one of over a hundred I have written and I'm very happy to have my favorite poem published. This poem was inspired by Edgar Allan Poe's "Annabel Lee," which is the best love poem I have ever read. I dedicate this to Alton, Jean, Sharon, Joanne (my family) and to Nikki, who the poem was written about.

UREN, BARBARA
[tile] "When the Wind Blows" [pers.] I'm 15 years old and I have special needs because of my autism. I'm very proud I achieved this. This poem is very special to me, because I wrote it for my mom.

URRUTIA, LUCY
[title] "Then Came You" [pers.] This poem is dedicated to a person I fell in love with, who brought happiness and sunshine into my life and who also brought me closer to God. Thank you for coming into my life.

VANNESS, RON
[title] "Saying Goodbye . . .Duchess" [pers.] I hunt and show dogs, and have done it so that bound dogs enjoy the wide open spaces. Nature has a lot to say and I'm inclined to listen. I was blessed with Duchess, a red bone coonhound, and she had my heart from the get-go. Then I lost her. This poem is a splinter of the loss in life that endows us with appreciation for the gains in life.

VARGAS, CESAR
[a.] Brooklyn, NY [title] "The Three Most Powerful Words in the World" [pers.] Thank you for your interest in my poem. I appreciate your kindness! This is only the beginning of a long and appealing journey. Passion is the number one motivator behind my poetry, and my heart uses my mind to put what I feel into words. Life, and an indescribable feeling of enlightenment, have led me to write a fine collection of songs and poems. I'd also like to thank God, my family, and everyone who has supported and encouraged me to expand my talent.

VARNES, MICHAEL
[title] "Kelly" [pers.] This poem was written for Kelly. She is my heart and soul. She inspires me in so many ways, and that's why she is my guardian angel. Just wanted to say to her thank you. Also, more importantly, I love you!

VAUGHNS, REBECCA M.
[a.] Miami, FL [title] "The Voice of Life" [pers.]

I've been writing poetry since I was 10 years old. It's conversation from my soul. "Voice of Life" was inspired by Jane and Jackson. The poem is a compilation of songs from *Dreamstreet*, *Control*, *Rhythm Nation 1814*, *Janet (self-titled)*, and her latest, *Velvet Rope*. The art of any artistic nature one may possess is being able to stretch your ideas of creativity. I consider myself a "gumbo soup" poet. I write about everything, because everything has some form of life, depending on which window you're viewing from. Poetry to me is that second voice that speaks what one feels, but can't say.

VAUGHT, HAROLD
[title] "One Thousand Years" [pers.] I never really thought about this poem much; it just came to me. To be able to write something of beauty and put your love into it is truly God's gift and I'm thankful for the privilege. We all see the problems in this world of ours, and it really does need to be fixed. It will take the kindness of everyone to change things for the better, but I hope it doesn't take "One Thousand Years." This poem is straight from my heart and we do need to make our one and only world better for all.

VAZQUEZ, JUSTIN
[a.] Virginia Beach, VA [title] "The World Dies With Us, Unless . . ." [pers.] He loved writing poetry since the third grade, when he composed his first poem entitled "The Math Test." Ever since he began writing poetry, he has intrigued teachers and others alike with his speed and talent. Justin hopes to have more of his work published in the future. He was inspired to write this poem when he realized how much mankind is damaging the Earth. Justin hopes this poem will inspire others, as it did himself, to change their wrongful ways.

VEAUNT, AMBER
[a.] Mt. Morris, NY [title] "Time" [pers.] This poem is very important to me because it was written about my ex-boyfriend. I enjoy writing poetry, because it helps me to better understand my feelings. I am 17 years old and I think that I received my interest in poetry from my mother. Speaking of family, I have my parents, an older brother, and two older sisters. My hobbies include writing, drawing, sports, school, and hanging with my friends. I believe that I have achieved a lot in my life already and hope to continue to do so.

VEINOTTE, TERRI
[title] "A Moment's Grace" [pers.] Writing poetry is a way to release your inner emotions and open up your soul to others. There are so many things that I have experienced in my life (many good), and lots of challenges. I have become stronger, more passionate and value every second of my life and family. I have a wonderful husband, Larry and four beautiful children: Lindsey twelve, Chelsey eleven, Matthew nine, and Alissah, four. It is an honor to have my poem published and I can't wait to see it. I hope that it will touch or inspire others, because everyone needs a moment's grace.

VELEY, EUGENIA
[title] "Time" [pers.] "Time" occurred to me at the end of a philosophical thought I had—time has a way of happening when we are looking the other way or are otherwise engaged. Time doesn't stand still, and so the universe has to obey. I hope my poem brings to mind a familiar experience to all who read it.

VILLAMIL, JOHN
[a.] Quaker Hill, CT [title] "Dream Come True" [pers.] My poem is a proposal of marriage to Banita Rose, a woman like no other, that somehow inspired me to poetry. Banita came into my life at a time when I had just about given up on finding love. After years of heartbreaks and disappointments, Banita somehow found her way into a heart that was too scarred to love again. Banita and I

started as friends and co-workers. Over time, I had the opportunity to see her many sides; a mother, homemaker, nurse and, oh yes, a blackjack dealer. I have seen her laugh and I've seen her cry. Banita and her two daughters, Shelse and Aftin, have opened up their hearts and home to my son, Jason and I. Jason and I now feel like part of a family. Over time, Banita and I fell in love, and yes, Banita has accepted my proposal of marriage. We are planning a September 2001 wedding. Banita is to me a "dream come true."

VINES, ELIZABETH
[title] "What If" [pers.] This poem was written in memory of my mother, who passed away too early in life for me to have known her. I have always held her in my heart, knowing she is with me from day to day. The loss of that mother-daughter bond had inspired me to write many poems. I hope that each person that reads my poem feels something strong and emotional. I am honored to be able to share with all a poem this dear to me.

VINSON, RALPH
[title] "Life's Battle" [pers.] In my 84 years I've lived, as my poem states, I've been an owner and operator of a sawmill, a vice president of public relations and sales promotion, editor of weekly newsletters and monthly magazines of life insurance companies. I was also an editorial cartoonist for daily newspapers. I was a noncommissioned officer in the navy sea bees during WWII when I lost my two younger brothers. My 82 year-old bride, with a mechanical heart valve and pacemaker, lives with her younger sister. I am not physically or financially able to take of her. I live alone in an apartment.

VOBI, RIELLE
[a.] Cincinnati, OH [title] "My Pocket Holds Only Paper Dreams" [pers.] The idea of poetry as an art form didn't come naturally to me. In fact, it took some time before I realized it's beautifully inventive power—power to heal, entertain, awaken and rest. Poetry is limitless in art. From the writer to the reader, energy takes place, which is sometimes (most times) a mystery. I've chosen not to explain my poem. However, I'll explain my pseudonym. It is a tribute to my three best friends. From the names Valerie, Michelle and Bobi, Rielle Vobi was birthed. I am Rielle.

VON COLDITZ, VIRGINIA
[title] "Sea Bound" [pers.] Holding her mother's hand, one summer afternoon in 1921, three-year-old Virginia first waded into California's Pacific Ocean. It was the beginning of her life long affinity for the sea. But the sea is by no means her only love. She's an avid adventurer, world traveler, storyteller, seamstress, sailor, museum volunteer, artist (drawing sculptures), problem-solver and beloved mother, grandmother and great-grandmother. Today, in her eighties, every summer means the beach and her ever-expanding family gathers to join her in diving waves and floating on the green sea. This is her first published poem.

VONBULOW, NICOLE
[title] "what is heaven?" [pers.] My name is Nicole Christina Vonbulow. I am eleven years old and in a few months, I will be in sixth grade. My hobbies are soccer, track, dancing, reading, story writing, playing with my stuffed animals, and writing poetry. My mom and dad are Sophia and Butch. I wrote this poem because I was wondering how life is after death. Do our souls disappear? Or do we emerge in Heaven? When I was younger, I used to get teased a lot, and I started thinking about Heaven. I thought it is a nice place for good souls. Heaven is an unsolved mystery. The poem just popped into my head. Sometimes I think I want to be a writer.

VOYLES, BELINDA
[title] "Love" [pers.] This small verse is dedi-

cated to my children, Jim and Jennifer. My love is with them always.

VRELITS, JEANETTE
[title] "Once More" [pers.] "Once More" is a dedication to life. I believe that a sunrise, though it appears every day, is one of the most beautiful wonders of nature. It is such a magnificent moment of every day that I just had to describe in words what kind of effect it has on me to have been given the gift of sight, and therefore, the gift of being able to witness the beginning of a new day that arises by the touch of light.

WADE, JIMMY
[a.] Cabot, AR [title] "The Lighthouse" [pers.] "The Lighthouse" by Jimmy Dead Wade is dedicated to Nancy Wade, my wife of 19 years. From the Island of Pharaohs stood the oldest and to the North Carolina Shores, Cape Hatteras stands the tallest; not to speak of them would be to douse their lights. "Give me a ray of hope," cried the vessels to every lonely shore, and the lighthouses boasted most diligently, "Come home, come home; my shores await thee. Safe by my light shall you come home to thy love's warm, tender kisses."

WAGGONER, MARJORIE
[title] "Friends and Neighbors" [pers.] To date, I have composed very few poems. One would come to mind, often in the middle of the night, only to be forgotten by morning. I submitted this poem to the resident newsletter where I live, hoping it might lift some spirits, and I feel it has. We are seniors, and at times, suffer from depression and loneliness. I have two sisters in New York, Irene Smith and Evelyn Hamilton, also in their eighties, whom I adore, and I am ordering an extra copy for them to share. I am thrilled to have my poem included in *Rainstorms and Rainbows*.

WAITES, TRIER
[title] "Lost in the Mist" [pers.] This poem created a second voice for me. At the time that I wrote it, I was going through an emotionally abusive relationship and the poem was my voice of reason. It helped me to get up and get out. It has been my guiding light to the beautiful relationship that I am currently enjoying.

WALKER, BETSY
[title] "Innocence" [pers.] I wrote this poem in hope of awareness. I wish to dedicate this to all those with a hope of love, and to those who turned away yesterday's dream, today's hope, for tomorrow may never come.

WALKER, LAURA
[title] "Dad" [pers.] This poem was written for the only man I knew as my father. My real father died when I was four years old. This man was already a father of twelve, and when I married his son, he accepted me as his daughter and loved me as his own until he died. He was always there for me. He loved sports, and he loved people. He died before I could tell him goodbye. I miss him still. I work as a supervisor at the United States Postal Service. I have three children and nine grandchildren. I'm called "The Card Lady," because I express feelings in verse.

WALKER, MELANIE
[title] "Out of Touch" [pers.] This poem is about a very special person in my life. His name is Gage. Gage is my friend Terri's nine-month-old baby. I spent a lot of time with him, and we formed a really close bond. One day Gage was taken out of my life, and my poem is an expression of the feelings I felt when it happened. I really enjoyed all the time I got to spend with Gage, and I'll treasure those memories for the rest of my life. No matter where he goes and how far away he is, he'll always be close in my heart. I love you.

WALKER, SHERYL
[title] "To My Darling Daughter" [pers.] My daughter is my miracle on Earth, and something I never thought I'd be blessed with. I believe I experienced true love for the first time when she was born.
My poem was inspired by her and my life renewed with love and joy. Being a mother is the greatest blessing I could ever ask for. I will love her until the end of time. I would like to thank my parents for their belief and influence in my life. My health is not the only thing I have now, but also a beautiful daughter to cherish forever.

WALLACE, COURTNEY
[title] "Rising" [pers.] Poetry to me is the bare essence of someone's soul who has the courage to share it with the world. I'm a PCA for Englewood Medical Hospital Center in Englewood, New Jersey. Writing poetry is my down time, the way I relax. I have always been a big fan of Maya Angelou and Nikki Giovanni. They have thought me how to express myself in the deepest way without anger and negativity. I hope when people read my poetry, they will be able to look into my soul and appreciate what I have to share, for words are the most powerful thing to use.

WALLACE, LISA
[title] "Smell of Sorrow" [pers.] Limitations of words causes numerous thoughts. My poetry is inspired by the feelings I have and the thoughts that go through my head. I have a light cast of morbidness in most of my writing. It is a sensation that is unknowingly brought about. Being only 15, I am ecstatic to get as far as I am. This is my first publication, and I want to thank my parents. Without them, I would be nowhere.
I love you. I also want to thank my family and friends for their support and encouragement.

WALLACE, PETE
[title] "Worried and Hopeful" [pers.] These are the thoughts that go through my head every time I sit down to write. I enjoy my poetry, but for me it never comes easily. (Does it for anyone?) Hopefully, with practice and patience, this battle between my head and heart will lessen. In doing so, I will be able to write more for my friends and family to enjoy. I hope you like it.

WALLS, SHERRY
[a.] Dallas, TX [pers.] My mother (who is in Heaven) often told me, "I had one child that would sit in a corner reading a book; another would sit in the middle of the floor writing in a book." With this in mind, it only reveals to me that writing has been my passion and talent from the beginning. Therefore, I must give all praises to God, from which comes my gift, knowing that without him, I can do nothing. I am very appreciative for the opportunity to share with the world and receive recognition and honor from the publication of "My Heart."

WANG, DAVID
[title] "See You" [pers.] What can I say? Love has always been the poet's bread and butter. Though I'm young, I think I know what I'm talking about, or at least I hope I do. This poem was written at 3:26 am, and it's about this girl I know. She still doesn't know my feelings for her (it's been years) but hey, here's to hoping!

WANG, PHYLLIS
[title] "Scared" [pers.] This poem is very special to me, because it tells how I felt when I was young. I want to dedicate my poem to my mother, who urged me to continue writing poems, to my aunt Emma, who first made me realize my talent, and to my teacher, Mrs. Masamori, who inspired me to be creative.

WARD, TIM
[a.] Simsbury, CT [title] "The Reel Truth" [pers.]

There were numerous influences that guided me in writing this poem, which included Ray Davies, a noted English songwriter, the movie "It's a Wonderful Life" and comedy from Firesign Theater. Poetry and writing have always been a way to express what I think and feel. Everyone likes to be creative and this is something I enjoy doing for myself. If this enables others to know me better, then I have accomplished one goal. Each life is a gift; make a positive difference in someone else's life. Thanks, Karen, for being part of my life.

WARREN, ANNIE
[title] "Love" [pers.] I enjoy life, people and treasure old friends and family. Most of my spare time has been shared preparing meals and feasting on conversations that follow small gatherings in my home. I sincerely get involved with the heart and soul of my contacts. Someone well-traveled or someone living on a mountain top raising 18 children opens my mind, my heart, and cultivates my imagination. When inspired to write, I can unlock the stored feelings and memories I've been so fortunate to collect and share them with a listener.

WARRICK, JEAN
[title] "Summer Serenade" [pers.] This poem is a tribute to my father. He truly taught me to listen to nature's songs. Summers in my small hometown in Nebraska were special times, as Dad and I rocked gently on that old porch swing, listening to summer evenings and waiting the arrival of the wonderful song of the cicada.

WASHINGTON, LAURADEE
[title] "The Starlight" [pers.] The stars, your eyes—who are you? My name is Lauralee Washington. I am a native of Trinidad and Tobago. This poem is dedicated to my parents, Gloria and Henry, sister April, Lucanda King, Dionne Nebblett, Valarie Samuel, Gary, and Avalon Pantin, the entire Niles family. A special thank you to my dearest, Hapta Tecle Murray.

WATSON, DANIEL
[title] "Strength in Yourself" [pers.] The above poem is a self-esteem builder for one's heart, soul, and mind, to overcome adversity such as things that I have come across in my life. If this helps anyone who reads this poem to become stronger for the challenges we must meet and overcome, I will only say you're welcome and God bless our existence on this Earth and how you live is from your own creation.
See what you want to see and become it.

WATSON, DUSTY
[title] "But" [pers.] I love to write about whatever takes my fancy at the time. The day I wrote this one was a day that no matter what I did or said, someone gave me a "But." Writing both stories and poetry flows through my veins, passed on from my mother, who only wrote poetry from tragedy. I had taken a twenty-year break and never wrote a single line. Now, it seems that all I'm doing is writing poetry and stories. I guess I'm making up for lost time. My heart soars with pleasure when I'm writing, but I frantically look for writing material when the mood strikes. I usually carry them with me, but unfortunately there are times without implements and I can't remember all the lines for very long. It is a great thrill to be published!

WATTS, CLEMENTINE
[title] "Timeless Love" [pers.] There are many ways to express one's emotions. I cannot always express opinions adequately to the outside world; therefore, I say it in print. Timeless love is my way of honoring a brother that died several years past. In a sense, I have given him some sort of immortality. His face and voice fades daily, but the love I feel will never cease. Written in loving memory of Gerald Ray Brewer. Clementine Watts, age 43, resides in Walnut Cove, NC., and has been married

16 years to Daniel Watts. They have two daughters, Brooke and Whitney.

WATTS, D.
[title] "My Church" [pers.] I was born in Winchester, Ontario, Canada. I've written 40 poems of a home- spun type, one of which was published. I live in Kawata, Ontario, Canada, with my wife, Anne, to whom I've been married for 40 years on July 30. I prefer poems that rhyme.

WEBER, CRYSTAL
[a.] Eastam, MA [title] "Teenage Puppy Love" [pers.] The kind of person who sings along to every word of a song and not care what she might sound like, Crystal knows the steps to take, and doesn't mind what others think of her stride. Red, bouncy curls match her personality. Purple and silver butterflies and fairies float in her aura. Crystal has aspirations of a Chicago-style life, directing film and performing arts, making the best of her natural organization and management skills. She would like to thank Kathy, Bill and family for making this publication opportunity possible, and to fellow poet, "kar."

WEBER, MICHAEL
[a.] Charlotte, NC [title] "The Shot" [pers.] This poem represents the dreams we all have in our hearts. We have to hold on to our dreams because they can come true. I owe a lot to my grandparents, who helped a lot of my dreams come true. I hope people and kids will read this poem and accomplish their dreams.

WEHNER, STEPHAN
[title] "What Are Friends" [pers.] This poem means so much to me, because it's real. It can happen to anyone at anytime, and it does happen to some people. I feel that people going through this have hard times. Fortunately, this never happened to me, but I feel it will someday, sometime. This poem brings out my innermost, deepest feelings, the feelings I didn't express until now. I am pleased to hear this poem will get published and people will see how I feel. I would like to thank Howard Ely and staff for keeping me updated. Thanks Poetry.com.

WELCH, SANDY
[a.] Baker, LA [title] "Can You See Me?" [pers.] I wrote this poem about my eating disorder. These words describe what many, if not all, of the people who suffer from all types of eating disorders feel. We constantly hide our feelings, for fear that if we show how we really feel, no one will love us. This poem is for all who suffer from an eating disorder. I hope that this poem will also help those who know someone with an eating disorder understand what they are going through and how they feel.
God bless all.

WELLS, KATHLINE
[title] "Houston" [pers.] I enjoy writing poetry, and I delight in expressing my views of the world as it evolves. Composing text with a poised language expresses rhythm, feeling, spirits and emotional effect that is from prudence of literature of a particular time, city, country and region. Recalling literature rich in aestheticism is exciting, yet devotional, to the domestic life of everyday living. Cognizance of an outer world of drifting volatile forms creates coherence and significance, authenticity without delusions. Experience the world with liberal consumption and exploitation of literature as it really is.

WENDELL, SUE
[title] "Once Again . . ." [pers.] This poem was written in commemoration of my husband, Captain William "Billy" Wendell. His wishes were to become a part of the waters where he worked for 30 years. Before his death, my husband encouraged me to write. His confidence in my ability to express myself through writing gave me inspiration. A lot of my poetry originates from many philosophical

talks we shared. The presence of his spirit is with me when I attempt to create poetry. My home is in Altamonte Springs, Florida. However, I have a small motor home that takes me to the ocean, mountains and nature in general. A natural environment enhances my ability to create.

WENTZEL, BRENDA
[a.] Tucson, AZ [title] "Spirit Wind" [pers.] This poem came flowing out of me very swiftly. Sometimes poetry is like that, and other times it can be like pulling teeth. I have always loved the sound and touch of the air as it moves around me and in nature. It recalls to me those times my family and I spent high in the mountains. I like words, especially those that sound exactly as they mean. With this poem, I wanted to capture that rushing sound the wind makes, and I think I actually did. I am very happy with it.

WHALEN, RITA
[a.] Freeland, WA[title] "Behind a Child's Eyes" [pers.] This poem is about my grandson, Anthony Lukjanowicz. It reflects the broken heart of a four year-old child, young yet wise, during a time of personal loss. His emotions and stoic strength remain with me always. My family and my country mean everything to me. From my experiences come the emotions. I put these into poetic verses and essays. I dedicate my work to them for their love and support. I live on beautiful Whidbey Island, in Freeland, Washington. Surrounded by water and mountain views, it's nature at its best. I hope my work reflects the peace and beauty given to my heart by the environment in which I live.

WHISTMAN, SCOTT
[a.] Wenatchee, WA [title] "Restraint" [pers.] I wrote this poem during high school. I'm sure that most people who have been through this experience can identify with having the urge to leap out of your skin and do something contrary to your character and conscience. This poem was fashioned from my feelings of frustration with having to restrain myself from acting on those urges.

WHITE, BEATRICE
[title] "Rue Words" [pers.] The title is intended as "Rewards." It was written from the perspective of a very long life with plenty of time for reflection and writing, most of it in prose. My first book was "Reluctant Pioneer," the life of my great-grandmother. The second was "Not on a Silver Platter," which carried the story up to 1904. Both have been well-received.

WHITE, LAWRENCE
[title] "The Empty Cross" [pers.] As I study the scriptures with the help of my teacher, the Holy Spirit, some of the most meaningful facts of my salvation come to life within my spirit. This is when "The Empty Cross" has full meaning to me. My savior and Lord died on that cross for my sin. As I call out to him, he comes to me. I ask him to forgive me and he does. He gave me a new life and promises me he will never leave me or forsake me. He is free for the asking. Just kneel down and ask him to come in.

WHITE, MELISSA
[title] "When I Was Just a Little Girl" [pers.] My whole life I've had a dream to be a writer. Although I've lacked the confidence to take that first step, my mother took it for me. You see, I wrote this poem for her, and she entered it in a contest. Now to see my writing published is a dream come true. In my poem, you will know what she gave me as a child, but what she has given me as a woman is a truly remarkable thing. Now, as a mother myself, I hope to achieve my ultimate goal, which is to write children's books. Thanks for the confidence Mom, I love you!

WHITE, SCARLETT
[a.] Gordon, GA [title] "Memories" [pers.] When I sit and write, sometimes I don't even know what I'm writing about. I always ask God to help me in my writing and he never fails. God laid this poem on my heart when my cousin passed away. I just felt like I had to do something, and my poem came to me. I wanted to have something that I could share with family and friends through this difficult time. I was asked to read it at the service. Lawana was like my sister. We shared a lot and I wanted people to know that her memories will always be in my heart, no matter where I go or what I do. I hope my writing will comfort those that are having a difficult time when losing someone. Memories are forever, and I've always got mine.

WHITNEY, THOM
[title] "Mother's Day Wish" [pers.] I wrote this poem for my mother to express to her how I felt and how much I love her for all she has done for me all my life. I will never be able to repay her for everything. Mom, I love you. Your son, Thom.

WHITWORTH, ROBERT
[title] "A Greener Field" [pers.] Several years ago, I received a Christmas card, which featured Santa Claus bestowing a gift upon a very surprised snowman. The inspiration read: "I couldn't have a better friend, if I had made one myself." "A Greater Friend" was the result of my attempt to restate this wonderful compliment in my own words, and return it with all the emotion and sincerity I possessed to its wonderful sender. I hope that someday she will read it, and know that I too, could not have had a better friend.

WIEDEL, TRACY
[title] "Courage" [pers.] To me, poetry is special. It's your feelings and your innermost thoughts. Anyone can write poetry—you just have to find your subject. Hi, my name is Tracy Wiedel. I'm 15. I wrote this poem when I was going through a rough time. Anyway, thanks. Thank you so much.

WIKRAMANAYAKE, MARISA
[title] "Fallen Angels" [pers.] My writing has become just one of my many outlets for my anger. But I also find that my poetry has meant a lot to others and has even inspired them to start writing. I write about the darker side of reality, as well as fantasy and emotions, such as hate and anger. It is amazing how many people relate to my writing. I get surprised every day. "Fallen Angels" not only mirrors the fall of Lucifer from Heaven, but also a feeling of helplessness and betrayal in people in normal, everyday life.

WILCOX, ANDREW
[a.] Rockford, IL [title] "Some Times and Others" [pers.] Going through high school, I found that poetry was a great form of escape. This poem is dedicated to all those in a situation in life that is confusing or just new.

WILHAMENA,
[title] "Holy Life" [pers.] God has visited me since 1980 and writes his love to me and all life. I see him and Jesus, and God speaks to me. Holy amen. God draws and writes his loving poetry through this poem!

WILHITE, MEGGIAN
[title] "Once Knew" [pers.] I am currently living in White, Georgia. I am 14, and a volunteer at the library. I love to swim, read, play basketball and soccer, and ride my bike. I am currently writing two novels. I hope to see them finished by the time I am 18. I love to draw and write poetry. This school year, I will be entering 9th grade at Woodland High School. My poem is about a very important person—Jesus! Jesus is the Lord of my life. Jesus is awesome! Jesus is the man in "Once Knew." He died for our sins.

WILKINS, MILDRED
[title] "The Answer" [pers.] My love of poetry began in my early pre-school years, when my mother read nursery rhymes to me. That love continued into my school years when we studied and memorized many poems by famous writers. However, had I then been given an assignment to write a poem, I would have panicked. Only in recent years have I attempted to write, first with simple little rhymes before branching into something with more meaning. I wrote "The Answer" based on Psalm 12:1-2 (King James Version), one night while watching an episode of "Touched by an Angel."

WILLEY, MARY
[a.] Ware, MA [title] "Reflections of Reality" [pers.] For me, writing and poetry bring the soul to a higher consciousness of one's own spiritual growth. "Reflections of Reality" is just that. Inspired by my soul mate, and written with enormous amounts of understanding, compassion, and love, it embraces the spirit's need to connect with one's self, to others, and to the God of understanding. I would like to thank Steve Cullen for all the love, inspiration, and support that he brings into my life. His presence truly enhances my spiritual development. I love you for now, forever, no matter what.

WILLIAMS, DOROTHY
[title] "I'll Take the Blame!" [pers.] This poem, during my time of stress, brought natural healing for me emotionally without medication. I was trying to find a quick antidote to a very emotional experience. Through my tears, emotional pain, and deep concentration, I found my relief, by walking through the words of "I'll Take the blame!"

WILLIAMS, FRED
[a.] Houston, TX [title] "Love" [pers.] I begin writing poetry when I was nine years old, and my parents and friends have really enjoyed my poems. I am thankful for my talent of poetry, and very grateful that love poem was chosen because God is love. I wrote this poem when I was twelve because of my closest family and friends' ups and downs in love. I am so blessed and honored for the publishing of my poem.

WILLIAMS, GARY
[title] "Through Baby's Eyes" [pers.] This poem has special meaning to me, because it's my first. I do most of my writing in the early morning hours. Many times, I awaken with thought and ideas. I also write and sing southern gospel music. There's nothing I enjoy more than praising the Lord with words and with songs. God has truly blessed me in many ways. I feel this poem is one of hope and of love. Regardless of our age, we can look forward to the day of being in our Heavenly Father's embrace.

WILLIAMS, HELEN
[a.] Nassau, Bahamas [title] "Graffiti" [pers.] Most of us would like to punch the culprit for marking up and defacing our walls. My husband, Fenton, wishes to catch him in the act so that he could minister to his wrath and outrage with society. He often says: "The popular, 'No Luv' scrawling signifies both our academic and social failings." I wrote this poem for him, hoping he would set it in rhythmic pattern for a rap. Now, I get a chance to submit my feelings so that others may stop, think seriously and be motivated to curtail this volatile expression.

WILLIAMS, MARION
[title] "Passing Through" [pers.] I have been writing since I was a child. My parents were forced to suffer through reams of childish creations and detective stories, but did so with smiles of encouragement. When I was in my teens, I learned that one of my ancestors was Henry Wadsworth Longfellow. (It must be in the genes!) Unfortunately, because my husband is infirm, I cannot spend as much time working on material as I would like, but having a piece of work accepted has given

me such encouragement, that I plan to devote more energy to this field in future.

WILLIAMS, NICHOLAS KENT
[title] "When the Sea is Black" [pers.] Nick Williams is president of Incentive Dimensions, Inc., a motivation travel firm headquartered in Greensburg, Indiana with sales offices in Ohio, New York and Florida. Nick has visited and operated large group travel programs to over 120 countries during the past 35 years. Nick was first published in the 1966 anthology *Timeless Treasures*. He has written hundreds of poems and short stories and is currently finishing a book to be titled *Tales of a Traveling Shepherd*, detailing funny and serious events he experienced worldwide. Nick is a loving and loyal father, brother, uncle, grandfather, friend and jovial neighbor.

WILLIAMS, RONDA
[a.] Forsyth, GA [title] "Wondering Tonight" [pers.] I was inspired to write "Wondering Tonight" when my dad retired and moved to Alabama. He and I have always been close. When I go visit him, we would sit on the deck of his house, looking out over the lake, talking and reminiscing. It is at times like this when I realize how much I miss him.

WILLIAMS, SHARON
[title] "We Were Lovers Once" [pers.] I am mother of six; four boys and two girls, ranging from age five to twenty-four. I also have a granddaughter, eleven months old. My poetry usually expresses my passions, frustrations, and expectations on my journey through life, or how I perceive others feel in their particular circumstances. It is not just therapeutic, but a hobby I find very enjoyable, and at times, a great challenge.

WILLIAMSON, SHEILA
[a.] Detroit, MI [title] "Blue Light Special" [pers.] This poem came into play after my girlfriends and I had another one of our "love summits," discussing what we want in a relationship. Some of the things we discussed made me laugh. Between fits of laughter, I said, "It sounds like we're man-shopping at K-mart!" That's when I grabbed a pen and note pad and wrote my observations of our love quest. "Blue Light Special" is dedicated to my late sister, Phyllis M. Jones, and my sisters worldwide looking for Mr. Right. Keep looking, ladies—he's out there. Siempre hay esperanza!

WILLIS, BRIANA
[a.] DeSoto, TX [title] "Friends" [pers.] I would like to dedicate "Friends" to my parents, Harold and Janice Willis, because I was deeply inspired by each of them to write this poem and to always do my best at whatever I do. My brothers, Allan and Roderick Turner, are also an influence in my life and we are the best of friends, as well as family. I am a 4th grade student at Brookhollow Christian Academy and my closest "Friends" and classmates are Erin O'Quin and Daycha Turner. Daycha, Erin and I are Christians and are sisters in Christ, and we will always be "Friends."

WILLOCK, PAMELA
[title] "What is Friendship?" [pers.] Born and educated in Antigua West, Indies. I have three brothers and one sister, and they all have supported me in my desire to write. Registered nurse, both in the UK and Canada. "What is Friendship?" is indicative of the special bond I share with my friends, near or distant. I thank God for giving me the judgement to choose my friends wisely and carefully. I'm especially honored that I've had most my friends for over thirty years.

WILSON, CHERYL
[a.] St. Louis, MO [title] "I Am The Resident" [pers.] For the last four years, I have had the honor to be a professional advocate for residents in long-term care facilities. It saddens me see how society treats the elderly. People need to stop talking about the elderly and start talking to them! This

poem is my first attempt to express the deep respect and love I have for the elderly. Someday, I hope to have the gift of time so I can continue to write about this population of people that I believe society has forgotten.

WILSON, KIMBERLY
[title] "Black Woman" [pers.] To my mother and every black woman in my life, I dedicate this poem. I thank you for all that you have done to allow me to express myself without ridicule. I am a third-year college student, majoring in elementary education. I hope to inspire my students to express themselves.

WILSON, MONDRE
[title] "A Man's Weaknesses"[pers.] Well, I guess I can start off by saying that I'm not some love-struck man who's been hurt and wrote a poem about it. I am a young man by the age of twenty-two who was born and raised in the heartland of Kansas. My poem is from the heart, and what I've seen in my life. I do know that beyond physical pain, the only weakness and true pain to the human man is a lost or broken heart by the human woman. There's no pain like the pain from a woman. Women are a paradox, women truly do have our hearts . . .we're just not man enough to admit it!

WILSON, TONI
[title] "Toys" [pers.] After retiring from a career in business, I took a job teaching at a private preschool because I love children. The children in my class range from six weeks to two years old. All of them are marvelous individuals. I write every lessons as a game so the children have fun while they learn. At certain points during the day, we have played with so many toys, we have to clean up. I teach self-help skills that makes cleanup fun. This poem originated from these thoughts and the prompting of my professor, Dr. Gitomer.

WINEIGER, LOIS
[title] "Song of the Windmill" [pers.] I'm seventy five, mother to secretary Sharon, nurse Carolyn, my pastor, Scott, and artist, Stephanie. I found country living was a wonderful place for ideas. I'd sit on a stump very early in the morning and watch the day come alive. At night, solitude, bobcats, and coyotes sent chills up my spine. I'd lie in bed, listening to wind and windmill talk and sing to one another. At times, they seemed unhappy, but the sounds inspired me to express their relationship through this poem. I'm thankful for the blessings of poetry.

WINSTEAD, ALETHA
[a] Greenville, FL[title] "Hear God" [pers.] I love a variety of literature books and poems. I've written several poems, but this is my favorite. God is my inspiration for all my writing. This poem was written at a time in my life when I questioned my faith and the very existence of God. Nothing was going right in my life. The harder I tried, the worse things seem to get. I finally realized God has been with me all the time, and always will be. I hope my poem inspires you to, as they say, "stop and smell the roses." God is there. He is listening and ready to talk, but sometimes I think he wants us to start the conversation. So God bless and never give up. Life is a war—fight it one battle at a time, and always use God as your armor.

WIXSON, SARAH
[a.] Everett, WA [title] "Nickies Youth" [pers.] "Nickies Youth" is a screaming reflection of the confusion I felt at that moment. Writing has always been a way to clear jumbled thoughts and give answers to my problems. Poetry has also been a fine line between passion and frustration. When my daughter was born, she too became a great inspiration, full of life and love. She gives me moments to present on paper.

WOHLGEMUTH, MICHAEL
[title] "Own Life" [pers.] The title comes from a Newspeak term in George Orwell's *1984*. The term

means to stray from the rest of the Communal Party, "doing your own thing." Scheduling your activities around a scheduled time of a show who's slogan is to find your "friends,"on the station that airs the program, is what I'm working at getting across. Personally, I loath the telescreens and feel that human interaction or personal is far more important than the superficiality of the movies. Read a book! It's one of my messages; my life is my other. Poetry equals expression.

WOLF, PATRICIA
[title] "Hope's Journey" [pers.] At the age of "40-something," I found the strength to overcome a lifetime of being stifled and trampled on. I never would have had an inkling that I possessed a creative side. But by gaining that strength, I began painting and writing. "Hope's Journey" is the story of what's most important to a girl named Patricia. I'm a Pisces and a hopeless romantic—aren't all poets? I wrote what my soul feels. I wrote about the beauty of life and the people who make that beauty a reality for me.

WOLFE, GWENDOLYN
[a.] Covington, VA [title] "Wedding Day" [pers.] When my daughter, Missy, got married, I searched everywhere for the perfect gift. Then it occurred to me to give something from the heart, something special that no one could give but me. I will always cherish this poem, as it holds special memories for me and my daughter.

WOODALL, WOODY
[title] "Whittling Man" [pers.] A dying mother-in-law inspired my writings. It was like a virus, a poetry virus, that come over me. I love to write because it is relaxing, and keeps the mind clear. I am a retired Vietnam veteran, with a GED for education. Presently, wife and myself are leaseholders on a original 1947 model Silver bullet (Diner) in Aalen-Germany (the Diner is from New Jersey). My hobbies are writing, fishing, and cooking.

WOODARD, C. V.
[a.] Portland, OR [title] "Feeling Lost Again" [pers.] Poetry exists everywhere in and around us all, extending beyond any known boundaries . . .even death. It may be simply stated or possess an infinite texture of complexity within the arrangement of words upon paper. I am attempting to capture emotion so that others may openly share the experience. The frosting of this poetic cake is the meaning found by others as a direct or indirect link with my initial emotion, now relating specially to your own emotions. Death caused me to feel lost; what has caused each of you to feel the same?

WOODS, NATHANIEL
[a.] Baldwin, NY [title] "Indignation" [pers.] In reflecting upon my love for poetry and its influence on my life, I am consistently aware that this development is an outgrowth of a stronger love for music, which helped to reinforce many of my growth experiences as a younger person attempting to cope with reality while living in a ghetto environment located in central Harlem. As far back as I can remember, in addition to experiencing ofttimes hauntingly beautiful and emotionally penetrating feelings from spirituals in church, the blues, jazz, opera, swing, country and western music, most of my favorite songs appeared to be composed with lyrics, which inevitably seemed to address many critical aspects of my personal relationships with family members, peers, and member of the opposite sex. Since these lyrics were generally written in such manner that each line would rhyme with the preceding one, while exuding declarations of unrequited love, manly pride, the impact of beauty, and numerous humanistic concerns resounding in poetic patterns, they also provided much reinforcement toward my development of sensitive listening skills and ego defenses against youthful emotional insecurities. Recognizing that

both intellectual and emotional feelings are expressed in music and poetry, which makes it difficult to separate them, I nevertheless am of the opinion that certain poems I read as a teenager also helped me to internalize many positive attitudes, notwithstanding my ethnicity as an Afro-American residing in a Caucasian-dominated area in the United States which categorized blacks as "second class" citizens.

WORTHEY, ANITA
[title] "To Move On" [pers.] The particular person whom this poem is about encouraged me to write. It is the first entry in a journal he gave to me. Although he is no longer the subject of my verse, he still encourages me to write. After a decade, it is nice to be able to say thank you, Ken, for being both my inspiration and my friend.

WRIGHT, JAN
[title] "Just Passing Thru" [pers.] I am a mother of five and a grandmother of five. My husband and I live in the small historic town of Granbury, Texas. I write a column in a weekly paper here. I love to write poetry, and I use it every chance I get. I find it easy to express emotions or feelings by writing it in poetry. I wrote this poem when I decided to go back to work after being retired for 15 years.

WRIGHT, MARY
[a.] Owensboro, KY [title] "The Corner Stool" [pers.] Poetry to me is an emotional outlet, a way of releasing the feelings in a productive manner. This poem does just that for me by marking a very significant turning point in my life. It is an expression of my own emotional state as I began the difficult journey through a divorce. I had lost my entire life, including my two children, who had been my reason for living the last five years. My life had fallen apart at my feet, and I ran across the country to pick up the pieces and start over.

WRIGHT, PRISCILLA
[title] "The World by Way of Wal-Mart" [pers.] I have been writing poetry since I was a very small child. To me, the words seem to be given by a divine source, because the words come as inspiration in a way that I couldn't think of on my own. Poems are a gift, and life itself is poetry. I hope others feel this when they read the words that I am given to write. I live in a rural area of Tennessee, and draw much on the feelings that come when I take time to appreciate nature. Also, I draw on the love that I have for my family.

YANCEY, JAMES
[title] "Come On 2 Me" [pers.] I am inspired by visions and ideas that enlighten me and I feel it is a duty of mine to express and share them with everyone. Every vision and idea with which I am enlightened, I express each one as perfectly as I see and feel. I am hoping that one day that will connect with someone, somewhere, along the way and then I might feel complete. It is my hope that you will enjoy this expression of my art. You can look forward to more of my work yet to be published and others yet to be written. Enjoy the ride!

YATES, ZACHARY
[a.] Austin, TX [title] "My Sock" [pers.] I have been writing poetry for only one year. I published my first book of poetry through a program at my parochial school. My encouragement for my writing has come to me through my teachers, librarian and my parents. I also love to read poetry, as well as spiritual prayers. I love to make people happy by dancing and writing special poems just for them. Some day I would like to author my second book of poetry for all to enjoy!

YERYAR, DEBORAH
[a.] Lapel, IN [title] "And God Whispered" [pers.] My husband is always doing nice things for me, whether it is bringing me flowers or just opening the door. When he does these things, he'll smile and tell me it's just because he loves me. I realized God does the same thing by all the wonderful things he

gives me every day. That is where I got my inspiration for this poem. I find that most people are so busy trying to see the big picture that they miss the details, which create and reveal the poetry within each of us.

YORK, BENJAMIN
[a.] Salt Lake City, UT [title] "The Woman Master" [pers.] This poem is a tribute to the many women who have practiced the martial arts over the centuries. Martial arts history has not named many of these great women, but their influence and contributions are enormous. I dedicate this poem in honor of my grandmother Cleo, Mother Lauralee, my wife, Joyce, and women everywhere.

YOUNG, CHRIS
[title] "Remembrance" [pers.] It's truly a blessing when someone special enters our lives, and it's unfortunate when they must leave as quickly as they came. As long as they're remembered, they'll always be in our hearts. Therefore, this poem is dedicated to a dear friend, Christian Carrasco. It was an honor to have known her and even though it saddens me that she's gone, I take strength knowing she is now "free." From all your family and friends at Barnes, we miss you Christina . . . we'll remember you always.

ZANELLA, JILL
[a.] Mississauga, ON [title] "Vanity Destroys" [pers.] When I wrote "Vanity Destroys," I wrote it as a reminder of what I'd not want to become. Vanity is in everyone, and if we are not careful, we can forget what it means to be human.

ZAWADZSKI, KATHRYN
[title] "The Clown" [pers.] The clown portrays a man who feels better about himself and feels accepted by others as long as he hides behind a disguise or mask. All of us tend to apply a mask when trouble reigns, or confidence and faith eludes us. Time has a way of stripping away this mask to reveal our true self. My mother always told me to be myself. Thanks to her encouragement, support and faith in me, I have found my true self through poetry. If not for Mom, I wouldn't have had the courage to send the poem.

ZERA, CHRISTINA
[title] "Treasure Love" [pers.] I wrote this poem about a hope, a wish, a possibility. May it reach the farthest hearts of Earth, and may it come true for all who read it.

ZIESKE, KAYLA
[title] "I Am" [pers.] Although I'm 12 years old, poetry in my life has already become a big thing to me. I love to write as much as possible, and often relate my work to daily situations and life. My poems just say a little about what goes on in my mind, and how I usually feel day by day. Getting these poems published has been a gift from God, and it's one whole step closer for me to actually follow my dream. Just as it says in my poem "I Am," I dream one day to become well-known.

ZIMMER, DAPHNE
[a.] Lutcher, LA [title] "My Brother Derek" [pers.] I had to write a poem as an assignment by my teacher in English class. My first and only thought was to make the poem about my brother, Derek. Derek is very special to me because he wasn't as fortunate as my older brother and me when he was born. He was diagnosed with a rare and terminal disease and faces many obstacles. I will be there for him every moment to make everyday life as easy as possible. He isn't any different in my eyes. Derek is 17 and I am 12, and I intend to always be by his side.

ZIVANOVIC, NATASA
[title] "Mario" [pers.] This is a poem I wrote for my last year's 5th grade class all the kids liked it, so I entered and I am glad!

Index
of
Poets

Index